Due Date	Return Date	Due Date	Return Date

Aesthetic Experience and Its Presuppositions

Aesthetic Experience and Its Presuppositions

MILTON C. NAHM
Bryn Mawr College

NEW YORK / RUSSELL & RUSSELL

REISSUED, 1968, BY RUSSELL & RUSSELL
A DIVISION OF ATHENEUM HOUSE, INC.
BY ARRANGEMENT WITH MILTON C. NAHM
L. C. CATALOG CARD NO : 68-10933
PRINTED IN THE UNITED STATES OF AMERICA

To Elinor

Contents

Preface

THE title of this essay of the Aesthetic of Empirical Idealism is intended to indicate, as precisely as possible, the scope and boundaries of the work. It will be evident that it owes much to analyses of the fine arts and to critical essays intended not only to interpret specific works of art but also to investigate the rules governing particular arts. The present essay stops short, however, of detailed analyses of the specific symbols of art or of the rules of art except in instances in which the argument plainly requires their inclusion. It should not be inferred from this that the author entertains any doubt whatsoever concerning the value of the many contributions made by aestheticians to these fields. Indeed, my introduction to Aesthetic was made as a student of Dr. Louis W. Flaccus, whose book, *The Spirit and Substance of Art*, is a masterly illustration of the possibilities afforded by empirical analysis. My own interests would have led to the extension of this book to include at least a brief empirical study of one of the fine arts, had it been possible to develop within the scope of one volume certain implications of earlier chapters. That I did not do so is owing not only to the truth of Dr. Johnson's remark that "He that runs against time has an antagonist not subject to casualties," but to the fact that from the beginning of my work in the subject it has appeared to me that much of profound significance has remained for speculation after the various critical and expository aspects of art and of its experience had been examined. It appeared to me, moreover, that those problems lay principally in the realm of aesthetic experience and its presuppositions and in the subject of the generic symbols of art.

It should be remarked, however, that while I have found the principal problems of this book in these fields, it may well be that the title of this essay promises more than the inquiry will perform. Its subject is properly aesthetic experience and such of its presuppositions as mainly concern the generic symbols of art and the feelings. In consequence, such presuppositions of fine art as are discoverable in craft and materials are scarcely touched upon. I need hardly add that the interested reader will find in Dr. Flaccus' study, in Samuel Alexander's *Art and Instinct* and *Beauty and Other Forms of Value*, D. W. Prall's *Aesthetic Judgment*, and Max Dessoir's *Ästhetik und Allgemeine Kunstwissenschaft*, the detailed analyses which these problems deserve.

The present essay falls within the confines of Professor Edgar A. Singer, Jr.'s philosophical system of Empirical Idealism. My dependence upon that philosophy will be evident to all who know Professor Singer's writings. But my indebtedness to their author for what in this volume derives from his thinking goes beyond my dependence upon his systematic philosophy, precisely as it transcends adequate acknowledgment in a preface. He suggested the central problem of the essay and, throughout the time I have spent in an effort to solve that problem and to meet its derivative difficulties, his suggestions and encouragement have been invaluable. I must add, however, that the responsibility for errors in the interpretations of the philosophy of Empirical Idealism is my own.

Among the classical writers on philosophy of beauty and art, I shall mention but briefly the three to whose writings I have gone most frequently. As will be plain, Plato's Dialogues have been the most fertile sources of suggestions of an essentially aesthetic character. Kant's writings in aesthetic present what appears to me to be the most interesting single problem attacked in the history of the subject. I have come to value Hegel's *The Philosophy of Fine Art* little for its display of dialectic skill at the same time that my respect has grown for the illumination its author gives to fundamental ideas. In this connection, it may be well to suggest that, despite the critical method used in the earlier chapters of this book, I do not hold the writers in question in less esteem than their contributions to philosophy of art warrant. Any contrary impression, if it occurs, may be attributed to the fact that a critical method abstracts writings from their contexts, whereas only the writings as a whole may be justly evaluated. Moreover, one has a tendency to interpret other men's thought in the light of one's own hypothesis, however one may labor to avoid doing so. But while there is scarcely a writer mentioned in this essay whose stature is not greater than it would appear to be in consequence of this process of "abstraction," it is nonetheless true not only that it is impossible to quote an author entire but that the philosophers in question almost certainly were not fully cognizant of all the implications of their own writings.

I am indebted to many contemporary aestheticians, critics, philosophers of art, and artists to a degree greater than references in footnotes will indicate. I regret that if they read this book they may encounter difficulties in terminology, as well as others originating in the analysis of problems which appear at first sight to lie beyond the limits of aesthetic theory. As regards terminological difficulties, I should perhaps content myself with the remark that, while speculation upon the beautiful merits beautiful expression, speculation and expression need not necessarily imply each other. But it appears to me also that philosophical problems may be solved only if philosophical tools are employed. As regards the problems which are dealt with in this book but which appear to lie beyond the range of philosophy of art, I conclude that no apology need be offered, precisely because it is the loose usage of such words as "feeling" and "form", derived from non-aesthetic fields, that mars many otherwise excellent studies in this subject.

I owe much to colleagues and others who have given generously of counsel and information. In particular, I am indebted to Professors S. J. Herben and T. R. S. Broughton, of Bryn Mawr College, for invaluable technical advice; and to Mr. and Mrs. W. Wallace Clark for the meticulous care they have exercised in editing this book for the press.

I have published in various journals articles concerned with the content and conclusions of several chapters in this book. The inclusion of the material of those essays in the present systematic account has been accompanied by alterations in form and presentation to a degree that warrants their mention only in the appended bibliography. It may be helpful, however, to note two specific instances of prior publication which I should except from the previous statement. The first, "The Philosophical Implications of Some Theories of Emotion," appeared in *Philosophy of Science* and was intended to present in detail the theory of feeling which, with some considerable alterations, underlies the argument of the latter portion of the present volume. The second, two lectures on "Form in Art" and "The Function of Art," appeared in *Art: A Bryn Mawr Symposium* and presented in brief scope some of the principal issues raised in this book.

I dedicate this book to my wife, Elinor Amram Nahm. Her encouragement and criticism have been equally helpful, inasmuch as each has been given at the moment only the most judicious mind could select.

M. C. N.

Department of Philosophy
Bryn Mawr College

Acknowledgments

The following acknowledgments are due for permission to use copyrighted material: J. H. Bernard, *Kant's Kritik of Judgment;* A. C. Bradley, *Oxford Lectures on Poetry;* Davies and Vaughan, *The Republic of Plato;* Walter Pater, *The Renaissance;* Norman Kemp Smith, *Kant's Critique of Pure Reason;* by permission of The Macmillan Company, publishers.

Sir Charles Sherrington, *Man on His Nature;* Cambridge University Press and The Macmillan Company, publishers. R. Trumbull, *The Raft;* H. Bergson, *The Two Sources of Morality and Religion;* E. A. Singer, Jr., *On the Contented Life;* Henry Holt and Company. K. Hamsun, *The Growth of the Soil;* Alfred A. Knopf and Company. H. S. Langfeld, *The Aesthetic Attitude;* Harcourt, Brace and Company. John Palmer, *Comedy;* Martin Secker and Warburg, Ltd. J. Maritain, *Art and Scholasticism;* Charles Scribner's Sons. Rebecca West, *Black Lamb and Grey Falcon;* The Viking Press. G. Richter, *The Sculpture and Sculptors of the Greeks;* E. R. Goodenough, *Religious Tradition and Myth;* Yale University Press. Ingram Bywater, *Aristotle on the Art of Poetry; The Works of Aristotle, Translated into English;* Clarendon Press, Oxford. *The Note Books and Papers of Gerard Manley Hopkins, The Letters of Gerard Manley Hopkins to Robert Bridges;* Oxford University Press. Plato, *Symposium* and *Philebus* (1925); Longinus, *On the Sublime* (1939), *Loeb Classical Library;* Gilbert Murray, *The Classical Tradition in Poetry* (1927), reprinted by permission of Harvard University Press, Cambridge, Massachusetts. *Picasso, Forty Years of His Art;* The Museum of Modern Art. *Divine Providence and The Problem of Evil* (A Translation of St. Augustine's *De Ordine*); The Cosmopolitan Science and Art Service Co. Stephen Mackenna's *Plotinus;* The Medici Society, Ltd., and Sir Ernest Debenham, Bt. Edna St. Vincent Millay's "Sonnet XXII," from *The Harp-Weaver and Other Poems;* by permission of the author.

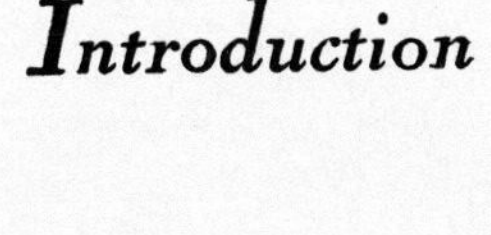

Introduction

Chapter I

The Problem: Antinomies in Art and Aesthetic Experience

But nevertheless let us admit, that, if the poetry whose end is to please, and imitation, can give any reasons to show that they ought to exist in a well-constituted state, we for our part will gladly welcome them home again.

—Plato

THE central problem of this essay of aesthetic experience and its presuppositions issues from a conflict. Art is compounded of apparently incompatible elements and the analysis of its experience seems destined to lay bare only an unresolvable antinomy. This conflict is integral to art and to aesthetic experience and does not merely reflect perplexities which adhere to speculation upon fine art and aesthetic experience because that speculation falls within the pattern of general philosophical inquiry. It is true, by way of illustration, that as pre-Socratic philosophers searched for general explanatory principles by analyzing objects and external events, such fragments of speculation upon art as remain of the writings of Heraclitus and Empedocles similarly relate to the objective problems of technique and beauty. It is no less true that once Greek speculation in general is thrust by the emergence of Sophism into an inquiry upon the "subjective," philosophy of art accompanies philosophy in general. But while ethical theory, epistemology, and cosmology likewise reflect these evident tendencies of metaphysical and physical speculation in general, the conflict revealed by the history of philosophical inquiry into art is unique to art and to its experience.

Seizing upon one aspect of the phenomena constituting art and of the factors in its experience, Plato concluded that he had revealed a source of grave discontent:

> And poetical imitation has the same effect on lust and anger and all those experiences of desire and pleasure or pain which, we believe, accompany all our actions. For it waters them and makes them grow when they ought to starve with drought; and it gives them power over us when we ought to subject them, and so to make ourselves better and happier instead of falling into misery and wickedness.

Seizing upon the opposing aspect of the phenomena constituting art and of the factors in its experience, Longinus in *De Sublimitate* concluded that he had revealed a source of profound exaltation. The products of genius are "far from unerring." Other qualities "prove their possessors men, sublimity lifts them near the mighty mind of God." And as Longinus answers the question, "What then was in the mind of those demigods who aimed only at what is greatest in writing?" the classic antithesis to Plato's conclusion rings forth:

> Among many other things this, that Nature has distinguished man, as a creature of no mean or ignoble quality. As if she were inviting us rather to some great gathering, she has called us into life, into the whole universe, there to be spectators of all that she has made and eager competitors for honour; and she therefore from the first breathed into our hearts an unconquerable passion for whatever is great and more divine than ourselves. Thus within the scope of human enterprise there lie such powers of contemplation and thought that even the whole universe cannot satisfy them, but our ideas often pass beyond the limits that enring us.[1]

As it is with this conflict that the present essay begins, so the study follows through the centuries the history of its changes of form and of its attempted reconciliations, to end with its own interpretation of the problem and its own offering in the reconciliation of ostensibly incompatible elements. We shall observe the tendency toward extreme disparity in the grounds for evaluation of art consistently maintained throughout the history of aesthetic and of

[1] Longinus, *On the Sublime*, XXXV. (Reprinted from W. H. Fyfe's translation in the *Loeb Classical Library*, Harvard University Press, Cambridge, 1939.)

criticism: The objects and events called art have been judged to be entertaining but, nonetheless, worthy only of a "surface attention, such as might wipe from a fruit a drop of rain or a speck of dust." Contrariwise, the same objects and events have been judged to be of serious import and to them have been assigned the tasks of revealing and symbolizing the most profound of metaphysical, practical, scientific, and moral truths. Nor does this divergence in evaluation affect judgments upon art alone. Aesthetic experience, as will be evident, has likewise been dismissed as merely entertaining playfulness, or analyzed with minute care as a form of knowing at that presumably highest level in which knower and known are mystically united.

Before taking up the history of the problem, it is interesting to inquire how there came to be a problem that came to have a history. The extremes of theory, in assigning to art and aesthetic experience the most deleterious, the most frivolous, or the most serious functions, have occasionally suggested to philosophers of art that a dialectic process has been in operation throughout the centuries of speculation on the subject. For our purposes, dialectic may be dismissed, in view of the sufficiency of the assumption that speculation has been satisfied with no solution offered to the problem simply because the experience of art is identical neither with play nor with the revelation of religious, moral, or scientific truth, although the hard fact remains that fine art is of such nature and character that aesthetic experience is integrally related both to playful and to serious activities and interests.

It is natural, in consequence, that speculation since Plato has sought to ascertain the precise need for aesthetic experience. Nor is it strange that speculation proceeds with this task, having inferred at once that there is a unique end for the art which evokes the experience and that the artist makes possible the satisfaction of a profound need by forming or making, in objects, events, or symbols, unique instruments for the achievement of that unique end.

It was Plato who believed that we should be "gainers" if what we now call fine art could be proved to be "profitable," but it is philosophy that must specify, if possible, the unique need satisfied by art both in artistic creation and in aesthetic experience. To do this, the philosopher of art must determine the unique end for fine art. In its assumption that fine art evokes aesthetic experience, this book does not contend that either natural or primarily technical objects or events lack potentialities which, when actualized, may move us as does fine art. It does assume, rather, that nature and technical art not infrequently do inadequately or accidentally what fine art does adequately and because of the artist's purposes. It also assumes that the perceiver may become, for the moment, the artist who does as well as lies in his power what the fine artist does in consequence of insight and training. But both assumptions, which derive from the original hypothesis that fine art is definable in terms of a unique end and that it satisfies one of man's profound needs, lead us to inquire how fine art came to be distinguished from technical art. Concerning the latter, the question of need is answered by an accurate estimate in terms of utility. Concerning fine art, however, there has always been the question of its use, its utility, and its value.

These questions have been answered variously in the course of history—in terms of the inexhaustibility of interest or the intensity of feeling which works of fine art induce, of the familiarity and uniqueness they manifest, of their structure, of the materials employed to make them, the techniques used to produce them, and the symbolisms that endow them with meaning. In the present study it is assumed that aesthetic experience is at least conditioned by feeling evoked by fine art. More, it is assumed that the presupposition of the diverse descriptive aspects of fine art is the capacity of the artist's product to move us profoundly and, by means of conative experience, to open paths for creative imagination.

But as we turn to inquire how there came to be a problem that came to have a history, some encouragement for the general limitation of the subject matter of this book to fine art and its preconditions to feeling is discovered in a field of inquiry in which these initial assumptions have in large part been denied. The differentiation frequently assumed to mark off classical philosophy of art from modern aesthetic theory provides the case in point. It will be of value to turn to a consideration of the validity of that differentiation.

II

HISTORIANS of critical and aesthetic theory have grown accustomed to an approach to their subject by which Greek and modern philosophies of art are distinguished on the ground that the former has no term corresponding to "fine art." They have not infrequently agreed with the inference drawn from this lack in classical theory, namely, that because ancient speculation uses no such term as "fine art" the thinkers had no conception corresponding to it. That the inference should have been assumed to be valid is strange in the light of the most cursory consideration of the facts and, in particular, of the obvious effort to distinguish beautiful and technical objects as well as to classify various arts. Plato, and Socrates before him, made an effort to set apart a "beautiful in itself" from a relatively beautiful and to describe "absolutely beautiful forms" in contrast to artifacts. Aristotle, in *Politics*, classifies kinds of music and explains the experience of tragic poetry and "enthusiastic" modes of music in terms of *katharsis.* Moreover, the inference appears to ignore Longinus' effort to analyze the sublime in poetry.

These illustrations from classical theory—and they could be multiplied—suggest that the differentiation between ancient and modern philosophies of art on the grounds of the occurrence of the term "fine art" or its equivalent is merely nominal and of negligible significance. It is, however, a differentiation that in fact ordinarily presupposes more than a distinction between "fine art" and "art"; and it is significant, if at all, on the grounds that by "fine art" the modern philosopher means "expressive" art, and that the Greek, since he does not know the connotation, does not have a name for the connotation and means by art only "technical" art. Whether art was regarded by the Greek merely as τέχνη is a subject for later consideration, as is the question whether "expression" implies that what is "expressed" requires no embodiment in material. The immediate issue is raised by the meaning of "expression" and its use, within that meaning, to distinguish ancient and modern aesthetic theory. As will be plain, it is not necessary to identify ancient and modern philosophies of art or to discover forms strictly analogous to "fine art" or "expression" to show that, despite differences in terminology, both assume that feeling is fundamental to aesthetic experience and that, in this connotation, "expression" does not serve to distinguish Greek from modern.[2]

Were the aesthetician's concern merely logical, the technique of an *organon* would stand him in good stead in differentiating "expressive" objects from artifacts. It is evident, for example, that the modern theory of "expression" implies that Greek speculation fails to recognize that, while products of technique are non-aesthetic in the sense that they are "non-expressive," others are "expressive" or aesthetic and, of the latter, some or all, it may be, are "non-expressive" as well. But neither this logical classification nor the denotative method of a Hippias of Elis is of value unless a specific connotation is given to the term "expression." To identify it with "art" is tautological and merely repeats the problem, except insofar as it evidences the intention of the modern to dissociate aesthetic from the so-called technical process of "making."

In this regard, it is worthy of note that most modern "expressionists" give to "expression" significance in terms of "imagination" or "feeling."[3] But it is apparent that while a meaningful theory of imagination may be offered to ground the proposition "art is expression," the significant problem is to determine whether or not "imagination" and aesthetic "expression" are identical. That it is difficult to maintain that they are identical is evident from the restrictions which have been placed upon so-called "expressive imagination." The particular restrictions are of less importance than is the reason

[2] "Feeling" is the fundamental issue, despite the fact that the problem in question is often resolved on the basis of *mimesis* in contrast to symbolism. Plato does imply that the artist "mirrors" nature, but it is difficult to interpret the philosophy of art of either the *Symposium* or *Philebus* in these terms, and Aristotle's suggestions concerning "imitation" of character and the problems of probability and possibility in art clearly show that *mimesis* meant more than mere "copying."

[3] For example, Croce, Bosanquet, Collingwood, and Lipps.

for their employment; the latter is sufficiently obvious. If "expression" is ultimately "imagination," if art is the artist's "expression" in terms of "images," whether or not embodied in material, it is clear that if the poet and the painter are of imagination compact, so, too, are the lover and the madman. So, too, in a meaningful sense, are the moralist and the scientist. It would be palpably absurd to ground a theory intended to explain beauty, art, the aesthetic experience, and the artist's creativity in terminology of such unrestricted generality.

It is not surprising, therefore, that aestheticians have come to write of "expression" in the more restricted terminology of "aesthetic imagination" or, again in an effort to avoid tautology, of "sensuous imagination." The use of the latter phrase, however, shortly reveals theory's true intent, inasmuch as "sensuous" is clearly a correlative of conation.

It is at this point that the demarcation between modern and classical theory following upon a differentiation between "expression" and *τέχνη* clearly disappears.[4] It is precisely in terms of feeling that the relevant Platonic and Aristotelian philosophies of art distinguish such poetry and music as transcend classification in terms of arts which produce utilitarian tables, beds, and chairs.[5] Plato does attack the poet, the sculptor, and the painter because the products of their arts are twice removed from reality, i.e., are copies of the "useful" bed which in turn is a copy or imitation of the "ideal" bed. It is at least of equal significance, however, that although his argument asserts that the tragic poet, the rhapsode, the painter, and the sculptor produce mimetic objects, Ion is made to remark not only that "at the tale of pity my eyes are filled with tears" but also that the rhapsode's art "produce[s] similar effects on most of the

[4] It is certainly true that modern aesthetic since Croce has become more "expressive," if by that is meant more "subjective." But it is scarcely a triumph to achieve expressiveness at the expense of all analysis of art objects and, indeed, to deny the relevance of so-called "technical" processes to aesthetic expression.

[5] That the conclusions either commend or are critical of the object so distinguished is of no consequence. The significant fact is that the differentiation is implied.

spectators." So, too, Aristotle analyzes the poetic art and music in terms of a *katharsis* of emotions and in another context interprets the work of art as a "symbol" of the artist's feelings. Finally, Longinus describes the experience of sublimity in terms of joy and exaltation.

It may be suggested, then, that Greek theory's failure to coin a term analogous to "fine art" does not bespeak the individual philosopher's failure to distinguish aesthetic objects from artifacts. Nor does it signify such a lack of interest by the classical philosophers of art as will permit a contrast to the modern as regards the relevance of feeling to the experience of art. Indeed the so-called "expressiveness" upon which the modern theorist lays such stress does not actually distinguish him from the ancient, and this fact is of more than historical interest. However much it be insisted that Greek and modern differ in their interpretation of the term "feeling," it is significant that both apply the term to the stage of differentiation between artifact and "more-than-artifact" at which the experience of the latter is "profoundly moving." It is the contention of the present study that the agreement of classical and modern theory upon this point is neither accidental nor merely the consequence of a literary tradition. It is added evidence, rather, that the meaning and problems of the structure, symbolism, and end of fine art may be dealt with fully in philosophy of art only if feeling is regarded as their proper frame of reference.[6]

[6] To state the problem in this way is to invite the criticism that the consequent analysis must necessarily overemphasize the subjective aspect of aesthetic. It may be replied that aesthetic does not differ from other philosophical techniques and that whatever its starting point, a philosophical inquiry is completed ordinarily by touching upon many if not all aspects of the problem. It will shortly be seen that the work of art presents non-aesthetic factors other than the media and symbols which refer to feeling. Moreover, it is not any feeling that is "aesthetic." To be profoundly moved is to be established in a uniquely creative mood and this is consequent upon the experience of works of art with explicit and objectively definable characteristics as fine art. El Greco's "St. Francis in Ecstasy," Bach's Sonata in E Major, No. 6, the "Epitaph," with "The hour when earth's foundations fled," and Giotto's Campanile, to mention a few illustrations, have other than aesthetic values. These they share with other products of technique. But the latter lack the former's power to move us, and it is sufficient, at this point, to insist upon this fact. It should, however, be made plain at the outset that no attempt will be

III

ONCE feeling is assumed to be integral to any sound theory of fine art and aesthetic experience, the problems presented could be attacked by referring to them in the context of either classical or modern theory. Thus, Aristotle's suggestion that the artist "makes" a symbol of his feelings or Hegel's conclusion that "the poet operates upon the material supplied him by his emotions, projecting it into an image for the conceptual faculty" would serve equally well as a sound point of departure for fuller analyses.

Certain advantages accrue, however, to the statement of the problem in a preliminary way in the context of classical theory. Most important is the fact that the Greek tradition in philosophy of art, unlike much of modern theory, never seriously identified the end of art with "mere surface attention" or with "art for art's sake." It assumed, rather, that the experience we now call aesthetic is significant—whether for good or ill—for the individual and for the society in which he lives. No doubt, in its speculations upon beauty, it did confuse the aesthetic, the moral, and the metaphysical universes of discourse. Still, it is perhaps better to err in this regard than to divorce art from other human activities or to conclude either that it has its origin *ex nihilo* or that it continues to exist *in vacuo*.

Moreover, not the least advantage to be derived from a return to the Greek speculation upon art in order to present initially the problems of fine art's relation to feeling is this, that aesthetic benefits from the richness and acuteness of Plato's speculations upon the subject. Within a tradition that approached the theoretical and practical problems of art with profound seriousness, while its artists had given evidence of the significance of the objects of art for speculation in their own magnificent creations, Plato's thought appears truly as "the progenitor" which "contained the seed of all

made in this book to offer more than a necessary minimum of analysis of the specific symbolism of art.

within its loins." His Dialogues suggest, at times in rudimentary form, the greater number of significant aesthetic theories amplified in later history. More important for the moment, however, is the fact that the Athenian not only recognizes the fundamental importance of feeling for the experience of art but maintains, in large part in consequence of this recognition, that art is susceptible both to serious condemnation and to highest commendation.

The dualism in Plato's philosophy of art is best understood if we observe his systematic transformation into theory of art, of what his predecessors judged to be of primary speculative interest largely as illustrative of the problems of "appearance" and of conation. This is most evident in a comparison of Plato's approach to the issues with that of another artist and philosopher of antiquity, namely Empedocles. The philosopher of Agrigentum urges, almost at the outset of speculation upon art, that painting has the character of an "image." He implies, moreover, that the "image" may be deceptive. His view is properly understood in terms of the central metaphysical issue inherited by the Pluralists from Milesian speculation, the pre-Socratic search for a principle or "material substance" adequate to account for change and multiplicity in the phenomenal world. But it is well to remember, also, that speculation had invaded, between the time of Thales and Empedocles, provinces as diverse as sensation, perception, cosmology, morality, and evolution and that the problems of art and of beauty had not been neglected in that extension of explanatory principles. Heraclitus had selected the painter's art as an apt illustration of the theory that contraries produce harmony. In this he had been influenced by the Pythagorean philosophy of harmony and number which, in effect, explained the universe in terms analogous to those employed in music. There is ample evidence, moreover, that specific problems of artistic technique had been brought to the attention of theoretical philosophers.

The significant consequences, however, of Heraclitus' theory of "flux," of Parmenides' "being," and of Zeno's defense of Parmenides by the formulation of paradoxes led Empedocles to seek to explain being and change by resorting to a theory of the "elements"—earth, air, fire, and water. The mixture of the elements through "pores" produced the compounds, the "appearance" of things. On Empedocles' hypothesis, the "real," i.e., the being of things, is the elements. The world of "appearance" is logically the unreal or non-being. For the aesthetician, it is significant that Empedocles illustrates an aspect of this unreality by likening the "mixing" to the method employed by the painter, and the "mixture" of earth, air, fire, and water to the consequences of the mixing of colors:

> For from these [elements] come all things that are or have been or shall be; . . . And as when painters are preparing elaborate votive offerings—men well taught by wisdom in their art—they take many-coloured pigments to work with, and blend together harmoniously more of one and less of another till they produce *likenesses* of all things. . . .[7]

The philosopher of Agrigentum implies in this passage that painting produces "appearance" and that painters are concerned with the illusory. In addition, there is a suggestion concerning the conditions which force the painter to make "images" and likenesses. That the world of phenomena is itself a "mixture" and a "non-being," in contrast to the ultimate elements or "being," tempers somewhat the harshness of the inferences that suggest themselves. On the other hand, because the "saving of appearances" is an important task for the Pluralist, the antinomy manifest later in Plato's philosophy of art is implicit in his precursor's writing.

It remained for Plato, who as a young man is said to have written tragedy and who in his middle age exiled tragic poets from the ideal republic, to deliver a shrewder blow to art than that dealt by Empedocles. For Plato, the problem of art is considered in the context of fundamental philosophical issues and impinges upon the Platonic interpretation of the relation of universal and particular and of being and becoming. The theory of beauty and of particular beautiful things, once it is implicated in the philosophy of Ideas, invades the speculative cosmology of *Timaeus*, affects profoundly the pedagogical and political theories of the earlier books of the *Republic* and the *Laws*, is central to Plato's analysis of the good life

[7] M. C. Nahm (ed.), *Selections from Early Greek Philosophy*, p. 132; (italics mine). See also W. E. Leonard, *The Fragments of Empedocles.*

in *Philebus*, and is given poetic as well as philosophical expression in *Phaedrus* and the *Symposium.* The number of Dialogues in which the issues concerned with art and beauty are considered is paralleled by the diversity of philosophical solutions Plato offers for the problems. In his writings originate not a few of the long-lived theories of aesthetic: that absolutely beautiful objects are mathematical and formal; that beauty is transcendental; that art is play; that art is *mimesis*; that there are "aesthetic senses"; that poets are divinely inspired; and that the poet is a link in the chain of magnetic rings endowed with power to communicate to the aesthetic percipient.

Were no profound issues at stake, idle curiosity might tempt an inquiring mind to investigate the reasons for the diversity of Plato's assumptions and inferences concerning art and beauty. A long life and a fertile mind suggest only the conditions under which the diversity could have been forthcoming. For the theorist to whom the issue is significant, two passages in the *Republic*, following as they do upon Plato's condemnation of art, not only provide some clue to a conflict that underlies the philosopher's speculation upon the subject but suggest, as well, that the Platonic difficulty is far reaching: ". . . We are ready," he writes, "to acknowledge that Homer is the greatest of poets and first of tragic writers; but we must remain firm in our conviction that hymns to gods and praises of famous men are the only poetry which ought to be admitted into our state." Again, ". . . let us assure our sweet friend and sister arts of imitation that if she will only prove her title to exist in a well-ordered State, we shall be delighted to receive her—we are very conscious of her charms; but we may not on that account betray the truth." An older Plato writes, in *Timaeus*,[8] in similar vein: "So, if a man can tell us of a selection for the construction of these bodies more beautiful than our own, his triumph will be that of a friend, not an enemy. . . ."

It is a plausible inference from these and similar passages in the Dialogues that the diverse efforts Plato made to explain art and to analyze its experience, to discover forms of art beyond reach of

[8] Cf. also *Laws* 658-659.

criticism and to manifest the idea of beauty, to limit the subject matter of art and to make clear certain of its technical problems, are put forward by a creative thinker who loved and was strongly attracted by this noble effort of man but who was also profoundly convinced of its dangers. Plato's philosophy of art is dichotomous because its author beheld the consequences of a bifurcation in the experience of profoundly moving art, precisely as he was aware of the analogous potentiality of the work of art for value and disvalue. This inference suggests, however, but a portion of the truth. Plato's philosophy of art, elaborated upon and refined even in the latest work of his life, is evidence that this fertile mind never wearied of the task of formulating and examining theories as possible solutions for the basic problems which it had encountered early and which it had apparently come to regard as implicit in the nature of art and aesthetic experience.

IV

IT IS assumed, in the present volume that the foregoing inferences are plausible in explanation of Plato's philosophies of art and, more significantly, that his intuition of a serious difficulty in the explanation of aesthetic experience is correct. Plato's writings suggest, in fact, that there are unresolved antinomies in art and in aesthetic experience. The history of aesthetic merely magnifies the difficulty of the original problem which Plato's insight revealed, although it ordinarily places emphasis upon one or the other of the antinomies. Much of Plato's theory and that of his successors becomes clear once it is realized that a justification for art, which is enjoyable, encounters the problems inherent in fine art's apparent uselessness and in its appeal to conative rather than to rational experience. Similarly, a justification for aesthetic experience must counter the charge that implicit in the experience of fine art is not only exaltation but discontent as well. Plato's philosophy of art is a series of related efforts to formulate a theory to account for what evidently were for him warring aspects of art and of experience.

In consequence of his awareness of art's charm, of what he considered to be the reasons for its uselessness, and of its possible dangers, Plato's various conclusions concerning the aesthetic problem are invaluable. They are no less so because he never, on his own showing, appears to have satisfied himself that the problems had been resolved. We shall do well to glance at their statement in the context of Platonic philosophy.

Empedocles had implied, as we have observed, that the painter's art in producing "images" is analogous to the "mixing" of elements to produce a world essentially unreal. Plato's argument, in *Ion* and elsewhere, is more specific. He, as philosopher, insists that arts are differentiated by their subject matter and that each art comprehends the whole of its subject. The poet, the painter, the sculptor, and, by implication, all artists now called "fine artists" are, in his view, masters of no subject matter. They copy, imitate, and borrow the subject matter of other arts, which in turn copy Ideas. That the objects of art are twice removed from reality is but the introduction to the more fundamental attack. Plato, inferring that deception is inevitably implicated in the making and experiencing of the derivative arts, concludes that "the poet, as well as the painter, lays on a species of colours, in the shape of verbs and nouns, to represent the several professions, of which he only understands enough to be able to imitate them."[9] The consequence is that the "form of expression" induces the percipient to regard as true a represented subject matter, whereas the veracity of the subject matter in fact can never be demonstrated, known, or expressed by the artist qua artist: "So powerful," says Plato, "is the charm which these musical appliances naturally possess."

That Plato judges this to be a serious charge is evident. He does not, however, rest content with it. The issue is clear: he who "manufactures fantastic phantoms that are very widely removed from truth" likewise "implants an evil constitution in the soul of each individual, by gratifying that senseless part." Plato has coordinated the analysis of "images" with the more general principle that art, and in particular the tragic art, "waters the emotions." The artist

[9] *Republic* 601.

is responsible for inducing, by means of the product of his making, actions and states of mind destructive of the rational restraint and discipline essential for the proper conduct of the citizen in the city-state. Plato is primarily interested, in the *Republic*, in the moral effects of art in a state dedicated to justice, to temperance, to wisdom, and to courage. The stern and conservative lawgiver speaks particularly of tragedy and of the tragic poet:

> It is our duty to think over the event that has taken place, and to arrange our affairs to meet the emergency in the way which reason pronounces best . . . and, instead of hugging the wounded part, like children after a fall, and continuing to roar, we ought ever to habituate the soul to turn with all speed to the task of healing and righting the fallen and diseased part, thus putting a stop to lamentation by the aid of medicine. . . . Then the better part of us, we say, consents to be led by such reasoning.
>
> On the other hand, shall we not maintain, that the element which prompts us to think of, and grieve over, our misfortune, and which has an insatiable appetite for lamentation, is irrational and idle, and the friend of cowardice?[10]

It is, in part, because the imitator appeals to "a general gathering of all sorts of persons collected in a theatre" and utilizes "the peevish and changeful temper, since it is easily imitated," that Plato attacks the mimetic art. But primarily he condemns the imitative artist because "he excites and feeds and strengthens this worthless part of the soul and thus destroys the rational part."

Perhaps the following may be regarded as the crux of the Platonic criticism:

> If you consider that the part which is forcibly held down when those calamities of our own occur, and which has hungered for the privilege of weeping and bewailing itself fully and without stint, because it is its nature to covet this satisfaction,—is the very part that is fed to satiety by the poets, and delights in those descriptions; and that, meanwhile, that part of us which is naturally the noblest, from not having been sufficiently trained by reason and by habit, relaxes in its watch over this querulous part, because it is surveying

[10] *Ibid.*, 604C. (The translation is that of Davies and Vaughan. By permission of The Macmillan Company, publishers.)

the afflictions of others, and because it is not discreditable to itself to praise and compassionate another man, who professes to be good, though his grief is ill-timed. . . .

And in the case of love, and anger and all the mental sensations of desire, grief, and pleasure, which, as we hold, accompany all our actions, is it not true that poetic imitation works upon us similar effects? For it waters and cherishes these emotions, which ought to wither with drought, and constitutes them our rulers, when they ought to be our subject, if we wish to become better and happier instead of worse and more miserable.[11]

What we should now call "fine art" is for Plato, therefore, not only deceptive. The work of art is intended by the artist to play upon emotions, properly controlled by the "higher self," by man's rational nature.[12] It is disrupting and degrading to give way to the feelings—as we are the more tempted to do because the form of artistic expression is attractive. The experience is, in fact, as dangerous as is that of being under the sway of the mindless orator or of believing the magician, the soothsayer, or the sophist. All of these practitioners, including the artist, are ignorant of the arts they profess. The experience of moving art is characterized by a lack in self-control not unlike the impulsion that forces the traveler to gaze upon gallows-hung bodies at sight of which he sickens and yet for which he yearns. Plato believes that the artist's product destroys rational self-respect and true inner courage, because its appeal is to a faculty of soul the nature of which may be inferred from primitive and uncontrolled actions and behavior.

It should readily be admitted that Plato's condemnation of art and of the artist is expressed at once in extravagant terms and with singular vehemence. The conclusions are obviously affected by the fact that the philosopher considers the artist to be comparable to the sophist who was a literary man in the field of knowledge, and no less incompetent in the realm of morality and legislation. It may likewise be urged that the vehemence of the attack bespeaks Plato's

[11] *Ibid.*, 606. (By permission of The Macmillan Company, publishers.)

[12] That this conclusion is not due merely to Plato's desire to construct an ideal commonwealth but is integral to his general philosophy is plain from *Ion* 535, and *Hippias Major* 298 ff. Cf. *Phaedrus* 245.

interest in determining, if possible, the subject matter of what we should now call fine art. This parallels his similar interest, evident in *Lysis* and *Charmides*, in ascertaining what the subject matter of the science of knowledge may be. But whereas in *Cratylus* and the *Sophist* he does appear to have satisfied at long last the desire to solve the latter problem, the liberality of tone in *Timaeus* suggests that the analogous problem in the philosophy of art remained beyond solution in the later period of his writings.

Perhaps one could go further in an attempt to ascertain the reasons for Plato's vehemence in condemning art and the artist. To do so, however, would be of little value for our present purposes, because the fundamental issue would still remain. For what Plato expresses in exaggerated terms accords with a less extreme but widely held conviction that the experience of fine art induces a profound discontent. It is significant that men have constantly been led to attribute whatever of value they have discovered in that experience to the non-aesthetic factors in art, factors derived from morality, science, logic, history, and religion. It is no less significant that they have resorted to theories of genius to account for artistic production, in part because they have regarded as irrational both the maker and his product. Even the cults of symbolists, professors of unintelligibility and of technical perfection in art, bespeak this discontent. The situation in these instances suggests that makers and percipients alike, having discovered themselves unable to justify art in intelligible terms, have been forced to resort to the terminology and connotations of the esoteric.

Plato's expression of the widespread condemnation of art is tempered primarily by his obvious desire to solve its problems. Our interest in that expression is properly due less to its vehemence than to the fact that the philosopher not only condemns art but likewise attributes to it great value. Our interest is quickened once we discover that precisely in profoundly moving art's appeal to feeling are to be sought the factors that endow its experience with significance and value. This dualism is integral to Plato's philosophy of art. Affected though that philosophy obviously is by what is erroneously thought to be its author's general "conservatism" in politics and by his tendency to relegate all objects in the realm of appearance to a status inferior to that of forms or ideas, it yet remains true not only that in it the attacks upon art are couched in more forceful terms than those used to characterize analogous but non-artistic issues, but that the analysis also endows art with value in phrases bearing the ring of conviction, and of conviction sustained in one who revered tragedy and knew its power—and the power of other art—to exalt men's spirit.

Moreover, Plato's commendation of art is presupposed by the identical assumptions that lead elsewhere to its condemnation. The artist is the maker of "images," comprehends no whole subject matter, and is ignorant of the arts whose subject matter he borrows. The *Apology* plainly conveys Plato's conviction that tragic poets are incapable of comprehending the significance of either their "making" or the object made. The inference drawn is, however, contrary to that which is made in the attack upon art in the *Republic*. Poets are divinely endowed and their poetry manifests divine truth: "Not by wisdom do poets write poetry, but by a sort of genius and inspiration; they are like diviners and soothsayers who also say many fine things, but do not understand the meaning of them." Plato asserts, indeed, in *Ion* that "all good poets, epic as well as lyric, compose their beautiful poems not as works of art, but because they are inspired and possessed." It is well to note that the poet—that "light and wingéd and holy thing"—offers poems "not human, or the work of men, but divine and the work of God. . . ."

It could be argued either that Plato has placed poetry upon an explicitly different basis than the other arts or that he regards the poet primarily as a religious teacher. Still, it must be remembered that he judges poetry to be a mimetic art and that tragic poetry, i.e., poetry which evokes other than proper religious feeling, is banned from the ideal state. Moreover, as his references to arts other than poetry are examined, we find further evidence suggesting that there is an antinomy implicit in the making of art and its experience. All but two of the modes of music are excluded from the ideal republic. Yet, in *Timaeus*, we are informed that the function of melody is not pleasure but the bringing back to the soul of "order and consonance with itself." The faculties of sight and hearing permit us to imitate "the perfect pattern set by God." *Philebus* analyzes "absolutely beautiful objects" in the experience of which we are free of pain and not subject to the consequences of the passions induced by tragedy, by music, and by painting. In the *Laws* and the *Republic*, the Plato who is attempting to formulate a theory of education implies that youth is best trained in surroundings made effective for knowledge by objects of beauty. *Phaedrus* tells us, indeed, that "beauty is the most manifest and lovable of all things." The *Symposium* argues that the products of art and the beauties of men and of institutions are the initial particulars by means of which we ascend until we attain to the mystical union with beauty itself. It is no doubt true that in some instances Plato differentiates the exalting experience of art from that which induces discontent primarily in terms of the objects under discussion. This does not always occur, however, and the variety of artistic objects to which reference is made amplifies rather than diminishes the difficulty of the problem with which Plato grapples.

Plato argues, in fact, that art is of value. He concludes that some products of technique and some natural objects induce "pure pleasure." In the experience of some profoundly moving art there is, indeed, "ecstasy," a far extreme from the degradation of soul consequent upon the experience of art described in the *Republic*. The Socrates of *Ion* asks, "Are you not carried out of yourself, and does not your soul in an ecstasy seem to be among the persons and places of which she is speaking?" Art is, therefore, not alone to be condemned. The poet passes on to the auditor godlike values. The experience of art may be inspiring and exalting.

The historical consequences of this dualism in Plato's philosophy are of interest. The counterattacks begin in ancient times and continue to the present. It is significant that both aspects of Plato's philosophy of art are tacitly accepted. Plato's condemnation of art, produced in the greatest period of ancient creativity, leads Aristotle to defend music and tragic poetry. The Peripatetic philosophy calls attention to unity and to *katharsis* in defense of art and its experience. Aristotle's argument is well known, but it is often forgotten that Plato's praise of the divine aspects of art and of the exaltation consequent upon the experience of beautiful objects is evident in the assertion made by Longinus, that the aim of inspired writers is to show that "nature has set our human family apart from the humble herd of brutes, and has bidden us to the pageant of life and of the whole universe, that we might be spectators of the mighty drama and acquit ourselves as worthy actors there."

The seriousness with which later philosophers and critics took Plato's attack upon art and the equal seriousness with which they seized upon his suggestion that art has value are reflected in the history of literary and artistic criticism. The terminology of the praise or blame is not always Platonic, but the recurrence of the problem argues that men are troubled by the fact that profoundly moving art does evoke an experience curiously describable in terms of both discontent and exaltation. The evidence that men are aware of the antinomy is plain in the evaluations they have placed upon art. The Platonic condemnation of art on grounds that it is deceptive has a continuous history too well known to require detailed mention here. It should be noticed, however, that not a few have been discontented with art's evident employment of meanings derived from other arts, a practice too frequently defended on grounds that the artist intends neither to tell the truth nor to prove a point, or countered by the assertion that art is merely "imagination." It is equally evident that many have regarded art as an instrument that does reveal reality. It has been argued that such poetry as that of Aeschylus, Shakespeare, and Goethe is profoundly illuminating, or indeed that it contains sound guidance for solving the problems of men's lives, as well as teaching much of value concerning motives and character. Great artists have been condemned as agents of immorality, while ineffectual artists have been praised for their godliness. In its long history, the artist's "making" has, in fact, particularized the doctrine of Terence: "Homo sum: humani nihil alienum a me puto." The artist has with equal genius portrayed the vices, foibles, and wickedness of man in such art as that of Molière, Jonson, and Congreve, of Breughel and Goya, of Wagner and Stravinsky; and his virtues and goodness in the morality plays, in

Paradise Regained, in the symphonies of Beethoven, and in the paintings of Botticelli. The recognition of the fact that art is dual in character has frequently led to the demand that a moral subject matter save it, as it were, from its own sins. The "problem play" is but one consequence. Simultaneously, proponents of "art for art's sake" have upheld with equal fervor—and with logic quite as sound—the assertion that the various arts must be divorced from morality, from religion, and from science. Men have found in art the expression of their own humanity and the awakener of "new ideas that advance the spirit." Equally, they have argued that its products undermine morality and that they are the *bête noir*, opposed to science and opposed to custom, degrading man and pandering to his lusts.

It has become a trite dogma that the realms of art and of science are not merely discrete but contrary. To some, this dogma signifies the "salvation" of art. The conclusions implied, it is held, are of value for having forced criticism to find its "proper" vocation in the study of "concrete" and sensuous media, in the analysis of techniques, or in the preemption of the isolated realms by individual and specific artists or art objects. That the "salvation" of art has apparently implied amorality, illogicality, and a denial to the artist of the resources of science, religion, and morality has seemed to some a small price to pay for emancipation. To Collier and to the early Christian church the very tenets which led to such "emancipation" convicted art of the power to degrade.

Despite the efforts to avoid the issue, however, many significant aesthetic theories assume implicitly or explicitly that the problem Plato propounds is central and that the antinomic aspects of art and of aesthetic experience require resolution. Some theories, of which Aristotle's is one, suggest that a reconciliation is possible by admitting the truth of Plato's charge that art does appeal to the feelings and thereafter proceeding to elaborate on an alternative which the Athenian failed fully to examine. Others admit the force of Plato's argument in their valiant efforts to rule from the aesthetic universe of discourse objects and events which induce feeling, or at least the "disturbing" feelings. We shall shortly examine some typical theories of this character.

As will be increasingly evident, the present inquiry proceeds upon the assumption that Plato and succeeding generations of philosophers, critics, and artists have been correct in assuming or asserting that in art are implicit factors of both value and disvalue and that aesthetic experience is a mood comprised of both discontent and exaltation. It proposes to examine the grounds for this duality, to account for the facts of aesthetic experience, and to discuss the need for art in terms of the structure and end of fine art, as well as in the nature of the life of feeling. It will suggest a meaning for the assumption that fine art is, in fact, a "symbol of the artist's feelings" and it will endeavor to show that the reasons which led Plato to attack art are precisely those from which the aesthetic experience derives one of its significant sources of power and value, upon which the fine artist also may draw.

On the assumption that fine art is the "symbol of the artist's feelings"[13] and that it moves the spectator profoundly, it will be advantageous to state explicitly and fully at the outset of this book various aspects of the antinomies which philosophy of art encounters.

1. The structure and end of objects and events called fine art are of such nature that aesthetic experience is profoundly moving. As a "symbol of feeling," fine art evokes uncontrolled action. It effects discontent. This discontent is ultimately consequent upon the nature of feeling. Men deeply affected by feeling are swayed in a manner contrary to the dictates of reason. They accept in aesthetic experience symbols either odious or trivial, or meaningful only because the "signs" have been borrowed from other arts. Alternatively, lovers of art are induced to accept works of art as valuable solely on grounds of technique and form. Art's experience is atavistic and occurs on a primitive level because the artist appeals to feeling and directs his efforts to an aspect of man's nature ordinarily and correctly suppressed by reason.

2. The structure and end of objects and events called fine art are

[13] Cf. below, Chap. X.

of such nature that aesthetic experience is profoundly moving. As a "symbol of feeling," fine art ennobles and inspires. It liberates the imagination and elevates the mind which, as Longinus says, "swells in transport and an inward pride, as if what was only heard had been the product of its own invention." The aesthetic experience releases sources of energy and power: "And Art, as it createth new forms of beauty, awakeneth new ideas that advance the spirit." The experience of profoundly moving art exalts man to a new and higher conception of himself and is genuinely creative in its effects.

It will be argued that each set of statements may be demonstrated with sound logic and that each is antithetical to the other. It will be argued, furthermore, that if taken together, invaluable inferences concerning aesthetic experience may be drawn from the statements despite the apparent conflict resulting from their consideration in separation. It will be maintained, in fact, that in his experience of profoundly moving art, man does yield to his baser nature, but that in yielding he is exalted, is made aware of his superiority to the brute, and, partly in consequence of this yielding and awareness, becomes a creator.

V

THE argument intended to demonstrate that the opposing factors in art and aesthetic experience may be reconciled is best postponed for an examination of various alternative hypotheses which the history of aesthetic has offered. It is significant in this regard that one may interpret the quotation with which this Introduction begins in terms of Plato's own efforts to provide a satisfactory answer to the questions his philosophy of art raises. And it is significant, not alone because it argues the Athenian's interest in the philosophy of art and in the resolution of the antinomy implicit in his writings, but because many of the hypotheses put forward to account for the phenomena of art and its experience to which we shall now turn, are first suggested by Plato.

The fact that Plato did envisage various means by which art and aesthetic experience might again be accredited to an ideal republic or become part of the good life is of some importance. History has in most instances amplified his original suggestion, with the consequence that numerous inferences essential for the solution to the problem before us have been drawn in the traditional philosophies of art. Moreover, each relevant elaboration upon Plato's suggestion contributes to a needed clarification of problems arising from the central antinomy. Among the former are the creative aspects of art's production and the recreative aspects of aesthetic experience; the strenuous processes enforced upon the artist by the material of art, as well as the ostensibly contrasting freedom both in creation and in aesthetic experience that has strengthened the arguments that the aesthetic attitude is "play" or "imagination."

The immediately valuable consequence of Plato's own effort[14] to resolve the problems of aesthetic and of history's amplification of his attempted resolutions remains, however, precisely the opportunity afforded to examine alternative theories directed, in part, to the problem with which this book is primarily concerned. As such, they will be examined in the course of the present volume, and as such, the specific hypotheses in aesthetic will be analyzed and evaluated in terms of their more general classification, basic to Professor E. A. Singer, Jr.'s philosophy of Empirical Idealism, of ateleological and teleological theories. We shall turn in the next chapter to a brief statement of the significant differences between these types of philosophical explanation. This will be followed by a study of the principal specific formulations of each type of theory.

[14] Other than the Dialogues, in which he demonstrated the art he meant.

Book One

Ateleological Theories of Aesthetic

Chapter II

The Theory of Transcendental Ateleological Form

And the One above conception is inconceivable to all conceptions; and the Good above word is unutterable by word.

—Dionysius the Areopagite

IT WAS observed in the preceding chapter that in Plato's philosophy there are implicit significant antinomies of art and aesthetic experience as well as various explicit suggestions for their resolution. In the history of aesthetic many of these suggestions have been elaborated upon in specific philosophies of art which diverge as sharply as do the theories of art as play and as form.

Diverse as these historical philosophies of art may be, they are susceptible to classification in a book on the aesthetic of Empirical Idealism. The theories are either ateleological or teleological and it is possible to examine their cogency in terms of the differentiation implied, while we remain content to presuppose the systematic account of hypotheses and principles made explicit for Empirical Idealism by Professor Singer in his various writings.[1] The present essay is limited in its scope to an examination of aesthetic experience. As concerns that limited problem, it is sufficient at the outset to contrast ateleological and teleological theories in general terms as follows: Ateleologically defined philosophies of art put forward resolutions to the antinomies of art and its experience which are grounded on the assumption that selected objects or events are "absolutely beautiful,"

[1] Particularly in *Mind as Behavior*, as well as in the articles and books mentioned in the Bibliography at the end of the present volume.

without necessary reference to the purpose they may achieve or the end by which they may be defined. The resolutions offered by teleologically defined philosophies of art are grounded on the assumption that objects and events have aesthetic value because of the purpose or purposes they achieve or in terms of the end or ends that define the objects and events.[2]

It is with two most general types of ateleological theory in aesthetic that the present and the next two chapters are concerned.

II

IF TRAGEDY and comedy, the Phrygian and Lydian modes of music, painting, poetry, and sculpture that owes its significance to other arts, are flawed instruments, if they induce discontent or evoke irrational behavior and stir the passions in appeals the more perilous because the "form" of art is attractive, the ateleologist in aesthetic theory proposes an ostensibly simple solution to the difficulty. His theory is intended to influence men not yet—nor, indeed, ever—fully prepared to deny value to aesthetic experience. In a sense, his argument is analogous to that of the ascetic in morality. Both would sacrifice the pleasures of sense or passion for the higher values afforded in the life of reason. But the ateleologist, although he does ordinarily proffer for aesthetic experience a "rational" set of objects or events, is primarily intent by doing so to limit the aesthetic universe of discourse either to an "absolutely beautiful form" or to "absolutely beautiful forms" or to ground, as correlative to the forms, a universally valid judgment of taste. The ateleological argument implies that because tragedy and comedy are deceptive, they are means to knowledge and are "relative" to that end. Because various modes of music appeal to the passions, they similarly are instruments effective for arousing passion. If means and end, however, are not judged to be of primary significance, the ateleologist

[2] Specific theories which fall under each head will be examined in the first two parts of this book, in which sufficient additional explanation of the principles of defining will be given.

may resort to "pruning and pinching back the luxuriant growth" of all art. He is certainly not alone in adopting the "pruning" technique and, in so doing, in trusting that he may leave only objects or portions of objects the experience of which will not be susceptible to the metaphysician's, the theologian's, or the statesman's destructive criticism. Thus, by way of illustration, Plato in the *Republic* and the *Laws*, excludes all but decorative art, the strenuous modes of music, hymns and moral verses, and the dance and song of the Chorus. This, too, is the consequence of "pruning" to assure limitation, but it may be defended, if at all, on teleological grounds.[3] It is nonetheless true, however, that ateleological aesthetic tends to deny aesthetic value to the larger number of objects and events and that the severity of its method tends to place far lower in the scale of values those objects of art the beauty of which is not predicated by definition.

Ateleological aesthetics, considered as a whole, is a science of "absolute beauty." But as the specific formulations of the science are examined, it is evident that beauty, as the subject matter of that science, has been sought in two different but not always unrelated realms. In one tradition it is sought and discovered in a realm transcending art; in the other it inheres in natural objects and the products of art. In all likelihood, both traditions derive from Plato's Idea of beauty as it is presented in the myths of *Phaedrus* and the *Symposium*, and implied in *Hippias Major*.[4] The Idea in the Dialogues is given locus in a supra-sensuous realm among universals which admit of no irrationality, alteration, or deceptiveness. Its experience is described in terms of ecstasy. The second tradition has analogues in *Philebus* and *Hippias Major*, in which empirical beauties are described in terms intended to place them beyond the strictures of the critic.

[3] Cf. below, Book Two, Part I.

[4] Cf. *Symposium* 211, with *Hippias Major* 291 ff. Jowett does not consider *Hippias Major* to be the work of Plato. In this judgment, D. Tarrant, who edits the Dialogue (Cambridge, 1928), agrees. Tarrant concludes (*ibid.*, xvi-xvii) "that we have in the *Hippias Major* the work of a young student of the Academy in Plato's own time." It is interesting, however, that A. E. Taylor, John Burnet, and Constantin Ritter conclude that the work is Plato's. See particularly p. xi of Tarrant's edition.

In Plato's writings, the differences between the Idea of beauty and the "absolute" beauties described in *Philebus* and *Hippias Major* appear to arise largely in consequence of one of the central problems of the theory of Ideas: the relation between universal and particular, between class and individual, between being and becoming. In the philosophy of art, as we shall see, Plato appears, in contrast to some of his successors in the theory of beauty, to have been more intent upon explaining the beautiful objects of the empirical realm by means of the Idea than in separating universal and particular.

As the history of speculation upon beauty proceeds, however, the initial problem, the explanatory function of the universal, tends to be subordinated by individual philosophers as their interest turns either to the universal or to the particular. The interest in each case accords, ordinarily, with a divergence in metaphysical preferences. Those philosophers who ground an aesthetic in the *universalia ante rem* pursue the search for beauty primarily in a realm transcending art, and endeavor to discover the εἶδος whose essence is revealed variously by the Neo-Platonic "going forth and return," in the Augustinian subordination of reason to faith or by means of a theory of transcendentals in Thomistic philosophy. Those who ground an aesthetic in the theory of the existence of *universalia in re* pursue the search for the absolutely beautiful in the field of mathematics or, decrying and renouncing all mathematical objects and means, they may turn to a non-mathematical interpretation of objects and events in art and in nature. Triangles, flowing lines, the beauty of the human figure, and the delineation of flowers have to various ages suggested themselves as absolutely beautiful, and theorists have put them forward as the sole objects to which aesthetic analysis is relevant. As will be seen, it is the relation of the beauty in the empirical realm to the explanatory beauty in the transcendental realm that presents the initial problem. The precise nature of that relation has provided a subject for speculation for centuries. But the tendency toward complete separation of the two beauties proceeds until finally both realms and objects are driven apart.

There are other distinctions to be made between the first type of ateleological theory, in this essay called "transcendental," and the second, or the "formal." It is well to note at the outset that transcendental theory tends to describe the apprehension of beauty as an experience different in kind from the bifurcated experience of works of art and that it has been prone, likewise, to consider the former as a "communion" or experience of identification with the object. There is similarly an insistence among some proponents of formal ateleological aesthetics—although on this point there is less consistency in the tradition[5]—to assert that the experience of absolutely beautiful natural or artistic objects is different in kind from the bifurcated experience of relatively beautiful objects. In formal ateleological aesthetic, the supremely valuable experience of beauty is rarely described as a "communion" but rather is analyzed in terms of the "purity" of the pleasure evoked, the fact that it is "unmixed" with pain or passion or that it is not "pathological."

One additional implication concerning transcendental and formal ateleological theories should be anticipated. The strict limitation of objects which follows upon the application of ateleological method appears, at the outset, to be in sharp contrast to the amplification of the aesthetic universe of discourse consequent upon the transcendentalist's inclusion of the transcendent form of beauty. But the latter amplification is in fact specious and its most frequent consequence for aesthetic has been a stringent limitation of objects judged to have aesthetic value.

That these and similar distinctions may be drawn between transcendental and formal ateleologies is a fact of evident significance for the speculative philosopher of art. But the distinctions should not obscure the equally significant fact that both interpretations of ateleological theory pose a common problem. This is evident to the poet as his imagination overleaps metaphysical boundaries. When "sweet Spenser" sang

> That wondrous pattern wheresoe'r it be,
> Whether in earth laid up in secret store,
> Or else in heaven, that no man may it see

[5] See below, Chaps. III and IV.

he voiced faith in the existence and supreme value of beauty as such.[6] His words assume, as well, that the search, continued since Plato first apostrophized the εἶδος and insisted upon the discipline preliminary to its full experience, has been successful. We should do well to recognize, also, that it matters little whether that beauty be "in earth laid up"—"or else in heaven." The endeavor to define it is intended to provide the philosopher of art with a form whose absoluteness frees it from deviations in value. The deviations in judgment of other objects in aesthetic may be due to temporal or spatial change or to relativity of taste or of the beautiful object to what it symbolizes. Manifestly also, the absolute beauty is freed from the relativity implied in the means-end relation. And in this connection it should be said that some of the aesthetic theories judged in this essay to be ateleological are integral to teleologically definable philosophies. Their ground may indeed be teleological, but some defect in analysis of function or some misapprehension concerning the final cause may permit the concept of an absolutely beautiful form to assume an ateleological status.

To summarize this preliminary account, it may be said that both transcendental and formal ateleological theories in aesthetic postulate the being and supreme value of a form or forms beautiful without necessary reference to an end possibly subserved by that form. The object or objects called beautiful in each system *must* have a certain form and *may* have a certain purpose.[7] To the objects and events in the aesthetic universe of discourse is applicable the Platonic description of the Idea of beauty to which ateleologists have reverted throughout the ages: it "is not beautiful in part and in part ugly, nor is it such at such a time and other at another, nor in one respect beautiful and in another ugly."[8]

[6] Cf. *Republic* 592.

[7] Cf. E. A. Singer, Jr., *Mind as Behavior*, pp. 57-58.

[8] *Symposium* 211. The quotation raises a controversial issue concerning the use of the word "ateleological," since it is one of Plato's great contributions that he analyzed teleology and that he completed the ideal system with the genus, good, of which the Ideas appear to be species. The issue will be argued in the next chapter with reference to Plato's philosophy of beauty in *Philebus*. Plato's general view cannot be dismissed as merely "formal" in its aesthetic implications, as has at times been maintained. There are "formal" theories

III

TO KNOW the supreme beauty, which is neither mere name nor symbol but is rather an *ens realissimum*, the existence of which depends upon neither the purposes nor the apprehension of the perceiver and which is the source of whatever beauty is discernible in subordinate objects, is to apprehend ultimate truth free of the deception inherent in the experience of images. For the transcendentalist, it is also to achieve knowledge of truth by "communion" with the εἶδος. This aesthetic "communion," to which is ascribed supreme value as experience, implies that one loses oneself in the act of apprehension. It suggests, as well, that in the experience the knowing subject is unaffected by passions disturbing to the soul. Yet, while there is little hesitation among those who describe the experience to ascribe to it supreme value, for some the worth inheres precisely in the ecstasy, whereas for others it is due rather to the fact that one emerges from that state with "increased vitality [from which] there radiate[s] extraordinary energy, daring, power of conception and realization."[9]

In either case, as the experience is described one is left with little cause for surprise that Plato judged the pursuit of the "form" of beauty to be "of all inspirations the noblest and best." If the experience of tragedy is irrational and uncontrolled, if the feeling that comedy evokes is a mixture of pain and pleasure compounded in

---

which ascribe a unique function to beautiful objects, but Plato does not do this. His beautiful objects are not uniquely defined by the ends they achieve, inasmuch as other and non-aesthetic objects are likewise defined by reference to those ends. Moreover, beauty, as end, stands outside the relativism of the means-end relation and its experience occurs without deviation. The consequences are not essentially different from those occurring in the strictest Democritean theory of mechanism.

It is perhaps well, in addition, to forewarn the reader, as we turn to an examination of transcendental ateleological aesthetic, that our primary interest is in the "form" as a possible ground for an extreme limitation, in ateleological terms, of the aesthetic universe of discourse rather than in "form" as a description of the structure of art, a problem to be examined in Chap. VIII.

[9] H. Bergson, *The Two Sources of Morality and Religion*, p. 216. Translated by R. A. Audra, C. Brereton, and W. H. Carter. (By permission of Henry Holt and Company, publishers.)

the passion of envy, if the arts of painting and sculpture are deceptive, and the experience of the softer strains of music are so enervating as to appeal only to the effeminate nature of the auxiliary in the state, it is wiser to avoid "images" conducive to these unsatisfactory experiences and to seek beauty itself. Difficult though the pursuit may be, it leads, Plato maintains, to the process of "beholding apparitions innocent and simple and calm and happy as in a mystery; shining in a pure light. . . ."

To many who would subscribe to other aspects of Plato's philosophy, the suggestions made in *Phaedrus* and the *Symposium* derive too plainly from a largely unexamined assumption that mystical and aesthetic experiences are identical to permit unqualified acceptance. It is evident, also, that even for the mystic who discovers in Plato's philosophy the classical source for a theory of suprarational apprehension, there may be some hesitation in acquiescing to the possible consequence: one requisite for achieving the supremely valuable aesthetic experience is the sacrifice of values inherent in all other objects and events. This does not alone mean that the aspirant for the experience of beauty must undergo such sacrifices as are implicit in rigid pedagogical discipline. He must consent as well to the sacrifice of most objects of art which men have customarily cherished. Despite this, no age—classical, Greco-Roman, medieval, and modern—has lacked proponents of the theory, proponents not only content but indeed eager to turn from the products of exquisite craft and severe technique if only they are assured that the sacrifice will carry them further along the road to the apprehension of absolute beauty. Nor is this empty rhetoric. It describes, rather, the actual consequence of at least one specific tradition of ateleological aesthetic. In it, theorists relegate the fine artist to the status of mere craftsman. They either deny value to fine arts or account for the inferior value the work of fine art may have by referring to the "mystery" of "beauty." They assert that no necessary relation holds between art as technique and beauty as transcendental. Whether the value of the experience of supreme beauty suffices for these sacrifices remains a moot point.

With this brief anticipation of history in mind, it is doubly interesting that Plato, whose writings are the source of much that the history of the transcendental theory makes explicit, does not impose upon his own philosophy of art the limitation that history would suggest it requires. His philosophy, insofar as it does elaborate and define the great discovery of the theory of Ideas, at times drives the distinction between universal beauty and particular beautiful objects to the point that there is immanent a complete separation of beauty and art. But Plato's interest is not only to formulate the theory of Forms but to explain objects of opinion in the world of becoming by reference to the Ideas. The change in interest that affected the tradition in the philosophy of art which we shall examine is consequent on the Alexandrian superposition upon Platonic theory of the concept of a transcendent God. It is significant that Plato in his own writings, implies that the Idea of beauty bears a peculiar relation to particular beautiful objects. It is true that the apprehension of beauty presupposes an "ascent," described in the *Symposium*, not unlike that by which the philosopher approaches the good in the *Republic*. It is also true that Plato indicates that there is a science to be learned before we can achieve beauty.[10] The degree to which the final stage of the ascent is rational or mystical experience presents a problem less significant at the moment than that the object of the endeavor, the Form of beauty, is not alone substantival but is adjectival as well.[11] Beauty is beautiful and this is significant for our subsequent analysis of the history of ateleological aesthetic. Substantives other than beauty for Plato are adjectival as well. Wisdom is wise, as beauty is beautiful.[12] But it is im-

[10] *Symposium* 211C: "Beginning from obvious beauties he must for the sake of that highest beauty be ever climbing aloft, as on the rungs of a ladder, from one to two, and from two to all beautiful bodies; from personal beauty he proceeds to beautiful observances, from observances, to beautiful learning, and from learning at last to that particular study which is concerned with the beautiful itself and that alone; so that in the end he comes to know the very essence of beauty." (Reprinted from the translation by W. R. M. Lamb, *Loeb Classical Library*, Harvard University Press, Cambridge, 1925).

[11] *Phaedrus* 250D-E.

[12] See Theodore de Laguna, "Notes on the Theory of Ideas," particularly p. 452. See also next chapter, pp. 90 ff.

portant to note that Plato maintains that beauty alone, of all the Ideas, is seen on earth "shining through the clearest apertures of sense." It is plausible, in the light of the *Republic*, *Philebus* and *Timaeus*, to assume he meant that it is susceptible to mathematical demonstration.[13]

It would be an error to overlook that transcendental aspect of Plato's thought which did affect later theory and to ignore the admonition that "if beauty in general is his pursuit, how foolish would he be not to recognise that the beauty in every form is one and the same . . ." or to forget the praise of the form of beauty in the *Symposium*. It would be equally unwise, on the other hand, to overlook the implications of mathematical and rational demonstrability suggested in this philosophy in contradistinction to the inferences concerning supra-rational apprehension which do appear.[14]

Whatever Plato's conclusion, his writings provide his followers with the wedge to be driven between art and beauty. The initial gap widens as the significance of the correlative aspect in his philosophy of art, expressed in the *Symposium*, becomes basic to Neo-Platonic epistemology.[15] Plato implies that the final "rung" of the ladder of beauty is "not of a piece with" the other rungs. The "science of beauty," which has entailed a rational progression from particular instances to more universal and inclusive forms until in the final stage, the supreme form is reached, now is replaced by supra-rational experience, a "leap" beyond systematic science to union with the essence. It is the latter experience which has been described, in fact, as "vision" and "communion." For A. E. Taylor it means "having got beyond 'science' " into direct contact with "beauty."[16]

[13] See below, chap. III.

[14] The problem of Plato's employment of the myth should be considered at this point. See J. A. Stewart, *The Myths of Plato*, and P. Shorey, *What Plato Said*.

[15] See below, p. 40.

[16] A. E. Taylor, *Plato: the Man and His Work*, p. 230. See below, pp. 81-82.

IV

THE extent to which Plato's philosophy of beauty does culminate in mysticism presents a problem which needs concern us in this book less than it would otherwise, were the present undertaking a history of aesthetic. Transcendental ateleological aesthetic is the consequence not only of Plato's theory but of an accretion of problems and hypotheses in the Platonic tradition. Its full expression is affected by Plotinus, St. Augustine, and Dionysius the Areopagite, as well as by the author of the *Symposium* and *Phaedrus.* It is also the consequence of Neo-Thomistic philosophies of art of our own day and, in particular, of Jacques Maritain's *Art and Scholasticism.* Its problems are at once immanent in the initial bifurcation of works of art and "absolutely beautiful forms" which affected the Platonic tradition and in mysticism, that "getting beyond science" which has been characterized as the medieval solution to the "really unsolved conflict between the Platonic metaphysics and the Platonic religion."[17] The specific problems of concern to aestheticians in this tradition are the implied indefinability and uniqueness of the form of beauty, the incommunicability of its experience, the differentiation in kind between that experience and the experience of particular beautiful objects, and the analogous differentiation of beauty, the absolute value, from the defective or indeed negative value of art.

The conflict between metaphysics and religion, of which Taylor writes, left its discernible imprint upon the philosophies of Plotinus and St. Augustine. Their writings, as do Plato's, bear the imprint of minds at once trained for the subtleties of aesthetic speculation and sensitive to the value of art. Of necessity, the present treatment of their philosophies of art will be summary, because it is intended only to stress tendencies culminating in transcendentalism and ateleology. But summary as the treatment may be, it will be plain, as well, that the Platonism common to the two philosophies is a ground for apparently contrary inferences concerning aesthetic

[17] *Ibid.*, p. 232.

values in art. The convergences and the divergences of these philosophies are significant for later analysis. They may best be presented in a general statement concerning Plotinus' and St. Augustine's theories and a brief summary of their hypotheses in the aesthetic field.

The two philosophies of art diverge fundamentally because Plotinus is presenting a systematic account of Neo-Platonic philosophy, whereas St. Augustine is writing not only as a philosopher but as a theologian intent upon the problems of religion. In the philosophy of art, as such, the most obvious divergence between Plotinus' and St. Augustine's theories is the fact that the former is a non-mathematical, the latter a mathematical interpretation of beauty and art. "Can we doubt that beauty is something more than symmetry," asks the Neo-Platonic philosopher, "that symmetry itself owes its beauty to a remoter principle?"[18] But St. Augustine, following closely upon Plato's *Phaedrus*, holds that "reason, turning to the domain of sight, that is to the earth and sky, noticed in the world it is beauty that pleases the sight; in beauty, figures; in figures, measures; in measures, numbers."[19] As the two philosophies of art are examined more closely, however, it is evident that this divergence merits less attention than is due other aspects. It is less important than the fact that for both Plotinus and Augustine art is not of highest value and that its experience is principally worth while because from it one may turn to attain to knowledge of universal beauty. Moreover, it is less significant than the fact that Plotinus grounds his assertions concerning the non-mathematical character of art on .he contrast between matter and the One and thus introduces into the philosophy of art problems relating to the media and the technique with which the artist works. Similarly, in Augustine's writings, it is less significant than that difficulties arise as his philosophy of art interprets the form of beauty and that the difficulties are due to an ambiguity concerning predication. Perhaps the facts of most interest emerge in both systems with the identifica-

[18] Plotinus' *Enneads*, 1.6. Translated by Stephen Mackenna. (By permission of the Medici Society and Sir Ernest Debenham, Bt.)

[19] *De Ordine*, 2.

tion of the unified and the beautiful, and the consequent tendency to associate the work of art with diversity. Considerations of technique and medium affect the latter identification, as well as the assumption that beauty is the source of aesthetic value.

V

THE self-imposed frame of a non-mathematical interpretation of art still affords Plotinus ample scope within which to exercise an acute critical capacity. The Alexandrian's criticism is, it is true, only in rare instances purely aesthetic, but even when its connotations have decided moral implications the author's power is evident. The artistic and aesthetic implications of Plotinus' analysis of evil provide a case in point. "We are like people ignorant of painting," he writes, "who complain that the colours are not beautiful everywhere in the picture: but the Artist has laid on the appropriate tint to every spot. Or are we censuring a drama because the persons are not all heroes but include a servant and a rustic and some scurrilous clown; yet take away the low characters and the power of the drama is gone; these are part and parcel of it."[20]

In this criticism, the Neo-Platonic philosopher is plainly intent on the work of art, its internal factors and their interrelations. His attention is deflected but little by interest in a supra-sensible form of beauty, a fact of importance because complete reliance upon such a form as a basis for aesthetic evaluation would entail a denial of the contrast and diversity which, it is implied, are necessary for the work of art. The interest is nonetheless evident in perhaps Plotinus' best-known remark upon art: "Thus Phidias wrought the Zeus upon no model among things of sense but by apprehending what form Zeus must take if he chose to become manifest to sight."[21]

Illuminating as these and similar specific critical passages in the

[20] *Enneads*, III,2.11.

[21] *Ibid.*, V, 8. 1. It is interesting to note that Plotinus prefaces this by the suggestion that the arts "are holders of beauty and add where nature is lacking."

Enneads may be for our evaluation of Plotinus' critical capacities, the more significant implications of his philosophy of art are in fact evident only in the light of the Neo-Platonic theory of emanations from the One and of the correction proposed for what in that philosophy is regarded as an inadequacy in classical theory of knowledge. The former, the theory of emanations, is proposed to explain diversity, as well as the emergence and rationality of process in the universe. The return to the One is integral to the assumption that unity is a supreme value, an assumption that particularly affects Plotinus' philosophy of art. The procession from and the return to the One culminate in union with the One. The union actually remains beyond the powers of reason to effect or to explain. For Plotinus, rational thinking is implicated in a separation of knowing subject and known object, with consequent destruction of the unity characteristic of the One. This true unity may be restored, according to his theory, only by means of a supra-rational process, in the mystical and ecstatic union of knower and object known.[22]

It is in large part the mysticism and "other-worldliness" of Neo-Platonism that have made its contribution to art and to criticism

[22] The Plotinean suggestion for the solution to the problem may be stated fairly clearly by contrasting it to the Aristotelian. In the latter system's relation of particular to universal, species and genus are related by subsuming particulars under a more general principle, that more general principle under a still more general one, and by finally establishing the most general principle as the *summum genus,* to be subsumed under none. But Plotinus' conception of supra-rational "communion" affords grounds neither for rational definition of the One nor for the final subsumption to be integrally related to the preceding ones.

It may be well to note also that while our present treatment of the problem as beginning with Plotinus is justified because of the philosophical significance he accords to beauty and to art, a strong influence upon both Plotinus and St. Augustine was exerted by Philo Judaeus. Philo's fundamental conceptions are of a God who transcends reason and of a Logos that is at times an overflowing of God's power and at times an hypostatization. For Philo, since the locus of Ideas is the Logos, the transcendent God is known by supra-rational means. The Neo-Platonic One is similarly supra-rational and Nous, the first emanation, is similarly the locus of Ideas. St. Augustine, influenced by both Philo and Plotinus, vacillates between the conception of a transcendent God, a Philonic-Plotinean conception of Logos, and the God of the Scriptures. Moreover, for St. Augustine, reason is not truth but judges by means of truth. Aesthetic, in the philosophies we are about to examine, reflects some of the more important ways in which thinkers in the Middle Ages attempted to resolve the problem of the relation of reason to revelation.

significant for artists as divergent as Michelangelo and Spenser, Leone Ebreo and Shelley. These factors, too, have made of it an influential starting point for speculation in aesthetic. It is nonetheless true that the theory of beauty and art in Plotinus' writing is less radically affected by recourse to mysticism as a solution to the problem of knowledge than are some of the philosophies of art which Neo-Platonism in its turn influences. That Plotinean aesthetic avoids a complete cleavage of beauty from particular beautiful objects is due to the internal ordering of the philosophical system. The One, from which the emanations "flow," is beyond all categories and differentiations; but beauty, for Plotinus, is an idea or form, the locus of which is the first emanation from the One. Man knows beauty by means of Nous. This follows from Plotinus' assumption that the first emanation, Nous, is intelligence or spirit and is both intelligence and the intelligible world. Nous is, in fact, the locus of the Platonic forms and of individuals and, in consequence, is the locus of the form of beauty. It is from Nous that Psyche emanates, to account for the lowest grade of reality in the spiritual world and for the fashioner of the sensible world.

The consequence of the fact that beauty is a form or idea in Nous and is not predicated of the One beyond the categories is that the Plotinean philosophy is not driven to separate beauty from beautiful things. But their separation is immanent in Neo-Platonic thought, as we shall discover in discussing Plotinus' principal and relevant views. He argues that beauty is resident in the Ideal world and that in intelligible beauty the intelligible faculty considers the general characteristics of symmetry. The cause of emotions arising from beauty is neither figure, color, nor size but the "colourless invisible soul." The work of art is in that lower and material world which "we take to be the very last effect that has penetrated to its farthest reach," because something of the light of the Forming Idea has irradiated matter which "first lay in blank obscurity."[23] The "efficacy of the soul" holds the rationalizing power latently, molding it by the seminal Rational Principles "to the nature of the soul's own Real-Being."

[23] *Enneads*, IV,3.10.

Objects are beautiful in consequence of the forthgoing principle: "Whence shone forth the beauty of Helen, battle-sought; or of all those women like in loveliness to Aphrodite; or of Aphrodite herself . . . ?"[24] Their source is the Idea, "primal, immaterial, firmly a unity—Beauty." Plotinus holds that "there is in the Nature-Principle itself an Ideal archetype of the beauty that is found in material forms and, of that archetype again, the still more beautiful archetype in Soul, source of that in Nature."[25] External stimuli suggest this primal beauty. The musician, sensitive to forms and to the beauty conveyed by them, is drawn by form, rhythm, and design to things of sense.

The musician is "exceedingly quick to beauty" and answers immediately to the "outer stimulus," yet "he longs for measure and shapely pattern."[26] The dualism implicit in Plotinus' aesthetic begins, at this point, to make its presence evident:

> This natural tendency must be made the starting-point to such a man; he must be drawn by the tone, rhythm and design in things of sense: he must learn to distinguish the material forms from the Authentic-Existent which is the source of all these correspondences and of the entire reasoned scheme in the work of art: he must be led to the Beauty that manifests itself through these forms; he must be shown that what ravished him was no other than the Harmony of the Intellectual world and the Beauty in that sphere, not some one shape of beauty but the All-Beauty, the Absolute Beauty.

Plotinus tells us that this true beauty, once known, induces the artist to "disdain all that once seemed fair."[27] "This, indeed, is the mood of those who, having witnessed the manifestations of Gods or Supernals, can never again feel the old delight in the comeliness of material forms."

Here are anticipations of a dichotomy between absolute beauty and the "comeliness of material forms" which, in turn, leads to a limitation to be imposed upon aesthetic objects. The "disdain" of the artist for "all that once seemed fair" suggests their immanent

[24] *Ibid.*, V,8.2.
[25] *Ibid.*, V,8.3.
[26] *Ibid.*, I,3.1.
[27] *Ibid.*, I,6.7.

separation in what appears to be in Plotinus' writing a reiteration of Plato's condemnation of works of art that merely imitate reality. In this vein, he argues that the products of artistic technique are made by "earth-based" arts, inferior to the productive forms of the intelligible world which are free of earthly imperfection.

The imitative arts are, for Plotinus, "painting, sculpture, dancing, pantomimic gesturing."[28] Their inferiority is due to the fact that, being "on an earthly base, . . . they follow models found in sense, since they copy forms and movements and reproduce seen symmetries; *they cannot therefore be referred to that higher sphere except indirectly, through the Reason-Principle in humanity*."[29]

Yet the imitative arts *can* be referred to the higher sphere; and however much Plotinus may have been influenced by Plato's scorn of "images" twice removed from reality, Neo-Platonism concludes that the products of these arts ultimately owe their being to emanations from the real, i.e., they are "material forms." Because they are in that sense and to that degree "real," the charge of "imitation" carries little weight.[30] As arts they are nonetheless "inferior," but the conclusion follows upon other grounds. Logically these products are posterior to the Prior Unity which is their source. Moreover, they are implicated in "matter." It is the ambiguity of treatment accorded the latter term in Plotinus' philosophy that radically affects the evaluation of the "earth-beset" arts as well as their products.

Some of these tendencies in the *Enneads* are evident in the following passage:

[28] *Ibid.*, V,9.11.

[29] *Ibid.*, V,9.11 (italics mine). The remainder of the passage is of interest: "On the other hand, any skill which, beginning with observation of the symmetry of living things, grows to the symmetry of all life, will be a portion of the Power There which observes and meditates the symmetry reigning over all beings in the Intellectual Kosmos. Thus all music—since its thought is upon melody and rhythm—must be the earthly representation of the music there is in the rhythm of the Ideal Realm. The crafts such as building and carpentry which give us Matter in wrought forms, may be said, in that they draw on pattern, to take their principles from that realm and from the thinking There: but in that they bring these down into contact with the sense-order, they are not wholly in the Intellectual: they are founded in man."

[30] Cf. *ibid.*, V,8.1.

—Art is of later origin than soul; it is an imitator, producing dim and feeble copies—toys, things of no great worth—and it is dependent upon all sorts of mechanisms by which alone its images can be produced. The soul, on the contrary, is sovran over material things by might of Real-Being; their quality is determined by its lead, and those elementary things cannot stand against its will. On the later level, things are hindered one by the other, and thus often fall short of the characteristic shape at which their unextended Reason-Principle must be aiming; in that other world (under the soul but above the material) the entire shape (as well as the idea) comes from the soul, and all that is produced takes and keeps its appointed place in a unity, so that the engendered thing, without labor as without clash, becomes all that it should be. In that world the soul has elaborated its creation, the images of the gods, dwellings for men, each existing to some peculiar purpose.[31]

Here we discover not a mere tendency but a significant implication. The relevant inferences to be drawn from the Plotinian assertion that the Intelligible Principle is superior because it is logically prior may well be considered in turn as they relate to the specific arguments concerning, first, the priority of technique to the work of art and, secondly, the general argument that the Prior is the unified. The first argument begins with a consideration of "prime causes": "Every prime cause must be, within itself, more powerful than its effect can be—and so the art exhibited in the material work derives from an art yet higher."[32] As a conclusive aesthetic justification for the "superiority" of beauty to the work of art, the implied criterion is applied throughout Plotinus' writing, but perhaps nowhere more interestingly than in the assertion that ". . . the stone thus brought under the artist's hand to the beauty of form is beautiful not as stone . . . but in virtue of the form or idea introduced by the art."[33] The implications of this assertion are made sufficiently explicit because Plotinus also maintains that the form "is in the designer before ever it enters into the stone." The striking simile by which the point is illustrated has led many philosophers to accept the argument as if it were conclusive: the form imposed by the

[31] *Ibid.*, IV,3.10.
[32] *Ibid.*, V,8.1.
[33] *Loc. cit.*

art or technique is like the "seal" that can produce many impressions without diminution of its own effectiveness. But Plotinus' thesis is directed not so much to establish the need to evaluate art in terms of permanence as to support two suppositions, namely, that the beauty of the divine Intellect and of the Intellectual Cosmos is revealed to contemplation and that its revelation is due primarily to the fact that art or technique has value solely because of "form" and not in consequence of the medium of the work of art.

It may be argued, in fact and on empirical grounds, that Plotinus' contention is erroneous. He may assert its validity only because of the ambiguity in his use of the term "matter." It is evident that not any stone is "matter" for the beautiful statue.[34] Neither is the stone "mere" matter nor is it true that the "formal" qualities of the stone are "produced" by the designer in what "lay merely in black obscurity." The specific qualities of marble, granite, or basalt are potential in the stone and do not permit indiscriminate treatment of the media of art as "matter" to be worked upon. The individual and unique qualities of stone affect the texture and, consequently, the appearance of the complete work of art. To infer, as Plotinus appears to do, that the aesthetic qualities in the stone are consequent wholly upon the "form" and upon the "form" having been impressed on matter by a technique in itself prior and superior to the matter is to beg the question of the relevance of technique to artistic creation and aesthetic experience. The assertion that technique is superior to media or that the form is alone the aesthetic criterion in the making of the work of art can be made only if the artist

[34] The artist knows, if the theorist does not, that these qualities are not known a priori any more than a man would know, as Hume remarks, that a given stone will or will not split more easily in one direction rather than in another. The contrast between Plotinus' and the opposed view is clear if we consider, as an illustration of the latter, Sherwood Anderson's remark that he, as an artist, is concerned with "the story of a mind groping, in the end perhaps reaching expression in an art, of what then happens to the work of art itself, how it in its turn must grope, trying to find its own life." Theoretically, Plotinus' difficulty arises because "matter" is at times "non-existent" and at others only relatively so. In contrast, Aristotle regarded matter as the logical contrary to form; but, except in instances of logical abstraction or "privation," matter is always "informed."

knows fully the qualities and potentialities of the material before he begins to use the chisel.[35]

The failure of Plotinus' assertion to account for the empirical facts of artistic creation derives ultimately, however, from metaphysical and systematic difficulties and, in particular, from the ambiguity and inconsistency with which the term "matter" is used in Neo-Platonism. Both ambiguity and inconsistency are exaggerated as the philosopher comes to consider the work of art as the consequence of a "form" impressed upon a "matter." On the one hand, Plotinus argues that the beauty of the statue is due solely to the "form" or "idea" impressed by the art and the form is "in the designer before ever it enters into the stone."[36] This implies what Plotinus sometimes intends, that matter is unreal, non-existent, and beyond the irradiation from the One. But contrariwise, Plotinus argues as well that the material, i.e., the "stone brought under the artist's hand," is not "nothing."[37] It has its own potentialities and these the artist actualizes. No practicing artist underestimates the effect of the material on the form the artist proposes to impose upon it.[38] It is not "matter" as "nothing" that Plotinus describes as "resisting" the form but "matter" as the inferior and the derivative: ". . . that original beauty is not transferred; what comes over is a derivative and a minor: and even that shows itself upon the statue not integrally and with entire realisation of intention but only in so far as it has subdued the resistance of the material."[39]

However, it is well to note that the foregoing quotation begins with Plotinus' statement that "the artificer holds it [the form] not by his equipment of eyes and hands but by his participation in his art; . . . that original beauty is not transferred." As one seeks the ground for this statement, the specific problems of "matter" and of

[35] See below, Chap. XVIII.

[36] *Enneads*, V,8.1.

[37] Matter is actually subject to the Aristotelian categories. But it is also non-existent.

[38] Cf. Anthony Trollope, *An Autobiography*, the passage "in which Kate Woodward, thinking that she will die, tries to take leave of the lad she loves." Trollope remarks, "I had not the heart to kill her. I never could do that. And I do not doubt but that they are living happily together to this day."

[39] *Enneads*, V,8.1.

the making of the work of art must give way to a consideration of a metaphysical principle, the operation of which exaggerates Plotinus' already evident tendency to deprive the work of art of its value. For although, as was observed above, the knowledge of beauty is rational and not mystical for Plotinus, the trend of his thought moves away from the emanations and toward the supremely valuable One. The consequent hierarchies of value are evident in the philosophy of art and particularly so in the statement, "The beauty . . . exists in a far higher state in the art." This conclusion is maintained because the art is logically prior to its product and that which is the Prior is the *unified*; the Posterior is the *diverse*.[40] The supreme value of the One is then a criterion of value for the objects in the realm of the "many."

The aesthetic argument proceeds on the assumption that the Prior or the unified is "the unmingled Beauty of the divine world." Plotinus in fact asserts: "This then is Beauty primarily: it is entire and omnipresent as an entirety; and therefore in none of its parts or members lacking in beauty."[41] This is clearly a different criterion than that applied to art objects.[42] Moreover, one may scarcely forbear to point out that the Neo-Platonic assumption that the beautiful whole must be composed of beautiful parts is a curious retrogression to a view that Plato, a greater formalist than Plotinus, knew to be fallacious.[43] This is, however, not the fundamental issue.

[40] *Ibid.*, V,8.1. "Art, then, creating in the image of its own nature and content, and working by the Idea or Reason-Principle of the beautiful object it is to produce, must itself be beautiful in a far higher and purer degree since it is the seat and source of that beauty, indwelling in the art, which must naturally be more complete than any comeliness of the external. In the degree in which the beautiful is diffused by entering into matter, it is so much the weaker than that concentrated in unity; everything that reaches outwards is the less for it—and so beauty [is] less beautiful." Cf. Jacques Maritain, *Art et Scolastique*, p. 49 (*Art and Scholasticism*, p. 31, hereafter referred to as "E. T."): "God is beautiful. . . . He is beautiful by Himself and in Himself, absolutely beautiful. He is exceedingly beautiful (*superpulcher*), because there is pre-existent in a super-excellent way in the perfectly simple unity of His nature the fountain of all beauty." (By permission of Charles Scribner's Sons, publishers.)

[41] *Enneads*, V,8.8.

[42] See above, p. 39.

[43] Plato not infrequently forgets this principle of art expressed in the *Republic*.

The basic problem is to determine whether or not unity is adequate as a principle for limiting the aesthetic universe of discourse. To this issue we shall return in the next chapter.

Of more immediate significance for an understanding of the transcendental theory toward which Plotinus' arguments tend is the evaluation of technique and art made on the ground that the world soul is both intelligent and intelligible. Plotinus argues that art, the efficient cause of the work of art, is beautiful. Indeed, it is urged that absolute beauty is "the image" of art's own nature and content. However, the implication that the technique or craft or art by means of which works of art are produced is "beautiful" is ordinarily metaphorical and implies that an instrument works "beautifully," meaning that it achieves in a successful manner the end for which it is fitted. Here Plotinus implies that any impediment or obstruction may be attributed not to the instrument but to the resistance of matter. The cogency of the argument depends, again, on the interpretation to be put upon "matter." But to infer, as Plotinus does, that "art" as a technique is more "beautiful" than its products not only introduces into aesthetic theory the irrelevant problem of the order of artistic creation as a basis for evaluation but also confuses permanence with aesthetic value. "Technique" or "form" or both may be more permanent than the product that results from the artist working upon the medium, but permanence does not imply beauty in this sense; and to argue that form or technique is beautiful without reference to the matter each impresses is to make a false abstraction. There are minimal structural conditions[44] for objects of judgment in aesthetic, and Plotinus' hypothesis, at least in this reference, ignores them.

The difficulties inherent in Plotinus' philosophy of art arise principally, as we have observed, in consequence of the Neo-Platonist's ambiguous inferences concerning "matter" and, specifically, concerning its connotations for art. The philosophy does begin to come to grips with unity as an aesthetic criterion and with technique and its place in theory. In contrast, St. Augustine's philosophy of art—

[44] See below, Chaps. VIII and XVIII. See also Chaps. III and IV on the problem of form as structure.

like Plotinus', considerably influenced by Plato—appears in the history of transcendental ateleological aesthetic to raise issues that are due less to "matter" than to a systematic difficulty concerned with predication. Moreover, the mystical experience of beauty is more explicitly implicated in the philosophy of art, once the locus of the Platonic Ideas presents the issue encountered in Augustinian speculation.

St. Augustine, as a critic of art, is no less acute than Plotinus, whose philosophy influenced him.[45] But the Patristic, in contrast to the Neo-Platonic philosopher, is interested in the significance of mathematics for art. This is evident in the reminiscence of *Phaedrus* that pervades *De Ordine*, not alone in the statement of the hypothesis that "reason turns to the domain of sight," to a domain in which "it is beauty that pleases the sight, in beauty, figures; in measures, numbers,"[46] but also in the specific analysis of harmony in architecture:[47] "We cannot but be displeased because (in considering carefully the parts of this very building) we see one doorway towards the side and another situated almost, but not exactly, in the middle." While such disharmony "seems to inflict, as it were, a kind of injury upon one's gaze, . . . the fact that three windows inside, one in the middle and two at the sides, pour light at equal intervals on the bathing place . . . delights and enraptures us. . . . In our own terminology, architects themselves call this *design*; and they say that parts unsymmetrically placed, are without *design*."

The principle of *design* to which St. Augustine attributes our pleasure in architecture is "very general" and "pervades all the arts and creations of man." Thus, it is true that in *De Ordine* (Book I, Chapter 7) it is urged that "the beauty of all things is in a manner configured, as it were, from antitheses, that is, from opposites." In general, however, the predominant tendency of his analyses of art is toward a preference for homogeneity of the parts comprising the

[45] Cf. Portalié on St. Augustine, in Vacant and Mangenot's *Dictionnaire de Théologie Catholique*, Vol. 1, Col. 2327 ff.

[46] St. Augustine, *De Ordine*, 2, Chap. XIII.

[47] *Ibid.*, 2, Chap. XI, 34. The translation is by R. P. Russell, O.S.A., in *Divine Providence and the Problem of Evil.* (By permission of The Cosmopolitan Science and Art Service Company, publishers.)

work, a tendency perhaps most evident in the mention in *De Vera Religione* that the balance of equal arches "pleases because it is beautiful, and it is beautiful because the parts are alike and are brought by a certain bond to a single harmony." It is, however, in the resumption of the Platonic search for the most beautiful figure that the tendency most clearly influences theory. St. Augustine weighs the possibility that the circle rather than the triangle provides the solution to the problem, "Quæ figura præstantior."[48] The argument makes evident the claims of the circle to satisfy the conditions of the problem, "sed dic, quæso, quænam tibi figura melior videatur et pulchrior?"[49] Equality, the entire concordance of the circumference, the absence of angles and the equidistance of the center from the circumference—all, it will be noticed, functions of the figure's unity—are pressed into service for the argument. Augustine is impressed by the circle's indivisibility and by the value of this factor.[50] Finally, however, the point rather than the circle, it is argued, satisfies the conditions of the problem because the point is indivisible, unified, and conceptual.

Again, philosophy of art is offered aesthetic value in the form of unity, both in itself and as an implied principle for a limitation of the aesthetic universe of discourse. But in the discussions of beauty the circle and the point are presently significant because they evidence once again the tendency of transcendental theory to leave the sensuous realm in offering a solution to aesthetic problems. The preference for conceptual rather than sensible criteria for aesthetic evaluation merely introduces the significant dichotomy in theory between transcendental beauty and art which is evident once theological issues are raised. Augustine's careful consideration of the mathematical factors in the work of art ultimately assumes minor significance in his own writings, for while there are beautiful mundane objects which derive their beauty from God ("Nulla essent pulchra, nisi essent abs te"), there is as well a condemnation of art

[48] *De Quantitate Animae*, Chap. IX.

[49] *Ibid.*, Chap. VIII.

[50] *Ibid.*, Chap. XI, 18. "Hoc ergo quod jam te intelligere video, potentissimum omnium, quæ demonstrata sunt. Siquidem hoc est, quod nullam divisionem patiatur."

in consequence of the necessary subordination of human arts to those of the Creator. The beautiful is "temporal, carnal, and a lower kind of good." It may be inferred that this conclusion follows from the adherence to the view that unity gives aesthetic value—a view similar to that suggested by Plotinus but given a mathematical interpretation: the beautiful is implicated in variety through the employment of the number series.[51] One inference is obvious and this Augustine apparently draws:

> What numberless things, made by divers arts and manufactures, both in our apparel, shoes, vessels, and every kind of work, in pictures, too, and sundry images, and these going far beyond necessary and moderate use and holy signification, have men added for the enthrallment of the eyes; . . . following outwardly Him by whom they were made, forsaking inwardly Him by whom they were made . . . But I . . . do hence also sing a hymn unto Thee—because those beautiful patterns, which through the medium of men's souls are conveyed into their artistic hands, emanate from that Beauty which is above our souls, which my soul sigheth after day and night . . .— And I, . . . impede my course with such beauties. . . .[52]

There is, however, evident reluctance in making explicit the implications of complete other-worldliness. Indeed, justification for the analysis and experience of the world's and of art's beauties is found, despite the supreme value of beauty, in St. Augustine's saying that we should judge of each object according to its own nature. Everything has its measure, its form, and a certain harmony in itself.[53]

It should be noted, however, that the bifurcation of beauty and art is latent in Augustine's Platonism. It becomes explicit once the history of medieval speculation brings forth a clarification of what in Augustinean writings remains a dual interpretation of the nature of God. In contrast to Plotinus who, as we have observed, gives the Platonic Ideas locus in the first emanation, Nous, St. Augustine, in the words of Svoboda, has identified "l'Idée suprême de Platon

[51] Cf. *De Musica.*

[52] *Confessions,* Book X, Chap. XXXIV, 53. Cf., *De Div. Quaest.,* LXXXIII, and *De Civ. Dei,* Book XV, Chap. XXII. (The translation from *The Confessions* is by J. G. Pilkington in *The Nicene and Post-Nicene Fathers,* Vol. I.)

[53] *De Civ. Dei,* Book XII, Chap. 4. Cf. *De Vera Rel.,* 21: "in quantum est, quidquid est, bonum est."

avec Dieu."[54] It is no less significant that the Platonic Ideas are now given locus in the mind of God. Moreover, the divergent influences of the Old and New Testaments and of Plato's, Plotinus', and Aristotle's philosophies affect St. Augustine's system of thought to the extent that, while he holds that God is transcendent, beyond the Aristotelian categories and describable not as substance but as *essentia*, nevertheless God is the Creator of the world in time and space.[55] The difficulty which besets Augustine's philosophy of art is one of predication, i.e., whether predicates may be asserted of God and, if so, whether such predication is literally true.[56] The problem is crucial, for it is God in Whom the Ideas are and He is transcendent. Yet we are told that God is the absolute unity to which the finite aspires and as such "omnis pulchritudinis forma unitas est."[57]

Different as are the tendencies which incline the later interpretations of Plato's philosophy of art toward transcendentalism and ateleology, there impends in both Neo-Platonism and in Augustinean philosophy a devaluation of art and of its experience. The tendencies become actual trends in the tradition under consideration, once the implications of mysticism for philosophy are conclusively expressed in the writings of Dionysius the Areopagite. The latter in turn

[54] K. Svoboda, *L'Esthétique de Saint Augustine et ses Sources*, p. 199. Cf. A. E. Taylor, *op. cit.*, p. 232: ". . . the supreme reality which is apprehended in the culminating vision is never said in Plato to be God, but always the supreme 'form.' It is the *good* which is the Platonic or Socratic *ens realissimum.*"

[55] The consequences for aesthetic are apparent in *De Musica*. Simple sights and sounds are not primarily aesthetic, since they are in space and time. Moreover, sensuous perception is inferior to reason, the object of which is God. As regards numbers, personal taste does enter into our aesthetic preference, but the form of numbers is universal. Numbers provide the variety necessary in the form; unity is provided by God, Who is not in space and time.

[56] Cf. *De Trin.*, V. ii; *Confessions*, XI, 26 ff.

[57] *De Vera Rel.*, 21 ff.; *De Lib. Art.*, 2, 9, ff. Cf. Svoboda, *op. cit.*, pp. 11, 43, 51, 101-102, 109, 133, and, especially, 195-196: "A la longue, ses idées se spiritualisent, elles se débarrassent des éléments sensualistes, elles se tournent de la beauté sensible à la beauté intelligible et de l'artiste d'ici-bas à l'artiste-Créateur; c'est là une influence évidente du christianisme." See also p. 43: "L'idée suivante d'Augustin, que toutes les choses ici-bas ne sont belles que par l'imitation de la beauté suprême et qu'elles sont laides, comparées à elle, provient de la distinction de deux mondes." See also, p. 16: "La plus belle unité est l'unité suprême, le bien; le contraire en est la mal, la division."

affect the philosophy of St. Thomas Aquinas. The author of *Concerning Mystic Theology* and *Concerning Divine Names* holds both that God is beauty and that God transcends reason. No predication may be made concerning Him. The supreme aesthetic value is apprehended by means of mystical union. In the mystical theology, the theory of beauty has got, through theology, "beyond science and beyond reason to the truth of faith and of revelation."

Dionysius' statement of the transcendental and mystical argument presupposes Platonic grounds now familiar to us. But it is interesting to note, as well, the Philonic implications made explicit in this later view. The locus of Platonic Ideas is God, but God is above all reason. The Scriptures afford knowledge of Him. The names of God, derived from His beneficent and divine emanations, are not descriptive of His own nature. Rather, they describe corresponding qualities in us. God is, in fact, Nameless and the Many-named: "As pain does not grieve and joy does not rejoice, so the primitive life does not live and original light is not illumined." Cause is not similar to effect, although "effects assume as much as they can of cause and try to become similar to it." Thus comes to be interpreted[58] Plato's suggestion that Ideas or Universals are both substantival and adjectival.

For aesthetic, Dionysius' philosophy, built upon Platonic and Philonic foundations as well as theological theory, has twofold consequences of importance. There is, first, a sharply drawn dualism between beauty and the beautiful, following upon the interpretation of God as both Nameless and Many-named, and beauty becomes absolute and transcendental. As Idea, beauty is described in Platonic terms, but to ascribe beauty to God or to predicate it of Him is to ascribe a term to the Nameless. Beauty, as the beautiful, is the source of all beautiful objects.[59] Beauty and good and being are

[58] This is an anticipation of the argument of "analogous concepts." See below, pp. 73-74. For Plato's view, see above, pp. 35-36.

[59] *Concerning Divine Names*, Chap. III, Sec. 7, pp. 39-41 (translation by J. Parker): "This Good is celebrated by the sacred theologians, both as beautiful and as Beauty—and all the other Divine Names which beseem the beautifying and highly-favored comeliness. But the beautiful and Beauty are not to be divided, as regards the Cause which has embraced the whole in one. For, with regard to all created things, by dividing them into participations and par-

identical in the Areopagite's teaching. The "being-in-itself" is neither a divine nor an angelic substance which is the cause of all things. "Being in itself" means, in one sense, the one super-original and super-essential principle and cause of all things. But in another sense it signifies that there are providential powers issuing from God in Whom participation is impossible. It is in these providential powers that existing things participate and they are called beautiful for that reason.

The chief implications of this first consequence of Dionysius' argument will be indicated as we consider the ateleological aspects of the tradition as a whole.[60] The second consequence of his philosophy has an historical importance which it is of value to indicate at once. Because God is transcendental, both sense and intellect must be abandoned in apprehending Him. Only in an absolute ecstasy, by standing outside the self in all purity, "wilt thou be carried on high to the superessential ray of all darkness":

ticipants, we call beautiful that which participates in Beauty; but beauty, the participation of the beautifying Cause of all the beautiful things. But, the super-essential Beautiful is called Beauty, on account of the beauty communicated from Itself to all beautiful things, in a manner appropriate to each, and as Cause of the good harmony and brightness of all things which flashes like light to all the beautifying distributions of its fontal ray, and as calling (καλοῦν) all things to Itself (whence it is called Beauty)(κάλλος), and as collecting all in all to Itself. (And it is called) Beautiful, as (being) at once beautiful and super-beautiful, and always being under the same conditions and in the same manner beautiful, and neither coming into being nor perishing, neither waxing nor waning; neither in this beautiful, nor in that ugly nor at one time beautiful, and at another, not; nor in relation to one thing beautiful, and in relation to another ugly, nor here, and not there, as being beautiful to some, and not beautiful to others; but as Itself, in Itself, with Itself, uniform, always being beautiful, and as having beforehand in Itself pre-eminently the fontal beauty of everything beautiful. For, by the simplex and supernatural nature of all beautiful things, all beauty, and everything beautiful, pre-existed uniquely as to Cause. From this Beautiful (comes) being to all existing things,—that each is beautiful in its own proper order; and by reason of the Beautiful are the adaptations of all things, and friendships, and inter-communions, and by the Beautiful all things are made one, and the Beautiful is origin of all things, as a creating Cause, both by moving the whole and holding it together by the love of its own peculiar Beauty; and end of all things, and beloved, as final Cause (for all things exist for the sake of the Beautiful) and exemplary (Cause), because all things are determined according to It."

[60] Cf. below, pp. 64 ff.

—but thou, O dear Timothy, by thy persistent commerce with the mystic visions, leave behind both sensible perceptions and intellectual efforts, and all objects of sense and intelligence, and all things not being and being, and be raised aloft unknowingly to the union, as far as attainable, with Him Who is above every essence and knowledge. For by the resistless and absolute ecstasy in all purity, from thyself and all, thou wilt be carried on high, to the superessential ray of the Divine darkness, when thou hast cast away all, and become free of all.[61]

Upon this eloquent note we may conclude a necessarily cursory presentation of some of the hypotheses, arguments, and conclusions concerning art and beauty that contribute to a complex tradition in which a central doctrine is that of a transcendental and absolute beauty but which nevertheless presents the aesthetician with a serious problem as he searches for the culminating philosophy of art. The philosophical tradition receives its most profound expression in the writings of St. Thomas Aquinas. But, as Maritain remarks, "The Schoolmen composed no special treatise with the title 'Philosophy of Art.' "[62] The lack has been overcome in some degree by the fact that in recent years the materials relating to philosophy of art, scattered among St. Thomas' writings, have been gathered and interpreted.[63]

Maritain remarks also that, "A full and complete theory of Art could . . . be composed from the materials prepared by the Schoolmen, if they were collected and worked over again."[64] The French philosopher's book does not do this but it does attempt "to indicate a few of the main features of such a theory." Moreover, Maritain speculates upon matters related to these "main features." By reference to *Art et Scolastique*—despite divergence of opinion among Thomists with regard to interpretations of Thomistic principles concerning art and beauty—we should be able to appraise the value

[61] *Concerning Mystic Theology*, Chap. 1, Sec. 1.

[62] *Art and Scholasticism*, p. 1. Translated by J. F. Scanlan. (By permission of Charles Scribner's Sons, publishers. References are ordinarily made to both the French and English texts, the latter ordinarily being referred to as "E. T.") Cf. also, Immanuel Chapman, "The Perennial Theme of Beauty" and M. de Wulf, *History of Mediaeval Philosophy*, pp. 308-309.

[63] A selection of relevant writings will be found in the Bibliography.

[64] *Op. cit.*, p. 2.

of one articulated philosophy of art drawing upon some of the aspects of the earlier tradition the direction of which we have indicated.

An appraisal of this kind making extensive reference to Maritain's book, encounters the following principal issues: the value of introducing transcendental beauty into the aesthetic universe of discourse, as well as the validity of the limitation imposed upon that universe consequent upon its introduction; the adequacy of mysticism as a philosophical technique (once a dichotomy between art and beauty has been made), as providing a meaningful account of beauty and its experience; and the difficulties inherent in the identification of aesthetic and mystical experience, an identification intended in part to resolve the antinomy of art. A systematic difficulty is presented, as well: there is required a consideration of the adequacy or inadequacy of mysticism and of its terminology for the statement and solution of philosophical problems, aesthetic or otherwise.

VI

WE MAY begin by presenting in abbreviated form Maritain's statement and interpretation of St. Thomas' theory of art and beauty. The theory implies, as Maritain states it, that art is, above all, intellectual, an *habitus* of the practical intellect bound to the object to be made.[65] The intelligible world is the natural site of art, upon which two conditions are imposed: Relative to the end of the work, integrity, proportion and light are essential to the unity that is the "form of all beauty." The second condition laid upon art is that the artist work in a "sensible" medium. The apprehension of art is due primarily to the "maxime cognoscitivi," i.e., to the senses of sight and hearing.[66] The function of art is to produce

[65] *Op. cit.*, pp. 30-31 (E. T. p. 20): "The Man of Learning is an Intellectual demonstrating, the Artist is an Intellectual operating (qui opère), the Prudent Man is an intelligent Man of Will acting well."

[66] *Ibid.*, p. 36; cf. p. 40 (E. T., p. 24): "So also man can certainly enjoy purely intelligible beauty, but the beautiful which is *connatural* to man is that which comes to delight the mind through the senses and their intuition."

delight and love, stir the desire for the good, elevate the soul, and give joy in knowledge.

What then of beauty? Maritain's interpretation, as it is in turn interpreted by an expounder of his theory,[67] makes plain the grounds for a possible separation of beauty from art and for the argument that beauty is absolute. Specifically, Maritain attempts to maintain two basic and related points: In the first place, beauty is a transcendental.[68] Secondly, some art is fine art. For Maritain, the transcendental nature of beauty has significant implications and his characterization of beauty echoes the words of St. Augustine and Dionysius. Thus, the propositions, "God is beauty itself" and "God is beautiful," are reminiscent of the substantival-adjectival description of the Idea of beauty which we met in Plato's philosophy and which recurs in different terminology in the writings of St. Augus-

---

Cf. also, *ibid.*, p. 36 (E. T., p. 23): "The natural site of beauty is the intelligible world: thence it descends. But it also falls in a way within the grasp of the senses, since the senses in the case of man serve the mind and can themselves rejoice in knowing: 'the beautiful relates only to sight and hearing of all the senses, because these two are *maxime cognoscitivi.*'" (By permission of Charles Scribner's Sons, publishers.)

[67] Cf. V. Burdwood Evans, "A Scholastic Theory of Art," *Philosophy*, October, 1933, pp. 397 ff. (Italics my own): "If beauty is thus perceived, is it subjective or objective? . . . On the one hand, it is indeed subjective in the sense that without mind, beauty would not be; this much follows from the dependence of beauty upon intelligence. On the other hand, it is objective in the sense that it is real: so long as there is intelligence, human or divine, there is beauty, *even if we imagine the world of sensible things destroyed, and as a pure spirit only remaining*, for beauty has been defined as essentially intellectual." Cf. *ibid.*, p. 399: "Beauty is essentially the object of intelligence; but because human-intelligence is not intuitive, whereas beauty must be perceived, for a human being the awareness of beauty naturally and usually involves the senses, which are related to their objects directly or by an intuition. . . . This form is seized in and through the senses . . . the appreciation of beauty is the very opposite of grasping scientific truth."

[68] *Art et Scolastique*, pp. 47-48 (E. T., p. 30): "If this be so, it is because the beautiful belongs to the order of *transcendentals*—that is to say, of concepts which surpass all limits of kind or category and will not suffer themselves to be confined in any class, because they absorb everything and are to be found everywhere . . . [parce qu'ils imbibent tout et se retrouvent partout]." Not all Neo-Thomist philosophers agree that beauty is transcendental. Cf. Cardinal Mercier, *Metaphysique Générale*. On the general problem of transcendentals, see E. H. Gilson, *The Philosophy of St. Thomas Aquinas*, Chap. XVII, pp. 347 ff. The translation of *Art and Scholasticism* is by J. F. Scanlan. (By permission of Charles Scribner's Sons, publishers.)

tine and Dionysius. Maritain lays stress upon one aspect of the problem implicit in the Augustinean philosophy of art, the interpretation which makes of beauty a divine attribute.

We learn, however, that although God is beautiful, His beauty is distinguished from that of created things in that in it there is no alteration or increase.[69] Moreover, His beauty is neither relative nor particularized although from it the "essence of beauty shines on matter in an infinite variety of ways." Yet, although it is argued that from God all beauty is imparted[70] to beautiful objects, it is asserted that the artist's task is to produce a work of art. The artist is a craftsman whose technique does not necessarily produce a beautiful work of art and who does not produce beauty. Beauty produces beautiful objects but art (with the exception of fine art) is not necessarily implicated in its production.

It is evident, therefore, that the relation between beauty and art is not necessarily reciprocal. But the restriction placed upon the artist would not appear to be absolute because, as we shall see, it is the artist working in *sensibilia* who produces in every "making" a product in which the form shines "on the proportioned parts of matter" ["sur les parties proportionnées de la matière"].[71] Maritain characterizes the result as it is described in St. Thomas' philosophy: "Beauty for him begins to exist as soon as the radiation of any form over a suitably proportioned matter succeeds in pleasing the mind" ["Il y a beauté pour lui dès que le rayonnement d'une form quelconque sur une matière convenablement proportionnée vient faire le bien-être de l'intelligence. . . ."][72] In consequence, not even the reservation that created beauty is "in a manner relative,"[73] obscures the fact that by definition all "works" in sensuous media are to some degree beautiful, if only because they have "form," i.e., *unity*. As a matter of fact, all "making" must, by definition, be formal.[74]

[69] Cf. Plato on the Ideas, in *Symposium* and *Phaedrus*.

[70] *Op. cit.*, p. 44, (E. T., p. 28). Cf. St. Thomas, "*Ex divina pulchritudine esse omnium derivatur.*"

[71] *Op. cit.*, p. 38 (E. T., p. 25).

[72] *Ibid.*, p. 46 (E. T., p. 29).

[73] *Ibid.*, p. 47 (E. T., p. 29).

[74] *Ibid.*, pp. 11-12 (E. T., pp. 7-8): "The work of art has been pondered before being made, has been kneaded and prepared, formed, brooded over, and

It would appear, therefore, to be valid to infer that all works of art must be to a greater or less degree beautiful. Moreover, since it is the human mind that concentrates upon the unification and upon the formal element, one would suppose that, at least in this limited sense, it is the function of the artist to produce beauty. Indeed, one wonders how, in forming *sensibilia*, the artist can avoid doing so. Maritain argues, however, that "Manual dexterity . . . is no part of art, but merely a material and extrinsic condition; . . . art remains entirely by the side of the mind."[75] Moreover, presumably, the condition holds not only for the art as technique but for the work of art as its product. It is asserted, as well, that because the artist is in the world, "where he is condemned to wear himself out among bodies and live with minds,"[76] he must content himself with good workmanship. God is beauty. Plotinus and St. Augustine tend to turn from values in the realm of art for the supreme value in the transcendental realm. Maritain makes the tendency an explicit move: "And the Parthenon and Our Lady of Chartres, the Sixtine Chapel and the Mass in B Minor are also rubbish, destined to be burned on the Last Day. 'Created things have no savour.' "[77]

One discerns reasons for not insisting upon too literal an interpretation of Maritain's conclusion that there is no value in created objects. Thus, the aesthetician could interpret the conclusion perhaps on the grounds that its doctrinal implications are relevant not only to art but to all transitory things, that it reflects the tradition of other-worldliness in Christian religion, or, on the specific ground that Maritain obviously does not intend his words to be taken

matured in a mind before emerging into matter. And there it will always retain the colour and the savour of the spirit. Its *formal* element, what constitutes it of its kind and what makes it what it is, is its being controlled and directed by the mind . . . If this formal element is in the least degree lacking, the reality of the art becomes correspondingly dissipated. *The work to be done* is merely the matter of art, the form of it is *undeviating reason*. [Pour peu que diminue cet élément formel, pour autant se dissipe la réalité de l'art. *L'œuvre à faire* n'est que la matière de l'art, sa forme est la *droite raison*."] (English translation, by permission of Charles Scribner's Sons, publishers.)

[75] E. T., p. 13.

[76] *Op. cit.*, p. 56 (E. T., p. 35).

[77] *Op. cit.*, p. 59 (E. T., p. 36).

literally, since he immediately proceeds to write about art. Yet it is scarcely possible to underestimate the aesthetic implications of Maritain's assertions, that "created things have no savour" and that "the production of beauty belongs to God alone as His true property."[78] They exact a noticeable toll, particularly because it is difficult to entertain a theory that lays down as a condition of artistic making the impressing of a form on matter, the possibility of producing a beauty "connatural with man," and the need for a sensible and material existence for art, and then proceeds to deny to the artist the capacity to produce a beautiful as well as a workmanlike object.

It is no easier to entertain the consequences of the absolutism that comes to divide beauty and works of art, particularly in the light of the argument Maritain uses to make and to defend the dichotomy. The distinction between "purely intelligible beauty" which "man can certainly enjoy" and "the beautiful which is *connatural* to man," ostensibly rests upon an argument with theological implications, namely, that "the part played by the senses in the perception of beauty becomes in our case enormous and well-nigh indispensable, because our mind is not intuitive like the angelic mind."[79] But, if only because the general tenor of the book is philosophical, the reader has some grounds for assuming that an additional argument will be forthcoming to show that a necessary relation holds between beauty and *sensibilia.* And this assumption is more plausible because, as the essay proceeds, some of the objects produced by *art* belong to the realm of fine arts and do transcend the realm of mere "making." A more explicit argument would be the more welcome, also, because there appears to be nothing in Maritain's conclusion that "the beautiful *connatural* to man delights our mind through the senses" that adds, either to Plato's original inference that sight and hearing are the senses implicated in the experience of the beautiful, or to the more soundly argued conclusion of the system of thought (to which Maritain refers as "shoddy Hegelianism") which defines art, in part, in terms of sensuous

[78] *Op. cit.*, p. 57 (E. T., p. 35).
[79] *Ibid.*, E. T., p. 23.

media.[80] In other words, what one looks for and does not discover in Maritain's philosophy of art is a clear statement concerning an integral relation between the transcendental theory of beauty and the structural presuppositions of art.

The distinction between "intelligible beauty" and "the beautiful *connatural* to man" is the more significant because it suggests a systematic difficulty. Maritain's theory at this point is a formulation of the theory implied in Plato's writing that beauty is both substantival and adjectival.[81] It is to be interpreted in the light of a tradition to which, as we have observed, Plato, Plotinus, St. Augustine, and the Areopagite, among others, have contributed. For Maritain, God is both beauty and beautiful. In consequence, *Art and Scholasticism* is led to a serious impasse—if the reader expects to discover in it dependence alone upon "scientific" or "logical" argument concerning art. This is evident in Maritain's essay, "The Frontiers of Poetry."[82] As we have observed, St. Thomas' theory has been interpreted by Maritain to imply that art is primarily intellectual, an *habitus* of the practical intellect. Because, as we have likewise been told, the formal qualities of works of art are primarily intellectual, it would appear to follow that the more "formal" and "intellectual" the work of art, the closer would be its accord with beauty, or the more fully would beauty have been imparted to it. It would also seem plausible, since *art* is an *habitus,* to assume that its perfection as an aspect of practical intellect would be desirable. But if we accept at their full value arguments concerning "abstract art" in "The Frontiers of Poetry," it is evident that neither of these presumably plausible inferences is actually to be drawn.[83] It may be argued that "abstract art" is a contradiction in terms and that art, because it is in material, does not permit the abstraction of form

[80] See below, Chap. IV, pp. 164 ff.

[81] Cf. above, pp. 35-36.

[82] *Op. cit.*

[83] It must be remembered that this essay presents Maritain's own view and is not necessarily implicated in the preceding analysis of Thomistic theory of art. It does appear, nevertheless, to make explicit implications which Maritain has before taken to be basic to the Thomist arguments concerning art and to beauty.

from matter.[84] Indeed, Maritain suggests this argument in his analysis of the metaphysical reasons which have impelled "our generation to search for *abstract music*, *abstract painting*, *abstract drama*, *abstract poetry*." These attempts he describes as the "ordering of contemporary art *to exist* as abstract art, discarding every condition determining its existence in the human subject." It may be agreed, in passing, that no such complete abstraction as that against which Maritain inveighs is possible. It is not, however, the conclusion that is significant. The crucial issue emerges in the author's analysis once it is asserted that "abstraction" in art implies an encroachment by art upon the metaphysics, with consequences of which he writes as follows:

". . . To order contemporary art *to exist* as abstract art, discarding every condition determining its existence in the human subject, is to have it arrogate to itself the aseity of God [c'est vouloir usurper pour lui l'aséité de Dieu] . . . To particularise: the whole discussion resolves itself into this, that art is faced by an antinomy (it is not alone in such a situation) between the supreme postulates of *its essential being* considered in itself and transcendentally [entre les suprêmes postulations de l'*essence* prise in en soi et transcendentalement], and the *conditions of existence* demanded by this same being as it is realised on this earth [et les conditions d'*existence* appelées par cette même *essence* selon qu'elle est réalisée ici-bas].

"Where would the notion of 'abstract art,' driven to its furthest logical extremes, lead? To an art completely isolated from everything which was not its own peculiar rules of operation and the object to be created as such—in other words, separate and exempt from, and perfectly disinterested in regard to man and things [parfaitement désintéressé de l'homme et des choses]."[85]

This, it may be inferred, means that no aesthetic object is completely definable in terms of the end of knowledge, that end being implicated in the function of entities definable by logical or metaphysical sciences.[86] Or, to put it otherwise, the apparent intent of

[84] The problem is discussed in Chaps. III and IV of this book.

[85] *Op. cit.*, pp. 148-149 (E. T., pp. 90-91).

[86] *Ibid.* (E. T., p. 56). Cf. below, Chap. III. Maritain remarks that if knowledge were art's task, "it would be widely inferior to geometry." (By permission of Charles Scribner's Sons, publishers.)

the "abstractionist" is to make art a means to knowledge at the expense of the sensuous structure of art. But the passion behind Maritain's attack upon the "abstractionist" leads him, at this point, to lay less emphasis than is requisite upon the fact that art, on the presuppositions of his theory, belongs to the intellectual realm of activity and that the artist in his art produces "an idea *formative* of things."[87] It is true that the writer insists that this "idea" of making differs from the speculative concept. It is also true that he denies validity to the Aristotelian dictum that art imitates the universal. Art, on the contrary, symbolizes and in consequence does not give an "*exact reproduction or representation of a given reality*."[88] But that the artist is concerned with knowledge is nonetheless evident: we learn that art never stops at shapes and colors or at sounds and words "considered in themselves and *as things* . . . but considers them *also* as making known something other than themselves."

If, as is granted, the artist does concern himself with knowledge, however true it may or may not be that his primary task is with the structure of the work of art in its symbolical form,[89] it is not clear precisely why the "abstractionist" should be charged with "arrogating to himself the aseity of God." It may be true that he is attempting to perform a task better entrusted to the logician and the metaphysician, but it is also true that he is "making" and must "make" in a sensible medium, and that the object made is a "symbol" of something other than itself.[90] The artist is, in effect, committed in dealing both with objects of knowledge and with "structure" to a task to which every artist including the "abstractionist" is likewise committed. Insofar as the "abstractionist" is "making," he is an artist dealing with "structure." Insofar as he labors in the intellectual world, he does what all other artists do, i.e., he symbolizes.

However, the "aseity of God," with the arrogation of which the "abstractionist" is charged, is a metaphysical principle. It is implicated in the clarification of theological issues with which, rather than with aesthetic analysis, the transcendentalist is primarily concerned. The

[87] *Ibid.* (E. T., p. 89).
[88] *Ibid.* (E. T., pp. 56-57).
[89] Cf. below, Chap. X.
[90] See below, Chap. VIII.

limits in terms of logical analysis to which Maritain's actual aesthetic theory—in contrast to the theological—are susceptible become evident once we return to his inference that God is both beauty and beautiful. And this we may do, bearing in mind the strictures that Maritain himself lays down for art. The artist is charged with "arrogating to himself the aseity of God" in "transcending" art and in attempting to solve metaphysical problems. It is, however, the metaphysician who has laid down the condition that the existence of art, in contrast to its essence, is implicated in *sensibilia.* Moreover, some art is fine art, is beautiful, and transcends mere craftsmanship. But if God is both beauty and beautiful, the predication of "beautiful" to Him is clearly not identical with the predication of that term to fine art, since Maritain has argued that His beauty is in a "pure" and "infinite" state and that it is not "like the beauty of things, which have a particularized beauty." Furthermore, God is "absolutely beautiful" and beauty is "essentially the object of intelligence." Whatever may be implied in addition, the propositions that "God is beauty" and "God is beautiful" are not intended to assert that God's beauty is conditioned by *sensibilia.* It would appear, in consequence, to be less "arrogant" for the artist to work to reveal the knowledge—since his art is symbolical and is implicated in knowledge[91]—than it is for the metaphysician both to permit in aesthetic discourse a dual meaning to persist for the word "beautiful," and to introduce an objectively real beauty, the meaning of which transcends our rational understanding, as the entity transcends all conditions of "making." It is important, moreover, to consider the implications of the metaphysician's rather than the artist's "arrogance," once it is evident that the application of the metaphysical principle actually introduces into art an antinomy, . . . "une antinomie pour l'art . . . entre les suprêmes postulations de *l'essence* prise en soi et transcendantalement, et les *conditions d'existence* appelées par cette même essence selon qu'elle est réalisée ici-bas."[92] The antinomy, it will be noted, holds only if "l'art pur"

[91] The larger issue of the function of non-aesthetic factors in the work of art will be considered in Book Two.

[92] *Op. cit.*, p. 148 (E. T., p. 91). See above, p. 62, where reference is made to the English text.

be taken literally to mean "un art parfaitement isolé de tout ce qui n'est pas ses propres règles d'opération . . . exempté, parfaitement désintéressé de l'homme et des choses. . . ."[93] If "pure art" is antinomic, so, likewise, is the conception of God as beauty and beautiful, as substantive and adjective, if the latter terms are predicated *univoce* of specified objects, made and evaluated as objects of fine arts.

It is at this point in Maritain's philosophy of art that the presumably insuperable barrier between art and beauty is imposed. This becomes an actual barrier once the implications of transcendental ateleological aesthetic are made explicit. Beauty, "abstracted" from art, is neither a goal to be attained nor to be approximated by the artist as he devotes his mind and craft to the task of imparting ideas to matter. It may be argued, indeed, that beauty is without significance for art because it is neither the ground for the latter's sensible condition nor is it properly explanatory of art's function. Regarding the latter issue, it is sufficient to remark that, for Maritain, beauty ostensibly performs functions too numerous to be of unique or precise significance for Aesthetic, particularly because "it is *being* itself considered from one aspect" and because "each kind of being *is* in its own way, is *good* in its own way, is *beautiful* in its own way."[94] Thus no ground is provided for adequate definition within a teleological system of the unique function of art. Moreover, the plurality of beauty's functions permits subordination of a possibly autonomous Aesthetic to a religious or metaphysical[95] universe of discourse.

One may, in fact, question the value of the inclusion of absolute and transcendental beauty in an aesthetic theory.[96] It has been ob-

[93] *Ibid.*, pp. 148-149. The issue is not whether or not works of art are in sensible media but whether any work of art by definition is "pure," i.e., not in *sensibilia*. There are degrees of sensuousness but Maritain appears to imply a difference in kind in "abstract" art.

[94] *Op. cit.*, (E. T., p. 30). Some of the reasons for this statement are suggested in the present chapter, pp. 72 and 75 ff.

[95] See below, pp. 75 ff.

[96] But to deny the value of this specific interpretation of the universal does not necessarily imply that there is no universal beauty. The latter need not be an object. It may be a process. See below, Chap. XIX.

served that the transcendental interpretation and its inclusion in the philosophy of art degrades the value of art. Moreover, as regards a similar underevaluation of technical skill, the consequent situation for artistic analysis recalls Hegel's remark upon the abstract idea of perfect duty, "Because the universal ought to be carried out, nothing good is done." Since it is assumed that there exists an absolutely beautiful beauty, it is made to appear that the artist can produce little that has value as beautiful.

It is profitable in consequence of these difficulties, to inquire further concerning the distinction made by Maritain between art's "postulates of its essential being" and the "conditions of its existence." In explanation, we are told only that art must accept and master the conditions laid upon it by *sensibilia*.[97] But, it may be asked, to what end? Not to the end of beauty, for the realm of beauty is ostensibly closed forever to the artist, inasmuch as it is beyond *sensibilia*, the condition for art's existence. The difficulty is implicit in the assumption that the universal beauty differs from the beautiful not in degree but in kind.[98] This was implicit in Plotinus' theory of emanations and in Dionysius' conception of ascending and descending entities. In Maritain's philosophy of art, it is made explicit and is reflected, in part, in the mysticism attendant upon the experience of beauty, a mysticism in contrast to the specific and definite emotions of joy and delight experienced in the apprehension of beautiful objects. This statement of transcendental ateleological theory discovers, as we have observed, that beauty is beyond rational or intellectual approach by the artist. If this is the conclusion of history, if beauty performs no specific and unique function for art, if art is forever doomed to be "worse than rubbish" in contrast to

[97] *Ibid.*, p. 151, (E. T., p. 93): "Such is the profound conflict which art cannot escape. The solution is no doubt clear to the philosopher. Art must acquire that ideal independence, the desire for which is engraved upon its nature, in regard to the material obligations involved in its conditions of existence; it must turn these obligations to account, master them, show itself strong enough to shoulder them without stooping; it must not refuse them —that would be an admission of weakness." (By permission of Charles Scribner's Sons, publishers.)

[98] Some art, i.e., fine art, is, for Maritain, beautiful. The problems involved in its transcendence of the realm of craft will be examined below, pp. 67 ff.

the "eternal archetype," it appears also to follow that aesthetic includes art merely to satisfy intellectual curiosity or for the purpose of directing perception to a contemplation of the eternal verities. The analysis and evaluation of particular works of art become acts of supererogation.

That this is, in fact, not actually the conclusion to which transcendental aesthetic arrives is evident. Maritain's philosophy does discuss works of art and, more significantly, works of fine art. The latter are contrasted to the products of "making," it is true, because art, as has been insisted, is a *habitus* of the practical intellect. "Art in general tends to make a work," writes Maritain, "but certain arts tend to make a work of *beauty* and thereby differ essentially from all the rest."[99] In consequence, it would appear that access to beauty is not forever to be denied the artist nor is the derogation of art, hitherto implied in the argument, intended to be conclusive.

Because the inference concerning the aesthetic value of some art appears to run counter to Maritain's theory concerning art in terms of craftsmanship, and because it also ostensibly runs counter to the assertion that the artist is "doomed" to work in *sensibilia*,[100] it is obviously important to determine the ground for the distinction between "fine art" and "art" as mere "making." The inference that fine arts tend to produce beauty[101] is evidently grounded on the assumption that they enter upon the realm of transcendentals. "Their contact with being and transcendentals creates for them . . . a quite

[99] *Op. cit.*, E. T., p. 33.

[100] *Op. cit.*, pp. 32-33 (E. T., pp. 19-20).

[101] *Ibid.*, pp. 53-54 ff. (E. T., p. 33): "Art in general tends to make a work. But certain arts tend to make a work of *beauty* and thereby differ essentially from all the rest [tendent à faire une œuvre *belle*, et par là ils diffèrent essentiellement de tous les autres]. The work which involves the labour of all the other arts is itself ordered to the service of man and is therefore a mere means: it is completely enclosed in a definite material *genus* or kind [elle est tout entière enfermée dans un genre matériel déterminé]. The work which involves the labour of the Fine Arts is ordered to beauty: in so far as it is beautiful it is an end, an absolute, self-sufficient; and if, as work to be done, it is material and enclosed in a kind, as beautiful it belongs to the realm of the spirit and dives deep into the transcendence and the infinity of being [et si en tant qu'œuvre à faire elle est matérielle et enfermée dans une genre, en tant que belle elle appartient au règne de l'esprit, et plonge dans la transcendance et dans l'infinité de l'être]." (By permission of Charles Scribner's Sons, publishers.)

peculiar condition," we are informed; the activity is primarily "contemplative." Although fine arts are ordered to beauty, "the work as such, realized in matter, is in a certain kind, *in aliquo genere*: and it is impossible for a kind to exhaust a transcendental."[102]

But the significant issue is not whether works of fine art exhaust a transcendental but in what manner they enter upon its realm. Maritain maintains that the work of fine art, "insofar as it is beautiful . . . is an end, an absolute, self-sufficient." It is thus, as an end, contrasted to the product of art in general which is a means. Nor is the solution to the problem made easier by the fact that Maritain likewise holds that the work, "as work to be done is material and enclosed in a kind" while yet, as "beautiful," "it belongs to the realm of spirit and dives deep into the transcendence and infinity of being."

But the issue is immeasurably complicated if one recalls, in this connection, the fact that the artist has been condemned for attempting to produce "abstract" or "pure" art on the ground that such art transcends *sensibilia.* The work of fine art "dives deep into the transcendence and the infinity of being," but yet, presumably, remains material. The solution suggested by Maritain for this difficulty requires some consideration of symbolism. Although the artist is to be deterred from producing "abstractions," he presumably does make "symbols."[103] Precisely why a work of fine art is a symbol and not an imitation is difficult to explain.[104] The trend of Maritain's thinking on this subject should be evident, however, from the following passage:

What is required is not that the representation shall conform exactly to a given reality, but that through the material elements of the beauty of the work there shall be transmitted, sovereign and entire, the brilliance of a form [la clarté d'une forme]—of a form, and therefore of *some truth*; in that sense the great phrase of the Platonists, *splendor veri*, abides for ever. But if the joy produced by a work of beauty proceeds from *some truth*, it does not proceed

[102] *Ibid.*, (E. T., pp. 45-46).

[103] Cf. Eric Gill, *Art Nonsense*, p. 147: "So of a beautiful thing we may say that it has Truth for it conforms to its archetype in the mind of God."

[104] Cf. *Art et Scholastique*, p. 91 (E. T., pp. 56-57).

from the truth of *imitation as a reproduction of things*, it proceeds from the perfection with which the work expresses or manifests form, in the metaphysical sense of the word, . . . it proceeds from the truth *of imitation as manifestation of a form.* There is the *formal element* of imitation in art, the expression or manifestation, in a suitably proportioned work, of some secret principle of intelligibility shining forth [l'expression ou la manifestation, dans une œuvre convenablement proportionnée, de quelque principe secret d'intelligibilité qui resplendit]. There the *joy of imitation* in art is brought to bear. And it is that which gives art its *universal* value.[105]

There are manifest difficulties in establishing the soundness of this conclusion, nor is the argument offered in its support in *Art and Scholasticism* especially convincing: "And the things made present to the soul by the sensible symbols of art . . . are themselves merely a material element of the beauty of the work, just like the symbols in question; they are the *remote matter*, so to speak, at the disposal of the artist, on which he must make the brilliance of a form, the light of being, shine."[106] Maritain adds that, "to set up the perfection of imitation materially considered as an end would therefore involve ordering oneself with a view to what is purely material in the work of art; a servile imitation absolutely foreign to art."[107] Once we discern the meaning of these conditions, we may be forgiven a desire for specific details concerning the manner in which works of fine art are, in fact, produced. For if the artist is able to produce them it can presumably be only by denying art's "condition of existence," i.e., the material conditions, and by affirming those of its "essential being."

It is clearly implied that there *is* some method at the disposal of the artist by means of which fine art transcends *sensibilia*. It makes little difference, however, whether the transcendence is achieved by "abstraction" or by "contemplation." In either case, and *ex hypothesi*, the realm of matter must be abandoned.[108] If works of "fine

[105] *Ibid.*, pp. 95-97 (E. T., pp. 59 ff.). (By permission of Charles Scribner's Sons, publishers.)

[106] *Ibid.*, E. T., pp. 58-59.

[107] *Ibid.*, p. 59.

[108] If it is maintained that "abstract" or "pure" art is "wildly inferior" to geometry, so too is fine art "wildly inferior" to metaphysics. What must be meant is that the artist who creates a work of fine art does not intend to be a

art" are symbolizations of the truth and because of this they transcend their material conditions, so too, do the "abstract drama" and the "abstract music," which symbolize, let us say, the truth of mathematics. Insofar as any art is sensible, it incompletely reveals the truth and insofar as it transcends its sensible condition it denies the essential conditions of its existence. And if it does not transcend the *sensibilia* and is beautiful, this is explicable only on the grounds of "mystery," "grace," "faith," or "chance."

There remains, therefore, a critical ambiguity in Maritain's philosophical analysis of the production of works of fine art. There is a curious intermingling of theories which hold, on the one hand that the work should be controlled "*by the artistic habit*" and that "everything is beautiful as everything is good, at least in a certain relation,"[109] with conclusions which follow such as assumption, and, on the other hand, that grace is of primary importance for the artist. The Christian artist is, in fact, warned: "Do not *separate* your art from your faith. But leave *distinct* what is distinct."[110] Some lines further along in the essay, however, it is urged that the soul of the artist should control his work only by the "*artistic habit.*" But "it [art] will be Christian, it will reveal in its beauty the interior reflection of the brilliance of grace, only on condition that it overflows from a heart possessed by grace." There is liberality displayed in the interpretation of the phrase, "Christian Art": Maritain writes that "wherever art, Egyptian, Greek or Chinese, has attained a certain degree of grandeur and purity, it is already Christian, Christian in hope, because every spiritual splendour is a promise and a symbol of the divine harmonies of the Gospel."[111] But the liberality does tend to obscure the analysis insofar as the latter is concerned with a strictly technical issue. The first alternative, that "everything is

metaphysician but by grace or unexplained genius is able to cause what is essentially sensuous to transcend the sensuous and enter upon the realm of beauty. Maritain does argue (Cf. p. 67 above) that art conflicts with "the narrowness of the work to be done" and that "the work as such, realized in matter, is in a certain kind . . . and it is impossible for a kind to exhaust a transcendental," i.e., to exhaust beauty.

[109] *Ibid.*, E.T., p. 30.
[110] *Ibid.*, (E.T., p. 70).
[111] *Ibid.*, (E.T., p. 69).

beautiful" within certain relations, breaks down the barrier between "abstract art" or even technical art and "fine art," and negates the distinction between art and beauty. The second alternative, that the artist should not propose to reveal beauty but that, if he is granted grace or if he has "Faith,"[112] he is enabled to make a work of fine art, takes too little account of the discipline required by art. Moreover, it does not do full justice to the artist as a craftsman or as a maker of objects, since it implies that objects or events made by craft require as well the occurrence of a miracle in order that they may transcend the condition of their sensible existence.

In the autonomous realm of art, artists in fact do make objects of fine art. By means of their craft, artists are able to produce objects at once profoundly moving as well as aesthetically and non-aesthetically meaningful. Technical mastery of tools, knowledge of the potentialities of material, effective use of symbols in order to communicate meanings, these are ingredients in artistic creation of the work of fine art. Maritain's philosophy of art, it is true, is not in fundamental disagreement with these statements. It is nonetheless a fact, contrary to his view, that artists do propose to make and do succeed in making works of fine art. These objects and events are not merely well constructed. But if and when the artist fails to produce a work of fine art, it is not because he has proposed to make a beautiful object. To argue, as Maritain does, that artists succeed in producing beauty by "revealing God's truth, but without *doing it on purpose*" is not only to ignore the need to discriminate a unique function by which to define fine art, but is also to confuse aesthetic and theology by giving the former a significance only as means in terms of the latter as an end.[113]

[112] See *ibid.*, (E.T., pp. 66-67).

[113] Maritain does offer an analysis that, in part, avoids this difficulty. "The conclusion is that in the case of the painter, the poet and the musician, the virtue of art, which resides in the intellect, must not only overflow into the sensitive faculties and the imagination, but also requires the artist's whole appetitive faculty, his passions and his will, to be rectified in relation to the end of his art." But the author argues, in the same paragraph—*Op. cit.*, (E.T., p. 48) —that this "rectification" and "exaltation" of desire and emotion in the artist must be "in the line of beauty, whose transcendence and immateriality are superhuman."

VII

It SHOULD be evident by now, however, that any further effort to discover—in this version of transcendental ateleological aesthetic—a solution for these problems solely in terms of philosophy of art or, in particular, to ground the distinction between art and fine art in philosophical terms alone, should best be abandoned. It is a philosophical issue of importance to consider the validity of such assertions as, "beauty is beautiful," "God is beauty," and "God is beautiful." As de Laguna suggests,[114] an acceptance of statements of this kind encounters the paradox of the "third man." Moreover, if it is urged that, to avoid the paradox, there must be a ground for the means-end relation in an end that is not in its turn a means, another formidable issue emerges.

It is not, therefore, because the issues raised are philosophically insignificant that, in the present instance, it appears wiser not to examine their implications more closely. Rather, the course is adopted because it is plain that neither the propositional statement of these problems nor a strictly philosophical analysis of their implications is the primary interest of either Maritain or of at least some of his predecessors in this tradition. In postulating an absolutely beautiful form of beauty that transcends art, and in accepting a description of an experience that similarly transcends non-aesthetic perception and understanding of art, it is clear that the theorists under consideration do not place sole reliance in their arguments upon the efficacy of either reason or logic.

To attempt to discover a wholly consistent system of aesthetic in these writings is to ignore—as has been done intentionally in this essay up to this point—the numerous signs indicating that the theory is grounded in other than philosophical presuppositions. Because there are quite other grounds, the conclusions that have been reached—that the introduction of transcendental beauty both degrades art and sets up a barrier between art and beauty insurmountable by logical argument alone; that there is a difference in the pred-

[114] *Op. cit.*, p. 452.

ication of beauty of God or to fine art and to art; that beauty has been considered as a transcendental rather than as a limiting conception; that symbolism, no less than imitation, concerns knowledge—these conclusions would scarcely impress the theorist who works with this tradition of transcendentalism.

That this is true is evident once we retrace the steps by which these conclusions were reached. The truth of imitation is the manifestation of "some secret principle of intelligibility shining forth."[115] "The human artist or poet whose mind is not, like the Divine Mind, the cause of things, cannot draw this form complete out of his creative spirit."[116] As the Areopagite urged that effects do not resemble their causes, so we learn from Maritain's writings that the beautiful belongs to the order of transcendentals and is, like other transcendentals, "essentially *analogous*."[117] "Analogous concepts," it is maintained, "are properly predicable only of God." The "beauty" predicated of God is predicable in a "pure and infinite" state and is unlike "the beauty of things, which have all a particularized beauty."[118]

It was remarked, at the beginning of this chapter, that the transcendental theory of ateleological beauty is not only a metaphysic of beauty but that it states an epistemological problem as well. Maritain remarks that "there is a real inspiration . . . whereby the first Mind gives the artist, when it pleases, a creative impulse transcending the limits of reason."[119] In this connection, he has maintained,[120] moreover, that "the perception of the beautiful is . . . not so much a kind of knowledge as a kind of delight." The beautiful "produces love" and this in turn "produces ecstasy, that is to say, makes the lover beside himself: an ec-stasy of which the soul experiences a lesser form when it is gripped by the beauty of a work of art, and the fullness when it is absorbed, like dew, by the beauty of God."

[115] Maritain, *op. cit.*, E.T., p. 60.
[116] *Ibid.*, p. 62.
[117] *Ibid.*, p. 30.
[118] *Ibid.*, p. 31.
[119] *Ibid.*, p. 69.
[120] *Ibid.*, pp. 26-27.

It is evident, from these and similar statements, that transcendental beauty is not only an "analogus concept" but that its apprehension is judged to be supra-rational. The suggestion of mystical union with the One, seized upon by Plotinus to break down the distinction between the knower and the object of knowledge in "the greater vision,"[121] a suggestion brought to the realm of beauty by Dionysius,[122] has been made integral to principles of the later philosophy of art. At this juncture, it is helpful to recall details of the earlier historical background of this philosophy. Discernible in its mysticism are reminiscences of the "circular movement of the soul," described in the Areopagite's words[123] as the state of "having become single, uniting with the uniquely unified powers, and thus conducting to the Beautiful and Good, which is above all things being, and One and the Same." It is thus that one experiences ecstasy, one characteristic of which is[124] the closing of "all perceptions of knowledge." He to whom "surpassing beauty"[125] is revealed, "enters into the altogether impalpable and unseen" and is thus,[126] "by inactivity of all knowledge, united in his better part to the altogether Unknown, and by knowing nothing, knowing above mind."

Correlative to the assumption of the transcendence of beauty, therefore, is the supra-rational "knowing above mind." Not all religions maintain that ultimate knowledge is consequent—to the degree that it is attainable by men—upon mystical experience. Nevertheless, religious belief constantly faces the issue whether or not the tenets of faith are susceptible of rational demonstration. The solution to the problem must necessarily impinge on theology. The identification of mystical and aesthetic experience does present one aspect of that theological issue but it has been made nonetheless an aesthetic problem, and in its consideration among the problems faced by philosophy of art, aesthetic may assert its right to autonomous judgment.

The reasons for the identification of mystical and aesthetic ex-

[121] *Op. cit.*, V,8.2. Cf. above, pp. 40-41.
[122] Cf. above, pp. 54 ff.
[123] *Concerning Divine Names*, Chap. 4, Sec. IX.
[124] *Concerning Mystic Theology*, Chap 1, Sec. III.
[125] *Ibid.*
[126] *Ibid.*

perience are comprehensible, it has been said, on theological grounds. It is less easy to account for the fervor with which writers—among whom are many less interested than Maritain in theology and metaphysics—have accepted the identification in the face of the formidable considerations that weigh against it. If it is argued, for example, that philosophy of art is implicated in metaphysical or religious problems, it may be replied that, while all general philosophical problems eventually seem, to the metaphysician, to require validation in metaphysical or even in theological terms, there are, nevertheless, autonomous universes of discourse, among which is the aesthetic. The objects in the latter field, as well as its principles, are precisely definable and it is unnecessary to revert continuously to the metaphysical origins or implications of aesthetic or beauty to argue its relevant problems. It may appear necessary to do so in those instances in which the artist, as he has often done, derives the representative content or the symbolic meaning of the work of art from the realm of metaphysic or theology, or on occasion when the object of art is used—as a triptych may be—for religious purposes. The issue of non-aesthetic ends in aesthetic will be considered later in this essay.[127] It is sufficient to point out here that not all works of art have sacred themes or subject matter nor are they all theological symbols. Even with reference to those which do have such significance or value, the theological purposes of the artistic object or event have no more intrinsic aesthetic significance and do not present a different or more difficult problem for philosophy of art than do the non-aesthetic purposes of a non-theological work of art.[128]

It is evident that this is true. It was suggested above that the transcendence of God and the identification of beauty with good and with being in Him serve merely to deny to beauty any claim to be determined in terms of a unique function. The conception of an absolute beauty is ateleological for precisely this reason. Aesthetic value is ateleologically defined by the assertion that there must exist an absolutely beautiful form—the additional characteristics of

[127] Cf. Chaps. V-VII.
[128] Cf. Chap. XVIII.

which are in this instance indefinite—and the additional inference that this form may have a function. It is, however, simply untrue that aesthetic experience is wholly definable in terms of the acquisition of knowledge concerning absolute being or absolute truth. It is an experience of objects and events which may effect such knowledge in consequence of the presence of non-aesthetic factors in the work of art, but the work of art is not properly or completely definable in non-aesthetic terms alone.[129]

Finally, mystical and aesthetic experience differ not only regarding objects but regarding ends as well. The essential value of the mystical experience is conviction of belief in God. Its object is God, the Being Who gives meaning to the inspiration and exaltation of the experience. The essential value of the aesthetic experience is, on the contrary, neither the analogous object, the artist, nor the conviction of belief in the artist. It is, rather, the "total structure" of the work of art, the medium, the symbolism, the experience, and the end.[130] The artist is of consequence for aesthetic experience only to the extent that the object is a symbol[131] and that knowledge and understanding of the maker may assist our comprehension of art—its meaning and value. But even if we suppose that the work of art is a symbol of the artist's feelings concerning objects, ideas, events, and situations,[132] as aesthetic percipients we are under no obligation to believe in the maker or to accept his convictions in order aesthetically to experience the work of art.

This last differentiation between religious and aesthetic experiences is sufficiently plain to make the frequently asserted identification of the two the more puzzling. Yet, if we consider the problem in the light of the antinomy of art and of aesthetic experience stated in the introduction to the present essay, the reasons become clear. It is evident, for example, that the predication of truth, being, and beauty to the absolute beauty, if it is demonstrable, diminishes the force of the charge that works of art, as particulars, are deceptive

[129] See Book Two, Part I.
[130] See below, Chap. IX.
[131] Cf. Chaps. X and XVIII.
[132] Cf. Chap. X.

and lacking in reality, since the tendency of the aesthetic theories committed to this hypothesis is to limit aesthetic to absolute beauty. There is, moreover, another issue of more significance for aesthetic. As we have observed, Plato charges that the artist appeals through his art to the passions, to man's irrational nature. If it may be shown that mystical and aesthetic experience are identical, the relevance of the experience of particular beautiful arts to true aesthetic experience may be denied and the universe of discourse called aesthetic conceivably may be restricted to the object or objects of the mystical experience.

The fundamental issue, therefore, is the latter identification of mystical with aesthetic experience. As we proceed to inquire whether the identification is sound, it is of no little value to remember that similarity is not infrequently confused with identity, a revelant point inasmuch as aesthetic and mystical experience are both manifestations of profound feeling. Indeed, one may urge that because the experiences are in this generic respect identical it has been assumed that they are likewise identical rather than similar in their specific characteristics.[133]

This is, however, to anticipate. We shall do well to pause for a moment to determine specifically, if possible, the more important reasons for the identification by asking what, in mystical experience, the mystics themselves value. In general, it may be said of the *experience*, in contrast to the values attaching to its objects, that those who value mystical experience assert its worth is owing either to the "communion" itself or to the consequences following upon the union with the object.[134] Similarly, if we may anticipate, aestheticians have discovered the value of the experience of profoundly moving art to lie either in the experience itself or in its consequences. Thus, the play-theorists in aesthetic stress the valuable consequences of the experience.[135] while theorists of other schools—and Tolstoy[136] is an instance—judge the "communion" itself to be of first importance. More specifically, it is well to note that among

[133] See below, p. 78 and fn. 137.
[134] Cf. above, p. 33.
[135] See below, Chap. VII.
[136] See below, Chap. XII.

the consequences of being profoundly moved either to mystical religious ecstasy or in aesthetic experience are augmented creativity and increased energy.[137]

It is noteworthy that students of mysticism do attempt to determine the worth of the mystical experience, despite the fact that the experience itself is judged to be "ineffable." It is easy to assume that aesthetic and mystical experience are identical, if it is assumed as well that both are "ineffable." But this easy way implies the acceptance of an argument by negation at the same time that it ignores the fact, already noted, that value has been attributed to the experiences, not always because of their presumed intrinsic worth, but because of their valuable consequences. However, before aesthetic experience is identified with a "communion," an identification that presumably places it beyond analysis in terms of reason, it is advisable to examine in more detail the alternative evaluations of mystical experience and the implications of its "ineffability."

One clear expression of the argument that mysticism's significance derives from the consequences and effects of the experience is presented by Bergson in *Les Deux Sources de la Morale et de la Religion.*[138] This is implicit in the French philosopher's conclusion that the Christian mystics were the true mystics who, in contrast to those individuals of ancient times for whom the ecstatic experience was the "culminating" phase, "merely passed through" the experience. Bergson judges that the "true mystics" were bracing themselves "for an entirely new effort," that "they burst a dam; . . . from their increased vitality there radiated an extraordinary energy, daring, power of conception, and realization."[139] In this, the philosopher attests to the inspiration derived from the profound emotionality of mystical experience. It is no less true that exaltation and inspiration are derived from feeling in aesthetic experience, and

[137] As was suggested above, it is probable that the confusion of the two experiences derives from a confusion of generic and specific aspects of feeling. This implies that the specification of aesthetic experience precludes the identification of the two conative experiences, just as it precludes the identification of playful and aesthetic experiences. See below, Chaps. XVII and XVIII.

[138] *Op. cit.* (E.T., pp. 216 ff.).

[139] *Ibid.*, p. 216.

that the energizing and creative power derived from the mystic's communion with the object of his search is a factor in aesthetic experience that has not been overlooked. Nor is its significance to be underestimated.[140] But if it is assumed that the value of mystical experience does derive, as Bergson maintains, from these consequences, does it follow that the aesthetic experience which also derives a profound exaltation of spirit from feeling, is identical with it? It is sufficient to assert, at this point, that the two experiences are different and to prove the truth of the assertion as the essay proceeds. There are other points to be noted, however, at this juncture. It may be urged, for example, that the experience of the religious mystic is inspired by a Promethean, a forward-looking, attitude toward a goal in which there is no defect. The imperfection and bifurcation implicit in the experience of art is, in this, in contrast to the mystical experience, which presumably transcends the realm of negative values. Moreover, the mystical feeling evokes creativity and energy which, in Bergson's view, is canalized into religious devotion or further communion with the object of mystical union, not infrequently for the purpose of knowing God. But, as Schiller properly insisted in the *Aesthetic Letters*, aesthetic experience does not incline the will toward a specific activity or end.[141] In fact, it has long been urged that the experience of art is not aesthetic if the perceiver, submitting to the artist's coercion, undertakes a particular or specified task in consequence of the experience. This lack of specification of end does not, however, make it impossible to define the end of art. The "ecstasy" which Maritain describes as "making the lover beside himself" does imply, as Professor Singer argues in another context,[142] that "art moves us *out of ourselves*" and this "can mean primarily nothing more than to be thrust into a new class of those classes teleologically defined. It is, then, *to be changed as to one's purpose*; it is to enter on a world in which things are revalued." It will be evident that this revaluation

[140] See below, Chap. XVII ff.

[141] See below, Chap. VII for Schiller's principal arguments.

[142] "Esthetic and the Rational Ideal," pp. 31-32. (By permission of Henry Holt and Company, publishers.)

is explicable in terms of conation.[143] It is not evident that because mystical and aesthetic experiences are both conative they are, therefore, identical.

To this conclusion, the mystic, intent solely upon the intrinsic value of the experience rather than on its consequences, may well reply simply that the two are identical in an essential "mystery," in what Gerard Manley Hopkins has well termed an "incomprehensible certainty."[144] Indeed, the "incomprehensible certainty" has its analogues in the literature of aesthetic as well as in the writings of the devout. It will be recalled that Plato maintains that the artist is not master of the content of the art he imitates. The poets write "by a sort of genius and inspiration" but "are like diviners and soothsayers who also say many fine things, but do not understand the meaning of them."[145] It is of interest to recall that the *locus classicus* for what may be called the mystical interpretation of beauty is found precisely in Plato's magnificent description in the *Symposium* of the ascent to beauty.[146] Some portion of what this ascent has suggested to those followers of Plato less inclined than was their progenitor to accept philosophical demonstration will shortly be evident. But it is of interest to note that, for their proponents, both the religious and aesthetic instances of "incomprehensible certainty" imply that the experiences do reveal reality.

The inferences drawn from this aesthetic grounded in "incomprehensible certainty" are well within the tradition of a philosophy that attributes to feeling the function of "immediate" knowing. They also come within the tradition which holds that feeling is indefinable. Both inferences are important for aesthetic but their

[143] See below, Book Two, Parts III and IV.

[144] *The Letters of Gerard Manley Hopkins*, pp. 187 ff. Hopkins, writing to Robert Bridges, says, "You do not mean by a mystery what a Catholic does. You mean an interesting uncertainty: the uncertainty ceasing interest ceases also. This happens in some things; to you in religion. But a Catholic by mystery means an incomprehensible certainty: without certainty, without formulation, there is no interest . . . the clearer the formulation the greater the interest." (By permission of Oxford University Press, New York.) My attention was called to this passage by Professor K. Gilbert.

[145] *Apology* 22.

[146] See below, Chap. III, pp. 93 ff.

consideration must await a later chapter.[147] Our more immediate task is to consider the validity of the identification of mystical and aesthetic experience on the ground that no predication may be made of the object of either experience. The inference is evident in Dionysius' terminology. For the Areopagite, the issue is the union of the self with God. For the mystic in aesthetic it is union with beauty or with the object of fine art. The experience in either case is described as an "ineffable union" with the object and both experiences have in fact been described as a "knowing above mind."

A. E. Taylor, in his study of Plato,[148] has made explicit some implications of the "knowledge" said to be derived from these profound conative experiences. He judges the mystical experience to signify, as we have seen, a "having got beyond 'science' itself," into "direct contact." It is an "actual possession and being possessed by" the object. Taylor further describes the mystical experience as one which may not be had "without the long preliminary process of travail of thought."[149] Yet the knowledge is neither discursive nor "knowing propositions which can be predicated of" its object. In addition, "all the mystics insist on the point that the direct vision of supreme reality is not only incommunicable, it cannot even be recalled in memory when the moment of vision is passed. You can be sure that you 'saw' it; you cannot tell what you saw even to yourself."[150]

Professor Taylor suggests that, "It is just in this conviction that all 'knowledge about' is only preparatory to a direct *scientia visionis*" that Socrates reveals the fundamental agreement "of his conception with that of the great mystics of all ages."[151] But it is also precisely in this regard that some aestheticians reveal their fundamental agreement with mysticism. They have urged that beauty is ultimately indefinable and that its experience is incommunicable. They judge as well that the creativity of genius and the recreativity of aesthetic apprehension are similarly "rich in un-

[147] See below, Book Two, Part III.
[148] *Plato*, pp. 230-231.
[149] *Ibid.*, p. 231.
[150] *Ibid.*, p. 232.
[151] *Ibid.*, p. 231.

disclosed mystery." This has been most evident for aesthetic is the reiterated assertion that the experience of works of genius is "immediate," a statement in accord with the more general view that aesthetic experience and its object are beyond the possibility of analysis in terms of rational discourse because "all communication takes the form of predication."

A consequent silence on the part of aestheticians who hold this theory would be a salutary and consistent attitude. But the presupposition of such a silence would have small attraction for one who believes that both experience and objects may be analyzed. Moreover, the latter's hesitancy in accepting the mystic's alternative would be accentuated, once he realized that "ineffability" and its attendant implications are neither the sole nor the most fruitful alternative speculative hypotheses presented to him. One alternative is that proposed by Professor Singer and is directly applicable to the problems of the supposed indefinability of beauty and of the incommunicability of its experience. Singer's argument, which appears to the present writer to be conclusive, asserts that whatever "exemptions from outside criticism" beauty and its experience may warrant as "subjective" and "immediate," they "must be given some place in experience":

> Insofar as a judgment lays claim to truth, insofar does it pretend to have grasped an objective reality, and insofar must it be capable of confirmation or refutation from an indefinite series of other points of view. The average of these observations (though never quite static) is the only result to which either the connoisseur of beauty or the scientific investigator can point as the fact he is in search of. In the comparison with such an average the truth of the "subjective appreciation" appears . . . its freedom disappears. That which has led history to separate the truth of a judgment of beauty from that of a judgment (say) of size is the relatively large "variable error" of the former which masks the nature of the average. We have not yet found a type of judgment that does not involve a question of fact, and statements of fact are capable of a continuous treatment throughout the whole range of experience.[152]

[152] *Mind as Behavior*, p. 197. (By permission of R. G. Adams and Company, publishers.)

The alternative offered in the foregoing quotation suggests that the aesthetician must accept the possibility of greater error in his judgments than is likely to occur in judgments in other fields. But it denies the impossibility of making a judgment in aesthetic. That the alternative is applicable to mystical and aesthetic experience is further suggested by the fact that the term "communion" is, in practice, employed by mystics not primarily to characterize an experience said to be "ineffable," but to describe distinct and discriminable experiences. The use of the term in aesthetic has lent it a distinct and specific meaning: it is rarely used to describe the union of the percipient with the *ens realissimum* but rather to suggest his oneness with the races and cultures of men of the past.[153] Merely to state the matter in this way is to imply that among "ineffable" experience are those which may be analyzed in terms of their objects, as well as in terms of the conative factors involved.

VIII

THE inferences that the object of aesthetic experience is neither transcendent nor beyond definition, and that the experience itself is not wholly "ineffable" affect to a lesser degree, perhaps, our consideration of the main current of artistic and critical theory by their reference to what is, after all, a narrowly accepted tradition of transcendental and ateleological aesthetic, than to the more widely held theory of the "genius" and his "perfect art." "Mystery" has at times dominated opinion concerning the nature of artistic creativity to the degree that great artists have been judged to possess "god-like" potentialities for "creating." From this, the inference is easily made that the products of artistic creativity are sacrosanct and, therefore, in some sense, beyond analysis. The argument comes full circle with the corollary that the recreation of the object of art in aesthetic experience is likewise the consequence of divine powers and thus is to be put beyond rational explanation.

[153] Cf. below, pp. 364 and 366-367.

The denial that it is true that profoundly moving works of art are beyond both analysis and criticism, or that artistic creation or aesthetic recreation is incomprehensible, does not imply that makers of fine art are not more acute in their powers of observation, more fully "aware" of their own feelings, or more skilled in technique, than are either ordinary men or technical craftsmen. Neither does it assert that, because the products of great art are comprehensible and may evoke aesthetic experience, their perceiver could produce comparable works of art. Rather, it simply maintains that the problems of creation and recreation in philosophy of fine art are not different in kind from those implicit in science. The scientist who grants without question that Newton and Leibniz invented the calculus does not ordinarily deny that other men can evaluate the inventors' technique and comprehend the mathematics of the calculus itself. To understand the calculus does not at all imply for them, however, that mathematicians who use its principles could invent it, were knowledge of the subject ever entirely lost.

The issue in aesthetic is analogous. There is no evident necessity that forces philosophy of art to transport the genius or his work to the realm of the incomprehensible and the inexplicable. The value of the artist and the product of his art depend upon no "mystery," nor do the evaluations made of them. And, if the first step towards a resolution of the problems implicit in aesthetic is made as we assume that its problems are not by definition impossible of solution, the direction of the second and the third steps is plain. The former concerns the corollary to "immediacy" and "inexplicability." Aesthetic should assume that there are no "perfect poems," "perfect symphonies," and "perfect statues," completely expressed or intuited by the artist, unless the poem, the symphony, and the statue is "expressed" and "made" in sounds, in notes, and in stone.[154] To urge, by way of illustration, that Coleridge created more of *Kubla Khan* than we now may read is to state the problem incorrectly: Coleridge's inability to complete the poem is the most telling argument against his having had the poem completed in his mind.

[154] The validity of the theory even in the latter circumstances is doubtful. See below, Chap. VIII, pp. 242 ff.

The third step is the assumption that speculation upon aesthetic experience may begin with the object of art and proceed to consider either the creative experience of the artist or of the aesthetic percipient. It need only be granted, until the contrary be proved, that artistic experience and aesthetic experience are not forever bifurcated, that they are at least analogous, and that the order of time that does ostensibly differentiate them regarding their relation to the artistic object does not distinguish them in kind.

What is suggested at the outset of an inquiry into the nature of aesthetic experience, and what will guide us through its course, is the initial acceptance of simple assumptions. Their simplicity does not diminish either the difficulties inherent in aesthetic theory or in its problems, but it does oppose the complete skepticism implicit in hypotheses which use such terms as "immediacy," "incommunicability," "ineffability," "genius," and "perfect expression," whether the hypotheses in question be integral to "intuitional" or "transcendental" philosophies of beauty.

An aesthetic theory comprehending art, objects of art, the creation of art and its recreation in aesthetic experience, and the end of art, need not neglect the problem of universals. But the theorist is well advised to test the soundness of the search for beauty by examining the relation between experience and art object before he embraces transcendentalism and encounters the problems consequent upon the acceptance of "absolute beauty" and its ineffable experience.

Once it is granted that the problems of art and of aesthetic experience are not to be put beyond the possibility of solution, philosophy of art most naturally begins with the object of art as its principal datum. From this datum as a starting point, it may proceed to investigate the creation of that object or its recreation in aesthetic experience. We shall shortly discover that this more direct method leads to a needed investigation of the "total structure" of art.[155] But complex as the problems of the "total structure" may be, they may be approached with some assurance that error in aesthetic judgment may be reduced if no fact relevant to aesthetic experience

[155] See below, Chap. IX.

is arbitrarily judged to transcend empirical analysis. This is a counsel of perfection but it is one that opens many avenues for research.

Of first importance among those avenues is that opened by the work of art as the datum. There are, in addition, many signs and suggestions proffered by the artist which enable us to clarify the datum's meaning by understanding the artist's intention and analyzing his technique. In this regard, two obstacles must be faced. The first is that the artist's purpose is not necessarily the purpose of art; the second, that the artist infrequently expresses his aesthetic or artistic theories with sufficient clarity to avoid at least the appearance of ambiguity. It would be an error to assume that the artist is ordinarily a dialectician. It would be equally erroneous to ignore, on that account, artists who have used language critically and philosophically. Wagner, Rodin, Michelangelo, Coleridge, Leonardo, Dante, Dürer, Tolstoy, Goethe, Schiller, Browning, Shelley, Housman, and Dryden are but a few of the many who have given sound expression to their views. Their writings and their notebooks are invaluable, if it always be remembered that the artist's primary mode of expression is the work of art. Thus, van Gogh's remark, "It's as interesting and as difficult to say a thing well as to paint it," is illuminating. It is, nonetheless, of less value than is his "*Self-Portrait.*" Picasso's is the truer word: "We give to form and color all their individual significance, as far as we can see it; in our subjects we keep the joy of discovery, the pleasure of the unexpected; our subject itself must be a source of interest. But of what use is it to say what we do when everybody can see it if he wants to."

The artist, it may be urged, does not always succeed in his effort to express himself. His failures are nonetheless illuminating for the philosophy of art. The poems that A. E. Housman did not publish in his lifetime, the disputed "*Gioconda*" in the Prado, the three *Leonora Overtures*—all are commentaries upon the intent of the artist. We gain in our comprehension of *Hamlet* by Shakespeare's comparative failures in *Measure for Measure* and *Troilus and Cressida*, as we add to our knowledge once we learn that Shakespeare punctuated dramatic poetry to enable the actor to place proper emphases upon the spoken words.

To the evidence internal to the work of art, aesthetic theory may well add all that criticism offers for the solution of its problems. The contemporary Ben Jonson criticizes Shakespeare, Dryden rediscovers the genius of Chaucer, Vasari recounts tales and anecdotes concerning the great and the near-great of the Renaissance. Each critic may be mistaken in his judgment, yet the possibility of error implies the possibility that a true judgment may be made.

This dependence of aesthetic upon "fact" is, perhaps, the most significant consequence of an analysis of transcendental ateleological theory. As we have observed, the most destructive consequence of that tradition is the diminution of, and, logically, the negation of the value of the work of art. No theory worthy of the name can with impunity exclude the product of the artist's technique from the aesthetic universe of discourse, degrade its worth by contrasting it to a standard at once indefinable and mysterious, or relegate its experience to the "ineffable" and the incommunicable.

IX

TO HAVE mentioned some of the consequences of the employment of principles in keeping with the transcendental theory of beauty does not preclude the possibility that there are "absolutely beautiful" objects or events or works of art "supremely valuable" without reference to end. The ateleologist may be and, in fact, has been, at times, as discontented as the teleologist with the indefinite "form" elevated by the transcendentalist to the status of absolute beauty. The ateleologist in the past has demanded not infrequently that theory turn from its absorption in beauty in a transcendental and supra-sensible realm to an inquiry into beauty in art and in nature. He is, on that account, no less an ateleologist, nor does he impose less stringent rules than does the transcendentalist for the limitation of the aesthetic universe of discourse.

It is significant, however, that the ateleologists with whose theories we shall be concerned in the immediately succeeding chapters, examine the aesthetic problem under conditions more nearly approximating those laid down by empiricism than do the transcendentalists. Historically speaking, the former has been prone to define beautiful objects and events, rather than to conclude, as does the latter, that they are indefinable. In fact, the ateleological theories which do apply their principles to art and nature not only take this first step but the second and third as well: they not only assume that there are objects and events either natural or made to which the predicate "absolutely beautiful" may be applied but they also assume that it is meaningful to relate artistic creativity and aesthetic experience to the natural object or to the object of art as a datum. They deny, however, that the datum is uniquely definable in terms of the means-end relation.

It is to an examination of various theories in which it has been maintained that there are absolutely beautiful objects and events, beautiful without necessary reference to the purposes they fulfill, that we now turn. Perhaps in this type of aesthetic we may discover a resolution to the antinomy of profoundly moving art's evocation of exaltation and discontent.

Chapter III

The Theory of Ateleological Form in Art and Nature

Wherefore we must endeavour to construct the four forms of bodies which excel in beauty. . . . Of the infinite forms we must select the most beautiful, if we are to proceed in due order, and any one who can point out a more beautiful form than ours for the construction of these bodies, shall carry off the palm, not as an enemy, but as a friend.

—PLATO

WE ARE told in the *Symposium* that, "the true order of going . . . to the things of love," is to "begin from the beauties of earth" and then to "mount upwards" until we know "what the essence of beauty is." The transcendental ateleologist in aesthetic, as we have observed in the preceding chapter, maintains that we may apprehend that essence only in union with the object of the search. In this getting "beyond science," there is "mystery." Indeed, even if it be granted that beauty may be predicated of objects of fine art, the transcendentalist tends to imply that this aesthetic experience likewise lies beyond the scope of rational philosophy's explanatory principles.

One consequence of transcendental aesthetic theory in its ateleological formulation is that the value of art becomes negligible in contrast to the supreme values attributed to the essence of beauty. The ateleological theories of form in art and in nature, some implications of which will be examined in the present chapter, are not transcendent. They are consequent upon the search for beauty "in earth laid up." Once the search is concluded, beauty in art and in nature is described or defined in terms far from mysterious and its experience and apprehension are judged to be susceptible to expression in the language of rational discourse.

In respect to the beauty of objects of art and nature, the tradition of ateleological aesthetic follows a course delineated by the same Plato whose theory of the essence of beauty culminates, once the complex demands of historical speculation are laid upon it, in mysticism. But it is the Plato of *Phaedrus*, rather than of the *Symposium*,[1] who directs his own search[2] and that of numerous successors to the world of art and nature. It is his successors who, in "correcting" Plato's original theory of absolutely beautiful forms, seek to "claim a friendly victory."[3] In *Phaedrus* Plato states the presupposition of the philosophy of beauty put forward in *Philebus*. The former dialogue belongs to the middle period of his writings but in its statement concerning beauty Plato turns away from the supra-sensible realm in which the essence of beauty exists with other ideal forms: "But of beauty, I repeat again that we saw her there shining in company with the celestial forms; and coming to earth we find her here too, shining in clearness through the clearest aperture of sense. . . . This is the privilege of beauty, that being the loveliest she is also the most palpable to sight."[4]

Indeed, aesthetic theory appears to be implicated by this statement in an empirical study of beauty. It will be plain, however, as we proceed, that the philosophies of art formulated by ateleologists from Plato onwards are *a priori* theories or derive from *a priori* principles. It would be equally erroneous to overestimate, not the liberality that accompanies Plato's bringing to birth of a theory of

[1] It should be mentioned, however, that in the *Symposium* it is implied that the abstract, colorless, motionless essence, described in *Phaedrus*, is made evident to living creatures by the intermediate δαίμων Eros. This power "spans the chasm" between gods and mortals. The good appears to men as the beautiful which men love and desire. Its comprehension results in a "single science, which is the science of beauty everywhere."

[2] *Phaedrus* 250. I have assumed that the Dialogue belongs to the middle period of Plato's writing. There is some evidence, however, that it is late.

[3] *Timaeus* 54.

[4] *Op. cit.*, 250. Cf. *Hippias Major* 299B-D.

beautiful forms, but that of his successors. The Athenian remarks that one who can point to a "more beautiful form than ours, . . . shall carry off the palm, not as an enemy, but as a friend." His successors, who are affected as profoundly as Plato is by the compulsion to define absolutely beautiful forms, are not eager to welcome such "friendly victory" by ateleologists with divergent views. Even less is their liberalism displayed in loosening the shackles placed upon art by transcendental aesthetic. Indeed, almost without exception, each ateleological aesthetic of forms in nature or in art puts forward, with its claim to adjudge objects to be either absolutely beautiful or subject to a universal judgment of taste, rules for the most stringent limitations upon what will be permitted the predicate "aesthetic."

It is the grounds for and the validity of these limitations that are of primary significance for the present essay because it is precisely these limitations that are integral to the efforts made by ateleologists to resolve the antinomies of art and aesthetic experience with which we began our present study. And again, because our interest does lie in the varieties of ateleological theory primarily as methods used in circumscribing the field of aesthetic rather than in their contributions to our knowledge of the structure of works of art, it should be made plain, even at the cost of repetition, that this type of philosophy of art is by no means the only one which lays down rules for restricting the aesthetic universe of discourse.

Although the current efforts of ateleologists to limit the predication of "aesthetic" or "beautiful" to the forms of circles or triangles, to the perfect curve, the flowing line, and the proportionate parts of the human body, are implicated in a ceaseless search at once to discover beauty and to exclude some products of artistic technique, other restrictions have been placed upon art objects. Figures in the drama have been relegated to "a world of themselves as much as fairyland." Theorists who have envisaged a realm in which art is "for art's sake" have laid down correlative limitations: "true" objects of art may be judged to be aesthetic only if they evoke "pure" pleasure, bring into operation "aesthetic" emotions, or stimulate artistic imagination.

But if accordance with ateleologically defined form is not, indeed, the sole limitation to which art has been subjected, it is nonetheless true that the principles held to explain beauty in formally defined objects or events have served most frequently to ground other restrictions. By way of illustration, "art for art's sake" in modern times derives from Kant's aesthetic of form.[5] Coleridge's theory of imagination in art similarly is grounded in a "form theory" and various views of "aesthetic emotion" have their presuppositions in interpretations which emphasize "form" as the substructure of art. It is well to note also that in the theory of form has been exercised not only the most rigorous principle of exclusion for objects from the field of art, but that in it philosophy has been provided with one of its most stimulating grounds for speculation upon art. The establishment of the validity of its implications has been a task set for themselves by the most eminent dialecticians. Should it be possible to demonstrate the objective beauty of aesthetic objects and events by the ateleological theory of form and to limit the field to them, the rigor of the method applied by the theory's proponents might conceivably be generalized to provide an incomparable technique for the solution to art's most perplexing problems. Whether the ateleological theory of form in art and in nature is sound and may bear the burden of this generalized task must be determined. At the outset, however, it is essential to be precise not only concerning the problem of the present chapter but, as well, in regard to the meaning of the term "work of art." To a preliminary specification of the meaning of the latter term, we shall proceed in the next section.

II

AT THIS point, where the present essay abandons the transcendental theory of absolute beauty in order to permit investigation of ateleological hypotheses which tend towards empiricism in aesthetics, the significant problem is to determine the meaning and

[5] See R. F. Egan, "The Genesis of the Theory of 'Art for Art's Sake' in Germany and in England."

application of "form" as the term refers to the "work of art." The "work of art" means, in this essay, the product of a maker's or an artisan's craft. The assumption that this product is the datum for aesthetic experience is made in the face of two possible objections. The first issues from the controversy concerning the aesthetic value of natural objects, a controversy, in fact, of little significance for the present study in which there is no particular reason for excluding the beauty of nature, precisely as there appears to be no particular reason for judging natural objects to constitute a special class of aesthetic entities. It is sufficient for our purposes to infer that natural objects or events are aesthetically valuable insofar as they are analogous to objects of art and to mean by this simply that their experience is made similar or identical to that of fine art by the creative "making" of the percipient without the intervention of the artist. The percipient is, in this instance, the artist. As an observer of nature, he adjusts his position to obtain the most satisfactory background or chooses the proper conditions of light and shade in order to make possible an aesthetic evaluation of the object under consideration.

The second objection to the assumption that the product of art is the datum for aesthetic experience is implicit in the Plotinian attempt, mentioned in the preceding chapter,[6] to establish the aesthetic superiority of technique or art over the work of art on grounds of logical priority and of unity, and in mysticism's assumption that aesthetic experience is identical with the experience of union with the object.[7] The contemporary controversy concerns both technique and the work of art. It is urged, in fact, that neither τέχνη nor the "work of art" produced by it is aesthetically valuable "art." Some of those who formulate the theory[8] maintain both that "art" is an "image" and that artistic creativity is "expression." With the latter, it is argued, craft or technique has nothing to do, inasmuch as the "image" does not stand in need of manual dexterity for

[6] Cf. above, pp. 43-48.

[7] Cf. above, pp. 73-75.

[8] Cf. Benedetto Croce, *Aesthetic*, and *The Essence of Aesthetic* and R. G. Collingwood, *The Principles of Art*.

its "expression." Thus, for Croce, intuition is the first stage of the philosophy of spirit and presupposes but is not presupposed by practical, theoretical, and economic activity. Art, intuition, and expression are identical. Intuitions are expressions of impressions, impressions which require for expression nothing derived from technical skill, if as "images," they are completely expressed.

Collingwood makes the issue clearer by separating the "work of art" as an "internal" or "mental" thing from craft understood in terms of means and ends. It should be pointed out that Croce, who influences Collingwood, is not unambiguous as regards the basic issue of the priority of intuitions. The general tenor of the Italian philosopher's writings is clear: Conceptions and practical activity are posterior to intuition. It is, however, not irrelevant to the question whether or not the artist is able fully to express his "feelings" or fully to intuit impressions without relating imagination to an "external" material or medium, that Croce does grant "the contention that the greater part of the intuitions of civilized man are impregnated with concepts."[9] Of more significance, however, is the inference that "those concepts which are found mingled and fused with the intuitions are no longer concepts, in so far as they are really mingled and fused, for they have lost all independence and autonomy. They have been concepts, but have now become simple elements of intuition."[10]

It is in the light of the foregoing that it is essential to follow Croce to his conclusion: "The whole is that which determines the quality of the parts. . . . Notwithstanding all these concepts the total effect of the work of art is an intuition."[11] If there may be intuitions "impregnated with concepts," while concepts are yet

[9] *Aesthetic*, p. 2.

[10] *Ibid.*, p. 2.

[11] The passages in question in *Estetica Come Scienza dell' Expressione e Linguistica Generale*, pp. 4 ff. are as follows: "Ma, checché si pensi di questi esempî, e posto anche si voglia e debba sostenere che la maggior parte delle intuizioni dell'uomo civile sieno impregnate di concetti, v'e ben altro, e piú importante e conclusivo, da osservare. I concetti che si trovano misti e fusi, non sono piú concetti, avendo perduto ogni indipendenza e autonomia. Furono già concetti, ma sono diventati, ora, semplici elementi d'intuizione." "Il tutto e quel che determina la qualita delle parti. . . . Ma, nonostante tutti quei concetti, il risultato dell'opera d'arte è un'intuizione."

posterior to intuitions, there appears to be no reason why there may not be intuitions "impregnated" with "practical activity," technical dexterity, and artistic skill, as well, provided only that the latter become part of "the total effect" of the work of art as an "intuition." Granted this, if it is argued that the "image" does not require for "expression" its "making" by "manual dexterity" into what is ordinarily called a "work of art," the consequences for philosophy of art are quite different from those which follow upon the hypothesis that art is "intuition," the logically prior activity or a knowledge which "has no need of a master, nor to lean on any one." For if the intuition may be an intuition which expresses the artist's technique operating upon material, the problems of craft and of requirements laid upon the maker by the material are presupposed in the "intuition," and the resulting theory need make no place for craft or the "work of art," in the ordinarily received meaning of "object or event made" because by a *petitio principii* it has included consideration of both.[12] The material has effected the "imagination" that makes or expresses the "image" or "intuition" and the act of "making" a work of art is presupposed in the act of "imagination."

There is, therefore, no need to "disabuse ourselves," as Collingwood advises, "of the notion that the business of the artist consists in producing a special kind of artifacts, so-called 'works of art' or *objets d'art*, which are bodily and perceptible things (painted canvasses, carved stones and so forth)."[13] While this may be the "technical" theory of art, in Collingwood's phrase, it is implicit in his own as well as in Croce's aesthetic. Its principles will be assumed and made explicit in the present essay.[14]

[12] Cf. Collingwood, *op. cit.*, pp. 146-147, on what the artist does. The author resolves the problem by use of Bernard Berenson's theory of "tactile values."

[13] *Op. cit.*, pp. 36-37.

[14] The theory of art as "intuition" or "expression," as contrasted to the philosophy of art that presupposes a "work of art" made, impinges upon the present essay in the problem of "feeling," as well. By way of illustration, Collingwood maintains that art is not a craft reducible to analysis within the meaning of the terms "means" and "ends." He argues that what the artist produces is "an 'internal' or 'mental' thing, something (as we commonly say) 'existing in his head' and there only: Something of the kind which we commonly call an experience." This, he urges, is "not anything that can be called

The aesthetic that identifies art with "intuition" or "expression" without reference to a work of art "made" and "formed" is not only logically fallacious but is, as well, inapplicable to practice. If the artist does express his "feelings" aesthetically, he does so in a work of art for himself, if for none other, as an observer. He knows the potentialities of his art as a technique because the latter are actualized in "making" in a material. In the process, the artist's "imagination" is subjected to requirements laid down for "images" in a medium.[15] It is Descartes, as an epistemologist, rather than Croce or Collingwood, who is the trustworthy guide in this aspect of philosophy: "Imagination" is contrasted in Cartesian theory to intellect which "in some manner turns on itself.[16] It is Bosanquet, as a philosopher of art, rather than Croce or Collingwood, who is the trustworthy guide in philosophy of art: ". . . Imaginative expression creates the feeling in creating its embodiment, and the feeling so created not merely cannot be otherwise expressed, but cannot otherwise exist, than in and through the embodiment which imagination has found for it."[17]

That embodiment is found in the "work of art," and the immediate problem is to determine, first, what is to be implied by this phrase, and secondly, to discern the significance of "form" as the latter term is applied to the "work of art." By the "work of art," as the term will be used in this essay, is meant the product of a maker's or an artisan's technique. That product may be either an object or an event. In general, a material—canvas, colors, stone, bronze, sounds, even the human body—has been painted, given a pattern, carved, poured, arranged, or decorated in such wise that certain of its potentialities have been actualized to produce a paint-

a work of art." This experience is conative but it is not a technique extended by psychologists to interpret "the essence of art to stimulation of certain reactions in its audience." Aesthetic experience is not, therefore, "a specific reaction to a stimulus proceeding from a specific type of external object" (p. 40). But, because Collingwood interprets "feeling" in purely subjective terms, *op. cit.*, Book II, his conclusion is unscientific and untenable. See below, Chap. X ff.

[15] See below, Chap. XVIII, pp. 495 ff.

[16] See *Meditations on First Philosophy*, VI.

[17] B. Bosanquet, *Three Lectures on Aesthetic*, p. 34.

ing, a statue, a poem, a symphony, a dance, or a drama. The completed work of art is a datum for an observer, who under certain conditions may be an aesthetic percipient. It is within this meaning of the phrase "work of art" that the implications of the word "form" must be ascertained in judging the validity of ateleological and "formal" aesthetic. These may best be determined by ascertaining (a) the general significance of the word form as it is used in aesthetic; (b) its usage by certain individual theorists and artists; (c) and, finally, its implications, if any, for the determination of the function or purpose of art.

Perhaps the clearest expression of the general significance of the word form as it has been used in such aesthetic contexts is to be found in *Hippias Major*,[18] one of the earlier dialogues attributed to Plato.[19] As the discussion proceeds in that work the effort to ascertain the meaning of "beauty" or of the aesthetic factors in art becomes a search for form as the *common.* This treatment of form as the universal, rather than the particular, is implicit in the definition offered: It is the "something identical which makes them [i.e., particular beautiful objects] to be beautiful, this common quality which pertains to both in common and to each individually." Plato is asking a simple and relatively straight-forward question: What is the proper means to the end, beauty? It will be observed that Plato does not discuss the problem of the beauty of this common factor or form which makes beautiful things beautiful. He does not apply the adjective, "beautiful," to the substantive, "beauty."[20]

The latter connotation of the term form emerges, however, in this Dialogue and it is a connotation retained by the word throughout centuries of speculation upon beauty. The formalist really desires to designate as form "the something of such sort that it will never appear ugly anywhere to anybody."[21] Form, it is implied, is no mere means to an end. If that were, indeed, its original connotation, the means is now judged to be beautiful. The Dialogue proceeds at this

[18] *Op. cit.*, 300A. (By permission of Harvard University Press, Cambridge, Mass.)

[19] See above, p. 29, fn. 4.

[20] Cf. above, p. 35.

[21] *Op. cit.*, 291D; cf. *Symposium* 211 ff. and above Chap. II.

point as if the purported discovery of the something identical to all beautiful objects which makes them beautiful had itself become the product of that making rather than the means to beauty's production. Once this step has been taken, the object is taken to be beautiful *in esse*. In effect, form has been interpreted not only in terms of the substantival-adjectival identity mentioned in the preceding chapter but has become the absolutely beautiful—absolute in the sense that its beauty is neither relative to nor dependent upon time, place, use, or personal taste.[22]

Two consequences of the latter interpretation of form are of immediate interest: In the first place, it follows that all "works of art" as products of the maker's technique which are not in accord with the form are necessarily denied a place in the aesthetic universe of discourse. A related consequence has been the acceptance of the beauty of equilateral triangles and the rejection of the tragedies of Aeschylus, the acceptance of the proportions of the *Doryphorous* of Polycleitus and the rejection of the elongated figures of statues made by Lysippos and Euphranor, and the acceptance of the beauty of the tulip and the rejection of certain kinds of music.[23] There has resulted, at one time or another as a consequence of the formal limitation upon art, the exclusion of tragedy, comedy, representative or imitative art, as well as the denial of aesthetic value to distortion as a technique in art. These limitations have been imposed upon art not only by theorists like Plato, Kant, and other classical philosophers but are also in accord with some influential modern critical theory and artistic practice. The denial of value to representation or imitation in such assertions of the worth of "pure form" in the Herzog's "Ich," in Kandinsky's "Komposition," in Picasso's "Paris" and, let us say, in the poetry of Mallarmé—these instances permit the inference that the artist as well as the theorist proposes

[22] Insofar as form is taken to be the common, it is obviously the designation of an aesthetic problem, the significance of which is not limited to ateleological theory. Insofar as the term is taken to be the absolute and unvarying exemplification of beauty, to the exclusion of all other natural objects or objects of art, the designation of a form must be justified for aesthetic theory. The justification presupposes the validation of any limitation placed by the particular formal theory upon the aesthetic universe of discourse.

[23] Each acceptance or rejection is examined in this and the two subsequent chapters.

to construct an object beautiful in and for itself without reference to an end.

It follows, in the second place, that once the beauty of the formal object is taken to be "absolute" and "not relative," art is defined ateleologically, i.e., without reference to purpose.[24] With this ateleological definition of art, a fundamental distinction is made between the ateleological formal theories of art and those philosophies of art which maintain that the aesthetic value in the product of the maker's technique is due to the latter's significance as a means related to the end subserved.[25] Theories which define art in terms of the end subserved are teleological theories. They attribute the aesthetic value of the work of art to one of three possible relations of means to end or to combinations of those relations: The work of art may subserve a non-aesthetic end, a unique aesthetic end, or it may be a means to both non-aesthetic and aesthetic ends. Upon the ateleological formal hypothesis, the work of art *must* have a certain delineation, shape, contour, and sequence of parts, or it *must* accord with a certain ratio, proportion, or dimension; it *may* be the best means to an end, such as pleasure, exaltation, or rationality.

To estimate the adequency of formal ateleological theory as an aesthetic in its elaboration upon the assumption that the field of aesthetic may be restricted to specified "absolutely beautiful" objects and events, would entail an evaluation of each systematic effort that has survived in the history of the subject. Theoretically, such an evaluation is possible but its worth in terms of completeness would be lessened because it would be impossible to anticipate specific interpretations of ateleological aesthetic which the future may bring forth. It is possible, however, to offer a classification of mutually exclusive theories such that no type of theory may escape the categories defined and to examine the most effective specific statements under each category. Let us assume, therefore, that all ateleological formal theories are identical in that the objects and

[24] See above, p. 32, fn. 8. It is, of course, "not relative" to other aspects of experience irrelevant to the present problem. But, specifically, it is neither "relative" to the taste of the subject nor to an external end which must be postulated.

[25] For other distinctions among teleological systems, see Book Two, Parts III and IV.

events are defined by reference neither to a unique aesthetic purpose nor to any end that distinguishes them completely from other and non-aesthetic objects, but that they are defined by the form held to be common to all objects or events. The specific theories may diverge in two ways: The form or the common may be mathematical or non-mathematical and it may be "abstract," i.e., non-sensuous, or "concrete," i.e., sensuous. Of the ateleological, mathematical, and "abstract" type of aesthetic theory, Plato's philosophy of art in *Philebus* and *Timaeus* is, for our purposes, the *locus classicus*. Of the ateleological, non-mathematical, and "abstract" type of aesthetic theory, Kant's *Kritik of Judgment* may be regarded as the *locus classicus*. Ambiguities in Plato's philosophy of art lead to the development of the ateleological, mathematical, and "concrete" aesthetic of form. Analogous ambiguities in Kant's analysis of aesthetic judgment are points of departure for a corresponding ateleological, non-mathematical, and "concrete" philosophy of form.

Each alternative formulation will be examined in this and the immediately succeeding chapters in sufficient detail to permit us to draw inferences concerning the validity of ateleological theory in general, as well as to estimate the cogency of the principles upon which each instance of the theory rests and from which is argued the right of its author to restrict the artistic and natural objects and events which may be called beautiful or judged to be objects of taste.

We shall begin with the ateleological theories of "abstract" form, of which Plato states the mathematical and Kant the non-mathematical hypothesis.

III

Plato and the Mathematical Hypothesis

THE sonnet beginning, "Euclid alone has looked on Beauty bare," expresses succinctly the judgment ordinarily passed by the ateleologist upon those not in accord with the theory of "absolute beauties":

Let all who prate of Beauty hold their peace,
And lay them prone upon the earth, and cease
To ponder on themselves, the while they stare
At nothing, intricately drawn nowhere
In shapes of shifting lineage.[25a]

But it is Plato, rather than Euclid, who "alone has looked on Beauty bare" because it is the philosopher rather than the geometer who knew he was searching for the abstract essence by which could be achieved "release from dusty bondage."

The quest for absolutely beautiful forms begins early in Plato's writings and culminates in the later Dialogues, *Timaeus* and *Philebus*. *Phaedrus* and the *Symposium*, as we have observed, evidence Plato's tendency to search for such objects and events in the world of experience as will satisfy the conditions of the problem. But it is in the *Republic* that the philosopher most clearly anticipates the theory of form which in *Philebus*, in particular, is stated with an air of finality.

In the latter Dialogue, Plato tells us what the "absolutely beautiful" objects and events are: "Beauties of pure colors, beauties of form, the straight line and circle and the plane and solid figures formed from these by turning-lathes and rulers and patterns of angles; . . . most odours and sounds" and, in particular, "those sounds which are smooth and clear and send forth a single pure note."[26]

However, neither the aesthetic problem of *Philebus* nor the theory of forms argued there is new. In the *Republic*, Plato does confess that as regards imitative poetry "we are conscious of being enchanted by such poetry ourselves; though it would be a sin to betray what seems to us the cause of truth."[27] But other remarks anticipate the "abstraction" of form from imitative content in the earlier effort to state what the poet does: for "the poet, as well as the painter, lays on a species of colours, in the shape of verbs and nouns, to represent the several professions, of which he only understands enough to be able to imitate them; so that if he writes in

[25a] "Sonnet XXII." From *The Harp-Weaver and Other Poems*, published by Harper & Brothers. Copyright, 1920, by Edna St. Vincent Millay.

[26] *Op. cit.*, 51 ff. Translated by H. N. Fowler. (By permission of Harvard University Press, Cambridge, Mass., 1925.)

[27] *Op. cit.*, 607.

metre, rhythm, and harmony, about shoemaking, or about generalship, or about any subject whatever, people who are as ignorant as himself, and who judge merely by the form of the expression, look upon his poetry as very excellent. So powerful is the charm which these musical appliances naturally possess. For I suppose you know what a poor appearance the works of poets present, when they have been stripped of their musical colouring, and are rehearsed in their proper nakedness."[28]

But if Plato in this passage implies that a separation of form and content is possible (he presumably makes no distinction between medium and representative content), it is also true that he anticipates in the *Republic* the technique employed in *Philebus* to resolve the antinomies of art. It will be recalled that the product made by the imitative artist appeals to the irrational rather than to that rational portion of the soul that weighs, calculates, and measures. An art that would so appeal to the rational soul is obviously definable in mathematical terms. The step needed to demonstrate this is taken in *Philebus* and *Timaeus*. Plato's meaning both in the *Republic* and in the later dialogues is best understood, however, in the light of the Pythagorean tradition that affected him.[29]

Aristotle writes of the Pythagoreans that "they assumed that the elements of numbers were the elements of all things, and that the whole heavens were harmony and number."[30] In general, Pythagoreans regard the *harmonia*, a term that originally signified the octave, as the "limited" or πέρας. More precisely, it is the "unlimited," τὸ ἄπειρον, into which number and measure have been introduced. The Pythagoreans had succeeded in expressing in mathematical and quantitative terms the hitherto qualitatively differentiated parts of the octave, the relations of the parts of which may be formulated in terms of the ratio 6:8, 9:12. This ratio expresses the relations in pitch of the tones produced by the vibrations of a measurable length of taut cord. The mathematical expression of

[28] *Op. cit.*, 601. Translated by J. L. Davies and D. J. Vaughan. (By permission of The Macmillan Company, publishers.)

[29] See above, Chap. I, p. 10. Cf. L. Robin, *Platon*, p. 307. See, particularly, *Philebus* 26A.

[30] *Metaphysics*, I, 5 and *De Caelo*, II, 9. 290 b 15.

qualitatively differentiated tones in terms of a ratio in which means and extremes are equal is a model of method for unifying and "harmonizing" ostensibly discrete and disparate "unlimited" factors.

The Pythagorean conclusion that there is "music of the spheres" is significant for later cosmogonies and becomes perhaps no less so as an image in poetry. But for philosophy of art the significant contribution of Pythagoreanism derives from the inference that the simple formula or "form" of the *harmonia* is the necessary and common factor by which is explicable the pleasingness of the harmony. The inference drawn in course of time that the mathematically definable relations of vibrating strings of varying lengths also completely define the "beauty" of music weds mathematics and aesthetic theory for over two millennia.

As we have observed, Plato in *Hippias Major* suggests that "the beautiful" is the common and the "something of such sort that it will never appear ugly anywhere to anybody."[31] One discerns Pythagorean influences in each suggestion, as well as in the Platonic hypothesis that the forms are mathematically definable. But it would be an error of first magnitude to argue that the aesthetic theory in *Philebus* is wholly Pythagorean. Throughout his writings upon art and beauty, Plato has brought the earlier theory within the confines of an elaborate and systematic philosophy. Beauty and beautiful objects are subjected to analysis intended to ground them ontologically and epistemologically within that system. Pythagoreanism not improbably influenced Plato most strongly in his later philosophy of art in drawing him from the pursuit of the *scientia visionis* to the realm of forms, mathematically definable and beautiful in themselves, as well as existent in the world of sight and sound.

Within this systematic philosophy, Plato specifies the objects and events to which he proposes to restrict the predicate "absolutely beautiful." He specifies, as well, the criteria by which they will be adjudged to be beautiful. For Plato, absolutely beautiful objects describable in spatial terminology are limited to simple geometrical

[31] Cf. above, p. 97. The coordination of issues in Plato's earlier and later dialogues presents vexed questions which need not be discussed here. It is sufficient for the purposes of the present discussion to assume that the Dialogues were written by Plato and that he is a systematic philosopher.

figures or to combinations of such figures.[32] Of this class are "the straight line and the circle and the plane and solid figures formed from these." Similarly, absolutely beautiful "events" (a terminology that will be adopted to denote entities describable in temporal terms) mentioned by Plato are "pure" and "unmixed." To this class belong single notes of sound. The philosopher mentions absolutely beautiful colors, presumably spatial, and smells, "a less divine class" and presumably temporal.

Both the temporally and spatially defined "forms" are beautiful without reference to a unique aesthetic end or purpose. Presumably they are all meaningful in terms of a common ratio or proportion of parts.[33] Finally, they are all "abstract," not only because they are "abstracted" from context and teleological reference but, specifically, because in their experience we are free of mixed pleasures and pains because of the object's minimal sensuous or mimetic content.

If we turn now to the detail of *Philebus*, we find that it accords with Plato's precise and mature speculation upon the beauty of "abstract" forms as geometrical figures and as mathematically definable tones, colors, and odors. It will be noted that Plato implies that some gradation of beautiful objects is possible. Not only do "odours" belong to a "less divine class" but the most beautiful of "visible bodies" is said, in *Timaeus*, to be the "triangle whereof a pair constitute an equilateral triangle."[34] We best approach the argument that is intended to substantiate these conclusions if we recall the words of the *Republic*[35] and assume that the objects in question are differentiated from the "whole art of imitation" and, by implication, rely upon "the better part of the soul" which "is likely to be that which trusts to measure and calculation."

It may be inferred that the absolutely beautiful objects, definable in non-imitative terms, are not "relative." Mimetic objects are relative precisely because they have their essences in other objects

[32] *Philebus* 51. Translated by H. N. Fowler, 1925. (By permission of Harvard University Press, Cambridge, Mass.)

[33] See below, p. 113, fn. 61.

[34] *Op. cit.*, 53D-54.

[35] *Op. cit.*, 603 ff.

of which imitations are "images." This point leads directly to the ateleological implication of Plato's philosophy of art. The philosopher denies to the mathematically defined objects the end of imitation, of representation, and of "what most people would understand by the words [beauty of form] such as the beauty of animals and of paintings."[36]

The tone of Plato's writing makes evident his intention to deny the relevance of ordinary ends or purposes to the beautiful forms of *Philebus*. They are, thus, "abstracted" from their "concrete" contexts.[37] Should the initial elimination of teleologically significant factors proceed to its logical conclusion, it may be supposed that the need to resolve the problem presented by the fact that the experience of art is one of discontent and exaltation, need not arise. That this is not entirely foreign to Plato's intention in *Philebus* may be inferred from the differentiation made between the experience of the mathematically definable forms and that of tragedy and comedy, as well as from the implication that the "beauty of form" is superior to the "relatively beautiful," to "what most people would understand by the words beautiful." The forms are not alone "abstracted" from the ends of imitation or representation and their beauty is not alone differentiated from "such beauty as that of animals or pictures." They are likewise "abstracted" from the class of objects that produce "pains of the soul,"[38] "anger, fear, yearning, mourning, love, jealousy, envy, or the like"—from all relation to the emotional and irrational experience induced by other art and against which Plato directs his attack in the *Republic*. It will be recalled that it is the artist's appeal to the emotional and irrational portion of the soul which, for Plato, explains the spectator's experience of tragedy and comedy. There is a reminiscence of this in *Philebus*: "You remember, too, how people enjoy weeping at tragedy? . . . And you are aware of the conditions of the soul at comedies, how there also we have a mixture of pain and pleasure?"[39]

[36] *Philebus* 50E.

[37] The terminology is Hegelian and is used by Bosanquet throughout his *A History of Aesthetic*.

[38] *Philebus* 47E.

[39] *Op. cit.*, 47.

It may be urged, however, that, granted Plato's evident effort to dissociate the "eternally and absolutely beautiful" mathematical forms from terminology definitive of such specific purposes as imitation, representation, or the evocation of emotional and painful states, his argument nonetheless does define them teleologically. Two problems require consideration, however, before this conclusion may be accepted. The first turns on whether or not *Philebus* does, in fact, specify a unique purpose for the beautiful forms in question. The second is a direct consequence of the first: If the unique purpose is not specified, does the purpose that is specified and with which the purpose of the beautiful forms is identified justify the acceptance of a teleological interpretation of Plato's theory of beauty in *Philebus*?

The ostensible teleology of the "eternally and absolutely beautiful" forms would appear to be explicable in terms of the capacity of the objects and events to induce in the perceiver an experience of "pure" pleasure. That Plato differentiates the pleasure derived from the experience of forms "absolutely beautiful by nature" and that characteristic of experience of other objects and events may scarcely be doubted. The former objects have "peculiar pleasures in no way subject to comparison with the pleasure of scratching . . ."[40] i.e., the pleasures are unmixed with pain. Plato's argument, offered to establish the ground for the differentiation, is given in the form of a general theory of the physiology of pleasure and pain. The process of repletion after the depletion of bodily tissues, Plato argues, is generically pleasurable and the contrary process of depletion after repletion is painful. Pleasures "arising from what are called beautiful colors, or pure forms, most of those that arise from odours and sounds" are "those felt by the senses, pleasant and unmixed with pain" because "the want . . . is unfelt and painless."[41]

[40] *Op. cit.*, 52D.

[41] *Op. cit.*, 51B, *arranged.* Cf. Taylor, *Plato*, p. 426: ". . . in any case where a 'subliminal' or unconscious process of 'depletion' is followed by a conscious process of 'repletion,' there will be an experience which is wholly pleasant. . . . These pleasures are not preceded by a painful sense of craving, like those of the satisfaction of hunger or thirst, and do not owe any part of their apparent intensity to contrast."

That the teleology presumably applicable to the beautiful forms is, however, merely ostensible will be apparent if we follow a specific line of criticism implicit in Plato's own discussion of the general problem and one relevant to the foregoing passage. The pleasure "unmixed with pain" that describes the experience of the "absolutely beautiful forms" is "in no way subject to comparison with other pleasures." In the light of the last part of the statement, it is difficult, if not impossible, to admit that the term "pleasure" is applicable to the experience. The *continuum* of pleasure and pain described in terms of physiological processes of depletion and repletion has no place for the sensation belonging to the experience of the beautiful forms if that sensation may neither be compared to nor, by implication, contrasted with "other pleasure." It is difficult, moreover, to believe that Plato intended to include the "pure" pleasures in the general class of pleasures and so to evaluate them by considering "whether the entire class is to be desired."[42] It is true that the latter consideration permits us to distinguish pleasure in general from the particular pleasures and pains which are sometimes desired and sometimes not desired. Despite this, however, it may be argued that both the general and the particular experiences have in common a factor, pleasure, requisite for their comparison and contrast. Pleasure is clearly said to be "generated," "if the harmony is recomposed and returns to its own nature."[43] Moreover, Plato adds that, "whenever in the class of living beings which, as I said before, arises out of the natural union of the infinite and the finite, that union is destroyed, the destruction is pain, and the passage and return of all things to their own nature is pleasure." Furthermore, it should be recalled that one of the most powerful denials of the truth of the hedonist's assertion that pleasure is the "highest good" is that given in *Philebus* in Plato's disproof on logical grounds of the identification of the "sensation" with the "third state," the "condition of animated beings who are neither in process of restoration nor of dissolution."[44] In fact, Plato remarks that "the great changes cause

[42] *Philebus*, 32D.
[43] *Op. cit.*, 31D. Cf. 25E and 32A-B.
[44] *Op. cit.*, 32.

pain and pleasure in us, but the moderate and small ones cause no pains and pleasures at all."

In consequence, although his initial suggestion is that "pure pleasures" belong to the class of the "limited" (i.e., that into which "measure" has entered), while "impure pleasures" belong to the class of the "unlimited," the tenor of the argument and of its conclusion tends to give the impression that there has been made a differentiation in kind rather than in degree. But even if we disregard this impression, the use of the same terminology to describe presumably disparate experiences of differentiated objects leads to a lack of clarity not unlike that which confronts the reader of Mill's argument in support of qualitative distinctions in pleasure.[45] Confusion is worse confounded because Plato has suggested that the "mixed life . . . is not composed of any two particular ingredients, but of all the elements of infinity, bound down by the finite," that is to say, by the imposition of "limit" upon "pleasure" and presumably upon any pleasure.[46] Since "limit" may be imposed upon any "pleasure," the application of the term "limited" to the pleasures had in the experience of the mathematical forms does not designate a unique function, *qua* their production of pleasure.

The dilemma in Plato's argument presumably may be traced to a desire to describe the experience of beauty at once as unique and as identical to the pleasurable experience of knowledge.[47] Plato argues that "pleasures of knowledge if they appear to us not to have hunger for knowledge or pangs of such hunger for their source" are similarly "pure" and "in whatever we find this freedom from pain, I regard it as a mark of similarity to those other pleasures."[48] Insofar

[45] Cf. Plato's own argument in *Protagoras* 356: "What measure is there of the relations of pleasure to pain other than excess and defect, which means that they become greater and smaller . . . ? There can be no other measure of them."

[46] *Op. cit.*, 28; cf. *E. N.*, 1173 a 15. Aristotle writes in criticism of the argument in *Philebus* that, "They say that the good is determinate, while pleasure is indeterminate, because it admits of degrees. . . . But if their judgment is based on the various pleasures, surely they are not stating the real cause (of the badness of some pleasures) if in fact some pleasures are unmixed and others mixed."

[47] Cf. *Philebus* 52A.

[48] *Ibid.*, 51E.

as a proximate end may be attributed to "absolutely beautiful forms," it is identical with the "pure pleasure" derived from the experience of knowledge. It follows, therefore, that all objects of such knowledge are beautiful or all objects called "absolutely beautiful" are also objects of such knowledge as does not have "hunger for knowledge" as its source.[49] Plato does not argue the implications of the former hypothesis but the acceptance of the alternative is implicit in the inference that the beauty of the mathematically beautiful forms is "absolute" and "not relative." The inference follows from the explicit differentiation drawn between the "absolutely beautiful" forms and "other things," including by implication, painting, the representation of organic life, tragedy, and comedy. The differentiation may be understood, perhaps, to signify that the mathematical "forms" are superior to "relatively beautiful" objects and events because the former not only educe "peculiar pleasure" but because, unlike imitative arts, they are not deceptive. If the forms are "absolute" in beauty, they are so because they are not "images." They contain their own essence.[50] Their essence is not in another or, in an Aristotelian sense, the "forms" have their truth immanent in them.[51]

Plainly, however, the objects and events brought forward in *Philebus* to satisfy the requirements of the "mixture" in inducing "pure pleasure" are not, as mathematical "forms," essences. An interpretation that took full account of Plato's philosophy could scarcely ground their beauty except in terms of imitation, representation, or "images" of the mathematical forms which, in the *Republic*, are objects of understanding. Plato does not qualify the statement that some of the objects are "turned off from lathes." These "forms" remain in what he ordinarily refers to as the world of opinion or becoming. Nor should it be forgotten that the author

[49] It would appear to be easier to argue that Plato does distinguish the relation of the "beautiful forms" to "pure pleasure" from that holding between "sciences" and "pure pleasure" had he given a more detailed analysis of the "forms."

[50] They may be arts of production rather than arts of imitation. Still, because they are in the world of becoming, they are percepts of concepts and not concepts themselves.

[51] Plato may mean that the "forms" are self-sufficient objects of knowledge.

of the *Republic* argues that mathematicians are "really endeavoring to behold those abstractions which a person can only see with the eye of thought."[52] Indeed, as he adds, of the geometers it may be said that: "They summon to their aid visible forms, and discourse about them, though their thoughts are not busy with these forms, but with their originals, and though they discourse not with a view to the particular square and diameter which they draw, but with a view to the absolute square and the absolute diameter, and so on." In accordance with Plato's doctrine of Ideas, as it is expressed in the Dialogues of the middle period of his writing, the mathematically definable spatial "forms" of *Philebus* are "relative," as, by implication, are the temporal "forms." The spatial "forms" are visible triangles and circles. Insofar as they are visible and "made," they are "images" whose essence is in another. In the light of Plato's usual arguments, they are not and cannot be "absolutely beautiful," if by this it is intended that we draw an essential contrast between them and the objects termed "imitative." The "eternally and absolutely beautiful forms" of *Philebus* are objects classified ontologically and epistemologically in the lower portion of the upper half of the quadripartite line of the *Republic*.[53] However much value they may derive from their direction to "the better part of the soul . . . which trusts to measure and calculation,"[54] they remain sensible objects inferior in Plato's scheme to the ideal "forms" in the comprehension of which is required no visible representation.[55]

It would appear, therefore, that the "absolute beauty" of the

[52] *Op. cit.*, 510D. Translated by J. L. Davies and D. J. Vaughan. (By permission of The Macmillan Company, publishers.)

[53] *Op. cit.*, Books V and VII.

[54] *Ibid.*, Book X.

[55] Cf. *ibid.*, 529C. "It makes no difference whether a person stares stupidly at the sky, or looks with half-shut eyes upon the ground; so long as he is trying to study any sensible object, I deny that he can ever be said to have learned anything, because no objects of sense admit of scientific treatment. . . . Since this fretted sky is still a part of the visible world, we are bound to regard it, though the most beautiful and perfect of visible things, as far inferior nevertheless to those true revolutions, which real velocity and real slowness, existing in true number, and in all true forms, accomplish relatively to each other, carrying with them all that they contain; which are verily apprehensible by reason and thought but not by sight." Translated by J. L. Davies and D. J. Vaughan. (By permission of The Macmillan Company, publishers.) For a contrary interpretation, see John Burnet, *Greek Philosophy:*

geometrical forms is wholly explicable neither on grounds of a unique purpose subserved by pure colors, odors, sounds, or figures, nor of an unsurpassed value in the science with which its teleology is ostensibly identified. In consequence, it is still necessary to seek a ground for Plato's statements that the "forms" merit the predicate, "absolutely beautiful," which presumably permits their inclusion among the goods that constitute the good life.

It should be made clear that whether the effort to ground what in this essay is interpreted as a theory of ateleological mathematical and "abstract" forms succeeds or fails, the dialogue, *Philebus*, is evidence of Plato's acceptance of a hypothesis fundamental to aesthetic, a hypothesis integral to the argument concerning the One and the Many. As this issue of unity and diversity develops, it becomes more and more evident that the theory of "absolutely beautiful forms" at least implies that Plato is speculating upon the possibility that aesthetic objects in general have an objectively definable unity and are self-sufficient.[56] It is not necessary to consider at

Thales to Plato, pp. 317 ff. Burnet writes that "It is clear, then, that numbers are unique forms, and we have some reason for thinking that they are forms in a pre-eminent sense." Still, it is well to recall Plato's remark, *Philebus* 59: "Let us say that the stable and pure and true and unalloyed has to do with things which are eternal and unmixed, *or if not, at any rate what is most akin to them has.*" (Italics mine).

[56] *Op. cit.*, 64 D–E. Burnet, *op. cit.*, pp. 322-323, proposes an interpretation of Plato's theory of numbers which is of interest in this reference. He holds that Plato in *Epinomis* presents the developed view that Geometry is "an assimilation by reference to surfaces of numbers not similar to one another by nature." Burnet proceeds to interpret *Theatetus* 148A "to the effect that certain numbers are incommensurable 'in length'" but commensurable "by means of the surfaces of which they are roots." He concludes that, "What is new here is the assumption of a material element even in the forms, though that element is nothing more than abstract continuity. The importance of this is that it tends to make the intelligible forms less disparate from the things of sense." Burnet, in examining *Philebus* (*loc. cit.*, p. 331), "which must have been written while he [Aristotle] was a member of the Academy," infers that the "Mixture alone is truly being. The process of mixing is indeed a 'becoming,' . . . but it is a becoming which has being for its result . . . and the mixture itself is being, though a being which has become. . . ." He concludes that, "As the form-numbers are themselves a mixture, it follows that even sensible things may be real in spite of the fact that they are mixtures." Despite this, however, it must be remembered that *Philebus* is a "practical" dialogue dealing with the good of man "and not of the Gods" and that its metaphysical substructure does not, in that sense, affect the Platonic theory of Ideas of the middle period.

this point the significance of unity in the structure of the entire Dialogue.[57] But that unity is the basic explanatory principle for the "eternally and absolutely beautiful forms" is evident if we consider the following aspects of the general argument:

1. Plato holds that the experience of "absolutely beautiful forms" is describable in terms of "pure pleasure." "Pure pleasure," it is argued, must be distinguished from such pleasure mixed with pain as is associated with the experience of objects for which the want or desire is not only precedent but of which the percipient is likewise conscious. The desire for the "beautiful forms," it is maintained, is "subliminal" and unfelt. "Pure pleasure" is not conditioned by contrast to previous pain and is, in consequence, self-sufficient or self-explanatory. Moreover, by implication, the experience of "pure pleasure" is not integral to the process of "repletion" which is called "pleasure." Insofar as it is "pure," the pleasure must be contrasted to the process of "repletion," since the latter is "becoming," is for the sake of something else, and, consequently, is incomplete. Moreover, "pure pleasures," because they are "limited," do not vary infinitely in intensity. It may be inferred from Plato's argument that "pure pleasure" is an "index" of unity. But the inference is of little significance for what it adds to Plato's analysis of "pleasure," because, as we have already concluded, "pure" pleasure is not commensurable with "mixed" pleasures or with what may be called generic pleasure.[58] It is significant, however, in its implication of unity in the experience effected in the percipient by the "forms."

2. It was remarked earlier[59] that it is difficult to accept the inference sometimes made that Plato meant in *Philebus* to assert that the "absolute" forms do not imitate essences but are, rather, essences themselves. Despite this difficulty, it is plain that the "absolutely beautiful forms" are remarked upon as if they were, in fact, neither representative nor imitative of percepts or of the objects of productive art and, whatever may be the conclusion concerning the larger issues of *Philebus*, the "forms" do not borrow their "subject matter"

[57] See above, pp. 102-104.
[58] Cf. above, p. 108.
[59] See above, p. 110, fn. 55.

from other arts.[60] Their unity is, therefore, intrinsic. Their value is in practice, if not in theory, independent of the value of the concepts or opinions or "images" of objects in other arts. Because they are self-sufficient unities, their significance is owing neither to accurate nor inaccurate imitation of what is external to them.

3. It may be inferred that Plato judges simple geometrical figures, pure colors, and pure tones to be the "absolutely beautiful" forms in part because their unity is that of objects and events, the components of which he conceives to be most nearly homogeneous[61] or which are most nearly "harmonized" in terms of mathematical ratios. The triangles and circles are specific and precise spatial delineations. They "limit" the "unlimited," and, if one may take cognizance here of an argument in *Timaeus*,[62] are individuated in the "receptacle." Thus, in *Philebus* we are told that pure colors are beautiful and it is remarked that "pure color" is "the most unmixed," because it is "that in which there is no trace of any other color, . . . not the most numerous or the greatest is both the truest and the most beautiful of all whitenesses."[63] A similar inference appears to be implicit in the attribution of beauty to "pure tones." It is recognized that "single pure notes" are compounds of successive parts, but it is argued in *Timaeus* that successive notes appear to be either dissonant or consonant depending upon the regularity possible when: "The slower motions . . . catch up with those of earlier and more rapid tones; . . . when they thus overtake them, they do not perturb them by the superposition of a fresh motion, but supply the beginning of a slower motion uniform with the more rapid, which is ceasing and so produce a single effect, blended of acute and grave."[64] It may be added that Plato, consistently, in

[60] See, Introduction, p. 14.

[61] See A. E. Taylor, *A Commentary on Plato's Timaeus*, particularly p. 370. Taylor remarks, in commenting upon *Timaeus* 54A-1-B2, that Plato regards the particular triangle under discussion as beautiful because "the ratio of the two acute angles is 2:1, the simplest of all ratios after the ratio of equality (1:1) which obtains between the acute angles of the isosceles right-angled, and again the ratios of the acute angles to the right angle of the triangle are 1:3 and 2:3, the simplest of all ratios except 2:1 and 1:1."

[62] *Op. cit.*, 48 ff.

[63] *Philebus* 52E, 53B (*arranged*).

[64] *Op. cit.*, 80 A-B. Translated by A. E. Taylor.

the same Dialogue argues that pleasant odors and perfumes, which we recall are beauties of a "less divine class," owe their "pleasantness" to the fact that "the process of depletion and evacuation is gradual but that of repletion sudden."[65]

Plato tacitly identifies "form" and unity or self-sufficiency[66] and has initiated analysis of a principle that occupies a central place in aesthetic. But it is not only history that recognizes the significance of unity in art and in aesthetic experience. Plato himself does more than recognize the basic value of unity, and proceeds so far as to distinguish the "unity" or "form" of "absolutely beautiful objects" from that of mere aggregates or "jumbles." That the "forms" or unities must have measure and proportion[67] is plainly, in his view, a proper corollary to the general principle. This is evident in the fact already mentioned,[68] that aesthetic objects are unified by "measure" which harmonizes the most nearly homogeneous parts into wholes or units in terms of a simple ratio.

Plato's is a significant contribution, yet the difficulty that follows upon his assertion that these "forms" or unities are "absolutely beautiful" is no less evident. One need but recall passages in *Protagoras*[69] to anticipate the crux inherent in this absolutism. Plato implies in this earlier Dialogue in the questions concerning the meaning of the relation of "parts" to the "one virtue," that two means of unifying diverse parts must be considered. One is the unity of identical parts, as grains of gold are identical, the other, unification of diverse parts, as is illustrated by the mouth, nose, eyes, and ears as parts of the face.

In *Philebus*, Plato appears to consider only the first alternative. His reliance in the Dialogue upon mathematical measure as applied to nearly homogeneous parts to insure unity and, in consequence, to explain the unity of "absolutely beautiful forms" is the more curious if we recall alternative suggestions made in other Dialogues which imply that the absolutism is not required by the argument.

[65] *Ibid.*, 64-65.
[66] I.e., the form or unity of entities with diverse parts.
[67] *Philebus* 63.
[68] See above, p. 113, fn. 61.
[69] *Op. cit.*, 329 ff.

In *Gorgias*,[70] by way of illustration, Plato grants that artists may produce "regular and systematic wholes" from wholes the parts of which are considerably diverse, inasmuch as the artist "compels one part to harmonize and accord with the other part." There is given, too, in *Phaedrus*[71] a description of the unity of rhetorical art which implies a principle generalized in Aristotle's *Poetics*. In *Phaedrus*, the whole described is in its unity analogous to the unity of the organism: "Every discourse ought to be a living creature, having its own body and head and feet; there ought to be a middle, beginning and end, which are in a manner agreeable to one another and to the whole." Clearly, in this instance, the parts of the whole may be far other than homogeneous. Their unity is that implicit in a function common to diverse parts. It is not suggested that, because the organism and the rhetorician's discourse are by implication unified by their relations to ends, the teleological method of unification in itself presents either any particular hindrance to the effectiveness of the means or that it diminishes the value of the unified object simply because the parts it does unify are heterogeneous if contrasted to unity derived by means of form and ratio. Plato does grant, in fact, in the *Republic*,[72] that the beautiful in sculptured wholes is not necessarily the consequence of the sculptor's making each part most beautiful. The sculptor makes the parts proportionate to the beautiful whole. It is well to recall that the *reductio ad absurdum* of the implication that the beauty of the "single" pure notes and of similar spatial and temporal entities which follows upon the requirement of homogeneity is offered by Plotinus.[73] The Neo-Platonist's criticism is the more interesting because he, too, maintains that unity is of fundamental significance for beauty.[74] Plotinus explicitly denies that symmetry explains beauty: "Almost everyone," he writes, "declares that the symmetry of parts towards each other and towards a whole, with besides a certain grace of color, constitutes the beauty appealing to the eye,

[70] *Op. cit.*, 503-504.
[71] *Op. cit.*, 264; cf. below, Chaps. IV and IX.
[72] *Op. cit.*, 420.
[73] *Enneads* I, 6.
[74] See above, Chap. II, pp. 44-48.

that in visible things . . . and in all things else, usually . . . to be beautiful is to be symmetrical and fashioned after a certain measure." Plotinus' comment upon this is just: ". . . by this teaching, of necessity, only a compound can be beautiful, never anything simple."[75]

Despite the passages which permit us to infer that Plato was well aware that there is a variety of means by which unity may be secured, he nonetheless arbitrarily selects exemplifications of mathematical "form" or unity for identification with "absolutely beautiful forms." But it may be argued, even if it be granted that unity is a necessary condition for the beauty of objects or events, no *a priori* necessity compels the theorist to accept unities definable solely in mathematical terms and to reject all other unities, including those functionally definable. It follows, therefore, that if we evaluate Plato's argument solely in terms of its identification of "form" with unity, mathematical unity does not provide a valid ground for the stringent limitation placed by this ateleological theory upon the aesthetic universe of discourse. It thus remains a possibility that the objects and events discussed in *Philebus* are in fact beautiful. It is beyond Plato's powers to prove that they are the only beautiful objects, if the proof rests solely on the argument that their form is unity. *Philebus* is aesthetically significant because it calls attention to the problem of unity as a necessary condition of aesthetic experience.[76] It fails to establish the grounds for "absolute beauty," as it fails to offer sound principles for restricting the field of aesthetic objects.

Moreover, against the *a priori* hypothesis implicit in *Philebus*, may be brought telling objections. The "absolutely beautiful" forms in *Philebus* and *Timaeus* are empirical and perceptible objects and events and not, as Plato appears to imply, solely conceptual in nature. Whether or not they satisfy the basic condition that they are beautiful is a question best answered on empirical grounds. To venture to predict *a priori* that their aesthetic qualifications are

[75] And Plato, it will be recalled, does use "single" metaphorically. A "single" tone is composed of successive and diverse parts.

[76] It is not suggested that this bald statement *is* the sole Platonic argument. But it is important to recognize that the subjective-objective criteria together are comprehensible primarily in terms of unity.

adequate to satisfy even the trained taste is impossible. Whatever initial interest they may educe, the enjoyment to be got from the experience of triangles and squares is not inexhaustible. Not only objects of more enduring interest but sounder arguments than those intended to ground "pure pleasure" as aesthetic experience are needed to justify the arbitrary elimination from the aesthetic universe of discourse of tragedy, comedy, sculpture, painting, and representation. It may be argued, indeed, that Plato's interest in simple forms and their combinations at the expense of a more complex art culminates in a formalism so lacking in variety as to induce sheer boredom. His concentration upon "form" as unity has led his philosophy of art and that of many succeeding theorists[77] to identify the simplest unity with the most perfect beauty. That critic is ill-advised who is content to assert that the deficiencies of Plato's theory of formally beautiful objects and events are owing to insufficient diversity of objects or events or to a lack of heterogeneity in the factors entering upon them. This is true simply because, while the inference is sound, it leaves unanswered the question why diversity in unity is a dictum by which the antinomies of art implicit in Plato's philosophy may in their turn be more effectively resolved than by Plato's use of the principle of homogeneity of parts.

Plato's effort to resolve the problems for art and aesthetic experience, which he himself has propounded by limiting the aesthetic universe of discourse to "absolutely beautiful forms" with internal factors as nearly homogeneous throughout as is possible for craft or nature to produce, is in fact, doomed to failure.[78] The failure is owing primarily to a defective analysis of the structure of art in relation to the end of art.[79] Form does not sufficiently define this structure. Moreover, as we have observed, Plato's effort to relate the "absolutely beautiful forms" to "pure pleasure" fails because what under other circumstances might have led to sound analysis at least of the formal factors in the work of art presupposed by a

[77] See above, Chap. II, particularly with reference to St. Augustine.
[78] Cf. below, Chap. IV, pp. 166 ff.
[79] Cf. below, Chaps. IV, VIII and XVIII.

teleological aesthetic culminates in an assertion that the object or event in question is "beautiful," whatever its "external" relations may be or, indeed, even if it be totally unrelated to percipient or end.[80]

The forgoing assertions merely anticipate issues pertinent to later chapters of this essay. For the present, it will suffice to assume that the difficulties inherent in Plato's ateleological theory result from the fact that the objects and events called "absolutely beautiful" are "abstract" or that they have been identified with mathematical "forms." Kant, an "abstractionist" in philosophy of art no less rigorous than was Plato, brings the latter criticism to bear upon the mathematical tradition in aesthetic. He grants that "geometrically regular figures, such as a circle, a square, a cube, etc., are commonly adduced by critics of taste as the simplest and most indisputable examples of beauty."[81] But he denies that "critics of taste" are correct in this judgment. In fact, Kant urges that "All stiff regularity (such as approximates to mathematical regularity) has something in it repugnant to taste; for our entertainment in the contemplation of it lasts for no length of time, but it rather, . . . produces weariness." And he adds that a man "need only have made the experiment of spending one day in a pepper-garden, to have been convinced that . . . the object will not entertain for long, . . . nay rather it will impose a burdensome constraint upon the Imagination."[82]

Although the force of Kant's argument is not expended upon *Philebus*,[83] it is improbable that most critics would exempt Plato's triangles, spheres, pure colors, and sounds from inclusion in the former's charge that such objects "produce weariness." The em-

[80] Whether even the more adequate analysis of the structure of the object of art is alone sufficient to resolve the aesthetic problems involved is discussed in relation to the theory of "aesthetic surface." See Chapter VIII.

[81] Immanuel Kant, *Kritik of Judgment*, Sec. 22, J. H. Bernard's translation, p. 97. This translation is quoted throughout. (By permission of The Macmillan Company, publishers.) In references to Kant's writings, I have used the usual abbreviations for titles of his works, i.e., *K.d.U.* for *Kritik of Judgment*, *K.d.r.V.* for *Kritik of Pure Reason*, and *K.d.pr.V.* for *Kritik of Practical Reason*.

[82] *Ibid*., p. 99.

[83] For the historical influences on Kant's aesthetic theory, see V. Basch, *Essai Critique sur l'Esthétique de Kant*.

pirical criterion implied by the author of the *Kritik of Judgment* provides a weapon for use against Plato's "abstract" theory and analogous arguments because by it is implicitly evoked the significant criterion of the inexhaustibility of interest implicit in objects of true aesthetic experience. It would, however, be no less serious an error to suppose that Kant's own selection of beautiful objects and events is intended to obviate boredom than to infer that the stringent limitation he places upon the aesthetic universe of discourse follows merely upon a denial of the mathematical presuppositions of beauty. Kant proposes an alternative aesthetic no less "abstract" and restrictive of objects and events than that formulated by Plato. Moreover, it is part of a system of philosophy no less complex than the theory of Ideas. Its nature and validity will be considered in the following section of this chapter.

IV

Kant and the Non-Mathematical Hypothesis of "Abstract" Form

THAT Kant does inveigh against the mathematical interpretation of beauty is significant for his aesthetic theory, as is the fact that he is critical of a philosophical tradition which, while it influenced his own thought, interprets beauty in terms of "hidden harmonies." However significant these facts may be, to dissociate Kant's arguments against the mathematical interpretation of objects of aesthetic judgment from his general rejection of an aesthetic of concepts is to misapprehend the meaning of perhaps the most influential writing upon philosophy of art produced in modern times.

The temptation to abstract such specific arguments from Kant's general aesthetic is ever present and the fact is illuminating. Hegel remarks that the *Kritik of Judgment* is both "instructive and remarkable." The difficulty lies not in accepting this evaluation but in limiting it to Kant's aesthetic theory, inasmuch as the analysis of aesthetic judgment is but a portion of the context of the third and last of his great Critiques. The issues raised in it are not only profoundly difficult but also, in many instances, so various as to fall outside the scope of aesthetic. It will be necessary, therefore, to limit our problem. We shall not be concerned here, except as either directly influences ateleological "abstract" and non-mathematical philosophy of art, with the success or failure of Kant's attempt to establish the *Kritik of Judgment* as the mediator of its predecessors. Nor shall we be concerned, except as they impinge on our problem, with the various specific mediations implicit in Kant's table of the "higher" faculties according to their systematic unity.[84] However, working within the confines of a systematic philosophy like Kant's, we must be prepared to gauge the consequences for the aesthetic problem of hypotheses and conclusions not always specifically relevant to it. Equally, even in the specifically aesthetic problem it will be necessary to limit the discussion primarily to Kant's analysis of the judgment of taste in relation to the beauty of natural forms and largely to forgo analysis of his views on art and genius.

A statement of Kant's theory of "abstract" ateleologically and non-mathematically defined forms is, at the outset, largely one of negations because of the philosopher's own effort to distinguish the judgment of taste from other synthetic judgments implicated in feelings of pleasure and pain. Nevertheless, in general, the formally beautiful objects of the judgment of taste to which Kant restricts the field of aesthetic may be characterized as follows: Spatial entities which are objects of the judgment of taste, and, consequently, components of the aesthetic universe of discourse, are restricted to specified shapes or delineations interpreted independently of any mathematical value they may have and apart from any mathematical significance they may display in another context.[85] Temporal entities, i.e., "events," judged to be beautiful are restricted to unified wholes which as objects of the judgment of taste are not definable in terms of mathematical formulae. Neither the spatially nor the temporally defined objects of the judgment of taste are signifi-

[84] *Op. cit.*, Introduction, IX.

[85] That they may have significance in non-aesthetic contexts seems to be implied by Kant. Cf. below, pp. 126 ff.

cant in relation to a specific or a uniquely aesthetic function or purpose. Moreover, they are specifically distinguished objects defined in terms of non-aesthetic teleologies. Consequently, considered ateleologically, they are "abstract," i.e., abstracted from function or purpose. However, with reference to them, the term "abstract" implies as well an absence or reduction of "sensuous" factors. In consequence, objects of the judgment of taste are "formal."

Among the specific "forms" called "aesthetic" by Kant are such spatial entities as flowers, birds, sea shells, delineations *a la grècque*, foliage for borders of wall paper, and the ripple marks on the sand by the sea. The "events" or entities temporally characterized include "sensations of color and tones" which "have a right to be regarded as beautiful only insofar as they are pure," "musical fantasies (pieces without any theme)," and "all music without words."

We have observed that Kant offers an empirical argument against the frequently stated interpretation of beauty in terms of mathematical regularity. The burden of his protest is, ostensibly, that triangles and similar objects "produce weariness" in the percipient. It is not beside the point, therefore, to anticipate a judgment that it is doubtful that the "forms" Kant himself selects would "entertain" for long. Actually, he rarely invokes such empirical criteria as boredom and weariness in evaluating beauty and the objects and events he does hold to be beautiful are consequently little affected by the criticism. He does hold that we "*linger* over the contemplation of the beautiful," but he does so for other than empirical reasons. The issue is truly joined once it is plain that Kant's criticism of regular mathematical figures derives from the fact that they are "mere presentations of a definite concept which prescribes the rule for the figure."

A significant, if negative, criterion is in operation at this point and is used by Kant to mark off the field within which it is fitting that the judgment of taste discover and assess its objects. Its significance is evident, not so much because it directly operates to include or exclude specific objects and events but rather because, as the argument is followed, one ascertains the reasons for Kant's answer to the question, "Why have mathematical objects so frequently been judged to be aesthetic?" He holds, in fact that the determination of a mathematical figure is "a purpose in respect of cognition and we derive satisfaction from the achievement of this end."

Kant argues that pleasure, which accompanies the solution to mathematical problems, is subsequent to the essential interrelated functioning of the faculties in the judgment of taste. In any case, although the determination of mathematical figures and the experience of beautiful objects may both be pleasant, they may and must be distinguished. But a second source of confusion, it is asserted, is found in the fact that "the regularity which leads to the concept of an object is indeed the indispensable condition . . . for grasping the object in a single representation and determining the manifold of its form."[86]

Kant's denial of conceptual character to the objects of the judgment of taste, as well as his evident preoccupation with the problem of the pleasure associated with aesthetic experience, suggests the need for an analysis of the ateleological structure of the theory and of an evaluation of Kant's success or failure in grounding the objects logically in that system. This requires that other distinctions between aesthetic and non-aesthetic objects and events made in the *Kritik* be mentioned, since Kant does not mean only that the objects of taste are not objects judged in terms of concepts. He intends, as well, to show that they are not proper objects of judgments concerned with interest, agreeableness, satisfaction, or utility. Moreover, the judgment of taste is not implicated in the problem of perfection. Neither does it relate to the capacities of objects or events to arouse emotion nor does its competence raise the issue of ontological status. In addition, objects of the judgment of taste are not mimetic, have no relation to an ideal or canon, and may not be defined in terms of organic function. The accompanying argument is intended clearly to dissociate them from teleological definition.

Kant proceeds to examine the problem implicit in the ordinary association of pleasure with the experience of beautiful objects in

[86] *Ibid.*, p. 98. Cf. below, pp. 133 ff.

terms of the "free interplay of the faculties." It is upon the implications of the latter phrase that his argument for an ateleological aesthetic rests. To understand what he means by "free interplay of the faculties," it is well to remember that Kant insists that the objects of taste must be "formal" and, with this in mind, return to the relevant Kantian interpretation of conceptual knowledge in the form of mathematics.[87] Kant holds that in the case of geometrical regularity "the Understanding gives the law." The Imagination can do no more than to "proceed according to a definite law." The product of this cognitive process is "determined by conceptions as to what it ought to be." But objects of taste are not judged in terms of "oughtness" and the procedure of Imagination "according to a definite law" runs counter to a primary requisite for the judgment of taste, i.e., the freedom of the faculties.[88] We are led by this argument to the generalized formulation of the nature and conditions of aesthetic judgment, of which the following is a summary.

In other than aesthetic judgment, the Imagination holds up the sensuous manifold for the Understanding. The determinant Judgment subsumes the latter as a representation under the proper Categories of the Understanding. However, as the argument continues:

> In order to distinguish whether anything is beautiful or not, we refer the representation[89] not by the Understanding to the Object for cognition, but by the Imagination (perhaps in conjunction with the Understanding) to the subject, and its feeling of pleasure or pain. . . . Every reference of representations, even that of sensations, may be objective (and then it signifies the real [element] of an empirical representation); save only the reference to the feeling

[87] I.e., in the *Kritik of Judgment.*

[88] Kant does insist, however, despite the fact that "the *beautiful* is that which without a concept is cognised," it is yet "cognised as the object of *necessary* satisfaction." He says that "The *imaginative power* should be *free* and yet *of itself conformed to law.*" *Ibid.*, p. 96. Compare Sec. 49, p. 198. Kant argues, as usual, for freedom as autonomy and not for freedom as freedom from restrictions. Translated by J. H. Bernard. (By permission of The Macmillan Company, publishers.)

[89] Cf. *K.d.r.V.*, A104, A135, A197, i.e. A representation is an appearance determined by space and time. An Object is a representation determined by the laws of thought.

of pleasure and pain, by which nothing in the Object is signified, but through which there is a feeling in the subject, as it is affected by the representation.

Kant holds that the Imagination synthesizes the manifold of sense and he calls this faculty "a blind but indefinable function of the soul without which we should have no knowledge whatsoever." Its function is apprehension.[90] The Understanding functions to find the principle of unity in the manifold synthesized by Imagination. The function of Understanding is recognition and by its perceptions [representations] are referred to concepts.[91]

Kant's argument proceeds on the hypothesis that, upon the occurrence of cognition, there is a harmony of the faculties with each other and presumably with the object cognized.[92] Specifically, however, he maintains that the "accordance of the cognitive powers" must be such that "this internal solution (of the faculties) by which one mental faculty is excited by another, shall be generally the most beneficial for both faculties in respect of cognition (of given objects). . . ." The interrelation of the faculties Kant describes as a "harmonious interplay." The fact that it occurs, he holds, can be determined not by concepts but only by feeling: the "feeling" of "free play" is aesthetic. The representation "of the state of *free play* of the faculties by which an object is given" does not relate to the conceptual significance of the object. It does represent the harmonious interplay of the faculties.[93]

This "subjective relation" for cognition in general, must be valid

[90] But see Kant's description of *apprehensio* and *comprehensio aesthetica*, *K.d.U.*, Sec. 26, p. 111.

[91] Cf. *ibid.*, Sec. 21, p. 93: "(Cognition) . . . actually always takes place when a given object by means of Sense excites the Imagination to collect the manifold, and the Imagination in turn excites the Understanding to bring about a unity of this collective process in concepts." Cf. *ibid.*, p. 64, Sec. 9.

[92] Cf. below, p. 125.

[93] *Ibid.*, Sec. 9, p. 64: "This State of *free play* of the cognitive facilities in a representation by which the object is given, must be universally communicable; because cognition, as the determination of the Object with which given representations (in whatever subject) are to agree, is the only kind of representation which is valid for everyone.

"The subjective universal communicability of the mode of representation in a judgment of taste, since it is to be possible without presupposing a definite concept, can refer to nothing else than the state of mind in the free

for everyone and therefore "universally communicable."[94] Because it is assumed that all men cognize, Kant concludes that the conditions essential for aesthetic pleasure may be presupposed for all men. The subject of aesthetic experience may assume, if he assures himself that the feeling in question is not the consequence of judgment upon the good or the satisfactory, and that his satisfaction is owing neither to the egoistic desires nor to the achievement of any end, that the judgment of taste will be universally valid.[95]

In his presentation of the argument, Kant unquestionably emphasizes the significance of both the harmony and interplay of the faculties. Equally without question, he does not intend to deprive his aesthetic theory of objects. He maintains, in fact, that "this accordance of the cognitive powers has a different proportion according to the variety of the Objects which are given."[96] Furthermore, criteria for the aesthetic value of the "Objects" are specifically stated to be the "immediacy" of the experience they evoke and their capacity to invite and hold contemplation.[97] Presumably in accordance with these criteria, Kant mentions in the *Kritik* the limited number of objects and events to which reference has already been made. Presumably, also, they are "immediately" and "easily" perceived and productive of a "harmonious interplay" of the faculties. Kant insists that they are describable in formal rather than in "sensational" terms.[98]

---

play of the Imagination and the Understanding (so far as they agree with each other, as a requisite for *cognition in general*)." Translated by J. H. Bernard. (By permission of The Macmillan Company, publishers.)

[94] Cf. *ibid.*, note to Sec. 38, 166: . . . "The subjective conditions of the Judgment . . . are the same in all men. This must be true, because otherwise men would not be able to communicate their representations or even their knowledge . . ."

[95] *Ibid.*, Sec. 8, p. 63 "He can [i.e., in making a judgment of taste] be quite certain of this [parity] for himself by the mere consciousness of the separating of everything belonging to the Pleasant and the Good from the satisfaction which is left." This, of course, runs counter to the claim for "immediacy."

[96] *Ibid.*, Sec. 21, pp. 93-94.

[97] *Ibid.*, Sec. 34, p. 159. "For I must immediately feel pleasure in the representation of the Object." Cf. Sec. 22 and Introduction VII, p. 30. Kant is not consistent, however, in his various arguments.

[98] *Ibid.*, Introduction, VII, pp. 31-42: "In the case of the object whose form (*not the matter of its representation, or sensation*), in the mere reflection upon

It is at this point that we may profit by making explicit other suggestions that may cast additional light upon Kant's interpretation in terms of form, of aesthetic objects and events. One is led to do this in part because to do otherwise implies the acceptance of the *Kritik* as if its author were intent wholly upon arguing the problems of universality and necessity as they relate to the judgment of taste. Important as are the latter issues for Kant throughout the whole of his philosophical thinking, it may be maintained that their significance comes to be largely ostensible, once the specifically aesthetic problems of the *Kritik of Judgment* are encountered. This is evident once we make an effort to apply his criteria to the "parrots, the humming bird and bird of paradise" or to flowers. The latter, he argues, are "free natural beauties" because "hardly anyone but a botanist knows what sort of thing a flower ought to be; and even he, though recognising in the flower the reproductive organ of the plant, pays no regard to this natural purpose if he is passing a judgment on the flower by Taste."[99] That this argument is only ostensibly an effort to prove that the judgment of taste is universal and necessary becomes plain if we attend to an aspect of Kant's theory that has as yet been barely mentioned. The flower obviously has a dual function. It is an object the ontological status of which poses a not irrelevant question. Kant grants that it does have an end, namely, in the process of reproduction. It is also definable in functional terms as an object of the judgment of taste. Kant argues, as regards its latter status, that the

it (without reference to any concept to be obtained of it), is judged as the ground of pleasure in the representation of such an Object, this pleasure is judged as bound up with the representation necessarily; and, consequently, not only for the subject which apprehends this form, but for every judging being in general. The object is then called beautiful. . . . For since the ground of the pleasure is placed merely in the form of the object for reflection in general and, consequently, in no *sensation of the object*, and also without reference to any concept which anywhere involves design . . . it is only the conformity to law in the empirical use of the Judgment in general (unity of the Imagination with the Understanding) in the subject, with which the representation of the Object in reflection, whose conditions are universally valid *a priori*, harmonises." (Italics my own.) Cf. Sec. 15, p. 77 ff. Translation by J. H. Bernard. (By permission of The Macmillan Company, publishers.)

[99] *Ibid*., Sec. 16, p. 81.

flower's ontological meaning and its natural purpose are equally irrelevant. He does entertain alternative possibilities in considering the issue: the person judging the object aesthetically may have no concept of the natural purpose or "else abstracts from it in his judgment."[100] To permit "abstraction" of this kind is, however, to destroy the possibilities of limiting the aesthetic universe of discourse. To grant that the percipient does "abstract from it in his judgment" would permit *any object* to be an object of the judgment of taste. One need only "abstract" form from material content. Kant does entertain the possibility but he clearly is confronted by difficulties. In order to surmount them, he is forced to assume that there are two kinds of beauty, one of which he calls "free," the other "dependent."[101] The former is "pure," the latter, impaired.[102] The point is that once by implication any object can be made "formal" by "abstracting from it in . . . judgment," Kant is forced to argue explicitly that only "free" beauties are truly "formal."

The reasons for Kant's emphasis upon specific formal objects and events are not unlike those that influenced Plato and led him to assume a not dissimilar hypothesis in the *Republic* and *Philebus*. Once the reasons are recognized, Kant's effort may be evaluated as one in part intended to resolve the antinomy of art and, moreover, one put forward to circumvent the charge that aesthetic experience has aspects of disvalue as well as of value. In this light, Kant's limitation of the aesthetic universe of discourse to beautiful forms[103] is a significant consequence of his assumption that objects to which we are attracted and by which we are pleased because of "sensuous" or "material factors" may induce in us a "pathological state."[104]

The important implication of the so-called *necessitatio per stimulos* holding in the latter "state" is succinctly expressed in

[100] *Ibid.*, p. 83.

[101] *Ibid.*, Sec. 16, p. 81. "Free beauty" is *pulchritudo vaga*; "dependent beauty" is *pulchritudo adhaerens*.

[102] *Ibid.*, pp. 83-84. Kant regards flowers as "free natural beauties" but he fails to avoid the dilemma by doing so.

[103] Omitting, for the moment, the problem of the sublime.

[104] Cf. *K.d.U.*, Sec. 5, p. 53.

Kant's *Lectures on Ethics*: "If the will of all beings were so bound to sensuous impulse, the world would possess no value." There are, as we have observed, basic systematic reasons for Kant's actual statement of his aesthetic theory but the hypothetical proposition just quoted is evidence of perhaps the most compelling reason for his limitation of the aesthetic universe of discourse to formally defined objects. Kant wants at once to guard the judgment of taste from consequences of art's antinomic character and to safeguard the value he holds to be intrinsic to beautiful objects by identifying the beautiful with the formal and non-sensuous. If the effort proves successful, the charges implicit in the term "pathological" may not be leveled at experience of the beautiful forms.[105]

At this point, in accepting hypotheses stated in the Cartesian theory of "automatism of brutes," Kant is by implication contending that if the judgment of taste is related to "content" or "matter" rather than to "form," the will is implicated in actions *per stimulos* or in "pathological necessitation," in which action is motivated solely by feelings of the pleasant or unpleasant.[106] Kant explicitly maintains that the judgment of taste "is different from all cognitive judgments . . . if we at the outset abstract from all content, viz.,

[105] There is extreme subjectivity in certain of Kant's deductions of the judgment of taste. It is significant that Kant does argue that, in contrast to his analysis of the beautiful, "no sensible form can contain the sublime properly called." (*K.d.U.*, p. 103.) It is even more significant that Kant is enabled to discuss the sublime and to assume that there are no sublime objects or events because he has recourse to Reason, with "its claim for absolute totality" and with its function as a practical faculty and a ground for the moral law. He grants that in the judgment of the sublime we are concerned with emotion. This state of feeling must be compensated for if we are to judge the representation of our own state of mind to be sublime. But there are no sublime forms. There are, however, beautiful forms and Kant implies that the "pathological" implications in the judgment upon the beautiful are negatived (a) by making pleasure subsequent to the "interplay" and (b) by urging that the forms are wholly formal. As will be evident, however, the "abstraction" of form from matter is untenable. But more significantly the implied bifurcation of "feeling" into pleasure as "sensation" (Cf. *Ibid.*, p. 49) and "emotion" is equally untenable. The consequence is that the forms are sensuous and related to feeling. Both the beautiful and the sublime should properly be related to "feeling" and the argument proceed from that point. The issue is discussed in the present essay on pp. 353 ff. of Chap. XI.

[106] *Lectures on Ethics*, p. 16.

from the feeling of pleasure."[107] This dependence in aesthetic upon form is analogous to Kant's procedure in ethical theory:[108] he regards the determining ground for moral judgment to be a "law divorced from all matter" after which "nothing is left but the mere *form* of a universal legislation."[109]

In consequence, one compelling motive that leads Kant to interpret aesthetic in ateleological and formally "abstract" terms is not far to seek: An aesthetic of objects and events in which beauty is owing primarily to sensation or to feeling not only devalues the object but makes the subject one who acts because the primary motivating spring or power is "pathological necessitation." So moved, the willing subject is brought to the level of the brute. The reversion to a "*bruta necessitas*" through the instrumentality of "material" *stimuli* is one to the level of instinct by which both brute and man are driven.

Kant offers, in fact, an obvious solution to the problem as he envisages it. He turns to a theory of form for the objects and he denies teleological reference to aesthetic experience. He concludes that there are certain objects and events which, without need for a conscious process of "abstraction" on the part of the percipient, induce a "harmonious interplay of the faculties." With reference to these objects, one may "impute" to all men an identical judgment of taste, i.e., the objects must be absolutely beautiful.[110]

It may be asked, however, whether these objects and events are not in fact teleologically definable and, indeed, whether they do not fulfill a unique aesthetic purpose. Kant's argument is certainly not unambiguous on either point. Some part of the ambiguity derives, as has been suggested,[111] from the use of the term "abstrac-

[107] *K.d.U.*, Sec. 31, p. 153.

[108] Cf. *K.d.pr.V.* (Abbott's translation), p. 114.

[109] Cf. H. J. Paton, *Kant's Metaphysic of Experience*, Vol. I, pp. 137-143, on *K.d.r.V.*, A20-B34: "Kant believes it is possible to consider form and matter in abstraction from one another." It may be added that there is, for Kant, "satisfaction" in the taste in the beautiful. It is, however, "disinterested and free" satisfaction, i.e., favor. It is neither inclination for the pleasant nor interest in the good.

[110] Kant does not call them "absolutely beautiful" but he does imply that all men properly experience them as beautiful.

[111] Cf. above, pp. 127-128.

tion." The primary source of confusion may be traced, however, to Kant's suggestion that "*the judgment of taste has nothing at its basis but the form* of purposiveness *of an object* (*or of its mode of representation.*)"[112] He offers, as a general definition of the "purposiveness of form," "the agreement of a thing with that constitution of things, which is only possible according to purposes."[113] "The concept of an Object, so far as it contains the ground of the actuality of this Object," on the other hand, is the "*purpose.*"[114] This suggests that he at least ostensibly makes a distinction between the potentiality and the actuality of the object. One observes, also, that we "will therefore speak of the beautiful, as if it were a characteristic of the object." But it is plain that Kant maintains that neither the pleasure accompanying the representation of the object, the representation of perfection, nor the concept of the good, can contain the determining ground of the judgment. He states specifically that neither "subjective purpose" nor a "representation of objective purpose" can lie "at the basis of the judgment of taste.[115] The "determining ground" is not *purpose*. Rather, "the mere form of purposiveness in the representation by which an object is *given* to us, . . . constitutes the satisfaction that we without a concept judge to be universally communicable; and, consequently, this is the determining ground of the judgment of taste."[116] Thus, if the attempt were made to describe the object of the judgment of taste, it might perhaps be said the judgment is made upon an object as if the latter were designed through its form for cognition in general and for the interplay of the faculties.[117]

It should be added, in this connection, that Kant's view appears sometimes to require the hypothesis that the judgment of taste is

[112] *K.d.U.*, Sec. 11, p. 69.

[113] *Ibid.*, Introduction IV, p. 18, *et passim.*

[114] *Loc. cit.*

[115] *Ibid.*, Sec. 11, p. 69.

[116] *Ibid.*, p. 70. Translated by J. H. Bernard. (By permission of The Macmillan Company, publishers.)

[117] *Ibid.*, Sec. 23, pp. 102-103, "Natural beauty (which is independent) brings with it a purposiveness in its form by which the object seems to be, as it were, pre-adapted to our Judgment, and thus constitutes in itself an object of satisfaction."

presupposed by cultural progress. This is suggested specifically in the illustration offered of the man on a desert island whose concern, Kant surmises, would be not at all with beauty but only with the practical necessities requisite for survival.[118] Had this line of speculation been elaborated in the *Kritik*, it would probably have been necessary to bring the theory into accord with teleological principles for defining the beautiful in art and nature. The actual obstacle to an interpretation of the beautiful in terms of means and ends is implicit in the systematic demands Kant made upon his aesthetic. Had he been able to argue that the "harmonious interplay of the faculties," the pleasure, or the enhancement of imaginative powers in the aesthetic experience occurred "for the most part," a need for an initial ground for a teleology of beauty might have been evident to him. But he cannot argue for the occurrence of aesthetic judgment of beautiful objects and events less than all the time for the specific reason that the "interplay of the faculties" is actually a ground for Kant's theory of "cognition in general."[119]

The relation of cognition and the "harmony of the faculties" turns, in part, upon the status of pleasure in the analysis. The pleasure implicated in the judgment of taste follows on the "harmony of the faculties," provided that the object is not attended to as if it were intended for knowledge but only for the subjective harmony. The pleasure is a sign or index of the occurrence of the "interplay." Since all men cognize, the condition of being pleased is taken to indicate the harmony which may be presupposed for all men.

It is clear, in consequence, that Kant proposes to solve aesthetic

[118] *Ibid.*, Sec. 2.

[119] *Ibid.*, p. 165, footnote to p. 166; cf. pp. 238-239. More particularly, p. 165: "The Judgment, as regards the formal rules of its action, apart from all matter (whether sensation or concept), can only be directed to the subjective conditions of its employment in general (it is applied neither to a particular mode of sense nor to a particular concept of the Understanding); and consequently to that subjective [element] which we can pre-suppose in all men (as requisite for possible cognition in general). Thus the agreement of a representation with these conditions of the Judgment must be capable of being assumed as valid *a priori* for everyone." The phrase "must be capable" shows some wavering on Kant's part. But, I think he refers only to the misjudgment of the beautiful of which he makes mention in the earlier sections of the *Kritik*. Translated by J. H. Bernard. (By permission of The Macmillan Company, publishers.)

and epistemological problems in terms of each other and at one and the same time. It need not be maintained that aesthetic judgment must be divorced from knowledge but insofar as this specific argument turns upon the fact that the agreement "must be capable of being assumed as valid *a priori* for everyone," it does follow that certain objects and events will always and for all men be beautiful, without necessary reference to purpose or end. The occurrence of the judgment in question will follow, in consequence of its relation to cognition in Kant's writing, as mechanically, one would suppose, as if the object affected the percipient *per stimulos*. One alternative to this conclusion is that all objects are beautiful or may be made so by "abstraction" but the latter alternative Kant does not permit.

If one now attempts to determine the aspect or aspects common to objects and events which, as representations, Kant judges will satisfy the subjective conditions laid down for aesthetic experience, one or two illustrations drawn from the treatment of objects to which aesthetic value is denied will be helpful. "Human beauty" is a case in point.[120] Such claims as its proponents make that it is properly an object of the judgment of taste are rejected because it "presupposes a concept of the purpose which determines what a thing is to be, and consequently a concept of its perfection."[121] It is implied that, in this instance, the basic reason for the rejection is that object and concept are separate. That the implication is correct is made the more probable by Kant's inclusion in aesthetic of "natural beauty (which is independent)" on the ground that it "brings with it a purposiveness in the form by which the object seems to be, as it were, pre-adapted to our Judgment."[122] Conversely, ornaments (*parerga*) are rejected because they are classed with things "which do not belong to the complete representation of the object internally as elements but only externally as complements."[123] Ornaments, such as frames of pictures, draperies of

[120] Cf. the discussion below, Chap. IV, of the canon of beauty.
[121] *K.d.U.*, Sec. 16, p. 82.
[122] *Ibid.*, Sec. 23, pp. 102-103.
[123] *Ibid.*, Sec. 14, p. 76.

statues, and colonnades of palaces injure "genuine beauty" and are objects of the judgment of taste only if, as ornaments, they "consist in beautiful form."

One clue to the significance of Kant's arguments is to be found in a statement that follows the rejection of complex colors and tones as beautiful. Purity of tone and color do "not supply a homogeneous addition to our satisfaction," the *Kritik* adds, but rather "they do so, because they make the form more exactly, definitely and completely intuitible, and besides by the charm [excite the representation, whilst they] awaken and fix our attention on the object itself."[124] Clearly, Kant assumes the validity and argues in favor of the formal hypothesis in aesthetic because he judges unity to be the *sine qua non* of beautiful objects and events. Form and unity, for him, appear to be identical in the aesthetic context of his philosophy and that he does mean to identify them is implicit in the significance of two passages in the *Kritik*. In the first, Kant discusses painting, sculpture, the formative arts, architecture and horticulture, "so far as they are beautiful arts." The criterion of the beauty of the objects included in these arts is "simple delineation" or "definite boundary":

> . . . the *delineation* is the essential thing; and here it is not what gratifies in sensation but what pleases by means of its form that is fundamental to taste. . . . Every form of the objects of sense (both of external sense and also mediately of internal) is either *figure* or *play*. In the latter case it is either play of figures (in space, viz., pantomime and dancing), or the mere play of sensations (in time). The *charm* of colours or of the pleasant tones of an instrument may be added; but the *delineation* in the first case and the composition in the second constitute the proper object of the judgment of taste.[125]

The second instance follows upon the distinction Kant makes between the beautiful and the sublime:

> The Beautiful in nature is connected with the form of the object, which consists in having [definite] boundaries. The Sublime, on

[124] *Ibid.*, Sec. 14, p. 76.

[125] *Ibid.*, Sec. 14, pp. 75 and 76. Translated by J. H. Bernard. (By permission of The Macmillian Company, publishers.)

the other hand, is to be found in a formless object, so far as in it or by occasion of it *boundlessness* is represented, and yet its totality is also present to thought.[126]

The unity and totality attributed by *subreption* to the object judged to be sublime is actually owed to Reason. The unity of the beautiful object or event is objective.

The form or unity which Kant regards as one condition for "universal communicability" in contrast to the particularity of communicability initiated by the "quality of sensations" is evident in objects and events as "boundary," "delineation," or "composition." It is stated explicitly[127] that the unity or form that gives "genuine beauty" implies the inclusion of the parts as elements internal to the representation. But, as Bosanquet justly argues,[128] the theory that form is the shape of visible bodies [i.e., boundaries or delineations] leads to difficulties once Kant attempts to apply a similar hypothesis to the aesthetic of color. Actually, in the latter instance, Kant abandons the conclusion that the principle of the unity of parts holds for instances of "genuine beauty" only if the representation has no "elements" external "as complements." The abandonment of the theory is evident once Kant suggests that the unity is perceived, not immediately, but by reflection. The result, if the latter suggestion were consistently argued, would be to interpret the experience of the beauty of color in terms more nearly applicable to the analysis of the sublime than of the beautiful. The passage in question is sufficiently important to quote:

> If we assume with Euler that colours are isochronous vibrations (*pulsus*) of the æther, as sounds are of the air in a state of disturbance, and, . . . what is most important, . . . that the mind not only perceives by sense the effect of these in exciting the organ, but also perceives by reflection the regular play of impression (and thus the form of the combination of different representations) . . . which I very much doubt—then colours and tone cannot be reck-

[126] *Ibid.*, Sec. 23, pp. 101-102. Translated by J. H. Bernard. (By permission of The Macmillan Company, publishers.)

[127] *Ibid.*, p. 76.

[128] *A History of Aesthetic*, p. 269.

oned as mere sensations, but as formal determination of the unity of a manifold of sensations, and thus as beauties.[129]

Not the least significant aspect of the quotation is evident to Bosanquet: "here we pass into a confusion between metaphysical 'form' as the relation of parts in a significant whole, and 'form' as the shape of visible bodies."[130]

As in the case of Plato's attempt to ground a formal and ateleological aesthetic, we discover that Kant's argument is broken-backed at a crucial point. Once what Bosanquet calls "the relation of parts in a significant whole" is used as a principle explanatory of form, the theory of abstract ateleological non-mathematical form proves to be inadequate for restrictive purposes in aesthetic speculation because a hypothesis of unity of a quite different order impinges upon the theory of "abstract" form. In the case of Kant's aesthetic, the difficulties arise from three sources. In the first place, Kant argues on the whole as if form as unity were necessary and, at times, as if it were both necessary and sufficient for beauty, whereas, in fact, his argument is that unity or form is a necessary condition for the cognition of objects of taste.[131] Secondly, Kant's aesthetic, like Plato's philosophy of art, but even more explicitly, requires that a sharp dichotomy be made between *form* and *matter*, despite the fact that the objects of taste are perceptible and, consequently, "sensible" or material. One interpretation of *form* and *matter* is pertinent in the circumstances: perceptual objects vary, as regards the degree of their formal elements. To assert that they are "forms" and to imply that they are not to some degree "sensuous" implies a differentiation not of degree but of kind and is invalid.[132] Thirdly,

[129] *K.d.U.*, Sec. 14, p. 74. Translated by J. H. Bernard. (By permission of The Macmillan Company, publishers.)

[130] *Op. cit.*, p. 269.

[131] I do not mean that he has not undertaken to give other characteristics to the object of the judgment of taste, i.e., characteristics such as immediacy, etc. Fundamentally, however, these are functions of *unity*. I do mean that Kant's argument does not demonstrate that a specific kind of form or unity is "essential," although that is obviously what he proposes to do.

[132] Cf. Kant, *K.d.r.V.* b 207-208: "Perception is empirical consciousness, that is, a consciousness in which sensation is to be found. Appearances, as objects of perception, are not pure, merely formal, intuitions like space and time. For in and by themselves these latter cannot be perceived. Appearances

Kant's assumption that "immediacy" is implicit in aesthetic experience has as its correlative absolutely beautiful objects. But aesthetic experience is reflective—and not only when evoked by color—and once this is granted the formalism that turns on elements "internal" to the aesthetic object proves inadequate.[133]

The latter issue is complicated but with reference to Kant's aesthetic its implications may be expressed simply: Unless reflection is integral to the judgment of taste, it is difficult to determine how the "immediacy" of pleasure in the experience of the representation is compatible with the recognition that the representation is, for example, of sea shell *qua* sea shell or, indeed, the recognition of the "form" as an object or event.[134]

The consequence of Kant's procedure is evident in the author's famous statement concerning the sight of the starry heavens. While it is true that the illustration relates to the Analytic of the Sublime, its implications concern the present argument because it relates to our knowledge of the object, in Kant's words, "just as we see it":

> We must not place at the basis of our judgment concepts of worlds inhabited by rational beings, and regard the bright points, with which we see the space above us filled, as their suns moving in circles purposively fixed with reference to them; but we must regard it, *just as we see it*, as a distant, all-embracing, vault.[135]

Precisely how these judgments, the one presumably conceptual,

---

contain in addition to intuition the matter for some object in general (whereby something existing in space or time is represented); they contain, that is to say, the real of sensation as merely subjective representation, which gives us only the consciousness that the subject is affected, and which we relate to the object in general." Translation by N. Kemp Smith. (By permission of The Macmillan Company, publishers.) It may be suggested that the majority of "abstract" formal theories, including those of Plato and Kant, use "form" as though it were separable from "matter." But "matter" is the correlative term that gives "form" its significance. It may be granted that Aristotle uses the terms as though they were separable but it must be remembered that even the *substratum* is only logically differentiated from form. The failure to recognize this has frequently been the cause of invalid aesthetic hypotheses.

[133] No object is comprehensible outside some frame of reference, since comparison and contrast are essential in cognitive processes.

[134] The issue is evident in the Introduction to the *K.d.U.*, VII, pp. 31-32. See the passage beginning, "For since the ground of the pleasure is placed merely in the form of the object for reflection in general. . . ."

[135] *Ibid.*, pp. 137-138. (Italics mine.)

the other aesthetic, are differentiable, it is difficult to determine and the difficulty is the more pronounced in Kant's counsel that: "To call the ocean sublime we must regard it as poets do, merely by what strikes the eye; if it is at rest, as a clear mirror of water only bounded by the heaven; if it is restless, as an abyss threatening to overwhelm everything." There may be "immediacy" in the experience but if reflection, as well, does not enter upon these so-called aesthetic judgments, one is hard put to it to ascertain the precise point at and manner in which it does become significant.

V

IT HAS been suggested thus far in our study of Kant's aesthetic of form, that nothing has been argued enjoining us to infer that unity is more than a necessary presupposition for aesthetic objects.[136] No argument brought forward by Plato or Kant has proved that either philosopher's specific selection of "forms" or "unities" does satisfy the conditions which in turn are intended to impose a stringent limitation upon the objects or events permitted entry to the aesthetic universe of discourse.

It is true that both philosophers maintain a position in aesthetic that is predominantly ateleological. It would be absurd, however, to maintain that either argues the position consistently or that the sole intention of their writings is to delimit the field of speculation in art and beauty. It will be evident, in fact, that the very ambiguities of their accounts are significant for later speculation. Plato's theory tends to become one of "unique aesthetic function," as is

[136] Cf. above, p. 135. Taken in conjunction with Kant's suggestion that the "harmonious interplay of the faculties" is basic not only for the aesthetic experience but for "cognition in general," the analysis of "form" as "beauty" suggests reasons for the constant recurrence of this type of theory. There is the clear recognition that unification is essential for perception and cognition and that without it the external world would be inchoate and beyond our comprehension. The elevation of this principle, a presupposition of perception and cognition, to a necessary and sufficient presupposition for aesthetic experience, affects and vitiates much that is of value in theories as divergent as Plato's, Kant's, and Croce's.

evident in his arguments concerning the "pure pleasures" evoked by the forms. Moreover, there is the specific suggestion that the aesthetic senses are those of sight and hearing. Similarly, once it is granted that "abstract" and non-mathematical forms are not the only unities evocative of aesthetic experience, Kant's phrase, "purposiveness without purpose," as applied to objects of the judgment of taste, may be interpreted to mean that certain objects and events have aesthetic values over and above those ordinarily defined in terms of non-aesthetic teleologies. This, in fact, Kant does suggest specifically in his analysis of the function of imagination.[137] In consequence, the most convincing account of aesthetic experience proffered in Kant's writings is implicit in that analysis and in his account of the relation of Imagination to the Understanding. For he holds that the Imagination, at least in the genius, is a "productive faculty of cognition," a "powerful agent for creating, as it were, a second nature out of material supplied to it by actual nature." In its productive or dynamic capacity, "we get a sense of our freedom from the law of association." Equally suggestive is Kant's view that, despite the inapplicability of the laws of association, there is involved in aesthetic contemplation "an inherent causality, that, namely, of *preserving a continuance* of the state of representation itself. . . . We dwell on the contemplation of the beautiful because this contemplation strengthens and reproduces itself."[138]

These suggestions will be of value to our later consideration of imagination,[139] as will be the Kantian inference that while the Imagination is not completely autonomous in its operations, it "should be both *free* and *of itself conformable to law*."[140] But our present interest is in the strictly ateleological implications of Plato's and Kant's aesthetic theories. And, if we attempt to summarize our

[137] *K.d.U.*, Sec. 49, pp. 198-199.

[138] *Ibid.*, Sec. 12.

[139] Cf. below, particularly Chap. XV ff.

[140] The argument supporting this is presumably that given in Sec. 35. Kant writes that the "harmonious accordance of the two powers of representation (i.e., Imagination and Understanding)" in the case in which "no concept of the Object underlies the Judgment" can only consist in the "subsumption of the Imagination itself . . . under the conditions enabling the Understanding in general to advance from intuitions to concepts. . . ."

conclusions concerning ateleological theories of "abstract forms," it is evident immediately that Plato and Kant interpret the term "form" as unity. It has been implied, furthermore, that various other "abstract" formal theories make a similar reduction of form to *unity*. If we defer considering the implication of this identification until we encounter other theories of art,[141] it may be urged immediately that the ambiguities inherent in these strictest of ateleological aesthetic theories arise largely from the impossibility of maintaining that an aesthetic object or event may be such an "abstract" form. The criticism holds for either the mathematical or the non-mathematical type of theory. On the grounds of their own philosophies neither Plato nor Kant can claim validity for their inferences that "abstract" unities are truly immaterial or non-sensuous. Kant's analysis presupposes the unification by Imagination of a sensuous manifold and the "forms" he proffers as beautiful in fact force him to make a false "abstraction." He suggests, for example, that upon making a judgment of taste not even the botanist looks upon the tulip as the reproductive organ of the plant (i.e., what the flower ought to be) but, by implication, merely as a congeries of line. The argument, if carried to its logical conclusion, would not permit us to attach a name to any object since it would not account for its recognition in terms of concepts. Plato, despite his contention that the mathematically defined objects in *Philebus* are "absolutely and eternally beautiful" and despite the additional inference that they are neither imitative nor representative, denies the presuppositions of his own philosophy of Ideas.

But the difficulty inherent in both Plato's and Kant's methods of abstraction raises an issue, which is, as we have observed, more fundamental still. In both aesthetic theories, "form" is used as though it were a term separable from "matter," the term in relation to which "form" is significant. Granted that form and matter logically may be abstracted from each other, it is quite impossible to permit theory to separate them as we consider objects of the empirical world, in which objects are always combinations of the formal and material elements. In the empirical realm, objects are

[141] See the following chapter, pp. 167 ff.

both "sensuous" and productive of sensations in us and are stimuli for our auditory, tactile, visual, and other senses.

This is true of linear or "abstract" art, as well. Objects of experience in the empirical realm are sensory and our reactions to them are reactions of sensation and feeling.[142] In the lines of the outstretched arms of Kolbe's *Adagio* and in the choreographic effect of the massed figures in the ballet of *Le Sacre du Printemps*, the flow of lines is inevitably interpreted in terms of flow and check, and flow and check of our "feelings." Indeed, in experiencing arches, triangles, and delineations, it is evident that Santayana[143] is correct in his suggestion that "the impression of a straight line differs in a certain almost emotional way from that of a curve, as those of various curves do from one another." One may infer that any theory of "abstract" form is and must be a characterization of a difference in the degree of formal elements embodied in various objects. It is never a characterization of a difference in kind.

Once "form" is identified with "unity" and the hypothesis of "abstract" form as unity is proved to be untenable, the truth or falsity of propositions that there are "absolutely beautiful forms" or that there may be made a universally valid judgment of taste in respect to specified objects or events—without necessary reference to teleological description—can be proved only by demonstration in terms of aesthetic theories of "concrete" or "sensuous" unities or "forms" which lay claim to satisfy the conditions of the problem within the limits of ateleological defining.

In the preceding chapter, it was shown that the ateleological theory of absolute and transcendental form is untenable. In the succeeding chapter, we shall examine the claims of certain ateleological theories which, accepting "form" as the "common"[144] proceed to discover the "absolutely beautiful form" in the unity common to specified complex objects and events. It is of interest to note, before turning to an examination of the claims of ateleological "concrete" theories of form to describe the "absolutely beautiful

[142] Cf. below, Chap. XI ff.
[143] G. Santayana, *The Sense of Beauty*, p. 84.
[144] Cf. above, p. 97.

form," that the two traditions with which we shall be concerned owe their origin and much of their interpretation to the fact that they derive from ambiguities in Platonic and Kantian statements concerning the nature of unity in art and nature. It is equally significant that theorists who follow upon Plato in their search for "concrete" beauty ordinarily employ mathematical principles of explanation, while those who are influenced by Kant most frequently interpret beauty in organic and non-mathematical terms.

Chapter IV

The Ateleological Theory of "Concrete" Form in Art and Nature

These they [the Egyptians] fixed, and exhibited the patterns of them in their temples; and no painter or artist is allowed to innovate upon them, or to leave the traditional forms and invent new ones. To this day, no alteration is allowed either in these arts, or in music at all. And you will find that their works of art are painted or moulded in the same forms which they had ten thousand years ago; . . . their ancient paintings and sculptures are not a whit better or worse than the work of to-day, but are made with just the same skill.

—Plato

PLATO in *Philebus* permits the "pure" pleasures had by experience of "abstract" and absolutely beautiful mathematical "forms" to enter upon the "mixture" of factors constituting the good life. Plato in the *Laws* grants that the more complex arts of dance and song have a proper place among the institutions of a well-governed state. A consequent investigation of the latter arts leads Plato to describe the genetic theory of play and to account for the rationalization of playful activities. Both aspects of his writing have exerted profound influence in a significant tradition of the philosophy of art.[1]

It is evident, however, that in the *Laws* Plato is not content merely to describe the kinds of art which may be "consecrated." He implies that these arts should be embodied in "a fixed and legal form."[2]

[1] See below Chap. VII for a discussion of the "play-theory."
[2] *Laws* 657. Cf. *Republic* 424.

Uppermost in his mind, evidently, is the prospect that if unchecked, "love of novelty which arises out of pleasure in the new and weariness of the old" may corrupt "the consecrated song and dance, under the plea that they have become antiquated." The precedent for his judgment is in his own philosophy the exile of the fine artist from the *Republic*. The precedent for the "fixed and legal form" of art he hopes to establish is discovered in the "laws of Egypt"[3] where "they have a tradition that their ancient chants which have been preserved for so many ages are the composition of the Goddess Isis."

Plato is no less convinced in the *Laws* than in the *Republic* that the products of art may be harmful and that those permitted in the state must be selected with care. He inveighs, in what is probably his last Dialogue, against novelty in art. He is forceful in drawing the auditors' attention to the dangers attendant upon the experience of "unconsecrated forms." His resolution of the problem of art in the *Laws* differs, nonetheless, in a significant way from that in *Philebus*. Song and dance may be interpreted in terms of mathematical harmony and rhythm but they are not "abstract," as are the "forms" in the latter Dialogue. Nor are they artistic or natural unities the factors of which are as nearly homogeneous throughout as are the components of triangles and "pure" colors. No less significant, however, is the fact that in the *Laws* Plato's interest is evidently caught and held by the possibility that the artist, the work of art, and the experience of art may be brought under the legislator's control if recourse is had to a canon of beauty.

It is of interest that Plato makes the suggestion of a possible imposition of artistic sanctions in much the same context as that in which he considers the exile of the artist and his arts in the *Republic*. But in the tradition of aesthetic theory the more significant point is that the inferences drawn with regard to the canon have notable consequences for that development in ateleological aesthetic in which the theory of mathematically definable "concrete" and beautiful forms in art and nature is formulated. It should be made clear, however, that the specific theory of the canon has had other

[3] *Ibid.*, 657.

applications. It has been formulated frequently to satisfy the compelling need to denote "absolute beauty" and thus to resolve the antinomies of art and of aesthetic experience. It has also served other and diverse purposes. It has been as useful to artists as a "rule-of-thumb"[4] for "making"; it has been no less valuable to a speculative philosopher of art like Hegel who presupposes some of its attendant criteria in his dialectical analyses[5] of the aesthetic adequacies and inadequacies of the forms of minerals, plants, animals, and man.

In view of this diversity of uses to which the theory of the canon has been put, it would be difficult to formulate principles which would be sufficiently general to account for all of its artistic significance. But in the specific circumstances in which it is integral to the ateleological tradition of "concrete" forms, the principles of the canon may be stated in terms of the more general theory: "Beautiful" entities, whether spatial objects or temporal events, are judged to be "forms" of complex unities. They are, in fact, said to be complex "varieties in unity" and their selection as "beautiful" presupposes the principle of subordination of parts to the whole. The beauty of the objects or events is attributed to their form, i.e., to the complete unification of parts in conformity to a mathematical principle of ratio or harmony or to the coherence of the parts of a living being.[6] The forms are assumed to be beautiful without reference to a unique aesthetic function or purpose, although they may in other connotations be describable in terms of ends or purpose, i.e., as flowers, plants, or living men. No "abstraction" of "sensuous" or "material" factors is required within this tradition and, consequently, the integration of the form may be effected by the use of such divergent means as color, symbolism, subject matter, composition, or sound. It is ordinarily asserted by theorists that a specific form is "the most beautiful." The principle presupposed to explain the beauty of a specific form is generalized to explain the beauty of

[4] W. M. Conway, *The Literary Remains of Albrecht Dürer*. Cf. Dürer's remark, p. 175 (Quoted below, p. 156.)

[5] Cf. below, pp. 163 ff.

[6] Cf. Aristotle, *Poetics* 1451 a 30.

art and nature. There is ordinarily a consequent limitation placed upon the aesthetic universe of discourse.

In the elaborations of Plato's and Kant's philosophies of art, the emphasis upon form as unity, in combination with the initial requirement that the form be "abstract," leads theory to an untenable position. The present hypothesis, as was mentioned above, places no restrictions upon objects and events in the aesthetic universe of discourse on grounds that the "sensuous" or "material" concomitant must be diminished or completely "abstracted." A stringent limitation does apply, however, to objects and events and its imposition is owing to motives little different from those impelling "abstractionists" to employ for art a similar Procrustean method. If the ateleological assumption is correct and there is a "perfectly beautiful" form, the bifurcation in the experience of other art needs concern theorists little because the factors which induce discontent in the work of art not in accord with the "beautiful" by definition, place the object itself beyond consideration in aesthetic estimation. This follows from the hypothesis not infrequently assumed that the "perfectly beautiful" objects in question are unique not alone in their beauty but in the experience they induce.

It is interesting to note, however, that few theorists of art, whether they belong to the ateleological or teleological tradition in aesthetic, have been content simply to assume this arrogant attitude. It is no less significant that in the writings of those who have given the impression of arrogance, various implications have led other writers to the elaboration of theories intended to absolve art from charges of "sensuousness" and "irrationality" by examining the grounds for the terms "sensuous" and "feeling." Thus, although Plato examines some complex unities in the *Sophist*, he still charges that some art of this kind is "appearance" and "deceptive." Aristotle, however, elaborates upon the kind of unity suggested by Plato and re-examines the problem in the light of the structure of the work of art and in terms of the *katharsis* of emotions.[7]

[7] Cf. below, Chap. IX.

The case is not dissimilar in the post-Kantian tradition of aesthetic, with which we shall be more briefly concerned. By way of illustration, Schiller[8] accepts many of Kant's aesthetic principles but reinterprets them in terms of "living form" rather than "abstract unity," and of "play" instead of judgment. Hegel's philosophy of art provides another illustration. In it is postulated a sensuous medium for art but Hegel[9] holds that the aesthetic percipient is enabled by fine art to become "conscious of feeling as of something external to him, towards which he must now enter into an ideal relation."

Diverse motives lead men to search for "absolute beauty." Even more diverse, however, are the objects and events which at one time or another theorists and artists have elevated to the status of the supremely beautiful. It would be of little value to list even a portion of the specific "concrete" unities for which theorists in the ateleological tradition have urged the palm of victory. It will be sufficient for the purpose of appraising the adequacy of the general theory to examine some implications of the recurrent interpretation of complex unity by reference to its specific statement in terms of the canon of the human form.

II

Plato and the Tradition of the Canon of the Human Form

PLATO writes in *Timaeus* that, "Copying the figure of the universe, which was round, the gods bound the two divine revolutions in a spherical body, that we now call our head, our divinest member and sovereign of all the rest.[10] It is of interest to recall that in the same Dialogue,[11] he maintains that the universe thus copied, is made by God who proposed "to make it most nearly like the every way perfect and fairest of intelligible things" and

[8] Cf. below, Chap. VII.
[9] Cf. below, pp. 164 ff.
[10] *Op. cit.*, 44D. Translation by A. E. Taylor.
[11] *Ibid.*, 30D.

"fashioned one visible living creature." The universe, as[12] "the perfect living creature," is single but it is made up of the elementary substances and "there must be a bond between them to bring them together."

Thus, the head is the "microcosm" of which the universe is the "macrocosm" and the latter is the "fairest of all intelligible things." We learn in addition that the elements of the universe are brought together by "the fairest of all bonds . . . that which makes itself and the terms it binds together most utterly one, and this is most perfectly effected by a progression."[13]

We are, at this point in *Timaeus*, introduced to issues beyond the scope of this essay. For our own problem, however, it is important to note that Plato elaborates upon the analogy between beautiful objects and events and complex organic unities, and that in this analogy it is the human head that is selected as the copy of the fairest work in the order of nature. In this, his theory resembles that of many writers in the tradition of the canon who make the "measures" of the head basic to the other proportions of the figure.

What implications for a specific canon there are in Plato's remark that the "fairest of all bonds" is that "which makes itself and the terms it binds together most utterly one"[14] are of particular significance here because the diversity of the universe implies the correlative diversity of the parts united in the microcosmic organic unity, the head. We shall see evidence of Plato's interest in a specific canon of the human figure in the *Sophist*. *Timaeus*, itself, is interesting not so much because of the possibility that Plato may have intended to offer the specific proportions for the canon as that it is an early and notable illustration of the tendency of theorists in aesthetic to select as the exemplar of complex "concrete" beauty the most developed and complex organism—man.

Since classical times, it has been again and again the beauty of the human form—because "whole for whole, of things visible nothing without understanding would ever be more beauteous than with

[12] *Ibid.*, 31B.

[13] *Ibid.*, 31C. Cf. *Hippias Major* 300A, and see above, pp. 97-98.

[14] *Ibid.*, 31C. Cf. for the "progression," A. E. Taylor, *A Commentary on Plato's Timaeus* and F. M. Cornford, *Plato's Cosmology*.

understanding"[15]—that ateleologists have seized upon the "perfectly beautiful figure." Ascertain the *measure* applicable to the relation of the parts of the whole structure called "man" and the problems of beauty and of form are solved—or so the ateleological theorists have held from the earliest times. Small wonder, indeed, that Dürer wrote[16] that he would rather be shown what is meant by a canon of proportion than "behold a new kingdom."

Let us observe various of the efforts to formulate the canon which becomes part of the ateleological theory of "concrete" form, undertaking the task in the light of a controversy reflected in Plato's *Sophist.* In the discussion in that Dialogue, Plato divides[17] imitative art into that of making "likenesses" and that of "phantastic art or the art of making appearances." The specific problem under discussion in the Dialogue follows upon an investigation of perspective in sculpture and painting. The contrast is drawn between "likeness-making," in which there is produced "a copy which is executed according to the proportions of the original" and "phantastic art" in "works either of sculpture or of painting, which are of any magnitude." In the latter art, ". . . there is a certain degree of deception; for if artists were to give the true proportions of their fair works, the upper part, which is farther off, would appear to be out of proportion in comparison with the lower, which is nearer." The conclusion is drawn that sculptors and painters who follow the "phantastic" mode "give up the truth in their images and make only the proportions which appear to be beautiful, disregarding the real ones." The suggestion has been made[18] that Plato believed that artists could display the truth by following a true canon of proportions. Schuhl holds[19] that Plato is expressing in the *Sophist* his adherence to the principles implicit in one of the great traditional theories of the "most beautiful forms"—the canon of Polycleitus[20]—

[15] *Timaeus* 30B.
[16] *Op. cit.*
[17] *Op. cit.*, 234-236 (*arranged*), trans., Jowett.
[18] P. M. Schuhl, *Platon et l'Art de son Temps*, pp. 6 ff.
[19] *Ibid.*, pp. 8 ff.
[20] Polycleitus' Canon, defended by implication by Plato, is, as is evident from the *Laws*, neither the first nor the last of attempts of this nature. It should be ted that Plato uses, in the *Sophist*, the word μορφή for "form" in his refer-

which is ordinarily supposed to have been incorporated in the *Doryphore*. This canon of proportions had been altered by the newer artists, Lysippos and Euphranor. Plato's praise of the fixed pattern of the arts in Egypt provides additional grounds for the assumption that the introduction of "novelties" had affected him adversely.[21]

Plato's defense of the Polycleitean canon is but one of the many enunciations men have made of their faith in the possibility of discovering the clue to "perfect beauty," i.e., to a beauty explicable through form alone with no reference to function. Nor has the search for the clue been limited to the theory and practice of sculpture. The Platonic-Polycleitean tradition has found its way into

---

ence to sculpture, while in *Hippias Major* he employs εἶδος. The earliest known canon is the Sanskrit *Silpa Santra* in which the length of the hand is contained in the body seven and one-half times. (See B. C. A. Windle, *The Proportions of the Human Body*.) The Egyptians, according to Diodorus Siculus (1.98; Cf. Ch. Blanc, *Grammaire des Arts du Dessins*, Chap. 7) had developed a canon which was presumably so accurate that two sons of Thocus, each working separately, constructed by means of it a single statue which was integrated perfectly. For the details of the Egyptian canon, see C. R. Williams, *The Tomb of Per-nēb*, pp. 7 ff.; Herbert Senk, "Der Kopf als Einheit des Ägyptischen Proportionskanons"; and Ernest MacKay, "Proportion Squares on Tomb Walls in the Theban Necropolis." However, although not the first, the canon of Polycleitus is of particular importance, not alone because of the quality of the sculpture produced at this period, but because it is the beginning of a great tradition and one of the standards of comparison in classical times. (See J. Schadow, *Polyclet*, p. 11, particularly the quotations from C. Galen, *De Temperencia*, 1.9: "Carvers, painters, sculptors, and artists in general, strive to paint and represent the most beautiful forms they can find, whether of human beings or animals. Such a form is exemplified by the 'Canon' of Polycleitus. The statue owed its name to the fact that its parts are of perfect proportion, and in harmony." Cf. Cicero, *De Clar. Orat.*, c. 86. Concerning the practice of the artists, cf. Eugene Guillaume, "Doryphore" in *Monuments de l'Art Antique*, p. 4 and R. Carpenter, "The Spirit of Classic Art," *Historical Aspects of the Fine Arts*, pp. 9-11.) Of the context of the Canon there are some traces: Cf. Ch. Blanc, *op. cit.*, Chap. 7, quoting C. Galen, *De Placitis Hippocratis et Platonis*, liv. 5., p. 255, (ed., Ven., 1563): "Pulchritudinem vero non in elementorum sed in membrorum congruenita digiti vidilicet ad digitum, digitorumque omnium ad palmam et ad manus articulum, et horum ad cubitum, cubiti ad brachium, omnium denique ad omniam positam esse censet; perinde atque in Polycletis norma litteris conspicitur." Compare I. Mueller's edition of Galen's *De Placitis*, Vol. I, p. 425 and H. Diels, *Die Fragmente der Vorsokratiker*, Vol. I, pp. 391 ff. for material on Polycleitus.

[21] Cf. *Laws*, 656.

the theory of architecture by way of writings as diverse as those of Vitruvius and Hambidge, among others, and into painting through theories proposed by Leonardo and Dürer.

Dürer's faith in the canon[22] is but one instance of the belief that theorists may ascertain by means of the science of mathematics the solution to the problem of an absolute beauty. Yet, as the history of the theories offered to ground the belief is examined, it is significant that the various "measures" formulated were disregarded in practice and that Plato opposed the very innovations which tended to alter the Polycleitean norm.[23] Cicero remarks, for example, that, "Other artists did not allow the perfections of such statues as those of the Olympian Jupiter and the Doryphorus to discourage them from the attempt to produce something greater."[24] It is precisely against such innovations in practice that Plato inveighs,[25] although the newer sculptors are merely demonstrating that com-

[22] Despite his conviction that only God is beautiful and that the Fall of man resulted in the destruction of the "perfect form," Dürer retains faith that a geometrical demonstration of such beauty may be possible. *Op. cit.*, p. 245. He writes that, "We are considering about the most beautiful human figure conceivable, but the Maker of the world knows how that should be. Even if we succeed well we do but approach towards it somewhat from afar." (*Ibid.*, p. 251.) He attributes the difficulties attendant upon our limitations to "differences of perception" and holds, as well, that although "it seemeth to me impossible for a man to say that he can point out the best proportions for the human figure . . . if a man can prove his theory by Geometry and manifest forth its fundamental truth, him must all the world believe, for one is so compelled."

[23] Cf. Guillaume, *op. cit.*, pp. 13-14: "But it would be an error to believe that while being a rule *par excellence*, it was considered to be an absolute rule. The type that he formulated could not be applied to each individual instance. . . . The Greeks did not seek to establish a unity which had been the ruin of art. Assuredly, they were capable of conceiving the absolute, but liberty was necessary to them and they could not sacrifice it to any particular rule, however perfect it might be." See also, Carpenter, *op. cit.*, pp. 9-10: "Although some of our sculptors may have honestly believed that it was possible to find the one, single, and perfect embodiment of the naked beauty of our race and kind, a sort of unsurpassable formula for pose and proportion and muscular articulation, nonetheless I notice that even these sculptors sought their idea by improving on their predecessors and not by merely copying and recopying a purely traditional standard and concept of perfection. Even if we believed that beauty could be reduced to its true forms and hence to formulas, still we never said that such formulas were inert, unchanging abstractions."

[24] *Ad Brutum*, Chap. 2.

[25] Schuhl, *op. cit.*, pp. 8-9. Cf. *Laws* 656.

plete adherence to a rigorous rule at least in part intended to assist the production of "absolutely beautiful form" is empirically impossible. This is evident in the case of Lysippos whose chief contributions to the art of sculpture, Pliny tells us, were

> . . . in his vivid rendering of the hair, in making the heads smaller than older artists had done, and the bodies slimmer and with less flesh, thus increasing the apparent height of his figures. There is no word in Latin for the canon of symmetry which he was so careful to preserve, bringing innovations which had never been thought of before into the square canon of the older artists, and he often said that the difference between himself and them was that they represented men as they were, and he as they appeared to be.[26]

It is equally evident that Euphranor, while he first gave "heroes their full dignity and mastered the theory of symmetry," ignored the canon. It is reported that "he made the body, however, too slim and the head and limbs too large."[27]

These and similar evidences offered by the practice in various arts suggest that craftsmen refuse to be bound by theory and that "principles" are ignored if they prove inadequate for "making." It is no less true, however, that hope persists that a mathematical rule may be formulated and that by its application the artist will be enabled to produce "perfect beauty." Perhaps Guillaume expresses not only the desires of the proponents of the *Doryphore* but those of all ateleological theorists:

> . . . The *Doryphore* was of still more considerable interest: it had been, so to speak, constructed according to a mathematical rule. It constituted a system of proportions such that one might infer from the dimensions of one of its parts the dimensions of the whole and reciprocally from (the dimensions of) the whole the measure of the least of its parts. It is what the Greeks called symmetry.[28]

[26] *The Elder Pliny's Chapters on The History of Art in the Historia Naturalis*, trans., K. Jex-Blake, xxxiv. 65.

[27] *Ibid.*, Pliny, *N.H.* xxxv. 128.

[28] *Op. cit.*, p. 7. See Gilbert and Kuhn, *A History of Esthetics*, pp. 29 ff. for an account of other innovations which may have caused Plato's conservatism in art to receive expression in this form. Concerning music, Plutarch writes: "Now the music appropriated to the harp, such as it was in the time of

Neither Plato's conviction that the forms of art should be "consecrated" nor the skill with which he wields the weapon of dialectic does, in fact, influence the practice of sculpture. The "love of novelty" prevails. But the tradition he entered the lists to uphold nonetheless affects the imagination of later theorists. It is a "fixed" but not a "legal" form, however, that gives promise of providing the rule in which Vitruvius hoped to discover the clue to the "perfect buildings" of the ancients. The anticipated rigor of the rule also leads Leonardo to attempt to ascertain the results in painting of an application of the principles of the "divine number." It is profitable to examine, however briefly, this later tradition.

In Vitruvius' *De Architectura*, there is a continuation of the investigation of the analogy between the work of art and the unified, complex organism.[29] The work of art is an organic whole, he implies, and is susceptible to mathematical analysis. The "fundamental ideas of measure" applicable to it derive from the measurements and relations of the members of the body: "These they apportioned so as to form the perfect number."[30] The standard for architecture is that based upon the proportions of "a well shaped man." The most important factor in the measure, presumably, derives from the fact that "The head from the chin to the crown is an eighth."[31]

It is this passage in Vitruvius' *De Architectura* that Leonardo da

---

Terpander, continued in all its simplicity, till Phrynis grew into esteem. For it was not the ancient custom to make lyric poems in the present style, or to intermix measures and rhythms. For in each nome they were careful to observe its own proper pitch; whence came the expression *nome* (from νόμοs, *law*), because it was unlawful to alter the pitch appointed for each one. At length, falling from their devotion to the Gods, they began to sing the verses of Homer and other poets. This is manifest in the poems of Terpander." (*De Musica*, 6. Translated by John Philips.)

[29] *Op. cit.*, Bk. III, Chap. I, translation by M. H. Morgan. Cf. mention of St. Augustine's *De Ordine*, above, Chap. II, p. 49, and Svoboda, *L'Esthétique de Saint Augustin*, pp. 105 ff.

[30] *Ibid.*, III, Chaps. 1, 5 and 9. Cf. 1,2.1. "Order gives due measure to the members of a work considered separately, and symmetrical agreement to the proportions of the whole. It is an adjustment according to quantity . . . by this I mean the selection of modules from the members of the work itself and, starting from the individual parts of the members, constructing the whole work to correspond."

[31] *Ibid.*, III, 1.2. Cf. above, p. 147.

Vinci quotes with approval.[32] With this, also, Dürer is in accord in general. Neither Leonardo nor Dürer is, however, in complete accord with the details of Vitruvius' theory. Indeed, there are interesting divergences between the Italian's and the German's interpretations of the canon due in part to metaphysical presuppositions made explicit in Dürer's writings and in part to varied difficulties each painter encountered in applying the measures. The consequence of Dürer's metaphysical and ateleological theory is a curiously ambiguous statement of the problem. He holds that the "perfect form" was destroyed by the Fall of man and he implies that it may be in part recovered by the geometrician. There is an illuminating effort to reconcile these views by a method that suggests that Dürer thought of the problem in terms of an ideal: "We are considering about the most beautiful human figure conceivable, but the Maker of the world knows how that should be. Even if we succeed well we do but approach towards it somewhat from afar."[33] But his opinion is perhaps most consistently expressed in these words:

I believe that no man liveth who can grasp the whole beauty of the meanest living creature; I say not of a man, for he is an extraordinary creation of God, and other creatures are subject unto him. I grant, indeed, that one man will conceive and make a more beautiful figure and will explain the natural cause of its beauty more reasonably than another, but not to such an extent that there could not be anything more beautiful. For so fair a conception ariseth not in the mind of man; God alone knoweth such, and he to whom He revealeth it, he knoweth it likewise. That only, and nought else, containeth the perfect truth which is the most beautiful form and stature of a man that can be.[34]

Dürer's words reflect the dilemma of those committed to transcendental beauty who maintain that there are two "perfect forms," one for God and the other for man. But Leonardo's enthusiasm for the tenets of the canon is tempered, on the other hand, by the increasingly evident inapplicability of the measures in practice. He

[32] *Trattato della Pittura*, Sec. 343, ed. J. P. Richter, I. 182.
[33] *Op. cit.*, p. 251.
[34] *Ibid.*, p. 244.

does attempt its application to the art of painting: "The length of the hand," he writes, "is ⅓ of a braccio [eight inches] and this is found nine times in man. And the face is the same and from the pit of the throat to the shoulder, and from the shoulder to the nipple, and from one nipple to the other, and from each nipple to the pit of the throat."[35] Leonardo's faith in the efficacy of the canon of the perfect beauty of the human form is, however, on the whole, half-hearted. Richter remarks that "the sketch [accompanying the measurements], as we see it, can hardly have been intended for anything more than an experimental attempt to ascertain relative proportions. . . . The proportions of this sketch are not in accord with the rules which he usually observed."[36]

Leonardo's attitude is susceptible to explanation on no very complicated grounds. It is evident that his interest in science and mathematics led him to assume that a canon may be formulated while his skill as a craftsman must soon have convinced him that absolute beauty could not be attained and that a technique enslaved by fixed measures is not compatible with the rules of art. It is clear, in any case, that in practice two serious problems implicit in the canon confronted Leonardo in his efforts to apply its principles. The first, noted by Schadow,[37] concerns the fact that while dimensions of length may be determined, those of thickness and breadth cannot be so determined owing to the immense variety of nature (*immensa misteriosa natura*). The nature of the second problem is made sufficiently clear in Leonardo's own words: "These rules are of use only in correcting the figures; . . . but if you try to apply these rules in composition you will never make an end, and will produce confusion in your works."[38]

It is evident that Leonardo judged that the canon's use is limited to the negative task of "correction" and that it fails if the artist attempts to derive from it affirmative or productive principles. What is equally true but plainly is not so evident to Leonardo is the

[35] *Op. cit.*, Sec. 309. Other proportions are given by Leonardo in the sections which follow in the *Trattato*.

[36] *Op. cit.*, note to Sec. 313.

[37] *Polyclet.*

[38] *Op. cit.*, Sec. 18.

significant fact that his theory is itself flawed. It will be recalled that he introduces his problem with the admonition, "therefore take a man of three braccia in height and measure him by the rule I will give you." But, as he proceeds, he warns, "If you tell me that I may be mistaken, and judge a man to be well proportioned who does not conform to this division, I answer that you must look at many men of three braccia, and out of the larger number who are alike in their limbs *choose one of those who are most graceful and take your measurements*."[39] It is plain that Leonardo's practice is consequently implicated in the use of a mere average. This is in marked contrast to Vitruvius' assumption that the measures provide a standard so absolute that it accords with ten, the "divine number." It should be noted, moreover, that Leonardo's conclusions are not unambiguous as regards the "measure." "Every part of the whole," he maintains, "must be in proportion to the whole."[40] He does make an effort to interpret "whole" as the "whole" of the figure.[41] It is evident, nonetheless, that the proportions in question are relative as well to the "whole," i.e., to the entire composition of which the given figure is a part except in the instance of a single statue in relief.[42] Of more significance, however, is the fact that Leonardo actually uses a standard other than that of mere "measure." His practice presupposes, at the outset, merely the selection of "many men of three braccia" in height. He quickly stipulates, however, that *in addition* the selection must be made among "those who are most graceful," i.e., judged to be most beautiful by criteria extrinsic to the measurements either applied to or derived from use of the canon.

[39] *Ibid.*, 309 (Italics mine).

[40] *Ibid.*, Sec. 366.

[41] *Ibid.*, Sec. 366, ed. Richter, p. 192: "*Every part of the whole must be in proportion to the whole*. Thus, if a man is of a stout short figure he will be the same in all his parts; that is with short and thick arms, wide thick hands, with short fingers with their joints of the same character, and so on with the rest. I would have the same thing understood as applying to all animals and plants; in diminishing, [the various parts] do so in due proportion to the size, as also in enlarging." (Italics mine.)

[42] Contrast more particularly Michelangelo's statement that "the artist must rely on his own eye as surest guide to correct proportion." Michelangelo actually painted some of the stooping figures in his compositions as much as twelve "heads" in height.

There is little need to enter upon the details of Dürer's effort to succeed in the task at which Leonardo failed. Like Leonardo, Dürer was interested in Luca Pacioli's *De Divina Proportione*[43] and also, as did da Vinci, he turned to Vitruvius as a source of information and inspiration.[44] Of the latter's theory, Dürer writes that "Vitruvius has brought the human limbs together in a perfect proportion, in so satisfactory a manner that neither the ancients nor moderns are able to overthrow it." The application of Vitruvius' theory is, however, no less difficult for Dürer than for Leonardo. Despite the care exercised in his adaptation of the canon,[45] difficulties hinder his effort.

Dürer writes, for example, that "no two fingers have the same form; anyone who searcheth amongst men will find that out. . . ."[46] The painter attempts to derive the measures from groups but soon abandons this method for that likewise used by Leonardo: "Further, in order that he may arrive at a good canon whereby to bring somewhat of beauty into our work, thereunto it were best for thee, it bethinks me, to form thy canon from many living men. Howbeit, seek only such men as are held beautiful and from such draw with all diligence."[47] Granting freely that he has failed to formulate a canon for the "perfectly beautiful figure" but accepting defeat with an accompanying liberality reminiscent of Plato's remarks in *Timaeus*, Dürer at last transfers the burden of the task to future artists:

[43] Published in Venice, 1509. Professor E. Panofsky informs me that Dürer was actually little influenced by Pacioli.

[44] W. M. Conway, *op. cit.*, p. 165.

[45] Dürer proceeded on the hypothesis that the figure of a normal man is eight of his own heads in height. He divided the body into three principal lengths: from the neck to the hip, the hip to the knee, and the knee to the end of "shin bone" and suggested that the first length is to the second as the second is to the third. The details, as given by F. W. G. Foat, in "Anthropometry of Greek Statues," are of interest: Heights marked for lower leg in profile against a vertical line are (600) 168, 154, 143, 70, 62.0 and 17 or 28%, 25%, *ca.* 24%, *ca.* 11.3%, *ca.* 10.3%. "To examine one or two parts in detail: his head in height is 78/600 i.e., 13%. This indicates that the stature is about 7¾ heads; his foot is in length 93/600, which is 15½%." Professor Panofsky tells me that this "Regel" is not a general one. It applies to only ten out of twenty-six figures and all ten are in the First Book, written prior to 1523.

[46] *Op. cit.*, p. 239.

[47] *Ibid.*, p. 246. Cf. p. 179.

"Good" and "better" in respect of beauty are not easy to discern, for it would be quite possible to make two different figures, one stout the other thin, which should differ one from the other in every proportion, and yet we scarce might be able to judge which of the two excelled in beauty. What Beauty is I know not, though it adheres to many things. . . . I do not highly extoll the proportions which I here set down, albeit I do not believe them to be the worst. Moreover I do not lay them down as beyond improvement, but that thou mayest search out and discover some better method by their help.[48]

The foregoing instances of efforts to ascertain and set forth the mathematical "concrete" ateleological "forms" suffice to show clearly some of the difficulties which confront those followers of Dürer who hope to "discover some better method." In large part, the obstacles are empirical in origin. It is significant in this regard that neither Leonardo's nor Dürer's practice is in accord with their own theoretical canons. It is no less significant that to Vitruvius' canon constant exception has been taken[49] and that the writer on ancient architecture proffers sound—and it may be unconscious—reasons for disregarding the principles by means of which he tries to derive a canon for the most beautiful form.[50] It may be argued,

[48] *Ibid.*, p. 179. I have altered Conway's translation, at Professor Panofsky's suggestion, from "dependeth upon" to "adheres to." As Panofsky remarks, beauty to Dürer is a quality found in many individual phenomena.

[49] See D. S. Robertson, *A Handbook of Greek and Roman Architecture*, p. 149: "The subject of proportions is always difficult and elusive, but this temple [of Athena Polias at Priene] well illustrates the general character of fourth-century and Hellenistic design. The architect seems to have aimed at a proportion of length to breadth approximating to 2:1. It is mathematically impossible to produce a stylobate of exactly these proportions without abandoning the principle of the equality of all intercolumniations, but a peripteral scheme of six by eleven (in which the number of *intercolumniations* on the flanks is double that on the fronts) gives one of the nearest possible approximations to this relation."

[50] See, for example, *De Architectura*, Book IV, Chap. III: "Some of the ancient architects said that the Doric order ought not to be used for temples, because faults and incongruities were caused by the laws of its symmetry. . . . This is not because it is unlovely in appearance or origin or dignity of form, but because the arrangement of the triglyphs and metopes (lacunaria) is an embarrassment and inconvenience to the work. . . . However, since our plan calls for it, we set it forth as we have received it from our teachers, so that if anybody cares to set to work with attention to these laws, he may find the proportions stated by which he can construct correct and faultless examples of temples in the Doric fashion."

indeed, that no canon has been formulated that has not undergone some alteration believed by practising artists to be essential. It may be argued as well, however, that no serious objection may be made to the hypothesis implied in the canon, merely on the grounds that its measures are not applied. It might be assumed that some future artist-mathematician may formulate the perfect canon and may succeed in applying it. There is, however, one telling blow that may be dealt the hypothesis that a "perfect unity" may be evolved. It has been observed that neither artists nor theorists have derived the actual "beauty" of their art from the "measures" applied. Leonardo assumed, as we have observed, that a "well-shaped man" must be selected as the model from which the "measures" may be abstracted. Clearly, the principle of beauty is a presupposition of the very instrument the application of which is intended to make it manifest.

It is evident also, that the significance of the phrase, the "most beautiful form"—and here we may use the canon of the human form as an illustration—has not been sufficiently determined by the theorists who employ it. For the most part, the various canons put forward in history have ignored variations of race, age, and occupation, as well as differences in the proportions of male and female figures.[51]

It may be urged, however, that these difficulties are no more insuperable than are those presented by other empirical issues which have been mentioned. The case is not, however, the same because the difficulties in question suggest a systematic problem implicit in any effort to discover an absolutely beautiful form or unity. It is to this systematic problem that the present argument may now turn. It is evident that the various canons of human beauty result from collections of data relating to the proportions of large numbers of

[51] Cf. Schadow, *op. cit.*, on statistics relating to this problem in the army and in various occupations. Cf. also, Kant *K.d.U.*, Sec. 17: "If now in a similar way for this average man we seek the average head, for this head the average nose, etc., such figure is at the basis of the normal Idea in the country where the comparison is instituted. Thus necessarily under these empirical conditions a negro must have a different normal Idea of the beauty of the [human figure] from a white man, a Chinaman a different normal Idea from a European." Cf. also, Dürer, *op. cit.*, p. 246.

individuals of a given type, age, height, and race. It is apparent, also, that these resultant and derived proportions represent the *average* proportions of groups of individuals in question. There is little doubt that the figures relating to the proportions presented by Leonardo in the *Trattato*, for example, are accurate. Nor need the critic doubt that statistical averages may be absolutely accurate. The probability is that the proportions agreeable to the greater number of percipients may be ascertained and that they may be expressed with mathematical accuracy. This probability is precisely the presupposition of Vitruvius', Dürer's, and Leonardo's various searches. But deviations from the average must be anticipated in considering the individual instance, precisely as deviations from the average in the individual case must be looked for in an effort to determine accurately the statistics of the death rate in any given instance. The unity sought by Polycleitus, for the retention of which Plato argued in the *Sophist*, and which for so long has been the object of interest among mathematically-inclined artists—this absolutely beautiful form is simply and solely the *norm*. The statement of such an average or *norm* can be given with exactitude in mathematical terms, i.e., in terms of measured probability.[52]

The very factors which have often been taken to deny to the ateleologist the exactitude he requires of a demonstrable beauty are in reality such as strengthen the claims of the teleologist. The deviations from the *norm* which Vitruvius, Leonardo, and Dürer encountered indicate a rule that holds for the theory of averages[53] as applied to the beauty of human figures. Within the range of these averages may be found the most pleasing form. What the earlier theorists expressed in somewhat inexact language or, rather, what may be inferred from their failure to discover or to demonstrate the absolute beauty of one organic form may be stated precisely once the problems are examined in the light of the more exact expression of formal theory in modern times by such writers as Fechner and Hambidge.[54] If we turn to Hambidge's theory of

[52] Cf. Singer, *Mind as Behavior*, pp. 64-68.

[53] Cf. particularly Dürer, *op. cit.*, p. 246.

[54] See respectively *Vorschule der Ästhetik* and *Dynamic Symmetry*.

dynamic symmetry to illustrate the point, we discover that its author undertakes the task of supplying a ground for "some correlating principle which could give artists a control of areas." As such, the principle is opposed to "static symmetry or proportion." The primary requirement of dynamic symmetry has been concisely put by Carpenter:

> For the curvilinear area of a vase a simple rectangle is substituted. This is the containing rectangle, of which the sides are parallel to the vertical axis and the base-line of the vase. It is, as it were, the smallest rectangular frame into which the whole vase will fit. . . . If this rectangle can be split up into rectangles of similar and related shape and if these smaller rectangles can be used to determine recognizable elements of the vase, the occurrence of dynamic symmetry is held to be established. . . .[55]

The requirement is that "the whole rectangle may be completely subdivided into squares and rectangles similar to the original rectangle or of closely related shape." The hypothesis of dynamic symmetry is propounded to make explicit the means by which the sculptor constructed his figures. It is not implied, indeed, that this is a ground for a theory of aesthetic experience but it is argued that in a symmetrical sculptured whole will be found a beautiful form constructed on the principle of an organic whole. Upon examination, however, as Carpenter has pointed out, the principle of dynamic symmetry is a reiteration in complex terms of the ratio approximating 5:8 which "has in all ages been a recurring favorite in artistic composition and artistic design. It is the famous 'divine section' or '*Phi* proportion'. . . . Somewhere in the neighborhood of that ratio man has an inveterate tendency to localize his sense for beauty of proportion."[56]

The aspect of Carpenter's inference that is significant for the philosopher of art is implicit in the words, "in the neighborhood." Hambidge has given additional proof that the artist knows that the highest average of reaction to the beauty of proportion will occur in relation to objects approximating to this ratio. The statistics for

[55] "Dynamic Symmetry: A Criticism," pp. 21 ff. (*arranged*).
[56] *Ibid.*, pp. 34-35.

such reactions have been collected by Fechner and other experimentalists. Hambidge has shown that the artist—probably unconsciously or as a "rule of thumb"—constructs vases in the proportion of 5:8. Fechner has inferred from experiments upon large numbers of observers that this proportion represents the probable *norm* of appreciation. The psychologist, conducting the experiments with care to avoid idiosyncrasies of personal taste and selecting the subjects of the experiments from varied groups, has provided an empirical test to determine the proportions of the figures for which most but not all the subjects would express their preference. Deviation from the *norm* was not only anticipated but required.[57] Moreover, the statement that the preference falls "somewhere in the neighborhood" of the proportion 5:8 is a simple statement of fact, of what happens under certain controlled conditions.[58]

It must be emphasized, however, that *norms* or averages of this kind are descriptive only of what occurs and that, as descriptive, they provide only data for but no conclusive answer to the philosophical questions, the "why" this or that average proportion pleases or "why" this or that rough average pleases more perceivers than does the average proportion of the measures of another group of objects. Philosophical analysis intended to answer these questions begins with the implication that the statistical averages in question are statements of "measured probabilities." The probability, however, that a certain number of individuals will prefer a form of a given kind or proportion, with proper compensation for deviation in the statistics, is not a description of the kind of mechanical re-

[57] Cf. G. D. Birkhoff, *Aesthetic Measure*, p. 11: "Such aesthetic comparison of which the aesthetic measure M is the determining index, will have substantial meaning only when it represents the normal or average judgment of some selected groups of observers;" cf. *ibid.*, p. 47.

[58] Something, too, must be added concerning the objects ordinarily subjected to the measurement. In the investigations by Hambidge and by Birkhoff, the measures are not limited to the actual object but in the case of vases, for example, include the spaces under the lip of the vase. Cf. Carpenter, *op. cit.*, p. 23: Hambidge presents us with "an orthogonal projection of the vase upon a single vertical plane." This involves the inclusion of "rectangular air-spaces with others which overrun the edges of the vase." This tendency to include in the ratio elements that go beyond the artistic object is evident in Vitruvius' writings, as well as in the writings of modern ateleological theorists.

sponse implied by Plato[59] in his assertion that "pure pleasure" is had in the experience of "absolutely beautiful" objects or events. Nor is it a description, like that of Kant,[60] in support of his intended proof that certain forms are the objects of a universally valid judgment of taste, are intrinsically beautiful because all men cognize, and that the faculties involved in the experience of beauty are presupposed in cognition. It is, rather, descriptive of response in teleological terms, a statement that the artist in a given instance succeeds in constructing a work of art which in turn succeeds in affecting the perceiver in a certain way "for the most part" and that for only an average of the individuals implicated.

This conclusion suggests, however, not only the systematic error of ateleological theories which posit an "absolute beauty" definable in terms of the "measures" of the canon without reference to unique function but the sound reasons as well for assuming that form as unity provides no valid ground for the stringent limitation of aesthetic to objects and events in accord with the ateleologist's theory. From the latter suggestion it may be inferred that objects or events are wholes or forms which may be unified as adequately by reference to end or purpose as by identity or similarity of parts. This is perhaps the most significant inference that may be drawn from the speculation upon the theory of "concrete" non-mathematical forms which occurred in historical attempts to restate Kant's "abstract" theory. To a brief statement of the artistic implications of the relevant point of that speculation, we shall turn in the next section of this chapter.

III

Kant and the Post-Kantian Hypothesis of Non-Mathematical Form

AS WE again consider the canon of the human figure as a specific instance of the "most beautiful" form expressed in "concrete" and non-mathematical terms, it is significant that Kant rejects[61] the

[59] See above, pp. 106 ff.
[60] See above, pp. 125 ff.
[61] *Op. cit.*, Sec. 17, pp. 88-89.

possibility that such a "rule" as is implicit in "the celebrated *Doryphorus* of *Polycleitus*" may be "the whole *archetype of beauty*" or that the "forms" in question can be an object of the judgment of taste. This Kant does on systematic grounds. It is no less significant that Hegel, whose philosophy of art is in many aspects a profound elaboration of Kant's principles, implicitly rejects the canon at least in part on grounds implicit in the work of art.

Kant, whose *Kritik* is, as we have observed, the *locus classicus* for non-mathematical aesthetic, argues that the human figure is inadmissible as an object of the judgment of taste. The reasons for this conclusion are complicated by Kant's assumption that a judgment upon a work of art or a natural object of this character would rest upon empirical and, therefore, *a posteriori* principles and consequently could not be universally valid. But Kant offers a criticism that is, in fact, more fruitful for our present argument. Implicit in the numerous canons of perfect beauty is one factor, "the stature of the beautiful man." This, Kant argues, is the average obtained by the imagination reconstructing a thousand separate individuals as one—the "form constituting the indispensable condition of all beauty, and thus merely correctness in the [mental] presentation of the race." Kant holds that the pleasure associated with such a presentation is not a consequence of taste but follows solely "because the representation contradicts no condition under which alone a thing of this kind may be beautiful."[62]

The argument is not only integral to Kant's theory but it touches upon the fundamental issue of the *norm* or average. Still, however sound the argument, neither point impeded the search by followers of the Critical Philosophy for an ateleological non-mathematical form, manifested in the beauty of the human figure, a search carried on in the assumption that the form might resolve basic aesthetic problems. The post-Kantian idealists entertain the possibility but it is also in this tradition that the possibility is rejected on grounds so conclusive as to satisfy the most critical analyst. It is Hegel who writes that, in the evolution of the art-stages through which *Geist* proceeds dialectically and which are regarded as its manifestations

[62] *Op. cit.*, Sec. 17, p. 89. Kant adduces moral and conceptual grounds to support the conclusion.

in concrete sensuous *Gestalt*, form and content are completely united for the first time in the history of art. This occurs in the representation of the human body,[63] in the sculpture of the classical Greek period.[64] In sculpture, Hegel maintains, the Classical stage of art has found "the free and adequate embodiment of the *Idea* in the shape that, according to its conception, is peculiarly appropriate to the *Idea* itself."[65] Moreover, it is in the artistic representation of the human form that the *Idea* thus manifests itself most integrally as form and content in art.

Our acquaintance with the inferences drawn throughout the history of the ateleological tradition in aesthetic may conceivably have led us to expect that Hegel would be forced to conclude that such perfection and union of form and content in the sculptured human figure would constitute the highest stage to which art could attain in the production of "beauty."[66] The motives that might have led to such a conclusion are plain from the history of the canon. Equally plain are the possible bases for such a conclusion either in the assertion that the "measure" or uniting principle is perfect or that the product is not "relative." Hegel, indeed, had argued in an earlier passage in *The Philosophy of Fine Art*[67] that the human form is the "most direct illustration" of truth "in its unravelment as external reality," on grounds that it allows the "animating soul or the unified totality freely to appear."

For all that, however, Hegel—and it is not solely because he is working within the confines of a systematic philosophy—concludes in fact that classical art, in its dependence upon the organic unity of the human body for its effect, is inadequate. He offers two reasons for the inadequacy. The first is that in this stage of Spirit too

[63] The validity of the more general hypothesis, that the unification of the art-object makes it self-sufficient and self-referent, will be examined later. See below Chap. VIII.

[64] "We must claim for sculpture, that it is in it that the inward and spiritual are first revealed in their eternal repose and essential self-completeness." *The Introduction to Hegel's Philosophy of Fine Art*, (Bosanquet's translation, p. 199).

[65] *Ibid.*, p. 184.

[66] He does, in fact, grant that "formal beauty" is achieved in this stage.

[67] *Op. cit.*, Part 1, Chap. 3, p. 209 (Osmaston's translation).

great a limitation upon the external manifestation is required. This is to say that too great restriction is placed upon the scope and extent of art itself. The second reason is that too great a limitation is placed upon the spiritual content manifested in that shape.[68]

Hegel does assume that the human form, in consequence of its "externality," is "alone capable of revealing the spiritual in sensuous guise."[69] From that form, because of the clarity with which the Greeks beheld *Idea*, as well as because of their skill or technique, has been eradicated all that is accidental and incongruous. Nevertheless, he argues, with reference to the gods who are manifested in classical sculpture, that, "The seriousness of the gods becomes a grace, which does not agitate with violence or lift a man above his ordinary existence, but suffers him to persist there tranquil, and simply claims to bring him content."[70] The philosopher implies that the profound feelings integral to the experience of fine art are not awakened by these lifeless forms. Thought is "dissatisfied in a reality which is no longer adequate to express it."[71] The movement, strength, and variety of the objective world force themselves upon the artist. Human emotion and thought demand expression and the most perfect technique in sculpture is inadequate for their manifestation in sensuous media. By implication, the form of the human body even in its most perfect artistic exemplification must fail to display them. It is true that Hegel's assertion that the most beautiful form does not represent the highest stage of art presupposes the formidable philosophical system as well as the dialectical method by which its philosophical truth is unfolded. Nevertheless, once Hegel permits the work of the Dutch painters, the sublime and, by implication, the ludicrous, the comic, and the grotesque significance in his aesthetic, an end to ateleological defining for the purpose of discovering an "absolutely beautiful" form or unity is near.

[68] *Ibid.*, p. 186. "The outer shape must be purified in order to express in itself a content adequate to itself; and, again, if the conformity of import and content is to be complete, the spiritual meaning which is the content must be of a particular kind."

[69] *Ibid.*, Vol. 2, p. 177.

[70] *Ibid.*, p. 259.

[71] *Ibid.*, p. 260.

For, once the theory of the canon is before us and once the point of Hegel's refusal to accept some of its traditional implications is grasped, it is possible to deal with the general problem in summary fashion. A primary characteristic of art may be unity, as the ateleologist properly contends. Certainly, the foremost contribution of ateleological theory to aesthetic is its theorists' recognition of the importance of unity and coherence in the object of art. However, the arguments put forward by these same theorists are intended not alone to ground unity but to demonstrate that unity is not only a necessary but a necessary and sufficient condition for the explanation of all the *phenomena* of art and experience. Once the latter hypothesis is permitted to stand unassailed, the procedure has ordinarily been, as is evident in transcendentalist theory of aesthetic,[72] to argue that absolute unity is logically prior to the diverse forms which are assumed to depend upon it and, on grounds of logical priority, to assume that absolute unity and beauty are identical. The conception of form as unity is not only ambiguous but, most certainly, is insufficient to serve as a limitation upon the aesthetic universe of discourse.

It has been argued that, precisely as the ateleological theory of transcendental beauty rests for its validity finally upon the hypothesis of unity, so, too, both non-mathematical and mathematical ateleological theories of "concrete" form likewise convert "form" to unity. It has been implied, as well, that the ateleologist who holds that the aesthetic universe of discourse may be restricted to "absolutely beautiful" forms or to objects of a universally valid judgment of taste must likewise assume that unity is both a necessary and sufficient condition for that beauty. The question then is whether or not the universe of discourse called artistic or aesthetic may be limited to absolutely beautiful unities. And in considering the issue, it is well, at this point, to recall that ateleological aesthetic not uncommonly converts the "common" to the "absolutely beautiful."[73] The original search for the "common" is continued despite an interpretation of the term as "absolutely beautiful" and, in

[72] Cf. above, Chap. II, particularly with reference to Plotinus, pp. 47 ff
[73] Cf. above, pp. 97 ff.

consequence, an examination of the adequacy of "unity" as the "common" should satisfy us concerning the ambiguity implicit in all ateleological theories of this type in which it is proposed to limit the aesthetic universe of discourse by the introduction of "absolute beauties."

"Forms" which owe their unity to the reiteration or variation of a given "measure" or to a given proportion, and "forms" which are unified by the relation of their parts to the whole upon analogy to an organism are limited classes of unities. Variety may be unified not only by ratio or boundary and by complex variations of ratios and proportions but also by the end or ends subserved, in the instances in question, by the object of art. The repetition of a common "measure" may serve, it is true, to bind together the elements of a particular work of art. The success of this method does not permit the theorist, however, to assume that the type of unity in question may provide a ground for a strict limitation upon objects and events in the aesthetic universe of discourse. The elements of a specific art-object may be bound together by their collective subsumption under one end. And in fact the diversity of elements in works of art, as the latter are ordinarily considered by theorists not committed to "formal" hypotheses—the non-aesthetic elements of material, representative content or symbol, and form in the simplest interpretation of the "structure" of the art-object—makes it initially more plausible to suppose that the latter principle of unification is, in fact, the one most widely used. To call the "measure" beautiful or "absolutely beautiful" is an error made by ateleological aesthetic but one implicit, as well, in other erroneous philosophical assumptions concerning the substantival-adjectival relation. The parts of a work of art are beautiful only if the part of the particular work of art subsumed under an end is considered to be a whole in itself. Plato is a sounder aesthetician in his suggestion[74] that the eyes of the statue need not be painted a beautiful color because it is the beauty of the whole that is desired, than he is in his attempt to limit painting and sculpture by use of the measures of the canon or to imply

[74] *Republic* IV.

in *Philebus* that there are mathematical forms which are "absolutely beautiful."

It is the ambiguity in the term "form," as it is interpreted to signify "unity" but which does not specify the two methods of unification that has led theorists committed to ateleological defining to the invalid conclusion that objects of art may be restricted to such as display a common measure. It is evident, contrary to their view, that "unity" provides the ground for no such strict limitation, as it is also plain that to use the term "form" as "unity" is merely to recognize the demand that coherence be admitted to be a necessary presupposition to aesthetic experience. In consequence, the hypothesis that "an art-object *must* have a certain form; it *may* have a certain purpose" proves to be untenable. The alternative, "an art-object *may* have a certain form; it *must* serve a certain purpose" remains to be investigated and it should be remarked at the outset, that the latter, the teleological hypothesis, lays down no *a priori* grounds for a limitation upon the objects which may be found to serve the purpose that binds the diverse parts together.

Certain additional consequences of the analysis of "form," are of interest. Ateleological theories of form as statements that the diverse must be unified merit no consideration as regards their *a priori* right to impose such conditions as will satisfy this requirement for unity. Specifically, no categorical demand need be heeded for unification in terms either of complex proportions derived from the relation of the parts to the whole of the human figure or of the coherence of the parts on analogy to the coherence of the parts of a living being. Nor need it be granted that objects unified by either means are necessarily beautiful because they are unified.

If this is granted, it follows that solely in terms of "form," it may be concluded only that the object must be unified, whether in terms of proportion, organic integration, content, symbolism, or of end. Within the limits of this requirement of unification, it may be argued that the object may be distorted or irregular in its proportions. However elongated the limbs of a figure by El Greco or whatever may be the exaggerations in a statue by Epstein, if the art-object is unified, the lack of precise "form" does not preclude the possibility that the object may be beautiful. Conversely, the regularity of the lines in a painting of a Madonna by Raphael or in the classical proportions of a Polycleitean statue assures the object in question only unity. The judgment that the unified object is beautiful must still be made. It may be urged, moreover, that art may be representative, imitative, or symbolical because, on hypothesis, mathematical measure or proportion or non-mathematical coherence of parts on analogy to the organism are principles of unification intrinsically no more effective, superior, or relevant than are those concerning the ends of pedagogy, morality, perfection, or desire, if the issue is one concerned with the means to the unification of art-objects. Harmony, rhythm, and proportion are merely the most obvious and "clearly demonstrable" means to the end of unity.

It must be emphasized, however, that this conclusion follows primarily in consequence and in the light of the assumption of the ateleologist that the aesthetic universe of discourse may be limited to "absolutely beautiful" forms or unities. Unity is not in fact a principle of limitation worthy of further consideration. It does have, however, a significance of another kind for art that explains at once its misuse by formalists and its recurrence in formal theories of art. The ostensible superiority of "form," as it has been used in this chapter, over the unification provided by ends in art is suggested by two remarks. The first is this, that since Kant wrote, "art for art's sake" has denied the relevance to fine art of non-aesthetic ends. It will be argued shortly, however, that every work of art is in fact at least partially definable in terms of such ends.[75] Secondly, and more immediately at issue, is the fact that "form," as it functions variously to unify by means of harmony, rhythm, proportion, and the like, is a structural and not a limiting term. Its usurpation of the place of sole criterion of the value of art is a consequence in part of reiterated efforts to describe the work of art solely in terms of such *structural* hypotheses as "living form" or "sensuous *Gestalt*" or "sensuous *media*." The significance of the structural interpretation of form will be clearer once we examine the bald statement

[75] Cf. below, Book Two, Chap. V ff.

of the "structuralist" that the object of art is, because of a unique interrelation of form and content, a "symbol of itself."[76]

To repeat, it is impossible to rule from consideration the numerous non-aesthetic ends of art, among which are representation, imitation, and symbolization, on the ground that "form" may properly delimit the aesthetic universe of discourse. If the ends in question be truly relevant to the value and experience of fine art, it must be because they, with "form" itself, are properly comprehensible in terms of a unique end of art. But, more specifically with reference to form, Rabelais' writings and Joyce's *Ulysses* are "formless" on grounds put forward by either Plato or Kant. Yet, if only in terms of non-aesthetic ends, these works of art are unified, the one in terms of a Gargantuan humor and joy of life, the other in terms of the relations of divergent individuals who wander through the city of Dublin in the course of twenty-four hours. It may well be argued, moreover, that the unifying factor in El Greco's "Toledo" is the unearthly light that permeates the painting. A statement of this kind with reference to any one of these works of art does not, indeed, tell the entire story. It does, however, plainly suggest the errors into which formalism and ateleology have recurrently led aesthetic theory.

It follows, finally, from the analysis of ateleological "form" as a *norm* or average, that there are no "absolutely beautiful" objects or events. It follows, moreover, that there can be no universally valid judgment of taste, if by this it is implied that an infallible and accurate prediction can be made that any specific object or event will always be judged to be beautiful. In both aesthetic judgment and experience, not only must errors of perception be anticipated but it must be granted that there occur periodic alterations in taste. Because the relation of art to science and morality and religion is intimate,[77] art itself is subject to alteration, and changes in aesthetic judgment may be be expected in consequence of altered attitudes towards the ideals held to be desirable in the culture in which the work of art is evaluated. Taste, notwithstanding

[76] See below, Chap. VIII.
[77] See below, Chaps. X-XIV.

the canons proposed by Plato and others, does seek novelty. Artistic usage "stales" to the point that "fixed and legal forms" would merely be ignored, were they ever imposed.

A surer criterion for greatness in art than universal agreement in judgment or continuity of taste is recurrence of interest. Ultimately, however, the judgment of taste is not universally valid because neither the object of fine art nor the aesthetic experience is describable in mechanical terms. Both are describable, rather, in terms of teleology.

Form, as is evident, is not a description of "absolutely beautiful objects" to which the dogmatist may limit the field of aesthetic. It is, rather, the name for a problem. The term merely suggests the basic requirement that unity be postulated as a necessary condition for fine art and for aesthetic experience. The use of the term is necessary primarily because it emphasizes the need for the theorist to examine the conditions for unity in both art and aesthetic experience before the sufficient conditions for fuller explanation of fine art and its experience can be made explicit.

IV

THE problems of aesthetic experience are too complex to permit uncontrolled application of Procrustean methods in their solution. The consequences of the method are aggravated if, as in the ateleological theories of aesthetic, either art or aesthetic experience is endowed with supreme value on no very sound grounds or on grounds assumed to be sound without complete investigation. The problems are, in fact, too complex to assume the correctness of a hypothesis in which the "material" aspects of the work of art are arbitrarily omitted from consideration or in which the correlative conative aspects of experience are neglected.

The price paid for "pure pleasure" and similar descriptions of "aesthetic experience" is exorbitant if we are left only with "forms" which preclude tragedy, comedy, the beauty of the human form, representative, or symbolical art. The price need not be exacted if, as has but rarely been done in classical ateleological theories, analyses of the aesthetic potentialities of media, form, feeling, symbols, and end be substituted for an arbitrary definition of "form." Nor should it be forgotten that the ateleologist avoids by the use of "form" the task of examining the implications of exaltation and discontent in the experience of profoundly moving art. In consequence, no sound resolution to the antinomies of art and aesthetic experience may be expected in a theory that fails to state the problem properly.

For these and for the other reasons evident in these chapters on ateleological aesthetic, we turn to the teleological theories of art. In this class of theory, we shall discover that adequate attention has been paid to factors neglected by the ateleologist. In fact, the history of aesthetic provides numerous instances of theories put forward to resolve the antinomies in question by use of ends intended both to unify art and its experience and to provide value in a realm otherwise not infrequently suspected of bringing its dwellers only discontent.

Book Two

Teleological Theories of Art and Aesthetic Experience

Part I

Non-Aesthetic Teleological Theories of Art and Aesthetic Experience

Chapter V

The Artist's Interests

For we shall be gainers, I presume, if poetry can be proved to be profitable as well as pleasurable.

—Plato

IT IS remarked in Boswell's justly celebrated *Life*, that, "There is no arguing with Johnson; for when his pistol misses fire, he knocks you down with the butt of it." The teleologist in aesthetic who concludes that he will achieve "mastery of the field" by default may profitably consider the counsel underlying this hyperbole. The learned Doctor's peremptory "talking for victory" bespeaks the conviction that affirmation is essential to the proof of a thesis. Few men are convinced solely by the disproof of an alternative theory.

There is no need for the scientist of ends to adopt Johnson's practice of fighting "with all weapons," including "rudeness and overbearing." But, as he grasps the "guiding thread" of a science of ends, his expectation that it will lead through the maze of aesthetic often attempted but never traversed by the ateleologist will be fulfilled only on condition that he offer an affirmatively formulated philosophy of art. Ateleological aesthetic does fail—as it must always fail—in its two-fold task: The firmest advocacy of an aesthetic that ignores ends is powerless uniquely to define the objects and events in that universe of discourse. It is equally incapable of hindering the incursion of the most varied "making" into a sanctum too often circumscribed for "absolute beauty." Neither deficiency of ateleological aesthetic, however, absolves the teleologist from the obligation that he in his turn must fulfill.

In satisfying that requirement he faces a formidable task and enters upon a field "still much vex'd." He may make no such simple initial assumptions as are implicit in ateleological aesthetic. In the latter systematic accounts of beauty, the aesthetician's task is reduced to its simplest terms. However complex even Plato's and Kant's philosophies of art may be in their final formulations, that task comprises a search for, an examination, an elimination or retention of objects assumed on *a priori* grounds to be beautiful in themselves. Before the "high *priori*" road the teleologist himself places bars and he does so precisely because he knows that should he travel that highway he will still encounter no objects that are not "relative to" persons, to time, and to place, and that he will chance upon no "absolutely beautiful" works of art.

That the task is difficult, there is no doubt. But the teleologist's hope that he may dispatch his mission is sustained throughout by an assurance that only by the introduction of means and ends into philosophy of art may life-blood and vitality be restored to a corpus of argumentation drained by abstraction and formalism. Moreover, if of necessity simplicity is sacrificed in forsaking ateleological aesthetic, the science of ends offers its own compensations. Not the least of these are freedom from the galling restrictions of the *a priori*, and release from fruitless attempt to validate judgments presumed to hold universally. These are, however, but derivative from the larger liberality implied in teleology's premise that no limitation may be placed upon the objects or events which may be found to serve the end that binds the diverse parts together.[1]

Many aestheticians, attracted to teleology by the theory's statement in terms of comparative liberality, may well hesitate to adopt its explanatory principles, once they discover that the science of ends imposes its own restrictions to ground the freedom it procures. But were its restrictions actually more galling than they prove to be, the science of ends would yet offer aesthetic analysis more permanent rewards than those afforded by mechanism. This is true because a sound teleology of art assumes that art and its experience are integral to or are presupposed by man's vital and end-seeking

[1] Cf. above, p. 168.

activities. It is the dialectician who has placed the rewards of teleological explanation within the grasp of the philosopher of art and it is well to clarify the issue raised by his technique. The dialectician has discerned in formal theories of art oblique and ostensibly inadvertent or accidental references to truth, to morality, to cognition, to utility, and to similar non-aesthetic ends. Their mention suggests an incursion of metaphysical processes into the stronghold of an aesthetic ill-prepared to explain their presence. From the point of view of the ateleologist, purposive references have little significance because the ends so casually mentioned are insufficient to define art objects. For the dialectician, on the other hand, these ends first serve to destroy the arbitrary limitations of ateleological aesthetic. They thereafter come to be the essential ground for constructive metaphysical theories of art.

Aesthetic owes no small debt to the dialectician. Its obligation is due, however, less to inferences that have been drawn concerning the operation of metaphysical processes than to the dialectician's conviction that purposive references, far from being incidental, are integral to philosophy of art. The impact of this conviction has led to the scrutiny of art in terms of fundamental problems: the precise significance of form, the relevance of content and representation, and the character and value of symbolism.

Of still greater value, however, is the fact that the dialectician has considered these problems in relation to the more fundamental issue that confronts a philosophy of art: if, as the critic correctly insists, "Art is not a plaything, but a necessity, . . ." what, then, is the need for art? A systematic teleology of art pays due attention to ends, to means, and to their interrelations and it does so in order ultimately to answer this question. It is this issue that is encountered by the present essay but, as will shortly be evident, the present level of its argument requires analysis of the partial answers afforded by historical non-aesthetic teleologies in which theories present ends and means as if they could be separated or as if the dominant value of one or the other called for slight consideration of its complementary terms.

Partial and distorted replies have been the results of these inadequacies. But it is soon evident that teleology has often been employed to satisfy a primarily systematic and aesthetic need rather than to answer the larger question. Theories of ends and theories of means[2] may be isolated one from the other but, no less than their ateleological counterparts, they have both been employed to resolve those antinomies of art and of its experience which proved so disturbing to Plato and which have confronted philosophy of art since his time. The reasons for believing that a science of ends will satisfy that need by resolving the antinomies are not far to seek. As moralists have at various times argued that the value of the end justifies the means, the aesthetician has likewise maintained upon occasion that the value of the end presumed to define the work of art compensates for whatever inadequacy the latter may exhibit as a technical instrument and for whatever irrationality its experience may evoke. It has been hoped that a proper consideration of the end of art may so transform the discontent integral to aesthetic experience that the dis-ease aroused by its failure as a means will become the ground for a mood at once inspiring and exalting.

The reasoning that has pervaded non-aesthetic teleologies in this regard is straightforward. If some aspects of all art are deceptive and evoke discontent and if a genius like Pascal may cry out against the "vanity of painting" and hold that the theater is the most dangerous recreation the world has invented, may a stronger defense be made than that which discovers the ground for art's value and for the inspiration it induces in a *telos* either of unique aesthetic value or one identical with or subsumed under the good, the true, the useful or, at the least, the playful? If, indeed, art has value—so runs the argument of the ages—this condition obtains because the musician reveals mathematical truth or for the reason that his composition is, indeed, a form of mathematical inference; that the craftsman reinforces in bronze or marble sound moral or religious teachings; that the painter gives permanent form to historical events; or that the poem affords a useful or playful means by which one may ex-

[2] One theory that emphasizes means almost to the exclusion of ends is analyzed in Chap. VIII. As will be evident, the theory in question is essentially concerned with "proximate ends."

pend surplus energy, or offers escape from life's ordered and serious commonplaces. The artist may offer a flawed or defective instrument in the work of art. He may fulfill his task less well, as Plato insists, than does the trained and expert mathematician, theologian, or historian. But that he succeeds to some extent is, on the present view, the redemption of his art and that redemption derives from the value of the end of that art.

Historical statements of teleology in art have rarely failed to assert that it is primarily in consequence of an alliance with the ends of morality, religion, productive craftsmanship, magic, play, or man's other numberless purposive non-aesthetic activities that sufficient value accrues to art to compensate for its disvalues. It is precisely the adequacy or inadequacy of non-aesthetic teleologies to explain art and aesthetic experience that is in question and an examination of this point will be significant as an initial step towards the formulation of a teleology of art.

II

As HISTORICAL instances of the teleology of art are examined a fact of some importance for our later consideration becomes evident. It has not infrequently been assumed that it is possible to formulate an aesthetic of such liberality that little or no heed need be paid to restrictions arising from the possible structural homogeneity of the works of art regarded as means to the end subserved.[3] But the more immediate problem is equally evident. However capricious may be a treatment of means in a teleology, the particular aesthetic system that emphasizes ends undergoes limitations immediately it is formulated. The selection of any end to define art presents the same difficulty to the teleologist as that which meets the ateleologist. Both philosophers of art must limit the aesthetic universe of discourse. The ateleologist, as has been observed, has ordinarily regarded form as the limiting criterion. The teleologist, in his turn, restricts objects and events by their relation to the end

[3] Cf. below, Chap. VIII.

they subserve. It is true that the teleologist may select from an almost unlimited variety of specific ends, with reference to which art, in his theory, is defined. These may be moral, religious, scientific, decorative, historical, archaeological, and so on. The end he does select, however, will be subsumed in its turn under one of three well-defined teleological classes. On the most general teleological theory, the work of art may be regarded as aesthetic, first, because it serves a non-aesthetic end; or, secondly, because it serves a unique aesthetic end; or, finally, because it serves both non-aesthetic and aesthetic ends. The cogency of the teleology of art is primarily concerned with the discrimination and adequacy of these ends. We shall consider at once the first possibility which is fundamental to the non-aesthetic teleology of art.

III

THE assumption that objects of art are definable, not in consequence of their relation to a unique aesthetic end but rather because they function as means to non-aesthetic ends, implies that the aesthetic universe of discourse is either identical with or is included within a non-aesthetic universe of discourse. It has already been suggested that the preponderant motive for history's predilection for this alternative has been a need to counter criticism adverse both to art and to its experience. There are, however, more immediate motives that impel thinkers to weigh its value. We may ignore theorists driven to its acceptance by blind conviction that no unique aesthetic end may be defined for art; we may overlook, also, those who, like Charles Lamb, have by its adoption justified the pleasure they have felt in a human activity that lies beyond the scope of their understandings to defend upon aesthetic grounds alone. Neither the blind sceptic nor the equally blind lover is the most urgent and compelling protagonist of the non-aesthetic theory. Rather, the strongest argument is implicit in the writings of critic and philosopher led to a non-aesthetic teleology and convinced of its cogency by the nature of art itself.[4] The direction of that argument is most easily indicated by considering the aesthetician's interpretation of one of philosophy's most venerable problems, the status in the work of art of the craftsman's selfish interests.

Much has been written in support of art's "impersonality" and the artist's "selflessness." It remains, however, no less difficult for the philosopher to accept without demur the conclusion that a technician labors to make a work of art without desiring to do so or without "interest" in it, than it is for the moralist to entertain the argument that an act may be done solely from other-regarding motives. But if it be urged that the individual artist does satisfy some selfish interest in the making of a work of art, may it be denied in consequence that the work of art is definable in non-aesthetic terms?

A definitive reply to this question not unnaturally awaits the most precise analysis of the relation between the artist and his product.[5] But a preliminary and necessary presupposition of that analysis is afforded by those theories of craft which encountered its difficulties in analogous fields long before a formal distinction between technical and fine art was made. One of its most interesting and suggestive formulations in fact is implicit in the earlier books of Plato's *Republic*. There the argument touches closely upon the remark made earlier in the present essay[6] that the artist is only rarely a dialectician and that, in consequence, his motives and purposes are revealed primarily in his work. It may be inferred quite simply that the completion of any technical task "achieves the end" set by the craftsman for himself and that the work of art is the "proof" of the effort's success or failure. It may be asked whether or not a differentiation may be made between the *telos* of art and the many ends the artist as a man proposes to attain by non-artistic activities.

It is possible to adduce both general and specific statements that

[4] The importance of their arguments is not limited to the present problem. Cf. Chap. X and Part III of this book.

[5] Cf. below, Chaps. X and XVIII.

[6] Cf. above, Chap. II, pp. 86 ff.

deny the possibility of such a differentiation. To illustrate the more general thesis, one may mention briefly an inference which Maritain draws from the assumption that art is an *habitus*. In an essay, "Christian Art," the French philosopher[7] remarks that a separation of faith and of art is not only undesirable but is, in effect, impossible. This he maintains on the ground that the integrity of the artist necessarily affects the "making." Yet it is not clear that this suggestion may not imply that the integrity of the artist is not to be directed wholly and solely to the work of art and that the latter may not be distinguished, to some degree at least, from its religious or moral frame of reference.[8] It may be urged, indeed, that the requirements of the work of art are sufficiently compelling, for example in tragedy and in comedy, to necessitate a delineation of character such that from a moral or religious point of view the latter is either vile or diabolical. Few would regard Vittoria Corombona as an exemplar of morality but Webster undoubtedly found her very wickedness essential to his dramatic purposes. It may be argued, contrariwise, that even the genius of Shakespeare fails to achieve true tragedy in *Measure for Measure* in part because the author is unable to control dramatically the eminently virtuous but essentially inflexible central character, Isabella. It may be urged, indeed, that the artist who does ignore the demands of the work of art denies his integrity as an artist and that in this he is no less hypocritical than is the man who fails of virtuous conduct in resolving a moral dilemma. One may accept the fact that there always is in art some reference to *mores* and yet deny that a specifically moral attitude must be adopted by the artist. The problem becomes an aesthetic issue only if one encounters a lifetime of artistic activity devoted solely to the depiction of depravity and luxuriance, for where this occurs without reference to context or end, the making is analogous to gluttony, the vice of the man who eats whether hungry or not. But in an instance of this kind, it is evident that the context of art is ignored.

[7] *Art et Scolastique*, Chap. VIII.

[8] The extent to which this is valid is considered in the present essay in the chapters on artistic symbolism. Cf. Chaps. VIII, X ff.

One consequence of the frequent interpretation of artistic integrity wholly in terms of non-aesthetic value has been the occasional ascription to craftsmen of whatever of "immorality" or "irreligion" appears in their works of art. The villainy of Iago, the lust of a Tarquin, and the passion of the sonnets have been attributed to Shakespeare, precisely as various critics have seen in Epstein's *Adam* and *Eve* clear evidence of the sculptor's presumed psychoses. Yet it is evident, to take the instance of Iago, that while Shakespeare necessarily "imagined" this character, he did so within the context of a potentially tragic situation that is in turn engendered by Othello's jealousy and Desdemona's character. For Desdemona was

> . . . A maiden never bold;
> Of spirit so still and quiet, that her motion
> Blush'd at herself; . . .

It is the characters, in all their complexity, caught in the trap implied by Othello's words,

> She lov'd me for the dangers I had pass'd,
> And I lov'd her that she did pity them . . .

that demand of Shakespeare the portrayal of a villain, although the requirement placed upon the dramatist is still wholly inadequate to account for the subtlety of Iago.

It would seem then that there is an integrity to art that transcends the subjective *habitus* of the artist *qua* man, an integrity that influences the artist *qua* artist. It is his recognition of this truth that adds value to Aristotle's remark that the poet "should prefer probable impossibilities to improbable possibilities," inasmuch as the "probable impossibility" allows for the operation of laws of art and of the art-object.

The more specific form of the argument that the artist and the man may not be differentiated as regards ends is given baldest expression if it be assumed that, because the poet or musician is a man and a social being, it is his livelihood that provides the predominant motive for his work and is, therefore, the end of the art.

An assumption made only less frequently is that the artist, since he must live, is influenced primarily in his work as the holders of the purse-strings dictate.

The consequence of either argument would be that the end of Michelangelo's art is that imposed, let us say, by the patron who commissioned the Medici Chapel or that Rodin sculptured *Balzac* solely to obtain the fee offered by the *Société des Gens de Lettres*. Critics persuaded of the soundness of this assumption would discover in some chance particular or personal relationship between Velasquez and Philip IV the full artistic meaning of the portrait of Sebastian, or would discover the purpose of *The Faerie Queene* to be the desire for advancement that may have inspired Spenser to dedicate the poem to Elizabeth. The wooing of a particular woman, the petitioning of a favor, the satisfaction of ambition, or the desire for a monetary reward—each has been regarded as the significant end of particular works of art.

It is a fact, nonetheless, that the thesis—the work of art is constructed wholly as a means to non-aesthetic ends whether these be the ends of the artist or of his patrons—rests upon no very firm foundation. Each instance cited in proof that an artist has been influenced in this way may be countered by a biographical instance of one not so coerced. Brahms and Wagner compose symphony and opera in the face of severe contemporary criticism. Vasari's anecdotes concerning Michelangelo make it clear that the great sculptor and painter was peremptory in the face of his patrons' critical and artistic pretensions. Rodin forthrightly rejects the demands of a *Société* which refuses to accept the *Balzac*. It is at least conceivable that artists are dominated by their determination to avoid all compulsion except that of "artistic purposes."

But if arguments and counter-arguments at this level are rarely convincing, a sounder consideration of these identical problems, raised by the artist's satisfaction of his own interests, is implicit in the discussion of τέχνη in the *Republic*.[9] Plato is forthright in his opinion. He maintains not only that it is unnecessary for an art to "investigate its own interests," since it has an integrity of its own,

[9] *Op. cit.*, 341 ff.

but also that no art, whether it be the physician's, the pilot's, or the ruler's, is intended to satisfy the practicing individual's own selfish interest. The arts have severally no "other interest to pursue than their own highest perfection."

The end of the perfection of the art itself and its care for its own subjects touches upon the present discussion. For if the conclusion[10] to the chapter on the ateleological theory of "concrete" form in art is recalled, it is evident that "subject of the art" is the material unified or formed by the artist. This "unified material" is the "end" of art, its "end-term." If Plato's argument is elaborated, it is plain that it is implied not that the satisfaction of the selfish interest but rather the product with which the artist's creativity is completed, constitutes the "end."[11] The end of the pilot's art is navigation. The pilot's selfish end is his livelihood. The navigation, the event produced by the "making," may be differentiated from the selfish end, as the art required for navigation is to be distinguished from the art that satisfies the need for subsistence. Plato's argument is, by implication, one that distinguishes the selfish and subjective interests of the artist who practices the art from the objective end of the art.

The production of the object of art does make an essential distinction. It is essential to distinguish among the arts which have their own perfection and so to indicate that an art separate from "making" is required to satisfy the artist's selfish interest. Such a distinction is of use later in differentiating fine from technical art. But the latter distinction lies beyond Plato's intention, since he certainly always reduced what may be called an aesthetic end to non-aesthetic ends. A more immediate complication is encountered, however, as one considers the practice of art in contradistinction to its theoretical justification. In practice, the product of the technique, the "end-term," may be a means for either the producer or the person for whom it is made. "Making," in other words, produces an "end-term" that may enter again the realm of "acting."

[10] See above, pp. 169 ff.

[11] Aristotle clarifies the point by his distinction between "acting" and "making." Cf. *E.N.*, VI. 4 and *Physics*, 191 b 1, 192 b 25.

The important implication of Plato's argument for the present is not its distinction between subjective and objective interests but its relevance to the question, whether there is or is not a unique aesthetic end for art. Plato's bifurcation of subjective and objective interests by means of the product of technique does not signify, however, that the artist is completely isolable from the object produced or that the art-object is completely isolable from the artist's interests. The selfish interest need be neither entirely subjective nor the solely relevant end of art. Solipsism in art needs for its establishment a complementary thesis to the effect that the selfish interest is subjective or that works of art are unrelated particulars.[12]

It is apparent that the so-called selfish interest may be regarded as wholly subjective only upon the supposition that it does not in any way affect the work of art. Plato's argument is, in fact, too extreme a statement of the case for the objectivity of the work of art and the subjectivity of selfish interest. If the work of art is unaffected by the selfish interest, subjectivity entails aesthetic incomprehensibility. There is, however, nothing in the argument to show that the selfish interest does not affect the object of art or that it is not in its turn displayed in it. In fact, the object may be used as a means to satisfy the selfish interest and in order for this to be possible, the subjectivity must have been objectified and have become one of the many possible non-aesthetic factors in the work of art. If its presence there is not evident, i.e., if it is not identified with some objective value, the incomprehensibility entailed applies to all attempts to know its meaning, including the efforts of the craftsman who made the object. It has been argued *ad infinitum* that the meaning of art may be expressed only in artistic terms and by this has been meant, all too often, expressed only in subjective terms. But there are few who would welcome solipsism to aesthetic once it is realized that the object is by it rendered no less incomprehensible for its maker than for others.

The means by which the subjective interest does affect fine art will be considered later.[13] At present, it is only necessary to point

[12] Cf. below, Chaps. XI-XIII.
[13] Cf. below, Chap. X.

out that the artist's selfish interest may be a factor omnipresent in the work of art. It does not necessarily follow, however, that a particular artist's end in "making" is necessarily identical with the selfish interest. Most important of all, it may be asserted that the Platonic differentiation of product and maker objectifies the selfish interest. The end-product of the artist's making is, in its completion, evidence that the work of art is potentially free of the wholly selfish interest. As such, it is an object to be judged, evaluated, examined, and appreciated. It is structurally of such nature that it and every product of artistic skill, in whatever art, have common characteristics apart from those pertaining to self-interest.[14] Moreover, it will be argued, it is a symbolism comprehensible within various cultures or even within the race.[15] These characteristics provide the criteria of differentiation between the selfish and unselfish interests.

If the object made may be a means to ends both selfish and unselfish and the former end is no less objective than the latter, the teleology of art as it has been considered thus far in terms of the artist's interests, may be thought of as a subform of the inclusive hypothesis that art is explicable wholly in non-aesthetic terms. "Making" produces an object or event usable as a means to moral, religious, or scientific ends. The difficulty lies in ascertaining whether or not every product of artistic "making" is definable wholly in terms of these and similar non-aesthetic ends.

The non-aesthetic theory of art, to which the problem of the artist's interests is subordinate, would signify, provided that it could be validated, that Giotto's frescoes in the Santa Croce and at Assisi present and are intended solely to present for contemporaries and for posterity the character of St. Francis by the representation of his kindly acts; that Bach's Cantatas are celebrations of religious ceremonies or aspirations; that Milton's *Paradise Lost* justifies "the ways of God to man"; and that *Hamlet* was written by a young

[14] The separation of artist from work of art is of value for a later consideration of objectification of feeling. See below, Chap. XVIII, pp. 503 ff. Fine art presupposes this separation and is itself "freeing" art, liberating the artist and the percipient from the interests or demands of morality, science, and religion. See below, pp. 502 ff.

[15] See below, Chaps. X-XIII.

genius whose pockets were being filled by just such productions, despite the outcries of Greene against the "young Shakescene." Michelangelo served his own interest in commemorating the Medici and obviously he served the interests of the ruling family. In each instance, the assertion that the work of art may perform a non-aesthetic function is true. It is true, as has been implied, in a more primitive sense as well. In both the spatial and temporal arts, the products of the artist's technique are objects *embodied* and material in the one case, and are events in the other. Verrocchio's *David* may decorate a garden or the primitive representation of a Crucifixion may become one of a myriad of adornments on the façade of the cathedral at Salamanca. Leonardo's "The Last Supper" may break the monotony of a blank wall in Milan. Each statement is valid, in precisely the sense that it is true that, as Raphael's "Madonna della Sedia" and Titian's "Transfiguration" may serve religious purposes, so Velasquez's "Surrender at Breda" may serve a secular, historical end, and that the latter painter's portraits in the Prado perpetuate the likeness of noblemen and noble ladies. The music of Tschaikowsky's *1812 Overture* may celebrate the founding or destruction of empires, as *Perpetuum Mobile* may illustrate or satirize one of man's recurrent fantasies. Similarly, music may hearten men in battle or lull children to sleep. As every object of art is produced by man in society, it may be urged in addition that both the artist and the work of art influence and are in turn affected by social interests. All art, on this hypothesis, has a social connotation and is therefore non-aesthetic.[16]

The particular ends of men's actions and the motives that impel them are many and various. It would be a dull task, even were it possible, to exhaust by denotation the list of ends attributed to art in non-aesthetic teleologies. Nor is it necessary to undertake the enterprise. One need read but briefly in aesthetic and artistic literature to discover that there are two principal kinds of non-aesthetic theory to which history has had constant recourse to explain various works of art. A quotation will suffice to suggest both the nature of

[16] The definitiveness of such a statement has too often in aesthetic history been argued *modus tollens ponendo*.

these theories and one of the interesting techniques that has made their relevant data available for analysis. In *Hunters and Artists*,[17] the Late Caspian style of primitive art leads the authors to remark that from it "we can glean much information as to the customs, clothes and weapons of the people." But this in turn suggests a difficulty "as to the motives which led to the production of these artistic displays." Concerning this problem, it is confessed, "there has been much difference of opinion. Some have suggested merely *joie de vivre*, others the need for some occupation during periods of enforced idleness; but the majority of anthropologists see behind these paintings a religious motive."

Joie de vivre is, however, but one reflection of the historically important theory that art originates in play, while religion is similarly but one of the many serious ends by means of which the artist's craft, both in its genesis and in its maturity, has been explained. The playful and the serious non-aesthetic teleologies of art are, in fact, recurrent theories the examination of which provides a test of the validity of the non-aesthetic hypothesis itself. Not only do they present at least ostensibly contrary evaluations of art and of aesthetic experience, but their respective historical formulations also complement each other in a valuable way. The non-aesthetic serious hypothesis for the most part directs attention to art's content, the play-theory to the experience of art. Finally, in these theories, art lends itself to examination, as the title of *Hunters and Artists* suggests, by use of a technique often adjudged superior to aesthetic analysis. Among the soundest analysts of art and of the significance of its experience in terms of non-aesthetic teleologies are those made by anthropologists, archaeologists, and ethnologists. Their writings are the more valuable because in them mere theory has been bulwarked by sound empirical investigation.

It is to but one aspect of anthropological research—and that within the briefest possible scope—that this essay will turn in order to test the cogency of the theory that art is wholly definable in non-aesthetic terms. But this one aspect—the genesis of art—is

[17] Harold Peake and Herbert John Fleure, p. 92.

integral to much that anthropology has contributed to aesthetic. Whether that contribution is sufficiently corroborated by the scientist's findings to convince the aesthetician that art needs for its analysis no reference to a unique aesthetic end is one of the primary considerations of the two succeeding chapters.

Chapter VI

The Genetic Theory of Art (I): The Serious Hypothesis

At liquidas avium voces imitarier ore
ante fuit multo quam levia carmina cantu
concelebrare homines possent aurisque iuvare.
et zephyri, cava per calamorum, sibila primum
agrestis docuere cavas inflare cicutas.
inde minutatim dulcis didicere querelas,
tibia quas fundit digitis pulsata canentum,
avia per nemora ac silvas saltusque reperta,
per loca pastorum deserta atque otia dia.
haec animos ollis mulcebant atque iuvabant
cum satiate cibi; . . .[1]

—LUCRETIUS

POETIC imagination has often revisited the rustic scene at which the arts quicken to life in rude imitation of nature's sounds and motions. A not dissimilar vision of a world yet young has hovered before the eyes of the classical philosopher of art, who dreamed a

[1] H. A. J. Munro translates the lines from *De Rerum Natura* as follows: "But imitating with the mouth the clear notes of birds was in use long before men were able to sing in tune smooth-running verses and give pleasure to the ear. And the whistlings of the zephyr through the hollows of reeds first taught peasants to blow into hollow stalks. Then step by step they learned sweet plaintive ditties, which the pipe pours forth pressed by the fingers of the players, heard through pathless woods and forests and lawns, through the unfrequented haunts of shepherds and abodes of unearthly calm. These things would soothe and gratify their minds when sated with food. . . ."

golden age peopled variously by yokel or corybante dancing or singing in mimicry or in play.

The dream no longer serves to describe art's origin, however tempting it may be for the Rousseaus of aesthetic. Its force has been dissipated by science, in contrast to which the speculations of classical philosophers upon the genesis of art suffer both in scope of the material observed and in the precision of its classification. Lucretius' *De Rerum Natura* is of negligible value in comparison to the findings of the anthropologist, not only in these respects but also in the integration of the arts with the specific cultures from which they are derived.

It is true, nonetheless, that both the poet's vision and the scientist's conclusions, despite their palpable divergences, present the same problem for the aesthetician. A genetic theory of art may begin with speculation upon the aesthetic implications of rustic hilarity for art or it may be formulated in consequence of analyses of artifacts, potsherds, wall paintings, tribal songs, or carved figurines. In either case, it has aesthetic significance only if at some stage in its elaboration the question is raised whether or not art and aesthetic experience originate in the satisfaction of non-aesthetic needs or interests. Furthermore, if to this question an affirmative answer is given, the theory must consider whether art and its experience are so completely determined by the conditions attendant upon their origin as to be explicable wholly in terms of non-aesthetic ends.

That these problems are implicit in ancient as well as in modern genetic theories of art and aesthetic experience is evident in the purposes attributed to artists by philosophers and anthropologists alike. It is in part his interest in the motives of the artist that is evident in Plato's earlier Dialogues as he elaborates the theory that art begins in *mimesis* and it is his concern with the artist's contribution to pedagogy and political practice that is presupposed by the suggestion in the *Laws* that certain of art's forms originate in play.

The familiar modern phrases, "to hold, as 't were, the mirror up to nature" and, "Man should only play with Beauty and with Beauty he should only play," are, in fact, reminiscent of the Academy. But it is Aristotle who infers that the aesthetic connotations of genetic theory are implicit in the experience of art as well as in its creation. In *Poetics*[2] he offers, in consequence, what is perhaps the first well-rounded theory of the origin of art. Aristotle writes that *mimesis* is natural "from childhood." Man is "the most imitative creature in the world." To this mimetic instinct, Aristotle not only ascribes the origins of poetry; he adds, wisely, that, "It is also natural for all to delight in works of imitation."

As the theory of *mimesis* is predominant in classical speculation upon the origin of art and its nature,[3] so the hypothesis that art begins in play and is to be understood in playful terms underlies the aesthetic of modern evolutionary theory. But while the anthropologist has adopted both imitation and play as factors significant for the beginnings of art, his research has suggested that many other non-aesthetic motives enter, as well, upon that genesis. In consequence, his consideration of the problem presents the artist, as the latter brings his technical skills into operation upon stone or wood, upon sound or color, as "making" for such specific ends as utility, ornamentation, and decoration. The product of his technique is explained, as well, as an instrument for communication or is described in terms of religious, magical, or moral values. The artist's particular purposes have been variously classified as commemorative, expressive, patriotic, or technical and his art has been grounded in the resolution of theoretical or practical problems, in the revelation of reality, or in the achievement or maintenance of social solidarity.

Nor has the anthropologist failed to present the corollary proper to his theories of the origin of art. It has been variously maintained that aesthetic experience is likewise implicated in non-aesthetic ends. More specifically with reference to the life of the "primitive," it has been argued, not that the art-object is a mere thing or event, but rather that it is an "image." As such, the product of "making" effectively stimulates percipients to recognize the object imitated or represented; to understand the significant facts the artist proposes to communicate; to evoke religious feelings; to evaluate the object's efficacy as an instrument for religious, mathematical, or moral ends;

[2] *Op. cit.*, 4. 1448 b 4 ff.
[3] But cf. above, Chap. I, pp. 5 ff.

or to allow primitive man to "express" himself in the experience of the art-object.

It may be doubted, at the outset, that the multiplication of motives attributed to the artist by modern science has improved, in one respect at least, upon classical genetic theory. Valuable as it may be to distinguish mimetic, playful, technical, or pedagogical art, there remains the possibility that not all the ends attributed to the artist are barren of aesthetic connotations. Imitation, decoration, and "expression" appear, indeed, to transcend the limits at least of the serious non-aesthetic genetic theory.

Philosophers of art have implied, however, that these at least ostensibly aesthetic connotations are not inconsistent with their general theory. They interpret the terms in question to denote means rather than ends of "making." In this sense, the ethnologist suggests that "imitation" is only ostensibly aesthetic but is in fact properly understood to explain primitive man's reproduction of an object's appearance for the sake of "sympathetic magic." Similarly, ornamentation and decoration come to be regarded as functions of sexual attraction and, ultimately, of the preservation of species. Nor, it is argued, does the primitive musician merely "express" himself. Rather, he invokes a tribal deity, precisely as the poet glorifies a totemic tradition to serve the ends of social intercourse.

The problem remains, therefore, whether on these grounds the assumption that the serious non-aesthetic theory of the origin and nature of art is competent fully to account for each and every product of craft. Its claims to such competence are immeasurably strengthened by the fact that some objects of primitive art are indefinable in aesthetic terms. Whether this is true of all "making" and its products, even though it may be shown that all artistic objects do have non-aesthetic value, is the crucial issue of the serious non-aesthetic teleology of art.[4]

[4] Only data and conclusions strictly relevant to this problem will be considered in what follows and even then the ethnological material will be used sparingly. The scope of the material that bears on the problem is so extensive that I have included in the bibliography only some of the more important general writings on the subject and have selected articles and books which I have found to be of particular value in describing the arts and crafts of the

II

IT MAY be asserted that, with few exceptions, the arrows and lance-heads, hammers, and ax-heads of neolithic cultures are properly defined and are completely explicable as useful implements.[5] It is doubtful that there are exceptions among the so-called "eoliths" which call for the use of aesthetic principles for their full explanation. Most comparatively simple weapons and implements of primitive man are susceptible to description in terms of non-aesthetic ends and are properly called "artifacts."

It would appear, indeed, that the more complex products of artistic handicraft in cultures more advanced than the pre-Chellean and Acheulian may likewise be fully defined in terms of similar technical and non-aesthetic ends. The *bâton de commandement*, which was presumably a badge of office in Magdalenian cultures, apparently served only that useful function.[6] The technician who produced the steatopygous Venus of Willensdorf in all probability was invoking by its means a goddess of the harvest to ensure fertility for the fields and for the women of the tribe. The Cro-Magnon painter who drew the bison at Salnoiu de Niaux and the sculptor who modeled the beast in the Cave of Tuc d'Audobert did so,[7] according to the anthropologist, either to ensure by "sympathetic magic" that spears thrown at the "image" would facilitate the killing of the living animal or "to express the wish that there be many bisons."[8]

Ethnological research among living primitive tribes suggests much the same explanation of art and in this field the technique of the science certainly presupposes fewer reconstructions of cultures and

---

African Negroes, the Eskimos, the Mayans, the Maoris, and various of the North American Indian tribes. The majority of these writings are not specifically referred to in the present volume but have influenced its conclusions.

[5] See Y. Hirn, *The Origins of Art*; G. G. McCurdy, *Human Origins*; and W. J. Sollas, *Ancient Hunters*.

[6] See Sollas, *op. cit.*, pp. 359 ff.

[7] *Ibid.*, pp. 379 ff.

[8] See Hugo Obermaier, *Fossil Man in Spain*, p. 259; and H. Peake and H. J. Fleure, *Hunters and Artists*, p. 92.

motives than in its investigations of the art of pre-history. Among the tribes of American Indians most closely studied is, by way of illustration, the Navajo whose *Night Chant* is an important ceremonial. Some of the words from the ceremony follow:

In Tse'gíhi,
In the house made of the dawn,
In the house made of the evening twilight,
In the house made of the dark cloud,
In the house made of the he-rain,
In the house made of the dark mist,
In the house made of the she-rain,
In the house made of pollen, . . .

Oh, male divinity!
With your moccasins of dark cloud, come to us.
With your leggings of dark cloud, come to us.
With your head-dress of dark cloud, come to us.
With your mind enveloped in dark cloud, come to us.
With the dark thunder above you, come to us soaring.
With the shapen cloud at your feet, come to us soaring.
With the far darkness made of the dark cloud over your head, come to us soaring,
With the far darkness made of the he-rain over your head, come to us soaring,
With the far darkness made of the dark mist over your head, come to us soaring.
With the far darkness made of the he-rain over your head, come to us soaring. . . .
With the far darkness made of the dark cloud on the ends of your wings, come to us soaring.

With the near darkness made of the dark cloud, of the he-rain, of the dark mist and of the she-rain, come to us.
With the darkness of the earth, come to us.
Happily may fair white corn, to the ends of the earth, come with you
Happily may fair yellow corn, to the ends of the earth, come with you
Happily may fair blue corn, to the ends of the earth, come with you

Happily may fair corn of all kinds, to the ends of the earth, come with you.

In beauty (happily) I walk.
With beauty before me, I walk.
With beauty behind me, I walk.
With beauty below me, I walk.
With beauty above me, I walk.
With beauty all around me I walk.
It is finished (again) in beauty,
It is finished in beauty,
It is finished in beauty,
It is finished in beauty.[9]

There is no evidence that the *Night Chant* is performed for other than therapeutic purposes or that the *Shaman* regards it in any other light than as a cure for disease. Among the nomadic Navajos, it is customary also to construct sand-paintings of intricate design for similar purposes and as instruments for the invocation of Gods of the thunder, the rain, the lightning, and the six directions. The complex symbolism of the *Night Chant* and of the sand paintings is paralleled in the dance rituals performed by the agricultural Pueblo Indians, who are neighbors of and were once prey of the Navajos. Many Pueblo Indian dances are performed to induce rain to fall and to bring its fertilizing and life-giving effects. Other ceremonials are totemic in origin. Among the most interesting of these is the Snake Dance which recapitulates the legend of Tiyo. The Butterfly, Buffalo, and Eagle dances are undoubtedly totemic and mimetic in origin, while other ceremonials are phallic, derisory, or playful in character.

One of the best known ceremonials among the North American Indians is the Sun Dance, which, the Arapahoe believe, functions to heal the sick. The Tlinkit commemorates his ancestors in carved wood and the totemic symbols produced may be either human or animal. The African Basuto carves wooden figurines and masks to imitate natural objects, to represent men or to commemorate

[9] *The Night Chant*, translated by Washington Matthews: "Rite of the Atsá-Lei or First Dancers," p. 143, Sec. 613.

events of importance. The Polynesians tattoo and scarify the human body to increase sexual attractiveness or for obscure reasons of health. Mayan codices serve largely to date events, and Aztecan carvings likewise function as calendars.

Art, throughout the wide geographical range in which its more primitive forms have been studied, appears to have originated primarily in the satisfaction of non-aesthetic needs and interests. It seems to retain functions identical with or similar to those it satisfied by its origin. But granted this, it is nonetheless patent that a study of most complex primitive art couched solely in terms of serious non-aesthetic ends gives evidence of inadequacy. The decorated Zulu spear is *qua* spear no better than one undecorated merely because its handle is minutely covered with interlaced designs. The efficacy of the Navajos' *Night Chant* is not augmented by poetic imagery or the repetition of evocative words. The fact that the carver has unified the details of the figure increases not a whit the efficient functioning of the African Congo fetish[10] *qua* fetish. Yet, some compulsion to unify has led the artist to distort the legs of the figurine to a degree that would render a living person a hopeless cripple. It is doubtful that the small figure[11] brought out of the Maritime Congo is more useful as a handle for a bell or rattle because "the rear view affords a remarkable example of the tendency . . . to seize upon and manipulate physical features so as to produce a pattern quite geometrical in appearance and yet not departing in essentials from the actualities of bodily conformation." Nor would it appear possible to explain wholly in terms of serious non-aesthetic ends the deviations evident in the bâton from Loanda.[12] The sculptured head of the bâton is remarkable for the exaggeration of the size of mouth and eyebrows. It is noticeable, however, that the line of the mouth repeats that of the jaw and that the shape of the face duplicates in reverse that of the helmet. Similarly, the prow of many a Polynesian canoe is curved, originally, no doubt, to add to the craft's speed. Nevertheless, the elaboration of that curve and the

[10] See H. U. Hall, "Congo and West African Wood Carving," pp. 75 and 78.
[11] *Ibid.*, p. 82.
[12] *Ibid.*, p. 69.

continuation of its line in a decorative pattern adds neither seaworthiness nor swiftness.

The aesthetic problem implicit in primitive art is made explicit by Thomas Wilson:

> It does not appear that he [man] considered himself in any way better off by having these objects decorated than he would have if they had been plain. There are many hundreds of them which are entirely plain, of equal value for service, evidently utilitarian, without ornament or decoration, and apparently serving as weapons of the chase or war equally well with those highly decorated. Therefore, these objects, beautifully designed as they may have been, were no addition to his wealth or his power, and as for information he was not busying himself with that.[13]

But if primitive man considers himself "no better off" because his weapon or his bowl or his figurine is decorated, how then may the theorist account for the deviations and elaborations that do occur in art? And how explain the interest, at least comparable to that which spurs him to produce an efficient instrument capable of fulfilling serious ends, that enters upon the inclusion of these "useless" additions? That there are "idealizations" in art and that the serious non-aesthetic teleology of art would appear to be incompetent to account for their presence seems obvious.

It is of interest, however, that philosophy of art has not always been forced by these "deviations" or "idealizations" to accept the alternative that the artist is influenced by either playful or aesthetic ends. It has been urged, indeed, that the serious non-aesthetic ends of art are quite adequate to their explanatory task, provided proper attention be paid to the requirements or "dictates" of the stone, wood, colors, or words used by artists as "materials." It is evident that this opinion carries to its logical conclusion the suggestion made in the last chapter[14] that the artist's interests are affected by the "demands" of the art-object, that craft is integrity to the object made.

If it is maintained that "idealizations" originate because of the

[13] "Prehistoric Art: or the Origin of Art as Manifested in the Works of Prehistoric Man."

[14] See above, pp. 182 ff.

problems presented by the material, we do have an elaboration of the non-aesthetic and serious teleology of art. The completed theory would begin by explaining art in terms of non-aesthetic ends such as self-preservation or utility. It would conclude with a study of the technique or craftsmanship requisite to "form" properly a recalcitrant material into an instrument competent to achieve that purpose within the limitations of the material available for making the instrument in question. The knob-like hair of archaic Greek sculpture would owe its origin on this view, to the hardness of the stone available to the sculptor and the "decorative" element would be explained by the need to use emery rather than a drill.[15] Similarly, the *bâton de commandement* unearthed in the Grotto of Montgandier[16] would owe its incised representations of eels to the peculiar shape of reindeer horn. One might cite many instances of Magdalenian art in which the curve of the horn permits the shoulder but not the legs of the animal to be represented. The implications of the suggestion are well illustrated in Eskimo sculpture. The art of this people suffers from the obvious limitations placed upon it by the shape of the walrus tusk, widely used by the native artists as material for carved knives and spear handles, miniature sledges and kayaks and similar objects. The distortions of animal and human figures represented in the material are sometimes attributed to the limited potentialities of the tusk itself. A still more interesting instance is afforded in various descriptions of pottery-making. On bowls produced by some potters, there is found a formalization of the natural objects represented—mountains, clouds, raindrops, and trees. But it is suggested that these formalizations are affected by the vestigial ridgings and coilings no longer functionally useful for the molding of the unbaked material. It has been urged, further, that the pottery remains true in design to the shape of the gourd that was its prototype. As more permanent clay replaces the gourd, the gourd-shapes are retained and so affect the decorations.[17]

[15] S. Casson, *The Technique of Early Greek Sculpture*, pp. 36 ff.

[16] Musée d'Histoire Naturelle, Paris.

[17] The argument is used by Gottfried Semper in *Der Stil in den Technischen und Tektonischen Künsten*, to explain the origin of the art of geometric style. Pots, etc., made from skin and fiber were replaced by clay and the old forms

There is plausibility in the argument that the origin of the object affects the product and the design evolved. That it does not fully satisfy the conditions of the problem is evident, however, if its claim is expanded to the degree that the theorist may then define art wholly in terms of serious non-aesthetic ends. The argument may not be generalized simply because the artist by lively imagination, increased technical skill, or newly discovered instruments, has not infrequently in the history of art dominated the recalcitrant material and has molded it into shapes and designs which, within limits, run counter to the material's dictates. One Magdalenian artist, for example, represents a stag running with horns held almost flat against the shoulders.[18] African sculpture in wood sought a different solution, inasmuch as the problem imposed by this material presents the carver with technical difficulties not met with in ivory or in metal. The wood-carver discovers that limited effects of contrast are possible because sharp definition of outline and edge is difficult to produce. This limitation has, however, apparently only served as a challenge to one African primitive sculptor.[19] He has achieved an intended contrast not only in the representation by portraying a face with pointed chin and broad forehead, but by actualizing the potentialities for light and shade in the close grained wood itself. A cruder attempt is illustrated in one mask-maker's effort to give a unified impression of three-dimensionality. He has fastened four masks together but his original problem was complicated beyond complete solution by the need to leave an entrance for the wearer's head. Hall cites one instance,[20] in which a portrait was obviously

---

were utilized in the new material, the potter being sufficiently unintelligent to imitate the seams and markings of the prototype. The influence of conditioning factors in art is more intelligently appraised by Ernst Grosse in *The Beginnings of Art* (E.T., p. 106). In explaining the genesis of personal decoration among primitive groups, Grosse holds that two aesthetic principles are expressed in the decorative form, i.e., symmetry and rhythm. Symmetry, he holds, is "subject to the nature of the body" and a symmetrical form "compels a symmetrical arrangement of the decoration." Grosse adds, interestingly enough, that asymmetrical arrangements in this instance are consciously used "to produce terrifying or ludicrous effects through the employment of the unusual and the unpleasant."

[18] See Wilson, *op. cit.*, p. 399, Fig. 57.

[19] See Hall, *op. cit.*, Fig. 3, p. 63.

[20] *Ibid.*, pp. 64-66.

required. The sculptor satisfied that condition by giving the "impression" of his model and then proceeding to take full advantage of the material's potentialities, repeating "the ridges of the eye-lids by incising a second heavy double curved line within the true outline of each lid. . . . Symmetrical repetition is seen in the bold curve of the ear repeated in the sharply curving salient of the line of the hair beside the temples, this second curve being reversed so that the two represent a perfect S."

The development in Greek archaic sculpture suggests what is in fact implicit in the entire argument.[21] The technical means by which figures may be undercut to take full advantage of light and shade are available to sculptors in various of the Greek islands. But one artist may produce merely a technically interesting figure. Another may have produced a figure of grace and beauty. In each instance, the technical resolution of the problem of handling material is the presupposition of art. The opinion that deviations and "idealizations" owe their origin to the divergence from serious non-aesthetic ends only because of the problems presented by the material converts a necessary presupposition into a necessary and sufficient explanation.

III

BUT if alterations and deviations in objects of art are not to be accounted for *in toto* either by the operations of serious non-aesthetic ends or by the laws of the material, it is scarcely to be wondered that "idealization" has been attributed to "aesthetic indirection." The phrase is no doubt ambiguous but one may be permitted its use to summarize the tendency of theorists who, recognizing the need for an aesthetic or playful teleology, yet regard the operation of these ends to be beyond the artist's intention. It is somewhat in this vein that Herbert Read reconstructs the technique of the primitive potter:

> . . . the larger pots were formed by first coiling a rope of clay round a sandy core or matrix which was afterwards scooped out. In

[21] Cf. Casson, *op. cit.*, and Carl Blümel, *Griechische Bildhauerarbeit.*

the process of coiling and smoothing the clay, markings of a geometrical character would be made at first involuntarily, and from these suggestions the potter afterwards developed a geometric ornament of a more conscious character. . . . The artist became so slick in his work that he tends to repeat his designs without much thought or accuracy. His designs are copied by other artists and further distorted, and a stage may be reached at which the craftsman is repeating a motive of which he no longer knows the significance.[22]

The opinion that geometric designs in pottery are vestiges of techniques that have disappeared but are repeated by the artist who "no longer knows the significance" has its analogues in numerous theories purporting to explain the presence of elements in many arts no longer directly related to serious purposes. It should be noted that if the conclusion of the argument is that a unique aesthetic end is operative, that end is either wholly determined by the serious non-aesthetic ends of the technique or else its emergence is, as Read suggests, fortuitous.

The first alternative, that the possible unique aesthetic end is wholly determined by the non-aesthetic factors, has been shown to be invalid. The second alternative, that the artist uses technique without conscious intention and in a haphazard fashion, is likewise invalid. It is precisely the artist's effort to make an artistic entity that cannot be described wholly in serious non-aesthetic terms that is most frequently evident in art and it is precisely the settled intention of the artist directing his effort that belies the implication of "indirection." The artist intends not only to escape the full tyranny of the useful, the moral, and the religious ends. His work is evidence also that he proposes to use all his skill to overcome the impositions of the material.[23] It is patent, by way of illustration, in a field other than primitive art, that one may scarcely attribute to a process of "indirection" such exquisite instances of bucolic English humor as the dramatist gives in the morality play, *Noah's Flood*. The playwright employs, in fact, the precise means used by Shakespeare in

[22] *Art and Society*, p. 26. It should be mentioned that Read does not use the terms "aesthetic indirection."

[23] See, however, below, pp. 505 ff.

Henry IV to escape the rigid historical frame in which the dramatic plot is implicated. Falstaff, Bardolf, and Mistress Quickly are deviations in the material of the original story but their introduction and the development of their characters are certainly not explicable either on grounds of chance or of history. The view that this is "indirection" is clearly fallacious. The artistic skill required to portray Noah's wife's obstinacy, an obstinacy that causes her husband to say

> Lorde, that wemen be crabbed aye,
> and non are meke, I dare will saye,
> This is well seene by me to daye

is of high order, both technically and imaginatively. Shakespeare's belabored Sir John, "larding the lean earth," must surely have presented the dramatist with a task that called for skill no less exacting in its expression than that which satisfied the demands for historical accuracy.

It is quite impossible to account for the facts of art by recourse either to the serious non-aesthetic theory of the origin and nature of art or to the thesis that its emergence and development came about by chance. Neither theory has greater merits as a complete aesthetic than has that of the artist's interests.

IV

IF ONE may conclude that such a painting as El Greco's "St. Francis in Ecstasy" transcends explanation wholly in terms either of the artist's selfish interests or of the religious ends it ostensibly fulfills, one may likewise conclude that the "horns" on Michelangelo's "Moses" may not be fully accounted for by the chance fact that the artist accepted as fact a mistranslation or that, fortuitously enough, there was sufficient marble to hand to enable him to solve a technical difficulty. One may insist that the serious non-aesthetic teleology of art is defective as a complete aesthetic theory. Its proponents do not succeed in justifying art by asserting that the value of the art-object as a defective instrument derives from a non-aesthetic end. The theory does, however, make evident one important fact: the aesthetician must not forget that all works of art, even if it is demonstrated that they are related to a unique aesthetic end, may and do function non-aesthetically as well. At the present level of the argument, it is sufficient to reiterate that this conclusion follows because every work of art is "made" and is, by its "making," an object or event, occurring at a particular time, in a particular place, and for a specific purpose. The ends that at least partially explain any work of art are serious and non-aesthetic. The fault of the serious non-aesthetic teleological theory of art is not that it is without foundation in fact. It errs, rather, because its proponents have not realized that some products of artistic craft may be at least bifunctional.

To such objects as are bifunctional and are in consequence indefinable wholly in terms of serious non-aesthetic ends may be given the name "fine" or "freeing" art. It remains to be determined whether or not they are completely definable in terms of a unique aesthetic or of a playful end. In either case, however, it follows that if there are objects that are "fine" or "free" art in part because they are not wholly definable in terms of serious non-aesthetic ends, they are nonetheless susceptible to analysis in non-aesthetic terms. It is precisely this fact that permits the archaeologist to consider the parapets of the Parthenon in archaeological and technical terms and the historian of religion to evaluate them in religious terms. It is also precisely because of this that the aesthetician must show how the non-aesthetic factors affect and become components of objects definable as fine art. The presupposition of fine art is the non-aesthetic function that the work of art may always perform.[24]

The non-aesthetic presuppositions of fine art may be the technical functions of the object or the multifarious interests of the artist or of society. But the doors constructed by Ghiberti for the Sacristy in Florence are no less objects possible of description in aesthetic terms because through them may have walked worshippers, because they are extraordinary examples of technical skill in the working of

[24] Cf. Geoffrey Scott, *The Architecture of Humanism*, pp. 59 ff.

bronze, or because the artist may have received a fee. Nor are they the less religious objects and technical objects because the stories from Scripture appear upon them in evidence of infinite artistic skill and care. One may infer that if there is an aesthetic end of art it is not reducible to non-aesthetic serious ends. One may also infer that to apply the term *fine* to art is to mean in some sense a *freeing* art that has potentialities for liberating us in aesthetic experience from the domination of non-aesthetic ends or practical interests. But it may be inferred, as well, that the non-aesthetic interests are omnipresent, that they become in some way effective in that experience and are implicated in all such experience.[25]

Of the truth of the fact that we are freed from the compulsion of serious non-aesthetic ends, we may be made aware in quite simple fashion. This lady, to whom Robert Herrick wrote

> Bid me to live, and I will live
> Thy protestant to be;
> Or bid me love, and I will give
> A loving heart to thee . . .

may, indeed, have lived, and most certainly, if she did live, she has since died. This world whose complexity threw into such amaze the poet who cried, "I saw eternity the other night," was a world compounded of Galileo's and Bruno's and Copernicus' science. Rodin *did* commemorate the surrender of Calais. The truth or falsity of the propositions that may be inferred from the poetry or sculpture may be corroborated and the science that inspired the artist is a science to be understood. However, if that were the entire value of these works of art and if our experience were analyzable in these terms alone, it is apparent that for accuracy one might turn for precise information rather to the dustiest tome in the most decrepit library than to the realm of rhyme and of stone. At times, the object of art is the sole source for information concerning a period, a science, or a culture. Then it is that the non-aesthetic function of the work of art may not unnaturally be accorded precedence in both our evaluation of the object and our attempt to

[25] Cf. below, Chap. XI ff.

ascertain its true nature. It may be said for the most part, however, that if pedagogy were the sole end of the artist, Plato is undoubtedly correct in his argument that art is the best means for teaching children. As a source of information, he contended firmly, it is less rigorous as a discipline than are mathematics and science. Similarly, although art may often serve moral ends, it does so with a bias and admixture of other factors distasteful to the moralist who does well to examine moral truth or falsity in the form of propositions.

V

THERE is every reason to conclude, therefore, that many philosophers and critics are in error in inferring from their painstaking analyses of art that the product of the artist's τέχνη may be understood wholly in terms of serious non-aesthetic ends. The aesthetic universe of discourse is neither conterminous with nor may it be wholly included within those realms in which such serious but non-aesthetic purposes as morality, religion, science, practical technique, or history are adequate to explain objects and events. It has been urged, however, that this failure to resolve the problems of art and of aesthetic experience is of value. To discard the theory is to do so in the face of the fact that the non-aesthetic function of art is omnipresent. Not the least consequence of the effort and conviction of the scientist of ends is that a proper interpretation must be made and a place must be found for the non-aesthetic function of art in a complete aesthetic.

The three succeeding chapters will consider theories that have attempted to explain the "freeing" of fine art from the restrictions of serious non-aesthetic ends. The play-theory of art, is, like its serious counterpart, primarily an analysis of ends. The theory of the structure of art, is more precisely a hypothesis of means. Both belong to the history of non-aesthetic teleologies.

Chapter VII

The Genetic Theory of Art (II): The Playful Hypothesis

Art is not a plaything, but a necessity, and its essence, form, is not a decorative adjustment, but a cup into which life can be poured and lifted to the lips and tasted.

—Rebecca West[1]

IT MAY be said of the play-theory of art that its vitality is attested by its survival since Plato's time, and that its value for speculative purposes is witnessed by the interest it has aroused in thinkers as divergent as Plato, Aristotle, Schiller, Hegel, and Spencer. It is true that each philosopher found it necessary to interpret "play" in the light of a different metaphysic but the persistence with which the term has been used in aesthetic is nonetheless remarkable. The theory's recurrence would be the more remarkable were it not that the identification of play and art provides an obvious ground for liberating fine art from the ends of morality, religion, science, and utility.

From the hypothesis that art is definable in consequence of its relation to the end of play has developed, however, not only a fruitful tradition in aesthetic history, but an ostensible paradox as well. It appears, indeed, scarcely less paradoxical that a serious genetic theory of art should be called "play" than, for example, that Zeno should contend that the arrow "in flight" is stationary. That the play-theory of art is serious, whether judged by the intentions of

[1] From *Black Lamb and Grey Falcon.* Copyright 1940, 1941 by Rebecca West. (By permission of The Viking Press, Inc., N. Y.)

its authors or by the artistic material which it comprehends is evident. The play-theorist knows that artistic technique is severe and exacting; he has analyzed in terms of play or art the most profoundly moving of man's creations and he has rarely meant by the activity "play" (with perhaps one exception in the first formulation of the theory) such aimless bodily or vocal activities as are ordinarily associated with animal or infantile sounds or movements.

It is nonetheless true that a paradox is hinted in the very triviality implicit in the theory's name, a name which usually recalls such judgments as Aristotle's that, "To exert oneself and work for the sake of amusement seems silly and utterly childish . . . ."[2] It is well to dispel the appearance of paradox at the outset, because in the process the true nature of play-theory's aesthetic principles begins to emerge. It is truly paradoxical, in the light of Greek mathematical theory, for Zeno to conclude that the arrow in flight must be motionless, since it can move neither where it is nor where it is not. It does not pass belief, however, that an aesthetic may be called "play" and still attribute to artist and percipient alike the most serious intentions if, as is the case, its suggestion of triviality pertain to little other than the name. The paradox of play-theory in art is nominal and persists because its proponents, eager to free art from the implications of such non-aesthetic ends as the moral, the useful and the religious, have incorrectly given their theory a name signifying the contrary to the "serious." The fact is that the aesthetic connotations of "play" make of it a hypothesis not contrary to but mediating between the "serious" teleologies of art.

The play-theory, properly understood, bridges gaps between several of the extreme accounts put forward in classical aesthetic with which the present inquiry has dealt. Systematically, it has mediated theories elaborated in terms of the alternative ends available for teleological definition.[3] One extreme form of speculation has maintained that art is definable solely by its relation to a unique aesthetic end. The other extreme, the validity of which has been

[2] *E.N.X.* vi.6. Aristotle commends the alternative, ". . . play in order that you may work."

[3] Cf. above, pp. 179-180.

tested in the preceding chapter, asserts that art is definable wholly by its relation to non-aesthetic ends. The first alternative has led, not unnaturally, to the conclusion that "art is for art's sake." The second has been used to bolster the Platonic contention that the artist always borrows the content of his art from the sciences and that he practices the crafts integral to the practical arts.

The nerve of the non-aesthetic teleological argument, as we have seen, is that all art, not excluding fine art, does display non-aesthetic characteristics. This has sometimes checked the aesthetician's too uncritical acceptance of the assertion that art is actually "for art's sake." On the other hand, if the proponent of a teleology of unique aesthetic ends encounters this obstacle, it is evident from the argument presented in the preceding chapter that his opponent meets one no less formidable in the incapacity of non-aesthetic serious ends to account for artistic variations, deviations and "idealizations."

It is commonly sound practice in philosophy to seize both horns of a dilemma. Yet it is an onerous task to construct a philosophy of art that not only considers fine art to be at least bifunctional but also proposes to show precisely how the aesthetic and non-aesthetic ends are interrelated. The historical alternative to that onerous task has frequently been the elaboration of a play-theory of art. And, indeed, if the teleology of fine or "freeing" art is inadequately defined in terms of life's more serious ends—in teleologies which attribute to art powers to control nature, promulgate the dictates of morality, or to display the prescriptions of religion—although non-aesthetic factors are present in the work of art; and if that teleology, by the presence of these very non-aesthetic factors, apparently transcends complete definition in aesthetic terms, it is at once natural and obvious to assume that fine art is structurally and teleologically identical with play. For "play" signifies both activity and objects freed from restrictions of serious ends but still definable in non-aesthetic terms. Explicitly, while it denies the competence of serious non-aesthetic ends to account for fine art and aesthetic experience, the theory implies that the value of play, a non-aesthetic end, is necessary to counteract the disvalue adhering to art because the latter is either a defective instrument or because it induces discontent.

II

THE play-theory has fulfilled, however, not only a systematic function in reconciling extreme teleologies of art; "play" itself is regarded as a mediator of factors within the "play-theory." We shall later be concerned with the interpretation of the "playful object" as one aspect of this internal mediation to explain artistic "idealization" in terms of a presumably unique structure. Of more immediate significance is the theorist's interpretation of "play" itself as the rationalization of feeling. It is in "play's" presumed reconciliation of reason and passion that one finds the basis for the theory's liberation of art from serious non-aesthetic ends. It is, moreover, in this aspect that its more perceptive advocates have properly discerned the play-theory's strength. The play-theory is, indeed, one of aesthetic history's foremost resolutions to the antinomies of art and aesthetic experience.

The assumption that "play" mediates the antinomic factors of reason and feeling in aesthetic experience is implicit in the first formulation, in Plato's *Laws*, of this genetic theory of art, precisely as it is explicit in its most influential elaboration in Schiller's *Letters upon the Aesthetical Education of Man*. For Plato, the rationalization of feeling is due to mathematical science. But Schiller, under the influence not only of Plato but of Kant's *Kritik of Judgment*, adopts a non-mathematical interpretation to resolve art's antinomy. A preliminary consideration of these divergences is of value for a later estimation of the play-theory's adequacy as an aesthetic.

Plato's account of the origin of dance and song in the *Laws*[4] suggests in its terminology rather than in its context in the Dialogue that "play" may afford a possible solution to the difficult problems presented for philosophy of art in the *Republic*. The genetic theory logically, if not historically, mediates the systematic extremes of teleological and ateleological aesthetic found elsewhere, as we have

[4] *Op. cit.*, 653 ff.

observed, in Plato's writings. It bridges the gap between the sharp attack in the *Republic* upon the irrationality and emotionalism of imitative art, and the theory of "absolutely beautiful forms"[5] and their correlative experience of pleasure unmixed with pain in *Philebus*. The objects analyzed by Plato vary in the three Dialogues as the imitative, formal, and playful—but feeling presents the central problem for an understanding of Plato's treatment of each form of art.

Plato first considers "play" in its integral meaning as the presupposition of dance and song. It is an activity specifically associated with "right discipline in pleasures and pains."[6] In its primitive manifestation, play is common to man and animals: "every young creature is incapable of keeping either its body or its tongue quiet, . . . leaping and skipping and delighting in dances and games, and uttering, also, noises of every description." However, while the higher forms of art have their origin in this aimless instinct for movement and sound, their actual emergence presupposes a capacity discoverable only in man. To him is possible "the pleasurable perception of rhythm and harmony . . . whereas all other creatures are devoid of any perception of the various kinds of order or disorder in movement."

It is notable that Plato judges the choric song and dance to be valuable for the community he constructs in the *Laws*. It is even more notable that playful delight in movement and noise comes to be one of the instruments for building that community in consequence of man's "pleasurable perception of rhythm and harmony." Rhythm and harmony are principles of Pythagorean mathematics and astronomy and the genesis of the arts of song and dance, in Plato's theory, presupposes the employment in "play" of man's rational powers.

There is here an obvious analogy to the more extreme mathematical philosophy of art of *Philebus*. It is true that Plato's technique in the latter Dialogue leads for all practical purposes to feeling's extirpation, except in the form of incommensurable "pure pleas-

[5] Cf. above, Chap. III.

[6] *Laws* 653-654.

ure."[7] In the *Laws*, in contrast, the pleasurable but presumably valueless actions of spontaneous play are brought under control rather than extirpated. But both the ateleological aesthetic of *Philebus* and the play-theory of the *Laws* are implicitly resolutions to the antinomies of art and its experience, resolutions grounded in a possible rationalization of feeling by means of mathematical science. The first Dialogue attributes explicitly, the second implicitly, a value to mathematically definable objects of nature or art superior to that accorded the irrational imitative arts in the *Republic*. It is well to recall in this connection that the latter arts are censured by Plato precisely because they appeal to "the inferior elements of our nature," to that "part of the soul, whose opinion runs counter to measurements." The imposition of "limit" upon the "unlimited" leads to the postulation in *Philebus* of "absolutely beautiful forms." The pleasurable perception of "rhythm and harmony" leads in the *Laws* to the choric dance and song. Both Dialogues, however, convert irrational aspects of experience into possible "images" for rationalized feeling.

Plato suggests in this way a problem that has proved to be of primary importance for play-theory and indeed for all aesthetic. But if both the problem and its solution remain largely implicit in the *Laws*, the implications of Plato's theory of "play" for the resolution to art's antinomy are made explicit by Schiller[8] and his successors.

Schiller's analysis of the "play-instinct"[9] is intended to ground "freedom in phenomenal appearance." The poet holds that it may do this because "play" is an ideal union of the "sensuous" and the "formal" instincts which, in its mediating capacity, enables man to experience his world in both its sensuous and rational aspects. In play, man need submit neither to the extreme abstracting power of the instinct for form, nor to the compulsions to passion consequent upon the operations of the "sensuous instinct."

[7] Cf. above, pp. 107 ff.

[8] Cf. Constantin Ritter's remarks in *Die Kerngedanken der Platonischen Philosophie*, pp. 307-309.

[9] He uses the term *Spieltrieb*. The "formal instinct" is *Formtrieb*, the "sensuous instinct" is *Stofftrieb*.

"Man only plays when in the full meaning of the word he is a man," Schiller maintains, "and *he is only completely a man when he plays.*" The "form-giving instinct" has for its objects shapes, formal qualities, the law, and all relations of reflection. The "sensuous instinct" has for its objects, in turn, all material existence and all that is immediately present to the senses. The first reveals reality, the second, appearance. Man, a creature of both instincts, needs the objects of each for his full experience and he may enjoy those objects without sacrifice of his complete humanity only as aesthetic man. Only in the satisfaction of the "play-instinct" are the dangers implicit in a too extreme rationality or an equally extreme sensuality obviated. On Schiller's hypothesis, exclusive rationality divests appearance of its richness, while exclusive sensuality deprives experience of its reality. Aesthetic experience, which is playful experience, mediates reason and feeling in beauty: "Man shall only *play* with beauty, and with *beauty* he *shall only play.*"

Schiller uses the term "trieben" to characterize the instincts or impulses in question because "they impel us to realize their object, urge us onward to the solution to the double problem of realizing the necessary within us and of subjecting the reality outside of us to the law of necessity." The "sensuous instinct," he holds, emanates "from man's physical nature." It "seeks to make him a thing of time and matter, not to give matter to him, for this already presupposes freedom of action on the part of the personality that receives matter and distinguishes it from the permanent identity." It is this instinct that reveals change and reality in time, that "alone awakens and unfolds the capacities of human nature." It is likewise true that man's too great dependence in experience upon this instinct "makes the fullness of his development impossible," inasmuch as "with indissoluble bonds it binds the aspiring spirit to the world of sense."

Schiller regards the "formal instinct" as the impulsion of man's rational nature. It emanates from man's "absolute existence." It is true that this instinct tends to set him free. It is also true that it tends "to harmonize his various phenomenal determinations and to preserve his personal identity in spite of all changes." But too complete dependence upon the "form-giving instinct" as a guide to experience produces the abstract lawgiver under whose rule all reality escapes.

To Schiller, the conflict between the man of theory, blind to the enrichment of "concrete" experience, and the man of passion, dominated by nature, is intolerable. Its resolution is made possible by recourse to beauty and to the experience of play. One obstacle presents itself as Schiller discovers that beauty has itself been charged with "error and wrong." For "pressing the mind into the dangerous direction of neglecting all reality," to it has been attributed error; for "sacrificing morality and truth to a charming exterior," it has been charged with wrong.

In that very beauty, however, which has been attacked so bitterly, the poet finds the resolution to the antinomy of reason and feeling and, in turn, in the resolution to that antinomy by a consideration of play, beauty escapes the charges of error and wrong. Beauty is, in effect, in its widest sense the entirety of the aesthetic qualities of phenomena. Its experience mediates the opposed instincts in the exercise of the third instinct, play. In the playful or aesthetic experience, man may *at once* enjoy the consciousness of freedom and the feeling of existence, may both know and feel. In play, without conflict, perception receives and form produces its object.

Schiller attempts to free art from the charge that it is irrational, sensuous, and deceptive by postulating play as the highest activity of which man is capable. The exercise of the sensuous and the formal powers to their fullest extent is "free play," an activity whose value is not derived from the serious non-aesthetic ends of ordinary experience. In consequence of implicating it in the ends of logic and science are derived the charges that beauty is error and immorality. Schiller holds, on the contrary, that these ends are irrelevant to aesthetic experience. In contrast to activities defined in terms of serious ends, those of the aesthetic man are "free." The man who "plays" with beauty is freed from the tyranny of the specific end, as well as from the bondage of the universal. Neither law nor the morality of the ought coerces him and liberation from "all exigent determinations" permits man in "play" to relax as well from the strain of emotion in the experience of phenomena. Aesthetic experience is likewise a freedom from physical needs: in it, "the beautiful becomes for its own sake an object of his [man's] endeavor."

Schiller's "play," at once the instrument by which man is freed from serious non-aesthetic ends and the beauty by which man achieves humanity, is the vision of a poet in whom the imaginative powers that created the vision exceed the dialectical skill needed to establish the philosophical theory.[10] Whether the play-theory he offers to his successors is for them a sound guide to the promised land of an aesthetic freed from the domination of serious and non-aesthetic ends is one of the considerations of the present chapter. But if Schiller did not achieve all that he proposes to do and if Plato does not fully develop his account of the origin of art, it is nonetheless true that they have presented for consideration some of the primary problems of play-theory. Two of these problems are of immediate interest.

III

THE first problem appears to be largely terminological, although it conceals a more serious difficulty. The second concerns an issue more fundamental to the determination of play-theory's adequacy for speculation in the aesthetic field. The terminological difficulty arises because few proponents of the theory have been precise in applying the term "play." The word has been employed indiscriminately to denote an object, spectacle, or event, the activity either of "playing" or of observing the spectacle of others "playing," and an end said to be "playful." To discriminate play as object and play as activity may indeed be of assistance in dealing with certain problems falling beyond the scope of the present chapter.[11] But since the primary problem is to determine the relevance of play to aesthetic we may be permitted, on the whole, to follow the lead of the aesthetician with reference to two aspects of play: if the acts of artistic creation and of aesthetic recreation are taken to be funda-

[10] The argument in Letter XX by which the author proposes to ground the play-instinct as the aesthetic instinct reconciling reason and feeling is, for example, obviously fallacious.

[11] See for example, Chap. XVII, pp. 479 ff.

mentally the same, the act of playing and the observation of play may be held to be similarly identical. At the present stage of our analysis,[12] we may assume, as Aristotle did of music, that we can "form a correct judgment from hearing others."

The second and more fundamental problem concerns the precise relation of play to art. Is play identical with art or is it propaedeutic to art? If the latter, is it propaedeutic to other activities as well? The difficulty is sufficiently evident in both Plato's and Schiller's play-theories to permit its illustration by reference to them. It may be said, in general, that for Plato playful activity is propaedeutic to art. For Schiller, at least at the outset, play and art are identical. Yet, upon closer examination, neither writer is unambiguous. Plato, as has been indicated, suggests that play, as an activity indulged in by all young creatures, must be regulated by rhythm and harmony if it is to become the arts of song and dance and, ultimately, in the union of song and dance, the festival dances. Yet the argument is sufficiently ambiguous for Constantin Ritter to maintain[13] that, for the author of the *Laws*, "Every artistic activity is free play" and that art is the most distinguished kind of play. Moreover, play as art is propaedeutic to higher activity: Plato writes that music is properly described as "the process of drawing and guiding children towards that principle pronounced right by the law and confirmed as truly right by the experience of the oldest and most just."

It has been implied that Schiller also argues that play and ideal art or beauty are identical. Yet, as the poet's final letters are read, it is evident that it is not the first wild excesses of the play-impulse that are artistic, but rather the ordered functioning of the play of imagination which seizes upon and is in turn controlled by its proper material.[14] In fact, Schiller tells us that, "In its first attempts the aesthetic impulse of play will hardly be recognizable, since it is continually absorbed by the caprices and wild desires of the senses." Only when the "influence of form" finally takes possession of man, when "the emancipated impulse of play finally frees itself entirely

[12] The differentiation of artistic creativity and aesthetic experience is examined below, pp. 317 ff. See also, pp. 337 ff. and Chap. XVII.

[13] *Op. cit.*, pp. 313 and 315.

[14] Letter XXVII.

from the fetters of physical need," and "the beautiful becomes for its own sake an object" of man's endeavor is the "lawless bound . . . changed to the harmonious dance." And if this be insufficient to suggest the difficulty presented to the play-theorist in his attempt to free aesthetic from the domination of serious non-aesthetic ends, it may be added that, for Schiller, play or beauty is propaedeutic to morality.[15]

To inquire whether play is propaedeutic to art and to other activities or is identical with fine art is, in reality, to ask a question, long-delayed, concerning the significance of play and one implicit in the elaboration of Kant's ateleological theory. Since Kant's time, at any rate, "disinterestedness" has been taken to be perhaps the primary characteristic of playful activity initiated by the object, play.[16] "Disinterestedness" is a term signifying primarily play's freedom from serious ends and purposes. It is consequently not unfair to examine the question in the light of the significance of this term, especially since lack of "serious" interest is one of the ostensible connotations of playful activities. Are the playful and aesthetic experiences, then, identical in being characterized by "disinterestedness"?

Concerning aesthetic experience, it may be argued that the term "disinterest" can be applied to the aesthetic experience in at least one important, if restricted, sense. It has been urged in this essay[17] that the artist's selfish interests find expression in the production of any work of art and may be concomitants of our experience of the object. Equally clearly, however, the end-product of the artist's craft is by its nature and completion freed from the selfish interest,[18] and is an object to be judged, evaluated, and examined without especial reference to the artist's selfish interest.

But may the same assertion be made concerning play? To the

[15] Karl Groos' consideration of play is interesting as a combination of Plato's and Schiller's views on this issue. In *The Play of Man*, he considers play first as the satisfaction of instinct, secondly as having serious intent, and finally, as being a stage of conscious self-illusion.

[16] For example, in the writings of Groos, K. Lange, Spencer. Compare Kant's view, above, p. 122.

[17] Cf. above, Chap. V, pp. 181 ff.

[18] *Ibid.*, pp. 185 ff.

modern exponents of the theory who have analyzed specific games, it has become apparent that not all so-called "play" is "disinterested." Lange's opinion[19] is of value as illustrating a somewhat general attitude. The author of *Das Wesen der Kunst* undertakes a classification of the forms of playful activity. He enumerates intellectual games, games of chance, games of skill, "sense-games," and games of motion. To take but one instance, he regards games of chance as pleasurable, although they are not "disinterested." It may be argued, however, that the artist, no less than the gambler, is intensely interested in success or failure; that the "making" of a work of art involves hazard and the possibility of loss; that there are rules of art no less stringent than rules of gambling or chance; that the "game" after it is played is "objectified" and comprehensible to a spectator; that the material with which the artist works is recalcitrant and imposes its own laws upon the maker, no less than do the roulette wheel and the card table. Still, it may be urged that the analogy is only an analogy and that the artist's interest, unlike that of the gambler, is objectified in the product rather than in the technique. It may be added, likewise, that permanence is a value for art but it is one of like consequence for games of chance. Games of chance may be repeated, as the dance is repeated, and there are reconstructions of bridge games.

It is more significant, however, that the game of chance is a matter of such predominantly selfish interest that it is difficult to regard the gambler as truly "playing." It is evident, moreover, that the selfish interest in gambling augments the difficulties of objectifying the meaning of the activity or of introducing the idealizations which make art something more than a mere instrument for serious non-aesthetic ends.

It is the latter consideration that receives Groos' attention: only the addition of a "disinterested aesthetic attention" in the players is needed, he holds, to change "instinctive" into "artistic" activities.[20] He means, it may be assumed, that the technique has become an

[19] *Das Wesen der Kunst* (2nd ed., 1907), particularly Chap. 21, "Kunst und Spiel," pp. 613 ff.

[20] *Die Spiele der Menschen* (English translation). See particularly pp. 389-395.

object of contemplation analogous either to the dancer's activity or to the product of "making." But how one is to introduce "disinterested aesthetic attention" into a game to which selfish interest and the excitement of personal risk are integral is precisely the problem in question. This is not to suggest that it would be impossible to do so. Rather, it is to suggest a reason for the constant adoption of the alternative, which is to restrict the objects included in the hitherto presumably identical universes of discourses of play and art.

Such a restriction of the playful and artistic universe of discourse is implicit in Lange's suggestion that the problem presented by games of chance may arise not from the identification of art and play but rather from the fact that these games are not play. Since the aesthetician constantly employs, as we have seen in our consideration of ateleological aesthetic, this Procrustean method of limiting the aesthetic universe of discourse, he may scarcely deny to the play-theorist a similar privilege, provided that the selection of objects is meaningful with reference either to their end or structure or both, inasmuch as these are the determining factors in the theory that play and art are identical.[21]

What is the end of play? Plato presents with clarity a view that has been dominant throughout centuries of speculation: "He who is a good builder, should play at building children's houses; . . . those who have the care of their education should provide them when young with mimic tools. . . . They should learn beforehand the knowledge which they will afterwards require for their art."[22]

Modern play-theory has followed the general pattern of Plato's thought. Its divergences are largely due to its association with evolutionary theory. Herbert Spencer's elaboration[23] of a suggestion in Schiller's *Aesthetic Letters* provides an interesting instance both of the tradition and of its alteration. The poet illustrates in his twenty-fifth letter play's freedom from compulsion:

[21] This is to anticipate a terminology used later in the present argument, particularly in Chaps. VIII and IX. The inference is, however, required by the inadequacy of "form" uniquely to define the object. Cf. above, Book One and Chap. V, pp. 178-179 and fn. 2 to p. 178.

[22] *Laws* 643 (Jowett's translation, *arranged*).

[23] *Principles of Psychology*, Vol. 2, pp. 627 ff. Spencer does not acknowledge his debt to Schiller but it is nonetheless an obvious one.

When the lion is not tormented by hunger, and when no wild beast challenges him to fight, his unemployed energy creates an object for himself; full of ardour, he fills the re-echoing desert with his terrible roars, and his exuberant force rejoices in itself, showing itself without an object.

Thus, too, the beautiful becomes for man "for its own sake an object of his endeavor."

Spencer takes a necessary step in differentiating "play" and "aesthetic activities"[24] but assumes that both emerge in the process of organic evolution. It is in this way that Schiller's suggestion, "the animal *works* if its activity is stimulated by want, and it *plays* if its activity is the result of an inherent excess of power," undergoes elaboration. Spencer holds that as superior animals evolve they require less energy to satisfy their immediate brute needs. The surplus is expended in leisure and in play, the latter a condition characterized by the union of feelings and actions.

But this alteration of the poetic theory of play to coincide with the Darwinian hypothesis calls attention, not only to the augmentation of energy and its release for other than practical purposes in the course of evolution, but to the playful or artistic object and to the conditions which permit the latter to serve the end of play. Spencer remarks that "every one of the mental powers [is] subject to this law, that its organ when dormant for an interval longer than ordinary becomes unusually ready to act." Under these conditions, he adds, "it happens that *a simulation of those activities is easily fallen into, when circumstances offer it in place of the real activities.*"

It is both because the organs "become unusually ready to act" and, by implication, because there are "simulated" images that "play of all kinds" is possible. To "*this tendency to superfluous and useless exercise of faculties that have been quiescent*" may be traced the origin of play and aesthetic. The artificial exercise of the once useful powers gives rise in animals to the mimic chase and to playful combat. In the young of humans, it emerges in nursing and in "the dramatizing of adult activities." Play, for Spencer, is a function of "various lower powers," aesthetic of "higher powers."

[24] Schiller also distinguishes aesthetic from non-aesthetic play.

Play, the object, retains its status as a "simulated image" throughout much of the history of the alliance between play and evolutionary theory. The end defining that "simulated image" alters as individual interpretations of play-theory alter. Groos, however, offers an interesting opinion and one fairly typical of the main trend of evolutionary play-theory. It shows clearly a similarity of Plato's original hypothesis. Groos, concluding that "play," the object, is a "simulated image" describes "play," the activity, as the agency used to develop crude powers and to mature them for life's uses.[25] The child, helpless at birth and cared for by its parents, develops gradually its capacities to meet the problems and difficulties of life. This gradual development is consequent upon the child's playful activities. Play, in turn, depends upon "the elaboration of immature capacities to equality with perfected instinct," the "evolution of hereditary qualities to a degree far transcending this [perfect instinct] to a state of adaptability and versatility surpassing the most perfect instinct." Added to this, there is the impulse for imitation "which gives selection the opportunity to strengthen the hereditary foundations of the activity imitated."[26]

It is evident that Groos regards "play" not as the single instinct such as it was for Schiller, but as constituted of "various instincts called upon when there is no occasion for their serious exercise." The potentialities of the child are actualized by means of "preparatory practice" and "imitation." The boy plays at fighting and engages in mimic warfare in preparation for the career of soldier. The girl plays at nursery games in anticipation of and preparation for motherhood.

Whether the conclusion follows from the Platonic or the more detailed evolutionary formulation of play, however, the identical problem still must be faced. If, as is clearly implied, by "preparatory practice" is meant specific training for later serious activity, play is propaedeutic to a specific serious activity. The playful object, "fictitious opportunity," or "simulated image," is offered "if a real

[25] *Op. cit.*, pp. 375 ff. (English translation).

[26] Groos attempts to maintain his theory in accord with the hypothesis of the germ cell formulated by Weismann.

opportunity is lacking." The end of play is thus describable in pedagogical terms.

This is not to maintain that play-theorists have not offered at least another alternative or that a more significant explanation could not be given that might, perhaps, allow avoidance of the issue.[27] But it may be asserted that, whether the stimulus to play be "real" or "simulated," whether the preparation be regarded as occurring within the lifetime of the individual or within the history of the race, play considered as propaedeutic to a specific art or science is clearly to be differentiated from the function of fine art. To maintain that play is initiated by a "simulated image" is merely to imply that play mistakes the symbol's significance; that is to say, that the player is in error in his judgment of what the image "stands for" and that the consequent activity is truly useful and would be judged to be so by one capable of a correct opinion despite the mistake by the player. In determining the true significance of play, it is of less consequence to find that the player misapprehends both the meaning of the "image" or "symbol" and of the end of his action, than to discover that "image," activity, and end are properly to be understood in terms of the master arts, let us say, of warfare, religion, or morality and that they derive their significance from the master arts in the same way that any other subordinate art similarly derives its meaning. In this sense, play is propaedeutic to a specific art and is non-aesthetic. It would be difficult seriously to contend that, in aesthetic terms, the experience either of the sculptor who labors to copy Donatello's *David* or of the spectator who stands before the statue in enjoyment, would be exhaustively analyzed were that experience interpreted solely as preparatory for the technical art of stone-cutting or for the science of physiology, even if it were

[27] That the traditional theories examined here are wholly sound analyses of the function of play may be doubted. It could equally well be argued, for example, that play affords an opportunity for activity without serious purpose and that the activity, on the evolutionary hypothesis, is meaningful in the phylogeny of the race. It need scarcely be argued that the child who plays with toy soldiers is preparing specifically for a military career. It could with equal cogency be argued that the "play" rids the individual of that particular combative impulse, satisfying it, and acting as a general training for muscle and mind. This would make the theory more properly a therapeutic one.

argued that both individuals mistakenly took what they were doing to be other than what they were actually doing. But what is invalid with reference to aesthetic is valid in this respect with reference to play. For it is evident that, considered in terms of teleology, the propaedeutic theory of play, although offered to explain the fact that fine art escapes complete identification with non-aesthetic objects, merely presents other non-aesthetic ends in disguised form. As a consequence, one of the principal arguments which has led aestheticians to adopt the play-theory of art throughout its long history is seen to be without foundation.

IV

THAT play is propaedeutic in this sense, and that fine art is not, would appear to be so obvious that one is tempted to urge either that play-theorists who identify art and play have misunderstood their own hypothesis, or that they have put forward a teleological theory of the preparatory function of play as a merely ostensible argument in support of a view primarily concerned with the proximate conditions of the presumably identical activities. To support the latter interpretation, it would be necessary to maintain that the play-theorists proceed upon an assumption contrary to a generally received analysis of activity expressed by Plato in *Gorgias*: "If a man does something for the sake of something else, he wills not that which he does, but that for the sake of which he does it."[28] If this assumption contrary to the accepted view is made by the play-theorist, he must mean that it is precisely for the sake of the activity of play and the experience it offers that men do play and that it is precisely the nature of the activity rather than the end that leads to the identification of play and aesthetic.[29] As will shortly

[28] *Op. cit.*, 467.

[29] This appears to be the meaning of Spencer's statement (*op. cit.* Vol. 2, pp. 627 ff.) that "those actions of them [i.e., the faculties bodily and mental] which constitute play, and those which yield the aesthetic gratifications, do not refer to ulterior benefits . . . the proximate ends are the only ends." Cf. above, p. 178, fn. 2.

be seen, the suggestion is an impossible one to entertain, but in ascertaining the grounds put forth for its acceptance by some aestheticians, certain facts important for an analysis of aesthetic experience do emerge.

If it be assumed, as we have done for the sake of the present argument, that play as observed and play as an activity are identical and that the artist's creativity and the experience of the art created are like in kind, it may well be asked what in this would most patently suggest the identification of the playful and the aesthetic experiences. It is not unimportant to remark in this connection that Aristotle, despite his unpromising characterization of amusement or play as an end as "silly" and "childish," offers certain illuminating observations concerning the value of play as an activity: play is "a sort of relaxation and we need relaxation because we cannot work continuously. Relaxation is not an end; for it is taken for the sake of activity."[30] Moreover, as he writes in *Politics*, "Amusement is for the sake of relaxation, and relaxation is of necessity sweet, for it is the remedy of pain caused by toil."[31] The application of Aristotle's views concerning play and relaxation to art may be inferred from his remarks upon music as plays or amusements which we should introduce "only at suitable times, and they should be our medicines, for the emotion which they create in the soul is a sort of relaxation; and from the pleasure we obtain rest."[32]

It would not be unfair to interpret Aristotle's remarks concerning

[30] *E. N.* 1176 b 33 (Ross's translation).

[31] *Op. cit.*, 1339 b 15 (Jowett's translation).

[32] *Op. cit.*, 1337 b 40. As the context shows, Aristotle obviously has in mind his theory of *katharsis*, which he promises to amplify in *Poetics*. This theory will be discussed in Chap. IX but there are several relevant points to be noted. Music, as pastime or amusement, is but one form of that art subjected to analysis by Aristotle. (Cf. S. H. Butcher, *Aristotle's Theory of Poetry and Fine Art*, pp. 244-245 and W. L. Newman, *The Politics of Aristotle*, Vol. 3). As regards the obvious criticism that it is unwise to apply Aristotle's analysis of music to other arts, it is of interest to anticipate Bywater's remark, with reference to *Poetics*, "that a cathartic effect is not peculiar to Tragedy. . . . Aristotle recognizes there [i.e., in *Politics* 8.7] a catharsis of 'enthusiasm' effected by certain kinds of music, as well as a catharsis of pity and fear effected by Tragedy. . . ." (*Aristotle on the Art of Poetry*, p. 152). Bywater adds that a similar analysis of Comedy may have been written.

play and certain forms of art by William James' term, "energizers."[33] Play and art are not unlike in the refreshment and relaxation they afford,[34] and in this, Aristotle's analysis is eminently correct. To art and to play men have gone constantly for the sources of power to pursue their appointed tasks, just as the mystic has found resources of energy[35] in his experience of unity. It is essential to observe, however, that Aristotle implies that what is now called fine art is productive of an experience transcending the merely therapeutic effect which is the common function of play and some "inferior" art. Although his analysis does not avoid the dominant moralism attendant upon Greek theory of beauty, Aristotle does maintain that music may provide not only refreshment and relaxation but that it may have a nobler use: certain kinds of music inspire "enthusiasm," "an emotion of the ethical portion of the soul."[36] It is well to note, also, that Butcher[37] interprets Aristotle to include in music certain forms which have the end of "higher aesthetic enjoyment."

It is not important for the present argument to examine in detail the significance of Aristotle's differentiations of the kinds of music.[38] It is sufficient for the discussion of play-theory to proceed upon the inferences that both the playful and the aesthetic *are* "energizers" of man's spirit, and that both are sources of power and, finally, to ascertain whether, in spite of these common characteristics, the experiences may be differentiated.

Of the characteristics common to the playful and the aesthetic activities, perhaps the most apparent is this, that as play relieves us of fatigue by its release of pent-up feeling and may quiet us by the concentration of our energies for that *katharsis*, so too, it is evident that a dramatic spectacle or a symphony may have a similar therapeutic effect. Play and art may provide, in this way, alleviation

[33] Cf. below, Chap. XVII, pp. 480 ff.

[34] Cf. *Politics* 1339 b 28: ". . . whereas men rarely attain the end, but rest by the way and amuse themselves, not only with a view to a further end, but also for pleasure's sake, it may be well at times to let them find a refreshment in music."

[35] See above, Chap. II, p. 78.

[36] *Politics* 1340 a 10.

[37] *Op. cit.*, p. 244.

[38] See Chap. IX.

from past toil, and may further afford relaxation and refreshment. Both appear to be, as was said, "energizers" for further effort. Both may, moreover, rid us of the need to repeat for practical purposes the action which play feigns or which art depicts.[39] But an important empirical fact to be observed is that the activity of play is re-creative of the activity it "simulates," while aesthetic activity is, as the ablest critics of all ages have argued, truly creative. The "divine inspiration" which, entering upon the work of the profound artist, is in turn a *sine qua non* of the experience of profound art. Its product, creativity, is no merely meaningless phrase inherited from Plato and Longinus. To ignore the creativity of the aesthetic experience is to ignore one of the distinguishing characteristics of that activity and one that makes it truly antinomic. To seek its ground or source by an analysis of play merely makes more manifest the recurrent dilemma with which the play-theory is faced. If its exponents concentrate solely upon the activity, the actions described remain discrete and disparate, indistinguishable from any other aggregate of reflexes, reactions, instinctive movements of the body, and impulses to produce sounds to which no common name may be applied. Indeterminate activity of this kind is not "free creativity." It is the merest capriciousness, which can only be rendered artistic, as Plato and Schiller both imply, by the imposition of order, or rule, or reason, and by a comprehension of the aesthetic potentialities of the material upon which it may operate. Completely purposeless activity may not even be called "playful." It is, rather, meaningless.[40] Such activities are not truly describable without reference to the end which becomes operative and which at least partially determines the nature of the activity.

If, however, the exponents of the theory of play concentrate upon the end, the activity is, as has been observed, propaedeutic. It is propaedeutic, furthermore, only for the specific technique or art of which play, as the object, is the "simulated" image. At the conclusion of the muscular and intellectual activity, the end of play is fulfilled in the muscular and intellectual coordination achieved,

[39] Cf. above note to p. 223, fn. 27.
[40] See below, pp. 433-434.

in the relaxation which follows upon effort, and in the reproduction of the serious activity simulated. The differentiation between the experiences of the objects, play and fine art, may be expressed more precisely in terms of "imagination." Here may be anticipated what a later part of this essay[41] will elaborate. Play, in terms of "images," is describable entirely within the range of "reproductive imagination," and must remain propaedeutic only for the specific technique of art of which play, the object, is the "simulated" image. And this in each case is truly understood as a serious end.[42] The end of fine art, in contrast, is only partially describable in terms of "reproductive images." Its effectiveness presupposes "productive imagination,"[43] as well as "reproductive imagination." Play reproduces the "image" of which it is propaedeutic. Aesthetic experience, as will be seen,[44] transcends the experience of the art object. The end of art presupposes not alone the energizing of the will for the possible repetition of the technique of the art but it places creative capacities in operation. The aesthetic experience, in contrast to the playful experience, provides no specific training for any one activity nor does it direct the will to the repetition or pursuit of any specific activity, aesthetic or non-aesthetic, although its non-aesthetic factors *may* permit it to do so.

Clearly, therefore, in view of divergences of end and of activity, play and fine art are separate universes of discourse. These universes of discourse, however, may have objects in common; and this may explain Plato's and Schiller's ambiguity in the matter of the identity of the two, an ambiguity which is clarified by Spencer. But if there are common objects, it may be inferred that play and art may have a common source or play may, in some instances, presuppose artistic creativity and fine art.[45] That one may "play" with serious art and imagine that this is the sole characterization of the aesthetic experience may be evidence, indeed, of the vestigial characteristics retained by fine art in its evolution from objects definable solely in

[41] Part Three, Chap. XI.
[42] Cf. above, p. 223.
[43] Cf. below, Chap. XVI.
[44] See Chaps. XVII and XVIII.
[45] See Groos, *The Play of Man*, pp. 394-395.

teleological terms. The emergence of the aesthetic from the merely playful would appear to occur not infrequently, particularly in the ceremonial dance. The Corn Dance of the New Mexico Pueblo Indians, by way of illustration, is basically non-aesthetic. It is religious and moral in significance and it is performed for the specific purpose of fertilization. Yet there appear in this and in similar ceremonies *Koshares* or funmakers whose ostensible function is to ward off the forces of evil. As the group-dance proceeds, however, the activity of the *Koshares* comes to be in every sense playful—free, unhampered, and dependent on the ingenuity of the individual dancer. There is, also, a "free play" in the movements of the communal groups—an instinctive grouping and a movement of hands and feet foreign to the set ritual. The latter kind of "play" obviously is a function of social solidarity. It may be, too, that the group-dance does afford, as Lange argues, an opportunity to stimulate the auditory organs and so to preserve and develop a function otherwise little used in everyday life. But the movements of the *Koshare* are inexplicable, wholly non-aesthetic ends, whether these are ends of social solidarity or of the preservation of the sense organs. At certain moments and by express intention, the dance of the *Koshare* comes to be choreographically inexplicable in non-aesthetic terms, either serious or playful. This, in itself, is not extraordinary, as will shortly be evident.

It was argued in the preceding chapter,[46] on the more "onerous" hypothesis, that fine art is bifunctional and that every object of fine art which has an aesthetic function is also definable in terms of a non-aesthetic end. It may be inferred that the play which "simulates" fertilization or sexual activity takes on an aesthetic aspect and is subsumed under the aesthetic end. This may imply that the evolution of art is by way of play or it may mean that the phenomenon occurs more frequently in play because the playful image is a "simulated" one. But this is to say only that a change of emphasis is necessary, whether the object is originally treated as serious or playful, since both ends are non-aesthetic. But what, it may be asked in the simplest terms, has undergone alteration?

[46] See above, p. 205.

It is of utmost importance to note that in specifying what has undergone alteration, play-theorists have contributed to philosophy of art various terms and phrases descriptive of art's structure. Plato's "certain images and very partial imitations of the truth" have their modern counterparts in Schiller's "living form" and *Schein*; in Spencer's "simulated images"; in Groos' "whatever furnishes immediate pleasure to the eye and ear in esthetic appearance"; and in Lange's "illusion-play."

Each phrase implies that "play" that has come to be art is of a unique structure which accounts wholly or in part for its unique aesthetic value. The terms mentioned above have been sufficiently significant to be adopted by writers other than play-theorists. There nevertheless remains the question, what, in the structure of the work of art, causes the emergence of the aesthetic from either the serious or the playful? Lange's term, "illusion-play" serves well to show at once the impasse of play-theory and the structural factors in art seized upon to resolve the difficulty. Lange begins by defining the experience of "illusion-play" as a capacity in part innate and in part acquired. In its experience, man gives himself and others a pleasure grounded in illusion. The illusion is free from any conscious aim other than that of immediate satisfaction.

Lange further maintains that not all play is art but all art is "illusion-play."[47] Chess, for example, is not "illusion-play," since it is "intellectual." "Illusion-games," it turns out, are certain "visual or auditory activities." But from this set of distinctions it may be inferred that play and art are identical only in an interrelated universe of discourse in which the end-products of artistic technique are made with primary attention paid to the sensuous media of the non-aesthetic factors as entering on or incorporated in the work of art. This must mean, however, that "play" is not the actual criterion for differentiating aesthetic and non-aesthetic objects. If the playful is, as Lange suggests, "more akin to art" because it is "sensuous," the differentiation between non-aesthetic and aesthetic playful objects follows, not from the fact that the latter is "playful," but that one has a "sensible structure" or a "sensuous medium" lacked by the former.

[47] *Op. cit.*, p. 623.

Lange's phrase, "illusion-games," is not an isolated instance of nomenclature implying that structure is the *sine qua non* of play-theory. It was remarked that Schiller abandons the strict identification of all art with play and comes to treat as aesthetic objects those that appeal to a cultured imagination. Schiller's thesis is in fact ultimately an aesthetic of imagination. The correlative to the imagination is not "play" but "image" or "stimulus" to feeling. Schiller's concern with the problem of the rationalization of feeling adds force to the inference that the true intent of his philosophy of art is an aesthetic of imagination or conation.

Granted, however, that Schiller's theory is truly grounded in an analysis of imagination rather than in one of "play," is it not true that the consequences for aesthetic remain the same? Kant's suggestion that aesthetic is freed from the laws of association of ideas certainly influenced Schiller to regard the imagination as having "her own freedom of motion and her material play, where she enjoys her inherent power and freedom without reference to form." In a word, is it not in conformity with Schiller's meaning to speak of the "aesthetic play" of imagination, despite the fact that the analysis of imagination offered by the poet at the conclusion of the *Aesthetic Letters* differs profoundly from the description of the instinct of play with which the book begins?

The fact is that the "play of imagination" is, as it stands, merely a metaphor. A sound aesthetic of "imagination" will show that the latter's operations are differentiated from those of "fancy" not by the rules of play but by the laws of the materials and by the possible techniques of art with which it works.[48] A sound aesthetic would ask, moreover, whether there are kinds of "imagination," whether and in what precise ways imagination is differentiated from feeling, and what relation "images" bear to reality.

The mere mention of "images" suggests one aspect of "imagination" that has appealed to play-thorists, the aspect of "illusion."[49] It remains to be proved, however, that the art-object is illusory and aesthetic experience is certainly not describable in terms of illusion. The experience of fine art may presuppose serious non-aesthetic

[48] See below, Chaps. XVII-XVIII.

[49] Cf. above, pp. 230-231.

ends and may occur only after a culture has developed means by which utilitarian interests may be satisfied. It does not follow, however, that the priority of non-aesthetic purposes makes the purposes that do emerge as aesthetic any the less serious, once they have emerged.

The relations of "sense-games," "sensuous media," and "living form" to imagination or to the senses; the fundamental place occupied by the rationalization of feeling in an argument like Plato's or Schiller's; and the incapacity of "play" actually to account for aesthetic experience; all have important consequences for the evaluation of play-theory. In the introduction of the terms "sense-games," "living form" and "*Schein*," however, there is implicit a hypothesis of art's "structure" that is no more integral to play-theory than it is to many another aesthetic. It is a matter of arbitrary nomenclature whether we choose to call objects to which this terminology is applied either "play" or "art." "Play" is no more the correlative to these "structural" terms than are morals, religion, or science. The proper correlative is "feeling" or "imagination." And if on the hypothesis under consideration, "play" on occasion is "art" it is art in precisely the same sense and for the same reasons that any other non-aesthetic product of artistic technique is similarly art and is similarly potentially or actually aesthetic.

The theory of play fails as a mediating hypothesis in aesthetic. It provides no true resolution either to the antinomy of art or to that of aesthetic experience. Because the theory's very nature is to mediate and because of its dependence upon the hypothesis of proximate ends, it fails likewise to free art and aesthetic experience from the "tyranny" of serious non-aesthetic ends. This is not to conclude, however, that the theory itself has not exerted a profound influence upon philosophy of art. Indeed, many suggestions made later in the present essay derive from implications, the significance of which are not wholly evident to play-theorists but which are evident in their writings once the end of play as the end of art no longer dominates the theorist. The play-theory itself remains a non-aesthetic hypothesis of the origin and nature of art and its experience. As such, it fails to satisfy the conditions of the aesthetic problem.

V

THE failure of play-theory repeats that of the serious genetic hypothesis. Neither teleology of art succeeds in defining fine art wholly by its relation to non-aesthetic ends. One fact, however, beyond all others, both hypotheses do enforce upon the attention of the aesthetician, despite their failure to resolve the essential problem. No aesthetic, led by the inadequacies of non-aesthetic teleologies to entertain the possibility that art is definable in terms of a unique aesthetic end, may ignore with impunity the non-aesthetic factors in fine art. A sound philosophy of art must redefine these non-aesthetic factors in art and make evident the manner in which they assume aesthetic connotations. The theory of the artist's selfish interests and the serious and playful genetic hypotheses suggest that aesthetic may well consider seriously the counsel, *mutatis mutandis*, Wallace once offered to students of religion: "They [the ancient Jews] knew," he writes, "some things which it would have been well if the later ages had not lost sight of. They knew that even if religion is not a matter of meats and drinks, meat and drink are no trifles which religion may ignore. They knew that religion is intimately wrapped up with the tillage of the field, the pasture of the flocks, the rules and modes of wedlock, the customs of the market, with sanitary rules, with the treatment of disease."[50]

As religion is "not a matter of meats and drinks," so aesthetic is not wholly a matter of either serious or playful non-aesthetic ends. But these ends are not "trifles" the aesthetician may ignore with impunity and to the ethnologist and the anthropologist are due no small debt for having overestimated their value.

The most obvious inadequacy in non-aesthetic teleologies which lay emphasis upon the value of ends is sound analysis of the work of art and its structure. It remains a question whether philosophy of art need postulate a unique aesthetic end, provided only that a

[50] William Wallace, *Lectures and Essays*, p. 162.

theory of structure, perhaps elaborating upon suggestions in play-theory, be developed. There has been no dearth of such suggestions in the history of aesthetic criticism. Their interest for the present essay is twofold. First, there is the question of the validity of the attempt to justify art's value without reference to an external *telos*. Secondly, the theory of structure provides a wider setting for considering the possibility that the freedom of art and aesthetic experience may be secured by considering means related solely to proximate ends. The theory of structure does derogate from the value of ends, precisely as the non-aesthetic teleologies minimize the value of means. But while an analysis of non-aesthetic teleologies would be incomplete without an examination of a theory of means as well as one of ends, the former analysis is integral, as will be seen, to the problem of structure itself. It is to this larger problem that the next part of this inquiry will be devoted.

❋

Part II

The Structure of Art

Chapter VIII

The Theory of "Aesthetic Surface": The Work of Art as "Symbol Equivalent with the Thing Symbolized"

What any music I like expresses for me is not thoughts too indefinite to clothe in words, but too definite. . . . If you asked me what I thought on the occasion in question, I say the song itself precisely as it stands.

—MENDELSSOHN

THE merging of deep passion, speculative skill, and broad learning that makes *The Provincial Letters* an attack upon casuistry unique in moral philosophy, has had no counterpart in the literature of aesthetic. The battle has not, however, gone by default. It is true that philosophy of art boasts no figure comparable to Pascal to defend it against the doctrine, *respice finem.* There have been, however, many artists, passionate in their utterance, as well as numerous critics, skillful in their essays, eager to heap scorn upon the aesthetician's resort to ends to illuminate the experience of poetry, painting, or music.

The craftsman's attacks have more often than not been ill-tempered and the critic's essays have at times sacrificed consistency to dexterity. These are facts of less significance, however, than this—that it has fallen to the lot of the "maker" and the appraiser of "making," rather than to the philosopher of art, to defend a theory of art as a means against the incursions of an ill-balanced doctrine of ends. But significant as the fact may be, it is not inexplicable.

The artist, in his writing, may subscribe to a doctrine of "credo quia impossibile" and the critic may belie yesterday's principles in today's pæan of praise. Yet, each subscribes to the doctrine of integrity to the "work to be made" and expresses his faith by efforts to master and understand the materials, technical processes, tools, and symbols that make possible the work.

It is not surprising that the artist's attitude is best expressed in the work of art and that the critic's defense is similarly implicit in the technical factors that interest him. For the artist, the poem or the painting expresses the conviction that the work of art is free from the compulsion of external ends. The craftsman has never hesitated to attribute a seashore to Bohemia, despite the geographer's strictures; to make "his Hector quote Aristotle," despite the historian's protests; or to elongate heads in massive sculpture, in spite of the anatomist's or the "realist's" injunctions. Nor has he felt the need, in perfecting a technique that may further weaken the claims that art is explicable in terms of non-aesthetic ends, to conceal his own serious intention in "making." So rarely, indeed, has he entertained the notion that the end-product of craft is propaedeutic for any other art that he has constantly practiced a doctrine of "proximate ends." Moreover, he has done so while free from the yoke of such a specious theory as handicaps the play-theorist in the latter's attempt to conceal the serious ends implied for art in his principles.

To some artists, bent upon speculation, the absorption of their interests in "making" has called for justification. To such of their writings as cast light on the problem, we shall shortly refer. It may be said of the critic, also, that he has become increasingly occupied with analyses of brush-stroke, preoccupied with the problems of the precise function of tools evolved to work stone of a given hardness, or immersed in mapping geographical distributions of materials to trace the spread of "styles" or techniques. These preoccupations have often operated to the detriment of an interest in more theoretical issues. Nevertheless, there has been much reflective criticism, scattered, it is true, and far from uniform in its terminology. Despite these obstacles, it is possible to gather evidence that critics have recognized the need to justify both the artist's practice of disregarding all but the "proximate" ends of craftsmanship, as well as the spectator's assumption that the end of art is immediate enjoyment.

By way of illustration, Clive Bell has urged not only that the "contemplation of pure form leads to a state of extraordinary exaltation and complete detachment from the concerns of life," but also that "the emotion that artists express comes to some of them, so they tell us, from the apprehension of the formal significance of material things."[1] We discover that these views rest upon the thesis that "the formal significance of any material thing is the significance of that thing considered as an end in itself." It is plain that Bell judges the work of art to be an "end in itself" once it no longer is considered as a "means to practical ends or as a thing related to human interests." Nor has the point been argued solely to provide a theory for the general philosophy of art. A. C. Bradley has maintained for a particular art that while poetry may have an "ulterior worth" its true nature is to be a "world of itself, independent, complete, autonomous."[2]

The reasons for the artist's concentration upon the work of art and the critic's usual attention to technique are thus evident. The reasons for the philosopher of art's lack of interest in the work of art as a mere means are no less clear. It is not that the latter does not esteem both the artist's and the critic's loyalty to the work of art. He has, in fact, not infrequently subscribed to their statements and has joined them in support of the thesis that the art-object is properly to be understood only if it is freed from the domination of external ends. Nor has history shown him to be less prone than either artist or critic to defend assertions that the artistic and relevant ends are "proximate" or that the operation of all such ends may be "postponed" to artistic creation or aesthetic experience. The philosopher's hesitation in regard to this larger issue may be ascribed, rather, to his discovery in artistic practice and critical speculation of a more significant problem than either the aesthetic counterpart of moral casuistry or that of "proximate ends." Some artists and critics are at this point in agreement with the aesthetician.

[1] *Art*, pp. 68-69.

[2] *Oxford Lectures on Poetry*, p. 5.

They have gone beyond mere practice or assertion and, as will shortly be seen, their writings parallel those of some aestheticians in asserting that the presupposition of the freedom of the work of art from external ends is a sound theory of the structure of art. The philosopher simply carries the argument to its logical conclusion: Art because of its "structure," may be freed not alone from ends but, as well, from all external relations.

Critic, artist, and philosopher have joined at times in their efforts to designate the elements entering upon a unique structure for the work of art. For some, the search has run its quarry to earth by means of phrases that vary but which nevertheless express a common intention. It is the common intention that is of interest and in the present chapter, the implication will be discussed by reference to an *omnium gatherum* term, "aesthetic surface."[3] For others, the search has led to a still more inclusive hypothesis, that of the "total structure" of art which will be illustrated in the chapter following by reference to certain historical interpretations of Aristotle's theory of *katharsis*.

II

THE implications of "structure" are evident in aspects of play-theory to which "aesthetic surface" owes an indebtedness that goes beyond that already suggested by its use of the words, "proximate ends." It will be recalled that Schiller strove to establish the unique impulsion of the play-instinct by arguing that the man who plays simultaneously thinks and feels. The playful experience is one characterized neither by external relations derived from the abstracting capacities of reason nor from a process which owes its character to feeling. More important for our present consideration, however, is the implication that the object of the play-instinct is likewise unique.

Schiller's and Lange's conclusions that the playful object is unique in that in it are completely integrated both formal and material

[3] Its usage here has no relation to D. W. Prall's interpretation of the phrase in *Aesthetic Judgment*.

elements would be of little moment were it not that the end, "play," is the proper correlative neither for the art-object nor for aesthetic experience, which they, as theorists, analyze. Their proper correlatives, as was indicated in the preceding chapter,[4] are, on the one hand, "image" or "sensuous medium," on the other, "imagination" or "feeling." Play-theory is scarcely precise in its definition of these terms and its ambiguity has suggested that, since the structure of art characterized as "play" is separable from its ostensible end, "play," it is likewise separable from all external ends, including "imagination" or "feeling."

It is not alone the ambiguity of "play-theory" that has led to the development of "aesthetic surface" as a theory of the structure of art. Other historical problems inherited by modern aesthetic have affected this hypothesis as well. The impact of Kant's third *Kritik* upon succeeding aesthetic theories was profound but, as we have observed, it laid severe restrictions upon objects to which the judgment of taste was applicable. Indeed, the limitations of the system in this regard were so rigorous that various attempts were made to reaffirm the aesthetic value of non-formal objects and by means of sounder analysis of art-objects to insure wider application of Kant's general principles. One consequence was that Schiller's suggestions concerning the sensuously defined "form"—the "living form"—tended to satisfy a historical demand transcending the specific needs of play-theory itself. One essential problem for the newer aesthetic was the specification of a possibly unique structure of art to which judgments of taste would apply.

"Living form," "aesthetic surface," "concrete sensuous *Gestalt*," "formed sensuous medium," are but a few among many terms offered to characterize such a unique structure. Each, in its context, suggests the attempt to free art from the charges of discontent, immorality, falsity, and irrationality which followed upon judgments that the work of art is properly evaluated in terms of non-aesthetic external ends. The ateleologist, it is true,[5] has attempted to meet the same difficulty by predicating "absolute beauty" of specific "forms." The

[4] See above, pp. 232 ff.
[5] Cf. above, Book One.

theorist of structure disregards this method, since he is little concerned either with *a priori* judgments of taste or their universality. In fact, he is launching an attack upon the restrictive method of the ateleologist who proposes to delimit the aesthetic universe of discourse and the point of the attack is precisely the "abstraction" of form from matter and the over-estimation of the former's value which are typical of ateleological theory. For the structuralist, the ateleological theory makes a false "abstraction" of form from matter, an "abstraction," it is contended, that does not in fact characterize the object of aesthetic experience.[6]

The proponent of "structure" has not been content, however, merely to criticize ateleological aesthetic. In his turn, he has formulated a philosophy of art that puts forward a postulate no less extreme. Maintaining that "form" and "matter" are inseparable except by false abstraction, the "structuralist" infers that they are identical in the object of aesthetic experience. It is implied, in fact, that the production of a work of art upon which the artist may concentrate his entire attention presupposes the perfection of a means by which form and matter are indissolubly joined and made identical. In this, the naive "structuralist" again evidences his debt to Schiller who tends to imply at times that the structure of the aesthetic object reveals all that the latter is "on the surface."[7]

Various inferences have been drawn from the phrase, "on the surface," and it will be of value to examine some of them in detail as this essay proceeds. It will be sufficient for our present purposes to emphasize the common implication which variously named theories of structure make and which permits their interpretation in terms of "aesthetic surface." All imply that the aesthetic meaning and value of the work of art are made fully explicit "on the surface" of the object, so that no external frame of reference is required. The nerve of the supporting argument is that aesthetic experience is not characterized by "abstraction." The identity of form and matter

[6] The theorist of structure is equally uninterested in "absolutely beautiful" forms and the theory thus differs from that presupposed by Hegel's analysis of Greek classical sculpture. Cf. above, Chap. IV, pp. 164 ff.

[7] Cf. Listowel, *A Critical History of Modern Aesthetics*, p. 32.

is held to obviate the necessity for external ends, abstract principles, classifications, or categories to make meaningful the aesthetic object.

The theory of "aesthetic surface," in its implication that the work of art is its own frame of reference, eventually raises an issue more significant than the asserted identity of "form" and "matter" in the art-object. The implied self-reference of the work of art argues that the aesthetic object is a symbol, "a symbol equivalent with the thing symbolized." This specific interpretation of the theory that art-objects are symbols presents difficulties. But the introduction of symbolism into philosophy of art brings a salutary change from the terminology concerned with mere "images," objects, or events employed in non-aesthetic teleological theory.[8]

III

TO REGARD the product of artistic technique as unique in structure because of its "aesthetic surface" and to infer from this that the object or event is self-referrent lead to interesting consequences. They are consequences, however, which follow not alone from speculation divorced from art but which have their *fons et origo* in artistic and technical problems. The word "surface" has spatial rather than temporal connotations. It is not strange, therefore, that the philosophical implications of the theory are made explicit by certain problems inherent in spatial rather than temporal arts.

We touch at this point the "literal" meaning of "surface" but it is evident that the word in its aesthetic context has undergone considerable metaphorical extension of meaning. This fact has enabled philosophers of art to generalize "surface's" most literal implication —that relating to perspective in the spatial art of painting. The literal significance is clear, if one considers the difficult problems faced, let us say, by Raphael in painting the "Madonna del Cardellino."

The artist must present not only the foreground but the bridge

[8] Cf. below, pp. 277 ff. and Part III.

and towers in the middle and far background on a single two-dimensional plane surface. By use of perspective, he gives a three-dimensional representation of objects in space and he does this literally upon the "surface" of the painting. It is not evident that the artist requires any external "referrent" to clarify what he means by space or the objects in it. Similarly, to apprehend Raphael's meaning in the represented scene, it is presumably unnecessary for the perceiver to "abstract" from the context of the painting or to reinforce his understanding by reference to physical or metaphysical meanings of "space."[9]

This primitive and "structural" meaning of "surface" does not apply literally to the temporal arts. It is, in fact, only partially applicable even to the spatial art of sculpture. Donatello's *David* is three-dimensional, as is the model portrayed by the sculptor. Architecture, similarly, is inadequately described in terms of "surface." By way of illustration, the Campanile in Florence is three-dimensional and our experience of it includes the impression of masses and volumes as well as of surfaces. "Surface," if interpreted literally, would be basic to a theory of structure for arts to which the propositions of plane rather than solid geometry are applicable.

Despite the obviously restricted field in which the literal interpretation of "surface" is meaningful, it is significant that the important inferences of a theory strictly applicable to and probably originating in analyses of perspective should have been drawn not only from spatial arts other than painting but from temporal arts as well. The literature of sculpture and poetry amply illustrates the aspect of "aesthetic surface" that denies the need for or validity of "abstraction," as it equally well illustrates the attempts to ground the implications of the work of art's self-reference.

It will be of value in view of the presumed generality of the theory to consider at the outset the contrast between "abstract" and "concrete" to which the theorist of "aesthetic surface" denies validity in art. The structuralist is not intent at this point to elaborate upon either the physical or the mathematical *differentiæ* of two- or

[9] That the impression is not one of "real space" gives rise in part to the theory that art is "illusion." See K. Lange, *Das Wesen der Kunst* and above, pp. 230 ff.

three-dimensional space which relate to the problem of perspective. Rather, he hopes to show that the dichotomous method of analyzing the object of art into form and matter is unsound. The method he adopts to indicate that the bifurcation fails is illustrated if it be maintained, for example, that the form or delineation by which the figures are marked off in El Greco's "Virgen y Sta. Inés," is the product of color and is no less sensuous than is the yellow background of the painting. It could be argued, furthermore, that weight and density, for the painter, are never experienced in terms of an opposed "form" and "matter" or even in terms of a problem of numerical calculation. The theorist of "aesthetic surface" insists that these effects are necessarily given directly in the composition of compact figures or masses and that it is by means of similar technical devices that all so-called formal characterizations must be presented. Tempi in music are only derivatively mathematical and, as directly experienced, concern feeling. By way of illustration, it may be urged that while the so-called "germ-motif" of Beethoven's *Sonate Pathétique* may be written

this is a mere "abstraction" from the organized sounds and sequences in the audible pitch and tone which are the data of aesthetic experience. Similarly, the representation of a line of iambic pentameter has the "form" –′–′–′–′–′. It is, in abstraction, any one of the lines which follow:

> Under the Trees now trip'd, now solemn stood
> Nymphs of *Diana's* train, and the *Naiades*
> With fruits and flowers from *Amalthea's* horn,
> And Ladies of th' *Hesperides*, that seem'd
> Fairer than feign'd of old, or fabl'd since
> Of Fairy Damsels met in Forest wide
> By Knights of *Logres*, or of *Lyones*,
> *Lancelot* or *Pelleas*, or *Pellenore*.

But neither in the musical notation which sets down the "germ-motif" nor in the formalized scheme of accentuation of Milton's lines does "abstraction" give the datum for aesthetic experience. This, it is maintained, may only be presented as the timbre or intonation is expressed or when the imaginatively suggestive connotation inherent in the musical or poetic datum is sensuously apprehended. Similarly, the proponent of "aesthetic surface" does not mean by colors the "abstract" and variant wave-lengths which the physicist proffers in consequence of spectroscopical analysis but, rather, the rich flesh-color of the figures in Rubens' "Bacchantes," the tactilely experienced textures in El Greco's "El Despolio," or the hard and brilliant blue-back of Manet's "Dead Toreador." It is not the written but the spoken word in *Macbeth* that is integral to "structure," precisely as the accompanying gestures, the pomp and ceremony, the sound of martial bugles, the rich and varied costume, enter upon aesthetic data.[10] The aesthetic object is not an architect's blueprint of the Mosque at Cordoba but the blue of the myriad stone pillars which give the impression of a shady forest.

The metaphorical meaning of "surface" is implicit in these illustrations. The theorist understands the term to mean, in its application to arts other than painting or sculpture in relief, the immediately perceived sensuous datum which reveals its full significance without "abstraction" by the percipient. And, regarding this aspect of the problem, he maintains that "abstraction" is properly an epistemological technique—mistakenly employed in aesthetic—directed to the isolation of "form" presumed to be the object of knowledge rather than to the experience of *sensibilia*. The "struc-

[10] This is emphasized in an interesting fashion in a passage in J. O. H. Jespersen, *Growth and Structure of the English Language*, p. 205, in which the author quotes C. Alphonso Smith in the *Englische Studien*, Vol. XXX, on "The Chief Difference between the First and Second Folios of Shakespeare": " 'The supreme syntactic value of Shakespeare's work as represented in the First Folio is that it shows us the English language unfettered by bookish impositions. Shakespeare's syntax was that of the speaker, not that of the essayist; for the drama represents the unstudied utterance of people under all kinds and degrees of emotion, ennui, pain, and passion. Its syntax, to be truly representative, must be familiar, conversational, spontaneous; not studied and formal.' " But " 'the Second Folio is of unique service and significance in its attempts to render more "correct" and bookish the unfettered syntax of the First. The First Folio is to the Second as spoken language is to written language.' "

turalist" maintains, furthermore, that the object as object of aesthetic experience is the entirety of its "substantial form," attributes, and accidents. This unity, he urges, is destroyed in the effort to analyze the "form" as object of knowledge from the work of art as a "whole in sensuous media." The object of art, considered as a symbol, is thus complete and *sui generis*. The artist's "idea" must be expressed wholly in and through the medium of the art. In consequence, if the artistic efforts of "making" be successful, there is no need to verify the meaning of the object by turning attention to another "image" or set of "images." In fact, such verification by reference to "images" or contexts external to the art-object, the theorist of "aesthetic surface" would hold to constitute the techniques of art criticism, scientific procedure, or mere antiquarianism.

IV

IT IS not difficult to illustrate the theory of "aesthetic surface." Valuable suggestions concerning its implications are evident in critical parts of Hegel's, Schopenhauer's and Croce's writings. But it will be more profitable to turn to the conversations and essays of artists who have encountered structural problems in consequence of attempts to form material by technical means. Perhaps no better instance may be found than that of Rodin, whose conversations reflect the extension of a technical dictum into an embryonic metaphysic of the structure of art.

Rodin, as a sculptor, faces problems inherent in the carving of marble and in the techniques needed to form bronze. The more technical strictures he lays down are intended to apply not only to his own practice but to that of classical Greek sculpture as well. In technical terms, Rodin considers the primary problem of sculpture to be not merely the carving of surfaces as such but as "projectures of interior volumes."[11] His advice as a technician is as direct and cogent as are the instructions of an anatomist or a projective geometer: "When you carve, . . . never consider a surface except

[11] *Art*, p. 60. Translated by R. Fedder.

as the extremity of a volume, as a point, more or less large, which it directs towards you."[12]

At this point, the sculptor speaks literally of the carved "surface." He is led, however, to hint at and in part to come to grips with the philosophical problem of the relation of "surface" as "structure" to the "truth" that it represents. That there is a philosophical problem for him is evident: "To any artist, worthy of the name, all in nature is beautiful, because his eyes, fearlessly accepting all exterior truth, read there, as in an open book, all the inner truth."[13] In consequence, the technical dictum for the sculptor who is to regard surfaces as "projectures of interior volumes," is made to bear a wider meaning. The "surface" is taken to be a projection of interior volumes because, the sculptor contends, "the truth of my figures instead of being merely superficial" is the consequence of forces "expanding from within to the outside."[14] As he explains his technique in the light of this belief in the "truth of figures," Rodin remarks, "I forced myself to express in each bulging of the torso or of the limbs the 'upthrust' of a muscle or of a bone which lay deep beneath the skin."[15]

What is stated and what may be inferred from Rodin's theory and practice for "aesthetic surface" are significant for a theory of structure. It may be observed, at the outset, that the context of his writings shows clearly that the sculptor intended the "surface" of figures to manifest sensuously and for perception what, in fact, only the scalpel of the anatomist could lay bare. It would appear that he thought that this could be accomplished, however, wholly within the limitations laid down by the medium. The minimum requirement, for Rodin, was the sculptor's attention to and technical concentration upon the spatial superficies at which the muscular forces manifest themselves.

This remains, however, a restricted and technical application of

[12] *Ibid.*, p. 59.

[13] *Ibid.*, p. 46.

[14] *Ibid.*, pp. 60 ff.

[15] An interesting contrast to Rodin's view of the competence of sculpture in this regard is afforded by Galen's argument concerning the limitations of Praxiteles' and Phidias' art as compared to nature. See Galen, *On the Natural Faculties*, II, Chap. 3, 81 ff.

the principle of "aesthetic surface." The "'upthrust' of a muscle or of a bone which lay deep within the skin," illustrates a more general contention. The representation of "bone" is ordinarily merely a portion of the entire figure portrayed. The "truth" of this portion is usually but a modicum of the significance the artist intends to express. Not even in Rodin's own *Hand in Bronze*, however, does the artist display "on the surface" only structures of interest for the physiologist. Nor is the clenching of the fingers intended to represent merely the interactions of muscles, tendons and nerves. An even more inclusive aim is evident in Rodin's groups. *The Burghers of Calais* does manifest contorted and tense muscles "on the surface" of the figures. But it is patent that Rodin intends, also, to reveal "on the surface" the moods of the individual burghers. They face the hangman in an agony expressed as defiance, resignation, and animal pain. Whether, indeed, the "content" of what is expressed does not transcend even the metaphorical meaning of "aesthetic surface" is a matter shortly to be discussed.

It is evident, however, that whatever conclusion may be drawn concerning the limitations of the particular metaphor, the sculptor's practice elaborates a technical rule-of-thumb (by which a "surface" is to be considered "as an extremity of a volume") into a way of modeling. This, in turn, presupposes an aesthetic theory to explain and ground the direct presentation in formed media of non-aesthetic "truths." Nor is this a mere inference. Rodin abandons technical instruction concerning lines, planes, light and shade, and the relations of volumes to declare this philosophical inference drawn from his theory of modeling: "Lines and tints are only to us the symbols of hidden realities." He then adds that, "Our eyes plunge beneath the surface to the meaning of things, and when afterwards we reproduce the form, we endow it with the spiritual meaning which it covers."[16]

The statement that lines and tints are but "symbols of hidden realities" implies, however, that the former, the structural factors,

[16] *Ibid.*, p. 190 Cf. G. W. F. Hegel, *The Philosophy of Fine Art, Part 1*, Chap. III, pp. 209-210. English translation by F. P. B. Osmaston. Hegel's suggestions concerning the superiority of the human body over the tree or the animal for displaying the *Idea* present an interesting philosophical view of "surface." Hegel holds that the human form reveals the truth freely in ap-

"stand for" the latter, the content. The content symbolized by the structural factors presumably may be either the "feeling" or data represented or expressed in the work of art by the artist. Rodin's argument implies, therefore, in part, that the non-aesthetic factors implicit in the work of art which contribute to its conative, archaeological, moral, historical, scientific, or religious significance, are displayed by means of the artist's technique "upon the surface" of the medium in the lines, tints, hues, and textures.

Other formulations which may be regarded as statements of principles implicit in "aesthetic surface" make a suggestion more complex than Rodin's. The lines, hues, tints, and other structural factors constitute for certain theorists a sensuous medium to which attention is properly directed because the art-object is intended to refer to the perceiver's feelings. Because the structural components signify factors in a non-aesthetic "reality" ordinarily called scientific, logical, moral, or theological, it is evident that symbolization "on the surface" implies in addition that the artist replaces one mode of knowing by another in that he addresses the art-object to feeling rather than ordinary cognition. This assumption, that the sensuous medium functions to present conative as well as other non-representative or representative non-aesthetic content for feeling, has led some thinkers to maintain that the cognitive process in aesthetic experience should be characterized as "immediate" rather than "mediated."[17] But from the assumption that the "aesthetic surface" of art-objects presents the non-aesthetic factors for immediate rather than for mediated judgment or inference, it has been concluded

pearance. The "external covering of the human body" in contrast to that hiding the bodies of animals, reveals the "heart of life pulsing through and throughout it." It is superior to the animal form because "it is a totality of organic members each of which is penetrated by the notion, differentiated thus in every particular organ by some particular mode of activity and the specific motion congenial to it." He adds, after remarking that the human soul "appears as such in its entirety" in the eye, that "it can be asserted of art that it has to convert every point of the external appearance into the direct testimony of the human eye, which is the source of soul-life, and reveals Spirit."

[17] Cf. Walter Pater, "The School of Giorgione," *The Renaissance*, p. 138. (By permission of The Macmillan Company, publishers.) "Art . . . is . . . thus always striving to be independent of the mere intelligence, to become a matter for pure perception, to get rid of its responsibilities to its subject or material; the ideal examples of poetry and painting being those in which the constituent elements of the composition are so welded together, that the

(since the "reality" is revealed for "immediate" perception on the "surface" of these structures) that the total significance of the non-aesthetic factors is likewise presented and that there is no need, in the properly constructed work of art, for an external "referrent."

There are, therefore, for the more sophisticated elaborations of the theory's implications, two related but separable inferences. The first concerns the "immediacy" of knowledge in aesthetic experience and is argued in consequence of the sensuous structure of the work of art and its relation to feeling. The second asserts that the work of art as a symbol is a completely knowable object *sui generis*. The latter inference is arrived at by assuming that the structure of the work of art is an identity of form and matter or content. For convenience it will be well to consider these inferences in reverse order, leaving for later discussion the relation of structure to feeling.

V

RODIN'S conversation is of value principally because it reflects the conversion of an artistic technique into an aesthetic principle. Rodin is, however, not a systematic thinker and he fails to develop the argument for the identity of form and matter in the work of art. A well known essay on poetry, however, does raise the significant issues at the level of philosophical speculation. It is true that its author, A. C. Bradley, does not use the phrase "aesthetic surface" and that his writing concerns a different art and derives from another tradition than Rodin's. But in "Poetry for Poetry's Sake,"[18] he does maintain the identity of form and matter in poetry, as well as for other arts.[19]

---

material or subject no longer strikes the intellect only; but form and matter, in their union or identity, present one single effect to the 'imaginative reason,' that complex faculty for which every thought and feeling is twin-born with its sensible analogue or symbol." For the extension of Pater's view to translation and its problems, see "Style" in *The Writer*, Vol. XI, No. 1, p. 4.

[18] *Oxford Lectures on Poetry*, pp. 3-37. (The quotations which follow are printed by permission of The Macmillan Company, publishers.)

[19] *Ibid.*, p. 15: ". . . this identity of content and form . . . is no accident; it is of the essence of poetry in so far as it is poetry, and of all art in so far as it is art." For the opposed view, see George Saintsbury, *A History of English*

Bradley's specific arguments presuppose the general theory already outlined for the structure of art. The essayist, as we have observed,[20] maintains that while poetry may have an "ulterior worth," its true nature is "to be not a part, nor yet a copy, of the real world . . . but to be a world by itself, independent, complete, autonomous." It is asserted, furthermore, not only that poetic expression is autonomous but that analysis of the art-object which proceeds from outside is neither expression nor intuition, but science. It is in accord with this epistemological presupposition that Bradley weighs the consequences of giving predominant value either to form or content. To overemphasize either aspect, he remarks, results in heresies "which would make poetry a compound of two factors—a matter common to it with the merest prose, *plus* a poetic form, as the one heresy says: a poetical substance *plus* a negligible form, as the other says." Both heresies are regarded as injurious to the dignity of poetry and, indeed, to the dignity of all arts.[21]

Nor does the experience of poetry consist in the enjoyment of "a certain meaning or substance" and as a separate thing "certain articulate sounds." Bradley infers this because, for him, the "substance" and the "form" are no more apprehended apart "than you apprehend apart, when you see some one smile, those lines in the face which express a feeling, and the feeling that the lines express. Just as there the lines and their meaning are to you one thing, not two, so in poetry the meaning and the sounds are one."[22] Since

---

Prosody, III, pp. 74-77. The implied "immediacy" of knowledge as feeling will be considered below, pp. 271 ff. and Chap. XI.

[20] Above, p. 239.

[21] *Ibid.*, p. 24; cf. p. 25: "Poetry in this matter is not, as good critics of painting and music often affirm, different from the other arts; in all of them the content is one thing with the form. What Beethoven meant by his symphony, or Turner by his picture, was not something which you can name, but the picture and the symphony. Meaning they have, but *what* meaning can be said in no language but their own: . . . it [poetry], content and form in unity, embodies in its own irreplaceable way something which embodies itself also in other irreplaceable ways, such as philosophy or religion."

[22] *Ibid.*, p. 14. Bradley certainly maintains that the substance is the content or subject-matter. What he means by "form" is less evident but it would appear that he would make little distinction between the formed material and the verbal expression of that material.

neither extreme is descriptive of poetry or of its experience on his view, Bradley maintains that the aesthetic character of poetry and of the other arts consists in the union of form and content. The significance and the form are presumed to be identical and it is held, moreover, that once conjoined, form and content cannot be differentiated. It is implied that form can signify or symbolize the content in but one way, a way which Bradley describes by referring to a proposition formulated by Matthew Arnold: "The words are 'symbols equivalent with the thing symbolized', or in our technical language, a form identical with its content."

It is well to remark that Bradley's statement of the problem is not unique in critical literature. Not only has it counterparts in poetry,[23] but in music, in painting, and in architecture as well. Indeed, the argument is so pervasive in writings upon the latter art that Geoffrey Scott feels the need to attack its exaggerations as part of a "Romantic Fallacy." Scott remarks that, "for example, the Gothic building from being the 'expression' of 'ignorant and monkish barbarians' came to 'suggest' the idealised Goth . . . 'firm in his faith and noble in his aspirations' . . . and the forms of an architecture which later came to be admired as the lucid expression of constructive mathematics were about this time commonly praised as the

[23] Cf. for example, Walter Pater, "The School of Giorgione," *The Renaissance.* Pater is maintaining that "*All art aspires towards the condition of music*," which he regards as the "ideally consummate art." Perhaps the most significant single aspect of Pater's view is that "it is the constant effort of art to obliterate" the distinction between form and content. The obliteration actually occurs, he argues, only in music but "In the art of painting, the attainment of this ideal condition, this perfect interpenetration of the subject with the elements of colour and design, depends, of course, in great measure, on the dexterous choice of that subject, or phase of subject; and such choice is one of the secrets of Giorgione's school." Poussin hints, similarly, at this identity in painting and in other arts. Writing to Chantelou in 1647, he says that as regards "le tableau de Moïse," "voyés vous pas bien que c'est la nature du subiec qui cause de cet effet, et vostre disposition." He refers at some length to the ancient modes and suggests that in following them the artist is obedient to "une certaine manière ou ordre déterminé, et ferme dedens le procéder par lequel la chose se conserue en son estre." Poussin regards the Doric mode as "stable graue et séuère et luy appliquoint matières graues séuerès et plaine de sapiense," and "L'ypolidye continent en soy une certaine Suauité et Douceur qui remplit l'ame des regardans de joye. Il s'acommode aux matières diuines gloire et Paradis." (Letter 156, *Correspondance de Nicolas Poussin.*)

architectural image of primeval forests." Scott wryly adds that "When the romantic material entered, the conventional form of necessity disappeared. 'Quaint' design and crooked planning took its place. For here form and content were practically one."[24]

Scott's irony undoubtedly touches the general theory of the identity of form and matter in the work of art but its particular aim is to show the weakness of the usual careless ascriptions of significance to "content." One may grant its force and yet maintain that iconology does offer an instrument of such precision that erroneous ascriptions need not necessarily be the rule in the interpretation of artistic symbols. No specific complaint like Scott's need hinder a general acceptance of the inferences of "aesthetic surface." The critic is better advised to quarrel with the enthusiasm of "structuralists" in art who use without discrimination the terms "content," "significant content," "symbolized content," and "matter." But despite these and other imperfections, there is an initial plausibility in the contention that in works of fine art, form and matter are in a relation of identity. We have referred briefly to Bradley's speculations upon the theory and followed the elaborations upon Rodin's technical instructions to show the methods by which the identity may theoretically be achieved in sculpture. It will be of value to ascertain whether there are, in fact, works of art which do exemplify the theory.

History itself does suggest that some general concordance holds between content and form and is implicit in the singularly persistent poetic forms adopted and retained by poets for the expression of certain "moods." Both temperament and ideas do appear to seek particular modes of expression even among artists of linguistically differentiated groups. Some "moods" are most adequately expressed in certain forms as is suggested both by the spirit and by the content of the lyric and the sonnet. Gerard Manley Hopkins has suggested indeed, that "feet and rhythm have their particular character . . ."[25]

[24] *The Architecture of Humanism*, particularly pp. 54 and 73.

[25] Cf. "Rhythm and the Other Structural Parts of Rhetoric . . . Verse," *The Note-books and Papers of Gerard Manley Hopkins.* (By permission of Oxford University Press, New York.) Hopkins writes in part, pp. 230 ff., that ". . . in fact it is commonly felt and said that feet and rhythms have their

and Drummond of Hawthornden speculated long ago upon the likelihood that there seems to be something "already condescended upon by all nations, and as it were established *iure gentium* amongst Greeks, Romans, Italians, French, Spaniards."[26] In fact, Drummond went so far as to entertain the possibility that "Neither do I think that a good piece of *Poesie* which Homer, Virgil, Ovid, Petrarch, Bartas, Ronsard, Boscan, Garcillaso (if they were alive and had that language) could not understand, and reach the sense of the writer" suggesting, as it were, an unmistakable alliance between the signification and the poetic form.

The foregoing are statements too indefinite and general to support the weight of the "structuralist's" argument that "form" and "matter" are identical. The general thesis of "aesthetic surface" does gain strength, however, as it brings to mind specific works of art that make of aesthetic experience a memorable and profoundly moving occurrence. Lear, in the storm on the heath, mad and raving against the elements and against the iniquities of men, does not speak in the smooth and majestic iambic pentameter of which Shakespeare shows his mastery in the earlier scenes of a play that requires the portrayal of kingly majesty. As the sequence of mean-

particular character. In general when the short or light syllables go before the long or strong, as in the iamb, the anapaest, the ionic *a minore*, the third and fourth paeon, the rhythm is *forward* and expresses present action. When it is the other way, as in the trochee, dactyl, the ionic *a majore*, the first and second paeons, it expresses succession and suits narrative. . . . More in detail the iambic is near the language of common talk, as Aristotle says of Greek and the same holds for English, and as modern verse is essentially spoken, not sung, it is the staple rhythm in the Teutonic and Romance languages: the ancients use it for dialogue. The trochaic is tripping, *ut idem dicit*: it runs. It suits brisk narrative ('Twas when the seas were roaring'), especially when not doubled. When doubled it becomes grave and monotonous ('Ah distinctly I remember' and Hiawatha). The dactyl is like the trochee made graver without becoming heavier. . . . The spondee is solemn and slow. The pyrrich is very light. . . . The anapaest is grave and swift too. . . . The amphibrach has the most bound and canter . . . it leaps like waves. The antispast is rocking and tumultuous: . . . The cretic is brisk and tramping. The choriamb is liquid and eloping. In general then there are three descriptions of rhythm . . . *upward* or *climbing* (iamb, anapaest), *downward* or *dropping* (trochee, dactyl), and *central or rocking* (amphibrach, cretic, choriamb, antispast), the first suiting the drama, the second epic and narrative, the last lyric verse."

[26] Quoted by W. P. Ker, *The Art of Poetry*, pp. 4 and 5.

ing in Lear's words is broken by passion, the form of utterance itself is similarly broken:

> Pray, do not mock me:
> I am a very foolish fond old man

are the words with which the mood begins, but the coherence breaks, in

> Cordelia, Cordelia! stay a little. Ha!
> What is't thou sayst?—. . .

and again as the significance changes the form is altered. The words themselves appear to have been selected for their gentle and soothing sound:

> . . . Her voice was ever soft,
> Gentle, and low, an excellent thing in woman.

There are many similar instances.[27] The apparent union of form and connotation affects the rapid, light curveting of the prose in Faulkner's *The Hamlet*, a prose which superbly contains the wild rush of the unbroken Texas mustangs and seems as wild and flowing as the movements of the animals themselves. Mrs. Bloom's unpunctuated monologue, with which James Joyce concludes *Ulysses*, is in the artistic sense the precise counterpart of the half-dormant mind reminiscing with few restrictions upon its power to associate images. The connotation of primeval and cataclysmic nature finds proper expression in the harsh consonants of the monosyllables used by Padraic Colum in *The Ploughers*. The effect is amplified by the poetic device of accentuating the first rather than the second syllable:

[27] Dr. Samuel Johnson's essay (No. 94) on Saturday, February 9, 1751, in *The Rambler* is an interesting analysis of "The resemblances of poetic numbers to the subject which they mention or describe." Johnson cites an instance from Milton's *Paradise Lost* which may be noted at this point: "A sudden stop at an unusual syllable may image the cessation of action, or the pause of discourse; and Milton has very happily imitated the repetitions of an echo:

> . . . I fled, and cried out *Death*:
> Hell trembled at the hideous name, and sigh'd
> From all her caves, and back resounded *Death* . . ."
>
> *P. L.* ii, 787.

Earth savage, earth broken, the brutes, the dawn-
man there in the sunset,

And the plough that is twin to the sword, that is
founder of cities!

The harsh and cruel beginning of a world is similarly expressed in the drumbeats and the sounds of bass viols in *Le Sacre du Printemps.* It is of value to contrast either of these instances with Hamsun's coordination of significance and form in the effort to present, in *The Growth of the Soil*, the sowing of corn as though it were little less than a mystical rite:

> . . . and then he sowed his corn. For generations back, into forgotten time, his fathers before him had sowed corn; solemnly, on a still, calm evening, best with a gentle fall of warm and misty rain, soon after the gray goose flight. . . . Corn was nothing less than bread; corn or no corn meant life or death. Isak walked bareheaded, in Jesu name, a sower. Like a tree-stump with hands to look at, but in his heart like a child. Every cast was made with care, in a spirit of kindly resignation. Look! the tiny grains that are to take life and grow, shoot up into ears, and give more corn again; so it is throughout all the earth where corn is sown . . . a great wide world, and here is Isak, a tiny speck in the midst of it all, a sower. Little showers of corn flung out fanwise from his hand; a kindly clouded sky, with a promise of the faintest little misty rain.[28]

The smooth flowing prose, in the long sentences, as majestic in their unfolding as the rhythm of blank verse, seems to have become integral to concepts and ideas appropriate to religious ritual and, specifically, to the sowing and growth of seed, the richness of earth, man's dignity as a tiller of the soil, as well as to the slow, untiring mood that reaffirms man's acceptance of a relation that at once binds him to the earth and sustains him. Colum's sentences, on the contrary, appear to struggle as the thoughts and passions they convey conflict. The poetic form suggests the feeling of sublimity that arises from man's willing to combat a force, savage and resistant to his efforts, much as the words are similarly savage and resistant.

[28] The success of the attempt is evident even in translation. (The passage is quoted by permission of Alfred A. Knopf, Inc., publishers.)

On the contrary, only a Latinized structure, upon which Sir Thomas Browne's masterly prose is constructed, is appropriate to express the conclusion to *Hydriotaphia*:

> To subsist in lasting Monuments, to live in their productions, to exist in their names and prædicament of Chymera's, was large satisfaction unto old expectations, and made one part of their Elysiums . . . 'Tis all one to lye in St. Innocent's Churchyard, as in the Sands of Ægypt: Ready to be anything, in the extasie of being ever, and as content with six foot as the Moles of *Adrianus*.

One may recall with profit, also, that in the making of the different but equally superb prose of *Le Morte d'Arthur* Sir Thomas Malory sensed so thoroughly the need for interrelating form and meaning that "In some places he consciously refrains from translating the meaning and introduces English words that are similar in sound to the French."[29] The welding of form and content in this romance of the Round Table is evident in the elegy for Sir Launcelot:

> And then Sir Ector threw his shield, sword, and helm from him. . . . Ah, Launcelot, he said, thou were head of all Christian knights, and now I dare say, said Sir Ector, thou Sir Launcelot, there thou liest, that thou were never matched of earthly knight's hand; and thou were the courtliest knight that ever bare shield; and thou were the truest friend to thy lover that ever bestrad horse; and thou were the truest lover of a sinful man that ever loved woman; and thou were the kindest man that ever strake with sword; and thou were the goodliest person that ever came among press of knights; and thou was the meekest man and the gentlest that ever ate in hall among ladies; and thou were the sternest knight to thy mortal foe that ever put spear in the rest.[30]

The fundamental argument of "aesthetic surface" is bolstered, also, if one recollect the practice of the parodist, intent often upon bringing ridicule upon outworn pseudo-chivalric, pseudo-classic, and pseudo-romantic *genres*. He succeeds precisely because he has

[29] Vinaver, E., *Malory*, pp. 101 ff. Cf. *ibid.*, p. 107: "Malory knows, besides, the secret of slow and swift movements, which he alternates according to the meaning. The slow movement is used in solemn discourse, and the swift in narrative and description."

[30] *Op. cit.*, Book XXI, Chap. 13.

emasculated the work of art and retained a form suitable only for a content that has lost meaning or interest.

Nor is it alone in poetry and in prose that the argument of "aesthetic surface" for the identity of form and content appears to have validity. No extrinsic frame of reference would appear to be necessary for a comprehension of El Greco's "Agony in the Garden." The artist gives his meaning in part by the agitation of the robes upon the figures at the left, leaving the impression that they are given life by the spiritual struggle of the central figure. Similarly, Zuloaga's picador, fatigued and defeated, rides against a livid and threatening sky. It is the color that gives the tone of the painting. Vermeer's girl, weighing gold in a tranquillity of light and color, is drawn with a certainty and crispness of line that does not permit conflict to emerge. Rouault introduces a heavy black outline against garish red in "The Circus Dancer" and employs a harsh and virile technique to display the brutish central figure and the fat, uncouth manager at the left of the painting; Glackens's "Young Girl" is done, by way of contrast, with a delicate pointillist technique. The overtone of greenish-blue upon the body is precisely suited to the girl, whose serious but immature face is in keeping with the delicate and tentative mood of the entire portrait. Similarly, Marie Laurencin's "Young Lady in Pink," with its shading of pink, green, mauve, and the girl's startlingly black eyes are well adapted to be a symbol of fragility and innocence. Picasso's "The Absinthe Drinker," its central figure wasted and degenerate, with pointed nose and chin and emaciated face and wrists, is given in a contrast of red and black. There are sharply drawn lines to outline the face and the background, while in softer but no less morbid color, figures less distinguishable merge into phantasmagoria. Similarly, the passionate feeling for fields and flowers appears to find most suitable expression through van Gogh's passionate technique.

There are suggestions that this theory of structure equally well explains sculpture. Rodin leaves rough-hewn the stone from which Adam emerges newly made of earth. Mestrović adopts a somewhat similar technique for *Girl Playing the Violin.* The French sculptor achieves strength for his figures by the use of rough and contorted finish. The Serbian gives his figure its peculiar strength by signifying vitality of character through use of the long line and the smooth interrelation of masses. Each sculptor seeks to give a different idea of strength. As the ideas vary, each apparently can be displayed adequately in sensuous media only by techniques and in forms suitable to its significance.

Similar instances in music, architecture, and the dance, could easily be cited. Enthusiasts have used them to buttress the argument of "aesthetic surface" but the effort entailed in repeating them would scarcely be repaid. For each product of technique that appears to exemplify the theory that form and content are identical, there may be adduced another in which these factors are obviously not "bitted" to each other. Van Gogh strives often to express in his landscapes the "idea" of riotous growth and fertility: "It's more the intensity of the thought than the tranquillity of touch we are after," he argues, and the intensity of feeling would appear to require a technique of heavy brush strokes and palette knife. Yet, the actual technique he does use is little different from that employed by Cézanne for the portrait of an extremely self-controlled "Uncle Dominique." Laurencin paints with light brush strokes and delicate color to portray her frail ladies. Georgia O'Keeffe adopts similar technique and color to portray the skulls and roses in "Life and Death" and the barren mountains in "View from My Studio, New Mexico." It has been pointed out that Shakespeare uses the broken line to accentuate Lear's bitter sorrow and perturbation of mind. This is, however, scarcely the only technical device by which the dramatist expresses profound feeling. The almost unbearable scene in Macbeth, in which Macduff's son prattles to his mother before foul murder is done, derives much of its strength from the contrast between the even flow of the prose, the simplicity of the words, and the brutality of the murder.[31] Epstein's *Eve* expresses conception of a crude and primitive woman. Its medium is, appropriately, roughly

[31] Dr. Johnson, *op. cit.*, No. 94, offers a classic criticism at this point. "The critics . . . have struck out other similitudes [between form and content]; . . . Thus the propriety of each of these lines has been celebrated by writers whose opinion the world has reason to regard:

Vertitur interea cœlum, et ruit oceano nox. . . .

—Virgil, *Aen.*, ii. 250

finished. Yet, Rodin finds it unnecessary to employ either a similar technique or rough medium to symbolize the tortures of the damned at the *Gates of Inferno.*

If the foregoing citation of instances were the sole ground for the validity of "aesthetic surface" as a theory of aesthetic, philosophy of art might well conclude that its proponents are primarily interested in advocating the adoption of the most obvious artistic technique for the expression of "ideas." This is not their intention, certainly, and to infer that it is, is the consequence of the constant dependence of their argument upon a thoroughly unsystematic denotation. The truth or falsity of the structuralist's postulate may no more be determined by the citation of instance and counterinstance than the contentions of the Sophist, Hippias, could be maintained in the face of Socrates' reiterated admonition: ". . . he asked you, not what is beautiful, but what the beautiful is." It remains to be determined whether or not the theory of "aesthetic surface" is susceptible to proof by a sounder method than that which denotes instances of "what 'aesthetic surface' is."

VI

SOME suggestion of sounder method for evaluating the contention of "aesthetic surface" that the work of art is a unique and indissoluble union of form and matter is implicit in the proposition,

---

Meantime the rapid heavens roll'd down the light,
And on the shaded ocean rush'd the night.
—Dryden

Sternitur, ex animisque tremens procumbit humi bos.
—*Aen.*, v. 481

Down drops the beast, nor needs a second wound;
But sprawls in pangs of death, and spurns the ground.
—Dryden

Parturiunt montes; nascitur ridiculus mus.
—*Ars Poet.*, 139

The mountains labour, and a mouse is born.
—Roscommon

If all these observations are just, there must be some remarkable conformity between the sudden succession of night to day, the fall of an ox under a blow, and the birth of a mouse from a mountain; since we are told of all these images, that they are very strongly impressed by the same form and termination of the verse."

"The words are 'symbols equivalent with the thing symbolized'."[32] The point of Arnold's statement is best examined if, at the outset, the field of its application is limited to poetry, in which connotations are ordinarily more precisely ascertainable than in other arts. There are two obvious contexts in which to test the truth or falsity of the proposition, "words are 'symbols equivalent with the thing symbolized' "; the first, that of single words (if there be any single poetical words), the second, that of collections of words entering upon or constituting complete poems. In other words, let us examine the artistic elements that enter upon works of a particular art in order to determine whether or not these elements have a peculiar status because they are unique combinations of form and matter. Then, let us examine the work of art as a whole with the same end in view.

If there are single words which are fixed and precise symbols, instances of what Sir Walter Raleigh called "Language . . . bitted to thought . . . some kind of preordained harmony between words and things whereby expression and thought tally exactly, like the halves of a puzzle,"[33] one would naturally search for them in the poet's practice of onomatopoeia. The definition of onomatopoeia shows its suitability for the purpose: "imitating the sound of the thing or action which it signifies."[34] The term has not infrequently been applied to words in such fashion that "onomatopoeic" is identical for practical purposes with Arnold's "symbols equivalent with the thing symbolized." By way of illustration, Tennyson held that the effects of such imitation meant "the marriage of sense with sound."[35] J. P. Dabney, who cites the poet's practice and remarks that some alliterative poetical passages "are all more or less onomatopoeic," suggests Arnold's conclusion in his own opinion that in Tennyson's line, "The league-long roller thundering on the reef," "the prolonged vowel cadence" of league-long roller "could mean nothing else but what it does mean, and it is capped by the strong onomatopoeic word 'thundering.' "[36]

[32] See above, p. 253.
[33] *Style*, pp. 62 ff.
[34] *New English Dictionary*.
[35] According to J. P. Dabney, *The Musical Basis of Verse*, p. 122.
[36] *Ibid.*, pp. 115 and 121.

The instance cited by Mr. Dabney is obviously contextual. Whether there is actually a "preordained harmony . . . between words and things whereby expression and thought tally exactly" in single words presents difficulties, to some of which even the so-called "four-letter" Anglo-Saxon monosyllables are susceptible. In the first place, one may consider the difficulties inherent in words of different spellings and dissimilar meanings which are yet identical in pronunciation.[37] For "wail" and "waste," for example, may be substituted "whale" and "waist," as a "wag" once pointed out in remarking upon Swinburne's alliterative and onomatopoeic effort.[38] Secondly, words which originally may have had an onomatopoeic significance assume a metaphorical or derivative meaning which runs counter to the principle of identity of thought and expression. An example may be drawn from Milton's use of the word "jarring" as "an imitation of a sound associated with an action":

> On a sudden open fly
> With impetuous recoil and jarring sound
> The infernal doors, and on their hinges grate
> Harsh thunder, that the lowest bottom shook
> Of Erebus.

In *Paradise Lost*, at this juncture, "jarring" means "sounding with harsh or rough vibration." In Cowper's *Nightingale and Glow-worm*, on the other hand, the word in the context,

[37] Cf. Robert Bridges, "On English Homophones": "When two or more words different in origin and signification are pronounced alike, whether they are alike or not in their spelling, they are said to be homophonous, or homophones of each other. Such words if spoken without context are of ambiguous signification."

[38] Dr. Johnson, *op. cit.*, p. 118, after remarking that, "Every language has many words formed in imitation of the noises which they signify," writes that, "Words of this kind . . . are sometimes combined with great propriety, and undeniably contribute to enforce the impression of the idea. We hear the passing arrow in this line of Virgil:

> *Et fugit* horrendum stridens *elapsa sagitta;*
> *Aen.*, ix. 632."

But after attending to the problem and citing other illustrations, the learned Doctor concludes that, "The representative power of poetic harmony consists of sound and measure; of the force of the syllables singly considered, and of the time in which they are pronounced. Sound can resemble nothing but sound, and time can measure nothing but motion and duration."

Hence jarring sectaries may learn
Their real interest to discern,

means merely "disputing."

It is evident, therefore, that it is true not only of thought, as Raleigh suggests, but of expression as well that it "is not confined to one mate, but roves free and is the father of many children."[39] For words have metaphorical, allusive, and associated meanings which age and usage at times confer upon them.

It may be urged, however, that a similar variability in the meanings and expressions of words does not occur when the "factors" appear in precise contexts. If this can be shown to be the fact, perhaps the contention that form and content are identical may be regarded as established in its proper form. That meanings are more precisely fixed and determined in and by contexts than outside them is unquestionably true,[40] but a problem is raised, as will shortly be seen, once one attempts to determine the extent and limitation of "context." The latter difficulty, however, may be postponed for consideration until we have examined a presupposition of more immediate interest. It may be argued that Bradley and Arnold imply that the work of art, the poem, the painting, or the sculptured figure, is the sole or unique symbol for the significance or "idea." If the poem as a whole is the unique symbol of the "idea" or "thing" symbolized, it would appear to follow that the words which compose it are similarly "bitted" to thought under the compulsion of the whole of which they are part. Perhaps, if this inference is sound, some justification through context may be made for what Raleigh has attacked as the "illusion, called in France the doctrine of the *mot propre*—a will o' the wisp which has kept many an artist dancing on its trail."

Upon the consequences for aesthetic judgment of the argument that the work of art is unique, this essay has already touched. It is necessary at this point merely to repeat our previous inference that "the only absolutely free judgment is the meaningless one."[41]

[39] *Op. cit.*, pp. 62 ff.
[40] Cf. Milton's use of the phrase "blind mouths," below, p. 266.
[41] Cf. Chap. II, pp. 82 ff.

We are now interested in determining the validity or invalidity of the proposition that only a specific form may symbolize, or express, or be adequate, for a particular content. Croce's theory of aesthetic maintains, as an instance, that each expression is an intuition of "impressions" and is to be regarded as individual, unique, and incomparable. The "impression" is the "content" to be intuited and no inadequate "expression" of "impressions" is judged to be art. The presupposition of Croce's intuitionism is that the "impression" finds its adequate expression only in a particular expression, i.e., in one particular "form."

It is important to realize that theories like Croce's are valiant but unavailing efforts to attribute to the artist and the lover of art an originality to which neither may lay proper claim. To speak only of the artist, it may be granted that the poet, the sculptor, and the painter do give evidence of originality. Yet, neither they nor any other "maker" can assure for his art a uniqueness that would establish it as an unrepeatable expression of idea, substance, or content. The dramatist, from Aeschylus to Shakespeare, borrows themes and situations, the sculptor from Pheidias to Rodin appropriates subject matter, and the painter from Michelangelo to Cézanne derives his "ideas" from morality, theology, astronomy, religion, and nature. Neither does technique nor form necessarily originate with the great masters of a craft. The craft of sculpture has its origins in pre-history and painters have inherited, similarly, an immeasurably old technique. Remarking upon stylistic traditions in art, Professor Carpenter has maintained, indeed, that the "artist's greatest and most necessary illusion is the illusion that he is creating."[42] But despite its necessity, it is illusion nevertheless: "If the artist were wholly free to create, why should not each of his creations be completely unique, instead of showing a manner appropriate to a school or group, which in turn takes its ordered place within a phase or style pointing back to its predecessors and forward toward its successors?"

[42] Rhys Carpenter, "The Basis of Artistic Creation in the Fine Arts," *The Bases of Artistic Creation*, pp. 30-31. As will be seen, Professor Carpenter's view of itself is too extreme. Cf. below, Chaps. XVI-XVIII.

At this point, the problem posed by the possible identity of form and content in the work of art impinges upon a historic controversy in aesthetic. To it the opposing forces bring both truth and falsehood. The artist is, in fact, at once a creator and an heir to the ages. Regarding its specific aspects, his work may be creative; regarding its generic aspects, it uses a symbolism derived from a thousand sources in the sciences and the theologies of the past. Similarly, the artist is heir to modes of expression, to techniques, and to stylistic traditions. Keats adopts but does not invent the sonnet form which Wyatt and Surrey brought to England from Italy. He is inspired by Chapman's *Homer* and by Balboa's discovery of the Pacific and neither the content of the former nor an acquaintance with the latter fact is eclectic. The specific sonnet which begins, "Much have I travelled in the realms of gold," is nevertheless Keats' and only his.

These are, no doubt, the commonplaces of art criticism, easily repeated and difficult to substantiate. They do have, however, relevance at this point for our consideration of the problem of the identity of form and content. It is evident, with regard to this alleged identity, that it is generic and not the specific aspects of art that pose the crucial question. It is apparent that the identical generic "idea" may be expressed in many forms and that it is not "bitted to" one work of art. John Milton inveighs superbly against

> Blind mouths! that scarce themselves know how to hold
> A sheep-hook, or have learned aught else the least
> That to the faithful herdsman's art belongs!

The "blind mouths" is the product of individual powers of a high order. Only to a creative imagination, and probably only to one imagination, would have occurred such associations of the word *episcopus*. Generically, however, and as "content," Milton's attack upon the clergy is identical with John Skelton's indictment of the bishops in *Colyn Cloute*:

> The Churche is put in faute;
> The prelates ben so haut,
> They say, and loke so hy,

As though they wolde fly
Aboue the sterry skye.
Laye men say indede
How they take no hede
Theyr sely shepe to fede,
But plucke away and pull
The fleces of theyr wull,
Unethes they leue a locke
Of wull amonges theyr flocke;

And surely thus they say,
Bysshoppes, if they may,
Small houses wolde kepe,
But slumbre forth and slepe,
And assay to crepe
Within the noble walles
Of the kynges halles
To fat theyr bodyes full,
Theyr soules lene and dull,
And haue full lytell care
How euyll theyr shepe fare.[43]

Similarly it is true that *Troilus and Cressida* is a masterly psychological analysis, which only Chaucer could have done. Yet, the generic theme of that story of passion and faithlessness finds other and adequate expressions in Henryson's *Cryseida*, in Boccaccio's *Teseide* and in Shakespeare's tragi-comedy. Again, the themes of death, burial, and survival, dominate *Hydriotaphia.* Yet Browne's individual prose style expresses the generic idea that moves Housman to write,

We now to peace and darkness
And earth and thee restore
Thy creature that thou madest
And wilt cast forth no more.

Only Dunbar could write the moving *Timor Mortis Conturbat Me* but it is fundamentally the same fear of death that haunts Marlowe's Dr. Faustus:

Ah, Faustus,
Now hast thou but one bare hour to live,

[43] *Op. cit.*, ll. 70 ff.

And then thou must be damn'd perpetually!
Stand still, you ever-moving spheres of heaven,
That time may cease, and midnight never come;
Fair Nature's eye, rise, rise again, and make
Perpetual day; or let this hour be but
A year, a month, a week, a natural day,
That Faustus may repent and save his soul!
O lente, lente currite, noctis equi!
The stars move still, time runs, the clock will strike,
The devil will come, and Faustus must be damn'd.

No one expression of the theme of death is identical in form to any other. Yet no one is generically different from the others.

The "ideas," implicit in the content, in the "matter" of poetry show many similar generic identities. They are themes arousing love or passion, "images" of death and immortality, moods of lyric happiness and black despair. To argue that, as regards content or "matter," certain given poems are not generically the same is to run in the face of the facts.[44] To argue that the object's generic aspects are irrelevant to art or aesthetic experience and that each work of art is unique and individual in every characteristic is to err. It is to ignore the fact that however a Shakespeare may tower above his fellows, his poetry and plays are yet kin to those of Marlowe, Greene, Chapman, Tourneur, and Massinger in ideas expressed, in events portrayed, in the prosody employed, and in the contemporary aspects of Elizabethan and Jacobean life which enter upon the art. To recognize that this is both true and relevant does not imply that the specific aspects of art may be ignored with impunity. For while there are generic ideas presupposed in all, each work of art that is potentially fine art differs in its interpretation from each member of its class. It achieves this individuality through the artist's particularization of a generic technique and his specification of generic symbols.

[44] Cf. F. H. Bradley, *Ethical Studies*, pp. 167-169: ". . . identity and diversity, sameness and difference, imply one another, and depend for their meaning on one another; . . . mere diversity is nonsense, just as mere identity is also nonsense; . . . If, concerning two dogs allied in blood, I were to ask a man, 'Is that of the same strain or stock as this?' and were answered, 'No, not the same, but similar,' should I not think one of these things, that the man either meant to deceive me, or was a 'thinker', or a fool?"

That a work of art is neither a wholly unique nor a wholly generic expression of content or significance is a fact that has primary importance for the sequel to this essay in which is considered the relation of symbols of art to feeling.[45] Of more immediate consequence is the bearing the fact has upon the issue whether or not a given work of art is a "symbol equivalent with the thing symbolized." It may be asked whether, given the generic and specific aspects, the content of a work of art has been sufficiently adequately expressed "on the surface" so that the object as a whole is its own sufficient frame of reference. This is to ask whether the work of art can be "a symbol of itself."

Thus far, it has been argued that the formal and material components of a poem do not possess fixed symbolic meanings. Their connotations vary at least with context. This conclusion, it may be said, follows for "elements" of art other than poetry. The color red, for example, is not at all times nor in all places a symbol of danger. It has associations, occasionally, with royalty and with greed. It is not, as sometimes occurs, a symbol for regal splendor in El Greco's "El Despolio," in which the composition as a whole tends to fix the meaning of the component colors as symbols. To accord with the theory of "aesthetic surface," it must now be inferred, not only that the meanings of component factors are determined by the whole into which they fit, but that the significance of the work of art as a whole is determined by the whole. This is to argue that the work of art is the "total structure" and that the relation of the whole work of art to itself is such that in it is manifested such significance for the perceiver that the latter need have recourse to no external frame of reference for its comprehension.

We need no longer illustrate the problem in poetry but may turn to the art of painting in which the literal connotations suggested at the outset by the theory of "aesthetic surface" were evident. And in painting, iconology has come to guard the critic from dangers inherent in the loose interpretation of symbols and may, consequently, provide an answer to our question, whether the whole work of art is a "symbol equivalent with the thing symbolized." It

[45] These problems will be considered in Part III of this book.

would be difficult to discover an instance more likely to provide an answer to this question than Dr. Edwin A. Wind's analysis of Botticelli's "Derelitta."[46] Complex non-aesthetic factors are expressed in the painting and their elucidation has been Wind's contribution. Our problem presupposes the iconographical material but is directed solely to determining whether or not the "content" of the "Derelitta" may be analyzed "on the surface," so that the work of art may be regarded at once as "referrent" and that to which reference is made.

It is evident, in this as in any illustration of complex "wholes" in art, that proper caution should be practiced before one accepts the inference that the significance of the work of art appears completely "on the surface." In fact, the resources of wide scholarship alone enable Wind to conclude that the non-aesthetic "referrents" for the "Derelitta" concern Mordecai, who is represented "covered with sack cloth and rending his heart as he has rent his garments," rather than "the despairing Vashti, the queen whom Ahasverus deposed." It would be idle to argue that, as a specific symbol, the "Derelitta" did not require for its comprehension specific training and knowledge on the part of the observer—a fact the more evident if it is recalled that Wind's interpretation argues that the figure portrayed is that of a man and not of a woman. One may only infer that, with reference to the non-aesthetic factors in the work of art, the "Derelitta" is less informative than is the Book of Esther. The philosopher of art is forced to conclude that while the frame of reference for a portion of the painting may be the "whole," the "whole" context is not only the specific painting but, first, the "story of Esther as represented in the six panels of the two cassoni";[47] secondly, the fact that "the series of pictures as a whole was meant to convey a moral lesson suitable to a young married couple; the glorification of humility"; and finally that "the calling of Mordecai by Ahasverus to be dressed in the 'royal apparel' and the 'crown royal' (Esther, Chap. 6) is the choice by the heavenly bridegroom of his earthly representative."

[46] *Journal of the Warburg and Courtault Institutes*, Vol. IV, Nos. 1-2.
[47] *Ibid.*, p. 116.

As Wind indicates, at the time the painting was executed "the themes of pictures were not meant to occasion more or less fanciful flights of the imagination. They formed part of a precise set of ideas." One may perhaps conclude that the frame of reference for the painting is, in fact, the whole of the Old Testament and of its Renaissance interpretation. In any case, however, it is evident that no work of art can be its own frame of reference. The "referrent" of the work of art transcends the work of art itself.

The "structuralist" who maintains that "aesthetic surface" provides an adequate ground for the explanation of art has not necessarily denied that an external frame of reference is required to make explicit the religious, theological, moral, cultural, or philosophical implications of the work of art. He has consistently maintained, however, that the satisfaction of this requirement is irrelevant to the aesthetic problem because it ignores "feeling." The main outline of his argument is of interest and may be put briefly: the theorist of "aesthetic surface" would maintain that the non-aesthetic and cultural connotations of the "Derelitta" are not asserted in the form of logical propositions and are not intended by the artist to be treated as if that were their nature.[48] Their truth or falsity is of interest only to the scientist who, in order to test either, must convert the content into the form of logical propositions. The theorist would grant that concepts and ideas did influence Botticelli but would nonetheless maintain that the painter's expression of significance is in color and is intended to individualize the universal propositions in question. He would attempt to direct attention, not to the problem of truth, but to the aesthetic values implicit in the structural interrelations of the figure, the background, the cast-off clothes, and the colors employed.

Ultimately, however, the theorist of "surface" would contend that the figure of Mordecai is not intended by Botticelli to be either representative or symbol of bridegroom. Rather, the figure is to be interpreted as a symbol of "feeling," a fact immediately evident in the attitude of grief, anguish, or sorrow which characterizes it. Philosophically, the argument of the structuralist would rest upon

[48] Cf. above, pp. 250 ff.

the assumption that there are degrees of "formed matter" in works of art,[49] precisely because it is impossible in aesthetic experience to distinguish form from matter. But the nerve of the argument is this, that while it is true that for the scholar, at home in the plastic arts of the Renaissance and versed in the lore of the Bible, the distinction between Mordecai and Vashti is significant and may be made only by means of the *apparatus criticus* of science, the aesthetic meaning of the symbol of grief is generic and may be apprehended by all who know or have known sorrow. The catholic appeal of the symbol is owing, on this hypothesis, precisely to the fact that such generic symbols have their meanings in themselves, meanings which are immediately evident and which are the consequence of the artist's ability to reorganize concepts, ideas, situations and events in terms of novel and complete wholes to be understood in terms of feeling.

The issue raised by these and other illustrations is one that will be examined in detail in later chapters[50] and is of significance for any judgment upon the relation between generic symbols of art and the life of feeling. We are not concerned, at this point, with the structuralist's argument that truth and falsity are irrelevant to art because art is not expression in the form of propositions. Our concern is with the structural problem, with the possibility of maintaining either that the work of art is "symbol equivalent with the thing symbolized" or that the art-object's structure is unique in that its meaning is complete without an external frame of reference.

To the question whether either possibility may be maintained, the answer must necessarily be in the negative. Regarding the first possibility, it may be asserted that the definition in question is contrary to the nature of symbols of art. In regard to the grounds urged for the uniqueness of the work of art, it may be maintained that "feeling" is itself an external "referrent." We may consider these issues in their proper order.

The invalidity of the proposition that a work of art is "symbol equivalent with the thing symbolized" is evident. A symbol is a sign

[49] Cf. above, pp. 244 ff.

[50] Below, Chaps. XI-XIV.

that "stands for" something else and this fact negates the implication of "equivalence," whether that relation is asserted to apply internally to the factors of the work of art or externally to the art-object's context. The postulate of "aesthetic surface," that "form" and "matter" in the work of art are identical, implies that "form" is not a symbol but a replica of "matter." To argue that a portion of a painting is a "symbol equivalent with the thing symbolized" is likewise invalid, as an illustration will indicate. To identify the Mordecai of the "Derelitta" with Biblical or Renaissance religious beliefs or cultural practices is impossible, since he is obviously a "sign" symbolizing a much larger whole. To argue that a work of art as a whole is its own frame of reference would be to maintain that Botticelli's painting is fully meaningful within the limits of the six panels. This, it is evident from the foregoing argument, is likewise untrue.

The invalidity of the statement that a work of art is "symbol equivalent with the thing symbolized" may be shown more affirmatively. It will be recalled that the equivalence of symbol and thing symbolized is asserted by the philosopher intent upon freeing art from judgments apparently implicated by the art-object's non-aesthetic content in relations external to the "surface" of the object. It is, however, precisely the non-aesthetic aspects of fine art that prove the untruth of the proposition in question. It is past denial that non-aesthetic factors do affect the "Derelitta." It is true, nonetheless, and was made evident in our previous examination of non-aesthetic teleological theories of art,[51] that no work of art is explicable solely in non-aesthetic terms. It was observed that the artist selects and idealizes. "Symbol equivalent with the thing symbolized" incorrectly estimates the product of his selection and idealization. If we regard symbolization, for the moment, as a proximate end of artistic technique, it is plainly a method used at least in part to eliminate such non-aesthetic factors in object, idea, event, or incident to be expressed as would tend to destroy the form or unity of the work of art intended by the artist. It is true that to the work of art as a mere "object" or "event" among other "objects" or

[51] See above, Chap. VI.

"events" inhere primitive spatial and temporal characteristics simply because "objects" and "events" occupy space and are in time. It was observed in consequence that a painting may be used to cover a blank wall or that a sculptured figure may decorate a garden. It is also true, however, that once the artist has "made" the work of art, these spatial and temporal characteristics may properly be regarded as "accidents." The spatial and temporal relations of the work of art have potential aesthetic value and meaning, but once the object is made, they do so only if the artist has integrated spatial or temporal characteristics in the object or event. By way of illustration, mass and volume do enter directly into the aesthetic experience of the Cathedral of Seville. They do so because the builders of that edifice have depended for their effects upon the sheer weight of the stone as it is used in the symbol. Similarly, the artist may satisfy his selfish interests because the art-object may be used as an instrument in the economic world. These interests may be irrelevant to the work of art as a symbol but they are not so of necessity. They may be selected by the artist and objectified, let us say, in a portrayal of avarice, envy, or sloth.

That "equivalent with" signifies replica and is non-aesthetic, and "selected from" is characteristic of the making of symbols of art is evident if we consider the fact that it is impossible for a work of art to be identical with the something it symbolizes. There are, no doubt, differences in the subtlety of suggestion made by symbols. It would be difficult to discover a more determined attempt, for example, to produce a replica than George Puttenham's "making" of "prettie conceits." In one instance, the poem is made of "Her Majesties resembled to the crowned pillar."[52] It would be equally difficult to find an artistic symbol less like Puttenham's poem than Brancusi's, *The Bird*. Puttenham obeys the rules of realism to the extent that his poem is printed in the shape of a pillar. Brancusi, on the contrary, omits all details that might identify the brass figure with any bird known to the ornithologist. The sculptured figure is a symbol of "flight." Yet, despite Puttenham's effort to produce a symbol most closely resembling the "thing symbolized," the poem

[52] *The Arte of English Poesie*, p. 97.

as a pillar is described by the poet as one "*signifying* stay, support, rest, state, and magnificence."

Not only must it be denied that symbolism is "equivalence" but a negative reply must similarly be given to the question whether the work of art is unique in requiring no external frame of reference. At this point, we may limit our consideration of the problem to such generic symbols of art as appear to bear direct relation to "feeling."[53] There are indeed instances in which symbols expressing grief, fear, anger, remorse, and the like, appear to be comprehensible upon direct inspection. Strictly to maintain this postulate of a complete frame of reference in the work of art, the theory of "aesthetic surface" must describe the conative aspects of a given work in terms of "formed sensuous media." It would be difficult to ascertain what this would signify but if it meant anything it is likely that it would imply that aesthetic analysis could be completed by the study of the almost infinitely differentiated morphological characteristics of so-called "sensuous data," i.e., color, light, shade, harmony, and balance. It is evident that morphological factors are valuable for artistic analysis in distributive terms. It is nonetheless true that their full meaning for aesthetic experience is not known until the factors are evaluated in collective terms, as well. Once the "sensuous" factors are considered collectively, they relate to ends. They presuppose a "total structure" in contrast to the limited one described by the theory of "aesthetic surface." The "total structure" of art comprehends "feeling" or imagination and the unique aesthetic end for art. "Formed sensuous media," or the "sensuous aesthetic surface" presuppose the correlative terms "feeling" or "imagination."[54] The meaning of the latter terms transcends the work of art and implies an external frame of reference, precisely as the intellectual factors transcend the "surface" of the "Derelitta."

One may go further, even in a preliminary analysis of the "total structure" of the work of art. It would be an error to conclude from the statement that "feeling" or "imagination" transcends the

[53] The supposed "immediacy" of conative experience is further examined in Chap. XI, particularly pp. 353 ff.

[54] Cf. above, Chap. VII, pp. 232 ff.

object of art, precisely as do the intellectual factors, that even a work of art of the magnitude of Rembrandt's "Dr. Tulp's Anatomy Lesson" presupposes two distinct external frames of reference, the one scientific or philosophical, the other conative. Were that conclusion sound, art would be by nature rent asunder and aesthetic experience similarly would be bifurcated. The inference appears to follow only in consequence of an analytic procedure which erroneously "abstracts" the intellectual and the conative factors. "Feelings" are not "abstract" except as theory "abstracts" them. They are aroused by and are attached in experience to persons, ideas, situations, objects, attitudes, events, and incidents. In aesthetic experience, they are evoked by non-aesthetic symbolic "content"[55] and the effect of the "content" is heightened by the sensuous media, the means by which the artist expresses the "content." The artist does not feel *in vacuo* as he creates nor does the perceiver of art feel *in vacuo* as he recreates the artist's expression. Considered solely as a craftsman, the artist initially does appear to be distinguished by the attention he pays to the "surface" of the object and to its preparation for sensuous enjoyment. Regarded as a fine artist, however, it is evident that the craftsman's attention to the "surface" is, in point of fact, directed to the presentation in symbolized form of ideas and "images" derived from morality, philosophy, religion, science, and nature which refer to "feeling."

The artist may not be distinguished from the philosopher or the moralist or the scientist by asserting that the former does not employ philosophical, ethical, or scientific data. It has been shown that he does use that data. Nor may he be distinguished from them on the ground that only he pays attention to the "surface" of the object.

If it is recalled, however, that the correlative of "sensible media" is "feeling" or "imagination,"[56] it may be suggested that the artist may tentatively be distinguished from philosopher and moralist because he directs his efforts to the production of a symbol which may convey "feeling" concerning the non-aesthetic factors in the work produced. The most obvious inference to be drawn at this

[55] Cf. below, Part III, Chap. X ff.

[56] See above, Chap. VII.

point from "aesthetic surface" would be that the work of art is a "symbol of feeling." Whether the inference is sound and, if sound, the degree to which it assists in the solution to aesthetic issues, are questions which must be investigated.[57] But whether or not the inference may be validated, the work of art is certainly not a "symbol equivalent with the thing symbolized."

VII

IT IS impossible to conclude that the theory of "aesthetic surface" is adequate to perform the many tasks with which its proponents have entrusted it. The hypothesis does not provide either a sound or a complete analysis of art's structure. Its extreme assertions that "form" and "matter" are identical in the work of art and that the art-object is, in consequence, unique, are demonstrably false. Its proponents' conception of symbolism is unsound and their intention to free art from the intrusion of ends fails of achievement. As a theory of structure, "aesthetic surface" offers, in consequence, no sound resolution to the classical antinomies of art and of aesthetic experience.

It may be inferred that these incapacities and failures leave the theory a value derived only from the empirical analyses its advocates have contributed in the history of art. It would be idle to deny that "aesthetic surface" has enriched a field that lies beyond the scope of our immediate problem. It would be equally idle, however, to overlook the theory's contribution to the general problems of aesthetic. As a theory of structure, "aesthetic surface" is of primary value because it makes explicit the related issues of symbolism and feeling. The shortcomings of the theory's solution to the problem of artistic symbolism are evident but the very need for correction of its errors makes it obvious that the work of art is more than a mere "object" or "event." Moreover, if an analysis of "aesthetic surface" demonstrates the futility of restricting aesthetic to the object alone, that footless errand has not been without value: it has

[57] See above, Chap. X.

shown that in philosophy of art problems must be stated in terms not merely descriptive of "surface" but of "total structure."

It would be absurd to infer that the fundamental aesthetic problems could be solved without analysis of the work of art. It is no less absurd to suppose that the naïve approach of "aesthetic surface" suffices to resolve the antinomies of art. No mere amassing of descriptive and distributive details relevant to the work of art is adequate to that resolution. The media of the art-object, as well as other non-aesthetic factors which enter upon the aesthetic object, must receive proper consideration in a theory of the "total structure" of art. But the fact that these factors are necessarily transcended in aesthetic analysis suggests that a more inclusive hypothesis of structure takes cognizance not only of the end of art but of the relation between the end and the work as well.

We may defer consideration of the implications of a theory that properly takes the work of art to be a symbol.[58] "Symbolism" is integral to analysis in terms of "total structure" of art and the immediate and significant inference to be drawn from the structural theory of "aesthetic surface" is that "the work of art is a symbol of the artist's feelings." This inference, however, is presupposed by at least an introductory analysis of feeling. We thus return to the problem with which this essay began. We may recall that the incapacity of "abstract" ateleological aesthetic to cope with feeling was shown to result in that theory's failure to define beauty in terms of "form." We may also recall that it is in part the problem of conation that argues the inadequacy of non-aesthetic teleologies of art. It may be surmised, indeed, that in the relation of feeling to the symbols of art is to be discovered the source of, as well as the resolution to, the antinomies both of art and of aesthetic experience which presented the problem of the Introduction.

"Feeling" may be integral to the "total structure" of art and it may be the external frame of reference essential for the statement of the aesthetic problem. But the many avenues of speculation opened by its inclusion in the problems of philosophy of art scarcely lead forward unless we know not only what feeling is but are able

[58] See Part III.

also to indicate what proper relation it bears to the aesthetic object and to the aesthetic end. Some guidance for the approach to these particular problems of art's "total structure" is afforded by a selection from among the historical interpretations of Aristotle's theory of *katharsis*, to which we shall turn in the following chapter.

Chapter IX

The Theory of the "Total Structure" of Art: The Aristotelian Theory of Katharsis

"*Tragedy, . . . said by* Aristotle *to be of power by raising pity and fear, or terror, to purge the mind of those and such like passions, that is to temper and reduce them to just measure with a kind of delight, stirr'd up by reading or seeing those passions well imitated. Nor is Nature wanting in her own effects to make good his assertion: for so in Physic things of melancholic hue and quality are us'd against melancholy, sowr against sowr, salt to remove salt humours.*"

—John Milton

THE assumption that the work of art may be analyzed as a structure in isolation from either "feeling" or end is, as we have observed, ill-founded. It would occasion little surprise, however, if, at frequent intervals in the course of aesthetic speculation, the theory of "surface" were restated. One need consider the difficulties alone implicit in relating art-objects to feeling to realize that few aestheticians would willingly subscribe to the complex principles of the "total structure" of art if the aims of the simpler theory of "surface" were possible of achievement.

The nature and detail of the problems, peripheral and central to the analysis of aesthetic experience and inherent in the more complex theory, will be plain as this essay proceeds. The character of the principal problem presupposed in the relation of art to conation is evident from a question asked in the *Republic*.[1] Socrates remarks, after his initial condemnation of mimetic art, that "we have not yet

[1] *Op. cit.*, 605-606.

brought forward the heaviest count in our indictment." The "heaviest count," as we know,[2] is that poetic imitation "waters and cherishes" the emotions. There is a brief stay, however, before judgment is passed upon the poet—that "light and wingéd and holy thing,"—whose "making" of "images," on Plato's view, may imperil the well ordered state. It appears possible, indeed, that he may be freed from the sentence of exile because there is a yet unconsidered alternative to the argument that has led to conviction. May it not be wise, the alternative urges, to indulge that part of the soul which "has hungered for the privilege of weeping and bewailing itself fully and without stint because it is its nature to covet this satisfaction"? And may one not indulge it safely by means of poetry which "feeds the very part to satiety"?

The alternative is entertained only to be rejected: "For it is given, I think, only to a few to reflect that the conduct of other people must necessarily influence their own, and that it is no easy matter, after feeling the strength of the principle of pity upon the sufferings of others, to keep it under restraint when we suffer ourselves." Plato concludes, in effect, that indulgence in emotion, whether through the medium or the subject matter of art or by means of the self-pity engendered by misfortune in personal affairs, strengthens rather than weakens the passionate soul's demands. The black horse of *Phaedrus* must submit to "blow or spur."

Plato resolutely renounces all indulgence of the passionate part of the soul. He defends the decision on the grounds that "it would be a sin to betray what seems to us the cause of truth." But Aristotle's analysis of poetic and musical experience has its correlative theory of the *katharsis* of emotions and thus a variant of the rejected alternative comes to be a doctrine central to *Poetics.* One consequence of this historical disagreement is that a form of the theory that indulgence of feeling benefits the soul is expounded in perhaps the most influential single work written upon a particular art. One may recall, perhaps, at this juncture, that Aristotle studied for twenty years in the Academy. It would be a serious error, however, to assume that the theory of *katharsis* is merely a disciple's

[2] See above, pp. 14 ff.

reformulation of a master's teaching. The error is the more difficult to avoid because neither in *Poetics* nor in *Politics* does Aristotle state precisely how, on his view, the purgation of emotion frees poetry and music from the indictment brought against them by Plato.

It is essential to remember that *Poetics* is the first notable attempt by a thinker other than Plato and one, moreover, at least of equal stature, to resolve the antinomies of art and aesthetic experience implicit in Platonic philosophy. If in this instance, Aristotle's words are cryptic, either because the text is mutilated or the speculation was never concluded, it is nonetheless evident that they are integral to a philosophy of art that is more than a bare assertion that Plato erred. Aristotle does not maintain that all art effects a proper purgation of the emotions, nor does he assert that all purgations are aesthetic experience. He exercises care in classifying the kinds of music in *Politics*, and *Poetics* has been a model by comparison to which later analyses of single arts and their subject matter have frequently been evaluated. Aristotle's stature as a philosopher is no less evident in his writings upon art than elsewhere. The consequence is that *katharsis* of emotions is not properly evaluated if judged merely as a repetition of Platonism. It appears as part of a classic illustration of the treatment of art as a "total structure": the place and interrelation of objects, "feeling," and end in that structure are paid proper attention.

A study of *Poetics* as a whole is beyond both the scope or needs of this essay. The statement of the Aristotelian problem affords some opportunity to recapitulate and reinforce conclusions arrived at previously in this study, as well as to indicate the future course of its argument. But the primary purpose of this chapter is to discover, if possible, the grounds for the assumption implicit in Aristotle's philosophy of art that analysis of the emotions and of the change they undergo, accompanied by a systematic account of poetry and music, shows how the dangers imputed by Plato to the experience of art are mitigated. Approached in this way, the theory of *katharsis* appears at the outset to be merely an additional alternative to ateleological, to non-aesthetic teleological, and to structural hypotheses such as that of "surface," in philosophy of art. No doubt, one may regard this progenitor of innumerable "defenses of poesie" as if it were merely one more effort to satisfy Plato's demand that a philosophy of art prove its competence by demonstrating that poetry and other arts are "profitable as well as pleasurable."

Nor need one doubt that there is much in Aristotle's philosophy of art that may be justly evaluated on these grounds alone. Yet, the history of the theory of *katharsis* suggests that to judge it merely as one among numerous efforts to resolve the Platonic problem is to ignore its unique claims to the aesthetician's attention. It is no small gain for aesthetic, for example, that Aristotle's theory attempts to counter the charge in Plato's indictment on grounds as nearly like the Athenian's as is possible for a philosophy that has different metaphysical presuppositions. Aristotle in *Poetics* grants, by implication, that Plato is correct in assuming that "feeling" poses a central problem in the evaluation of art and its experience, that, in fact, the "heaviest count" against the artist may well be implicit in the statement that his art indulges the passions. In addition, the Aristotelian argument implies that the issue in question may not be evaded. The reader encounters here no arbitrarily limited aesthetic universe of discourse; no flight from the realm of art to the empyrean of transcendental beauty; no deviation from the assumptions concerning feeling which are relevant to *De Anima*, *Rhetoric*, and *Nicomachean Ethics*, altered to resolve difficulties considered unique for art; and no easy success attained by reliance upon "ostensible" ends to account for serious activities.

One is tempted, indeed, to infer more concerning the peculiar status of the theory of *katharsis*. The juxtaposition of Aristotle's analysis of music[3] in this theory and in that of play suggests that the Peripatetic philosophy of art tended to assign to passionate art the benefits it explicitly bestows upon the playful. It was inferred in the present essay,[4] that Aristotle makes art an "energizer" of man's spirit, as it was also inferred that the play-theory of art owes not a little as an explanatory hypothesis in aesthetic to its author's recognition of this fact. The implication recurs in the discussion of

[3] *Politics* 1337 b 40 ff.

[4] Cf. above, Chap. VII, pp. 225-226.

passionate art but with one important distinction: to the ends of the activity in question no longer pertain the slightest implication of lack of seriousness. Moreover, a structure not inappropriate to the end in question is analyzed at length.

The seriousness of the activity is beyond doubt, for Aristotle, like Plato, does consider the passions to be potentially dangerous. In *Politics*,[5] by way of illustration, we are informed that, "Since then music is a pleasure, and virtue consists in rejoicing and loving and hating aright, there is clearly nothing which we are so much concerned to acquire and to cultivate as the power of forming right judgments, and of taking delight in good dispositions and noble actions." Moreover, in the same book,[6] there appears the admonition: "Let the young practise even such music as we have prescribed, only until they are able to feel delight in noble melodies and rhythms, and not merely in that common part of music in which every slave or child and even some animals find pleasure."

The nature of the antinomic effect of the experience of passionate art, not unlike that derived from play or amusement, presents a more controversial issue.[7] There is little doubt that Aristotle believed that by means of passionate melody—and presumably by tragic poetry—not only is "healing" possible but that "all are in a manner purged and their souls lightened and delighted." It is not unlikely that he implies more than this: since it is the ecstatic modes and modes of action which are particularly appropriate for *katharsis*, one may infer that Aristotle assumed that, like play or amusement, the ex-

[5] *Op. cit.*, 1340 a 15. (B. Jowett's translation. By permission of the Clarendon Press, publishers.)

[6] *Op. cit.*, 1341 a 12.

[7] The controversy arises because Aristotle divides musical melodies into "ethical melodies, melodies of action, and passionate or inspiring melodies, each having, as they say, a mode corresponding to it." He proceeds to make distinctions among the various ends of music. "But now," as the problem is stated in F. Susemihl and R. D. Hicks, *Aristotle's Politics*, pp. 638 ff, "the question . . . has to be considered: the relation, namely, of *catharsis* to the two other ends previously recognised, recreation (ἀνάπαυσις) and the highest rational enjoyment (διαγωγή)." It is sufficient for the argument in this essay to point to Susemihl's and Hicks' concluding remarks: "*catharsis* is only a means to one or the other of these ends"; and "it is the ecstatic modes and those of action which are said to be specially appropriate for *catharsis*, and it is to the ecstatic melodies that the explanation as given applies."

perience of *katharsis* is a source of energy and like relaxation, "taken for the sake of activity."[8] If this inference is sound, we are again introduced to an attempted resolution of the antinomies of art and its experience formulated in terms that make art an "energizer" of man's spirit, without the mystical implications associated with that process in transcendental ateleological aesthetic and without the suspicion of triviality of end ordinarily attributed to play.[9]

These inferences are sufficient to recommend Aristotle's method and subject matter and to justify the assumption that his philosophy of art has special claims to our consideration. One fact, however, may argue a lack of wisdom in one who places reliance upon the theory of *katharsis* in aesthetic analysis. Aristotle wrote of *katharsis,* in *Politics*, that "we use [it] at present without explanation, but when hereafter we speak of poetry, we will treat the subject with more precision."[10] This promise is not fulfilled. The consequent lack of "precision" in *Poetics* has made the question of the significance of "purgation" a controversial issue in philosophy. Indeed, Zeller concluded that "as to the purifying effect of Art, we must admit that to this day, after all the endless discussions to which Aristotle's definition of Tragedy has given rise, no agreement has been arrived at upon the question wherein, according to his view, it consists and what are the conditions of its production."[11]

If Zeller's conclusion is sound, is not the theory's value for aesthetic analysis thereby nullified? To reply affirmatively magnifies a misfortune that undoubtedly has befallen philosophy of art. There are some considerations, however, which tend to compensate for Aristotle's failure to offer the "precise explanation." In the first place, as will be evident, Zeller's statement overemphasizes the scholarly disagreement as concerns Aristotle's meaning. Secondly, Aristotle's incisive statement of the problem suggests that he goes to its root. This directness, accompanying the riddle concerning his meaning, has educed interpretations of *katharsis* which tempt the philosophy of art to repeat Dr. Johnson's commendation of one of

[8] Cf. above, Chap. VII, pp. 225 ff.
[9] Cf. above, Chaps. II, pp. 73, 77-78 ff., and VII, p. 209.
[10] *Op. cit.*, 1341 b 37-38.
[11] *Aristotle and the Earlier Peripatetics*, Vol. 2, pp. 309-310.

Warburton's readings of Shakespeare: "This is a noble emendation, which almost sets the critick on the level with the author." Finally, and most significantly for the present essay, the lack of "precision" has been a challenge alike for Aristotelians and aestheticians to reconstruct the text and to bring every effort to bear to search out the meaning of *katharsis*. The consequence is that the modern interpretations, which begin in 1527 with Paccius,[12] may be used to provide a philosopher of art with a needed *organon*. As such, they will be helpful for the task of summarizing and reinforcing certain conclusions drawn in the preceding chapters of the present essay. But they will prove to be more valuable as a means by which one may classify and evaluate structural theories of art which emphasize the relation of the object of art to feeling. So varied and far-ranging have been the possible and improbable readings of *Poetics* and *Politics* on the subject of *katharsis* that few inferences concerning the possible relations of art to context, to end, and to conation have not been drawn from them. Varied as they are, however, the interpretations that do supply a basis for an *apparatus criticus* in aesthetic may be classified if two relevant factors are kept in mind: there must be approximate agreement upon certain presuppositions of Aristotle's theory, as well as a sufficient divergence in the emphases placed by authors upon one or more of the factors that enter into the "total structure" of art. An *organon* of the kind suggested is thus neither independent of nor wholly dependent upon Aristotle's original meaning. Its principal value in the present context is to afford an instrument for the analysis of the general problem of "feeling" and the specific problem of the function of "feeling" in aesthetic experience.

II

WHILE it is an error to suppose that Aristotle's philosophy of art is merely a heritage from Plato, it is unwise to conclude that the divergence in their estimate of the value of indulging

[12] Cf. the synopsis of versions and paraphrases of the relevant passages in *Poetics* in I. Bywater, *Aristotle on the Art of Poetry*, pp. 361-365.

the emotions in art is characteristic of their writings upon art as a whole. By way of illustration, we have already used at a crucial point the Platonic anticipation of Aristotle's distinction between "acting" and "making."[13] A similarity in approach more nearly relevant to the present issue concerns the artist's relation *qua* artist to his audience and the nature of the audience's reaction to the work of art.

In this connection, it will be recalled that Plato in *Ion*[14] tends to interpret the work of art as a "symbol" or "sign" for the poet's or the rhapsode's emotional state and concludes that the "symbol" effects a similar emotional state in the audience. Aristotle's interpretation is not dissimilar. Thus, in *Politics*, we learn that:

> . . . when men hear imitations, even apart from the rhythms and tunes themselves, their feelings move in symphony. . . . Rhythm and melody supply imitations of anger and gentleness, and also of courage and temperance, and of all the qualities contrary to these, and of other qualities of character, which hardly fall short of the actual affections, as we know from our own experience, for in listening to such strains our souls undergo a change. The habit of feeling pleasure or pain at mere representations is not far removed from the same feeling about realities.[15]

But while Aristotle's opinion in this regard does not differ substantially from Plato's, since the former intends to show that the feeling about "representations" is "not far removed from the same feeling about realities," there is a systematic difference in the philosophies that does affect the problem of "purgation." For Plato, the universal is *ante rem*, for Aristotle it is *in re*. We have previously met in the transcendental version of ateleological aesthetic one consequence of a phase of history's translation of Plato's theory of forms. It is sufficient, therefore, to remark at this juncture that the particular hypothesis influenced Aristotle's theory of poetry only to a limited degree. It introduced into his poetic theory some didacticism and led later theorists to defend, on supposedly Aristotelian

[13] Cf. above, pp. 185 ff.

[14] Cf. above, pp. 19-20 and below, Chap. X.

[15] From *Politics*, 1340 A 13 ff. Translated by B. Jowett. (Clarendon Press, Oxford). Cf. *Problems* XIX.

grounds, the position that art in copying the universal produces the typical.

More significantly, however, the theory of the universal in the thing and the attention paid to the process by which matter attains to its form lead Aristotle closer in analysis to the object "made" than Plato is brought by the philosophy of Ideas. Perhaps no less significant is the fact that Aristotle's interests were implicated in contemporary empirical science and more specifically in medical and biological techniques. One consequence of the systematic divergences in the two philosophies is that Aristotle concludes that the artist need not produce a work of art necessarily implicated in deception.

The famous definition of tragedy offered in *Poetics* is not prodigal of words in regard to *katharsis*: "A tragedy, then, is the imitation of an action that is serious and also, as having magnitude, complete in itself; in language with pleasurable accessories, each kind brought in separately in the parts of the work; in a dramatic, not in a narrative form; with incidents arousing pity and fear, wherewith to accomplish its catharsis of such emotions."[16] We may be less concerned by the cryptic character of the definition once we turn to *Politics* and observe there the consequences of Aristotle's interest in science. "Some persons," he writes, "fall into a religious frenzy, whom we see as a result of the sacred melodies—when they have used the melodies that excite the soul to mystic frenzy—restored as though they had found healing and purgation."[17] The philosopher's interest is not alone aroused by possible cures for frenzy induced by sacred melodies. "Those who are influenced by pity or fear, and every emotional nature, must have a like experience, and others in so far as each is susceptible to such emotions, and all are in a manner purged and their souls lightened and delighted."

In consequence of the divergence of interest in empirical science, what for Plato is merely an illustration given in passing concerning the "madness" of the corybantes and the means by which children

[16] *Op. cit.*, 6. 1449 b 24. Translation by Ingram Bywater, *op. cit.* (Clarendon Press, Oxford.)

[17] *Op. cit.*, 1342 a 8 ff. Translated by B. Jowett (Clarendon Press, Oxford.)

may be quieted becomes for Aristotle a theory by which indulgence both in drama and in certain melodies may be justified by reference to the curative powers which contemporary medicine attributed to "sacred melodies."

It is evident, from the passage in *Politics*, that a reconsideration is necessary of Zeller's conclusion that "no agreement has been arrived at upon the question wherein it [the purifying effect of art] consists and what are the conditions of its production." Controversy persists as to Aristotle's meaning but, since Zeller wrote, Bywater's *Aristotle on the Art of Poetry* has exerted its just influence and Bernays' theory[18] has received the benefit of the English scholar's commentary. In consequence of this and other investigations, there are points concerning Aristotle's theory upon which scholars are in general agreement. It is generally conceded, for example, that Aristotle does not limit the application of *katharsis* to poetry. He uses it to explain the effects of certain forms of music. He may have used it to explain the experience of comedy and perhaps he considered its relation to arts other than music and poetry.[19] It is also fairly widely agreed that the emotions in question are not limited solely to pity and fear. Since Bernays' time, there has been general agreement also that Aristotle's theory is an aesthetic specification of a medicinal and physiological interpretation of the purgation of evil humors and that in the latter aspect, the theory in *Poetics* was anticipated by Plato but given a different reference in the *Laws*.[20]

[18] *Zwei Abhandlungen über die Aristotelische Theorie des Drama.*

[19] Bywater, *op. cit.*, p. 152, points out that the translation, "its catharsis" removes many preliminary difficulties in the theory, "the implication being that a cathartic effect is not peculiar to Tragedy." This not only relates the passages in *Poetics* and *Politics*, "in which the existence of several forms of catharsis is affirmed" but "there is reason to think that a catharsis of laughter also must have been similarly posited as the effect and ultimate justification of Comedy." Bywater concludes that the theory is not limited to pity and fear but is applicable to this whole group of disturbing emotions. See also W. L. Newman, *The Politics of Aristotle*; Susemihl and Hicks, *op. cit.* E. Zeller, *op. cit.*; S. H. Butcher, *Aristotle's Theory of Poetry and Fine Art* and J. A. Stewart, *Notes on the Nicomachean Ethics.*

[20] *Op. cit.*, 790 ff. We are told that the restlessness of children and the frenzy of the Bacchic women are stilled, not by rest but by motion, not by quiet but by dance and music. Plato allies the cures for these apparently diverse states by his suggestion that both the affections of the Bacchantes and

The interpretations to which we shall now turn are in sufficient agreement upon these presuppositions to satisfy the conditions of the problem of the "total structure" of art. They are also sufficiently divergent in their emphases—since no sound analysis completely ignores any one element in the relation of object to subject—to encompass the more important variations in interpretation. Finally, each is sufficiently typical of other interpretations in the long tradition to permit speculation upon general aesthetic principles implicit in *katharsis*.

The interpretations in question are those presented in Bywater's *Aristotle on the Art of Poetry*, Butcher's *Aristotle's Theory of Poetry and Fine Art* and Zeller's *Aristotle and the Later Peripatetics*.[21] The first lays emphasis upon objective factors external to the work of art; the second centers attention upon the subjective factors in the relations of object of art and "feeling"; the third limits the relevant objective factors to those internal to the work of art and offers a theory in which subjective and objective factors are accorded equal importance. Butcher's and Zeller's analyses differ in another significant respect. The former implies that there is a possible generic differentiation between aesthetic and non-aesthetic "feelings." Zeller makes no such assumption.

A

Bywater's interpretation is one which emphasizes the primarily objective factors in Aristotle's theory of *katharsis*. Its resolution of the difficulties in the theory brings to the fore the problem of the

---

of the children are emotions of fear, springing from evil habits of the soul. An external agent, motion, is applied to a violent internal one and produces calm and peace in the soul. For the Bacchic women, Plato tells us, music and dance produce a sound mind to replace the frenzy. Both Plato and Aristotle give credence to the medicinal interpretation, in referring to Bacchic rites and to the devotees who are stimulated to a frenzy by dancing and by passionate music. Cf. Aristotle, *Politics*, 3.6, 1341 a 21 et 7.1341 b 19, 1342 a 31. Also see Stewart, *op. cit.*, Vol. 2, p. 439, as well as Susemihl and Hicks, and Newman, *op. cit.*

[21] Zeller's doubt concerning the possibility of agreement upon the problem need not preclude the use of his own interpretation. His view anticipates presuppositions and conclusions of later writers.

extent to which the "context" of the work of art may be included in aesthetic analysis and, therefore, within the "total structure" of art. The difficulty has been met before in this essay in the discussion of the frame of reference adequate for a description of the "Derelitta."[22]

The problem of context is raised in connection with the theory of *katharsis* once Bywater concludes that Aristotle replies to Plato's denial of the benefits of indulgence in emotion in poetic and musical experience by maintaining that "purgation" is beneficial because the occasional presentation of tragedy in the Greek city-state did not allow the generation of a "moral habit." The interpretation suggests[23] that Aristotle "would seem to have been mindful of the position of the Drama in Greek life . . . the dramatic performances in the theatre were not sufficiently frequent or continuous to generate a moral habit, or make a lasting impression for good or evil on character." But is is plain that the nerve of Bywater's argument is the allocation of a significant function to the lawgiver rather than to the musician or the poet. Regarding the latter, the interpretation holds that "the great function of the tragic poet, he [Aristotle] thinks, is to excite certain emotions, and procure us the pleasure that must accompany such excitement. . . . This pleasurable excitement of emotion, in fact, is with him the end and aim of Tragedy, so far as the poet himself is concerned." It is, rather, the role of the statesman or lawgiver that is of primary interest for Bywater at this juncture. "The statesman, however, viewing human nature and society as a whole, is able to look beyond all this, and see the ultimate justification of the existence of Tragedy. In the Politics, accordingly, Aristotle recognizes the usefulness of Tragedy, explaining that it supplies a natural want, as a sort of *catharsis* of emotion, which as emotional creatures men require from time to time to keep their souls in health and quietude."[24]

It is instructive to have before us this extended quotation from

[22] Cf. above, pp. 273 ff.

[23] *Op. cit.*, pp. 152-161. In what follows, Bywater's argument is either quoted or paraphrased. The quotations are printed by permission of the Clarendon Press, Oxford.

[24] The reader will note that this interpretation appears to carry to its logical conclusion one implication of the play-theory of art made explicit above, Chapter VII, pp. 223 ff.

the commentary's conclusion because its author maintains there it constitutes "a reasonable apology for Tragedy, and a sufficient answer to Plato's criticism." But to achieve the status of a "reasonable apology," it is evident that it must contend that the dangers inherent in emotional experience are alleviated by a means external to the unified work of art and that the antinomies of aesthetic experience implicit in Plato's philosophy of art may be resolved by recourse to legislative or religious means. It will be of value to examine the hypothesis at length.

The conclusion in *Aristotle on the Art of Poetry* depends, as we have observed, upon the discussion of music in *Politics*. Bywater argues that Aristotle, writing as a political philosopher, demonstrates that the function of the "enthusiastic" melodies is salutary, inasmuch as it restores to normal conditions of peace and calm those persons subject to excess enthusiasm, as if the individual had undergone a *katharsis* at the hands of a physician. *Katharsis* means in general Greek medicine the clearance or discharge of something which, if retained, would produce harm. Pity and fear are presumably of such character and they are elements in human nature, possessed by some men to a great degree. To such men, tragic excitement is necessary but it is good for all men to some degree. The soul is relieved of accumulated emotion and harmless pleasure is provided.

The reasons for Bywater's emphasis upon the occasional and infrequent use of drama[25] to produce such pleasurable excitement are made sufficiently evident: even if it is granted, he argues, that the "tragic excitement" of emotion is taken to have occurred with sufficient frequency to produce a habit, "we have no right to suppose that the habitual indulgence of strong emotion (e.g., pity and fear) will weaken its force or reduce it to just measure."

This is sound criticism and as a conclusion has a significance for other than Aristotelian studies on art. But because, according to Aristotle, habits are inculcated by activities, habituation by repetition would produce "a habit of strong emotion."[26] But, Bywater

[25] *Op. cit.*, p. 156.

[26] Aristotle, *op. cit.*, "A *catharsis* in the medical sense of the word is an ἰατρεία and only for occasional use."

argues, Aristotle means neither that the theater is a school, nor that the tragic poet is a teacher of morality. The Aristotelian position is, rather, that "the great function of the tragic poet . . . is to excite certain emotions." As we have observed, however, with reference to the legislator, it is suggested that Aristotle does mean that tragedy is useful inasmuch as "it supplies a natural want, as a sort of *catharsis* of emotion, which as emotional creatures men require from time to time to keep their souls in health and quietude."

The historian of Greek culture or the chronicler of the theater may well welcome Bywater's interpretation and commend its recognition that conditions attendant upon the performance of Greek drama may not be ignored. The problem of the present essay is, rather, whether from this "reasonable apology" may be derived a principle sufficiently general to resolve the antinomy of art and of aesthetic experience. The problem may be put and the question it evokes may be asked in this context, although it must be made plain that the general problem raised by the relation of art to feeling in aesthetic experience does not fall within the scope of Bywater's inquiry. It has been maintained, however, in the present essay that Plato states a theory central to general philosophy of art and that the antinomies implied in his writings are not merely consequent upon an interest in statecraft. Bywater's interpretation of Aristotle may be correct, precisely as A. S. Ferguson's argument[27] that Plato in the *Republic* is "concerned with the right of the poet to guide opinion" may be well founded, but the general aesthetic problem remains.

It is plain, at the outset, that this interpretation of *katharsis* as a "purge" prescribed by or with the tacit approval of the legislator admits that Plato's condemnation is valid in its conclusion that "indulgence" in emotion is harmful. Plato charges that poetic art "waters and cherishes" the emotions. Bywater concludes that Aristotle agrees that the "great function of the tragic poet . . . is to excite certain emotions." The "reasonable apology" is "reasonable" precisely because it grants that excitation of the emotions in the experience of art is dangerous, since "we have no right to suppose

[27] See "Plato and the Poet's ΕΙΔΩΛΑ."

that the habitual indulgence[28] of strong emotion will weaken or reduce it to just measure." It may be assumed, therefore, that Aristotle, no less than Plato, recognized potentialities for danger in music or poetry *per se*. Nor is there doubt that the passage in *Politics* is indispensable for the interpretation of the cryptic references in *Poetics*. The basic issue, however, is whether the analysis of *katharsis* in musical experience in its context in a treatise on politics may be transferred with the implications of that context to a passage concerned primarily with the art of poetry. The most obvious consequence of Bywater's concentration upon the passage in *Politics* is that a sharp distinction is drawn between *katharsis* as an instrument used by a wise statesman and the end of art induced by the poet's or the musician's capacity to "excite certain emotions." One tends to underestimate the importance of the fact that the homeopathic theory applied to feeling implies that the work of art must be "made" so that it can effect the end proposed by the legislator. Whether the latter's use of the object made is entirely compatible with the end for which the artist made it is another question. But if the distinction between legislator and poet is pushed far enough, one may infer that the artist has no concern with the proper evocation—the "just measure"—of emotion induced by his art. If this is Aristotle's opinion, the conclusion is forced that *katharsis* is but one of many historical non-aesthetic teleologies of art[29] and that it differs from others only in that it employs the end of political action to justify aesthetic experience and to explain whatever beneficial effects art may have. This is, in fact, implied in Bywater's words, "ultimate justification of the existence of Tragedy."[30]

The non-aesthetic teleological hypothesis of art has already shown flaws. Bywater's specific formulation, if the theory is considered a model for an aesthetic, adds to their number. If it is assumed that a *katharsis* of emotion is beneficial only if it is effected with sufficient

[28] On A. S. Ferguson's argument, *op. cit.*, one may go farther than this. Ferguson regards Plato's theory in *Republic* X to be the conclusion of the lawgiver concerned with the right of the poet to guide opinion. The emphasis here is obviously on the word "habitual." But it should be insisted that emotion may be "strong" without its exercise having become habitual.

[29] Cf. above, Chaps. VI and VII.

[30] *Op. cit.*, p. 161. Cf. above, p. 225, fn. 32.

infrequency to cause no habit of strong emotion, it does not necessarily follow that infrequency of emotional experience implies that the emotion in question and upon the occasion of its discharge is not powerful.[31] Pity and fear are not "mild" emotions, even if it is granted that habit has not yet made their occurrence customary. This, it would appear, is admitted by Bywater in his suggestion that the emotions in question are elements in human nature and are possessed by some men in great degree.

It would be absurd to deny that indulgence is not restricted by infrequency of emotional experience, or to argue that control of indulgence does not inhibit the growth of habit. These admissions do not affect, however, the dangers attendant upon any indulgence *qua* indulgence, once it is admitted that the emotion is dangerous and that music and poetry may be dangerous *per se*. It may be urged, in fact, that Bywater's interpretation does not concern the "reduction" of emotion to "just measure." Rather, it turns upon the control by external means of violent emotion in a citizen throughout his civic life. The point is evident if we consider the actual theory of the "reduction" of emotion offered by Aristotle in the *Nicomachean Ethics*. The issue, as it is presented in that text, is that of moral virtue and as Mure says, a "right ratio (λόγος) correlates response and feeling, and so renders the degree of response-and-feeling a mean between excess and defect."[32] It may conceivably be argued that the lawgiver's function in permitting or bringing about *katharsis* is analogous to that of "right reason" but, if so, the emphasis must be upon the word "analogous." On Bywater's hypothesis, habit is not strengthened and emotions are "purged." But the former does not diminish to "just measure" the strong feeling and only retards it from attaining its most extreme state; the latter presumably eliminates the emotion.

It may still be concluded that Bywater has recovered Aristotle's meaning and that the author of *Poetics* intended only to make a "reasonable apology" as one political theorist to another. But before this conclusion may be accepted, other facts that weigh against it

[31] Cf. Bywater, *ibid.*, p. 161.
[32] G. R. G. Mure, *Aristotle*, p. 141.

should be considered. In the first place, Aristotle specifically writes that concerning musical education "we shall only speak of it now after the manner of the legislator, stating the general principles."[33] But if the factors internal to the work of art bear so little upon the resolution of the Platonic problem, it is difficult to account for Aristotle's preoccupation with the details of poetry and music. Such a preoccupation might help to clarify the end for which the poet "makes" but it would be of little value because, in the light of the "ultimate justification of . . . Tragedy," there would be little to choose, for example, between drama and *saturnalia*, since either "purges" the emotions.

A second point, however, follows from the evident overemphasis in Bywater's interpretation of the passages in *Politics*. The dominance of the political context tends to confuse the statesman or lawgiver with the poet or musician. The former merely affords the "occasion" or effects the *katharsis* because he agrees that the experience is efficacious and because he anticipates benefits in purgation for the community. It may be true that the statesman discovers that infrequent performances of drama have beneficial consequences but it is the poet or the musician who produces what for the former is only an instrument useful to effect a *katharsis*. A nurse may administer a cathartic but what ensures that medicine's effectiveness may be quite beyond her knowledge. So, too, the statesman may administer the dramatic or musical cathartic but it is the poet who constructs what is administered.

There is evidence, certainly, that Aristotle regarded *katharsis* not merely as the function of the statesman but also that, regarding the most significant aspects of the theory, he attributed its effects to factors internal to the work of art. It has at times been argued that *Poetics* is a textbook for the instruction of dramatics. The "textbook" was written, however, after the tragedies of Aeschylus, Sophocles, and Euripides had been produced. Aristotle never appears to intend to deny that dramatists had supplied the ingredients for the "purge." Indeed, he writes that "the tragic pleasure is that of pity and fear, and the poet has to produce it by a work of imitation; it is

[33] *Politics* 1341 b 31.

clear, therefore, that the causes should be included in the incidents of his story."[34] He tells his reader, moreover, (and this would appear, also, to run contrary to Bywater's emphasis upon the infrequency of dramatic presentation) that "The Plot in fact should be so framed that, even without seeing the things take place, he who simply hears the account of them shall be filled with horror and pity at the incidents; which is just the effect that the mere recital of the story in *Oedipus* would have on one."[35]

It may be possible, indeed, to carry further the argument against the overemphasis of legislative and external factors. The instance to be cited is clearly not conclusive, since it suggests only an analogy. Nevertheless, it is significant that Aristotle admits that the "Spectacle" may arouse tragic fear and pity, "but they may also be aroused by the very structure and incidents of the play—which is the better way and shows the better poet."[36] The "external" factor of spectacle, it will be noted, may induce *katharsis* but there is little question concerning Aristotle's opinion of the merits of a poet who depends upon it to produce the tragic effect. One is tempted to suggest that there is implied too sharp a distinction in Bywater's interpretation between the legislator and the poet regarding their functions and that this is analogous to a distinction between the maker of the spectacle and the poet. An overemphasis in either case to the detriment of the poet would lead to confusion. One might be tempted also to argue the overemphasis on systematic grounds, as well, because to isolate the function of the "external" factor and to make much of the legislative benefits would appear to run counter to Aristotle's theory of the universal in the thing. That theory is operative in *Poetics* and affords Aristotle a means by which Plato's charge that art is deceptive may be met. It will be recalled, also, that Bywater himself assumes that Aristotle's *Poetics* is written on the assumption that "Poetry, as a distinct art, has an end, a procedure, and a correctness of its own.[37] It is difficult to entertain an

[34] *Poetics* 14.1453 b 14 ff.
[35] *Ibid.*, 14. 1453 b 4 ff.
[36] *Ibid.*, 14. 1453 b 1 ff.
[37] *Op. cit.*, p. 325. Cf. note to 1361 b 24, p. 352.

interpretation that appears to run counter to the emphasis Aristotle lays upon the unity of the work of art.

This conclusion should not lead, however, to an exaggeration of the importance in Aristotle's philosophy of factors "internal" to the work of art. It has already been observed that the spectacle may induce a *katharsis*. It should be observed, as well, that despite the differentiations between Aristotle's and Plato's philosophies of art which are consequent upon the former's principles of the *universalia in re*, the analyses of the work of art and of its experience in *Poetics* are not entirely free from either didacticism or moralism.[38] The interest in non-aesthetic teleologies in Aristotle's studies of art argues that caution is required before the "external" end attributed to the wise statesman is ruled from a consideration of the significance of *katharsis*. The evidence is far from conclusive but it may be that Bywater's offers a sound reconstruction of Aristotle's meaning. If so, the difficulty lies in Aristotle's incapacity to deal with the work of art as a symbol in which the non-aesthetic factors are unified and formed by the artist in a "sign" standing for something else.[39] We are left, therefore, with no conclusive statement concerning the limits of "context" in the "total structure" of art.

If Bywater is correct, however, Aristotle's theory of *katharsis* is not properly aesthetic. To apply the homeopathic theory of medicine to "feeling" and to explain aesthetic experience in terms of wise statesmanship is to reduce aesthetic to non-aesthetic theory. But even were Bywater's interpretation correct in its assumption that this is Aristotle's meaning, the aesthetic problem remains to be solved. We infer that Aristotle preferred that *katharsis* be effected by factors integral to the poem. We know that he was meticulous in his analysis of poetry and music. We know that he differentiated playful, purgative, and pedagogical music. We have every right to search for the factors that make tragic poetry and certain kinds of

[38] Cf. Bernard Bosanquet, *A History of Aesthetic*, particularly pp. 58 ff.

[39] Cf. *ibid.*, p. 61. It has been argued in this essay that no aesthetic object is without non-aesthetic significance. It will be argued, also, that politics, religion, science, and morality supply the objects and events symbolized by the artist. But the symbols must express the non-aesthetic factors unified within the structure of the work of art. They do have an external reference in feeling and in end but the object of art is itself unified.

music instruments the potentialities of which are actualized for *katharsis* on occasion by the statesman. Moreover, we must still learn what "just measure" implies for "feeling," what feeling is, and what "purgation" means.

The merits of Bywater's analysis are obvious. However, the political implications of Aristotle's theory have obscured a more essential problem by overemphasis upon external non-aesthetic factors. A consideration of the effect of the work of art as a unified form upon the emotions would appear to promise more for aesthetic analysis. Such a consideration is given the problem by Zeller, whose interpretation of Aristotle's *Poetics* will be briefly summarized.

B

Zeller's interpretation of *katharsis* in *Aristotle and the Earlier Peripatetics*[40] has much to commend it. Its author is judicial as he evaluates the place and significance of each factor in the "total structure" of art and the analysis is completed without overemphasis upon the value of subject, object, or end. The account recognizes the basic importance to the problem of factors internal to the tragedy or melody and is developed by reference to the Aristotelian theory of the universal in the thing. Zeller's conclusions concerning the purgation of emotion contrast sharply in some respects with Bywater's but not in regard to the generic character of feeling. Finally, and perhaps in consequence of Zeller's conclusion that Aristotle's original meaning had not been recovered, the interpretation commends itself to the aesthetician. There is offered, briefly, a philosophy of art which takes account of the laws of the art-object and presents *katharsis* in a way that makes plain the need for a sound analysis of feeling in an aesthetic adequate to its task.

We have observed that Bywater infers that *katharsis* is the reduction of emotion to "just measure." Zeller judges the term to imply the removal of expulsion of "unhealthy" affections. He assumes that Aristotle in the theory of *katharsis* had extended analogically to

[40] *Op. cit.*, Vol. 2, pp. 300-324.

poetry and music the meaning of a medical term. The German historian argues that, beginning with the literal meaning of *katharsis*, the "expulsion from the body of burdensome or injurious matter," Aristotle proceeded to develop the conception of "states of the emotions" and "came to connect with it, as he went on, the idea of deliverance from pollution and spiritual disease as well." In this way, the "purification" came to consist in "deliverance from some dominating excitement of passion or overwhelming mental depression." Zeller infers, however, that Aristotle's meaning was not that *katharsis* applied to "any purification within the soul of permanent affections, but [was] the removal from it of unhealthy ones."[41]

It is significant that neither Bywater nor Zeller believes that *katharsis* is the purification of the soul from a feeling or that a feeling is purified. Not only do their theories lack accord concerning what occurs to emotion but they are in fundamental disagreement in regard to the efficient causes effecting a proper purgation. Bywater, as has been observed, takes purgation to be primarily the tool to be used by the wise legislator. For Zeller the crucial issue is, "How does Art affect this removal?"[42] The nerve of his argument is that "this effect" of purgation "is not to be expected from all excitements indifferently, but only from such as are artistic . . . not that which produces the most violent emotion in us, but that which produces emotion in the right way."

The difficulty is obviously presented in determining the "right way" to purge the emotions. Zeller argues that the solution to the problem is to be inferred from Aristotle's theory of the universal in the thing. He urges that its application to art turns on the "peculiar nature of artistic representation itself." On his view, "the generic difference between art and reality" consists in this, that the latter presents us with the particular wherein chance rules. Art, on the contrary, presents the universal in the particular. The feelings aroused by art are purified and soothed: Art "delivers us from such [emotions] as are morbid or oppressive by exciting such as are subordinate to its law, directing them, not towards what is

[41] *Ibid.*, p. 314.
[42] *Ibid.*, p. 315.

merely personal, but towards what is universal in man, controlling their course upon a fixed principle and setting a definite limit to their force."[43] Tragedy tells us of the universal lot of man; music "calms mental excitement and holds it spellbound by its rhythm and harmony."[44]

There is specific criticism to which Zeller's analysis of the problem is susceptible. It is evident, however, that it does bring Aristotle's writing into an aesthetic context, which Bywater's interpretation of *katharsis* does not succeed fully in doing. Moreover, the unity of the work of art, exaggerated to the status of an absolute by some ateleologists,[45] is here properly evaluated in its relation to feeling and end. Zeller does draw too sharp a contrast between "reality" and "art" but he is correct in theory. Non-aesthetic teleological theories of art have demonstrated that no work of art is wholly definable without reference to non-aesthetic ends. Zeller, thinking in terms of the Aristotelian theory of the universal in the thing, judges that art is valuable precisely because the non-aesthetic events, incidents, and ideas are unified and formed in art. More significantly, they are brought under the "law" of art. In the terminology of the present essay, they are made part of the symbol called the work of art.

Zeller's statement of the problem, in fact, is a program for the theorist of the "total structure" of art, rather than a complete aesthetic. The "laws" of art and the "peculiar nature of artistic representation" must be made explicit if the difficulties are to be resolved. This is the more evident as one discovers that Zeller suggests no sound answer to the question: Why should attention to one rather than to a variety of causal series in tragedy alleviate the effects of harmful emotions?

If, as Plato argues and Aristotle tacitly agrees, the appeal of art is to the passionate soul and this may be harmful and disturbing, it may be urged that the very effort by the artist to unify the non-aesthetic factors to which feeling "attaches" in a sensuous medium

[43] *Ibid.*, p. 317.
[44] *Ibid.*, pp. 317-318.
[45] See above, Chaps. III and IV.

intended to increase the appeal to emotion, would similarly augment rather than diminish the possibilities for evil consequences in the experience.[46] The poignancy of profoundly moving poetry and music, from which irrelevancies and "chance" have been removed, is no less than that of events and ideas that affect us in non-aesthetic experience. This is not to suggest that unity may be ignored in an analysis of the aesthetic experience and the work of art. It is merely to maintain that unity is insufficient in itself to account for the "right way" in which "artistic representation" must affect "feeling." We must know precisely what must be made of the non-aesthetic conative factors before they are susceptible to analysis in terms of the "laws" of art.

Nor is this the sole difficulty implicit in Zeller's interpretation of Aristotle's theory of *katharsis*. The second major problem concerns the subjective aspect of the relation within the "total structure" of art. What does the historian mean by the "purging" of emotions? The issue is not now whether Aristotle's theory is basically one of "lustration" or of physiology; rather, it is whether "purification within the soul," explained in terms of "the removal from it of unhealthy [emotions]," is consonant with sound aesthetic theory. It is significant that both Zeller's interpretation in terms of expulsion of emotion and Butcher's hypothesis in which is implicit a theory of "aesthetic emotions"—which we shall examine in the next section of this chapter—assume that aesthetic experience is not identical with the abrupt and compelling emergency action called "emotion." It will be contended that they are correct in this assumption and that aesthetic experience does differ from emotional experience.[47] But Zeller's explanation of the ground for that difference is certainly erroneous. Oedipus' struggle against the fate that drives him to patricide and blindness, the conflict between Antigone and Creon, and Hamlet's tragic dilemma do not extirpate or remove the emotions of fear or terror. These emotions are not only presuppositions of our experience. They actually continue as "resultants" in the aesthetic experience. Their function may be changed but it

[46] As Bywater correctly suggests.

[47] Cf. below, Chaps. XVI-XVIII.

does not follow that they are expelled. It is certainly untrue that "unhealthy" emotions are "extirpated" while "healthy" ones are retained. Fear and terror remain fear and terror and if non-aesthetic factors in the work of art affect either or both of these emotions, they still, as "fear" or "terror," in some aspect continue to exercise their effect in the experience. No argument will support the theory of the removal of "unhealthy" emotions except one that maintains as well that the stimuli for such feelings in the work of art are removed as well. An approach to the problem is that "emotions" are not removed but that "feeling" is a generic term of which emotion is but one specific aspect.[48] The point will be considered more fully in an alternative to Zeller's theory formulated by S. H. Butcher in *Aristotle's Theory of Poetry and Fine Art.* The emphasis in the latter interpretation is upon the subjective experience in contrast to the objective factors in art. Butcher's conclusions are typical of numerous efforts to resolve the antinomy of art, in that they raise the issue of a possible distinction in kind between "aesthetic" and "non-aesthetic" emotions.

C

Butcher's essays in *Aristotle's Theory of Poetry and Fine Art* are analyses of such divergent subjects as, "The Generalizing Power of Comedy" and, "The End of Fine Art." For the aesthetician, the book's conclusions may be evaluated as an aesthetic theory not only because of this general character but also because its author evidently infers that the arguments in *Poetics* and *Politics* present implicitly a theory of fine art. For our present purposes, it is necessary only to examine the implications of the essay called, "The Function of Tragedy."

Butcher's interpretation of *katharsis* diverges fundamentally from Bywater's and Zeller's, despite its author's assumption that the process in question is one of "clarification" in which painful and disquieting elements are expelled. Despite evident similarities to the interpretations previously examined, Butcher's essay on the function

[48] Cf. below, pp. 313-314, Chap. X, pp. 325 ff., and Chap. XI.

of tragedy proposes neither reduction of "feeling" to "just measure" nor an "expulsion" of "unhealthy" emotion. It tends to interpret "clarification" to signify a transformation of the emotion fear into what would appear to be most precisely called an "aesthetic emotion." The argument raises another issue, as well, inasmuch as it suggests that emotion is the generic term for "feeling."

Butcher relies in his interpretation of *katharsis* upon the definitions of emotions given in *Rhetoric*. It will be well to follow his argument briefly. Fear, Aristotle writes, is "a species of pain or disturbance arising from an impression of impending evil which is destructive or painful in its nature."[49] Pity is "a sort of pain at an evident evil of a destructive or painful kind in the case of somebody who does not deserve it, the evil being one which we might expect to happen to ourselves or to some of our friends, and this at a time when it is seen to be near at hand."[50] Pity turns to fear when the object is so nearly related to us that the suffering seems to be our own.[51] Fear and pity are, thus, "strictly correlated forms."[52] Butcher contends that the conditions of dramatic representation and the fact that both feelings are affected by tragedy modifies the emotions. Pity, it is argued, is not essentially altered. Fear is transformed, however, primarily because the artist transports the objects arousing fear to a world of imagination. The conditions under which this transformation occurs are threefold. Negatively, the change is due to the fact that there is no direct apprehension of misfortune impending in our own lives. Moreover, the fear is not caused by the actual approach of danger. Affirmatively, "fear" now becomes the feeling we have for the tragic hero, the ideal man, and is thus shorn of its narrow interest by the alleviation of pity. Artistic treatment expels the painful element from the emotional life by "universalizing" the emotions[53] and initiates the function of the imagination. In consequence, the tragedy may be interpreted in terms of an interplay of universal forces.

[49] *Rhetoric* ii.5.1383 a 21. Quoted by Butcher, *op. cit.*, pp. 251 ff.
[50] *Ibid.*, ii.8.1385 b 13.
[51] *Ibid.*, ii.8.1386 a 17.
[52] *Ibid.*, ii.8.1385 b 19.
[53] Butcher, *op. cit.*, p. 262.

It is significant that for Butcher, *katharsis* entails so complete a transformation of emotion that the generic character of the feeling appears to be altered in process. It is no less significant that "imagination" is likewise utilized in the account of ground art's universalization of the particular. The argument turns upon the issues involved in these two propositions.

Regarding the transformation of fear, Butcher maintains that Aristotle meant that as "tragic" this primary feeling "becomes an almost impersonal emotion," attaching itself not so much "to this or that particular incident, but to the general course of the action, which is for us an image of human destiny."[54] Moreover, in the experience of tragedy, "the events as they pass before us seem almost as if we were directly concerned," and yet, "the pressure of immediate reality is removed."

It is difficult to accept an analysis of fear, one consequence of which is that this impelling emotion becomes "almost impersonal" and which relates it to events "as if we were directly concerned." Neither characterization accords with customarily received accounts of terror. It is doubtful, however, that Butcher's usage is intended to be metaphorical. He takes the poet's task to be at least in part that of heightening the effect of the conative factors in the work of art and does not appear to doubt that the experience of poetry actually "clarifies" the emotion. It is certain that the "clarification" is not regarded by Butcher as a diminution of the feeling to "just proportion." Rather, his argument tends to imply that a qualitative differentiation between "fear" in ordinary experience and "fear" in artistic experience must be taken for granted, once the latter experience presupposes as well the activation of pity.

It may properly be assumed in consequence, that Butcher judges the resulting "fear" evoked by artistic presentation to be "pure" or "purified" rather than "moderate" or "moderated."[55] It is per-

[54] *Ibid.*, p. 258.

[55] Cf. *ibid.*, p. 264. He inisists properly that the effect of tragedy depends upon the fact that the "emotions of fears and pity are blended . . . that the essential tragic effect depends on maintaining the intimate alliance between pity and fear" (p. 258). But the "blending" is still regarded as "emotion," in "higher and more refined forms" of pity and fear (p. 249).

missible to conclude that the argument does imply that "purgation" induces a different "kind" of feeling than that experienced in non-artistic circumstances and because it is evident that the different "kind" of emotion is implicated in the experience of art, one may conclude, as well, that the "feelings" in question are in some sense interpreted to be "aesthetic emotions."

The principal ground for the conviction that there are "aesthetic emotions" is the fact that few would deny that there is a discernible difference, for example, between the "fear" we experience in observing Macbeth's reaction to Banquo's ghost and the fear felt by a small boy who flees a haunted house.[56] Yet, to admit that a distinction is required to account for these divergent experiences, does not mean that a theory of "aesthetic emotions" must be accepted to account for the aesthetic experience. There are obstacles to an acceptance of the theory, obstacles, in fact, difficult to surmount. It may be urged, by way of illustration, that to explain aesthetic experience in terms of "aesthetic emotions" is tautological and simply requires an explanation of the origin and nature of the "aesthetic" feelings. No less compelling is the argument, relevant here also, that has been brought to bear in this essay against Plato's use of "pure" pleasure to describe the experience of "absolutely beautiful forms".[57] Plato's account of aesthetic experience was criticized, it will be recalled, on the ground that the "pure" pleasures are incommensurable with the pleasures explained in terms of the physiology of depletion and repletion. "Aesthetic emotions" pose a similar problem. If the "fear" described by Butcher is different in kind from the fear as ordinarily defined, no generic definition of the emotion may be offered to permit comparison and contrast of the divergent conative states. If, by way of illustration, a general theory of the "feelings" presupposes physiological or neurological reaction, no necessity requires that "aesthetic" fear be defined in these terms. Bywater has expressed the ensuing difficulty succinctly: the theory of tragic pity and fear grounded on the assumption that the "emotions" are "pure" "confuses the ideas of 'pure' and 'moderate,' though there is no direct

[56] Cf. below, pp. 322 ff.
[57] See above, pp. 108 ff.

logical or other relation between them; excess or defect in certain matters may be a fault, but they cannot be termed 'impurities.' "[58]

It may be urged that Bywater is intent upon establishing the fact that Aristotle meant by *katharsis* a moderation of emotions and that his conclusion, in consequence, fails to recognize the merits of an interpretation assuming other premises. That the error is symptomatic of a more profound issue may be inferred, however, from the difficulties encountered by numerous aesthetic theories which have made assumptions similar to Butcher's. One such theory[59] underlies C. C. Pratt's *The Meaning of Music*, a brief glance at which will repay a departure from the historical interpretations of *katharsis*. The book comes quickly to the impasse to which "aesthetic emotion," as a theory, necessarily brings a philosophy of art once the question is asked, "Is music, then, language of emotion?"[60] The author is well aware that the answer "depends upon what one means by emotion" and he maintains that music is such a "language" if the "phrase is taken to mean that a given composition is capable of arousing a subjective feeling on the part of the listener." But whether or not this occurs, he infers, is irrelevant to the "character of music itself." The "characters of tonal movement," Pratt argues, have a "formal affinity to bodily movements" and are describable by "words which also denote moods and emotions." Much turns, in this statement, upon the specific meaning to be attached to the suggestion that auditory characters merely sound the "way *moods* feel." Pratt does not mean that "auditory characters" and "moods" are identical and, in consequence, his argument avoids some of the difficulties met by theorists of "aesthetic surface."[61] He does mean that there is a relation between "tonal movement" and "bodily

[58] *Op. cit.*, p. 160.

[59] A similar problem is raised by the long-lived theory that there are "aesthetic senses." (Cf. Plato, *Hippias Major* 298; *Timaeus* 47b; G. W. F. Hegel, *The Philosophy of Fine Art*, Eintheilung, yy). Sight and hearing have most often been granted a preferred position as "aesthetic senses," on grounds of their superior rationality. An argument may be offered on the ground that they are "distance receptors" and allow for "psychical distance" but one may be as fearful at the sight of impending danger as at the odor of death.

[60] *Op. cit.*, pp. 203-204.

[61] Cf. above, pp. 252 ff.

movement" but that the relation is not symbolical. Rather, "words" may be used to symbolize either the "tonal" or "bodily" movement. Pratt insists, however, that music cannot be the "language of emotion, . . . capable of arousing a subjective feeling on the part of the listener." He does accept an alternative that leads straightway to the following conclusion: "Music . . . Language of the emotions,—yes; but emotions removed from the sphere of bodily sensation and presented to the listening ear through the sensuous medium of moving, meaningless, wondrous sounds."

To infer that the meaning of music is implicated in "emotions removed from the sphere of bodily sensation" while they are yet presented to the "listening ear through the sensuous medium of sound" raises the crucial issue, one integral to the history of man's speculation upon the relation of mind and body. The reader may well inquire concerning the meaning that attaches to the terms and phrases and ask whether, in the light of that meaning, the argument is consistent. It may be pointed out that the "listening ear" undoubtedly receives impressions of stimuli and that sensuous media are stimuli significant with reference to correlated sensory perception. It may be added, as was observed in the preceding chapter,[62] that sensuous media actually require for their meaning "feeling" as a frame of reference. To grant this, it would appear necessary only to assume that percipients perceive and that there is some relation between perception and conation. Yet, if Pratt's conclusion is accepted, it is obvious that it would be impossible to offer a cogent theory relating "listening ear," "sensuous medium . . . of sounds," and "emotion," precisely because the theory supposes that "emotion" is "removed from the sphere of bodily sensations."

The argument is further complicated because Pratt's analysis of music does not make evident the grounds for his effort to differentiate generically the experience of "meaningless, wondrous sounds" from that of non-aesthetic objects or events. Whatever specific differences there are between music and noise, both are constituted of sounds. And because both are so constituted, it is impossible to distinguish the aesthetic from the non-aesthetic subject-object rela-

[62] See above, pp. 272 ff. Cf. above, pp. 231 ff.

tion on the ground that the former is initiated by a "language" directed to "emotion" dissociated from bodily sensation.

It should be made plain, however, that the argument directed against "aesthetic emotions" does not preclude the possibility that aesthetic experience may be a unique state of "feeling." In fact, the present inquiry concludes that our experience of profoundly moving art is a unique aesthetic mood.[63] But Pratt's theory, in which "emotions" are taken to be "removed from the sphere of bodily sensation," cannot come to a like conclusion because it presupposes a generic rather than a specific distinction to hold in the "life of feeling" between "aesthetic" and "non-aesthetic feeling." The presuppositions of audition are physiological and neurological structures. The presuppositions of music are "sensuous." But the "emotions" implicated in Pratt's theory of the experience of music presuppose neither context for conation. William James' conclusion concerning emotion is applicable to Pratt's analysis, as it is to similar hypotheses: "A purely disembodied human emotion is a nonentity . . . I do not say that it is a contradiction in the nature of things; . . . but I say that for *us*, emotion dissociated from all bodily feeling is inconceivable."[64]

The temptation is strong to attempt to solve the problems of artistic creativity and aesthetic experience by assuming that "feelings" may be "transformed" into the "aesthetic" or "pure" conation. It must be maintained, nonetheless, that to make the relevant "feeling" incommensurable with generic feeling or different in kind from "non-aesthetic emotions" is to misinterpret both art and aesthetic experience. Neither the object of aesthetic interest nor its experience is divine, pure, or sacrosanct. Those who maintain that "aesthetic emotions" are "pure" and "disembodied" are kin to those flatterers of Alexander the Great who asserted that the conqueror of the world was the son of Jupiter. It will be recalled that the wounded Alexander asked the pertinent question: "Is not this blood of a crimson color and purely human?"

Butcher's argument does not reach the impasse to which Pratt's

[63] See below, Chap. XVII.
[64] "What is Emotion," *Collected Essays*, p. 255.

theory comes, only because its author does not make explicit the implications of his interpretation. His essay on Aristotle's *katharsis* evidences both sound technique and analysis. It makes use, as we have seen, of *Rhetoric* to recover Aristotle's usage of the terms "fear" and "pity." More significantly, it implies that the grounds for *katharsis* are found in an interrelation of emotions in aesthetic experience which tends to reduce the intensity of single emotions and may serve to distinguish aesthetic from non-aesthetic experience.[65]

Small advantage ultimately accrues to Butcher's specific interpretation, however, from these presuppositions, primarily because the argument is itself bifurcated. Butcher does emphasize properly the fact of "idealization" in art and in this way makes an effort to surmount one of the principal obstacles to an acceptance of non-aesthetic teleological hypotheses of art. It will be recalled[66] that the latter hypothesis fails to account for the artist's idealization of material derived from moral, scientific, religious, or theological fields. In consequence, it is obvious that to assert that Butcher's interpretation is weak in this respect because there is a bifurcation in his theory between "imagination" and "idealization" does not imply that the use of either term, as such, presents an obstacle to sound theory of art or of aesthetic experience. *Aristotle's Theory of Poetry and Fine Art* presents, nonetheless, a weak form of the general theory precisely because it urges and fails to ground a hypothesis well-stated—only to be condemned—by Bywater: "The tragic pity and fear are regarded as pure, because they are aroused not by real suffering, but only by the imaginary woes of the theatre; so that there is no admixture of pain in them."[67]

It must be remarked in passing that the non-aesthetic factors in the work of art are not thus easily explained away. It must also be remarked that one falls easily into the habit of assuming that if the aesthetic feelings are "unreal," the factors comprising the work of art must be likewise "unreal." But once the assumption has been made that the disturbing effects of "strong" emotion may be miti-

[65] See below, Chap. XVII.

[66] See above, Chap. VI, pp. 198 ff.

[67] *Op. cit.*, pp. 159-160.

gated because the work of art is "unreal" and because the spectator enters upon the world of imagination, Butcher's argument rapidly encounters formidable difficulties. The realm of imagination is introduced to ground the generic differences between aesthetic and non-aesthetic "emotion" but it is evident that upon these differences the function of the imagination itself depends. Furthermore, Butcher's argument does not pause to inform the reader whether or not imagination and the state of "clarified" emotion are identical or, if not identical, what their precise relation may be.

It is not unimportant, in view of the later analysis in the present essay, to insist that the aesthetician's use of "imagination" for analyses of art and aesthetic experience has proved to be of value. In the "imagination," in fact, aesthetic discovered a means by which the theory of imitation could be replaced by a hypothesis in which artistic inventiveness and aesthetic freedom received adequate consideration.[68] However, neither the inventiveness nor the freedom may be purchased cheaply. To take the present instance as a case in point, Butcher's argument appears to assume the self-evidence of the proposition that the passions are less disturbing and dangerous provided that they are evoked by the universal rather than by the particular. It must be admitted that both universalization and objectification of "feeling" are fundamental to a theory of aesthetic experience,[69] precisely as it must be admitted that the work of art displays universal factors. But to prove the truth of these propositions is an arduous task. One need but recall Spinoza's *Ethics* and the relevant portions of Hegel's *The Philosophy of Art* to conclude, indeed, that too facile an assumption that one may obtain surcease from strong emotion through "play of imagination," if imagination remains undefined, merely places before us additional problems.

Perhaps the fundamental difficulty inherent in the aesthetician's dependence upon "imagination" derives from the thoroughly unfounded assumption that, because freedom from the restrictions of reality and from the compulsion of "emotion" have been secured

[68] See above, Chap. I, pp. 6 ff.
[69] Cf. below, Chap. XVII.

by its use, the scope of imagination may be as arbitrarily restricted as if one were considering a merely aesthetic faculty. Neither logic nor common sense will grant, however, that the use of a term may be appropriated to art and aesthetic alone, provided that its meaning is implicated in every field of man's endeavor, whether artistic or non-artistic, aesthetic or non-aesthetic. And certainly this is true of the imaginative faculties and processes.

It will be maintained in the present essay that imagination is not only creative but recreative. It may, perhaps, be unfair to be critical of the fact that Butcher's analysis of imagination ignores the Epimethean or "backward looking" function of this faculty, although it must be urged that sound analysis should suggest that not all "images" are "productive." It is not unfair, however, to require the aesthetician properly to distinguish "imagination" from "fancy" on grounds proper to art. Dryden was not in error when he wrote of "fancy" that "if it be not regulated, it is a mere caprice, and utterly incapable to produce a reasonable and judicious poem."[70] The most obvious regulation is that afforded by the medium of art. It is true, no doubt that the artist imposes "images" upon material but it is no less true that he may do so only within the potentialities of the material to receive them. It is in the proper interrelation of the laws of imagination and of material that one discovers the "law of art."[71]

III

IT SHOULD not be assumed, because no one of the alternative interpretations of *katharsis* is adequate to ground a theory of the "total structure" of art, that the *organon* implicit in the history of Aristotelian studies of the subject is proved thereby to be flawed, as was that other structural instrument, "aesthetic surface." The errors of "aesthetic surface" are consequent upon a systematic flaw in the theory. It is impossible to validate the argument that the artist devotes his energies solely to the forming of sensuous media

[70] *Essays of John Dryden,* Vol. 1, p. 299, ed. W. P. Ker.

[71] Cf. above, pp. 44 ff. and below, pp. 492 ff.

on the ground that the work of art is a "symbol equivalent with the thing symbolized" or because by concentration upon the "structure" of the work of art, he—or we—may ignore the "referrents" of feeling and end.

The inadequacies of the typical interpretations of Aristotle's views concerning *katharsis* examined in this chapter to determine whether or not they were explanatory of art and aesthetic experience are not owing to analogous systematic errors in the theory of "total structure." Certain of the difficulties emerge because each theorist tends properly to circumscribe his general aesthetic by reference to Aristotle's writings, whatever implications the problem may have for a general philosophy of art. Other difficulties are met in consequence of inconsistent analysis or unexamined implications. However, the fact that the interpretations do not provide a "reasonable apology" for art or its experience on the hypothesis of the "reduction" of emotion to "right measure," of the purification of the soul by the extirpation of "unhealthy" or "abnormal" emotions, or of the alteration of emotions into "aesthetic feelings," need not shake the conviction that the theory of "total structure" and the method of analysis it implies are sound. Whether an adequate aesthetic may be grounded in the theory is a question to be answered by the succeeding chapters of this book. In the meantime, there is the assurance that, whereas the structural theory of "aesthetic surface" is wholly unsound, that of "total structure" remains possible, if only because one alternative interpretation of "feeling" basic to the theory in question has scarcely been hinted at in the present chapter.

This is evident, once it is recalled that Bywater, Zeller, and Butcher tacitly assume that "emotion" is the generic term for "feeling" and that it is "emotion" which in some way is altered by *katharsis*. But if "feeling" is the generic term and "emotion" but one specific aspect of "feeling," "emotion" may be transformed into another aspect of "feeling" with no need to introduce such implications as "unhealthy" or "aesthetic" emotions. In this way, it may plausibly be argued that while aesthetic experience is initiated by stimuli effecting emotional reaction there is no need to assume that it remains describable solely in emotional terms. The dilemma into which the theory of "total structure" appears to have been forced by the failure of the interpretations of Aristotle's argument is thus seen to be no true dilemma. Whether the alternative in question is valid is a problem to be considered in the next chapter.

We have learned from the history of Aristotelian criticism that there is danger in formulating an aesthetic which postulates "feelings" incommensurable with each other; that a theory for generic feeling must be offered; and that feeling and imagination must be related. We have learned, as well, that the analysis of the work of art needs no less careful attention than does the problem of conation. Bywater's interpretation of *katharsis*, in particular, bespeaks the need for a study of "symbolism," with especial emphasis upon the status of the non-aesthetic factors in the work of art in their relation to "feeling" and to the end of art.

These problems, which arise in the study of the structure of art, are implicit in the assumption made in the next chapter that the work of art is a symbol of the "life of feeling." We shall turn in that chapter to the specific statement of the assumption that the work of art is a "symbol of the artist's feeling" and to a consideration of the respects in which it is superior to the initial teleological inference that the work of art satisfies the artist's interests.

Part III

Feeling, the Symbols of Art, and Aesthetic Experience

Chapter X

Feeling and the Work of Art as "Symbol of the Artist's Feelings"

The artist is a receptacle for emotions that come from all over the place: from the sky, from the earth, from a scrap of paper, from a passing shape, from a spider's web.

—PICASSO[1]

IT IS no idle fancy that discovers in Plato's Dialogue, *Ion*, a coping stone for the soundest and most consistent tradition of speculation upon the relation of the work of art to its creator and to those who, in turn, experience that creation. Artist, critic and philosopher alike have long been "seal'd of the tribe" of the Socrates of *Ion*, despite divergent presuppositions in the metaphysics of beauty and recurrent efforts to render more precise the words of the Athenian and the rhapsode. The reasons for the "sealing" are due in part, no doubt, to the dominant influence of Plato as a literary and philosophical figure. But Plato's words are in this instance persuasive because the argument in *Ion* goes to the heart of the problem. The rhapsode from Ephesus knows that he arouses in his auditors "various emotions of pity, wonder, sternness." These evocations, Plato explains, occur because the rhapsode speaks the words of a poet who has been "taken possession of." The auditor is the "last of the rings which . . . derive their power from the original magnet; . . . and the poet himself is the first link of all."

Behind the figure of the interlinked magnetic rings is a convic-

[1] From *Picasso, Forty Years of His Art.* (By permission of The Museum of Modern Art, publishers.)

tion that a necessary relation holds between feeling, artistic creativity, and aesthetic experience and that the work of art is "made" in order to communicate the artist's feelings to the audience. One of the most austere and celebrated poets of our times echoes this conviction: "And I think that to transfuse emotion," writes A. E. Housman, "—not to transmit thought but to set up in the reader's sense a vibration corresponding to what is felt by the writer—is the peculiar function of poetry."[2] That Housman should be kith and kin to Plato does not pass understanding but that Kant, the philosopher most intent upon establishing the universal validity of the judgment of taste, should subscribe to a theory of artistic communication not too alien to the Athenian's lends sufficient credibility to the truth lying behind the conviction that perhaps no additional illustrations need be brought forward from the writings of artists, their critics, or philosophers of art to support the contention.[3] Kant assumes that art is the consequence of "making," that it is a communication or expression of the genius' feelings, and that the presence of *Spirit*, the animating principle of the mind in an aesthetic sense, does not allow the poetic genius to "show how his Ideas, so rich in fancy and yet so full of thought, come together in his head, simply because he does not know and therefore cannot teach others."[4] It is on the grounds of feeling that the artistic genius and the great scientist are differentiated by the author of the *Kritik*.

But to speculate properly upon this distillation of the thought of two millennia means merely that the pressing problems which have received no resolution in philosophies of art previously examined in this essay are now to be submitted to the test of a new hypothesis. This is not to suggest that numerous philosophies of art do not accept the postulate called "emotional" or "sensational" or do not grant that the artist "makes" in order to communicate his feelings. But our task is to determine the significance of these suggestions with reference specifically to three issues: whether the work of art,

[2] *The Name and Nature of Poetry*, p. 12.

[3] The material has been set forth with a wealth of illustration by Julius Portnoy in *A Psychology of Art Creation*. Cf. also, Max Schoen *Art and Beauty*.

[4] *K.d.U.*, Sections 42-45.

intended to express the artist's feelings, is merely an object or event, as is assumed in non-aesthetic teleologies, or whether it must be granted another status; what "feeling" is to which art is related; and the precise relation that holds between the work of art and feeling.

A tentative reply to the first question is implicit in various conclusions to which the present essay has come. The inference most nearly relevant may be drawn from the failure of the limited theory of the structure of art called "aesthetic surface." The basic defect of "aesthetic surface" derives, as has been observed, from the theory's assumption that the work of art is a "symbol equivalent with the thing symbolized." The incorrectness of this assumption is of present significance, however, not so much because it invalidates the general theory of "surface," but rather, because the failure makes untenable either the assumption that the artist is merely a technician "making" for the purpose of forming or unifying sensuous media for the media's sake or that the aesthetic percipient is one whose sole function is analysis in terms of both "sign and referrent" of the product made. While the theory of "aesthetic surface" errs regarding the specific character of symbolism in art, it is sound in its assumption that the work of art is a symbol, if only because the meaning of the work of art is understandable in relation to communication. If, however, the product of artistic "making" is not "equivalent with itself," the new hypothesis must be adequate to cope with the question: What is the "referrent" for the artistic symbol?

It is plain, in consequence, that despite the theory's errors it has advanced the general aesthetic argument sufficiently to permit of a tentative answer to the latter question. If the work of art is not a "symbol equivalent with the thing symbolized," neither the media of the art object nor the artist's effort to form the media are ends in themselves.[5] Rather, the relation of media to work of art must be one of means to end. Moreover, the artist does not manipulate materials for their own sake but to produce an instrument. The question, therefore, may be reformulated. Granted this means-end relation, what is the function of the media? The correct reply is evident

[5] Cf. above, pp. 237 ff.

in the implications of the non-aesthetic teleological theories of art.[6] It was concluded concerning these theories that no sound aesthetic may deny that non-aesthetic ideas, events, situations, and objects become and remain factors in the work of art. It was inferred, as well, that the artist's forming or unification of the art-object is directed, in part at least, to the presentation in sensuous media of factors definable in terms of non-aesthetic ends.[7] Moreover, it is well to remember at this juncture that a specific argument among the many non-aesthetic teleological theories of art was designed to prove that the work of art is made solely to satisfy the "interests" of the artist. It was maintained that the theory was invalid. Of more significance, however, is the reason for its failure. The work made is separated from the artist in the "making" and thus may be a means or instrument by which are attained ends other than those selfishly desired by the artist.

If these inferences are now reordered in the light of the present problem, it is evident that the sensuous aspect of the structure of the work of art, the media, is a means used to present *in alio* the non-aesthetic ideas, events, objects, and situations. But this is to urge that the media are sensuous precisely because they are instruments by means of which the art-object is referred most directly to feeling. Constructed neither for the sensuous pleasure of manipulating material nor to satisfy selfish desires, the media become through technique the means by which the artist's feelings concerning non-aesthetic ideas, objects, situations, and events are fixed in concrete "images," presumably for proper transmission: "And the reason why poets clothe their philosophical expressions in concrete images is not because of any shame of the concept," as Dewitt Parker writes (and, in writing, reflects the tradition in which both Socrates and Housman may be placed), "but just in order the more easily and vividly to attach and communicate their emotion. Their general preference for the concrete has the same motive: for there are only a few abstractions capable of arousing and fixing emotions."[8]

[6] Cf. Chaps. V-VII.
[7] The quotation from Housman ignores this.
[8] *The Principles of Aesthetic*, p. 22.

Implicit in this conclusion concerning the status of media is the inference that the work of art is so far from being a symbol "equivalent with the thing symbolized" that it is actually a "symbol of the artist's feelings." The artist "makes" the non-aesthetic factors integral to a medium, thus forming and unifying the art-object, in part with reference to its formal structure or its end but ultimately in terms of both form and end. The work of art "made" is neither the artist's "feelings" nor his "feelings" about the non-aesthetic factors. The structure of art presupposes a medium differentiated from the structure of feeling. But, as we have observed in the matter of the "total structure" of art, the *sensuous* structure of the work of art has "feeling" as its proper correlate. It may be concluded that the work of art is a sign or symbol "standing for" the artist's feeling. As such, it may be a "sign" for the artist himself, who, once the art-object is made, becomes an aesthetically experiencing rather than an artistically creating individual. Because the object made is separated from the artist, no obstacle bars the assumption that if it is a symbol for the artist, it is potentially a symbol for percipients other than the artist. It may be inferred that as "symbol of the artist's feelings," as those feelings are attached to ideas, situations, objects, and events, the work of art is intended to induce in the perceiver feelings identical or similar to those experienced by the artist. Housman's suggestions will suffice for the moment: the work of art appears to be intended "to set up a vibration corresponding to what is felt" by the artist.

In what general sense the *Ion's* linking of artist, work of art, and aesthetic percipient may be accepted for this essay's later argument should be evident from the foregoing synthesis. Indeed, we may go further. The theory of the "total structure" of art links artist, object, and percipient and implies that there is a necessary relation between the work of art made by the artist and the effective stimulus or "image" that this product of making is intended to be for the perceiver. By attention to media and by the selection of comprehensible content[9] or signs the artist evidences his inten-

[9] Cf. below, Chaps. XII-XIII.

tion to convey a conative attitude towards the non-aesthetic aspects of experience. To urge that the work of art is a symbol of the artist's feelings is to accept "feeling" as a frame of reference not only for artistic creativity but for aesthetic experience as well. There must be, in some degree, a re-creation of the artist's feelings if the artist is understood to succeed or fail in the symbolization.

The question that most naturally suggests itself in any discussion that accepts the work of art as a symbol of the artist's feelings is whether *ex hypothesi* the maker is precluded from expressing the spirit of his age, culture, nation, or race. But the consideration of this question, to which we shall return in this and in later chapters, must be deferred. It is impossible longer to postpone the more significant issue which its answer presupposes. That issue is the nature of feeling.

II

ONE inference significant for aesthetic experience and drawn from the interpretations of Aristotle's theory of *katharsis* stands us in good stead as the issue of the nature of feeling is raised. It was stated abstractly in the preceding chapter that no generic distinction may be drawn between aesthetic and non-aesthetic feeling. Assured, therefore, that one theory of feeling must account for both aesthetic and non-aesthetic experience, insofar as feeling is the relevant issue, we may further be reassured as the concrete instances of art are examined. We know that if the question is, what is implied in such statements as, "We are afraid," "He is overwhelmed by horror," "This is a mood of melancholy, of joy, of sorrow, or of despair," generically the reply must be identical whether the object, idea, situation, or event that evokes the feeling is aroused by our own imminent danger or by Francisco's words, spoken at Elsinore: " 'tis bitter cold, and I am sick at heart"; whether our horror is aroused by vicious treatment of men under the knout, by Milton's description of Sin and Death, or by the words of the mad king upon the heath:

But yet thou art my flesh, my blood, my daughter;
Or rather a disease that's in my flesh,
Which I must needs call mine; thou art a boil,
A plague-sore, an embossed carbuncle,
In my corrupted blood.

We pity the ill and underfed. The feeling is not different in kind from that which pervades us as we look upon the sculptured portrayal of the gallows-bound burghers of Calais or hear Dante's words describing Ugolino:

. . . When a faint beam
Had to our doleful prison made its way,
And in four countenances I descried
The image of my own, on either hand
Through agony I bit . . .[10]

Similarly, the tranquillity and calm of the mood aroused at the sight of the English country-side in Devon or Herefordshire are of a kind with an aspect of our experience of a sunset by Turner or of Vermeer's "Girl Weighing Gold." We may be made gay by the antics of a kitten, by a country-dance, by Mozart's *Magic Flute*, or by Velasquez's "Los Borrachos." Exaltation of spirit is exaltation of spirit whether it is evoked by the attempt of a mother bird to protect her young, the mass of the Cathedral in Seville, El Greco's "St. Francis in Ecstasy," Bach's *B Minor Mass*, Giordano Bruno's courage in expressing his credo of "infinite universes," or John Milton's conception of a Satan who believes—in contrast to Belial's "Better these than worse,"—

So farewell hope, and with hope farewell fear,
Farewell remorse! All good to me is lost;
Evil, be thou my good: . . .

And if bitter sorrow and passionate anger dominate our reaction to the unending repetition of "man's inhumanity to man" in a world in which our experience is non-aesthetic, it is no less sorrow *qua* feeling that likewise is evoked by Michelangelo's figures in the Medici Tomb, by Malory's requiem for Launcelot, by the

[10] *Inferno*, Canto XXXIII. H. F. Cary's translation.

Graeco-Roman *Niobe*, or by Dante's tale of the ill-fated Francesca da Rimini. Anger, as feeling, is produced by the intricacy of Iago's machination, the treatment of Joseph by his brothers, and by the wretchedness depicted in Hogarth's and Brueghel's satirical paintings. However the "feelings" evoked by art may differ specifically and however the aesthetic mood differs specifically from "feeling" ordinarily aroused, generically, the emotions and moods aroused by art and by non-aesthetic objects, events, and situations are of a kind and may be compared and differentiated.

It is, however, not solely to substantiate this conclusion that there is offered at this point a description of feeling, accompanied by a minimum of supporting argument. The description will serve this purpose but it will also provide a point of reference for the necessarily detailed philosophical and psychological analyses of feeling which are, in turn, integral to the resolution of the antinomies of art and aesthetic experience.

The preliminary description of feeling need not be formulated *ab initio*. The preceding chapter affords more than the negative suggestion that aesthetic and non-aesthetic feelings may not be differentiated in kind. Aristotle's own theory emphasizes the significance of "emotion" rather than of "pleasure" and "pain" in the experience of music and poetry. To suggest this does not mean that *Poetics* ignores the significance of the "pleasure that accompanies the excitement" of tragedy. It is, rather, to assert that the central problem of *Poetics* is conative rather than hedonic—and that Aristotle is entirely correct in approaching the analysis of aesthetic experience on this assumption. It is not essential to the present essay's argument to present a minute analysis either of Aristotle's psychology or of hedonic theory. It is only necessary to mention the fact that *Poetics* does diverge on this issue from conclusions ordinarily attributed to "common-sense" and to remark, further, that "common-sense" has been notorious in its lack of precision in reducing to pleasure and pain such divergent "feelings" as joy, exaltation, contentment, sorrow, rage, melancholy, fear, love, hate, anger, and the like. The Aristotelian assumption that, because "pleasure completes activity" and because activities differ, pleasures differ among themselves, indicates at least a recognition of the complexity of a problem which may not be resolved by the use of vague hedonic terminology.[11] It may be stated, parenthetically, that the contribution of hedonism to aesthetic is amply recognized in the later development of this book, in so far as pleasure and pain are taken to be concomitants of conatively definable behavior which, respectively, achieves or fails in its end.

The more important problem of feeling lies in the explanation of the "activities" themselves, in the significance of the highly complex bodily reactions that constitute conative experience and in the purposes which that behavior attains or fails of achievement. That Aristotle did place pleasure and pain in a subordinate position in his *Poetics* is, as his arguments show, not accidental.[12] That he selected the emotions as the particular aspects of feeling implicated in the experience of poetry and music is, for the present essay, merely fortuitous, at once because in the ensuing description, "emotion" is the median range of the biological *continuum* to which the generic term "feeling" is applied[13] and because by reference to this median range, the descriptions of the other levels or dimensions and their variations within the *continuum* of feeling may most easily and summarily be given.

Assuming that emotion is the median range, the extreme dimensions of the *continuum* of feeling are "instinct" and "mood."[14]

[11] Cf. C. D. Broad's comments on pleasure and pain in the essay on Sidgwick, in *Five Types of Ethical Theory*, pp. 230 ff.

[12] Cf. *E.N.*, Books 7 and 10.

[13] Cf. my article, "The Philosophical Implications of Some Theories of Emotion."

[14] It is necessary to clarify two points. In the first place, the specific ranges of the *continuum* emphasized in this context are necessary and sufficient for the analysis of aesthetic experience, despite the fact that one peripheral range theoretically comprises reflex and tropistic action. Secondly, the differentiations within the "life of feeling" are logically posterior to the common factor which permits us to treat in integral terms the relation between an organism and the stimulus which "moves" it. The logically prior factor, identical throughout the *continuum*, is the ateleological aspect which provides also the potential factor in the experience of art. The logically posterior differentiations evident in the various manifestations of feeling are teleological factors, which permit the actualization of aesthetic experience. Therefore, in the following account, it is permissible to write of "feeling" at once in generic and in specific terms.

The "life of feeling" is considered, therefore, in distributive terms as "instinct," "emotion," and "mood." It is to be regarded collectively, however, as a *continuum* constituted of observable behavior.

Two significant variations characterize the observable behavior within the extreme ranges of the *continuum* of feeling. The behavior varies directly in intensity from overt action in the instinctive range to peripheral reaction in the range of "mood." Within these same ranges, however, the behavior varies in overtness or intensity in inverse proportion to the alternative stimuli or modes of possible action which the organism "imagines" or presents to itself.[15]

In the present usage, an "image" is a stimulus effective for the production of observable behavior in an organism. The behavior evidenced in the *continuum* of feeling is interpreted as the organism's capacity to present effective stimuli to itself. The *continuum* is, moreover, susceptible of further interpretation in terms of two diverse but interrelated operations: It is throughout the entirety of its dimensions an inherited biological and a derived cultural *Apperceptionsmass*. This aspect of feeling may properly be called "reproductive imagination."

In addition, the behavior of the individual who "feels" evidences

---

It may be added, with reference to the first point, that while some references to reflex action and tropism which are made subsequently are intended to clarify the meanings of the various stages of feeling, our present problem does not necessitate the inclusion of an account of such organic operations as Sir Charles Sherrington describes in *Man on His Nature*, pp. 175-176. It is only necessary to add that the so-called "tropism" as a range of action, like ateleologically defined feeling, is a portion of what Sherrington describes as part of "an ancient system of adjustments, present, variously stereotyped, in great numbers of our stock, forerunners of ourselves." The emphasis upon instinct in what follows in the analysis of feeling is thus quite arbitrary and is intended to distinguish this from more peripheral aspects of "feeling" with which instinct actually merges. To paraphrase Anaxagoras, tropistic and instinctive behavior are not "cut off from one another, as if by an axe."

[15] The terminology implies and is intended to imply that "feeling" and "imagination" are interchangeable terms. "Productive" imagination is potentially aesthetic and creative. But there may be designated a specific range of feeling within "mood" to which the term "aesthetic imagination" is applicable. I have adapted Kant's terminology, "reproductive" and "productive," to my own uses. Cf. below, pp. 358 ff. While it is necessary for analytical reasons to bifurcate feeling and imagination into "productive" and "reproductive," what may properly be called imagination is a whole. It reaches the actualization its name connotes only in the operation called "mood."

a capacity for the presentation of alternative stimuli or "images." This capacity is minimally operative in the range of the *continuum* called instinct. It is present, but less evident in reflex and tropistic action. This characteristic of feeling,—the organism's presentation to itself of alternative stimuli,—may properly be called "productive imagination."

The foregoing discrimination of reproductive and productive feeling nevertheless presupposes a more basic methodological differentiation of the observable behavior in the *continuum* in terms of ateleological and teleological definition,[16] a differentiation requisite for complete analysis of the factors implicated. The need for and the significance of ateleological and teleological definitions of feeling will be evident as the argument proceeds. It should be remarked at this juncture, however, that historical interpretations of the "life of feeling" have been grounded in one or the other of these two classifications, one consequence of which has been the tendency to conclude that the aspects of feeling which they define are mutually exclusive. On the one hand, theorists who maintain the ateleological hypothesis to the exclusion of the teleological reduce the connotation of "feeling" to a description of the reflexes of direct sensory-motor mechanisms involved in the experience of stimuli. But were the *continuum* of feeling explicable solely in terms of ateleological defining, its description would comprehend only types of act, couched in either physiological or neurological terms or in some combination of the two. The life of feeling, if one held exclusively to hypothesis, would be explicable without reference to any end which, on occasion, is subserved by the mechanically produced reaction or type of act.

To this mechanistic view has ordinarily been contrasted the teleological or vitalistic hypothesis of feeling. Theorists who adopt this, the teleological hypothesis, to the exclusion of the ateleological, reduce the connotation of "feeling" to a description of the means-end relation assumed to hold between act and end. They interpret the action solely in terms of the goal or end attained. But were the

[16] See E. A. Singer's treatment of this definition in "Beyond Mechanism and Vitalism."

continuum of feeling couched solely in terms of teleological defining, its description, comprehending the life of feeling in terms of goal, end or function, would ignore all reference to the type-of-act observed.

It will be maintained in the present essay that neither the *continuum* of feeling nor the aesthetic experience which is presupposed by it may be properly analyzed or understood if recourse is not had by the theorist to both ateleological and teleological definition and to the evidences of interrelations between the typical and the purposive reactions. The argument will be directed primarily to the task of ascertaining the relevance to aesthetic experience of both ateleological and teleological factors in feeling. But the specific intention of the argument merely fortifies the conviction that man's potentialities for the experience of art are presupposed by both aspects of feeling.

The course of the argument may be briefly anticipated. It will be maintained that in the ateleological aspect of feeling are grounded "reproduction" and the reinstatement of the past. To "reproductive" imagination, the experience of art owes familiarity with the content of art and from its operation art derives "images" which recur and are functions of that familiarity. In these generic aspects of feeling, also, are ascertainable the authentic grounds for the assumption that art is the symbol of the artist's feelings. In "reproductive" feeling are found, also, some sources of the artist's inspiration. For while artists have frequently made excursions to the realms of speculation upon their own creativity, too often they have concluded that the "fountain" of their powers is "I know not what." There is in "feeling" that to which the reflective artist is linked because "the old instinct brings back the old names." In reproductive imagination are found, as well, bases for that assertion reiterated by the lover of art who "knows what he likes," although he offers no objective reason for his liking. One may discover in this aspect of feeling, also, the source of the universal desire for art, which too frequently finds but partial satisfaction in inferior products of technique. Here also are discovered factors in aesthetic experience that lead to its and to art's condemnation, for to the operations of reproductive imagination may be traced the charges that art is deceptive and degrading and that its experience is irrational.

As we turn to the teleologically definable aspect of feeling, there is found the ground for "production," for the Promethean in contrast to the Epimethean in imagination. Productive imagination is the wellspring of the artist's creativity and of the creator's individuality. In it, consequently, are the sources for art's uniqueness. Here also are the sources for what in the experience of profound art is a mood of courage and exaltation, for the inspiration to effort that energizes man and "creates the creator." But the mood of aesthetic experience derives, more precisely, from the interrelations of teleologically and ateleologically definable factors in feeling. Art appeals to the entirety of man's imagination. Perhaps only within the relations of its "total structure" do the Promethean and Epimethean aspects of feeling interact so freely and with such significant consequences.

The remainder of this essay on aesthetic experience will be elaborated with reference to the general description of feeling given in this section, at the same time that the general description, in its turn, is amplified and implemented.[17] In the course of the inquiry itself, the antinomic aspects of art and its experience will receive the more precise expression required for their resolution. The course of the study is properly set once the meaning, implications, and limitations of the proposition—the work of art is a symbol of the artist's feelings—have been shown.

III

THE ambiguities of the proposition—the work of art is a symbol of the artist's feelings—have not infrequently led otherwise sound criticism and aesthetic theory into an error analogous to that

[17] The theory of feeling upon which the remainder of this book in part depends takes cognizance of much of the literature concerned with experimentation in a highly controversial field. It is not assumed, in the formulation of that theory, that continued experimentation and research will not alter the details and provide additional empirical data. It is assumed, however, that the more general principles and hypotheses of the theory will be in accord with the experimental data.

committed by the non-aesthetic teleologies of art. This is not because the assumption—the art-object is a symbol and, therefore, more than a mere object or event among other objects or events—does not place the argument on a level different from that which assumes that the artist makes in order to satisfy his own interests. To state the problem simply and on the assumption that the art-object is a symbol, it must be asked whether the poet, the painter, the sculptor, or the musician makes a sonnet, a symphony, a portrait, or a statue as a "sign" for his individual feelings or to communicate the "feelings" or spirit of a community, an age, a culture, or a race.

In critical writing, the issue is more explicit. In the arts in which the maker speaks for another, the feelings of the character in the drama, of the figure in the allegory, or of the subject of the portrait are at times interpreted to be those of the artist. Is, then, Hamlet's dilemma also Shakespeare's? Is the sorrow symbolized in El Greco's "Interment of the Count of Orgaz" the painter's, that of the contemporaries' portrayed in the painting, or of both? Research directed to the recovery of the artist's dreams and childhood memories suggest one reply. Ateleological theory has suggested quite another.

If, as we have assumed, there is a fundamental soundness in Socrates' figurative statement that the artist is the first in the series of magnetic rings which bind the maker, the object made, and the aesthetic percipient, it is to the reflective artist that we are likely to turn for illumination on these and allied issues. But artists' reflections on the problem show little agreement. The *Ion's* statement of the problem implies at once that the artist is a medium sensitive and receptive to objects and events that affect his feelings and that he is sufficiently skilled in craft to evoke by means of the work of art the original feelings. An echo of this classical theory is heard in the words of a distinguished contemporary painter. "The artist," writes Picasso, "is a receptacle for emotions that come from all over the place; from the sky, from the earth, from a scrap of paper, from a passing shape, from a spider's web."[18] Moreover, however "ab-

[18] "Statement by Picasso: 1935," p. 17, *Picasso: Forty Years of His Art.* (By permission of The Museum of Modern Art, publishers.)

stract" the work of art may be, the artist "must always start with something." More significantly, the painter holds that

> Afterward you can remove all traces of reality. There's no danger then, anyway, because the idea of the object will have left an indelible mark. It is what started the artist off, excited his ideas, and stirred his emotions. Ideas and emotions will in the end be prisoners in his work. Whatever they do, they can't escape from the picture. They form an integral part of it, even when their presence is no longer discernible. Whether he likes it or not, man is the instrument of nature. It forces on him its character and appearance.[19]

But what Picasso affirms, a no less distinguished contemporary denies. T. S. Eliot, examining the theory of artistic communication, concludes concerning "the experience that the poet is so bursting to communicate" that "by the time it has settled down into a poem it may be so different from the original experience as to be hardly recognizable."[20]

We need not necessarily infer that these conclusions vary because Picasso is a painter and Eliot a poet. The media of the arts do vary in their potentialities for "representing" specific objects or events. Music, by way of illustration,[21] does not permit the precise and specific "reproduction" of the object or event to which a painting as a symbol may refer. A "representation" is, however, a symbol and the exactitude with which the original stimulus is "reproduced" is of little consequence for the present issue which concerns the general theory of symbols in art. It may even be granted in so far as the present argument is concerned that artistic signs for "referrents" do vary to a degree that lends credence to the assumption that no natural relation may be specified in a given instance between symbol and object symbolized.[22]

Actually, Picasso's and Eliot's apparently conflicting statements must be evaluated in terms of two factors, the feelings presumed to be communicated by the work of art and the events or objects

[19] *Ibid.*, p. 16.
[20] *The Use of Poetry*, p. 131.
[21] See J. W. N. Sullivan, *Beethoven: His Spiritual Development*, pp. 149-150.
[22] Cf. J. A. Stewart, *The Myths of Plato*, pp. 256 ff.

to which the feelings attach. Assuming that Picasso's conclusion is correct, to argue from it that the art-object is a symbol of the artist's feelings would signify that "feeling" is evoked by or attached to every conceivable natural, historical, or artistic event, to situations, to ideas, or to objects of all possible variety. Nor is this a complete statement of the consequence since it is evident that, on this view, the object of art may also, "stand for" any or all of the artist's feelings of love, hatred, grief, and sorrow, as well as similar "emotions" evoked not only by objectively referred "facts" but by subjective states.[23] The "referrents" for the symbols would include, in consequence, not only the vast panoply of art, folk tales and legends, history, religion, science, economics, nature and natural science, theology and morality, but, as well, the artist's introspective state, his analyses or evalutions of that state, his dreams, hallucinations, illusions, delusions, and fancies.

But does the proposition, the work of art is a symbol of the artistic feelings, require either that the completed sign "stand for" the initial feeling or that the symbol need refer directly to the vast number of objects, situations, events, or ideas which may have evoked that initial "emotion"? It is evident that the artist may try to "symbolize his feelings" and propose to "reproduce" in the art-object the stimulus that originally aroused the "emotion." It is equally evident, however, that no necessity forces him to refer to the specific object, event, situation, or idea to which his feelings originally attached. A remark by Dali is not without value apropos of this possibility.[24] As a young student, Dali recalls that he was instructed to represent a specified object. He immediately drew what he calls "counter-images." Indeed, it is not difficult to infer from other and similarly self-revelatory comments that an expert technician may have produced a work of art deriving from Scripture without having been vitally affected by religious feeling. The symbol actually adopted may be selected because a commission specifies its use or merely because the artist adopts an accustomed mode for expressing his feelings in a particular age or tradition.

[23] *The Use of Poetry*, p. 131.
[24] In *Paintings, Drawings, Prints: Salvator Dali.*

There is ground for assuming, indeed, that the artist is at times repelled by the object or event about which he feels or by the original "feeling" itself. He may be repelled to a degree that makes improbable his use of the original as a symbol. Yet such repugnance may initiate the experience which in its turn may be expressed. Plainly, also, many artistic experiences which have been symbolized are initiated by content or in feeling either too intangible or too difficult to comprehend or to make comprehensible to permit of symbolization.

It may be inferred, therefore, that while Picasso is certainly correct in asserting that the artist's emotions "come from all over the place"—if one does not inquire too closely into the precise meaning of "emotions" in the quotation—it does not follow that the "referents" for the artist's feeling are retained as "signs" in the completed work of art or that the initial "emotions" are in fact those that the artist is interested to express. Moreover, because it is evident that the aesthetic percipient (for whom the art-object is the datum and comes to be the symbol) may be presented with a "counter-image" or indeed with a sign for a "counter-feeling," it is with the "sign," the work of art, that the problem must begin. It is not infrequently possible, as Picasso's statement implies, that beginning with the "sign," we may discover the original "referrent." To discover the initial "feeling" presents difficulties of a more complex kind. Leaving aside the fact that the inquirer faces the task, classically presented by Zeno as a paradox, of specifying the final term of an infinite series, it is evident that the presentation of the artist's experience in a medium of art is an obstacle to the recovery of the maker's original experience.

That the obstacle does present itself is evident. Cellini's well known account of casting the *Perseus* affords an instructive illustration. The reader of the autobiography may well inquire whether the statue actually symbolizes the obvious stimulus—the classical myth—or whether, on the contrary, it is not equally a symbol of the artist's feelings of triumph, evoked in the effort to control recalcitrant material. The latter inference would be in accord with a dominant contemporary interpretation of emotion which suggests that "feeling" necessarily implies conflict. On this interpretation, all profound moving works of art are symbols of the conflict resolved in the artist's soul and reflect experiences of the chagrin, the futility, frustration, or exaltation accompanying failure or success in conceiving the idea, forming the material, or expressing the self.

It remains for teleological theory to determine the specific significance of conflict for the function of feeling.[25] Consequently, any conclusion concerning that function in a symbolism of art must be deferred until a systematic account of the end of conation may be given. It is similarly irrelevant to the immediate issue whether the artist feels pride, dejection, exaltation, sorrow, or joy in "making." But whether he is frustrated or triumphant, it is evident and significant that the effort of constructing and of manipulating the material affects the artist's feelings. Those feelings enter, with the "emotions" evoked by the "referrents" of the symbol, upon the entire state of feeling which he proposes to communicate to the aesthetic percipient by means of the work of art. The work of art is, in consequence, a multiple symbol in regard to feelings for which it is a sign, and what is communicated in this respect must be said to derive from various sources.

Picasso is correct in assuming that the creative experience may originate in all manner of places, objects, and events. His assumption is not truly antithetical, however, to Eliot's conclusion that the experience "the poet is so bursting to communicate" may hardly be recognizable once "it has settled down" into the work of art. Due to the intervention of the media of art, the original experience must undergo alteration before the work of art becomes a proper symbol for the artist's feelings. It is noteworthy that Picasso does conclude that the original ideas and emotions are "integral" to the work of art but may be "indiscernible" in it.

We are now in a position to state more precisely the conditions under which the work of art as a symbol of the artist's feelings may be held to induce aesthetic experience. Here, our interests are principally twofold: In the first place, we must attend to the artist's

[25] Below, pp. 445 ff. and Chaps. XVI-XVII, particularly pp. 476-477.

"feelings," which derive variously from ideas, events, situations, and objects called "referrents" for feeling, as well as from the effort involved in "making" and from the manipulation of media. Secondly, the problem involves the sources and character of the symbol. The symbol is intended to fulfill its function in communication and cannot be solely the reproduction of the initial object or event that initiated the feeling.

Regarding the artist's feelings, Eliot significantly concludes that the experience actually communicated "may be the result of a *fusion* of feelings . . . ."[26] If the argument concerning the necessarily varied sources of the artist's feelings is sound the word "may", which Eliot uses, should be altered to "must." Yet, despite the fact that the art-object is not a symbol of a single "feeling," it is plain that, however complex works of fine art may be, the finished product of technique is unified. Variety in the work of art derives initially from the "referrent" of feelings and from the media. It may be inferred that the unity in the product has its correlative in the "fusion" of feeling. On grounds yet to be established, it may be concluded that a proper "fusion" of feelings is a "mood," presupposing the discrete states of feeling called instinct and emotion.[27] Once the state of "fusion" is achieved, discrete states of feeling are merged. The mood presupposes but is not reducible to its component conative factors. Further to characterize the mood, one may adopt Descartes' term, "conserving." The source of a mood may be discovered, as Picasso suggests, in "fear" or "sorrow." The mood need not necessarily be dominated by either one or the other of those emotions. But if it is so dominated, the mood itself "conserves" in the fearful or the sorrowful the discrete conative factors of which it is the end-product.

The "conserving mood" dominates the maker in his "making." The mood is characterized by a "temporal spread" sufficient to ensure the maintenance of feeling throughout the process of "making." The mood is not only "conserving," however, but "productive." Its productivity is actualized in the artist as he works with

[26] *Op. cit.*, p. 131.
[27] Cf. above, Chaps. XVII and XVIII, pp. 490 ff.

media appropriate for the various arts. To this extent, Bosanquet is correct in assuming that "imaginative expression creates the feeling in creating its embodiment. . . ."[28]

The mood or "fusion" of feelings that is at once conserving and productive is a factor significant for "making" and for a fuller understanding of aesthetic experience, because in the mood are the potentialities that give to aesthetic experience its antithetical character. Yet, although this will be shown to be a valid inference, the artistic symbol is communicable ultimately because mood is an aspect of feeling. Feeling, not its specific states, is presupposed in artistic symbolism and by it the artist is assured—to the extent that such assurance is possible—that the aesthetic experience of the percipient accords with what the artist intended to communicate.

The two significant, related, and relevant inferences are, therefore, first, that the work of art is a symbol and, secondly, that it is a symbol of feeling. Picasso's remark to the effect that the artist's "emotions" come from "all over the place" is plausible because it appears to be in accord with the wide range of meaning discoverable in the arts. Specifically, as we have observed, the meanings of art-objects are ostensibly coextensive with each and every object, idea, situation, or event to which the artist's feelings may conceivably attach. The implication is, therefore, that the range of meaning in art is inexhaustible in variety and extent.

It will be recalled, however, that the work of art is neither unique nor a symbol equivalent with the object symbolized. Moreover, the art-object is neither a mere object nor a mere event. It is a mode of communication and we have assumed, therefore, that it is a symbol. But a symbol is a sign that "stands for" something else. Consequently, the work of art, no less than any other symbol, must have a generic meaning. A poem, a building, or a sonata, no doubt "stands for" specific and individual aspects of the artist's experience. But to ensure communication, each individual expression must also stand for classes of objects, events, situations, and ideas to which feelings attach. Inexhaustible as the significations of art-objects may appear to be in the specific details of their representative or non-representa-

[28] *Three Lectures on Aesthetic*, p. 34.

tive meanings, their meanings are communicable only because they are generic symbols. Only because they are generic signs, are works of art comprehensible even to the artist, once the process of "making" has been completed.

It has been assumed in this chapter that the truth implicit in the *Ion's* interrelating of the poet, the poem, and the auditor may be made explicit in terms of feelings and symbols. We have now inferred that the presupposition of that relationship is the generic symbolism of the work of art. There remains to be considered the further inference that the presupposition of the work of art as an effective generic symbol is the generic and ateleologically definable aspect of feeling.

IV

BECAUSE each work of art is generic as well as specific in significance it is, *ex hypothesi*, a symbol of feeling adequate to "stand for" numerous feelings. The history of the arts is a chronicle of recurrent "mirrors of passion," generic symbols intended to effectuate the communication of the maker's feelings. It is unlikely that the symbols "mirror" the artist's original feeling. It is certain that they are not "feeling." They are, however, effective symbols for feeling because the artist who produces or adopts them has no need to reproduce the idea, event, or object which initiated his original feeling or the original feeling.[29] He need only make a generic symbol adequate to conform to his "conserving" mood in order to be assured of the efficacy of the symbol because feeling, considered ateleologically, is generic and typical behavior manifesting an organism's predisposition to react typically to generic situations, ideas, events, and objects. The percipient of the work of art is presented with a generic symbol of feeling. The sensuous media embody in artistic and symbolic form the non-aesthetic events, incidents, ideas, and situations to which feeling attaches and by which feeling is evoked. Aesthetic experience of the symbol is, thus far, the typical

[29] The "referrent" for the original feeling may, of course, accord with the generic sign.

behavior of a class of individuals to conative aspects of their environment.

In the various ranges of the life of feeling called instinct, emotion, and mood, there are particularized instincts of sex, hunger, self-preservation, and the like; emotions of love, hatred, fear, benevolence, anger, sorrow, and grief; and moods, variously called exalted, depressed, discontented, sentimental, sympathetic, and friendly. But specifically different as these aspects of feeling are, the *continuum* of feeling is generically identical throughout its range. All feeling is the behavior of an organism predisposed to react in typical ways to certain aspects of its environment, to ideas, events, objects, and situations. The symbol of feeling presented by the artist for communication is intended to evoke feeling in the percipient and the effectiveness of the symbol presupposes this predisposition to react in a typical way.

This is far from an assertion that aesthetic experience will be a necessary consequence of the reaction of the percipient to the symbol or that there is universal agreement upon the aesthetic merits of a given work of art. Moreover, works of art may be generic signs without being aesthetic, but all works of fine art are generic signs. Whatever warranty there is that these symbols will both convey the artist's mood and be the effective sources of the feeling presupposed in aesthetic experience derives either from the nearly universal attitude of humanity towards certain stimuli of fear, dread, love, and the like, or from the more limited attitude of individuals in a culture whose feelings are evoked by stimuli in a culture common to the artist and to his audience. Within a culture, the symbols are understood because the culture itself provides a predisposing factor. Because cultures have common practices and ideas it is probable that, in so far as divergent symbols have a common reference, the signs for their meanings may be understood by translation into the recognizable signs of another culture.

The artist, in order to communicate his feelings, must use generic symbols. In so doing, he avails his art of the common and moving heritages of both race and culture. These heritages provide him with situation after situation, event after event, object after object, and idea after idea to which feeling attaches and by which feelings may be evoked. These are the "referrents" for feeling, derived from the non-aesthetic teleologies, and they are likewise the "referrents" for the symbols of art.

It is because the symbols of art derive from the common and moving heritages of humanity or of particular cultures that they are not only adequate for the signification of the artist's feelings but also provide the *sine qua non* for the assumption that those who experience the art will understand it and be moved similarly by it. One such heritage is the tradition of the tribal leader, the "wintry slayer," common to Shakespeare's *Hamlet* and in the *Oresteia*.[30] Other "mirrors of passion" derive from cultural conceptions of the soul[31] and appear in the poetic accounts of Orpheus', Odysseus', Vergil's, and Dante's visits to the land of the dead. Art offers again and again the well-nigh universal theme of the barter of a man's soul to the forces of evil. The tales of martyrs and saints, the hunt, the chase, the shepherd, the horseman and the warrior, the struggle, man's love of his hearth, man's reverence for the gods—these are generally received symbols of pity and reverence, of combativeness, of loyalty, of aspiration, and of despair which become the symbols of profound art because in them innumerable specific feelings may find their adequate signs and because by their instrumentality the feelings may be expressed and re-expressed.

Because the character of the work of art as a symbol is considered at this juncture solely from the point of view of communication, it is not necessary to speculate upon the reasons for the artist's employment of generic signs in profoundly moving art. Those reasons are bound up with the issue of the end of art. It is, however, of interest and value to consider the problem in relation to the immediate end of communication. The artist is not isolated. He, perhaps no less than most men, seeks to be understood. All art worthy of commendation owes a portion of its value to its individuality and to the factors which *this* poet, *this* painter, *this* musician alone could contribute to it. To produce a work of art both recognizable and familiar is in some degree to grasp and hold the aesthetic perceiver's initial attention and to ensure interest in individual skill and interpre-

[30] Cf. below Chap. XII.
[31] Cf. below Chap. XIII.

tation. The symbol that must convey the artist's most individual and personal feelings is a sign whose structure and meaning are such that its generic meaning is recognizable. It not infrequently happens that if the artist does not convey the generic symbol clearly, the perceiver reinterprets the sign in terms of the familiar.

But if the personal and the individual in art presuppose the generic, it must in honesty be added that those aspects of sign and feeling that ensure familiarity and "immediacy" enormously complicate the artist's task in creating at the same time the unique and the individual. Yet is it true, as the chronicle of profoundly moving art shows, that such a generic symbol as the leader or great man has served, not only as symbol adequate to signify a great variety of feelings for a great variety of artists, but it has also been a more than adequate vehicle for great skill and for artistic imagination. In it, Milton gives the feelings of the great rebel and of the defeated who stood against the hosts of heaven. In it, also, Homer signified adeptness for craft, great sagacity, and the minutiae of the great Hellenic tradition. For the one poet, the symbol stands for the defeated leader, for the other, the leader and the wanderer. Great art has never hesitated to join in complex signs the symbols adequate to evoke a common conative experience.

But the artist desires not only to be understood. He adopts generic symbols for the expression of feeling in order to "fix the feelings" in concrete images. He derives from the signs an immortality impossible were the experience to vanish with organic changes. However extended even the mood may be, its continuation is but a moment in contrast to the permanence inhering in the symbol embodied in its proper materials. Horace's "exegi monumentum ære perennius" speaks for most masters of technique.

V

THERE is more to be inferred from the proposition that the work of art is a symbol of the artist's feelings than has been made explicit in this chapter and, as this essay proceeds to examine the teleology of feeling, some additional inferences, and in particular those significant for the understanding of aesthetic experience, will be drawn. At present we are concerned, however, only with what is implied in the proposition for artistic communication. The chapter is not intended to account either for artistic creativity or for the specific character of the symbols used in art.

It is necessary, nevertheless, to consider one additional implication of symbolization in art for which a brief anticipation of teleological theory is requisite. The *continuum* of feeling is generically identical throughout but it is specifically different in function in the stages of instinct, emotion and mood. It will be argued that artistic creativity presupposes these differentiations in feeling. By the same token, and notwithstanding the fact that the work of art is a generic symbol, artistic creativity is always evaluation. But while the artist's productivity implies evaluation, it does not create the "referrents" for art, the non-aesthetic objects, events, situations, and ideas to which feeling attaches.[32]

The larger portion of the conviction that the artist does create all of the aspects of his art probably derives from the fact that traditions in art sustain and maintain the non-aesthetic "referrents" for feeling long after the objects, ideas, events, and situations to which they refer have reached desuetude. The continued use of a given symbol in an artistic tradition does not prove, however, that the symbol itself originated in art. In fact, identical signs occur and recur in artistic traditions which are unrelated either historically or culturally. It is more plausible to assume that the generic symbols of art derive their meanings from non-aesthetic realms than that the maker invented or created either them or their "referrents."

Indeed, the Platonic argument that adds strength to the non-aesthetic teleological theories of art[33] is at this point a powerful instrument. It will be recalled that the Athenian urges that the subject matter of art is assimilated from other crafts and sciences; that the artist is never master of the subjects of his craft. The issue is not

[32] Whether he creates in the technique of his art is discussed by Rhys Carpenter in "The Basis of Artistic Creation."

[33] Cf. above, p. 14.

merely one for "subject matter," except as the latter is one aspect of symbolism. But even in regard to "subject matter," it would be difficult to name one idea, situation, object, or event to which feeling attaches and which appears in symbolic form in the art invented or originated by Shakespeare, Titian, Raphael, or Mahler as an artist. If that statement is too extreme, it may nonetheless be urged that no artist ever made in his art contributions to the frame of reference for the symbols he uses comparable to the contribution of a Plato or a Newton, an Alexander the Great or a Tamurlaine, a Whitney or an Edison. Shakespeare sought out generic symbols ultimately originating in Saxo Grammaticus, in Painter's *Palace of Pleasure* and in English history. Michelangelo's, Titian's, and Raphael's symbols derive from the religious and philosophical conceptions of Christianity and Neo-Platonism widespread in Renaissance thought. No one of these artists added original concepts to our philosophies or religions, laid the foundations for new theologies, or initiated a new science. Even the genius of Leonardo is content to accept in his fine art the fruits of the science of the past, although his inventive skill is manifest elsewhere than in the generic symbols of art. This is not to deny that art is creative. It is, however, to insist that artistic creativity does not extend to generic symbols or to the "referrents" for those symbols.

Significant, if negative, support for this argument is discovered in the fact that odium rarely attaches to the creative maker who is content to adapt from the non-artistic fields and from other artists the ideas, events, situations, and objects that enter upon the symbol of his own art. By way of illustration, scholars patiently searching for the sources and precursory ideas in Shakespeare's plays appear to do him no disservice. On the other hand, the discovery that either Newton or Leibniz had borrowed rather than invented the calculus would be ruinous to either mathematician's repute, whatever refinements of technique each may have effected. It is more significant, however, to recall that in recent aesthetic theory odium does attach to the artist if in his art he proposes and attempts to create new worlds of science, if he employs his art to moralize for the sake of man's ethical improvement, or to educate men in specific techniques.

We have observed, in fact, that the non-aesthetic teleological theories fail in part because the work of art may not be adequately defined in terms of these ends. Commercial art and illustration do not often move us profoundly because they concentrate too often solely upon these non-aesthetic ends.

The fine artist who attempts to achieve primarily non-aesthetic ends is said to have left the realm of aesthetic creation. But this implies only (despite the fact that the work of art definable in aesthetic terms is nonetheless bifunctional) that the fine artist is relieved of the need to create in these non-aesthetic fields. It is implied also, however, that he does always use for his symbols meanings definable in non-aesthetic terms. The conclusion is forced that the artist, in regard to symbols, recreates. It is because he does recreate by means of generic symbols derived from non-aesthetic realms that works of art are susceptible to use as instruments for teaching, for preaching, or for religion. But if the artist neither creates nor anticipates the non-aesthetic "referrents" of the symbols he employs, it is evident that the source of the symbols is in the science, in the religion, and in the morality presupposed by art.

Professor Singer suggests that "*Art* is the creation of a being in a society of beings already possessed of purposes definable without reference to art."[34] One may add, moreover, that the artist for the most part employs symbols the meanings of which derive, in point of time, from the past of his race and his culture. The "past," as it is intended here, is, however, not only a temporal but a logical presupposition.

The artist may and often does use the science, the religion, and the morality of an era that no longer exists for the profoundly moving symbols which "stand for" his feelings. He may equally well seize upon the static residue of the non-aesthetic techniques—static in the sense that they are accepted without active inquiry or without the critical creativity required to make science a living and dynamic search for the productive means by which man may best control his environment, explain the supernatural and organize the relations of man to man in society. In this sense the religious symbols used

[34] "Esthetic and Rational Ideal." *On the Contented Life*, p. 26.

by the artist ordinarily derive from solidly founded and accepted theological principles. The artist receives the doctrine and does not create it. Nor is the doctrine from which the symbols derive ordinarily in state of flux in which its proponents attempt to formulate or prove its theses. The mores of the society that provides the artist with the symbols by which he expresses his feelings are similarly those which time and custom have established and to which feeling has attached. The science he employs is *ex hypothesi* not a progressing one. Rather, it is one of the "images" which the dynamic technique of science has "discarded" in its infinite progress.[35]

The generic symbols of profoundly moving art derive from

> The fair humanities of old religion,
> The Power, the Beauty and the Majesty,

which "live no longer in the faith of reason!"[36] This Epimethean, backward-looking tendency in art, which induces its reversion to the past, implies a return to a world in which, as Hegel writes: "The columned temples are dead carcasses from which the living spirit of belief has departed and the words of hymns. The tables of the Gods are empty of spiritual meat and drink, their festivals no longer bring that joyous oneness with the heart of things." The artist does adopt symbols offered by "the fair humanities" which "live no longer in the faith of reason." But he does so because he knows that, ". . . still the heart doth need a language, still doth the old instinct bring back the old names . . ."

It is precisely in explaining the factors that lead the artist to heed "the old instinct" as well as our willingness to return to the past in the experience of his art that aesthetic comes to some of its most significant issues. There may not infrequently be pleasure in a return to the past. There may also be boredom or even sorrow. It is true that art makes alive the past that is irrevocably gone, that it gives spirit to concepts from which spirit has fled. It is also true, however, that it is not art alone that recreates in this fashion. Science, history, morality, as well as religions, have their pasts which

[35] Cf. below, Chap. XVII.
[36] *Wallenstein,* Act II, Scene IV, ll. 123 ff. Translated by S. T. Coleridge.

may also be made to come alive by the scientist, the historian, the moralist, and the theologian. Indeed, art, because its objects are idealized, has often appeared in its reinstatement of the past to be of negligible value in contrast to the sciences. The latters' recovery for far-ranging intelligence, employing the techniques of the historian, the mathematician, the physicist, and the philosopher, reconstructs the past accurately to understand a world that is dead, to compare and to contrast it with what is living, to salvage misunderstood but valuable contributions to man's history, to demonstrate the evolution of man's mind, mores, and society. The function of the artist in recovering the past is a different one and it is significant that the fine artist has not infrequently been accused of attaching his feelings to the past solely in order to escape the rigors and problems of the present.

If art only incidentally and, indeed, inaccurately makes the past valuable for science or history or morality; if it is incompetent to anticipate or to construct models of future worlds and societies by which the present may be directed towards a goal of improved science, religion, or morality; if art, being derivative in this sense, may not insist upon the intrinsic worth of the symbols it employs or contribute a new meaning for those symbols; if this is true, it may well be asked why the artist—and we—heed the "old instinct" which "brings back the old names."

The artist heeds the instinct—and we likewise heed it in our experience of the symbol of feeling—because in aesthetic experience there is satisfied a demand laid no less rigorously upon humanity than are the needs satisfied by science, religion, and morality. The artist reinstates the past in his symbols because fine art is implicated in feeling and feeling is in part reproductive. The artist's use of symbols drawn from the arts, the sciences, the moralities, and the religions of the past follows the pattern of feeling itself, which, in its reproductive part, is a reinstatement of the past. Within the dimensions of the life of feeling, from tropism, through instinct and emotion to mood, the *continuum* is a "traditional stair of life" which ranges "step by step to man." Feeling, as an instrument of science, "marks the way man has climbed," man whose rational life "is nothing more than the topmost rung continuous with related degrees below."[37] And because this is true of feeling, in art "the memory of falsehood is treasured even by those who love the truth."[38] But the aesthetic experience is also creative and "creates the creator." It is a paradox of art that the artist induces in us a reversion to the past of the culture and of the race and that in consequence of our experience of profoundly moving works of art we emerge in a creative mood. The paradox is no less paradoxical because the artist does not himself create the world in which is fully expended the creativity his art induces.

The paradox is but an aspect of the antinomy with which this essay began. The grounds for the antinomic aspects of art and of aesthetic experience will be shown in a more detailed analysis of the ateleological theory of feeling in the following chapter. It is well to turn to that theory, aware as we do so, that the grounds for the present chapter on the work of art as the symbol of the artist's feelings are to be sought there, as are the grounds for the relevant consequences of the reversion to the past implicit in aesthetic experience.

[37] Sherrington, *op. cit.*, pp. 181-188. The application of Sherrington's words to feeling is the present writer's.

[38] E. A. Singer, Jr., "Old Magic and New Art," *On the Contented Life*, p. 264.

Chapter XI

The Ateleological Theory of Feeling: Reproductive Imagination

There are, we have said, two memories which are profoundly distinct: the one, fixed in the organism, is nothing else but the complete set of intelligently constructed mechanisms which ensure the appropriate reply to the various possible demands. This memory enables us to adapt ourselves to the present situation; through it the actions to which we are subject prolong themselves into reactions that are sometimes accomplished, sometimes merely nascent, but always more or less appropriate.

—Henri Bergson[1]

IT IS the result of an inspired poetic imagination accompanied by the rarest speculative powers that philosophy of art is the heir to the image of the magnetic rings. One may hope that the philosophical truth Plato wished to express in the Dialogue between Socrates and Ion—that the work of art is the link of communication between artist and percipient—has been afforded a sufficient initial precision in the language of generic symbols to compensate for the loss in poetic richness that must inevitably follow upon reinterpretation of his original words.

But once committed to interpretation of the passage in *Ion* for the purpose of formulating a general aesthetic theory, one observes that Plato himself is not content to leave the problem with the suggestion that the poet and his auditor are "links" in a chain. Socrates

[1] Henri Bergson, *Matter and Memory*. (By permission of The Macmillan Company, publishers.)

alludes to the "power"—likened to that exercised by the stone of Heraclea—which attracts and imparts the "power" to attract and "makes one man hang down from another" in the chain of inspiration.

Precisely as the poetic figure of "rings" with the "vast chain of dancers and masters and undermasters of choruses, who are suspended, as if from the stone" gives way in aesthetic theory to the precise language of symbols, so the "power" of the original magnet which imparts the capacity to attract is replaced by "feeling." Nor is it incongruous that the counterpart to precise symbolism in the reinterpretation of *Ion* should be a theory of feeling evolved from Descartes' rational philosophy. Cartesianism takes "for granted that the human body is just as much a machine and as explicable by the ordinary laws of physics as any complicated piece of mechanism."[2] The precision that inheres in the science of symbols served as one of the primary goals in the formulation of the Cartesian theory of the passions. This is the more significant as we recall that the communicability of the generic symbols of art was asserted to rest upon the hypothesis that feeling is a generic attitude.[3]

The hypothesis of feeling in question is ateleological. Its immediately significant implication is that of "reproductive imagination." The theory itself will be presented in this chapter. We shall proceed, in the three succeeding chapters, to indicate the significance of the ateleological theory of feeling for the relation of art to aesthetic experience and the difficulties to which aesthetic explanation is led by a sole dependence upon its explanatory principles.

II

THE ateleologist interprets the feelings, presupposed in the communicability of generic symbols in art, to be the typical behavior of any "ego" with reference to an objective or subjective

[2] E. S. Haldane, *Descartes, His Life and Times*, pp. 374-375. Some aspects of the Cartesian hypothesis and its continuing influence will be discussed in Chap. XV.

[3] Cf. above, pp. 337 ff.

stimulus. This typical behavior he describes distributively in terms of physiological and neurological reaction. The description is intended to exclude from analysis of the life of feeling all reference to "purpose" or "end."[4]

Some reminiscence of the terminology used by the ateleologist in describing the typical behavior alluded to as feeling is discovered in Sir Charles Sherrington's *Man on His Nature*. Sir Charles does not conclude that the theory is adequate but he does present it fully and well and his words will serve to introduce the principal problems requiring consideration. Feelings for the mechanist are "trigger-like" reactions to stimuli and imply a preorganized nervous and physiological structure. The reactions, beyond the control of the agent, are regarded as "innate." Feelings are "extrinsically" produced reactions, with "activity . . . partly operated by nervous action arising spontaneously within the nervous centers themselves" and "so constructed that the world outside touches triggers for their doing."[5]

It is significant at once that Sherrington places some emphasis upon the fact that "the world outside touches triggers" for the "reactions" and that he interprets the ateleological theory to mean that there is an implied conversion of "the signal into a releasing force for an act." It is the latter implication, in fact, that sets the initial problem for any discussion of the ateleological theory of feeling. However minute may be the analyses of physiological and neurological structures, the explanation of the reactions presupposes an epistemological theory. The "signal" in order to be a signal must be "recognized" so that it may be "converted" into "a releasing force for an act." It is this connotation that permits us to treat the description of feeling in question as a hypothesis of "reproductive imagination."

More specifically, it is the epistemological significance of "signal" and "conversion" that has led classical ateleological theorists of feeling to maintain that the organism brings to its environment

[4] Cf. above, pp. 327-328.

[5] *Op. cit.*, pp. 180 ff. Cambridge University Press, England. (By permission of The Macmillan Company, publishers.)

and to its subjective states an *Apperceptionsmass* or predisposition for experience. At this point, it is of value to anticipate a fact of some significance for later discussion. The predisposition for experience closely resembles what Bergson regards as "pure memory." But in the present interpretation of the ateleological theory, it will be argued that "pure memory," as the biologically inherited *Apperceptionsmass*, is but a portion of that predisposition.[6] As feelings operate, there is evident, in addition to the primary, atavistic, and biological, a secondary and derivative cultural predisposition. The biological *Apperceptionsmass* is shared by man with the brute. The cultural predisposition of feeling may be limited, for the purposes of this exposition, to men. It operates upon the heritable past with which men are endowed through language, customs, and institutions.

The *Apperceptionsmass*, the presupposition of an ateleological analysis of feeling of mechanically defined behavior, is best analyzed against the background of the *continuum* of feeling itself.[7] The significant features of the *continuum* are most easily made evident, in their turn, by reference to William James' theory of the emotions, the "coping-stone" of modern controversy concerning "feeling."[8]

In so far as James did succeed in presenting a consistent analysis of emotion, his theory offers arguments basic to two important ateleological principles concerning the "life of feeling."[9] In the first place, his is the modern *fons et origo* for the assumption that the instincts and emotions are constituted of observable behavior.[10] Sec-

[6] The significance of this argument for art will be made clear in Chap. XIII.

[7] Cf. above, pp. 325 ff.

[8] *Principles of Psychology*, Vol. 2, pp. 449 ff. It is natural to turn to James' theory, not to amplify it but, rather, because it is a sound point of departure for analysis. Because it has been the historical storm center of modern theory of the emotions and because of James' own ambiguities in the statement of his views, succeeding theorists have benefited by the attempts to attack or defend it and by efforts either to validate or deny James' own attempts to make his theory consistent.

[9] The third important principle concerns the purpose of emotion. Cf. below, Chap. XV.

[10] Cf. the quotation, in Chap. IX, p. 309 (William James, *op. cit.*, Vol. 2, p. 452): "A purely disembodied human emotion is a nonentity—for us, emotion dissociated from all bodily feeling is inconceivable." As will be obvious, what James meant precisely by "bodily feeling" is difficult to ascertain. It is important, however, at the outset, to bear in mind that James regarded as

ondly, it is not unjust to his text to urge that James' meant to imply in expressions of the kind, "We are afraid because we tremble," that fear and other emotions are modes of "knowing involved in a total reaction to a situation or inner stimulus."[11]

It is significant, concerning the implication in James' theory that feeling (and in particular the emotions) is observable behavior, that it was to the striking phraseology of such statements as "We are afraid because we run" that popular attention was called to the James-Lange theory. But it was the extreme complexity which James attributed to the behavior that gave direction to the scientific research which followed upon his hypothesis. The extent to which James realized that "the bodily affections . . . characteristic . . . of any one of the standard emotion[s]" are "infinitely numerous and subtle" is evident in the following passage:

> The researches of Mosso with the plethysymograph have shown that not only the heart, but the entire circulatory system, forms a sort of sounding-board, which every change of our consciousness, however slight, may make reverberate. Hardly a sensation comes to us without sending waves of alternate constriction and dilatation down the arteries of our arms. The blood vessels of the abdomen act reciprocally with those of the more outward parts. The bladder and bowels, the glands of the mouth, throat, and skin, and the liver, are known to be affected gravely in certain severe emotions and are unquestionably affected transiently when the emotions are of a lighter sort. That the heart-beats and the rhythm of breathing play a leading part in all emotions whatsoever, is a matter too notorious for proof. And what is really equally prominent, but less likely to be admitted until special attention is drawn to the fact, is the continuous cooperation of the voluntary muscles in our emotional

---

crude the most frequently quoted statement of his theory. He had written (*ibid.*, pp. 449-450) that, "Common-sense says, we lose our fortune, are sorry and weep; we meet a bear, are frightened and run; we are insulted by a rival, are angry and strike. The hypothesis here to be defended says that this order of sequence is incorrect, that the one mental state is not immediately induced by the other, that the bodily manifestations must first be interposed between, that the more rational statement is that we feel sorry because we cry, angry because we strike, afraid because we tremble, and not that we cry, strike or tremble because we are sorry, angry, or fearful, as the case may be." In *Mind*, Vol. IX, pp. 188-205, James wrote in detail concerning the subtlety of the emotions and the difficulty of their analysis.

[11] "The Physical Basis of Emotion."

states. Even when no change of outward attitude is produced, their inward tension alters to suit each varying mood, and is felt as a difference of tone and strain.[12]

It is only necessary for the purposes of the present essay to indicate the general lines of the research which followed upon James' theory and which increasingly showed the complexity of any adequate and precise description of the physiological and neurological structures involved in feeling. Perhaps the most considerable impetus to the experimentation was given by Sherrington's researches,[13] the inferences from which were that James' theory was "competent" for "coarser emotions." As the efforts were continued to establish or to disprove James' hypothesis, two opposing schools of thought concerning the emotions came into being and are in process of development. The first accepts the suggestion that the important bodily reactions constituting emotional behavior are "peripheral." The second, largely associated with the name of W. B. Cannon,[14] denies the primary importance of the peripheral reaction and maintains that the emotional center is the optic-thalamus, the emotional response being a "pattern reaction" in which "impulses flash through peculiarly co-operating neuron groups of the central nervous system."[15]

It will be of importance to indicate later the consequences of this divergence of theory, the more so because Cannon maintains that there is a difference between "emotional behavior" and "emotional experience." At present, however, it suffices to remark, without entering into detail, that each interpretation, peripheral or thalamic, requires the most detailed analysis of observable behavior and that, despite divergences elsewhere, both interpretations agree that the feelings are primitive and atavistic in character.[16]

[12] *Mind*, Vol. IX.

[13] *The Integrative Action of the Nervous System*, Lecture vii, pp. 235 ff. and "Experiments on the Value of the Vascular and Visceral Factors for the Generation of Emotions," *Proceedings, Royal Society of London*, Vol. 66, May, 1900.

[14] In particular, *Bodily Changes in Pain, Hunger, Fear and Rage*. The controversy which Cannon's view aroused is in part touched upon in my article, "Philosophical Implications," pp. 465 ff.

[15] Cannon, *op. cit.*, p. 228; cf. p. 247.

[16] By way of illustration, see Cannon, *Feelings and Emotion*, p. 263, and *Bodily Changes*, VII. See below, pp. 433-434.

Concerning the second point, that feeling is a mode of knowing, it is necessary to make plain at the outset that James does not regard feeling as a "simple sensation" received by an organism for use as a "building block" in subsequent knowledge. He does not maintain this position consistently, however, and the ambiguity of his interpretation is of value in any effort to clarify the cognitive problem raised. In consequence of his own inconsistency, James gave a dual characterization of the emotions. "We are afraid because we tremble" rightly implies that fear is a way of knowing implicated in a total reaction to a situation or inner stimulus. The alternative, implicit in the *Principles*, is that emotion is the combination in "consciousness"[17] of the objects as sensation, simply apprehended as idea, to which is added perception, as complex sensations, of the alterations undergone by "muscle, skin and viscus."[18]

It is a matter of first importance to understand that these alternative statements plainly suggest James' occasional tendency to distinguish "object-simply-apprehended" and the "object-emotionally-felt" as if they were different in kind.[19] The issue is significant because the distinction cannot be maintained. James admits that "object-simply-apprehended" has its source in "an object fall[ing] on a sense organ" or in the inward excitation of the "cortical part." This simply signifies, however, that there occurs "sensation" as

[17] Cf. E. A. Singer, Jr., *Mind as Behavior*, pp. 6-9, 174-176, and 182 for an examination of James' views on "consciousness."

[18] *Op. cit.*, Vol. 2, pp. 473-474: "An object falls on a sense-organ, affects a cortical part, and is perceived; or else the latter, excited inwardly, gives rise to an idea of the same object. Quick as a flash, the reflex currents pass down through their preordained channels, alter the condition of muscle, skin and viscus; and these alterations, perceived, like the original object, in as many portions of the cortex, combine with it in consciousness and transform it from an object-simply-apprehended into an object-emotionally-felt."

[19] Traces of Locke's theory of "impressions" are to be found in the treatment of the "simply-apprehended-object." The contrasting view does make mind active rather than passive but it does more. The former theory interprets the *given* as the datum of experience and ignores the fact that, as H. B. Smith writes ("Postulates of Empirical Thought," p. 26), "the apparatus of sense . . . is itself an instrument . . . and is employed . . . in the business of ordering and comparing data." Smith observes that ". . . we might expect to gain some further insight into the physiological nature of man through a study of his instruments and tools, and similarly, some understanding of his conscious and unconscious habits of perception by analyzing his methods of experience and experimental technique."

reaction to stimulus. And James himself argues[20] that the emotions are "sensational processes," that "each emotion is the resultant of a sum of elements," and that "each element is caused by a physiological process of a sort already well known." All these elements, i.e., the "sensational processes," he regards as "organic changes, and each of them is the reflex effect of the exciting object." But what on this hypothesis is a stimulus? The implications of James' statements suggest close accord on this point with Adrian's precise definition: "any change in the environment of an excitable tissue which, if sufficiently intense will excite the tissue, i.e., will cause it to display its characteristic activity."[21] Plainly, therefore, "object-simply-apprehended" implies and involves bodily change. It is evident, moreover, that the phrases "object-simply-apprehended" and "object-emotionally-felt" do not and can not imply, regarding the occurrence of bodily behavior, a difference in kind. Such a difference would imply that "simple" perception is sufficiently "simple" to preclude bodily reaction to stimulus.

The supposed need to satisfy the demand for a difference in kind between "object-simply-apprehended" and "object-emotionally-felt" has led theory, in fact, to set up a false dichotomy between the two. But the distinction being untenable, the dichotomy need not be retained and in fact disappears upon the adoption of the alternative view. Crudely stated, the alternative is that, "We are afraid because we tremble." The alternative is also implied in the somewhat ambiguous statement that the emotions are "our feelings of the same [bodily] changes as they occur," if the term "feeling" is not taken to signify unsupported introspective analysis. For if either statement of the alternative is examined, the distinction between "object-simply-apprehended" and "object-emotionally-felt" is evidently no longer consequent upon the invalid exclusion from consideration of bodily reaction in perception, but upon observable differences (not in kind but in the degree) of bodily reaction implicated in the per-

[20] *Principles of Psychology*, Vol. 2, p. 453. It is also true that he takes the "sensational processes" to be due to "inward currents set up by the physical happenings."

[21] E. D. Adrian, *The Basis of Sensation*, p. 18.

ception of non-emotional and of emotional situations.[22] The point is that the adjustments of the body which constitute at least a portion of ordinary perception are, for the perceiver, in large part subliminal. Ordinarily, such adjustments are insufficiently overt to warrant attention from any observer other than the psychologist or the epistemologist. In the perception called "emotional," on the other hand, the reaction of the perceiver (who may or may not be the sole percipient) becomes a "threshold stimulus" for the experiencing individual, as a result either of the rapidity or extent of the change. "Object-simply-apprehended" is distinguished from "object-emotionally-perceived" by what, in Singer's phrase, *does not* affect the experiencing individual.[23]

Perception is not the collection or sum of "simple sensations." It is, rather, the adjustment or reaction of the organism to stimuli. In instances in which perception may properly be called "feeling", the adjustment is at least in part a typical reaction which, because of the intensiveness or extensiveness of the muscular, visceral and glandular change, is readily observable by a perceiver. Emotion is perception of a kind. For the observer, it is the pallor of the skin, the sweating, the capillary action of the hair, the trembling and palpitation, the clenching of the hands, the dilation of the nostrils, the blush. But one is, as well, afraid of the fearful object or overjoyed by a joyful object. The behavior called "feeling" is knowledge of the nature of the stimuli. In feeling, there has occurred a discontinuity in the external or internal world—or one supposed by the organism emotionally moved to have occurred—which calls forth emergency action. It is the magnitude or intensity of the emergency action that causes the reaction to become an obvious portion of the total perceptual situation.

The complexity of the experience called "feeling" results from the complexity of an organism reacting as a whole in a preadjusted way to its environment. Instinct, emotion, and mood are in this respect allied because the individual in each state of feeling manifests "familiarity" with the stimulus as an object or as a situation experi-

[22] See E. A. Singer, Jr., "On Sensibility," *op. cit.*, pp. 93 ff.

[23] *Ibid.*, p. 95.

enced. Limiting the present discussion to the operation of the *continuum* as a biological *Apperceptionsmass* and ignoring for the moment the reaction to cultural stimuli, the typical reaction occurs without previous training or discipline in the individual's experience. The reaction is, moreover, in varying degrees beyond the control of the individual.[24] It is in this sense that the ateleologist maintains that the *continuum* of feeling, in its divergent aspects of instinct, emotion, and mood, is properly understood as an *Apperceptionsmass* through which "every living thing is but a bundle of predispositions to react in particular ways upon the contact of particular features of the environment."[25]

The more significant inferences to be drawn from the ateleological description of the *continuum* of feeling (whether it is de-

[24] Cf. below, Chap. XV. A further point is that the behavior is taken to be common to a species or to a sex within that species.

[25] Cf. E. von Hartmann, *Philosophie des Unbewussten*, particularly Chap. 10, p. 302. It is of interest to note, at this point, that despite the controversy to which James' view has been subjected, the hypothesis of the *Appercepzionsmass* of feeling has been maintained even by some of the most severe critics of his theory. Cannon, the ablest exponent of the view explicitly opposed to that of James' on the two grounds of "quality" of emotions and of the significance of peripheral reactions, holds that, "Fear, rage, pain and pangs of hunger are all primitive experiences in which human beings share with the lower animals." He adds that the responses noted are "typical organic responses . . . evoked through inherent automatisms." (Cf. *Bodily Changes in Pain, Hunger, Fear and Rage*, Chap. VII and pp. 194-243; "Again the James-Lange and the Thalamic Theories of Emotion"; and "The James-Lange Theory of Emotions: A Critical Examination and an Alternative Theory." The crucial points of difference between James' view and Cannon's are treated in my article to which reference was previously made.) Cannon holds that "the neuro-muscular and neuro-visceral arrangement for the display of rage has its central control congenitally organized in or near a phylogenetically ancient part of the brain, the optic thalamus. The thalamus is not like the cerebral cortex in being a region where new relations with the outer world are registered and old relations are modified; it more nearly resembles the spinal cord—a region under superior dominance, where afferent impulses are received, regrouped, and redistributed either to the higher levels, or to neighboring motor neurons which promptly discharge to effector organs in stereotyped reaction patterns. The typical postures and attitudes which result from action of the thalamus are more complicated than those produced by spinal reflexes but are not essentially different. The physiological organization which establishes the reflex figure of rage I have detailed because it may serve as a prototype for other primitive emotional responses." (*Feelings and Emotions*, p. 263). It is obvious that, despite fundamental divergences between Cannon's theory and that of James', the men are agreed upon the primitive and mechanical reaction of "feeling" as an *Appercepzionsmass*.

scribed in terms of the peripheral or thalamic physiological structure) are best expressed for eventual use by the aesthetician in terms of "imagination." "Imagination" is not, as Butcher's analysis of Aristotle's theory of *katharsis* implies,[26] a faculty vaguely related to feeling. It is, as this essay has argued, the organism's effective presentation to itself of a stimulus. As Descartes properly maintained, imagination is, in contrast to intellection, eventually directed to the external world.[27] An "image," on the present hypothesis, is an "effective stimulus," a stimulus that effectuates observable behavior. Regarding their source, "images" may be subjective or objective effective stimuli. There are naturally, combinations of "images" which derive from both internal and external effective stimuli.

It is advisable to note, before elaborating upon feeling or imagination and before indicating the eventual distinction between "reproductive" and "productive images," that a stimulus sufficiently effective to become an "image" for an organism presupposes the activity of the organism in the latter's presentation of stimuli to itself. Imagination is never merely passive or receptive. The epistemological presuppositions[28] for the mind's "imagining" are such as to preclude the mind's resemblance to a *tabula rasa*, to a "mirror," or to an "empty cabinet." Each of these classical metaphors suggests a mind passively awaiting the operations of *sensibilia*. Despite this, however, it is nonetheless essential to emphasize the fact at the same time that in comparative degree the *Apperceptionsmass* of feeling, upon which familiarity in art is grounded and which presupposes the dominant epistemological operation common to all dimensions of the *continuum*, constitutes an "imagination" of primarily reproductive character. However essential to "imagination" the activity of the individual who feels may be for the presentation to himself of stimuli, the physiological and neurological "predisposition to react in particular ways upon the contact of particular features of the environment" presupposes the individual's "recognition" of the

[26] Cf. above, pp. 311 ff.

[27] *Meditations* V.

[28] The presuppositions are, among others, the capacity to compare and to contrast, as well as to individuate.

stimulus.[29] This follows because the stimulus (which in being effective comes to be an "image") is but a portion of a "total situation" from which the ego's selection of stimuli must be made. In the instance of typical reactions to stimuli ordinarily called reflex, instinctive or emotional, however, the behavior of the individual so moved is consequent upon no observable empirical training. Indeed, the ateleologist argues that the reaction is, in varying degree, beyond the subject's control. The actualized behavior must in consequence be potential to the the organism's physiological and neurological structure. In the reaction occurs the actualization of the structure's predisposition "to react in particular ways upon contact of particular features of the environment." "Re-cognition" is implied.

The inference that this recognitive aspect of typical behavior is a function of "reproductive" imagination suggests Kant's analogous argument concerning the "reproduction of representations."[30] It has been argued in the present essay that the "image" is but one of a "total set of stimuli" constituting a portion of a "total situation." The individual who feels, behaves, with reference to the effective stimulus, typically, generically, and with no need for previous training. In so doing, as his behavior shows, he "recognizes" the stimulus which is a part of that "total situation." The recognition presupposes for its occurrence on Kant's analogous argument, the "reproduction of representations,"[31] that connection of the imagination "with some one representation in preference to another." The

[29] He need not know that he recognizes but his behavior makes such recognition apparent to a reflective if not to the experiencing mind. The experiencing mind, however, may be reflective. See Edgar A. Singer, Jr., *op. cit.*, pp. 163 ff.

[30] The significant point is Kant's argument, not the similarity of the terminology employed. The force of that argument and the light it casts upon the problem of feeling make it advisable to adopt for a brief space Kant's terminology of "representative images," in turn inherited by the Critical Philosophy from Kant's rationalist predecessors. In this terminology, the effective stimulus which has been called here an "image" is a "representation" or a "representative image."

[31] *K.d.r.V.*, A 121. I am not here concerned with Kant's analysis of Imagination as it is integral to his system of philosophy, nor with Categories of the Understanding, nor with the "rule" which governs the "reproduction of representations." The problem under consideration is that of the presuppositions of "feeling" and not the *Appercepzionsmass* of experience in general.

stimulus has become a "representative image" but it can become such an image—i.e., it can be selected from among the total set of stimuli—because there has occurred a "reproduction" of a prior "set of representations," as well as the display of a preference.

The significance of Kant's point for the present argument is not the metaphysical ground for the "preference." Rather, it is the fact that Kant so plainly seized upon, that the process upon which the selection depends is essentially recreative or reproductive. In the case of conation, the "preference" displayed in the reaction by the organism for one among numerous stimuli of the "total situation" is explicable upon the assumption that the subject that feels possesses a predisposition which is a function of a physiological or neurological structure. This reproductive imagination, like Bergson's "pure memory," is "fixée dans l'organisme" and it reinstates or reproduces what a classical epistemology might term an inborn or hereditary "set of representations." Of this "reproductive imagination," one may perhaps write as Bergson wrote of "pure memory" that it "is nothing else but the complete set of intelligently constructed mechanisms which ensure the appropriate reply to the various possible demands."[32] In its operation, the reproductive factor in the biological *continuum* of feeling, "fixée dans l'organisme," makes possible, to retain Kant's terminology, the "reinstatement" of the necessary precedent "image" alongside the subsequent "image." The latter is the effective stimulus. The former is the precedent predisposition which in feeling supplies the connection of the imagination "with some one representation in preference to another."[33]

Terror, hatred, rage, love—the instincts, emotions, passions, and moods of the individual who feels—are, in conjunction with the end of the action and the stimulus to action, descriptive of the behavior of the moved individual. Our concern, in the present stage of the theory of feeling, is solely with that aspect of the behavior definable in ateleological terms. It is in this connection that it is requisite to ask, What is "reinstated" in this "preceding image," reproduced

[32] *Matter and Memory*, p. 195. Translated by N. M. Paul and W. S. Palmer. (By permission of The Macmillan Company, publishers.)

[33] I have again adopted Kant's terminology for the problem, without any intention of attributing the application to him.

alongside "the subsequent one," and essential to the explanation of the latter's effectiveness?

If we ignore the ambiguity in the term "image" as it is identified with the "precedent" predisposition,[34] it is possible to infer precisely concerning what is reinstated from the character of the "subsequent" image or effective stimulus. The effective stimulus for feeling is a particular situation, object, idea or event, one of numerous diverse particular stimuli potential in the "total situation." The stimulus evokes typical and generic behavior called feeling. Panic fear, flight, the clenching of the fist, the blush, the "start" of surprise—all may be initiated by a variety of particular stimuli. The actual behavior is, however, common to a class or to a group of a class. It is, moreover, generic and it may be described in universal terms despite the fact that a particular aspect of the environment effects it. The behavior is, as James, Cannon, and others have suggested, the operation of primitive biological mechanisms, in overt but nonetheless vestigial forms. The feelings are mechanisms which permitted man to adjust himself to his environment and must have been instrumental for the survival of both man and brute.

The *a priori* physiological and neurological *Apperceptionsmass* of feeling is basically emergency action. Throughout the ranges of the *continuum* of feeling, as is suggested by the immediacy of the compulsion to react to effective stimuli, there is every evidence that the typical and generic behavior is the primitive reaction of the organism to its environment. In feeling is discovered a necessary preadjustment to that environment.

The mere description of the types of reaction called feeling is incomplete without an understanding of the stimuli which transform the potential predisposition into actual behavior. These stimuli are events, objects, ideas, and situations in the "total situation." To be "signals" for emergency reaction they must be recognized. For recognition, a "precedent image" must be reproduced alongside the "subsequent one." Because the "precedent image" does not derive from the experience of the experiencing individual, it may be inferred that the "precedent image" is the past of the race. *Mutatis*

[34] "Formal idea" is the more classical terminology.

mutandis, the "precedent image" for feeling aroused by cultural, in contrast to racial symbols, is the past of the culture. As we shall discover, the teleological theory of feeling permits the inference that the "precedent image" is not only constituted of the past of the race but of its evolution or progress, as well.

The operation of the *continuum* of feeling in reproductive imagination is atavistic. Its pattern is reaction rooted in the common ancestry of man and brute. By means of his reason and through his science, man has evolved beyond the brute but to the status of the brute he reverts in the more violent of his feelings. He reverts more or less completely because conation has undergone change as man has evolved. But feeling in each instance of its occurrence "marks the way man has climbed."[35]

In the operation of "reproductive" imagination, as "subsequent" images reinstate "precedent" ones, it is clear that the effective stimuli evoking panic, fear, hatred, joy, sorrow, and the like, are of great variety. For ease of treatment, they may be divided into biological and cultural stimuli and for equal ease of handling they may be said to evoke reactions possible because of biological and cultural *Apperceptionsmassen.* The terminology employed, however, requires clarification. The distinction between biological and cultural stimuli does not turn upon a difference between natural and social "images." It does turn upon a distinction among stimuli which arouse feelings in man and in brute, and in man alone. Numerous social stimuli are experienced in common by man and by brute. Man is and has always been a "social animal" and the generic symbols of the den, the leader, gregariousness, and the like, are signs of experiences common to man and to brute.

[35] Whether the "reinstated image" argues a racial memory, i.e., whether content is passed on through feeling, is a question beyond the scope of the present inquiry. What is observable is behavior which indicates recognition of a situation as one understandable in terms of a generic category of experience. Whether there is "content" it would be difficult to say, but it is interesting that, despite the strictures of biology upon the inheritance of acquired characteristics, the problem of initial recognition by a perceiver appears to be inexplicable without some *a priori* presuppositions of knowledge. But whether the latter are formal or structural, material, or what not, is the task of the epistemologist to determine.

In the course of man's evolution, however, and because culture stores up much for conation through history, customs, and intellectual activities, feelings have attached to stimuli the experience of which man almost certainly does not share with others in the brute world. To these stimuli, for which birth and nurture in human society predispose feelings, appropriate reactions may be as little consequent upon individual effort, may be as atavistic and as binding as are reactions to the more primitive stimuli to which both men and beast are moved. Habit, training, discipline, language, education, and tradition—these too, compel the individual to "react in particular ways upon contact of particular features of environment" in non-human and in human societies and in aspects of each.

It is also well to observe at this juncture an additional point that will be of value for our subsequent study of the function of "biological" and "cultural images" in art. The stimuli for the biological predisposition in feeling are more nearly universally understood than are those affecting the "cultural" *Apperceptionsmass*, if only because the symbols affecting the cultural predisposition are frequently limited in reference. The symbols of feeling restricted to the experience of men—such as those which attach to "images" of the Deity and of man's immortal soul—vary both in detail and in connotation in various cultures. It is doubtful that many men are unaffected by cultural stimuli of this kind. But only individuals who inherit specifically the tradition, let us say, of the Pythagorean or Indian interpretations of *metempsychosis*, will be predisposed to react to symbols in the art of that tradition. These are, in fact, among the symbols of limited scope which arise in what Bergson has called "closed societies."[36] Some cultural symbols, such as that of light as a sign for divinity or for the immortality of man's soul, are sufficiently widespread to warrant the assumption that they are comprehensible in "open societies."[37] There are, however, means by which the meanings of symbols may be communicated to members of a "closed society" for whom there is no specific cultural predisposition. Thus, the man of the mountains may be made to

[36] See *The Two Sources of Morality and Religion*, Chap. II.
[37] *Ibid.*, Chap. III. Cf. below, Chap. XIII.

understand in art the dangers, the mode of life, and the feelings attached to both for the seaman.

Such, in broad outline, is the ateleological theory of feeling. It has been offered, with some anticipations of its relation to the generic symbols of art and to the problem of communication. We shall turn now, more specifically, to its implications for the experience of profoundly moving works of art.

Chapter XII

Reproductive Imagination and the Generic Symbols of Art (I): The Biological Apperceptionsmass

For the essence of humanism is that belief . . . that nothing which has ever interested living men and women can wholly lose its vitality . . . no language they have spoken, no oracle beside which they have hushed their voices, no dream which has once been entertained by actual human minds, nothing about which they have ever been passionate, or expended time and zeal . . .

—WALTER PATER

PLATO, in the *Laws*, as we have observed, commended Egyptian art and praised the rules by which "no painter or artist is allowed to innovate upon them, or to leave the traditional forms and invent new ones."[1] The Athenian's motives were no doubt mixed. We have commented upon the possibility that he judged that the Egyptian canon, like that of Polycleitus, provided one solution to the problem of "absolutely beautiful forms."[2] It is certain that he was convinced that conformity to an art of this kind would help to habituate young citizens "to forms and strains of virtue." It is significant, however, that he qualifies his opinion: "And therefore, as I was saying, if a person can only find in any way the natural melodies, he may confidently embody them in a fixed and legal form." Granted that this discovery may be made, "the love of novelty

[1] *Op. cit.*, 656-657.

[2] Cf. above, Chap. IV, pp. 143 ff.

which arises out of pleasure in the new and weariness of the old, has not strength enough to corrupt the consecrated song and dance, under the plea that they have become antiquated."

Whereas Plato urges conformity to ancient canons and decries novelty, Aristotle makes some suggestion concerning the problem of the familiar in art by calling attention to the pleasure consequent upon recognition in the experience of art.[3] Aristotle's inference is a natural consequence of the theory of *mimesis.* If the aesthetician insists that the "maker" is re-creative as well as creative in his art and that works of art derive their symbolical significance from the past, it is neither because he adheres blindly to Plato's faith in the canons of antiquity nor because he permits a conclusion which follows from Aristotle's adherence to a theory of imitation to influence his judgment. The aesthetician may be influenced, in some degree, by consequences in art which suggest that a curb is required for theory that has swung so far from *mimesis* as to accord the artist a limitless creativity he never possessed and could never exercise had he possessed it. These factors may influence his judgment but the immediate issues which lead him to analysis of recreation in art are communicability and actual communication. The ultimate issue is to resolve the antinomies of art and of aesthetic experience. And in the operations of reproductive imagination, as we shall discover, some of the reasons for the bifurcation in feeling and in art are implicit.

The present essay has been led to accept the work of art in part as a generic symbol, the significance of which is derived from the sciences, the theologies, or the moralities of the past. Its analysis of feeling has similarly been influenced by the ateleological theory to consider reproductive imagination's reinstatement of precedent images alongside subsequent ones and from this has been led to the hypothesis that feeling reinstates the past of the race or of a culture.

We are now in a position to undertake a more detailed analysis of the relation of generic symbols in art to feeling. For we may take advantage of the results of the analysis of art as a symbol of the artist's feelings and of the ateleological theory of feeling to clarify

[3] *Poetics* 1448 b 9 ff.

some initial problems concerning the conditions and nature of aesthetic experience. And here we may well begin with a phrase offered by a well-known literary critic, whose words are reminiscent of Plato's and Aristotle's. I. A. Richards suggests, in another context, that the "first characteristic" of the artist or, indeed, of the "adept in communication" is the "available possession of the past."[4] In the most primitive and fundamental sense, the "available possession of the past" is the artist's because he is essentially an individual who feels and who objectifies his feeling by means of his skill in a craft. In all men, "reproductive imagination" operates to permit recognition of the presented stimuli for feeling. But for the artist, its operation is attended to because generic symbols are requisite for the communication of feeling. The aesthetic individual, whether he is an artist or not, is similarly of "feeling-compact." In consequence, the realm of profound art is possible of production and of comprehension and comes to be the ground for aesthetic experience. The artist, in regard to feeling, is not different in kind from the non-artistic individual. Works of genius are the works of great men, of men endowed with pervasive imagination. The product of that imagination, however, displays a power that Tolstoy well describes as the "infectiousness of art"—the feeling that "the recipient of a true artistic impression is so united to the artist that he feels as if the work were his own and not someone else's." Something of this "power" of art Plato and Longinus divined long ago. But Tolstoy intends to attribute more than mere "infectiousness" to the experience: "Each is glad that another feels what he feels," the novelist writes, "glad of the communion established not only between him and all present but also with all now living who will yet share the same impression." But, moreover, "he feels the mysterious gladness of a communion which, reaching beyond the grave, unites us with all men of the past who have been moved by the same feelings and with all men of the future who will yet be touched by them."[5]

What Plato described in terms of "magnetic rings," Tolstoy calls

[4] *Principles of Literary Criticism,* pp. 181 ff.
[5] "What is Art?," *Tolstoy on Art,* p. 287. Cf. p. 274.

a "communion" uniting "all men of the past and with all men of the future." It has also been argued in the present inquiry that this relation is occasioned by the generic symbols of art and presupposes the operation of "reproductive" imagination. It is from the latter's power of reinstatement that the effectiveness of generic symbols derives and that power requires the operation of feeling as *Apperceptionsmass*, which makes possible the reproduction of the "available possessions of the past." The artist personalizes and individualizes the art-object. He does so, however, within a tradition of symbols which give his art power to induce generic and typical behavior. The perceiver brings to art a predisposition for the experience of the sensuously constructed works of art, precisely as he brings a predisposition to react to situations, objects, events, and ideas which evoke hatred, love and anger in non-artistic experience.

One consequence of the predisposition called feeling is the familiarity associated with aesthetic experience. This follows upon feeling's "reinstatement of the preceding images" and, more specifically, upon the reinstatement of the past of race and culture. In the realm of the familiar, occurs the "communion" through art with men of the past and of the future.

One encounters, at this point, however, one of the curious paradoxes of art. If the experience of profound art is one of communion induced by familiarity, what meaning has the statement, asserted time without number, that the artist knows not what he does? There is a tradition, it will be recalled, that Sophocles said of Aeschylus that he "does right without knowing it." Plato's *Apology* makes much of the poet's "inspiration": "Not by wisdom do poets write poetry but by a sort of genius and inspiration; they are like diviners and soothsayers who also say many fine things, but do not understand the meaning of them." A more recent tradition in criticism appears similarly disposed to accept the fact of the artist's "ignorance." The conclusion is no less paradoxical than was that of the ancients in view of the asserted familiarity of profound art. And yet, it is precisely in feeling that the criticism discovers the source of the artist's "unconscious" creativity. Carlyle inferred that "if aught be created, and not merely manufactured and communicated," that creation must take place "underneath the region of arguments and conscious discourse." Santayana suggests that the poet has dug "deep enough to tap the subterranean springs of his own life." Yet all agree in some sense with Hegel: The work of art provides for us an experience that permits men to "recognize in it their own dominating essential reality." Men have long believed, as did Lowell, that the poets—and other artists—

> . . . utter wisdom from the central deep,
> And, listening to the inner flow of things,
> Speak to an age out of an eternity.

But familiarity in aesthetic experience and the artist's presumed "inspiration" in creating actually stem from the same set of circumstances. One needs neither the theory of divine inspiration nor the mechanism of the magnetic rings of *Ion* to discover that there is no paradox here. The artist does not create the symbols he employs to express his feelings. He adopts or recreates in symbolic form generic situations, ideas, events, and objects derived from non-aesthetic teleologies and uses them in an effort to induce a typical experience in the aesthetic percipient. The artist adopts symbols but he is also a craftsman able to make a work of art directed in part to the primitive predisposing aspect of feeling, reproductive imagination. By means of art, the maker actualizes the symbols in sensuous media. Those who experience the art actualize in their own experience the predisposition to action which, in its primitive form, is the mechanical reaction of organisms behaving with some appropriateness to particular features of their environment.

Feeling aroused by art and converted in aesthetic experience does not retain all the characteristics of primitive tropism or reflex action. But aesthetic experience, which is a mood, does retain epistemologically significant aspects of all feeling, most evident in the direct and "unconscious" reactions called tropism or instinct. Among these are "immediacy" of recognition. Finally, it may be urged, because the artist employs the symbols of generic situations, objects, ideas, and events, he need not be an expert except in the technique of his particular craft. He need not be expert in the arts and sciences from which he borrows to know the content of each art and science to which humanity responds in the symbols of art. Such content is familiar because humanity is predisposed by feeling towards it. The artist, to take advantage of this, needs to be only a man of imagination. He stands in need of no divine inspiration to fulfill his function in "the chain of being." And he need offer only generic symbols in art to assure what he must assure, the initial recognition that in turn brings the aesthetic percipient into a familiar realm.

The history of art abounds in symbols used by the artist to communicate his feelings, such symbols as are comprehensible in the main to common humanity. Art deals with situations fraught with danger and with perplexity or endowed with hope or fear; events which turn upon hunger of the body and of the soul, upon murder, incest, sacrilege, adultery, patriotism, undying loyalty and devotion, youthful passion, treachery, violent death, and revenge; with ideas, the significance of which centers upon the experience of suffering and of death, upon such intimations of immortality as deny that death is man's ultimate sacrifice, upon the rival claims of obligation; with objects from the natural world of rain, sunshine, clouds, forests, mountains, homes, and the like. Profoundly moving art returns inevitably to these aspects of experience. Architecture, with its fundamental symbolism of man's need for shelter, its stylization of natural forms and its diversification of structure to embody symbols of aspiring or receptive religions, political or social ideals, provides symbols for memorial, religious, and ceremonial purposes. Music, less specific in its symbols, expresses a wide range of mood from aspiration to despair. Literature, sculpture, the dance, and painting presuppose in their symbols the "primitive" feelings of rage, hope, jealousy, fear, lust, aspiration, and joy. Art returns again and again to the "mirrors of passion," the flight and the pursuit, the combat of warriors, the threat of storm and destruction, the journey of the soul, and their cognates.

The first noticeable consequences of the artist's employment of symbols directed to the reproductive imagination are the familiarity of the "signs" and the recognition accorded the art. The importance of such familiarity in art, as we have seen, was recognized by Aristotle[6] who correlated it with imitation. Because, he believed, the delight in works of imitation is natural for all, Aristotle adds significantly that it may extend to objects which are "painful to see" and that "we delight to view the most realistic representations of them in art, the forms for example of the lowest animals and of dead bodies."

There is, indeed, pleasure in knowledge and some delight derived from familiarity. But it is more significant that familiarity and recognition secure for art an initial interest from the percipient of the work of art, as well as the beginnings of empirical agreement among men concerning its value. The agreement may concern only what the work signifies, since there are many factors in addition which enter upon the judgment of the aesthetic worth of art. Yet, the familiarity that follows upon the recognitive function of feeling presupposes the aesthetic judgment. That familiarity may well provide obstacles to the aesthetic evaluation of particular works of art is evident as well. Ennui and boredom with the familiar may not only impede interest but may also lead to the making and appreciation of the bizarre and the excessively romantic. Neither does the familiarity provided by generic symbols and feeling fully free experience from the possible misapprehensions of a perceiver lacking in "mother-wit," nor is the predisposition of feeling a guard, in times of emotional stress, against misinterpretation and misrepresentation. It may not run counter at all times in effectiveness to the dominant interest of the community which may be directed for the moment or for the decade so completely elsewhere that the initial impetus given by familiarity may be of little avail.

It is of interest, however, to observe that even in its failures, the familiarity is presupposed. Obstacles to its effectiveness do present themselves but, in general, profoundly moving art is perhaps man's most universal language. This it is because the artist expresses

[6] *Poetics* 1448 b 4 ff.

feelings concerning ideas, situations, and objects comprehensible by all humanity in generic symbols not created by his own craft but derivative from man's non-artistic activities. With aesthetic experience, in consequence, is associated an initial ease of comprehension alien, at any rate, to science. "Pugna magna victi sumus," writes the Latin poet and all who hear the words know their meaning. It is similarly the realm of the familiar and the recognizable that pervades Dante's tale of Paolo and Francesa, a symbol of passion individualized by the phrase, "that day we read no more." The tales of Tristram and Iseult, of Niobe, of the three searchers for death in the *Pardoner's Tale*, need no interpretation for an understanding of their basic meanings. They, too, are symbols of passion, of love, of sorrow, and of dread of the supernatural. We know with our inmost feelings the significance of the stories of man's forfeiture of his immortal soul, whether they occur in the numerous artistic presentations of Faustus' life or of Orpheus' search. We are similarly familiar with the story of the guilt-pursued wanderers, the Cains who reappear as the Flying Dutchmen, the Ancient Mariners and the Wandering Jews of a thousand written, sculptured, and painted forms. Of the latter, Lowes remarks truly that they belong to the "misty mid-region of our racial as well as literary inheritance, toward which we harbour, when the imagination moves through haunted chambers, the primal instinctive will to believe." They are "immemorial projections of elemental human questionings and intuitions," as are the storied and depicted travelers to the realm of the dead—Orpheus, Odysseus, Vergil, Dante, and their many followers.

The themes pervade every art. To list even the more important artistic instances of their occurrence would be tedious. It will suffice to suggest here that profoundly moving art employs the symbols of the hunt and the chase, danger, and vengeance, chicanery, death, old age, change, tales of the marriage of spring and winter, the passage of time and the seasons, chance and love, the ladder and the tree of life, the isles of the blest, the demons and the werewolves, of a hundred Beowulfs, and tales of horror; the beneficence of warm sun and soft rain, the marriage of heaven and earth, the havoc of storm, hurricane, earthquake, tidal wave, and typhoon, of pestilence, starvation, and war, the magic and witchcraft—all generic symbols of feeling and combinations of feelings in artistic themes as old as the tales of Diana and as new as *Bambi*, occurring in Greek vase painting and in the Bacchanalian oil paintings of Rubens, in Ovid's *Metamorphoses*, in the tales of Uncle Remus and in the Great Beast Epic, in *Endymion* and in Conrad's *Typhoon*. They are symbols expressing moods which, in turn, fuse feelings of love, greed, deceit, pride, jealousy, covetousness, sorrow, desire, fear, awe, joy, horror, hope, aspiration, pity, sympathy, and the numerous other conative states men experience.

It is because the artist's feelings may be communicated by generic signs that the art of the past is often more "immediately" known and is regarded as less alien to the modern mind than is the technical archaeological content of ancient civilizations. We know the meaning of the art of such civilizations because we know deeply and personally the feelings evoked by these symbols. We enter in art upon a familiar world. It is more accurate to say of the symbols of art than of political constitutions that men may borrow but will not retain what is alien to them.

The extent of such borrowing and lending of generic symbols is evidence both of the artist's need for generally understood signs to express feeling and of his insight and assurance that men are predisposed by feeling to recognize their meanings. But even the undoubtedly frequent recurrence in art of symbols commonly known in a culture, passed on in folklore, in mythology, in beliefs, and in literature and art—a recurrence and repetition sometimes attributed merely to the renown and dominance of a great artist—presupposes not so much a common artistic taste as a general predisposition to react to situations arousing feeling. This conclusion is borne out by the recurrence and repetition of symbols in art in instances in which research offers no evidence of borrowing. Many of these symbols derive from the basic stimuli for the biological *Apperceptionsmass*. There are numerous symbols of this kind in art—symbols of fear, of dread, of passion—which help to substantiate the hypothesis that the presupposition of aesthetic experience is a predisposition to react to non-aesthetic ideas, situations, objects, and events.

It will suffice for the present purpose to examine two illustrations of profoundly moving art which make evident use of generic symbols. The first, the central symbols common to *Hamlet* and to the *Oresteia*, is offered as evidence of the operation of the biological *Apperceptionsmass*. The second, the symbol of light by which western culture has recurrently signified the immortality of man's soul, is offered as evidence of the operation of a cultural predisposition. It is unnecessary to offer detailed analyses of the symbols of feeling which obtain in "closed societies." In many instances, they are specified examples of the biological and the cultural symbols which have taken on a provincial cast in a particular society.

We shall now turn to the generic symbols of art found in *Hamlet* and in the story of Orestes.

II

THE long-recognized similarities between Shakespeare's *Hamlet* and the tragic accounts of Orestes provide an interesting and valuable illustration of the recurrence of generic symbols in art and make explicit certain problems which the reiteration of those symbols of feeling raises. The most significant issues for the present discussion concern reproductive imagination and the ultimate source and character of the symbols employed to evoke it. In Shakespeare's *Hamlet* and in the *Oresteia*, there is the central symbolism of the leader and of his relation to a situation. The prototypes for the dramatic symbols are found in cult-worship and in the social organization of the higher primates. How much further the origins of the symbols could be traced, it is impossible to say but they may be followed sufficiently far to suggest the reasons for the recurrence of symbols in art and for the power exercised in the common experience of man and brute upon the presentation of generic ideas and situations.

It is past history, a mere legend stored up in chronicles by

Elizabethan times, that a prince of Denmark found the times "out of joint." If, indeed, the tale of murder and revenge is history, neither the particular situation following upon the death of Hamlet's father nor the particular dilemma that faced the murdered king's son was likely to recur within the life-span of any playgoer or reader of Shakespeare's tragedy. On the surface, Hamlet's tragic biography resembles the life of the average Elizabethan or, indeed, the life of the majority of men of today, less than the garb he wore resembles today's raiments. Yet, were he as alien to us in other respects as he is in the life he led or the fate he suffered, were he essentially as alien to us as are the bizarre incidents of that life, how fantastic would be the figure who stood upon the wind-swept ledge at Elsinore to pose questions to his father's departed spirit! Yet Hamlet is neither fantastic nor is his tragedy incredible.

It may be supposed, therefore, that Shakespeare uses in the tragedy "signs" comprehensible to all men, symbols for experience in their own lives in which "the times are out of joint." There is here a bloody tale of murder, fratricide, adultery, and incest, but one is left also with the conviction that this tragedy is ours or any man's. It is significant that in Greek tragic poetry the fateful story of Orestes turns upon a theme analogous to that enacted in *Hamlet* to a degree that has permitted critics to speculate upon the possibility that the Greek and the English versions derive from identical primitive sources. The similarities were noted by A. C. Bradley.[7] More recently, Gilbert Murray entered upon detailed analyses of the similarities between the traditions presupposed by the dramas.[8] There has been little suggestion that the likenesses are due to literary borrowing.

Perhaps no works of art have surpassed Shakespeare's *Hamlet*, Aeschylus' *Agamemnon*, *Chœphori* and *Eumenides*, Sophocles' *Electra* and Euripides' *Electra*, *Iphigenia in Tauris*, and *Orestes* in

[7] *Oxford Lectures on Poetry*, p. 77.

[8] *The Classical Tradition in Poetry*. I have followed Murray's essay closely and have often appropriated his words. The more technical account is Professor Murray's *Hamlet and Orestes; A Study in Traditional Types*. (The quotations from *The Classical Tradition in Poetry* are reprinted by permission of Harvard University Press, Cambridge, Massachusetts.)

either profundity or in power to move men. The dramas may well be said to have expressed every feeling and every shade of feeling. They fuse horror, pity, dread, sympathy, hope, aspiration, love, and terror into tragic moods because of their extraordinary implications concerning man's fate and aspirations. The extent to which the Greeks differ from the English dramatist in their conception of tragic conflict, indeed the extent to which the Greek dramatists differ from each other in their interpretations of the moving tale of an ancient family and the extent to which in each play, the marks of individual genius are evident, do not present the immediate problem. The issue is the significance for aesthetic experience of the reiterated and recurrent generic symbols by which each artist expressed feelings to which men of all times appear to be susceptible.

The significant symbol common to *Hamlet* and the *Oresteia* is that of the "leader." In integral relation in the tragedies to that central generic symbol are the following peripheral symbols of ideas, events, and situations:

1. In the northern and in the Greek versions, "the hero is the son of a king who has been murdered and succeeded on the throne by a younger kinsman. . . . The dead king's wife has married his murderer. The hero, driven by supernatural commands, undertakes and carries through the duty of vengeance."

2. In all the versions, the hero is in some way under the cloud of madness.

3. One of the greatest horrors about the father's death in both traditions is that he died without proper religious observances.[9]

These are striking analogies but there remains to be considered a factor of consequence common to both traditions. Its significance has been properly stressed by Murray, in view of the light it casts upon the primary generic symbol in the tragedies. Gertrude is "a wife who loves her husband and bears him children, and is then wedded to his slayer and equally loves him." In the version of the

[9] These points are given here as they have been summarized by Murray, *The Classical Tradition in Poetry*, pp. 209 ff. Murray gives other "coincidences" and similarities.

tale given by Saxo Grammaticus, Hermutrude, Amleth's wife, behaves in the same manner as his, Amleth's, mother has done. "In Thebes King Laïus and his wife Jocasta knew that their son would slay and dethrone his father. Laïus orders the son's death." The child is saved, however, by the Queen-mother. After the son slays and dethrones his father, he marries the Queen-mother.

It is well to recall that, on the evidence at hand, there is no conscious literary borrowing by northern from Mediterranean writers. And, although the reiteration of themes may conceivably be due to coincidence, the proof of separate origin of the symbols would not alter the general conclusion to be drawn from the fact of similarity. There is in the two versions evidence of a communality of interest more profound than that afforded by tradition. The dramas and their prototypes suggest, in fact, that the frame of reference for their analogous symbols is the primitive and biological predisposition common to men and brutes—the conative *Apperceptionsmass* of experience. It is here effectively brought into operation by the symbol of the "wintry slayer."

This conclusion is the more probable once evidence is sought for a *common* or analogous source for these basic situations and ideas in *Hamlet* and in the *Oresteia*. It has been argued by Murray, Jane Harrison, and others, by way of illustration, that the prototype for both the Greek and northern versions is the ritual story of the vegetation spirits, details of which Frazer gives in *The Golden Bough*.[10] We may well quote Murray's statement at this point: "Each Year-king comes first as a wintry slayer, weds the queen, grows proud and royal, and then is slain by the Avenger of his predecessor."[11]

Murray suggests that Greek tragedy has its origin in the *môlpe*, the ceremonial dance and song centering upon the cult-worship of the god, Dionysus.[12] The god, the life-spirit, combines in the cult-worship the qualities of the bearer of the fruits of the new year and

[10] See Sir G. B. Frazer, "The Magic Art," *op. cit.*, II, Chap 18.

[11] *The Classical Tradition in Poetry*, p. 229.

[12] See Murray on the Môlpe in *The Classical Tradition in Poetry*, Chap. II, and compare his "Excursus" in J. E. Harrison, *Themis*, pp. 341 ff., and F. M. Cornford, *The Origin of Attic Comedy*, particularly pp. 53 ff.

those of the Scapegoat, driven from the community and bearing away the sins of the people. The ceremonial depicts the god destroyed and the casting forth of his remains. In the spring, the god returns reborn and vigorous.

Concerning Hamlet, the suggestion had previously been made that its sources lie, in similar fashion, in a cult-ceremonial.[13] It is of value to ascertain both the basis and the implications of this suggestion. The earliest known reference to Hamlet to which the Elizabethans may have had access is that of Saxo Grammaticus. Gollancz holds that the earliest reference to Hamlet occurs in the *Skaldskapar-mál* of Snorri Sturlason, in a poem dating about the year 980. In this, he is in error.[14] In Saxo's version, it is well to note the main themes in the following passages:

"Most infamous of women," says Amleth of his mother, Gerutha, "dost thou seek with such lying lamentations to hide thy most heavy fault! Wantoning like a harlot, thou hast entered a wicked and abominable state of wedlock, embracing with incestuous bosom thy husband's slayer. . . . This, forsooth, is the way mares couple with the vanquishers of their mates.

"Pity also my stricken mother, and rejoice with me that the infamy of her who was once your queen is quenched. For this weak woman had to bear a two-fold weight of ignominy, embracing one who was her husband's brother and murderer.

"Disdain the dust of him who slew his brother, and defiled his

[13] Hamlet is at once "the murderer of his uncle and of Polonius and the saviour of Denmark. Orestes is the matricide and the redeemer of the House of Atreus." Cf. I. Gollancz, *The Sources of Hamlet*, pp. xxxv-xxxvi, who suggests that "the Hamlet story may very well have borrowed certain elements from the ancient Northern myths of the struggle between Spring and Winter; from this point of view, the most difficult element of the whole story, the part played by the hero's mother, becomes illuminated."

[14] The most detailed study of the problem of which I have knowledge is Kemp Malone's *The Literary History of Hamlet*, of which Part I, "The Early Tradition," was published in *Anglistische Forschungen* (Heidelberg, 1923). Malone suggests that the Danish vikings "brought the Hamlet story with them to Ireland." Malone traces the king to Beowulf. His argument is given in detail with considerable philological and phonological material to support the thesis. The volume is of particular interest here because of the references of some of the generic aspects of the story to vegetative and harvest cults (cf. pp. 87 and 118-119), and the associations of the primitive bestiality of the earlier versions with "the ram or goat" as a "fetish of the Scyldings" (pp. 255-256).

brother's queen with infamous desecration—and crowned patricide with incest. I have been the agent of this first vengeance; I have burned for this righteous retribution. . . . It is I who have wiped off my country's shame; I who have quenched my mother's dishonour; I, who have beaten back oppression; I who have put to death the murderer;—Acknowledge my service, honour my wit, give me the throne if I have earned it, for you have in me one who has done a mighty service, and who is no degenerate heir to his father's power; no fratricide but the lawful successor to the throne; and a dutiful avenger of the crime of murder. You have me to thank for the recovery of the blessings of freedom, for the release from the power of him who vexed you, for relief from the oppressors. . . . I have deposed the despot and triumphed over the butcher."[15]

And, strangely enough, as Murray remarks, Hermutrude marries Amleth despite her desire to be "united with her lord in death." Even more strangely, "she kept this rare promise ill; for when Amleth had been slain by Wiglik in battle in Jutland, she yielded herself up unasked to be the conqueror's spoil and bride."

There are, in this early version, clear analogies to the story of Orestes. But Saxo presumably drew his materials from *The Elder Edda*, which is held in its turn to be of dramatic origin. In her study of the Edda, Phillpotts has arrived at interesting and relevant conclusions:

There is no mistaking the significance of these scenes; the flyting, the slaying, the love scenes are the integral parts of the most widespread drama of the world. It represents the eternal contests of the Old and the New Years and has outlasted heathendom because the fulfillment of its aim is the age-long desire of the peasant. Its primary object is not commemorative but magical, and it is performed in order to induce the earth to bring forth abundantly. . . . The moral conflict, the family feud, the love-scene and the hint of rebirth . . . these are the tragic formulas with which we have to deal, and they are inexplicable except as springing from the soil of the ritual marriage and the slaying.[16]

[15] Saxo Grammaticus, *The Danish History*, translation by Oliver Elton, pp. 91 and 99.

[16] Cf. B. S. Phillpotts, *The Elder Edda*, p. 114: "The continual recurrence of stock scenes is, of course, characteristic of primitive drama. We hardly need to be reminded that the flyting, the love scene, the slaying and the resurrection are to this day the main scenes of folk-drama. . . . The Norwegian Eddic poems . . . are the actual shattered remnants of ancient religious drama."

From these studies of early material, some inferences may be drawn concerning the origins of the similar themes of *Hamlet* and of the legend of Orestes:

> Our northern Helgi plays, however rudimentary, however shattered, do afford another instance of Tragedy as an independent growth. There can be little doubt that this growth, though independent, springs from the same seed as Attic tragedy. The Fertility-drama bequeathed to both a plot which contained in germ the moral conflict, the sense of Destiny, and the religious background and the essential characters of Greek and Northern tragedy.[17]

On this hypothesis, *Hamlet* and the *Oresteia*, which present numerous similar situations, do so because in both are retained elements of a ritual drama derived from a fertility ceremony. It is inferred, likewise, that the great dramatic tragedies may owe their similarity to an original homogeneity of northern and southern peoples.[18]

But if, indeed, it may be argued that in *Hamlet* and the *Oresteia* are vestigial traces of the ceremonial usages of a primitive and homogeneous folk, it may equally well be contended that the latter as functioning religious ceremonials retain, in their turn, traces and vestiges of a more primitive life to which profound art reverts in its employment of generic symbols. There are presuppositions of the very homogeneity brought forward to account for the presence in the drama of the vestiges of a more primitive life to which profound art reverts in its employment of generic symbols; presuppositions which concern attitudes and feelings towards incest, murder and sacraments basic in their turn to the tragedies and to the cults themselves. The sociologist, the anthropologist, and the psychologist in their research have done a considerable service in making intelligible the non-aesthetic sources of these recurrent and familiar symbols.

It is, in fact, to the very foundations of society that the anthropologist goes to discover the prototypes for such vestigial elements of early rites and customs as are retained in *Hamlet* and in the *Oresteia*. For some students of man and his mores, these are survivals of the specific stage in the evolution of man's relations to

[17] *Ibid.*

[18] Murray, *The Classical Tradition in Poetry*, pp. 238 ff.

man at which the differentiations between matrilineal and patrilineal social structures emerged. To accept this hypothesis is to accept, as well, accompanying implications concerning property rights and inheritance, in addition to inferences concerning general regulations imposed to govern the familial and marital relations. On one such view, the vestiges of the tradition of the Winter King (the story for which the cult of Dionysus is the prototype) are the remnants in turn of a primitive human organization in society, itself prior to the matrilinear and patrilinear division of the social structure and suggesting a tribal hegemony under the *aegis* of a supreme individual called by Professor Elliot Smith "The Old Man." Concerning this hypothetical earlier organization, it is assumed that the primal horde is dominated by the father, who keeps all of the females for himself and drives from the group the growing sons.

The psychoanalyst interprets this situation in terms which have made the "Oedipus-complex" a familiar phrase. Freud, in *Totem and Taboo*,[19] reconstructs the destructive conflict that ensues in the society of the "horde": ". . . One day the expelled brothers joined forces," Freud holds, "slew and ate the father, and thus put an end to the father horde. . . . Of course these cannibalistic savages ate their victim. This violent primal father had surely been the envied and feared model for each of the brothers. Now they accomplished their identification with him by devouring him and each acquired a part of his strength."[20] To this deed of cannibalism, Freud argues, the young males add incest with their mothers: "They hated the father who stood so powerfully in the way of their sexual demands and their desire for power, but they also loved and admired him." Their consequent hatred and their remorse at having done the deed evolves, on Freud's hypothesis, into the totemic worship of the father. The new society, composed of equally powerful brothers, introduces the prohibition against incest, a prohibition requisite to guard against a reversion to the

[19] *Op. cit.*, p. 233.

[20] Compare the story of Dionysus Zagreus and the Titans, and of Manus and Zeus.

social usages holding for the primal horde, with the consequent breakdown of the newer mode of organization by patricide and cannibalism.

On Freud's view, the instinctive demands of hunger and sex come to be controlled by a religion and an ethic, in turn to be altered and finally abandoned as society enlarges and as its moral practices and concepts evolve. The more primitive methods and techniques of social control, as control, vanish. They survive, however, in "group memory," largely through the instrumentality of folklore. The vestiges of an ancient social instrument are regenerated in art, however numerous the restrictions placed upon the ancient practices by more developed religions and more refined ethical codes. There remains for art and in art, which is itself the product of a more advanced civilization, the *mythos* reminiscent of patricide, of totemic animal worship, and of the sacramental cannibalistic feast.

Elliot Smith's and Freud's speculative reconstructions respecting a primitive human horde aid us in various efforts to return to the sources and to comprehend the nature of the generic symbols to which art returns. By their theoretical re-establishment of one of the many primitive situations upon which profound art has drawn for its symbols of feeling, they have opened up an avenue of research. But even this speculation stops short of analysis of the social organization presupposed in the vestiges of the life of the horde which have been traced thus far. The power of the poet to move us by greater tragedy than ever occurred in Elsinore and in Mycenæ uses as an instrument, as has been observed, a symbol drawn from a ritual magic already rationalized into a cult. The religious significance of the cult centers around the concept of an external agent who died worn out but who returned regenerated. It was he who was needed to ensure fertility to the crops and it was he to whom the tribe turned as an agency through which prayers could be made effective.

But the predispositions of man to be moved to typical behavior by generic situations of this kind probably manifest themselves in pre-human groups before the development of a society of men centered upon the leader. Man is a late arrival upon the evolutionary scene and the predispositions he displays are found in primates cognate to him and presumably descended from a stock common to man and to other higher anthropoids. The relevant factors in the social practices of the cult and of the patrilinear organization are discernible, as well, among the anthropoid apes, cognate to men, and probably had their origin in a much more primitive common society of an anthropoid stock common both to man and ape. Several aspects of the behavior of the primates are of interest in this connection. Köhler recalls, in *The Mentality of Apes*,[21] that among the anthropoid apes there is strong group solidarity which it is meaningful to interpret in terms of the social behavior by which the actions of the tribal horde are explicable. The anthropoid's behavior is in fact analogous to that of primitive man.[22] Köhler implies that not only is the primate a social animal, demanding social solidarity but he is one which observes a well-defined principle of leadership.[23] The animals of these related but subhuman groups display in their behavior the rudiments of entreaty, and act, at times, as if there were an indebtedness to be paid. "Rogue" beasts are driven from the society, as the scapegoat is driven from human societies. There is even some suggestion, in the bargaining necessary to ensure return to the group, of group communion and ritual.[24]

[21] Cf. also, R. M. Yerkes, *Almost Human*, pp. 115, ff. E. A. Hooton, in *Up From the Ape*, pp. 154 ff., gives a concise and interesting account of Köhler's and Yerkes' experiments.

[22] Köhler, *op. cit.*, p. 293: "It is hardly an exaggeration to say that a chimpanzee kept in solitude is not a real chimpanzee at all. . . . The group connection of chimpanzees is a very real force, of sometimes astonishing degree. This can clearly be seen in any attempt to take one animal out of a group that is used to hanging together. When such a thing has never happened before, or not for a long time, the first and greatest desire of the separated creature is to get back to his group."

[23] *Ibid.*, p. 295: "It matters a great deal who the returned ape is. The oldest animal, who occupied a special position in the life of the community, was, on any such occasion, greeted by a universal welcome, such as was not accorded to others."

[24] *Ibid.*, pp. 293-295. Gerald Heard suggests in *The Social Substance of Religion* that the elements of ritual are very much present: If the group "remained indifferent, as is often the case, the separated animal stretched his arms imploringly towards them, and, as they did not respond, he threw small objects towards them, including often, portions of his own hair." Heard

Hamlet and the *Oresteia* are not isolated illustrations of themes recurrent in the history of art which owe their power to move us to symbols in which persist the vestiges of primitive science, religion, and morality. It has been suggested, by way of illustration, that *Jocasta* is susceptible to similar analysis, that Odysseus and the tale of his wanderings are survivals of memories of man's and of animal's hibernations and this theory is not too alien for application to Washington Irving's *Legend of Sleepy Hollow*. It has been maintained[25] that Robin Hood is, as are the prototypes of Hamlet and Orestes, a pagan god, "particularly associated with spring and vegetation" and that his successively unsuccessful fights are "suggestive of a system by which the king reigned from one May-day till the next, when he had to fight for his title." Perhaps, as M. A. Murray suggests, he fought also for his life and for his queen and his death is a sacrifice not unlike that of Orpheus and of other Spring Kings. Robin Hood had no Shakespeare to immortalize his deed but architecture has been enriched, according to Lady Raglan,[26] by "The Green Man." And Robin's prototypes of another kind, the good fairies and the "little folk" live in *A Midsummer Night's Dream*, in *The Tempest*, in Grimm's and Dunsany's fairy tales, in James Stephen's *Demigods*, in the endless variations of the theme of *Cinderella*, in the ballet, and in paintings as diverse as artistic renderings can make them. Opposed to these in nature but kindred in the matter of symbols of feeling are the forces of evil which recur in the Caliban, the deformed Cyclops, in Grendel and in his dam, in the old tales of Titans and other earth-gods, of chaos and of death. Endymion, Proserpina, Diana and Phaeton have their many proto-

---

asks, "Can we go deeper and learn anything from the ape group under normal conditions? . . . One of the best observed [examples of behavior] centered around food. . . . When one member, generally one of leading ability, was striving to attain food placed where only protracted effort could win it, sympathetic urgency was expressed by all others who looked on. They would sit around, and as the principal actor strained toward his objective, the arms of the others . . . waved and gestured in sympathy. . . . Here, clearly is the unreflecting urgency to express, the effective need which will create ritual, before any clear intention, any shadow of purpose can be present."

[25] Lord Raglan, *The Hero*.

[26] *Folk-lore*, 1939.

types in folklore and in art and have provided profound art with numerous recurrent symbols.

To list generic symbols in art would be an endless task. It is, moreover, rather with their significance as survivals in art than with their number that aesthetic is concerned. Concerning many of the instances in which familiar symbols recur in profoundly moving art, one may search in vain for evidences of literary or artistic borrowing, a situation paralleling that which appears to hold between *Hamlet* and the *Oresteia* or, more significantly, between the primitive myths and practices of Asia Minor and the north. In the latter connection, Murray concludes that their "fundamental identity still shows itself" although "the only point of contact [between the *Oresteia* and *Hamlet*] lies at their common origin many thousand years ago." But even a possible "common origin" would be little more significant for a full explanation of the problem involved than would be a hypothetical "common" literary source.

The significant issue is merely suggested if one considers the problem solely in the light of the possibility of literary influences or of a homogeneity of ideas or customs arising from the possibility of a pre-migration identity of peoples. The true issue is met only as one realizes that an essentially human and potentially tragic situation recurs and that the situation is vestigial of a once functioning science in both versions. Feeling is the predisposition for a comprehension of the theme which derives from circumstances experienced by the brute, by primitive man, and by modern man and which, in turn, are the "referrents" for the symbols employed by the artist. The "situation" presented by art "reinstates" in reproductive imagination a "precedent image" and the past of the race so reinstated is familiar because to be predisposed to it was once essential to the survival of both man and beast.

Generic symbols in art move us profoundly precisely because they are "signs for" the most primitive initiators of feeling, "signs" the significance of which the anthropoids know through feeling. In all probability, they are coeval with the emergence of at least the higher primates. Stimulated by such typical and generic ideas, objects, situation, and events, the *Apperceptionsmass* of feeling continues to operate as it operated from the beginning to make possible through recognition the struggle for the survival of man and of brute. The artist, who "listens to the inner flow of things," may not know fully what he does but his instinct tells him that by means of generic symbols he may communicate his feelings and effect a common experience in his audience. The symbols recur in the history of art because the artist knows that they appeal to man's common experience and humanity.

It has been a point of critical interest to discover some analogy for Hamlet's dilemma in Shakespeare's own experience, either in Stratford or in London. James Joyce reconstructs a tale of Anne Hathaway and of Shakespeare's son. Similarly, biographical details have been sought to cast light upon the events portrayed in the *Oresteia.* But Hamlet's problem, born of his father's murder and his mother's marriage to the fratricide, is not the man's, Shakespeare's, dilemma. It is still less the dilemma of his audience, as each century's theater-goers watch the unfolding of events upon the stage. Rather, it is not ours as spectators in the sense that we individually have experienced these tragic happenings. It is, however, ours generically. We are creatures of feeling and we have no doubt concerning the nature of the typical reaction the ideas and situations of which the drama is a symbol will call forth in man of action or in dreamer. An Orestes commits murder. Hamlet's will appears to be paralyzed. We understand the actions of both and we understand them more fully because the artist forms those actions into a whole of coherent experience. And, finally, because we are creatures of feeling and because the artist induces in us a mood describable as aesthetic experience, specific, personal and tragic experiences of divergent kinds, experiences upon which pain and lack of resolution may have been attendant, find their expression in the artistic symbol employed. For as Gilbert Murray writes:

> I suspect that a charm . . . lies in these stories and situations, which are . . . deeply implanted in the memory of the race, stamped as it were upon our physical organism. . . . There is that within us which leaps at the sight of them, a cry of the blood which tells us we have known them always. . . . In plays like *Hamlet* or the *Agamemnon* or

the *Electra* we have . . . a strange, unanalyzed vibration below the surface, an undercurrent of desires and fears and passions, long slumbering yet eternally familiar, which have for thousands of years lain near the root of our most intimate emotions and have been wrought into the fabric of our most magical dreams.[27]

Murray adds, "How far into past ages this stream may reach back, I dare not even surmise; but it seems as if the power of stirring or moving with it were one of the last secrets of genius." One may conclude, from the fact of reproductive imagination, that this "stream" flows from man's most primitive experiences, as it does from the experience of all sensitive and feeling organisms.

Clustered around the generic symbols of the "leader" are peripheral symbols in *Hamlet* and the *Oresteia* that provide further suggestions concerning the power of reproductive imagination to reinstate the past of the race. We are led, indeed, to a consideration of man's brutish origins and of the conflicts and resolutions of conflict which are a part of that past. Human sacrifice to free the tribe from contamination, from guilt, and from sin, find their cognates in practices of the subhuman anthropoids. The art in which such symbols are found gives evidence of the common ancestry of man and brute and its symbols have their "referrents" in ideas, situations, objects, and events towards which man and beast react generically in much the same fashion.

Yet, the generic symbols of art may arouse "a cry of the blood which tells us we have known them always" and still may not be such as have their "referrents" in ideas, situations, objects, and events experienced in common by man and brute. There are symbols of feeling, the frame of reference for which is comprehensible within the experience of man alone. *Hamlet* and the *Oresteia* contain some of these recurrent symbols, as is evident in suggestions of divine possession in madness and in the horror of death without religious observances. They represent another class of stimuli for feeling. In art, they become symbols communicable because they relate to the cultural *Apperceptionsmass* postulated by the ateleological theory of feeling. To their consideration, we shall now turn.

[27] *The Classical Tradition in Poetry,* pp. 238-240. (By permission of Harvard University Press, Cambridge, Massachusetts.)

Chapter XIII

Reproductive Imagination and the Generic Symbols of Art (II): The Cultural Apperceptionsmass

. . . *As the lyre trembles and sounds after the wind has died away, so the child seeks by prolonging in its voice and motions the duration of the effect, to prolong also a consciousness of the cause. In relation to the objects which delight the child, these expressions are what poetry is to the higher object. . . . Man in society, with all his passions and pleasures, next becomes the object of the passions and pleasures of man; an additional class of emotions produce an augmented treasure of expressions; and language, gesture, and the imitative arts become at once the representation and the medium, the pencil and the picture, the chisel and the statue, the chord and the harmony.*

—Shelley

IN PROFOUNDLY moving art, there recur generic symbols or signs for ideas, situations, objects and events which have meaning only for man in a human culture. In sharp contrast to such symbols as that of the "leader" which reinstate a past common to man and to brute, the meanings of these cultural signs depend solely upon the fact that man is "a thinking reed." All generic symbols of art are directed to feeling and are the means by which the artist communicates. They affect the reproductive imagination and reinstate "precedent images." But the past that is reinstated and for which men are predisposed by cultural symbols of art is the past of a culture in itself conditioned by man's ability to think.

In power of compulsion, the cultural *Apperceptionsmass* of feeling is no weaker than its biological counterpart. As we react to the idea of the leader and to the situations in which he acts, so we feel no less strongly towards conceptions of God and the immortality of the soul of which the brute world has no experience and for which it has no predisposition. By means of cultural conceptions of this kind artists have been inspired to produce some of their most significant and moving works and have been enabled to communicate for aesthetic experience. The artist has used them for his generic symbols and men have been predisposed for their experience by training, education, nurture and habituation in a culture.

It will suffice for the present purpose to examine briefly but one such cultural symbol, that of light as a generic sign for the divine and for immortality. The choice of this symbol follows in part from evidence of its capacity to convey and express in an easily recognizable mode the most divergent emotions. By the architect of Byzantine art, particularly in the iconostasis, it has been used again and again to signify the feeling of reverence before God. For El Greco, in "St. Francis in Ecstasy," it stands for the feeling of mystical oneness and union with deity. For Dante, it has symbolized a life of spiritual aspiration. To generations of sculptors and painters, it has been, in the aureole and the nimbus, a familiar means for expressing piety, sorrow, sympathy, and the like. For many, including Milton, it has been a sign for the power and glory of the forces of heaven.

The widespread use of light as a symbol of feeling in art presupposes meanings given to a natural phenonomen by men in a culture. However, the cultural *Apperceptionsmass*, here effective, presupposes the biological, and there is no need to postulate the "additional class of emotions" which Shelley suggests. The reactions which actualize predispositions of fear, hatred, aversion, love, sympathy, and the like, are by cultural inheritance directed to different stimuli and are brought into operation by means of stimuli immanent in language, human social usages, concepts, and conceptual systems constructed by human minds. These reactions are, for the ateleologist, no less completely explicable in terms of the neurological and physiological structures than are those evoked by biologically defined stimuli, the minute description of which is intended to comprehend all feeling as typical behavior.

It is of value to speculate upon the origin of the experience of these stimuli. The experience for which the cultural *Apperceptionsmass* predisposes us and by means of which the stimuli become "images" for reproductive imagination is roughly attributable, as Bergson suggests, to "intellectualism." Feeling in this aspect may be thought of, in part, as a "readjustment of our sensitive faculties to an intellectual representation." These "representations" are man's and man's alone.

II

THERE are discernible many variations of kind among the uniquely human cultural "images" or "intellectual representations" to which feelings attach. Our present interest is less in the minute differentiations which have given art such material as the ne'er-do-well, the miser, the nonconformist, the domestic crisis and the like, than in one distinction suggested by Bergson. Some of the "intellectual representations" belong alone to "closed societies," the "essential characteristic" of which is "to include at any moment a certain number of individuals, and to exclude others."[1] For art, by way of illustration, the symbols of the wheel, of democratic government, of the sea, of the machine age, of the age of chivalry and its relation to the culture of the horse, have an appeal restricted to individuals in cultures in which the "referrent" for the artistic symbol is integral to that culture. Eclectic or arbitrary mores, customs and usages similarly reinstate feeling but they do so only for members of the "closed societies" in which those practices have provided the grounds for predispositions. Some translation of symbols of this kind is no doubt possible and a study of contexts in works of art

[1] H. Bergson, *The Two Sources of Morality and Religion*, p. 22. I use Bergson's terminology but I do not necessarily accept either his illustrations or his detailed argument. The application to the symbols of art is not Bergson's.

may do much to suggest the specific feeling the artist is attempting to symbolize.[2]

Evocative of more profound interest, however, are the cultural symbols for "referrents" in "open societies," societies "deemed in principle to embrace all humanity."[3] Within the bounds of such "open societies," it is possible that "representations" common to all men may be found. And it is probable that such "representations" are those, among others, of God, the soul, immortality, such symbols as concern the movements of the heavenly bodies, and "signs" like soil, hearth, bread, or their cognates.

The origin of what in this essay are called the cultural generic symbols of "intellectual representations," is explained if we think of Pascal's words, the implications of which may be elaborated to cover all of the instances: "Man is but a reed, the most feeble thing in nature; but he is a thinking reed. The entire universe need not arm itself to crush him. A vapour, a drop of water suffices to kill him. But, if the universe were to crush him, man would still be more noble than that which killed him, because he knows that he dies and the advantage which the universe has over him; the universe knows nothing of this. All our dignity consists, then, in thought."[4] It is this power and this knowledge that distinguishes man from beast.

But Pascal might well have added, man not only "knows that he dies"; one of the most passionate of his beliefs is that he survives death. This "image" of an immortal soul is a "representation" which man does not share with the brute. It arises in the "open society" of man and is comprehensible to all humanity. Upon this "representation," art has elaborated in some of its recurrent and profoundly moving symbols. Yet, while the "intellectual representation" of the immortal soul may belong to the "open society," many specific symbols of that "representation" clearly are limited in significance to the frame of reference understood by members of "closed societies." As was observed above, for the initiate of the Pythagorean society or for the East Indian, the symbols of *metemp-*

[2] Cf. above, Part II.

[3] *The Two Sources of Morality and Religion*, p. 256.

[4] *Pensées*, Sec. 6, No. 347.

sychosis would be familiar. For one unacquainted with that cultural tradition the symbol might have little or no significance. But there is one symbol of the divinity of man's soul which is perhaps, for reasons shortly to be investigated, a sign understandable among the "open societies" of men: Light is so universally experienced as an event in the succession of day and night and has connotations for man so intimately related to the fire which early warmed and protected him that its symbolic association with divinity and power is well-nigh universal. From Egypt to Japan, religion and art reflect the symbol's significance. For historical reasons, light has become for Western Europe a more specific symbol of the soul. It has been understood, in contrast to more specific symbols of feeling, not only by Greek but by barbarian as well, not alone by Frenchmen but by the German, as well. It has become a symbol, in fact, for men in "open societies." A summary glance at this artistic symbol of the concept of immortality will suffice to indicate the operation of the cultural *Apperceptionsmass* of feeling as a presupposition of aesthetic experience.

III

TO ANALYZE even in a summary fashion one illustration of a cultural symbol and to determine its effect in the experience of profound art requires, however, some mention of an aspect of feeling that forces theory to break the rigid limitations imposed upon it by the ateleologist. The symbolism of light as a sign for the immortal and divine soul is inadequately presented unless there is likewise mention that a belief in immortality extends the scope of the sciences man has developed to achieve the end of self-preservation. This leads unavoidably to teleology and presupposes some mention of the teleologist's interpretation of feeling in terms of "emergency action."

Once it is remarked that it is impossible to understand the conception of immortality and the recurrence of its symbols in art without anticipating a teleology of feeling, it is equally evident that the symbol that affects the biological *Apperceptionsmass* of feeling must likewise be subjected to teleological explanation. It has been urged, already, that the symbols of art appeal to our innermost nature because their "referrents" are the science, the religion, and the morality of the past which, in the history of the race or of a culture, were techniques by means of which man satisfied the demands of his speculative self, conquered nature, and brought it under control. We have observed that art reinstates the primitive codes by which societies labored to satisfy mutual as well as individual desires. *Hamlet* and the *Oresteia*, as we have seen, retain in their symbols vestigial remains of men's brutish origins and of the conflicts that may be traced in the origin of a patrilinear society. They bear witness to human sacrifice by which the tribe is freed from contamination, from guilt, and from sin. They evidence the supreme importance, for the practical arts of agriculture and shelter, of the science which takes account of the succession of the seasons and they manifest a primitive religious regard for the continuity of nature. In them survive the practices of the spring festival. They cast back to a society in which the leader is dominant and arbitrary in his rule and they exemplify the grounds for the symbol of leadership which brings the Satan of *Paradise Lost*, the theory of *Sartor Resartus*, the story of Odysseus, the portrayal of kings and military leaders, and even the fabric of the great chivalric romances closer to our common understanding.

It is in accord with this that it was previously argued that the recurrent and persistent symbols of profoundly moving art are not the creations of the artist. The assumption that they are reproduced by the artist and that they originate in the non-aesthetic purposive activities of man must be made for the symbols of the cultural as well as of the biological *Apperceptionsmass* to which art turns. It is necessary to emphasize the point here because it is evident that cultural symbols are more often employed to ensure the perpetuation and propagation of particular beliefs than are those with a racial reference. This has been true of the belief in the soul's immortality, to which the great art of the Renaissance contributed beyond measure. It is, nonetheless, an error to attribute the invention of the symbol of the soul to the artist as artist or to regard this non-aesthetic use of profoundly moving art as its aesthetic end. The art truly significant for an understanding of reproductive imagination and, consequently, for the experience of profoundly moving art is the art that retains vestigial traces of content derived from a once functioning science.

With these brief anticipations of the teleology of feeling in mind, we may turn attention to the problem of light as the symbol of the immortal soul to speculate upon its origin and to mention some inferences which may be drawn from its widespread use in the history of art.

IV

THE conception of the immortality of man's soul and its divinity, as well as the symbolism of light used to signify that divinity, are manifestations of man's science. Many proofs of the soul's immortality have been formulated and numerous hypotheses have been offered to explain the widespread reception and the long persistence of the belief. Bergson, enlarging upon the significance of the quotation in Pascal's *Pensées*, offers a plausible account of the belief's probable origin among primitive people:

> Animals do not know that they must die. . . . But with man reflexion appears. . . . Seeing that every living thing about him ends by dying, he is convinced that he will die too. Nature, in endowing him with intelligence, must inevitably lead him to this conclusion. But this conviction cuts athwart the forward movement of nature. . . . Nature, then, looks as if she is going to stumble over the obstacle which she has placed on her own path. But she recovers herself at once. To the idea of inevitable death she opposes the image of a continuation of life after death; . . . religion is a defensive reaction of nature against the representation, by intelligence, of the inevitability of death.[5]

What Bergson calls a "virtual instinct" that leads primitive man to the belief in life after death is initially an extension of the scope of the instinct of self-preservation. Subsequently, it is elaborated

[5] H. Bergson, *op. cit.*, pp. 119-121. (By permission of Henry Holt and Company, publishers.)

to explain objects and events in a postulated realm beyond the visible world and in that elaboration becomes a vehicle for a science inclusive of theory of knowledge and of morality.

On Bergson's own view, the initial extension of the self-preservative function of the "virtual instinct" compensates for dangers arising from an excess of "intellectualism." It is unnecessary to accept either Bergson's metaphysics or his epistemology to acknowledge the value of his correction of Lévy-Bruhl's analysis of this belief as it is held by the primitive mind. Man's nature and activities hint at the tenacity with which he clings to a precarious existence in this world. This same tenacity is evident in equal, if not greater, force in the belief in an existence beyond the realm of the tangible, the visible, and the audible. For the present purposes, it is of no moment whether the majority of men affirm or deny the validity of this extension of the fundamental desire for life and its continuation. It is only necessary to reiterate that the "representation" of an existence continuing after physical death is one the compulsion of which all men feel whether that compulsion leads eventually to the acceptance or rejection of the "representation."

To light as a symbol of the soul's immortality, men of Western Europe have shown a continuous predisposition. The symbol itself, however, derives from early scientific speculation concerning the nature of the universe. The association of the two sciences, of the soul and of light, is in fact not limited to western culture. By way of illustration, the Egyptian theory of the soul as the *Ka* is thoroughly realistic but, as Maspero points out, this "double" is "recognisable at night by a pale light, which has won for it the name of Luminous *Khu*."[6] Moreover, it is probably the religion of Zoroaster that contributed the nimbus to the iconology of western culture. But light holds a firm place in the religious art of the West and it does so because the two great sources of the religious and metaphysical traditions of western culture, the religion of the Jews and the philosophy of the Greeks, associated it with divinity. Not the least of the reasons for its pre-eminent

[6] Sir G. C. C. Maspero, *Ancient Egypt and Assyria*, p. 43. Cf. below, for the figure of Aten, "lord of the beams of light."

importance, however, is that it is also fundamental, in the contrast of light and darkness, to the structure of painting, architecture, and sculpture and that it has a dramatic connotation of its own which has well adapted it for use in epic, lyric, and dramatic literature.

The scientific beginnings of the symbol for the West are clear. God's fiat that there be light and the consequent existence of light, as the story of Creation unfolds in Genesis, suggest numerous analogies in legend and in myth. But most significant is man's ordinary association of light, in contrast to darkness, with a definite act or instrument. Moreover, light has been widely thought to result from a direct act of divinity, as is suggested by the "burning bush" in the Old Testament and by the Greek attribution of it to the Sun or Apollo or to the Moon or Diana. There are, moreover, specific heavenly bodies which cause or bring light, while the agency of darkness is, in contrast, inferred to be negative. The conception has evidently stirred imagination from the beginnings of recorded time. It is reflected in the protective power of light as fire in the Greek legend of Prometheus, as well as in the numerous images of a struggle between light and darkness. It recurs in the Hesiodic poems, in the struggles between Zeus and the Titans, and in the tales of Demeter, Proserpina, and Pluto.[7]

The Septuagint made the Hebraic conception available for Western Europe. To this great influence may be added the widespread "representation" of light in folklore and belief and the essentially dramatic contrast between light and darkness already mentioned. But there was also in Western Europe the influence of Plato, in consequence of whose philosophical and imaginative power, light and the soul are joined as sign and object signified. On the subject of immortality, Shorey writes justly that "Plato was the first great prose writer to enforce it by philosophical arguments, or impress it upon the imagination by vivid eschatological myths. And the Platonic *Dialogues* remained the

[7] Cf. Gomperz, *Greek Thinkers*, Introduction.

chief source of the hopes and aspirations of the educated minority through antiquity."[8] But the association of immortality with light that was established for Western Europe by Plato's Dialogues is one already implicit in early Greek philosophy. Even if we disregard the writings of Homer and Hesiod, there is in Greece a tradition as old as Anaximenes that associated the soul with air, a light and radiant element in hylozoistic science. But in the philosophy of the Pythagoreans and of Heraclitus there are found the most significant and relevant contributions of early Greek philosophy. The ancient belief in a conflict of light and darkness comes to be central to the cosmology of the Pythagoreans. The central fire (Zeus) or light introduces limit into the universe by breathing in portions of darkness from the unlimited. Harmony results and this, as a principle, is adopted by the Heraclitean philosophy of fire or Logos to explain the measure of interchange for fire of factors basic to all flux and change. The Pythagoreans drew for their conception of man's soul from the beliefs of Orphism. This they interpreted to be an entity which had the power to achieve immortality if the individual adhered to the mysteries, lived temperately, and secured knowledge by means of religious practices and mathematics. Again, for Pythagoreanism, there appears, transformed, the myth of Dionysus Zagreus, with its reminiscence of the conflict of fire or light with earth or darkness. The Titans trick Dionysus and eat his flesh. The earth-gods are destroyed, in their turn, by Zeus. From their ashes, which contain the divine god, man is made and man is, in consequence, in part divine.

For much of early Greek philosophy, with its adherence to the theory of "natural place," fire was merely one of the elements, a physical body which, because of its lightness, ascended to the periphery above air, water, and earth. For Heraclitus, fire became the Logos, the rational law diffused throughout the universe, which directed the process identical with that universe. From fire, man's Logos derived its rationality and from the association of natural fire with the rapidly ascending flame and with the "picture images" of

[8] *Platonism Ancient and Modern*, pp. 67-68.

falling ash, came for Heraclitus the conception of fire as eternal and everlasting.[9]

The Heraclitean theory of the rational soul affected Plato as it affected the Stoic, Epictetus, who maintained that each individual has a spark of Zeus. But its influence on Plato's theory of soul is less effective than is that of the Pythagorean belief in *metempsychosis*, which becomes a presupposition for the theory of reminiscence. From these and many other sources, Plato drew for his development of the Socratic conception of soul, which for him is not alone an immortal visitor to the body but is, as well, an instrument by means of which we obtain knowledge of the Forms or Ideas. The highest of all knowledge is, however, of the Good, the Idea the nature of which is discussed in the *Republic* in terms of a myth.

It is Plato's envisagement of the Good and of the philosopher's search for this Form of Forms that once and for all seizes upon the imagination of the mystics, the philosophers, and the artists of western Europe and establishes the relation between light and the symbolism of divinity and immortality. Plato uses two figures to expound his theory: One is the myth of the Cave which describes the fire casting shadows in front of the shackled captives. The second metaphor likens the Good to the sun. Plato tells the auditors in the Dialogue that the two myths concern the same thing, for "the prison-house is the world of sight, the light of the fire is the sun, . . . the journey upward [is] the ascent of the soul into the intellectual world." But the philosopher further likens the soul itself to the eye, which possesses a power which "as a sort of effluence . . . is dispensed by the sun." The soul is like the eye more particularly because "when resting upon that on which truth and being shine," it "perceives and understands and is radiant with intelligence."

The assumption that the soul and the supreme Good are similar is maintained by Plato on the ground that the Good is the "cause of science and of truth insofar as the latter becomes the subject of knowledge," while "the sun is not only the author of visibility in all visible things, but of generation and nourishment and growth." But

[9] This Heraclitean doctrine affected the Stoic conception of souls and, ultimately, influenced Neo-Platonism and early Christianity.

as the sun "is not generation," "the good is not essence, but far exceeds essence in dignity and power."

This aspect of Plato's theory profoundly influenced the Neo-Platonists and, through them, the art of the west. From it came the symbol of the sun as the source of light, the conception of the identity of the soul, and the divine object of the mystical search for the One, of the difficulties of that search and of the ultimacy of the One. There came also, as has been previously mentioned,[10] the problem presented by the separation of the souls from their source and by an ultimate dichotomy in knowledge, which Neo-Platonism attempts to overcome by a theory of emanation and of mystical experience. In seizing upon likeness of the soul to the Good and of the eye to the sun, Plato offered his heirs a symbol. Its meaning rests upon the assertion that ". . . the power of elevating the highest principle in the soul to the contemplation of that which is best in existence," is comparable to "the raising of that faculty which is the very light of the body to the sight of that which is the brightest in the material world. . . ." The analogy which results, as Stewart writes, becomes the "equation 'φῶς in the sensible world'=ἀλήθεια in the intelligible world" and it "meets us wherever Plato's influence is felt."[11] The analogy of light is employed by Aristotle to explain the immortality of the actual intellect, for "it becomes all things . . . like a sort of definite quality such as light. For in a manner light, too, converts colours which are potential into actual colours."[12] It is central to that greatest intellectual influence upon the Renaissance, Neo-Platonism, and probably influenced, with Philonic philosophy, the Fourth Gospel.[13]

Panofsky maintains, in "The Neoplatonic Movement and Michelangelo," that "With the decline of classical civilization and the concomitant invasion of oriental creeds an interesting reaction [in Greek art] can be observed. Funerary art came again to be focussed on the future instead of the past. . . . Late-antique and Early Christian funerary art produced symbols anticipating their [i.e., the

[10] Cf. Chap. II, pp. 39-41.

[11] *Plato's Doctrine of Ideas*, p. 53.

[12] *De Anima*, 430 A.

[13] Cf. E. R. Goodenough, *Religious Tradition and Myth*, pp. 78-79.

dead's] spiritual salvation. Eternal life . . . was thought of . . . as an ascension of the immortal soul."[14] But that reaction in Greek art reflects a change that occurred in science and entered upon speculation concerning the universe. Goodenough writes that "not long after Aristotle" men came to be perplexed at "how the purely abstract God, who was perfectly self-contained and had no direct relation with anything outside himself . . . could still be in such relation with material as to have produced the material world."[15] Hellenistic thinkers, he continues, turned to the east "with its solar religion," which substantiates Plato's myth of the Good and of the Sun. For the sun "was the nearest thing they knew to self-sufficient and changeless existence. . . . It was the source to man and nature of life, warmth, and order. . . . The fact was that from the sun, by the very nature of its being, there streamed out a great flood of light and life and power. The stream went forth, for all its munificence, without decreasing the source at all."

But the Heraclitean conception of the Logos had, also, its profound effect, upon Hellenism. In it the rational word with fire had already been identified. And the Logos, which Goodenough translates as "utterance" in the following quotations, had for the "gloomy philosopher" similar associations with a stream. But "utterance" develops into "a stream which comes out from something otherwise inscrutable, the human mind. . . . Mind is never emptied by what it gives out. . . . So God's Stream of divinity, his Utterance, goes out without diminishing himself." But while "This Utterance (the Logos) was to be distinguished from God the source," it was itself divine. "It was light and its light was the life of men." Goodenough concludes that

> The Fourth Gospel brought the God of the Greeks, with his streaming radiation, into Christianity, or shows it already brought in. . . . The Mystic hoped to become one with God by becoming one with the Logos radiation. And the myths were to him just poetic

[14] E. Panofsky, *Studies in Iconology*, pp. 183-184.

[15] Cf. chapters on Greek philosophy and Hellenistic Judaism, E. R. Goodenough, *op. cit.*, and *By Light, Light*, *passim.* (The passages which follow are quoted by permission of The Yale University Press.)

fancies to make that conception real, the conception that though God is remote, he has actually made himself accessible to men by the merciful act of his Stream by his Light, his Life. . . .[16]

The significance of the figure of light is thus understood early in Western thought and finds an important place there. For the Greeks, baptism was illumination and the theologian Tertullian writes that the "ray of the sun is still part of the sun, there is no division of substance but only of extension." The Neo-Platonic stream of light from the One signifies that the souls caused by the source of light do not diminish the source but are yet of the same eternal substance as that source.

It would be of small value here to trace the spread of the two related symbols of light as a source and of the light as the sign of man's soul. The symbol of light is basic to the philosophy of Dionysius the Areopagite, finds its place in the theology of St. Thomas and, after Mirandola reawakened the poets and thinkers of Italy to Neo-Platonism and Platonism, becomes the common property of the Renaissance through the *Dialogues of Love* of Leone Ebreo, through the work of other poets, painters, sculptors, and philosophers of the day. It is, indeed, the task for the iconologist and for the mythologist to employ their skill and erudition in specifying the precise source and interpretation of the particularized symbols of Apollo, Diana, the Holy Spirit, the dove, and the nimbus employed by a particular artist in a particular age. But it is important for aesthetic to recognize that Plato's symbolism appealed to the Hellenic age, as Goodenough has pointed out, not as a final form of religion but as one of many myths—like that of the Orphics, of Persephone, of Attis and the Great Mother of Asia Minor, Isis and Mithra—which "told of the capture of divinity by lower powers, and then its restoration"—myths that were to the Hellene "poetic fancies to make that conception real, the conception that though God is remote, he has actually made himself accessible to men by the merciful act of his Stream, by his Light, his Life, which comes to us, seeking as Isis did for her lost and dismembered husband, or as Demeter did

[16] *Religious Tradition and Myth*, pp. 48-49, 63. (By permission of The Yale University Press.)

for her lost Persephone." There is here the "same story of deity imprisoned in material nature, and the hope of man in whom a particle of this divinity was present to escape back to God."

Light is a symbol familiar in "open societies." It is small wonder, indeed, that man's predisposition to extend the duration of his life and the scope of his knowledge should be actualized by the same "image" of light in divergent cultural environments. It is a familiar sign, whether it appears as the symbol for the God Amen, the "lord of beams of light," for the Ra of whom it is said, "thou dost renew thyself and make thyself young again under the form of Aten," or as the symbol of divinity, the nimbus of Byzantine and of north Italian painting. It is even less strange, if it is considered that the *mythos* ordinarily lays hold upon precisely those factors, light and darkness, which are basic technical means in representative art in the contrast of light and shade. Here is the double gift of the myth: to a symbol generally understood by the peoples of a culture and to the technique of art, a gift which it is of the nature of plastic art to exploit.

The diversity and variety of feelings for which the symbol of light as a sign for divinity and immortality has stood in art in consequence of its dual conceptual and structural potentialities, provides a study that passes beyond the scope of the present essay. But some hint of both is evident in artistic symbols less obvious technically than are those in which rays emanate from the sun, in the nimbus, or in the stream of light. The subtlety of expression to which the symbol lends itself is clear in such works as El Greco's interpretation of mystical union and reverence in "St. Francis in Ecstasy," in various of Tintoretto's ceilings, and in Giotto's representations of the stigmata; in the piety and humility signified in the two Annunciations, the one by a painter of the School of San Rocca, one by Bianchi; in the profound symbolization of divinity which overcomes all laws of mass and gravity in Dürer's "Die Sieben Pousaunenengel" and "Die Heilige Dreifaltigkeit"; in the feeling of aspiration lent, in part, by light to the Cathedral at Chartres, in contrast to the darkness predominant in the architecture of the cult of Mythras. Over against these symbols of divinity are the dark symbols of man's mortality, the darkness that recurs in Housman's poetry, in the shadows and downward mien in Kolbe's *Totentanz*, and in the recurrent association of black night with the representations of Sin, Death, and Chaos.

In conclusion, it will suffice to mention the pervading influence of this "intellectual representation" of light in two of the great epic poems of Europe in which the symbol stands for divinity and for the immortality of man's soul. The very structure of Dante's poem rests upon this symbolism and in *Paradise Lost*—perhaps the more so because of Milton's personal affliction—is displayed the constant struggle between the opposed elements of light and darkness. Milton, indeed, symbolizes almost every human emotion in terms of this sign. Woe and dread find their proper sign in

> A Dungeon horrible, on all sides round
> As one great Furnace flam'd, yet from those flames
> No light, but rather darkness visible
> Serv'd only to discover sights of woe,
> Regions of sorrow, doleful shades, where peace
> And rest can never dwell, hope never comes
> That comes to all; but torture without end
> Still urges, and a fiery Deluge, fed
> With ever-burning Sulphur unconsum'd
> . . . here their Prison ordain'd
> In utter darkness, and their portion set
> As far remov'd from God and light of Heav'n
> As from the Center thrice to th' utmost Pole.

Cupidity and pride, combativeness and avarice are symbolized in Mammon's suggestion that, with gems and gold, the fallen angels

> As he our Darkness, cannot we his Light
> Imitate when we please.

It is Uriel, on the contrary, who is called "regent of the Sun," "the same whom *John* saw also in the Sun," "Of beaming sunnie Raies, A Golden Tiar Circl'd his Head." And light throughout the poem is used to express Adam's hope, his joy, his power, and his immortality.

V

THE generic symbols of the "leader" and of "light" must suffice to illustrate the relation of profoundly moving art to ateleologically defined feeling. To multiply instances of generic signs would no doubt reinforce the argument that the artist recreates, that feeling reinstates the past of the race or of a culture, and that communication in aesthetic experience presupposes both processes. Similarly, to add illustrations of the recurrent symbols in question—the frequency with which, for example, the figures of Caesar, Tamurlaine, Alexander the Great, Lincoln, and Napoleon appear in art—might fortify the argument. One could also suggest avenues of investigation in the field of generic symbolism, indicating signs that have come to be basic to art and to signs that have, as yet, merely shown potentialities for so doing. To the first class belong the horse as a symbol[17] and the "image" of the Good Shepherd.[18] To the second, belongs the windmill, a sign for feeling familiar in meaning to those who have known the aspirations and sufferings of the pioneers of our own West.

It is more essential, however, for the argument of the present essay to turn at once to the problems and difficulties inherent for aesthetic experience in this hypothesis of generic symbols and of their conative presuppositions.

[17] Cf. S. Casson, *The Technique of Early Greek Sculpture.*
[18] Cf. V. Müller, "The Prehistory of the 'Good Shepherd.'"

Chapter XIV

The Ateleological Theory of Feeling and the Generic Symbols of Art: Difficulties and Limitations

So the elementary passions, pity and love, wrath and terror, are not in themselves poetical; they must be wrought upon by the word to become poetry.

—Sir Walter Raleigh

WERE ateleologically defined feeling to be identified with aesthetic experience or were the theory of generic symbols taken to be both a necessary and sufficient explanation of fine art, the most sympathetic critic could scarcely overlook the limitations patent in the present essay. Yet, the initial assumptions both of the theory of feeling and of symbols are sound. Aesthetic experience is conative and the feeling that defines it does not differ in kind from that in terms of which non-aesthetic instincts, emotions and moods are understood. Moreover, the artist does communicate by means of the work of art and the communicability of the product of his craft presupposes the use of generic symbols. Finally, towards the "referents" of these symbols men are predisposed by an *Apperceptions-mass* of feeling.

The limitations evident in the theory of aesthetic experience at its present development are not attributable to its presuppositions in symbols and in feeling. Rather, they are limitations only if it is concluded that the ateleological theory proffers not merely a necessary but a sufficient account of conation and if it is inferred either that the sole characteristic of art is familiarity or that the sole intention of the artists is communication. For the procedure of this essay, it needs, in fact, only to be granted that the work of art is a symbol as well as a mere object or event and that a presupposition of the symbol's aesthetic value is its communicability.

It will be apparent, as we proceed, that the ostensible limitations and difficulties, the precise nature of which will shortly be clear, concern factors in fine art and in aesthetic experience which in the light of the general theory are essential and valuable. We shall profit, however, by assuming for the moment that in them inheres no such value. In this, the inquiry is in accord with one tradition in the history of aesthetic and is by that tradition led to a more precise statement of the original antinomy of art and of its experience.

The first difficulty is best expressed in the form in which Hazlitt criticized Johnson's estimate of Shakespeare, the second in terms of Plato's conclusions concerning the effect of art upon the lover of poetry, painting, and sculpture. The English critic recalls that Johnson says "of Shakespeare's characters, in contradiction to what Pope had observed, and to what every one else feels, that each character is a species, instead of being an individual."[1] To much the same pass does the theory of generic symbols bring not only characters of the drama but all works of art.

In Plato's attack upon the artist in the ideal republic, this essay discovered a portion of its central problem and, in consequence, the reader is familiar with the details of Plato's conclusions. It is of value to recall, however, that the avowedly most serious indictment in the charge is that the artist releases from restraint the control properly imposed by reason upon the passions. For a more precise statement of this charge, the ateleological theory of feeling lays the ground. The *Apperceptionsmass* of feeling, brought into operation by the generic symbols of art no less than by other conative stimuli, is integral to action in a realm which Sir Charles Sherrington describes in the following terms: "the normal motor behaviour is operated relatively more and more by the 'extrinsic' processes with less and less of the 'intrinsic.' "

[1] William Hazlitt, *Characters of Shakespeare's Plays*, Preface, pp. xxxvi-xxxvii.

The object of the present chapter is to make explicit the implications of these not unrelated limitations and difficulties.

II

BOTH problems are implicit in the suggestion previously made in this study that the "referrents" for the symbols of art belong to the science, religion, and morality of the past. This is evident once we consider additional inferences to be drawn from the symbols of the leader and of light used to explain the operation of the biological and the cultural *Apperceptionsmass* of feeling.

The central generic symbol of *Hamlet* and the *Oresteia* is the vestigial figure of the "wintry slayer." This is one form of the symbol of the leader. The prototype is implied in much of the art of the Greeks, in the epics, in the medieval romances of Arthurian legend, and in traditions as diverse as those of Tamurlaine and Napoleon, Moses and St. Augustine, Pasteur and Lincoln. It is now the original and not the vestigial significance of the symbol and the frame of reference in which it functioned as an instrument, with which we are concerned. For the primitive peoples whose king had died and who had been replaced by the murderer, the myth and ceremony of the "wintry slayer" were science. They constituted one means by which man attempted, in formulating a theory of immortality and resurrection, to rid himself of the dread imposed by the cold of winter, by the death of vegetation, and by the cataclysms of nature which threatened them. The tale of the "wintry slayer" is not only a primitive account of the continuity and succession of seasons and of the vicissitudes and triumphs of an agricultural people aware of their dependence for survival upon the fertility of their crops. It bears traces as well of the ritual by which man hoped to control the partially alien forces which threatened him. The tale, as we have observed, penetrates the past more deeply still. In it is the detritus of a primitive social structure, built around a leader as part of a social instrument in which a patrilinear tyranny was implemented by the practice of human sacrifice. For the member of the primitive group there were impulsions of superstition and magic, as well as the more evident compulsion of force, directing the mind to conform to the practices imposed by this science in itself founded upon magic. But the compulsion imposed by the forms of this primitive society touches us but slightly as it similarly affected but slightly either the Athenian or the Elizabethan. For the former, the ritual had been supplanted by the gods of the Pantheon and only a vague reminiscence of human sacrifice disturbs even the Homeric poet. A rational philosophy and a reasonable religion had replaced the cult of the slayer in classical times. Even more remote were the traditions of the "wintry slayer" for the Elizabethans, while for modern man the magical science has given place to experiment and observation on the one hand, and on the other to ideals, at least, of more flexible and enlightened social practices. Yet the art still moves us profoundly.

The same perplexing problem emerges as we consider the recurrence in Western European art of the generic symbol of light. Plato's Socrates does hesitate to reply to the young Adeimantus' questions concerning the nature of the Good and finally agrees only to expound the Good's nature by using a figure, the "offspring" of that highest of Ideas. The "figure" of the sun which he does offer is no doubt a metaphor and to that extent removed from the highest sphere of science. Yet, Plato's description of the soul and of the Good in terms of light and of the sun is integral to Pythagorean philosophy and this, in turn, is presupposed by Plato's physics and astronomical science in *Timaeus*. Stewart is certainly correct in calling attention to the constantly recurrent "equation" between light and the physical realm and the Good and the intelligible realm. The generic symbol of light derives only in part from Plato, the artist. Its source is in the thought of Plato, the scientist, elaborating a theory of perception, knowledge, and physics. Not, indeed, the highest science, it is nevertheless derived from the highest science for which Plato at that moment has the terminology and power to present to his auditor.[2] It should be remembered, moreover, that it is not only in the physical realm that the soul, likened unto the sun, is integral

[2] He does, in the *Sophist* and in *Timaeus*, give it definite expression.

to Plato's science but it is presupposed as well by his theory of knowledge. The soul is like the Ideas it knows and has dwelt amongst them. Its power to know Ideas presupposes, for Plato, reminiscence of them.

Now not even the poet who sang

> I saw eternity the other night
> Like a great Ring of pure and endless light,
> All calm, as it was bright,
> And round beneath it, Time in hours, days, years
> Driv'n by the spheres
> Like a vast shadow mov'd,

subscribed to a Pythagorean physics. Nor did Drummond believe, as Plato did, in the theory of reminiscence. Yet he wrote

> Most true it is, for straight at the first Sight
> My mind me told, that in some other place
> It elsewhere saw the idea of that face,
> And lov'd a love of heavenly pure delight;
> No wonder now I feel so fair a flame,
> Sith I her lov'd on this earth she came.

Pythagoreanism was not Marlowe's creed nor was it believed in by the Dr. Faustus who recalls the music of the spheres. Vergil almost certainly did not hold as a religious belief the primitive theories of *metempsychosis* recalled in the *Aeneid*.

Similarly, for Plotinus, the theory of emanations from the One was not poetry. It was science. The Neo-Platonic philosophy certainly teaches that experience culminates in the mystical union with the One but its principal argument is logical and scientific. The theory of light as Plato and Plotinus expound it is science, a metaphysic with a correlative physics. It is impossible for us to accept that science, however many reminiscences of it there may be in modern times.[3] A science based upon experimental physics that began with Galileo and came to fruition in Newton and in Einstein has replaced it, as it has replaced the Ptolemaic cosmology.

Science has discarded these "images." Whatever is the moving power of the "image" of light, it does not hold the imagination because men seriously entertain the notion that immortality is either

[3] Cf. Sir William Bragg, *The Universe of Light.*

due to or is explicable ultimately in terms of an event that has meaning only in natural science. The instinct of self-preservation may indeed be "virtual." "Light" is no doubt an effective symbol of man's constant effort to extend the principle of self-preservation to a realm beyond mortal life. The scientific theory of light, however, is hopelessly inadequate to satisfy the demand—and we who are affected by it in art know rationally that it *is* inadequate. Art retains the "image" and the artist's recurrent use of it and of similar "images" argues the operation of a process essential to the understanding of aesthetic experience.

Shelley argued eloquently that "Time, which destroys the beauty and the use of the story of particular facts, stripped of the poetry which should invest them, augments that of poetry, and for ever develops new and wonderful applications of the eternal truth which it contains." This is, indeed, truth. But there are difficulties, as we may infer from the words of yet another poet. Robert Frost asks a crucial question in "The Black Cottage":

> . . . why abandon a belief
> Merely because it ceases to be true?

The poet suggests an answer:

> Cling to it long enough, and not a doubt
> It will turn true again . . .

This inference is certainly invalid. Schiller. in words already quoted, had the more profound insight:

> The intelligible forms of ancient poets
> The fair humanities of old religion . . .
> They live no longer in the faith of reason!
> But still the heart doth need a language, still
> Doth the old instinct bring back the old names.

The symbols of profoundly moving art not only live no longer in the "life of reason"; the very instinct that brings into operation man's predisposition toward them and is explanatory of their recurrence in art belongs to a side of man's nature by which, in fact, reason and rational activity are imperilled. The symbol of light in its association with the divinity and immortality of the soul derives its power to move men from the cultural predisposition. This, in its turn, owes much to Plato's philosophy and in particular to those contexts of his Dialogues which emphasize the close relation of the symbolism to the Good. It is at least debatable that Plato's separation of the Good from the sphere of man's moral activities has not been more harmful than valuable for ethics. The Platonic hypothesis has not infrequently influenced men, making a false and dangerous contrast between the ideal and all that is best in human nature, to choose an ideal and supreme value that is impossible not only of attainment but presumably of approach as well. Moreover, it is at least problematical whether Plato's attempt to justify Socrates' opposition to Thrasymachus by the theory of Good grounds obligation more soundly in moral principles than does the Sophists' out-and-out theory of power. Plato's view ignores, in its exaggeration of the function of knowledge in virtue, the significance of will and, consequently, overlooks the role of freedom in the moral life. The political system propounded to implement the theory takes so little cognizance of economic factors as to be palpably impractical and the citizen of the appetitive class would appear to enjoy "privileges" on a par with those of the slave. Finally, as the conclusion to *Phaedo* clearly implies, the ultimate sanction of this ethic of the Good is not self-enjoined duty but fear of punishment after death.

The art affected by the Platonic tradition of light is one for which men are predisposed. It ignores the defects in the theory of Good, defects which certainly argue strongly in favor of the abandonment of a belief so beset with error. It is unlikely, indeed, that the artists who follow in the tradition are aware of its limitations. And this retention in art of an outmoded morality suggests two crucial problems which an aesthetic presupposing reproductive imagination must resolve.

III

IF, AS has been contended here, the operation of reproductive imagination in feeling is a necessary presupposition in the experience of profound art, its substantiating theory must be prepared to encounter two related difficulties, one more particularly concerning the limitations which a sole dependence upon the theory of reproductive imagination implies for art, the second concerning aesthetic experience.

Regarding the first, it is unequivocally true that the theory of the reinstatement of images provides no ground for either the individual artist's creativity or for the uniqueness of the particular work of profoundly moving art. Moreover, while it is evident that a generic symbol may derive from the non-aesthetic teleological activities practiced in a culture or by the race, if no master of craft transforms the "referrents" by means of his art and brings them within the reaches of an individual and creative imagination, the sign is stillborn or subsists only in folklore. Thus, the airplane yet awaits the great artist, while the horse found its expression as a symbol in the great sculpture of Greece.

As we encounter the second difficulty, which primarily concerns aesthetic experience, it must be repeated that the theory of reproductive imagination apparently serves only to double in force Plato's castigation of the artist. The consequence of a sole dependence upon the theory is that aesthetic experience is inevitably a form of feeling in which man reverts to the primitive life of the brute and to a cultural level in which individuality and personality disappear under pressure of compulsions imposed by the collective spirit of the mob.

If it were conceivable that an adequate aesthetic could be grounded solely in the ateleological theory of feeling—and this is the inference which must be drawn if, as some theorists have declared, feeling is definable wholly in terms of typical behavior—that aesthetic would concern itself of necessity only with generic and typical similarities and differences in the symbols of typical and traditional works of art. For while ateleological theory provides some ground in its analysis of reproductive imagination for the familiarity of profound art, for its recognizability, and for the recurrence of its symbols, it provides and can provide no ground for the unique, the individual, and the novel aspects of works of art. If the theory were conceivably to be maintained and elaborated—and again it must be repeated that if art is the symbol of the artist's feeling either the ateleological theory is incomplete or there can be no aesthetic worth mentioning other than that of types—the obvious fact that works of art are individual and unique as well as generic and typical must be denied or ignored. Yet the issue is settled neither by denying these qualities to them nor by ignoring their existence. This is evident even to that most individual of poets, Shelley, who holds paradoxically that ". . . there must be a resemblance, which does not depend upon their own will, between all the writers of a particular age. They cannot escape from subjection to a common influence . . . though each is in a degree the author of the very influence by which his being is thus provided. . . . And this is an influence which neither the meanest scribbler nor the sublimest genius of any era, can escape." Yet, the very Shelley who holds that the poets "are compelled to serve" because it is in them that the power resides to communicate the "national will," knows that "the power" is "seated on the throne of their own soul."

It is precisely because generic signs are needed to communicate all art, whether aesthetic or non-aesthetic, and because all artists are subject to "an influence which neither the meanest scribbler, nor the sublimest genius of any era, can escape," that there is no mistaking the touch of the pre-eminently gifted individual upon the symbol of feeling in art. One may no more err in this respect than one may mistake the meaning of the individual work of art because of the generic aspects the same work of art displays. The bare bones of the themes common to *Hamlet* and the *Oresteia* could no more exalt us to genuine aesthetic experience did the dramas not also exhibit the power of a Shakespeare or an Aeschylus than could a familiar but prosaic account of diurnal and nocturnal sequence jotted down in the notes of the worst time-server. The art of genius is not that of the "meanest scribbler" but for the grounds of the necessary distinction between the two one searches in vain in the theory of reproductive imagination.

Nor is it wholly true, as Murray suggests that "in all these strangely characteristic speeches of Orestes, every line might have been spoken by Hamlet, and hardly a line by any other tragic character except those directly influenced by Orestes or Hamlet."[4] True it is, that only a man of the type of Orestes or Hamlet might have spoken lines like these. The lines themselves are the mint of the individual mind of Aeschylus, Sophocles, Euripides, or Shakespeare. Nor is this true because there are references in the dramas to contemporary affairs or inferences to be drawn concerning the individual artist's life and interests. It is in part a matter of the significant difference between the Greek conception of a fate external to the individual and the modern conception of fate consequent upon man's own actions and thoughts. This is well illustrated by the contrast between the words of Hecuba and Lear. Thus Hecuba of Euripides' *Trojan Women*:

> Lo, yonder ships: I ne'r set foot on one,
> But tales and pictures tell when over them
> Too strong breaks the o'erwhelming sea: lo, then
> All cease and yield them up as broken men
> To fate and the wild waters. Even so
> I in my many sorrows bear me low,
> Nor curse, nor strive that other things may be.
> The great wave rolled from God hath conquered me.[5]

The characters of Shakespeare's tragedies make their own fates. This, Lear knows:

> I am a very foolish fond old man,
> Four score and upward, not an hour more nor less;
> And to deal plainly,
> I fear I am not in my perfect mind.

But the attitude towards fate constitutes a generic cultural difference between Greek and modern conceptions of the world. Yet, even in this respect, there are at work among the Greek tragic writers forces which affect and alter conceptions as deeply imbued as is that of fate and of its power over mortals. The plays of Euripides reflect the influence of Eleatic philosophy, perhaps as it was expressed by Xenophanes: "There is one God, supreme among gods and men; resembling mortals neither in form nor in mind." The

[4] *The Classical Tradition in Poetry*, p. 212 ff.
[5] Gilbert Murray's translation.

conclusion that tragedy is consequent upon human weakness or excess and that the responsibility for it rests upon man and does reside wholly in fate appears, indeed, in Aeschylus' *Choephoroe*:

> The House itself can deliver itself,
> The House hath healing for its own bitterness,
> Tis here within.

Justice is substituted for vengeance in Sophocles' *Elektra*:

> Hads't thou the right to slay him? What high
> Law ordaining?

As for Euripides, as A. W. Verral writes, his creed "was that of a nascent philosophy, science and rationalism. . . . The duty preached by the philosophers, and by Euripides . . . was the duty of thinking on system, of not adopting without evidence or investigation, contradictory hypotheses on different days of the month . . . a duty which . . . would if pursued make it impossible to use at all such conceptions as 'Apollo' . . . and reduce even 'Zeus' to the position of an inconvenient and misleading name."[6] And so Euripides writes:

> Yet must I plead
> With Phoebus . . . What ails him? He ravisheth
> Maids and forsakes . . .
> And were it just then that ye should enact
> For men laws, and yourselves work lawlessness?

This is Euripides alone among the tragic poets. That his ideas are generic and derived from the philosophers is true. Still, he endows them with individual expression.

The issue, however, is more significant than this. Aeschylus alone is the master of words that reveal the workings of a world in which tragic conflict is reconciled with a belief in both justice and God—"God, whose law it is that he who learns must suffer." In contrast, Sophocles is one who looks upon the world dispassionately and writes with supreme perfection. Again, it is with human beings that Euripides is concerned:

[6] *Euripides, the Rationalist*, pp. 73-74.

Ah, what a death hath found thee, little one.
. . . Poor little child!
Was it our ancient wall so savagely hath rent
Thy curls—here where the bone-edge frayed
Grins white . . .

Perhaps there is no sharper contrast between men as artists than that evidenced in the individual techniques which wrought the conclusions to Aeschylus' *Libation-Bearers* and to Shakespeare's *Hamlet*. There is a divergence as sharp as individual genius can make it between Orestes' words, "I have ranged a homeless world, haunted by shapes of pain" and Hamlet's dying admonition to Horatio:

If thou dids't ever hold me in thy heart,
Absent thee from felicity a while,
And in this harsh world draw thy breath in pain
To tell my story.

This is still but to touch the suface of the matter. Aeschylus' profundity finds expression in succinct and austere phrase, as we learn from Orestes' condemnation of his mother.[7] Shakespeare's poetic and dramatic gift is in part the product of a power to perfect imagery, less direct in expression than is that of Aeschylus. And Shakespeare's *Hamlet* is the sickened reaction of the civilized man[8] towards incest. Aeschylus renders the images of poetic imagination objectively. Before Orestes, in the *Choephoroe*, come Gorgons with "snakes coiled with snakes." Before Hamlet is a philosophical dilemma and the consequence is a meditation upon man's existence and his future life.

What is true of the art in the tradition of the leader is no less true in that of the symbol of light. El Greco's suffused light, the symbol of St. Francis' ecstasy, is no less individually conceived than are the human figures which, in their very distortions, are elevated to proper place in a mystical context. The clarity of the emanating rays in Dürer's "Das Sonnenweib" marks the contrast between El Greco's mysticism and the German artist's penetrating and realistic mind. Between the light that shines invisibly in Milton's Hades and

[7] The *Choephoroe*, 973 ff.
[8] Act 3, Sc. IV.

the light that burns with glory in Dante's *Paradiso*, there is the difference that profound art manifests in highest degree in the capacities of individual minds to "imagine" creatively and productively and to feel uniquely as well as generically.

Again, one is tempted to elaborate the point by means of illustrations drawn from other arts. It will perhaps suffice, however, to conclude this, the present preliminary stage of the argument, with mention of Greek sculpture. So evident to the archaeologist is the fact of what have in this essay been called generic symbols that the author of *The Sculpture and Sculptors of the Greeks* has interpreted a passage in the *Republic* to support the theory that there are "foundation myths" to which sculptors and painters of classical times resorted.[9] It is interesting, in the light of the tenor of the present portion of this essay, to quote Richter at some length:

> Much of Greek religion consists of stories about gods and goddesses and heroes; and these manifold imaginative tales would naturally make a great appeal to the artist. They supplied him with the most varied material, which he used so constantly that definite standardized types soon emerged. Plato's words about literature apply equally well to sculpture and painting, "Art eschewed novelty and was framed after the pattern of those foundation myths which the poets have made familiar." So we must become conversant with these "foundation myths". . . . In entering this world of Greek fiction with its contests of Lapiths and Centaurs and Amazons, its wonderful deeds of heroes, and its manifold adventures of gods and goddesses, we feel very near the beginning of civilization. . . . We must remember, then, that the only symbolism we shall find in Greek art is the concrete one. . . . This practical symbolism was freely used, for such shorthand methods were useful and easily understood, and were thoroughly in line with the Greek tendency to simplification. . . . The almost total absence of historical representations (in the large mass of architectural sculptures) is striking. . . . The Greeks, in order to convey the strife and stress of their time, had recourse to mythological contests, or to the semi-legendary events of the Trojan war.

[9] Gisela M. A. Richter, *The Sculpture and Sculptors of the Greeks*, pp. 31 ff. Dr. Richter refers to *Republic* 377c. (Quoted by permission of The Yale University Press.)

It would be a serious error, however, to infer from this, or to suppose that Richter assumes, that the "standardized types" resulted in merely a generically interesting art. One need but glance at the illustrations of sculpture given in her book to be aware of the individual artist's firm grasp of technique and of his use of both symbols and technique for individual purposes. Perhaps one need simply mention, in this connection, Casson's characterization of the progress of Greek sculpture between 600 B. C. and about 540 B. C.:

> The following discussion will therefore aim at establishing in order of time the new fashions in the execution of detail and the introduction of new tools in the order in which they are introduced. . . . For by learning what they invented and when, we can get some insight into the aesthetic changes that were going on inside their minds and get some hint of the astonishing fecundity and imaginative power that was behind their work.[10]

As Casson remarks in conclusion, "For technical inventions may revolutionize the whole outlook and capacity of an artist. By the aid of a small invention he may suddenly find that a whole universe of power is opened to him." If he does, however, it is because there is in him a creative power and this is not identical with mere reproduction.

IV

THE theory of reproductive imagination poses more than the problems of the artist's creativity and the work of art's individuality. One encounters in its implications an equally serious difficulty, one, indeed, of which that of artistic creativity is a part. The problem of creativity is presupposed by it because there is raised here the issue of the adequacy of ateleological theory to account for aesthetic experience. If reproductive imagination affords a necessary and valuable generalization of Aristotle's conclusion that there is pleasure in the experience of art, it is likewise true that the theory of feeling which validates reproductive imagination offers a basis for a generali-

[10] S. Casson, *The Technique of Early Greek Sculpture*, p. 97.

zation of Plato's charge that the artist must be condemned because the experience of his art fosters irrationality.

For Aristotle, it is the recognitive, the epistemological, aspect of the experience of art that is of primary consequence. For Plato it is the instrumental value or disvalue of the same experience that is of first importance. Whatever the ultimate validity of the distinction between the epistemological and instrumental evaluation of the effects of feeling, the fact that the two thinkers emphasize different aspects is significant for a generalization of the implications of art's reinstatement of the past. A consideration of the value of the epistemological interpretation of feeling for aesthetic may be deferred. For the instrumentalist, however, art's appeal to feeling, as described by the ateleologist, is a perilous reversion for almost precisely the reasons that Plato put forward. The nerve of the Platonic argument is not, indeed, that the flute is stimulating or that tragedy is enervating, but rather that all profoundly moving art effects loss of control in the man who experiences it.

It is precisely the individual's lack of control over actions that is implicit in the theory of reproductive imagination. The artist uses the primitive initiators of feeling, symbols ensuring familiarity for his art. The "referrents" for the symbols are events, situations, ideas, and objects for which the *continuum* of feeling is predisposed to react. The symbols directed to its actualization, the consequence of which is familiarity, effect in the life of feeling the predisposition to react typically to stimuli. The reinstatement of a "precedent" image which is the presupposition for the recognition of a "subsequent" one is a typical and not an individual reaction. It is, in fact, a primitive means by which organisms exercise some control over their environment. The ateleologist proposes to describe this typical behavior entirely in terms of the operations of physiological and neurological structures, without reference to purpose. Such interpretation in terms of mechanism implies that the typical behavior is undeviating and that it varies only for mechanical reasons, i.e., its variation may be traced to the force of the effective stimulus or to the energy of the organism's reaction.

Typical reactions have been minutely described. The behavior includes panic, fear, unpremeditated flight, cowering, pallor, the clenching of the fist, the erection of the hair, and the secretion of adrenin. The pattern of this reaction is the operation of the *Apperceptionsmass* of feeling as the behavior of an organism whose reactions are consequent upon an inborn or acquired predisposition and is action judged to follow upon the effectiveness of stimuli without reference either to deliberation or to conscious control on the part of the individual.

The reasons for this implied inflexibility of behavior are evident in terms of the theory of reproductive imagination. For the recognition of the "subsequent image," a precedent one must be brought to the experience. But it is assumed that at this point the activity of the imagination ends. What occurs, in epistemological terms, is a "one-to-one" relation of external stimulus to reproductive "image." But the epistemologist infers from the organism's behavior that a reinstatement of the precedent image has occurred and that the behavior is automatic and inflexible. Rousseau, remarking behavior of this kind, concluded that "the Brute cannot deviate from the rule prescribed for it." It cannot deviate—nor can man if this theory of feeling be sound—because reproductive imagination provides no alternative "images" or modes of action. The man driven by panic-fear envisages no alternative but flight. His behavior is typical and implies, as Sherrington suggests, that "as receptor pure it signals to the motor individual pure." There is recognition of the stimulus. But the action may be unseasonable and, whether unseasonable or not, it is beyond the agent's control. He may be driven to react precisely as the lemming is driven to destruction by return to lands no longer above the sea. At the best, the organism is in the hands of fortune. At the worst, he is deprived of freedom and acts wholly in terms of the stimuli which his environment presents to him.

This holds true for the experience of stimuli presented either to the biological or to the cultural *Apperceptionsmass*. Feeling, for the ateleologist, is a "trigger" reaction. Feeling for the teleologist is a primitive instrument by means of which man survives. But the success of the instrument's operation is dependent upon the presentation in environment of appropriate stimuli and, negatively, upon the presence of no condition deleterious to the completion of the typical action. Either the "image" presented by the organism actually corresponds to the "stimulus" or the behavior is abortive.

One must not conclude from this that the stimuli to such reactions do not have some value. It is simply to urge that the organism so moved is able neither to reflect upon that value by comparing or contrasting it to that of others nor to be deflected from action by a comparison of its value with that of others. The man moved profoundly reacts unseasonably. The glutton is driven by desire for food in season and out, and the coward flees whether there be small danger or great. Spinoza holds that the brave man sometimes flees in the face of danger. He is eminently correct. The primitive reaction to the stimuli of feeling belongs to the life of the brute.

It is to the implications of speculation of this kind that an analysis of the experience of profound art brings us. We are moved by the symbols of the "wintry slayer" and by the symbol of light. Each symbol refers to ideas and organizations which have had value in the history of man's thought and evolution. The primitive "referents" for each, however, have been transcended. The artistic symbols recur and are contemplated with delight. The artist uses them to ensure the familiarity the percipient requires for complete aesthetic experience. But to ensure familiarity, the artist also appeals to an *Apperceptionsmass*, the actualization of which is inflexible behavior. Whether the leader be good or bad, cruel or kind; whether the symbol of light be the ancient error of the pseudo-philosopher or the fear of fire, the reaction, on this hypothesis, is identical and mandatory.

Art has depicted heroic leaders both good and evil, from the crafty Odysseus and the sublime Miltonic Satan, to Hamlet and Orestes. Art does not differentiate them in ethical terms as virtuous or vicious. It is in this sense that art could be charged with deception, if one were to judge it by non-aesthetic standards. The experience of art's symbols is implicated in a reversion to the past. Yet its lovers would deny that the consequence of the predisposition to react typically to the stimulus of the leader or of light as each is a symbol in art is comparable to that of the reversion that drives military hordes in blind adoration to commit abominations in the name of the principle of leadership. Similarly, they would deny that the recurrent symbol of light in art is comparable to the stimulus that drives the fanatic to massacre all unbelievers who adhere to cultural symbols to which he denies value.

There are strong arguments in support of the denial that art does degrade its lovers. Not the least of these is the denial of validity to the non-aesthetic teleological definition of art and, therefore, of the adequacy of art's explanation solely in terms of self-preservation. But perhaps the stronger argument is that the artist's realm is one in which a wide-ranging imagination—and one not only recreative—is creative beyond the predictions of ordinary experience. And one may insist that to explain creativity goes beyond the power of the ateleologist.

To this argument, based upon the fact that there is artistic creativity, may be added the other, that even the aesthetic experience, which to some degree re-creates the artist's feelings, is creative. For every Plato who attacks art there is a Pope who looks upon Homer as one who not only "opened a new and boundless walk for his imagination," but who opens a similar walk for our own. For every detractor of art, there is a Schopenhauer who maintains that tragedy elevates the soul, a Goethe who felt before Strasburg Cathedral that his "powers arose gladly at once to enjoy and understand," a Longinus who finds that "other qualities prove their possessors men, sublimity lifts them near the mighty mind of God." To read the following passages is sufficient to make the point, for any lover of art, that aesthetic experience exalts man to a realm in which experience transcends the atavism of feeling common to man and brute:

> The years like great black oxen tread the world
> And God the herdsman goads them on behind
> And I am broken by their passing feet.[11]

[11] W. B. Yeats, *The Countess Cathleen.*

Seven resistless captains o'er a shield
Blackbound with hide have slit a bullock's throat
And dipped their fingers in the bullock's blood
Swearing a mighty oath by War and Havoc
And Panic, bloodshed's lover.[12]

Ossa then upon Olympus they strove to set, then
upon Ossa
Pelion, ashiver with leaves, to build them a
ladder to Heaven—
Yea and indeed they had done it.[13]

But both denial and illustration drive against the rock of ateleological theory, against the rock of any theory which, like that of Descartes, reduces feeling to the behavior of *automata*. Descartes, however, merely fathers the interpretation with which begins a long tradition. Pavlow, for example, judges the Cartesian theory to be sound and the Russian scientist, in turn, has exerted widespread influence. Thus, it may be hoped, Pavlow writes, " . . . that some of the more complex activities of the body, which are made up by a grouping together of the elementary locomotor activities, and which enter into the states referred to in physiological terminology as 'playfulness,' 'fear,' 'anger,' and so forth, will soon be demonstrated as reflex activities of the subcortical parts of the brain."[14] But if this hope were fulfilled, the reduction of feeling to reflex action and mechanism would forestall any attempt to explain the creativity of the artist or of aesthetic experience.

The fact is that aesthetic experience cannot be encompassed within the range of reproductive imagination. That it is not wholly creative but that its adherents have written as though it were, has made the task of countering the arguments of mechanism the more difficult. These two aspects of feeling, reproductive and productive, are in fact interrelated and interdependent. The inspiration of aesthetic and the creativity of the experience presuppose the atavism of reproductive feeling. The exaltation of aesthetic experience presupposes

[12] Aeschylus, *Seven Against Thebes*.
[13] Homer, *Odyssey*, XI, 315.
[14] I. P. Pavlow, *Conditioned Reflexes*, p. 4.

the degradation implicit in automatic reaction. It is an error for aesthetic to assert that the operational aspect of feeling insisted upon in ateleological theory does not effect aesthetic experience. The constant and recurrent attacks upon art suggest the fact of its presence precisely as does the price exacted, not only for the familiarity of profound art but for a more profound function as well. There is, in aesthetic experience, a reversion to the past, to a more primitive existence. But the possible evil effects are mitigated and in that experience the primitivism is turned to good account, employed for a richer and more profound experience than could otherwise be had.

These are assertions which may be substantiated neither by conviction nor by faith, but only by re-examining the life of feeling. The grounds must be discovered for the productivity of aesthetic experience which, in conjunction with the reinstatement of the past and the primitivism, will account for the creativity and inspiration that have, along with the degradation, been in all ages attributed to the experience of art.

It is in the teleological theory of feeling, with its presuppositions that the *continuum* varies throughout its parts, that overt behavior diminishes, and that alternative "images" are possible, that there will be found a firm foundation for the analysis of the aesthetic mood, the resultant of both creative and recreative imagination. It is not to Descartes but to Kant that we turn for the presuppositions of the teleology of feeling which are, in turn, the presuppositions of creativity in aesthetic experience. It is Kant who rightly maintains the principle that the science of ends is requisite for a comprehension of biologically defined entities and that not even the "blade of grass" may be adequately explained upon the "mechanical principles of nature" alone.

In the subsequent chapters of this essay, the general theory of the teleology of feeling and its problems will first be examined. We shall then consider, in the light of both reproductive and productive imagination, the aesthetic mood, the artist's productivity, and certain of the artistic methods by which aesthetic experience is guarded from the full implications of the organism's reversion to atavistic behavior. Our first task is to examine the value of the ateleologist's contention that there can be no teleology of feeling.[15]

[15] The reader is referred to an article by Alden O. Weber and David Rapaport, "Teleology and the Emotions," for a somewhat vehement defense of the ateleological theory. Weber and Rapaport's article is primarily an attack upon my "The Philosophical Implications of Some Theories of Emotion." Although I should regard it as misinterpreting my general position in the matter as well as my particular argument, it has value in showing the tenacity with which mechanists maintain their thesis. In reading Weber and Rapaport, the reader should perhaps be warned that their principal arguments presuppose an unwarranted assumption that their opponent deliberately alters the texts he quotes, that their conclusion is susceptible to the identical criticism brought in my article to disprove the validity of earlier ateleological theories, and that there is a vast difference between their assumption that my argument is "an amplified version of James' theory of the emotions" and my original statement that "a sound point of departure for an examination of the emotions lies in the view propounded by William James."

Chapter XV

The Teleology of Feeling: Productive Imagination

And as a clock composed of wheels and counter-weights no less exactly observes the laws of nature when it is badly made, and does not show the time properly, than when it entirely satisfies the wishes of its maker, and as, if I consider the body of a man as being a sort of machine so built up and composed of nerves, muscles, veins, blood and skin, that though there were no mind in it at all, it would not cease to have the same motions as at present. . . .

—DESCARTES

There is surely a strange confusion of causes and conditions in all this. It may be said, indeed, that without bones and muscles and the other parts of the body I cannot execute my purposes. But to say that I do as I do because of them, and that this is the way in which mind acts, and not from the choice of the best, is a very careless and idle mode of speaking.

—PLATO

THE issue of a teleology of feeling is sufficiently significant for aesthetic theory to warrant, if it were possible to do so, concentration of attention solely upon the implications of purposiveness for art and its experience. This is the more evident as, in retrospect, we consider the status of the interrelated problems made integral to aesthetic theory by the ateleologist and left by him unsolved. At the outset, it is plain that the work of art is insufficiently defined as a generic symbol. Moreover, true as it may be that the artist recreates but does not create the "referrents" for the symbols of his craft, he is nonetheless creative and his creativity is evidenced in the products of technique. Finally, it is no less impossible to rest content with the conclusion that aesthetic experience is solely recognitive than to agree either that profoundly moving art exerts its influence only because of familiarity or that its experience is wholly analyzable in terms of reactions merely mechanical and automatic.

In view of this heritage of insufficiently analyzed problems, it is plain that a theory presupposing a hypothesis of feeling must discover in that hypothesis potentialities for explaining artistic creativity and aesthetic productivity. Otherwise the philosopher of art must seek elsewhere for the presuppositions of his subject. It has been a fundamental thesis of the present essay that only a theory which does take cognizance of both the ateleological and teleological implications of feeling is implemented adequately to account for the subtleties of art and for the divergent aspects of aesthetic experience. It is, however, precisely in the substantiation of that thesis that the purposiveness of feeling as it is related to philosophy of art is most evidently implicated in a more inclusive problem, that of mechanism and vitalism and of their interrelation in a general philosophy.

The postulates and implications of a general teleology have been stated clearly by Professor Edgar A. Singer, Jr., and the conclusions to which he has come in the elaboration of Empirical Idealism[1] are presupposed in the present study. But the issue between the mechanist and the vitalist touches upon artistic creativity and aesthetic productivity at a crucial point. The ateleological theory of feeling, as it was outlined in the preceding chapter, reduces conative behavior to mechanical response to stimulus, and precludes, in consequence, the presuppositions of freedom. The issue is the more clearly drawn inasmuch as the artist's "making" is a specific form of action and, for this reason alone, is more nearly crucial to the immediate problem of these concluding chapters than was its emergence in the analysis of ateleological theories of art.[2]

It will be necessary, in consequence, to examine in some detail the

[1] See *Mind as Behavior*.

[2] Cf. above, Chaps. II-IV.

contentions of those ateleologists who maintain that feeling is completely definable in terms of mechanism. That it is definable in those terms, but not completely so, is the alternative which appears to the present writer to be the conclusion forced by an examination of the facts presented by the mechanist. But the teleology of feeling is not assumed to be essential to theory solely because the ateleological theory fails. The facts of conative behavior, as well as those of aesthetic experience and artistic creation, presuppose the theory's validity. Plato judged that the mechanist's view implied "a strange confusion of causes and conditions." He did not maintain, however, that the ateleologically definable aspects of human behavior could safely be ignored. The latter are nonetheless insufficient, precisely as the aspects of the teleologically definable behavior in their own turn are inadequate for a complete analysis of conation. To show this, we may best begin with the consequence of Descartes' conception of the body as a machine and proceed to the opposed position, that there is no break between the feelings and mind.

II

THE precise character of the feelings becomes a pressing problem once it is evident, as we have observed, that ateleological theory offers no ground for the emergence of artistic or aesthetic productivity. The very terminology employed by the ateleologist likewise comes to be significant at this point because it indicates systematic difficulties in a theory which, forced to deny to feeling any function as "emergency action," denies to its adherents the use of any reference to a means-end relation.

These are consequences which follow because the ideal of the ateleologist, as we have observed,[3] is to describe feeling solely in terms of the relation assumed to hold between stimuli and the physiological and neurological structures predisposed to react within typical and generic patterns of behavior. The mechanical ideal, as it affects the problem of feeling and the consequent denial of the

[3] Cf. above, Chap. X, pp. 327-328.

relevance of the terms "means" and "end" to conation, presuppose, in their turn, an effort to secure what Pavlow, one of the foremost physiologists of this school, calls "scientific objectivity."[4] The eminent physiologist, in laying down this requirement, expresses the hope that a "genuine scientific conception" will follow upon the avoidance of phraseology like "fear" and "playfulness" to denote "some of the more complex activities of the body, which are made up by a grouping together of the elementary locomotor activities." These activities, he hopes, "will soon be demonstrated as reflex activities of the sub-cortical parts of the brain." It is precisely in order to undercut "the unscientific tendency . . . of speculation and teleology" that Pavlow demands increased terminological precision and it is precisely because teleology appears to him to be both an obstacle to progress in scientific methodology and to the achievement of the goal of reducing feeling to a science of "necessity"[5] that he suggests the elimination of purposive terms.

But Pavlow's presentation of the ateleologist's point of view suggests that more than a terminological difficulty has been encountered and that a sole dependence upon mechanism in the theory of feeling has, in fact, raised systematic issues. Indeed, as he and his followers express themselves more fully, it is plain that their intention is to limit analysis of feeling solely to minute description of structural behavior. It is equally patent that the ateleologist is prepared to attack two—for him—interrelated aspects of teleology which—again on his view—effect a lack of precision. The object of the first attack is the "finalisme theologique" which, it is asserted, an adoption of teleology forces upon the science of feeling.[6] The object of the second attack is to substantiate the teleologist's denial that all feeling may be reduced to concepts of "necessity," i.e., to explanation wholly in terms of stimulus and physiological and neurological behavior related in terms of cause and effect.

The first objection is sufficiently met by counterassertion. Numerous teleologists have had recourse to theology and, with it, to a

[4] I. P. Pavlow, *Conditioned Reflexes*, p. 7.
[5] *Ibid.*, pp. 48-50.
[6] G. Dumas, *Traité de Psychologie* (2nd ed.), p. 681.

doctrine of final causes. But neither the principles of logic nor the results of experiment drive teleology to the absolutism which the ateleologist fears. Indeed, Kant long ago demonstrated that the employment of purposive principles of explanation affords no ground for a proof of the existence of God.[7]

It is, consequently, the second of the ateleologist's objections to the introduction of purposive description into conative analysis that constitutes the nerve of his argument. The intention of the argument is to offer an explanation of feeling in terms of a "necessity" that accords with a systematic account of all behavior in terms of mechanism. The teleologist maintains, on the contrary, that some of the observed behavior called feeling, even if it is granted that it is evoked by stimuli definable in mechanical terms, is explicable as means to end and, in consequence, that some aspects of the behavior which the ateleologist judges to be the inevitable effect of a cause actually occur only "for the most part."

[7] The specific attack in the *Traité* is directed against Darwin and Spencer but it is implied consistently throughout that the conception of "end" or "purpose" inevitably involves theological considerations. The argument appears to rest upon the simple statement that "finalisme theologique" is consequent upon any departure from mechanical principles but it obviously is intended to guard against any possibility of introducing into "science" proofs of the existence of God based upon data indicating that there are purposive aspects in nature. However, simply because phenomena are interpreted teleologically, does not necessarily imply either (a) that all purposes in the universe are completely co-ordinated or (b) that they are co-ordinated by a deity. In fact, either implication entails an infinite regress which by definition excludes the final term. Kant, in his discussion of the physico-theological proof for the existence of God, has shown with sufficient clarity the fallacy involved. The author of the *Kritik* adds, moreover, the equally significant empirical objection to the argument, the fact that "we can never find in experience material sufficient to satisfy such a concept [the idea of God]. . . . We are not acquainted with the whole content of the world, still less do we know how to estimate its magnitude by comparison with all that is possible." But Kant holds with equal clarity that the concept "is never decisively contradicted by any experience," that "it contributes" as a regulative principle "to the extension of the employment of reason within experience, through the guidance which it yields in the discovery of order and purposiveness." *K.d.r.V.*, A 621 ff., *arranged.* Kant sums up the argument succinctly in the *K.d.U.*, Sec. 75: "On the question, therefore, whether or not any being acting designedly stands behind what we properly term physical ends, as a world cause, and consequently, as Author of the world, we can pass no objective judgment whatever, be it affirmative or negative." (Quoted by permission of The Macmillan Company, publishers.)

In any consideration of the respective merits of these two interpretations of feeling, one point must be insisted upon at the outset. However valuable and, indeed, basic the concept of "necessity" may be for the explanation of data in terms of the causal relation, the most indefatigable employment of ateleological definition will not suffice if it leaves unexplained significant aspects of the phenomena of feeling. That it does leave the phenomena without sufficient explanation may be inferred, as will be seen, from terminological difficulties. To this, however, the ateleologist has ordinarily replied that inadequacies in terminology signify merely deficiencies in the possible perfection of techniques developed to investigate the phenomena of feeling. He implies, moreover, that more minute analyses of mechanically defined stimuli and more detailed studies of the corresponding structures will obviate the need for introducing another type of description, the teleological. It should be possible to substantiate the claims of the mechanist that his principles are sufficient to explain the phenomena. The issue is itself sufficiently clear: Can the life of feeling actually be encompassed within the scope of minute analyses of the glandular, skeletal, and visceral behavior produced by mechanically defined stimuli without reference to the purpose of that behavior?

Nowhere has a more rigorous attempt been made both to define feeling ateleologically and to demonstrate experimentally its causal and mechanical implications than in the work of the French physiological psychologists whose hypotheses and experimental results have been published in Dumas' *Traité de Psychologie*. The *Traité* presents itself as a more adequate testing ground of ateleological theory, moreover, because in it are elaborated the interrelated traditional Cartesian theory[8] that the life of the passions is reaction of *automata* to stimuli and the Pavlowian theory of "scientific objectivity."[9] In addition, Dumas' and his confrères' efforts to establish the required "objectivity" is especially relevant to the present dis-

[8] Cf. *Med.* VI, *Passions of the Soul*, *Letter to the Marquis of Newcastle*, *Letter to Henry More*.

[9] See Pavlow, *op. cit.*, p. 7: "Our starting point has been Descartes' idea of the nervous reflex. This is a genuine scientific conception, since it implies necessity."

cussion because among its presuppositions is the acceptance, within limits, of the validity of significant aspects of James' theory of the emotions.[10] It goes without saying that the teleological implications of the latter's view are denied and that a more modern terminology than that used by Descartes for the mechanist hypothesis is employed. As an illustration, the Cartesian phrase, "expansion and contraction," in its application to the physiology of the passions, is replaced in the modern psychology by the terms "tonus" and "hypotonus." But the underlying motive is identical with a dominant one that led Descartes to formulate his conclusions upon the automatism of the brute: the explanation of passion solely in terms of physiological and neurological structures and of mechanical stimuli.[11] This is well illustrated by Barat who concludes as follows an analysis of the mechanical conditions for different expressions of emotion:

> If one is willing to accept our conception of excitation or depression, at the same time making reservations on those parts of our schematization which seem too dogmatic, one may fruitfully turn back to a large number of mimic expressions that Spencer, Darwin and Wundt have explained by their psychological principles and that are in reality the consequence pure and simple of variations of excitation and depression.
>
> We have already pointed out the importance of variations of muscular tone (*tonus*) in our affective tonality; these same variations do not fail to play a role in most emotional expressions, first by themselves and then because they facilitate or impede contractions more or less complicated, reflex, automatic, half or entirely automatic, which are part of the expressions of anger, of joy, of sadness and of fear.
>
> In joy, for example, simple tone can suffice to lift up the head, round out the cheeks, give to the entire countenance the well-

[10] G. Dumas, *op. cit.*, p. 681: "Tandis que l'expérimentation physiologique n'arrive pas à infirmer la théorie de Lange-James. . . ." A further stipulation is made, however: "l'observation psychologique et l'observation clinique permettent d'être plus négatifs." Dumas finds this to be particularly true in the problem of the "émotions délicates."

[11] *Ibid.*, p. 633. For example, concerning the expression of the emotions, it is said that "it is then indispensable to give a large place to the phenomena of excitation or of neuromuscular depression in the explanation of emotional expressions; many of these expressions are only phenomena of *tonus*, *hypotonus*, of excitation, of exhaustion, of inhibition. . . ."

known expression of satisfaction, and facilitate in that way all the contractions of the voluntary musculature by which the light excitation of joy is discharged. There is thus at the basis of joyous expression, however complicated, however mixed with mental representations it may be, a simple phenomenon of mechanics. . . .[12]

This and similar summaries suggest throughout the *Traité* that emotion may be reduced to an association "with an affective discharge of abnormally intense nervous energy."[13] It is significant, however, that in the above-mentioned quotation from Barat the demand for strict "objectivity" and the correlative denial of teleology make way for the assumption that simple phenomena of mechanics may be regarded as the *bases* for "joy." It would not be necessary for the teleologist to deny that this is the case. In fact, the assumption that simple phenomena of mechanics are the presuppositions of feeling must be accepted. It has been argued in the present inquiry that the additions made by the physiologists and neurologists to our knowledge of the structure and of the mechanical stimuli implicated in feeling are essential for the statement of the problem of conation. But the inference that simple phenomena of mechanics are "bases" for "joy" and kindred feelings is not identical in its implications with those of the assertion that teleological description is unscientific, lacking in objectivity, and inevitably influenced by theological considerations.

There are, indeed, sufficient indications that complete success has not been attained even by those who have employed the most rigorous mechanical techniques. Indeed, even the hope for such success has in part been abandoned. Dumas, by way of illustration, is content to suggest in the revised edition of the *Traité* that "from the facts and the laws . . . the strictly mechanist explanations of expression can go much farther than one might ordinarily think."[14] Indeed, he maintains that the sound conclusion to be drawn from the hypothesis and the experimentation intended to substantiate it is that one must lay "considerable emphasis on the psycho-reflex and instinctive

[12] *Ibid.*, pp. 629 ff.

[13] H. Piéron, "Emotion in Animals and Man," *Feelings and Emotions*, pp. 285 ff.

[14] G. Dumas, *op. cit.*, p. 200.

reactions which are mingled with the reactions of excitation and depression." He hastens to add, however, "but much less so than did Darwin." The limitation is added for an obvious reason. The last stronghold of mechanism must still be tenaciously held, whatever the breaches in the outer defenses. Thus, Dumas argues that "in the case of very simple emotions, such as passive sadness and active joy, one may stop here," i.e., one may rest within the limits of mechanist explanation.

But the entire ateleological interpretation of feeling must rest its case, not upon the possibility that simple rather than complex feelings are completely describable in mechanical or causal terms alone, but rather upon the demonstration that any feeling is adequately describable solely and completely in these terms. Consequently, it is essential to determine whether one may properly "stop here" even in the interpretation of "simple" passions. It would seem that the phrase, "very simple emotions," obscures by terminological means the extremely complicated bodily reactions which, as was previously suggested, constitute all behavior called feeling. It may be suggested, furthermore, that if one does rest content with causal description in the instances of very "simple emotions," it is only because a sufficiency of teleological connotation is associated with the terminology used by the mechanist in the discription of "sadness" or "joy" to satisfy the conditions of the problem. It may be stated categorically that, upon strictly mechanist grounds, terms like "joy" and "sadness" are without significance. It is precisely this inference that may be drawn from the statement previously quoted from Pavlow, expressing the hope that feelings would some day be reduced to description in terms of "reflex cortical action." The analysis made by the ateleologist is devoted to minute observation, enumeration, and description of muscular, nervous, and glandular action. This necessarily implies that his consequent description of phenomena will be offered in terms of the distributive factors in feeling, since it presupposes that "all" of the actions, considered one by one, do not add up to the collective "all," the totality of the reaction, with reference to which the terms "fear," "joy," and "sadness" are applicable. The collective term is descriptive of diverse actions and reactions, the unity of which is implicit in a common function. For the ateleologist to apply the collective term "joy" or "sadness" to minute enumeration and description of muscle, nerve, and reflex action is avowedly to ascribe to the former conative terms no more meaning than would have been implied in the use of the letter "x." If more is implied in such usage, the mechanist must grant that the collective term is employed because an end for the mechanical reactions is tacitly presupposed.[15]

This presumably terminological impasse raises again the fundamental problem for the ateleologist. The analysis of feeling he proposes to offer without reference to teleology must ultimately be accepted or rejected on grounds which concern the adequacy of the mechanical and causal descriptions and explanations offered. It is the ateleologist who issues the challenge and his is the task of proving the case. His view runs counter to common sense which considers it absurd to dissociate, for example, fear from self-preservation. It is admitted by the psychologists whose data and conclusions are under examination that mechanism is inadequate to the task of explaining the feelings. Moreover, the reasons offered to account for the inadequacy actually beg the question. Dumas writes, for example, that, "In reality, what prevents our mechanist explanations from being extended to all muscular expressions is that the active expressions of anger and of fear, like the entirely instinctive reactions of

[15] Some attempt, indeed, is made to avoid the consequences which follow upon the use of such terminology. Dumas argues, for example, that the expression of the feelings upon which teleological explanation bases its analysis "is not true expression either in the psychological or the biological sense of the term." This follows, it is argued, "since the subject who experiences the emotion has neither the intention nor the desire to express unless he adds imitation to his emotion. . . . It is the observer . . . who creates the term of expression and gives it a meaning . . . by making a symbol of a spontaneous reaction which was naturally linked to an affective state but which did not have for its purpose the signifying of it." (*Traité*, ed. 2, p. 201) But, clearly, Dumas finds it impossible to carry this argument to its ultimate conclusion, since even the mechanist responses are best analyzed by the observer of that behavior. Moreover, if as Dumas insists (*ibid.*, p. 201), it is solely the fact of their being visible which has caused these physiological reactions to be considered expressive, it is similarly only because they are perceptible to an observer that the reaction may be treated "scientifically."

defense and aggression, are too complex to be reëstablished as variations of excitation."[16]

It is not surprising that the ateleologist should attribute the inadequacy of mechanical explanation to a not yet attained refinement of experimental technique or to limitations upon the extent of the experimentation. But are these, in fact, the reasons for the incompleteness of the ateleological theory of feeling? One is reminded that the strongest motive for Kant's search for the ground of reflective and teleological judgment lay in what he regarded to be an *a priori* necessity. The third *Kritik* was written because it appeared to the author that "the forms of nature are so manifold" that the concept of purpose is indispensable if we are to arrive at a required unity of empirical principles.

That the "forms of nature" are so manifold as to require teleological as well as mechanical explanation is not mere theory employed to bolster a non-empirical analysis of the feelings, is evident from Singer's conclusions concerning Jennings' experimentation upon "sensibility" in paramecia.[17] Singer points out that Fechner's is the classic model of an inquiry which would lead to the attribution to these organisms of "sensations of different intensity." But one of the conditions that is demanded by Fechner's experiment is that "the intensity of the stimulus just noticeable by the organism under the same conditions of sensibility" be re-established as the experiment proceeds after the first application of the mechanical stimulus. But this is to say that the same conditions as those which produced the "just noticeable" difference in the sensibility of the paramecia in the initial experiment are required. However, as Singer maintains, this, "the third of our empirical data cannot in general be obtained," for in the particular experiment the temperature at which the reaction will recur will not be identical with that at which the "just noticeable" difference in behavior began. There follows, rather, "a sensation of the *same intensity* under conditions of 'over-estimation.'" The results may be tabulated statistically, the reactions are

[16] *Ibid.*, p. 200.

[17] Edgar A. Singer, Jr., *op. cit.*, pp. 86-87. Cf. E. D. Adrian, *The Basis of Sensation*, pp. 28 ff.

those ascertainable by observation of groups and not of individuals, and the statistics by which the results are tabulated concern collections. The predictions are necessarily given in terms of probability and not of necessity. The ateleologist is faced, indeed, in this classic experiment upon sensibility, with the impossibility of describing feeling in causal terms because there is no identity of the distributive effects.

The point may be put briefly in another way. It has been too often assumed that the introduction of teleology leads to the exclusion of mechanical explanation. But instinct, emotion, and mood presuppose typical reaction, including glandular and somatic distributive changes. These aspects of feeling presuppose, in fact, increase in glandular secretion, physiological and muscular alterations, and nervous excitation. Yet instinct, emotion, and mood differ as parts of the *continuum* of feeling and they diverge in respect to the overtness of the behavior which each displays as a level or range of the *continuum*. They are, nonetheless, identical in the end they subserve, however much they may vary in efficiency as means to that end, and however widely the gross descriptions of each level may differ as they are all referred to that end. Instinct, emotion, and mood are evoked by stimuli describable in mechanical terms and, as neurological and physiological analysis improves its techniques, the structural effects are likewise more minutely describable in ateleological terms. But some aspects of the reaction have purposive references and are neither predictable in terms of nor reducible to explanation in causal language. A full understanding of feeling, in fact, presupposes both ateleological and teleological description.

Concerning the adequacy of ateleological defining, Barat concludes "that in this part of psychology where so many facts still escape us, the greatest error that one can commit in presenting a theory of emotion would be to consider this theory as sufficiently explicative." One is tempted to conclude, however, that the insufficiency of ateleological explanation is not due to lack of precision in or perfection of technique but, rather, to its advocates' unwillingness to avail themselves of objective facts and inferences belonging to another but no less "scientific" order.

To the ateleologist, the substantiation of the hypothesis that the feelings are fully definable in mechanical terms may appear to await only a new technique or, in Kant's words, "another Newton." This is implied by Dumas, who concludes that certain emotional reactions are "too complex" to be susceptible to available mechanical explanation. But the feelings, like the blade of grass which Kant mentions in illustrating his more inclusive point, are susceptible to teleological and purposive as well as to mechanical description. To the assertion that they may be defined completely in terms ignoring this conclusion, one may reply in the words of the *Kritik of Judgment*:

> It is. . . . quite certain that we can never get a sufficient knowledge of organized beings and their inner possibility, much less get an explanation of them, by looking merely to mechanical principles of nature. Indeed, so certain is it, that we may confidently assert that it is absurd for men even to entertain any thought of so doing or to hope that maybe another Newton may some day arise, to make intelligible to us even the genesis of but a blade of grass from natural laws that no design has ordered. Such insight we must absolutely deny to mankind.[18]

III

IT MAY be concluded that no experimental ground has been established for the ateleologist's assumption that the analysis of feeling must be restricted to the description of factors taken distributively in inflexible behavior. It may be inferred, as well, that feeling is not merely behavior interpreted as the effect produced by a stimulus defined as a cause. The evidence that feeling is not definable solely in ateleological terms has led, however, to the counter-assertion that instinct, emotion, and mood are completely describable in terms of the means-end relationship which holds in teleological systems. It is not strange that the winds of the ensuing controversy have blown particularly in the realm of the extreme dimension of the *continuum* of feeling called instinct: the very word, instinct, is ambiguous. For some theorists, instinct is identical with mechanical

[18] *Op. cit.*, Sec. 75. (By permission of The Macmillan Company, publishers.)

reflex action. For others, it most clearly evidences the operation of "unconscious purpose."

Precisely as the French physiological psychologists have maintained the validity of the ateleological theory of feeling, the French philosopher, Bergson, interested in the function of feeling in his philosophical system of Creative Evolution, has given to instinct a widely influential interpretation in teleological terms. Bergson brings forward, to illustrate his theory, the description of the "instinctive" reaction of the beetle Sitaris which lays its eggs at the entrance of the underground passage of the bee Anthophora. The larva springs upon the male bee and remains until the "nuptial flight," "transfers to the female bee and waits until the eggs are hatched. It then eats the eggs and is metamorphosed to the insect." Bergson concludes that "everything happens as if . . . the Sitaris itself knew that its larva would know all these things."[19]

The inferences drawn from Bergson's argument and from the illustration of the reaction of the Sitaris imply that instinct is wholly purposive activity. The dissenters to this view, however, may well observe that the larva comes to be attached to any object which passes through the underground passage. In consequence, they need, apparently, only to reiterate the mechanical theory to confute teleology: this instance of "instinctive" reaction is a simple, mechanical reflex response to stimulus.

It is no less evident, however, that the instinctive reaction of the Sitaris is meaningful only if it is described in both ateleological and teleological terms. The structure of the Sitaris larva is such that its movements presuppose the operation of physiologically describable mechanisms. But the continuity of the Sitaris as a species presupposes the occasional success of the larva in attaching itself to the Anthophora and to the Anthophora alone. The behavior by which this end is achieved is observable, as are the mechanically describable and stimulated reactions. The purposively describable behavior occurs more than once and less than always. The conditions under which it occurs are describable empirically and to record and evaluate the success or failure which attends the achievement of end, the theory

[19] H. Bergson, *L'Évolution Créatrice*, pp. 158-159.

of probability is available. That description, requisite for a full analysis of the action, entails the assumption of a purposive but nonetheless objective realm in which the means-end principle operates. It is not necessary to speculate concerning the larva's knowledge or ignorance of the significance of its own action. The important facts are these, that the reaction of the Sitaris is on occasion meaningless in teleological terms alone, but that it is not even completely describable in mechanical terms alone, and that it is completely significant if both modes of description are utilized.

The instance afforded by Bergson's illustration of the reaction of the Sitaris is the more significant because it refers to instinct, the type of response that of the stages of feeling under consideration is most nearly analogous to complete mechanical action. The similarities have constantly tempted theorists to describe the reaction in terms of a simple conversion of "the signal into a releasing force for an act." But it is significant that Sherrington, whose words these are,[20] maintains that even the reflexiology of innate "protective reflexes"[21] which "instance the psalmist's 'wisdom of the body' . . . afford a measure of protection to their individual beset by a world of danger and damage." For our problem, Sherrington's most significant conclusion is that,

> The motor individual is driven from two sources. The world around it and its own lesser world within. . . . It can be regarded as a system which in virtue of its arrangement does a number of things and is so constructed that the world outside touches triggers for their doing. But its own internal condition has a say as to which of those things within limits it will do, and how it will do them. Its own internal condition is also initiator of some of its acts.[22]

Here it is suggested that to however primitive a level our observation descends in the animal scale, there is evidence that behavior is explicable in terms of both "extrinsic" and "intrinsic" processes. As Singer's inferences from Jennings' experiments upon paramecia

[20] *Man on his Nature*, p. 180. (By permission of The Macmillan Company, publishers.)

[21] *Ibid.*, p. 285.

[22] *Ibid.*, p. 181.

similarly suggest,[23] the interrelation holds for the behavior of the most primitive organisms. The field to which teleological description is applicable is coextensive with biologically definable entities.[24] It does so extend to the most primitive aspects of feeling behavior because, as was maintained in our initial description[25] of "reproductive imagination," even reproduction presupposes, in some degree, "productivity," and this is an "intrinsic process" needed to reinstate the "precedent image" appropriate for recognition.

The teleological argument assumes that feeling does "afford a measure or protection to the individual beset by a world of danger and damage." It assumes, therefore, that the *continuum* of feeling affords a primitive means to which the individual has access in his endeavors to control that same world. The predisposition to react to stimuli in the environment is not action describable merely as meaningful "extrinsically" and as part of a system in which "the world outside touches triggers for their doing"; the action is "emergency action" for which organisms are predisposed. This inference holds for the reaction induced by such a symbol as that of the leader in *Hamlet* and in the *Oresteia*, and to the extension of the instinct of self-preservation presupposed in man's feelings towards the idea of the soul's immortality.

It is of utmost importance, however, to make plain the fact that, while the entire *continuum* of feeling is significant within a teleological frame of reference in terms of emergency action, the dimensions of the *continuum*, instinct, emotion, and mood, despite their identity in ateleological terms, function variously as means to the common end of such purposive action. Some evidence for the differentiation of the dimensions in terms of means within the *continuum* will be of value for grasping the connotations of "productive imagination" and that evidence is again best presented by reference to emotion, the median range of the *continuum*, in its differentiation from instinct. Once that evidence has been presented, we may proceed to judge the entire "life of feeling" in terms of its efficiency

[23] See above, pp. 435-436.
[24] And to some of the products of their purposively describable techniques.
[25] Cf. above, pp. 326 ff.

as a means. To do this, we shall compare and contrast it, in the varied dimensions and by the same standard of effectiveness, to "ideal science."

IV

JAMES maintained that "emotional reaction usually terminates in the subject's own body, whilst the instinctive reaction is apt to go farther and enter into practical relation with the exciting object."[26] This differentiation of two modes of feelings appears merely to turn upon a somewhat general distinction between overt action and peripheral reaction. Piéron offers a more specific contrast between emotion and instinct:

> An animal is threatened; he gives a defense reaction, a stereotyped reflex, or a more plastic and better adapted response. This reaction is generally connected with an effective orientation of behavior tending toward flight or aggression. There is no reason for evoking an emotion. But, in addition to the defense reaction, the animal displays processes which are foreign to this reaction, and, like it, are aroused by the threatening stimulus. This is the emotional reaction.[27]

To the question whether the processes called "emotional" by Piéron are actually "foreign" to this [defense] reaction we shall return.[28] It will suffice for the moment to mention that the processes in question are peripheral behavior "aroused by the threatening stimulus" and are describable as the capillary action of the hair, dilation of nostrils, pallor, and sweating in fear. The instinctive process, on the contrary, is describable in terms of overt flight or aggression. The descriptions of both processes could be given in greater detail and with more precision but the primary question is, what does the differentiation of the processes signify for the teleology of feeling?

On the ateleological hypothesis, it could mean only that the mechanically defined stimulus which evokes instinctive action in

[26] William James, *Principles of Psychology*, p. 442.
[27] H. Piéron, *op. cit.*, p. 286.
[28] See below, p. 443.

the one instance is sufficiently intense to cause overt action, while a less intense stimulus or set of stimuli is sufficient only to effect the peripheral reaction of empirical behavior. But if we have been properly forewarned by the impossibility of verifying Fechner's hypothesis,[29] we shall adopt the sounder alternative provided by teleology and assume at the outset that it is sounder if only because it conforms to the so-called "all-or-nothing" principle of sensitivity.[30] On the teleological view, "feeling" may be discriminated into various "feelings" precisely because the reactions are taken to be "to stimuli of the same intensity under varying conditions of sensibility." Feelings do not vary merely in terms of "an organism's reaction to stimuli of varying intensity."

In the present analysis of feeling, the varying conditions of sensibility—the dimensions of the *continuum*—are instinct, emotion, and mood. The presupposition of their variation is the fact that stimuli which come to be effective as "images" in conative experience are never isolated but are always portions of a "total situation" or context which may be object, situation, event, or idea. The "intrinsic" factors in feeling-experience are augmented as we proceed from instinct to mood.[31] In instinctive action but one stimulus in the "total situation" is effective. In emotion, the increased number of stimuli made effective by the individual present possible alternative modes of action. The augmentation of effective stimuli is a function of the increase in productivity in the individual affected.

This augmentation of "intrinsic" and the diminution of "extrinsic" processes in the experience is sufficiently clarified for our

[29] See above, pp. 435-436.

[30] Cf. Adrian, *op. cit.*, p. 28 ff. "The stimulus, then, may be compared to the pressure on the trigger on a rifle: either it is strong enough to fire the bullet or it is too weak to do anything. . . . The force of the contraction cannot be controlled by altering the strength of the stimulus, and the latter is either completely adequate or completely inadequate. These facts are best expressed by the statement that there is an 'all-or-nothing' relation between the stimulus and the activity which it produces." See below, pp. 475 ff. for mention of Adrian's significant discussion of frequency, total number of impulses, and restrictions of "local conditions."

[31] I.e., the behavior varies directly in intensity from overt action to peripheral reaction and inversely with the alternative modes of action implied in the organism's "images" (i.e., effective stimuli).

immediate discussion if the scope of the problem be limited to a consideration of instinct and emotion as conditions of sensibility. The individual who is moved instinctively reacts overtly through the effectiveness of the one stimulus in the "total situation" to which the *Apperceptionsmass* predisposes him. The stimulus which, in this experience becomes the "preferred image," exerts its compulsion because the individual presents himself with no alternative "image" or, more precisely, makes no other stimulus or stimuli effective. The consequent minimal operation of productive imagination in instinctive reaction subordinates "intrinsic" to "extrinsic" processes and, as James suggested, the "instinctive reaction is apt . . . to enter into practical relations with the exciting object."[32]

It has previously been observed that James differentiated emotional and instinctive reaction on the ground that the former "usually terminates in the subject's own body." Emotional behavior is peripheral but it comes to be incorporated, because of the intensity of the "extrinsic process" and the speed of the reaction, with overt behavior. It is significant, however, that the peripheral reaction is evoked, as Piéron observes, by "processes . . . foreign to this [instinctive] reaction."[33] James himself held that "objects"—the primitive arousers of instinctive reflex movement—"take their place as elements in the 'total situation' " in which there are "other suggestions of which many prompt to movements of an entirely different sort."[34] If we return to the implications of Piéron's suggestion, we discover that this writer holds that ". . . we have in anger, in fear, in joy, in sadness and in emotional shock, . . . reactions of the mental and physical organism which are in no way implied in the notion of the principal inclination, although this inclination be the primitive and fundamental condition of the emotional complexus in which it is met, satisfied, unsatisfied, thwarted, paralyzed or excited." Pallor, sweating, the shrug, the aversion of the head, the capillary action of the hair, are "reactions" such as are "in no way implied in the notion of the principal inclination," despite the fact that they may

[32] *Op. cit.*, II, p. 442.

[33] *Op. cit.*, pp. 286, 290. Cf. W. B. Cannon, *Bodily Changes*, pp. 228, 234.

[34] William James, "The Physical Basis of Emotion", *Collected Essays*, p. 350.

be integrated in an instinctive reaction such as fear. But the significant inference is that if they do occur it is due to the increase in "intrinsic processes" by which the individual affected emotionally succeeds in presenting to himself alternative effective stimuli implicit in the "total situation." As Sherrington suggests in another context, in emotion the individual's "own internal condition" has become the "initiator of some . . . acts" to a greater degree than is true in instinct.[35]

One need not infer from this differentiation of emotion and instinct or from the grounds for it that emotional reaction guarantees the efficiency of the "emergency reaction" as an instrument. It does imply that in contrast to the range of instinct the median range of the *continuum* of feeling may not without reason be judged to be "higher" than the extreme dimension. The evaluation depends primarily upon a consideration of the capacity of organisms to present to themselves alternative modes of action by making effective the varying stimuli in a "total situation." Organisms which customarily make effective either a single "image" or a minimum of effective stimuli depend, in large degree, for the achievement of the end served by emergency action upon the presentation in environment of a stimulus appropriate to the presented "reproductive image." Such organisms act "instinctively" and are brought into action by "extrinsic processes."

Instinct is ordered teleologically as the "lower" stage of the *continuum* because, affected in this condition of sensibility, the individual's preservation depends for its successful achievement upon such presentation by the environment of an appropriate stimulus and of no stimulus either deleterious or useless to the completion of that purpose.[36] Instinct thus closely resembles "tropism,"

[35] *Op. cit.*, pp. 184-190.

[36] Similarly "lower" organisms are "lower" because their potentialities for adjustment are restricted by a limited capacity to present alternative "images." Consequently, they require for survival conditions in which a minimum of, or at least the less extreme alterations of environment occur. Thus, single-celled organisms require a moist or liquid environment, because the conditions of sensibility are such that a less constant medium would produce almost constantly unseasonable reaction—unseasonable beyond the possibility of proper response, adaptability or, indeed, of survival. Cf. L. B. Heilbrunn, *An Outline of General Physiology*, p. 397.

the reaction that occurs not automatically but for the most part in season and out of season and which ateleological theory interprets in terms of mechanical action. Emotion is a "higher" type of action than instinct. It implies "awareness" of stimuli in the "total context" and without the increase in productivity implied, as well, overt and often dangerous or largely unseasonable action would ensue. Such "awareness" presupposes the requisite adjustments to environments characterized by considerable variations in conditions. It implies a greater probability of success in the achievement of ends than does instinct, although the means to such success are not necessarily those afforded by bodily reaction.

Emotion, no less than instinct, is "reproductive imagination" and is to that extent describable in ateleological terms. It also evidences, however, an increase in the effectiveness and activity of "productive imagination." This is evident as one considers the previously mentioned "processes foreign" to the principal inclination. These, in turn, proffer significant data for an understanding of feeling, inasmuch as they are not always integrated with the instinctive movement. Most significant is the fact that there occurs, in the emotional stage of feeling, what Kant called a "checking and a recovery."[37] This is the so-called "emotional shock" and is evidence of the occurrence of such conflict as is not frequently a factor in instinct.

Conflict is the primary clue to the philosophical significance both of emotional behavior and of feeling in general. As Angell maintains, "Whenever there is conflict among the motor impulses called forth by any specific situation, the phenomena called the emotions are present."[38] One element of a "total situation" has evoked typical reaction but in emotion the "processes foreign to the principal inclination" have been made effective. These processes emerge, for organisms potentially able to respond to such stimuli, when "the reflex and hereditary responses of the organism are inadequate to cope with the demands of the environment."[39] With these processes emerges, as well, the "monitory function" of the emotions. By its

[37] *K.d.U.*, Sec. 15.

[38] J. R. Angell, *Psychology*, p. 323; Cf. William McDougall, *An Outline of Psychology*, pp. 325-326.

[39] Angell, *op. cit.*

means, the organism's instinctive reaction to the external stimulus on occasion may be checked at the limit of the agent's body. And it may be checked only because the individual aroused emotionally has actualized the potentiality for presenting to himself alternative stimuli or alternative modes of action implicit in the "total situation." The individual impelled to instinctive and overt behavior is blind to alternative stimuli. The "monitory function" of emotion is the "compelling announcement of needed adjustments."[40] It is a report of "unstable equilibrium"[41] and it may, as Bergson suggests, "express the fact that the disturbance is a systematic readjustment with a view to equilibrium on a higher level."[42]

The increased productivity and effectiveness of imagination in emotional experience thus makes possible for the moved individual the presentation of suggestions in environment other than those which effect in instinct the one-to-one relation of "subsequent image" or effective stimulus to "reinstated image." In inverse ratio to the augmentation of stimuli effective for imagination, overt behavior in the *continuum* of feeling diminishes.[43] This inverse relation of alternative effective stimuli to overt behavior expresses formally the assumption that emotional behavior is an "attitude,"[44] in which the clenching of the fist, the shrug of the shoulder, the pallor of the skin, either have superseded or now operate alongside the blind and overt acts of instinct.

Despite the diminution of overt behavior characteristic of emotion, emotional reaction is no less "emergency action" than is instinct. Productive imagination does characterize emotional behavior more fully than it does instinctive reaction. Emotion is "attitude" but it is also the predisposition to react without prior training or discipline, or, to cultural stimuli, in accord with an *Apperceptions-mass* But the difference between instinct and emotion turns largely upon this, that the "attitude" of emotional behavior has the greater

[40] *Ibid.*

[41] *Ibid.*, p. 323.

[42] H. Bergson, *The Two Sources of Morality and Religion*, p. 218.

[43] Cf. above, p. 326: The behavior varies . . . inversely in intensity from overt action to peripheral reaction with the increase in alternative modes of action implied in the organism's "images" or stimuli effective to it.

[44] See John Dewey, "The Theory of Emotions," p. 562 ff.

significance for the relation of the self to the object in the experience called feeling. The effectiveness of alternative stimuli in emotional behavior implies that action has come more completely into the power and under the control of the organism. The "contribution and participation by 'intrinsic' processes" has been augmented and the "operation of nervous processes of 'extrinsic' origin" has diminished as feeling alters from instinct to emotion.

As the *continuum* of feeling is examined in its successive stages from instinct, through emotion and mood, the alteration that gives the individual greater freedom is more evident in the tendency towards an inhibition of overt behavior and in the increase of reflection. Greater flexibility in action and adaptability to enviroment are consequences for the individual of this change in feeling. Accompanying these, there is an increase in the individual's potentialities for freedom in the control of nature. But while in emotion some of the compulsive "extrinsic" processes of instinct have diminished in force, the experience is likely to be disturbing in consequence of the monitory function, and action is to a considerable extent still under severe compulsion. It is in mood that productive imagination is active in such degree that aesthetic experience becomes possible. To that aspect of feeling, the mood, we may now turn.

V

THE condition of sensibility called mood is integral to the *continuum* of feeling. Mood, as are other dimensions of feeling, is susceptible to ateleological description. It is typical behavior, an actualization of the *Apperceptionsmass* by means of which precedent "images" are reinstated alongside "subsequent" ones. Similarly, its physiological and neurological description accords with the generic and distributive patterns applied to emotional and instinctive behavior.

With respect to its description in teleological terms, mood is a means, as are emotion and instinct. It is "emergency action" and serves the end common to all aspects of feeling. However, as emotion differs as an instrument from instinct, mood differs as a means from the two "lower" dimensions of feeling. Its most noticeable divergences from instinct and emotion are the incipient nature of the bodily reaction involved and the increased activity of productive imagination. Feeling, in the dimension of mood, is reflective and productive. Its productivity is marked by the presentation of vastly increased numbers of effective stimuli in the "total situation." This activity of the self is augmented, in turn, by association and by what Darwin describes as the power of "reacting similarly to analogous-feeling stimuli."

As emotion diverges from instinct in the operation of the monitory function, mood differs from emotion in that the strength of that function is reduced as conflict is diminished.

VI

WITH this brief and general characterization of the mood, we may conclude the formal investigation of the teleology of feeling, the significance of which for aesthetic experience may be made evident immediately. It has been possible to be brief concerning the description of the mood, although it is this range of feeling that is presupposed by aesthetic experience, because we are now in a position to examine the theory of empathy. Descriptions of empathy show its striking analogies to productive imagination. Equally significant, however, is the fact that the theory of empathy has been primarily put forward as an aesthetic theory. Consequently, we are able not only to continue our examination of mood but to consider its potentialities and deficiencies in providing a sound basis for an aesthetic theory.

Chapter XVI

Productive Imagination: Mood and the Theory of Empathy

It lies in the nature of aesthetic imitation that it aims chiefly at arousing the activity of the self.

—THEODOR LIPPS

. . . *Empathy exists or tends to exist throughout our mental life.*

—VERNON LEE

ONCE it is evident that the operation of feeling is not restricted to the "reinstatement of images," it is no less plain that the philosopher of art, who argues that artistic creativity and aesthetic experience are presupposed by conation, may disregard the possibility that for systematic reasons he may be forced to abandon his hypothesis. Teleology provides the necessary ground for productivity. In it, moreover, is implicit the significant inference that there are varying degrees of the self's activity. Because there are divergent dimensions of the *continuum* of feeling, the aesthetician is enabled to account in terms of productive imagination for the creativity manifested both in artistic creativity and aesthetic experience.

To determine the precise relation between productive imagination and aesthetic experience presents problems of proportions comparable to those encountered in relating reproductive imagination to artistic creativity and the symbols of art. Nor are the difficulties diminished by the current tendency in philosophy of art to identify the creativity of imagination with aesthetic experience. Whatever the historical conditions that influenced theory to replace *mimesis* by fancy, there has been an overemphasis of creativity in the analysis of art and its experience.[1] It will shortly be evident not only that productive imagination is not identical with the experience of profoundly moving art but that while the latter has creative aspects, it is essential to recognize as well its recreative presuppositions. This is to suggest only the most obvious of the difficulties encountered in an analysis of aesthetic experience but it does argue the advisability of returning for brief consideration to certain inferences implicit in the theory of art as a symbol of the artist's feelings. And we may preface the return by a comparison, faulty in some respects, of aesthetic experience to artistic creativity in terms of the image in the mirror as the counterpart of the object mirrored.[2]

In analyzing aesthetic experience, no less than in elaborating a theory of the communicability and the communication of the artist's feelings by means of generic symbols, the figure of the magnetic rings in *Ion*, linking poet, poem, and auditor, exerts its power over the initial consideration. But here one may be content with Housman's echo of Socrates' words. Having remarked upon the diction and movement of a few lines of verse used to illustrate the argument of *The Name and Nature of Poetry*, the poet concludes, "It is perfect." But he adds, significantly, "And nothing more than perfection can be demanded of anything: yet poetry is capable of more than this, and more therefore is expected from it." In support of this extraordinary suggestion, Housman argues that, "There is a conception of poetry which is not fulfilled by pure language and liquid versification, with the simple and so to speak colourless pleasure which they afford, but involves the presence in them of something which moves and touches in a special and recognisable way. . . ."

The poet, writing as critic, thereupon brings forward another illustration and in it discovers that "more than perfection" of which "poetry is capable." "There a new element has stolen in, a tinge of emotion. And I think that to transfuse emotion—not to transmit thought but to set up in the reader's sense a vibration correspond-

[1] This is evident, for instance, in E. Hanslick, *Vom Musikalisch-Schönen.*
[2] Cf. Plato, *Republic* 596.

ing to what was felt by the writer—is the peculiar function of poetry."

One may quote Housman without the hesitation ordinarily attendant upon taking literally poets' critical opinions. His judgment is that not only of a distinguished poet but of a profound and precise scholar. The difficulties that inhere in his writings arise neither from poetic vagueness nor are they consequent upon inconsistent critical principles. Rather, they are due to questions concerning the nature of the "vibration" identified with artistic experience and the precise character of the something "more than perfection" of which poetry is capable. Yet, we may be content with what we do have of Housman's thought, for the inference is sufficiently clear. The poet may create a formally perfect poem but the full meaning of poetic creativity is implicated in the fact that the poem is felt by the reader or auditor, that the emotion intended is transmitted. And one may generalize and conclude that the proper correlative of artistic creativity is aesthetic experience.

But if, as has been maintained in the present essay, artistic creativity and communicability are consequent not alone upon the evocation of reproductive imagination by means of non-aesthetic "referrents" and generic symbols, the aesthetic experience requisite to fulfill the significance of the art-object is likewise not alone the consequence of reproductivity and its attendant symbolism. The work of art is for the artist a specific and unique as well as a generic expression. It is for the percipient, no less than for the artist, a specific as well as a generic symbol. And while it is true that the presuppositions of artistic communication are reproductive imagination and the generic symbols, neither the predisposition of feeling nor the recurrence of symbols ultimately derived from the past account completely for the creative aspects implied in the experience of what is communicated. We need but recall,[3] to evaluate the significance of this portion of our problem, the extraordinary competence of play-theory to explain much of aesthetic experience precisely because of its emphasis upon productivity.

The elements essential to an analysis of aesthetic experience which,

[3] Cf. above, pp. 227 ff.

as Housman suggests, is no less integral to the poem than is the latter's technical perfection, are strewn throughout this inquiry and need only to be gathered together to supply the meaning of aesthetic experience and of the end of art. There is to hand the productivity of imagination, made available for aesthetic theory by the teleology of feeling. There is, likewise, the fact that the work of art is an "image" for the percipient whose aesthetic experience presupposes the ability to feel "stimuli of the same intensity under varying conditions of sensibility." We need recall, also, the operation of the reproductive imagination and its implications for art, the "referrents" of whose symbols are the science of the past. And, finally, there are the two as yet barely related descriptions of feeling, the one a teleologically defined emergency act, the other the ateleologically defined reinstatement of images. These must be integrated and their interrelationship in aesthetic experience made plain.

"To set up in the reader's sense a vibration corresponding to what is felt by the writer"—that is to say, on the assumption of this essay, to induce an aesthetic mood, is the "peculiar function" of the profoundly moving work of art. And because the generic characteristics of the mood are analogous to those of the experience called empathy or *Einfühlung* and equally as well because empathy, although it has been widely accepted as a description of aesthetic experience, fails to specify the "peculiar" and unique nature of the aesthetic mood, we shall turn in the next section to a brief presentation and evaluation of the theory of empathic experience.

II

IT WILL be of value for the purposes of the present essay to distinguish two traditions in the history of empathy or *Einfühlung*. They are, apparently, of independent origin.[4] One group

[4] See M. Rader, *A Modern Book of Esthetics*, Chap. VIII. The origins of the theory are traced by Gilbert and Kuhn to Aristotle. See also Listowel, *A Critical History of Modern Esthetic*. I have availed myself of Langfeld's translations of Lipps' writings, in most instances quoted. H. S. Langfeld, *The*

of theorists denies significance to action or behavior in aesthetic experience, the other holds the fact of "tentative" or "inhibited" action to be central. Theodor Lipps is the most noteworthy exponent of the first tradition. The writings of Violet Paget (Vernon Lee) and Langfeld present a sufficiency of relevant data and argument to clarify for our purposes the contribution of the second.

As we shall discover, one of Lipps' brief essays upon *Einfühlung*[5] offers a brief and satisfactory introduction to the general theory. *Einfühlung*, Lipps maintains, "can come about, only as we attribute to outer things our own feeling of force, our own feeling of striving and willing, our own activity and passivity. . . . The column seems to brace itself and raise itself, that is to say, to proceed in the way in which I do when I pull myself together and raise myself, or remain thus tense and erect, in opposition to the natural inertness of my body."

The crucial point of Lipps' statement is that "It is impossible for me to be aware of the column without this activity seeming to exist directly in the column of which I am aware." This "projection" of the self's activity into "outer things"—and it is essential to attend to the fact that it is the self's "feeling of force, . . . of striving and willing"—is regarded by Lipps as "unintentional." It is activity but it is an "activity of the self" that "can be satisfied in the mere perception of the movement" of the self. The ground of aesthetic satisfaction, Lipps' account continues, lies in "a feeling of inner activity." The active self, in its aesthetic experience, is "contemplative" and "exists in the lingering contemplation of the object."

This, in its briefest expression, is the fundamental argument in the theory of empathy. It would be an error to ignore the subtlety of detail with which Lipps implemented his interpretation[6] but the foregoing brief quotations suggest the main contentions: the activity of the self; the contemplative state in which the perceiver who "feels himself into" outer things is free from compulsions inherent

---

Aesthetic Attitude is quoted by permission of Harcourt, Brace and Company, publishers.

[5] Theodor Lipps, *Archiv für die Gesamte Psychologie.*

[6] In *Ästhetik.*

in non-aesthetic experience which direct action in terms of scientific, moral, or religious values; and the "vivification" of the objects experienced in empathic contemplation.

The essential problem of the present chapter is to determine whether aesthetic experience may be encompassed by the phrase, "feeling oneself into," as a specification of productive imagination. And the solution to this problem must be arrived at not only by evaluating the empathist's proper insistence upon creativity and the increase of contemplation but, no less, upon the significance attributed by some theorists to the correlative inhibited action in the experience called *Einfühlung*.

On the latter issue, Lipps' position is clear. What Housman has called a "vibration" is for Lipps non-aesthetic experience. *Einfühlung* is non-aesthetic if identified with "sensations of my own bodily state." More than this, Lipps asserts that "so far as I am concerned the sensations of my own bodily state are entirely absent in aesthetic contemplation." He does grant that "it may happen that I am conscious of such sense-feelings" but the general conclusions are clear: "It is the duty of scientific aesthetics and necessary for its sound development, that it gradually recover from this disease of preoccupation with sense-feelings."

It is, however, precisely what Lipps terms a "disease" that has been fundamental to the alternative interpretation of empathy and it has provided precisely the strength with which those opposed to Lipps and his tradition have endowed the theory. For the opponents it is the fact that empathy is an analysis of aesthetic behavior and that the behavior may be subjected to experimental analysis. Indeed, this it is that marks the potential value of the theory itself. In regard to the direction of that experimentation, we are little interested in the descriptions of gross "empathic" reaction given in detail by Vernon Lee.[7] The issue is not to be settled on the basis of introspective analyses, by way of illustration, directed to the "adjustment" of muscles in imitation of the "tenseness or slackness" of a statue's attitude. The essential problem centers upon the significance of the behavior called "feeling oneself into." For

[7] For example, in *Beauty and Ugliness.*

Lipps, the behavior is of no consequence and is merely inhibited. But for others—and noteworthy among them is Langfeld, to whose interpretation we are about to turn—it is precisely the fact that the behavior is "incipient" or "tentative" that is significant. It is in the investigation of the significance of this "tentative" or "incipient" behavior that we shall observe at once the contribution of the theory of empathy to aesthetic, as well as those of the theory's defects which arise from its identification of a generic with a specific activity of mood, its overestimation of the value of creativity, and its failure to consider the reproductive implications of feeling.

Langfeld has supplemented the traditional formulation of empathy with an analysis of motor attitudes and it is this analysis that the "mere perception of the movement" requires for its proper grounding. The author of *The Aesthetic Attitude* holds, properly, that the "perception of the movement" is basically one of the motor attitudes assumed towards the object. It is the "activity" involved in "adjustment in" the object.[8] This "movement" is interpreted as "a tendency towards movement" which may be described "as a motor act or pattern which must precede any overt act. . . . It must be repeated, in order that there shall be no misunderstanding, that in all such instances, the impulses may be so far in the initial stage that there is no movement produced and frequently not even a consciousness of strain or of other similar sensations. The nervous set is capable of influencing perception, even though it remains completely unconscious and is discoverable only when the conditions are suddenly altered."[9]

If we may be content with this brief and general statement of a theory, the elaboration of which has held the attention of many psychologists and philosophers, we may observe that it brings to the fore two important elements in empathic behavior. The first is the activity of the self as projected into an object, the second is the incipient or tentative peripheral movement descriptive of *Einfühlung*. The difficulties of the theory arise from implications

[8] *Op. cit.*, Chap. V, particularly pp. 117 ff.

[9] H. S. Langfeld, *op. cit.*, pp. 126-127. (Quoted by permission of Harcourt, Brace and Company, publishers.)

and inferences concerned with these initial elements. For if it be asked either how the generic activity of the experiencing individual who "feels himself into the object" may be identified with an aesthetic attitude or what constitutes the ground for a unique aesthetic satisfaction in contrast to the satisfaction afforded by playful or other non-aesthetic activity of the self, we are apt to receive answers at once various and inconclusive. Both Langfeld and Lipps suggest, by way of illustration of the similarity of the contrasted traditions, that one answer is afforded by the fact that "aesthetic imitation" is "unintentional." It is argued, in support of this inference, that empathic experiences are neither "felt as sensations within the body" nor do they come "to consciousness as sensations of our own movements at all, but influence the perception in such a way that the lines and figures themselves seem to have the force which is actually in us."[10]

But if the differentiation between generically defined perception and specifically aesthetic "feeling oneself into" turns either upon the fact that the latter is unintentional or that in aesthetic experience we are "not under the distraction of bodily processes," it is evident that the theory of *Einfühlung* is merely a reformulation of the hypothesis of "aesthetic immediacy." It follows that, on the ground of the specific differentiation, empathic experience is scarcely discriminable from a generic mood or, indeed, from other modes of feeling, such as instinct or emotion. All states of feeling are "unintentional" because they are, like mood, actualizations of predispositions to action.

It may be urged, however, that despite the fact that the terms instinct, emotion, mood, and "empathy" describe movements which are all similarly unintentional, only the two latter terms describe behavior that is "tentative" or "incipient." The point is significant and its implications, as will shortly be evident, are indispensable for an understanding of aesthetic experience. Yet, as it is specifically employed by Langfeld, the term "tentative" applied to movement suffers from an ambiguity. The behavior is either "tentative" in contrast to "overt" and, if so, is therefore a completed act, or it is

[10] H. S. Langfeld, *op. cit.*, p. 117.

actually "tentative" and, as Langfeld maintains, "preparation for overt action." On the teleological theory of feeling formulated in the present essay,[11] the former meaning is permissible, yet it is precisely the significance of complete incipient or tentative movement that the theory of empathy leaves unexplained. It is implied, certainly, that aesthetic objects evoke activity freed from the compulsion of practical necessity and from the influence of other nonaesthetic ends. To that extent, the theory is valid. But the same conclusion may be made concerning numerous activities of the self in moods which are not aesthetic. The proof of this is the application by empathists themselves of the adjective "contemplative" to the experience called *Einfühlung*. A contemplative state of feeling is, however, a characteristic of the generic mood. Its use implies the activation of numerous effective "images" in "total situations" but its specifically aesthetic connotations are undetermined.

The conviction is deepened that in the theory of empathy there is offered no ground for the requisite differentiation between what has in this essay been called the productive activity of feeling and that productivity as it is manifested specifically in aesthetic experience, once it is recalled that "feeling oneself into" an external object provides the basis for such general epistemological theories as George Mead's. Yet, Mead is wholly concerned with the problem of knowing the "interior" of things and not at all with the analysis of aesthetic experience or its objects. He holds that we know the "interior" of things by similarly projecting ourselves into them. One is forced to conclude that the theory of *Einfühlung* offers a useful account of our ways of knowing objects external to us by means of muscular and motor responses. It remains a question unanswered by the theorist, why, on the other hand, the generic motor attitude useful to explain perception in general is identified with aesthetic perception or experience.

The proponents of the theory of empathy have not been unaware of the problem. Lipps argues, it is true, that "It lies in the nature of aesthetic imitation that it aims chiefly at arousing the activity of the self," although it might well be maintained that all perception

[11] Cf. above, pp. 441-442.

does likewise. But Vernon Lee, on the contrary, has observed of empathy that, "It is, indeed, one of our simpler, though far from absolutely elementary, psychological processes, entering into what is called imagination, sympathy, and also into that inference from our own inner experience which has shaped all our conceptions of an outer world, and given to the intermittent and heterogeneous sensations received from without the framework of our constant and highly unified inner experience, that is to say, of our own activities and aims."[12]

One must not conclude, therefore, that the theorists of empathy have not themselves recognized *Einfühlung* as transcending aesthetic experience in its explanatory scope. Nor have they stinted their efforts to differentiate aesthetic and non-aesthetic empathic experience. The direction of these efforts has not in all instances been identical but the results serve to emphasize the consequences of an initial incompleteness of their theory's description of the experience of fine art. In general, the intended distinction has ordinarily turned upon the assumption that in aesthetic attitudes we "feel ourselves into" lines, delineations, and forms. It is implied, in consequence, that the activity of the self encounters no impediment in non-aesthetic factors in the work of art. The theory of empathy is, however, no more successful than other accounts of formal art in sustaining its initial abstraction of form from content.[13] It fails, in fact, as do other formal theories, because it cannot safely ignore the proper, if partial, characterization of fine art in terms of generic symbols of feeling. One infers from this that, insofar as empathy is a conative theory, it does not make explicit the implications in feeling of reproductive imagination.

The second general direction of empathic speculation leads its proponents towards the conclusion that unity is the criterion for the discrimination of aesthetic and non-aesthetic activities. But this direction, it turns out, offers little guidance to the theorist in aesthetic. It is evident that all objects we know by the process of "feeling ourselves into" are to some extent unified. It is plain that a

[12] *The Beautiful*, p. 68.
[13] Cf. above, Chap. III.

specific aesthetic unity is implied and it turns out, interestingly enough, to be the following: Objects do not please us aesthetically, that is to say, are not felt empathically, "unless they give rise to unified empathic responses because the nervous set requires such unification, and that is the ultimate reason why unity in the object is essential to beauty."[14]

That this does suggest the proper employment of unity in aesthetic experience will shortly be clear[15] but for reasons not made explicit by the theory of empathy. This is probably because empathists, absorbed in the speculative possibilities for aesthetic experience of "lingering contemplation," have failed to observe that all feeling-experience—*Einfühlung* included—presupposes conflict and consequent disequilibrium. The unification of experience that ensues and is integral to aesthetic experience is due to other factors in feeling which are actualized because there is a structure unique to works of fine art. A return to equilibrium is brought about in the individual moved profoundly by the work of art.[16] These aspects of aesthetic experience scarcely impinge upon the empathist's envisagement of the aesthetic problem. The initial analysis of aesthetic experience ordinarily reflected in their writings consistently overlooks the fact that feeling is not only productive but reproductive, that it is not only a mood of exaltation but also of discontent, and that the symbols of art refer to non-aesthetic activities rather than to the arts of form or to a world of "art for art's sake."

It must not be forgotten, however, that the theory of *Einfühlung*, in so far as it is a sound hypothesis, has been correctly grounded in the analysis of aesthetic experience as an attitude. In its various elaborations, there is a lack of conclusiveness upon the point whether the empathic movement is tentative, incipient, or inhibited. Moreover, whatever its description of the behavior, empathy certainly ignores the problem of the full significance of the negation of the practical relation that ordinarily holds between the subject and object in conative states. The proper evaluation of the

[14] H. S. Langfeld, *op. cit.*, p. 122.
[15] Cf. below, Chaps. XVII-XVIII.
[16] Cf. below, pp. 488-489.

behavior turns, as will be plain in the next chapter, upon its interpretation in terms of feeling as "emergency action." And only in this way is it possible to explain the end of fine art and the characteristics of the unique aesthetic experience.

In order to make explicit these implications of empathic behavior for aesthetic experience, we must examine feeling as "emergency action." This we may best do by evaluating it in comparison and in contrast to the instruments of "ideal science." Once this has been done, we shall be able finally to discriminate the aesthetic from the generic mood and determine more precisely the unique function of fine art.

Chapter XVII

The Aesthetic Mood

Science since Descartes has repaired the stair [the traditional stair of life ranging upward step by step to man] and finds it more significant than before. It marks the way that man has climbed. And it is the stair of mind as well as body, and it is without break, man's mind being nothing more than the topmost rung continuous with related degrees below.

—Sir Charles Sherrington[1]

"THERE is a fine art of passion," writes Schiller as he approaches the conclusion to the *Aesthetic Letters*, "but an impassioned fine art is a contradiction in terms, for the infallible effect of the beautiful is emancipation from the passions." Few poets have uttered words of more profound import for the artist and few philosophers have given more cogent expression to one of the central problems of aesthetic experience.

It is not without significance that one searches almost in vain in the voluminous writings upon *Einfühlung* to discover evidence of an understanding of the problem comparable to that displayed by Schiller. The empathist appears to be content to describe the generic mood, to identify it with the aesthetic attitude, and to characterize the experience of art in terms of contemplation and of activity of the self. Schiller, on the contrary, seeks to make evident the conditions under which empathy itself could be effective as aesthetic experience. It is upon "emancipation from the passions" that activity of the self depends, precisely as the creation of the work of art presupposes similar freedom.

[1] Sir Charles Sherrington, *Man on His Nature*. (By permission of The Macmillan Company, publishers.)

Thus, it may be contended that Schiller's general suggestion is sound. That some form of mood is identical with aesthetic experience accords with the facts and problems. The state of feeling minutely described in theories of empathy enables the aesthetic percipient to experience creatively the non-aesthetic "referrents" of feeling; permits the symbolization essential to the communication of the artist's feelings; and, finally, accounts for the exaltation implicit in the experience of profoundly moving art.

There is little to be gained by elaborating upon the contrasts between Schiller's theory of art and that of the empathist. The play-theory, as the poet presented it, has few peers if we consider only the intuitive grasp of problems it displays but it remains an aesthetic irremediably weakened because its initial hypotheses are unsound. *Einfühlung*, in contrast, is an embryonic aesthetic, an implicit philosophy of art, once an aesthetic specification of its analysis of the generic mood is produced. Nonetheless, it must not be forgotten, as we evaluate Schiller's theory, that for the poet man is only man when he plays and he plays only with beauty. It is well to remember this because, as the present essay will attempt to demonstrate, aesthetic experience, which presupposes "emancipation from the passions" while yet remaining feeling,[2] "marks the way that man has climbed." Its end is presupposed, moreover, in the ends of man's non-aesthetic activities. The creativity of its mood is essential for man's further efforts. To the proof of this, the concluding chapters of this volume will be devoted. Among the evident problems to be considered are how aesthetic experience does emancipate us from the passions; how, in turn, the mood is the consequence of this emancipation; and finally, how the antinomic aspects of the experience itself are explicable in terms of this freedom.

II

MOOD is an extreme dimension of the *continuum* of feeling. As feeling, it is implicated both in reproductive imagination's "reinstatement of images" and in productive imagination's

[2] Cf. above, pp. 313 ff.

teleological description in terms of "emergency action." In its productivity is manifested the "wisdom of the body."

There are numerous specific moods—the cheerful and the melancholy, the anticipatory and the reminiscent, and a host of others. Each implies activity of the self and each is characterized by peripheral in contrast to overt behavior. But whether we regard the mood generically or specifically, as activity or contemplation, one significant factor pertains to it that has as yet not received proper consideration, either in the theory of *Einfühlung* or in the present essay. We have been content, thus far, to consider feeling solely in terms of response to external stimuli. But it is no less true that we "imagine" or make effective the stimuli of our own states or conditions.[3]

It will be recalled, in this connection, that the present analysis of feeling took as one of the points of its departure the Aristotelian theory of emotion. It was remarked, at that point, that it was significant for Aristotle to write primarily of the emotions rather than of pleasure and pain in connection with the experience of poetry and music.[4] Aristotle does hold elsewhere, however, that pleasures and pains are concomitants of activity and his argument implies that the former are implicated in the proper functioning of the activity, the latter in its inadequacy or failure.

As was remarked before, the terms pleasure and pain are notoriously ambiguous and we may well ignore them, not only for this sufficient reason but, as well, because the significant inferences to be drawn from Aristotle's suggestion are implicit in feeling as emergency action in relation to ends. And because of this, it is possible to ground the "moods" which Professor Singer rightly terms "fundamental."[5] These "fundamental moods" are those of "exaltation" and "depression." Feeling, as emergency action, is related to ends. The successful achievement of the end is accompanied by "exaltation," the lack of success by "depression." Both moods are "images" of internal stimuli.

In the light of these new factors concerned with feeling, our

[3] See above, pp. 355-357.
[4] See above, pp. 324 ff.
[5] Edgar A. Singer, Jr., "Esthetic and the Rational Ideal," pp. 45 ff.

present problem may be more clearly envisaged. Mood is characterized primarily by activity or productivity. The theory of empathy has emphasized the "feeling oneself into" that is the most obvious concomitant of productive imagination. But we must now consider as well the consequences for aesthetic experience of our reflection upon our own condition or state as "productive imagination" operates thus actively.

It is essential to keep in mind, as we follow this line of investigation, that the symbols of profoundly moving art are the science of the past, that the mood is a complete act, and that all acts of imagination are at once reproductive and productive. It may be urged that the polar distinction between exalted and depressed moods makes it probable that the history of aesthetic and artistic criticism —in which attacks upon profoundly moving art because of its deceptiveness, its irrationality, and its appeal to man's brutish nature alternate with equally cogently argued professions of faith and theories of aesthetic, intended to show the value of art that moves deeply, its creativity, and its revelation of reality—reflect something of a mood in which depression and exaltation are in a unique relation.

Other aspects of the mood lend credence to this assumption. It has been maintained, for example, that the mood is an interrelation of the reproductive and the productive aspects of feeling. Insofar as the former implies a reversion to the past and to a primitive stage of culture, it is not inconceivable that in reproductive imagination is implicated the discontent of aesthetic experience. Productive imagination, on the contrary, marks the difference between "extrinsic" and "intrinsic" behavior, between organisms largely controlled by environment and individuals which in some degree control environment. It is likely that productive imagination sets men off from the brute and may well contribute to the exaltation of his spirit. Furthermore, because it is not accidental that art and aesthetic experience have been subjected to bifurcated analyses, it is all the more possible that abstract analyses of a mood which uniquely relates the extreme dimensions of feeling may result in exaggerated conclusions concerning one or the other conative concomitant.

III

ONCE the "fundamental moods" of exaltation and depression are implicated in success and failure in the achievement of ends, the mood and the aesthetic mood must be considered in terms of "emergency action." And for reasons that shortly will be plain, this may best be done by comparing and contrasting conation as an instrument with the means of "ideal science." It is in consequence of this analysis that the full significance of man's "emancipation from the passions" as a condition of aesthetic experience and as integral to the latter's antinomic character becomes clear.

If we describe feeling teleologically in terms of "emergency action," the various "conditions of sensibility," instinct, emotion, and mood, belong to the "apparatus of sense." Of this apparatus, H. B. Smith wrote that "physiologically considered", it "is itself an instrument, and is employed in essentially the same way [as experiment], in the business of ordering and comparing data."[6] That "experience" and "experiment" are not different in kind permits their comparison and contrast. "Experience of whatever sort is experimental in all its characters" but that aspect of experience called feeling is in one sense an inferior instrument and, in another, the precondition of more precise instruments. This will be evident in what follows.

The individual organism is a focus of desire. The goal of its activity is the attainment of any end in the world that may be desired. The primitive capacity for reaction upon the presentation in environment of appropriate stimuli is the *Apperceptionsmass* of feeling. The actualization of this predisposition to react, either because the stimulus attracts or repels, is a presupposition of all instruments available for the satisfaction of desire. The organism does not require training to use the instrument called feeling. Indeed, its typical and generic character as behavior makes possible under conditions of emergency the preservation of the individual.

Nevertheless, the reaction of an individual profoundly moved in

[6] In "Postulates of Empirical Thought."

the dimensions of feeling called tropism or instinct is largely inflexible. The action is, in consequence, as we have observed, often unseasonable. For organisms which do not develop beyond the primitive stage in which feeling is not only the primary but the sole instrumentality, survival is primarily dependent upon stable conditions in the environment and, metaphorically speaking, is possible to a considerable degree only because "nature" permits.

For more highly developed organisms, the inflexibility of reaction characteristic of ateleologically defined feeling has left traces in the *continuum* of feeling itself, not only in the retention of generic behavior throughout the *continuum* of feeling but also in the monitory function of feeling most evident in emotion. Whatever implications concerning the factors entering into the "rationalization of feeling" may be read into the emergence of the monitory function, the evidence of conflict in emotional behavior is undeniable. The disequilibrium which is evident in emotional shock is a warning that hereditary bodily mechanisms are inadequate. But, equally significant is the fact that conflict and disequilibrium both can occur only because in the stage of feeling called emotion, in contrast to that of either tropism or instinct, the organism has developed the power to present itself with alternative stimuli in the total presented situation. In emotion there has occurred an increase in the productivity of feeling and this operates to make effective stimuli other than the dominant one to which the organism is predisposed for action.

However inadequate emotion may be as an instrument in contrast to ideal means, it is a stage of "emergency action" more efficient than either tropism or instinct because the organism in its productivity makes manifest alternative images in the "total situation" and these may properly be considered to be alternative modes of possible action. It may not be possible for the emotionally moved individual to accept the alternative and, indeed, as we have observed, the alternative images may be merged into the dominant one. It is nonetheless true that the dominance of "extrinsic factors" has been mitigated for the organism and its own powers, inherent in "intrinsic" factors, have been augmented.

Once having observed that in emotion there is a monitory function, a warning that the hereditary mechanisms are inadequate to cope with the presented situation, it must be made clear that the emergence of emotion, with its corresponding increase in the activity of productive imagination, is correlative to a diminution in overt action. It is true that emotion and instinct may merge into an integrated overt act. It is no less evident, however, in consequence of the increase in productivity, that it may be inferred from the fact of alternative images even in this primitive stage of feeling that there is presented the possibility for the use of instruments other than bodily reaction to stimuli.

No less significant is the inference to be drawn from the diminution of overt behavior that other instruments for the attainment of ends have actually come into existence. The monitory function of the emotions is meaningless unless this is true. Feeling does not construct the new instruments of which, as productive imagination, it is a presupposition and which, in turn, diminish its instrumental effectiveness. But only because other and more adequate instruments for the control of nature are devised may the higher forms of living things survive and the primitive overt reaction of feeling diminish in significance.

Feeling, as the productivity of imagination, makes effective alternative stimuli as possible modes of action in a total situation. It is, as productive imagination, one of the presuppositions for the "ideal science" which E. A. Singer's Empirical Idealism takes to be "the condition of attaining any end in the world," i.e., "such control of the world's machinery as shall give you the power to get what you want."[7] Had not experience and, finally, man's experimentation provided more adequate science, the most primitive science, that of feeling, might well have continued to evoke behavior as inflexible as that instinctive drive which causes the lemmings to rush headlong into the sea to their deaths, as they traverse routes long since submerged.

In the alteration from overt to peripheral behavior, in the divergences of instinct, emotion and mood as "emergency action" and as

[7] "On a Possible Science of Religion," p. 109.

means to the end of man's control of nature, are reflected the hardships and triumphs, the story of man's progress. How frail a reed his animal ancestors must have been as they were confronted by the world's complexities and difficulties is evident from the vestiges of original inflexibility implicit in the one-to-one relation of stimulus to "reinstated image" which follows upon actualizing a predisposition of experience. Moreover, it is significant that however much man may progress, the "wisdom of the body" remains the last recourse in times of stress. Feeling suggests in peripheral behavior and in productivity long-forgotten primitive conquests of nature. For the inflexible action that persists is in marked contrast to the means of the ideal science which postulates flexible and variable means and the selection of the proper instruments to the end.[8]

This is to suggest, however, yet another inadequacy of feeling, of "emergency action," as an instrument of science. It is true that imagination, as its productivity increases, makes effective an increased number of stimuli in the "total situation." It is significant, however, that in feeling, due to its reproductivity, there is some retention of dependence upon "extrinsic factors" in experience. Feeling only partially fulfills and can only partially fulfill the task of science because in its operations, in contrast to those implicit in the methods of ideal science, there is no "gradual squeezing out of images proved non-permissible"[9] which on science's hypothesis, would render "every stage of our experimental knowledge in terms of that 'bundle of mechanical images,' any last experiment must have left permissible." Ideal science postulates infinite reduction of error. The productivity of feeling is the primitive presupposition of such a science but reproductivity conserves as valuable the "image squeezed out" by that progressive science itself. Feeling *qua* feeling is not implicated in error, since it operates merely as a natural reaction but it does serve as a profoundly conservative factor in civilization. To its conservatism fine art owes the constant employ-

[8] Edgar A. Singer, Jr., "Philosophy of Experiment," p. 160. It is the function of the experimental scientist, as Professor Singer writes, "to contrive endless experiments that shall bring him nearer and nearer to those single-valued answers his questions of fact demand."

[9] *Ibid.*, pp. 165-166.

ment of generic symbols, precisely because feeling is not an abstract process. It attaches to objects, events, situations, and ideas, as well as to persons, including the self that feels.

IV

THE foregoing account of feeling as "emergency action," as a primitive science essential for the control of nature but, nonetheless, a flawed instrument, leads directly to a consideration of the reasons which account for mood as peripheral behavior in contrast to instinct as overt action. Nor is it strange, in this connection, that Darwin's, *The Expression of the Emotions in Man and Animals*, provides still the guiding thread. Whatever the book's deficiencies, its author bases his explanations upon the theory of evolution, in the implications of which are found the reasons for the teleological differentiation of instinct, emotion, and mood as dimensions of the *continuum* of feeling. And, as will be evident, we shall discover here also the reasons for the ease with which the play-theory of art was also brought within the framework of evolutionary theory.[10]

Darwin interpreted emotional expressions to be vestiges of overt action, once wholly functional in significance, which, in the course of evolution, had diminished in strength.[11] He suggested, in accordance with the principles of the general theory of evolution, that as the human being evolved the physiological and neurological structures associated with feeling underwent atrophy as the need for them as means to the end of self-preservation diminished.[12]

James adopts the Darwinian hypothesis concerning emotion. In doing so, he supplies a teleological frame of reference for his own

[10] Cf. above, Chap. VII, pp. 221 ff.

[11] Charles Darwin, *The Expression of the Emotions in Man and Animals*, p. 363 *passim*. By way of illustration: "We may further suspect, notwithstanding that we have no support for our analogy, that our semi-human progenitors uncovered their canine teeth when prepared for battle, as we still do when feeling ferocious or when merely sneering at or defying someone, without any intention of making a real attack with our teeth."

[12] His argument is devoted primarily to emotions. It requires extension to account for the mood as a range of feeling.

theory of feeling.[13] The emotions become, for James, not only bodily reactions to stimuli but "*weakened repetitions of movements which formerly* (when they were stronger) *were of utility to the subject.*"[14] On this view, reactions like the capillary action of the hair may once have been significant for the mechanism of defense, increasing the apparent size of the individual as he faced danger.[15]

The ostensible obstacle to the acceptance of Darwin's theory of emotional expression in its original form or in James' interpretation is the criticism of the biologists who, since Weismann, have shown that acquired characteristics are not heritable. The difficulty is scarcely insuperable. It is unnecessary to regard emotion and mood as "phyletic contractions." They may well be later emergents potential in the organism and actualized in the process of evolution.[16] Mood and emotion, as levels or dimensions of the *continuum* of feeling, emerge as environment is more adequately controlled and as the conditions for control come to be better comprehended. They are, as well, alternative means for making environment susceptible to better control and understanding. Overtness in feeling never completely vanishes, but in man's evolution emerges the alternative peripheral reaction to the same stimuli that once only evoked overt movement.[17]

Evolution, in this respect, implies that in the emergence of an alternative to overt action the imperfect means of direct bodily action related to "arousers" of feeling has in some degree been replaced by better means and instruments. It has been implied, moreover, that the original function of feeling has been replaced by a function which was once its presupposition, inasmuch as feeling in the higher dimensions is directed primarily to productivity. The

[13] He denies teleology, as Rapaport and Weber point out ("Teleology and the Emotions," pp. 75-76). But James is a stimulating, rather than a consistent thinker and the teleological reference is obvious in the passage quoted in the text.

[14] William James, *Principles of Psychology*, II, p. 478.

[15] That an analogous tactic has been known and used by belligerents for millennia is evident from Tacitus, *de Germania*, XXXVIII.

[16] On an argument analogous to that offered by T. H. Morgan, *A Critique of the Theory of Evolution*, p. 21.

[17] That is, they are different conditions of sensibility requiring no difference in the intensity of the stimulus.

implicit progress of science of which feeling is a portion, is towards omnipotence and omniscience, towards the goal of the scientist, the "limiting conception of a mean reading with probable error zero."[18]

Ideal science postulates infinite time for its formulation. However, in the circumscribed period of time required for man to evolve to the stage in which mood has been actualized and does on occasion supersede emotion and instinct in the experience of profoundly moving objects, ideas, situations, and events, there has been actualized, as well, the massive and complex structure of man's culture and civilization with its codes of law and morality, its science, its religion, and its arts. In this progress, the developments in science have not been isolated from changes in religion, morality, and craft. The scientist who represents the advance of all science in the control of nature depends upon the social man to whom he is related in moral and legal societies. Societies not only permit the results of science to be utilized. In them are also prescribed mutual sacrifices of egoistic desires to desires common to all men in a community. In the realm of morality, the alteration in feeling, which is at once the consequence and presupposition of man's progress, manifests its evident effects in moral judgments and in human freedom. The possibility of choice among objects of desire implies that feeling, as productive imagination, has made evident alternative modes of action. In more primitive organisms, the "ought" cannot emerge from the "must." Only upon the assumption that man may select from alternative stimuli and may reflect upon the values of one mode of action in comparison to the one offered by another stimulus may sheer egoism—the inflexible reaction of an organism to a stimulus—make way for the sacrifice of goods essential for the common life of men among men. The primitive is more frequently enraged and drawn into overt action by inanimate as well as by responsible and animate beings in his environment than is the rational man. The primitive's action is in this respect more completely determined by feeling. He is primitive in this sense, that proper

[18] E. A. Singer, Jr., "On a Possible Science of Religion," p. 104.

judgments concerning alternative modes of action are not made, but rather operate still at the reproductive level.

V

NOWHERE in man's experience are the consequences of his evolution and of the increase in his control of nature and of his own brute nature more manifest than in the aesthetic mood. Profoundly moving art which evokes the mood, because of its sensuously defined structure and of the artist's employment of generic symbols of feeling, is designed to ensure the initial attractiveness and familiarity which emphasize in the experience significant aspects of reproductive imagination. As we have observed, the mood is likewise and for the same reason, a form of typical behavior, in which the artist is similarly implicated both by the nature of his craft and by the materials into which he projects the symbols in order to communicate his feelings.

It is, however, the mood which, of the dimensions of feeling, most markedly evidences man's evolution and the growth of imagination's productivity. The potentialities in craft, in material, and in symbols, which incline productive imagination towards the creation of fine or "freeing" art are, upon actualization, expressed in the work of art. The object made is, as Plato implies in the figure of the magnetic rings, a carrier of the power by which the artist communicates. We know that the power is feeling. And the object made, as the actualization of potentialities in craft, in materials, and in symbols, becomes the potentiality for the actualization of productive imagination in aesthetic experience. What the potentialities are is suggested by recalling a remark made at the outset of this essay. It was asserted that one of the important empirical criteria of profoundly moving art is its inexhaustibility. Our concern is not now with the "inexhaustibility" of the symbols of fine art derived from the non-aesthetic teleologies but, rather, with the meaning of the criterion of inexhaustibility itself as it relates to the product of the artist's technique.

The inexhaustibility of the work of fine art is a fact for those who return again and again to the experience of Michelangelo's "The Last Judgment," of Beethoven's *Eroica* or of Brahm's *First Symphony*, and it is a fact not only beyond contention but one that distinguishes at the outset the profoundly moving from the merely pleasant products of craft. The fact, however, bespeaks a permanence of interest for which the lover of art is dependent at once upon the artist's power to inform a material with the content of broad and deep human experience comprehensible to all the race or culture and upon a mastery of technical processes. The artist must make, to satisfy the conditions, an object or event marked by individual and personal interpretation in a material with aesthetic potentialities of its own.

The presuppositions of art's inexhaustibility are, in fact, primarily twofold: The work of art is a symbol of feeling and it is a symbol which "stands for" and "objectifies" feeling in material with complex requirements for the material's proper technical treatment. As a symbol, the work of art is completed as a complex system of interrelated symbols, selected at once to augment and fortify the effect of the primary symbol that ensures communicability and to diversify within the limitations of unity the experience of the integrated sign.

The second presupposition for the work of art's inexhaustibility derives from the material in which the symbol is expressed for aesthetic experience. The requirements of specific materials of art are diverse. They are perhaps most widely differentiated initially by the fact that the work of art is either an object or an event. In painting, by way of illustration, the artist encounters an initial spatial problem in the need to give the symbol a three-dimensional semblance within the restrictions of a two-dimensional surface.[19] In poetry, each word contributes individual significance and sonority to the meaning and consonance of a whole which unfolds in time. Once the conditions of the initial requirements are met—and they are not hard and fast since time is consumed in experiencing spatial objects —there is an infinity of particular requirements which the material

[19] Cf. above, Chap. VIII.

presents, perhaps suggested sufficiently for our purposes by the differing potentialities for sculpture inherent in wood and in bronze.

These general and particular aspects of the problems of symbolization in material, affected at once by the selection of the generic symbols and its individualization as well as by the projection of the symbol into a material with requirements of its own, afford the grounds for the widest variety within the unity of the work of art. Their first significant consequence for the mood, as the latter marks man's progress, is that the work of art is put beyond possible definition either as a mere object or event produced by merely unreflective activity induced in conation.[20] Formed as a symbol adequate to express the artist's feelings concerning non-aesthetic "referrents," the work of art is for the individual who experiences it the end product of the formative process. Reflection, in turn, discovers in the object made such evident characteristics of variety in unity as rhythm, harmony, and repetition. Moreover, the aesthetic experience is of a datum that has been selected because it can be made into an adequate sign, since the making of profoundly moving art is always an evaluation. Once the selection has been made, the object has been subjected (both regarding what it symbolizes and the material in which it is symbolized) to a process intended to include and exclude factors relevant or irrelevant to the whole.

The foregoing are certainly a minimum of the factors, the presence of which in the work of art are presupposed in both the process of its creation and in any gross description of the object or event. They are factors in themselves significant for the inexhaustibility of the art object in aesthetic experience and may perhaps be sufficient to allow us to offer an answer to the question: Why does fine art induce mood rather than overt behavior in aesthetic experience? The artist, in making the work of art, intends to move us or, as Housman suggests, the art object fulfills its "peculiar function" in transmitting feeling. As has been observed in the technical analysis of the teleology of feeling[21] already given, the rela-

[20] Cf. above, Chaps. V-VII.
[21] Cf. above, p. 442.

tion of stimulus to reaction falls under the law of "all-or-nothing." The reaction of mood is not partial. Consequently, the mood is not "preparation for action," inhibited instinctive reaction, or incipient movement. It is emergency action, full and complete as such.

The work of art is certainly more than a mere stimulus to feeling but what more it is, its conative characteristics condition but do not precisely determine. Consequently, since the art object is subject to the law of "all-or-nothing," its maker succeeds or fails as he either does or does not move us. But, because the work of art is a product of making, the artist uses his craft in part to induce various kinds of reactions by means of the products' stimuli. Under any circumstances, however, he is enabled to produce a work of art that in turn induces a mood because in the process of making he can control—again in technical physiological terms—not alone the total number of impulses, i.e., images, which affect the experience of the percipient but also the frequency with which the same stimulus or one intimately related to it is repeated within the structure of the object made.

But the latter consideration, suggested by the physiologist and the neurologist,[22] is to be understood in terms of the specific and limited structure of the art object or event. The formal aspects of art abstracted by ateleological aesthetic constitute precisely the most obvious factors in art objects which are significant at this juncture. Their meaning has not often been made evident but the principal point is that the primary generic symbol and the interrelated symbols, as well as the sensuous factors of the material, are in the work of art brought under the technical rules of art most frequently expressed in terms of the diverse functions of unity.[23] More specifically, they are brought under the rules of rhythm, harmony, proportion, and balance by means of which the stimulus is repeated in related but diversified ways. Zeller[24] is certainly correct in assuming that the intent of Aristotle's theory of *katharsis* presupposes primarily the internal structure of the tragedy. The modern tragic

[22] Cf. above, pp. 441 ff., particularly Adrian's writings.
[23] See above, pp. 166 ff.
[24] Cf. above, pp. 299 ff.

poet merely amplifies the scope of the method as he alternates comic and tragic scenes in drama to avoid too great concentration upon one stimulus and too great intensity of one emotion. Moreover, his knowledge of the potentialities of material permits further attention to the aspects of sound and relation of words which add further scope for diversity.[25]

The foregoing are among the most general reasons for assuming that the profoundly moving work of art induces a mood rather than either instinct or emotion. That the aesthetic mood is more specifically one of courage in consequence of discontent and exaltation, presupposes these general reasons. The consequent problem is the subject of the next section of this chapter.

VI

SYMBOLIZATION and the artistic satisfaction of the requirements of the material contribute to the inexhaustibility of profoundly moving works of art and are presuppositions of mood. But mood is itself generic and typical reaction and the aesthetic mood, as a specification of the generic mood, induces discontent. Not only are its symbols drawn from the past but mood is ineffective as "emergency action" because as behavior it is peripheral, although it retains traces of the monitory function of emotion which warns of the inadequacy of hereditary mechanisms to cope with presented situations.

There occur, however, neither "shock" nor "paralysis of will" in the aesthetic mood. The artist presents a symbol that requires no overt action and there is put forward no compulsion to choose between the dominant stimulus and others which productive imagination makes effective in the total structure of art. The conflict, which in emotion warns of unstable equilibrium and for which emotion is emergency action necessary for a return to equilibrium, has been almost wholly resolved by the artist in his production of the

[25] Cf. below, Chap. XVIII.

work of art.[26] The artist has not only expressed and objectified his feelings in the generic symbol but the very objectification of the feeling by means of craft in the material implies a resolution of the conflict in the emancipation from the passions. The selection and unification of the non-aesthetic factors entering upon the original conflict in the artist has taken place in the "fusion" of feeling that characterizes the creative mood and is presupposed in the symbol presented for aesthetic experience.[27] The evidence for this is the varied treatment of the symbol and materials, of the complex factors in the symbol, e.g., the variations in theme in music and the reiteration with difference in architectural motifs.

Finally, and most significantly in relation to the general problem of feeling, "mood" is characterized by neither "shock" nor paralysis of will, not only because of the objectification of feeling and, as we shall see, by the compensatory activity of the productive imagination, but also because discontent has supplanted depression. The admonition of the emotions is forceful primarily because emotions are the median range of the *continuum* and because the effectiveness of alternative stimuli presents for the organism a practical issue. The diminished overtness of the behavior in mood is correlative to the increase in the productivity of imagination. Specifically, the aesthetic mood is productive imagination at the height of activity and it is a complete exemplification of the exaltation that accompanies the achievement of the end. This the artist assures by his making. But the concomitant depression has been altered to discontent, to a mere diminution of the force of depression.

Nonetheless, the aesthetic mood is one of discontent and this fact is significant. As we have observed, in art persist the errors of the past, as well as its truth. It may be used to influence the will to evil as well as good causes. The art object is deceptive. More abstractly, it appeals to feeling and its experience is complicated, as are all operations of reproductive imagination, in the disequilibrium consequent upon the reinstatement of "images." That reinstatement is effective for the evocation of brute behavior characteristic of a level

[26] Cf. above, pp. 333-334, 445 ff.
[27] Cf. above, pp. 335 ff.

from which man has evolved. The disequilibrium, implying a reversion to the level of panic fears, dreads, hatreds, and lusts, reinstates a stage in which "extrinsic" factors in behavior are, however momentarily, dominant. And, as we have observed, inasmuch as productive imagination is operative at least to the extent of offering an "image" of the self as well, the individual so moved is aware of the discomfort and discontent attendant upon even an attenuated admonition that the dependence upon hereditary mechanisms implicit in generic and typical behavior is dangerous. The artist is the "messenger of discontent." The generic symbols of his art—for example in the blind adoration and following of the hero and the compulsions implicit in relations to the hero—are known by the percipient of profoundly moving art to be uncomfortably close to "arousers" of irrational fear and uncontrolled revulsion.

Discontent there is in the aesthetic experience. It is, however, but one aspect of that mood. The aesthetic mood is describable, not alone in terms of the reproductive, but of productive imagination as well. Here productivity is dissociated, however, from practical action. The work of fine art does not incline the will in a specific direction and in this differs from either rhetoric or oratory. The artist's making is not definable completely in terms of non-aesthetic ends and it may be inferred that the maker does not propose by means of the work of art to create ends for man's willing or to present speculation with apparatus or concepts adequate for the solution to theoretical problems.

The theory of empathy enlarges upon the fact that the work of art is primarily an object of reflection or contemplation.[28] That this undervalues the activity in aesthetic experience is true but *Einfühlung* does in this suggest the significant fact that in the aesthetic mood the "intrinsic" processes of imagination are at the height of activity. It is not strange that the corresponding decrease in "extrinsic" factors should have led empathists to assume that the mood is incipient behavior.

[28] Cf. above, pp. 457-458. For a version of the theory that the contemplative attitude towards art is sufficient, see Charles Mauron, *Aesthetics and Psychology*.

The significant inference to be drawn from "contemplation," "incipient" behavior, and productivity is that the practical, non-aesthetic relation of the subject to the object is in mood no longer essential for the individual's welfare. Emergency action is no longer required. The additional inference is that in the history of man, feeling as "emergency action" was once essential towards the "referrents" of the symbol, was evoked by man's relation to "extrinsic" factors in environment, and that it was so evoked to enable him to cope, however inadequately, with the situations in which was implicated the problem of his very survival. To be able to reflect freely upon the profoundly moving work of art, to be freed in its experience from compulsion to practical action while yet behaving typically and experiencing the discontent induced by the relation of emergency action to disequilibrium—action to some extent beyond our control and to that extent dangerous—these are the antinomic factors in aesthetic experience which now assume primary significance.

The aesthetic mood is comprehensible in the light of two factors implicit in feeling: The first of these is the reinstatement of man's brutish past and the accompanying discontent evoked by the warning of our weakness. The second is the reflection upon our progress beyond the stage in which man is driven by "extrinsic" factors and the exaltation attendant upon the experience of our own state, conditioned by our awareness of past progress. The crucial point is that overt action is no longer required. The aesthetic experience is made possible by man's progress in the control of nature. That progress itself produces the exaltation accompanying the achievement of ends and makes possible the utilization of feeling as a source of energy which, as Bergson says, is like the bursting of a dam.[29]

In consequence, the artist is not merely a messenger of discontent and the message he bears is borne not merely for its own sake. Aesthetic experience is unique as a mood primarily because it employs the reinstatement of the past and converts the discontent

[29] Cf. above, p. 78 and next chapter. The play-theory, as we have seen, emphasizes the abundance of energy available for both play and aesthetic experience. See above, pp. 221 ff.

attendant upon the disequilibrium of feeling into a source of strength for further effort in the conquest of nature. In this latter aspect, there is heard one overtone of play-theory. The long history of the hypothesis that art is play suggests that speculation was attempting to make clear the fact that play and aesthetic experience in common provide refreshment for body and mind. Moreover, thinkers whose speculation is concluded in attempts to limit aesthetic experience to the knowledge of a mystical beauty[30] are correct in their assumption that aesthetic and mystical experience are similar. Perhaps they may have been led to the assumption by the fact that both mystical and aesthetic experience release energies through profound feeling. For profoundly moving art is, to use again a term found in William James' writings, one of the significant "energizers" of man. But that energy, made available by means of feeling, may in non-aesthetic conative experience lead to danger or dis-ease. This is avoided in aesthetic experience because the same factors are given specific direction by the artist in making his work of art. In doing so, the artist by means of art evokes a mood of courage. This mood in turn "creates the creator."

Many factors enter into courage but few sound analyses of this virtue have failed to recognize that one of the effective grounds for heroism is either the recollection of past triumph over apparently insuperable odds or the memory of solutions offered for presumably insuperable problems. Thucydides offers a negative reason to account for the fact of courage in his remarks upon maritime skill: "Their want of practise will make them unskillful, and their want of skill timid." The strength of the courageous man is derived from knowledge. This is the tenor of Emerson's essay, in *Society and Solitude*: "It is he who has done the deed once who does not shrink from attempting it again." The facile orator at times obliterates by skill and a spate of words the power of the past to close the serried ranks, to energize man for further effort, to encourage the faint and weary. We forget this power until a master orator stirs us to the depths and a Churchill rallies a nearly spent England to indomitable courage by bringing to his people memories

[30] Cf. above, Chap. II.

of anguish met with fortitude by harassed men and women of another day.

Biblical chronicle and epic poetry, the words of the common man, the spirit of the nation and of the race attest this source of courage, as the memory of the past energizes man's spirit. Saul tells David "thou art a youth." Youth he is but, "The Lord hath delivered me out of the paw of the lion, and out of the paw of the bear. He will deliver me out of the hand of the Philistine." Odysseus "beat his breast" in despair. But he "reproached his fear," crying, "Endure, my heart, far worse hast thou endured." In this, the crafty Ithacan is kin to Aeneas who rallies his spent Trojans, off the coast of Libya, with the words:

> With me, the rocks of Scylla you have tried
> The inhuman Cyclops, and his den defied.
> What greater ills hereafter can you bear?

But he is kin also, to that pilot of a more modern craft who told Saint-Exupéry that, "you will be bothered from time to time by storms, fog, snow. When you are, think of those who went through it before you, and say to yourself, 'What they could do, I can do.' "[31] These are not merely literary devices, given birth in quiet reflection by Biblical and epic poets. One of the numerous tales of heroism born of the present conflict tells the same story in words used by ordinary men facing death. It recounts the same tempering of dread by the past. Three airmen are downed in the Pacific. They float on a raft for some thirty days. Cold, wet, burned by the sun, with little food or water, the words of the narrator of that experience are worth repeating: "sitting glumly about the boat, discouraged, the three of us considered the possibilities. . . . The thought of what we had already gone through—that clinched the argument. We all agreed that neither this nor any other disaster which could overtake us now was sufficient reason for giving up the fight we had been making. Again we shook hands all around, and vowed we'd go on."[32]

[31] Antoine de Saint-Exupéry, *Wind, Sand, and Stars*, p. 6.

[32] Robert Trumbull, *The Raft*, pp. 170-171. (Quoted by permission of Henry Holt and Company, publishers.)

The memory of past achievement stirs courage for renewed effort in the face of unknown or untried foes and of overwhelming obstacles. It does so, however, not only for the individual. Empires and states—the collective wholes—similarly draw upon the profound influence of the past in the lore and chronicle of their achievements. This is the core of Rebecca West's *Black Lamb and Grey Falcon.* It is this strength drawn from the past—and the lessons to be learned from a history that provides no such source of strength—that is uppermost in her mind as the consequences of the Serbians' defeat by the Turk at Kossovo are before her. It is, she concludes, the weakness of the defeated that there is for them no intricate and complex process of the past upon which their men may draw:

> What would England be like if it had not its immense Valhalla of kings and heroes, if it had not its Elizabethan and its Victorian ages, its thousands of incidents which come up in the mind, simple as icons and as miraculous in their suggestion that what England has been it can be again, now and for ever? What would the United States be like if it had not those reservoirs of triumphant will-power, the historical factors of the War of Independence, of the giant American statesmen, and of the pioneering progress into the West, which every American citizen has at his mental command and into which he can plunge for revivification at any minute?[33]

Poets know that their epic heroes drew upon the past for the sources of courage, as the common man, nations and empires likewise know and act upon that fact. But courage is essential for the culture and for the race, as well, and the reservoir upon which both draw in order to gird man's spirit is the identical reminiscence of past triumphs. This it is that is made explicit primarily in the experience of profoundly moving art. In the aesthetic mood, it comes like Blake's "lost traveler's dream under the hill." Art gives men courage in the same manner that Caesar instills valor into the Legion seized by panic at the report that "the Germans were men of a mighty frame and an incredible valor and skill at arms." Caesar asks, "What, pray, have you to fear? Why do you despair of your own courage or of my competence? We have made trial of this foe at a

[33] Rebecca West, *Black Lamb and Grey Falcon,* pp. 55-56. (Copyright 1940, 1941, by Rebecca West. By permission of The Viking Press, Inc., N. Y.)

time our fathers could remember. . . ." And Caesar adds, as he recounts the episode, that, ". . . a marvelous change came over the spirit of all ranks and an utmost ardour for action took possession of them."

Fine art is "freeing art." In reflecting upon our own state as we experience profoundly moving art and in contemplating the work of art itself, we are freed from the compulsion that once enslaved men to "extrinsic" forces and made of them creatures inflexible in reaction and to this extent unfree. That we are able to and that we do reflect upon symbols, the "referrents" for which are the objects, events, ideas, and situations which arouse feeling; that we are moved profoundly; that we know these symbols because they appeal to an *Apperceptionsmass* and yet that we may do so in such wise that our action is peripheral rather than overt; this is evidence that the "measure of the enemy" has been taken "at a time our fathers could remember."

Aesthetic experience is presupposed at once by aeons of hardship and danger and by the well-nigh miraculous triumph of man in his evolution to manhood. The experience itself, in its message of discontent, discovers one source of morale and courage. As Caesar's soldiers displayed an "utmost ardour for action," profoundly moving art affords in its experience exaltation of spirit. The measure of the enemy has been taken in the time our forefathers could remember. From the experience induced by reproductive imagination and hinting at discontent, but equally compact of freedom and exaltation induced by productive imagination, there is derived the courage essential to face new obstacles. Profoundly moving art, *sui generis*, does not teach, preach, or construct scientific systems. It does, however, endow man with the courage and it does release energy needed by artist, moralist, and scientist to keep each at his endless task in art, morality, and science.[34]

[34] It may be objected that if the aesthetic experience is a mood of courage, this is again a generic form of feeling while specific works of art induce feelings of pity, fear, sympathy, etc. The mood presupposes these emotions and is their "resultant." It is a fusion in which courage is dominant and generic but in which, also, as Picasso suggests, the feeling the artist intends to communicate may be retained and communicated by the specific nature of the symbol in question.

VII

ARTISTIC techniques which enable the craftsman at once to actualize material's potentialities as if for the latter's own sake and yet to employ those potentialities to communicate by means of individualized generic symbols, the objects, events, ideas, and situations with which all men of a race or culture are familiar through feeling, make possible the production of fine art which in turn is designed to fulfill art's unique function in the "creation of the creator." The symbols have their "referrents" in the science, the morality, and the art of the past. To such symbols feeling has attached and in them is the power to evoke typical physiological and neurological reactions of ateleologically defined feeling.

Man in his evolution has developed more efficient and flexible instruments ensuring his progress in the control of nature than those proffered by the ancient "wisdom of the body." The making of fine art is one consequence of the resulting progress. Neither in its making nor in its experience is fine art, as has often been contended, an escape from life. The function of fine art is one requisite for the continuance of man's efforts to control nature and satisfy his deepest desires. By means of aesthetic experience, inspiration, energy, and courage are proffered and these enable men to continue their efforts in non-aesthetic fields of endeavor. Defective art induces defective experience. Mass-produced art may substitute excitement for courage, the refreshment of play for the exaltation of aesthetic, or triviality for the profundity that touches—as both tragic and comic fine art must do—upon the basic interests of the race, the culture, and the individual. Yet the refreshment afforded even by defective forms of art deepens the conviction that aesthetic experience enables the scientist, the moralist, the theologian, and the "common man" to face the inexhaustible difficulties of their work with a courage in itself born of the remembrance of past triumphs in the conquest of nature by science, morality, theology, art, and the endless tasks of the "common man" in assuring the stability of the culture or society which presupposes his individuality.

It is to the scientist, the moralist, the theologian, the artist, and the "common man" who have gone before that fine art owes its symbols to which we, in turn, owe aesthetic experience. In this is the truth of Tolstoy's "communion which, reaching beyond the grave, unites us with all men of the past who have been moved by the same feelings and with all men of the future who will yet be touched by them."[35] Art inquires of each man, "What is there to fear?" Reproductive and productive imagination operating in the total structure of art suggest the reply, a reply implicit in the antinomic character of art and of aesthetic experience: "The measure of the enemy was taken in the days our fathers could remember," in the history of the evolving race, of the expanding and deepening culture. If the problems of the present appear to burden men with insuperable difficulties, the experience of fine art—which manifests the true "emancipation from the passions"—informs us that different foes, long since overcome, have given in the past the false appearance of invincibility. In part because it does recall past conquest, art effects "the marvellous change in the ranks," a change conditioned by the interrelation of reproductive and productive imagination and evidenced in the discontent and exaltation with which the experience of all profoundly moving art is instinct.

[35] Cf. above, p. 366.

Chapter XVIII

Productive Imagination and the End of Art

. . . The feeling . . . cannot otherwise exist than in and through the embodiment which imagination has found for it.

—BERNARD BOSANQUET

BECAUSE profoundly moving art reinstates the past and because in its experience the percipient also makes effective the stimulus of his own condition of sensibility—facts from which may be inferred the overcoming of obstacles in the past—the dominant feeling in aesthetic experience is one of exaltation. Exaltation is implicit in the courage that inspires to additional effort.

That the aesthetic experience is a mood of courage does not, however, fully describe the experience of fine art, although it does indicate the direction in which we must proceed in order to offer a more complete analysis. For this reason it is important to have well in mind the inferences that have been made in reaching the conclusions thus far set down. The first of these is that feeling, in all stages of the *continuum* including mood, is "emergency action." The second is that mood is the only dimension for feeling in which behavior is peripheral to a degree that theorists have characterized it as inhibited action, tentative reaction, or, indeed, "preparation for action." The final inference is that, while instinct, emotion, and mood are, as reproductivity, generically the same, they are also "varying conditions of sensibility." As the latter, they are divergent means to the end of the control of nature.

The emergence of mood bespeaks a corresponding diminution

of the need for a direct bodily relation to conatively definable stimuli. Moreover, although the capacity of feeling to make effective stimuli in a "total situation" is implicit in "recognition" and as such is a presupposition of the "wisdom of the body," this primitive use of productive imagination assumes a secondary role. In the course of man's evolution and in consequence of the diminishing need for direct and overt behavior, productivity has come to be, not a presupposition of but a primary function of feeling.

These inferences are significant for aesthetic theory, as are their consequences. Still, they provide only a partial explanation of the experience of profoundly moving art. Emancipation from the passions, the mood of courage, the "awareness" of man's progress, the feelings as a source of energy released in the experience of art, the productivity of feeling as it is directed to "awareness" of alternative stimuli—each plays its significant part in the resolution to aesthetic problems. But neither separately nor collectively do they provide the conclusive reason for fine art's "appeal to men's hearts and minds," nor can they provide that reason precisely because each suggests an instrumentality in its own turn significant only in terms of an end. The description of the structure of art, as we have observed,[1] is incomplete unless it is a description of the "total structure of art." The artist communicates and the percipient apprehends because the work of art is, in part, a symbol intended to serve as a means for effecting aesthetic experience. But the figure of the magnetic rings in *Ion* is insufficient to explain aesthetic experience unless it provides a final link—the *telos* of fine art.

II

THAT final link transmits its power because the artist, who moves men profoundly, is a "messenger of discontent." He must stir "the deepest depths of the soul" in order to initiate in aesthetic experience the productive powers of imagination. The presupposition for the discontent he does induce is the fact that feeling

[1] See above, Chap. IX, particularly, pp. 313-314.

effects a disequilibrium in the individual who is moved, a disequilibrium accompanied in the median range of feeling by warning that the bodily reactions—manifesting the "wisdom of the body"—are inadequate to cope with the crisis.

In mood, it is true, the monitory function of the emotions is diminished. There is not in the aesthetic mood an admonition sufficiently forceful to be the imperative injunction which, explicit in emotional shock, calls for readjustment. Yet in aesthetic experience there are overtones of warning. The artist is skilled in his craft. His skill bespeaks knowledge of the potentialities both of materials and signs with which he works to provide symbols which may induce aesthetic experience. Some of that skill is employed to induce reversion to "extrinsically" controlled experience and yet to guard the aesthetic percipients from the full force of feeling's power as a means to emergency action.

The artist's technical skill and his understanding of symbols are essential to produce an object or event suitable to ensure, insofar as it is possible to achieve it, an experience of this character. But the effectiveneses of craft and symbol is presupposed by the significant fact that the disequilibrium integral to deep feeling is not the sole possible consequence of the interrelation of reproductive and productive imagination in conative experience. The interrelation of these correlative aspects of imagination presages the proximate end of art in what Bergson, reflecting upon the meaning of another deeply moving experience,[2] correctly maintains is "a systematic readjustment with a view to equilibrium on a higher level."

The readjustment occurs in aesthetic as well as in other conative experience. But it will be argued that the "systematic readjustment" that fulfills aesthetic experience is but partially achieved in the direct experience of fine art and that the "equilibrium on a higher level" comes about in the achievement of the end of art, in what Professor Singer refers to as the "creation of the creator." The achievement of the end frees the aesthetic percipient from the restrictions of non-aesthetic ends. Aesthetic experience "creates the creator" but the fine artist neither formulates the ideals nor fixes

[2] Cf. above, pp. 78-79 and p. 446.

the ends which enter upon the non-aesthetic activities which the creator, in his turn, creates.

Aesthetic experience is thus implicated in the creativity or productivity of imagination as fully as it is in re-creativity or reproductivity. In fact, as we have observed, productivity of imagination affects the generic symbols of art both in the requisite reinstatement of a precedent image,[3] and in the evaluation made by the artist who selects from among his generic symbols that sign by which he hopes to communicate.

Fine art most markedly manifests the impact of productive imagination as each individual artist specifies the generic symbols, uses and forms the sensuous media of his art, and individualizes the techniques inherited from the tradition of craft in which he works. But the relation of productive imagination to the specific symbols of art is one that touches aesthetic as philosophy of art is implicated in fields so comprehensive as to include all the arts. In this domain, the special skills and studies of archaeologist, historian of art, and critic are of primary significance. An essay which from the outset has been directed only to the investigation of aesthetic experience and its presuppositions need impinge upon this vast realm of specific symbols only to the extent that for its findings a limited number of relevant illustrations may be used to illuminate its text.

Within these limits, the significance of productive imagination for our principal problems will be evident if we consider the inferences to be drawn from two statements. In expressing his creative powers, the artist works with materials and symbols in such wise that the work of art made evokes productivity in the aesthetic percipient. Secondly, the productivity of feeling thus evoked in aesthetic experience transcends the direct relation between the aesthetic percipient and the art object.

The creative function of feeling, implicit even in the dominantly one-to-one correspondence of stimulus and reinstated image characteristic of the lower stages of the *continuum*, is evidenced primarily in the capacity of productive imagination to make effective alternative stimuli or images in "total situations" as varied as ideas, objects,

[3] Cf. above, pp. 358 ff.

and events. It has been observed in this essay that the productive aspects of feeling are most strikingly actualized in emotion, specifically in the contrast of the latter stages to that of instinct. Emotion is feeling at a stage in which the individual makes effective for himself modes of possible action other than that mode required by the response to a dominant stimulus.

It has also been maintained that mood is marked by the augmentation of "intrinsic" over "extrinsic" factors in experience. The individual in this stage of feeling presents to himself the maximum of stimuli in the "total situation" and, as is true to a lesser degree in emotion, the consequent "images" include those evoked by his own condition of sensibility. In mood, therefore, is the most complete actualization of productivity. It is the "fusion" of feeling which, as we have observed in considering the artist's creativity,[4] allows for the "temporal spread" required to permit symbolization and making. The counterpart in aesthetic experience permits the recreation of the artistic symbol and induces other creative acts, the nature of which we shall now proceed to consider.

The work of fine art is constructed by the artist in such wise that productivity of feeling in aesthetic experience is sustained at its height. It is significant, however, that feeling operates thus productively within the limits of an object or event which introduces requirements and restrictions of its own and it is within these limits that productive imagination makes evident potentialities for aesthetic value in the material itself. As Housman implies, the creative act of the artist is incomplete unless the experience of the work of art is effected. In other words, the immediate end of the artist is to induce an aesthetic mood by means of the object or event made. To succeed, the artist must provide for the spectator's productive imagination a "total situation." The incorporation of generic symbols of art in material assures varied but organically united "images" to initiate productive recreation on the part of the percipient. The very symbolization of non-aesthetic "referrents" in materials suitable for fine art provides the initial diversity in unity which augments the tendency of productive imagination to create.

[4] Cf. above, pp. 335 ff.

This increase in productivity is also a decrease in overt behavior. Therefore, the technical efforts to maintain and strengthen contemplation by augmenting the "images" available in the work of art tend likewise to diminish feeling's originally unrestricted identification with overt behavior. Conversely, the artist's intention to diminish the possibilities for inducing overt behavior by means of the work of art are identical with his efforts to augment the activity of productive imagination in the aesthetic mood.

To assure success for these efforts, there are many means to hand which vary primarily in the degree of "internality" or "externality" of technique they employ. With the most obvious and external means at the artist's disposal, this essay is little concerned. The larger number of external techniques are best understood as means for ensuring for the percipient what may be called "aesthetic distance."[5] Their listing would include frames for paintings, stages intended to separate actors and audience, invocations to muses in poetry, suitable sites for buildings, as well as many other facile means of unification, for the most part external to the work of art. In many instances, the means produce "aggregates" rather than "organic unities" in the work of art. The title of Roy Harris's *American Symphony*, for example, has no integral relation to the music and cannot compensate for the lack of internal dominant theme.

These external means may best be regarded as initial steps in the direction of making the object or event into a symbol characterized by "aesthetic" rather than non-aesthetic "semblance." Their most interesting manifestations, apart from displays of technical skill and individual acumen, occur as the external technique itself develops into a technical art. This has occurred in various instances, in the construction and arrangement of the stage, in landscape gardening and similar arts which in turn lay requirements upon the artist making in the original art.

For all that, however, the method of "internality" has more profound significance for aesthetic experience. The principal means

[5] Cf. E. Bullough, "Psychical Distance as a Factor in Art and an Aesthetic Principle."

which permit the initiation and augmentation of aesthetic productivity and encourage the artist to strive to increase its operations are potential in the art object and may be considered under general rules concerning symbols of feeling and material, along with the techniques required to actualize the latter for experience.

The proper evaluation of these internal controls presupposes one general condition of making suggested in previous chapters. The work of art is a symbol intended to evoke feeling. But the symbol is not the original "referrent" for feeling and the material in which the sign is communicated is not conatively describable behavior. These conditions of fine art are converted by the artist into means by which he is, in turn, enabled to produce a new organic unity. This new unity is potentially a work of art in which the widest variety is attainable and in which materials, imposing necessary limitations upon technique, provide stimuli to be made effective in new "images" by and for productive imagination.

De Quincey remarks that the object of artistic creativity is to "reproduce in the mind some great effect, through the agency of *idem in alio*. The *idem*, the same impression, is to be restored, but *in alio*, in a different material . . . by means of a different instrument." This puts our present problem clearly, however much the term "impression" may differ from the language used in the present study. But we have already observed that what De Quincey refers to as the *idem in alio* implied in artistic communication presupposes both objectification of feelings and reflection upon one's state or condition of sensibility. Moreover, the actual making of the work of art, whether object or event, imposes upon the artist the requirement that the sign, by means of which are communicated his feelings concerning the non-aesthetic "referrents" for feeling, be made intelligible in material and integrated with it.

The frequent consequence is that by making, the central generic sign is related to other signs and that the meaning of the whole is amplified. Thus a variety of related emotional situations, objects, ideas, or events follow upon the elaboration and individualization of the generic symbol. But whether the elaboration and individualization is held within strict bounds or allowed free play, the *in alio* of the material means simply that there is an amplification of the "images" presented by the art object for aesthetic experience.

The merging of sign and material adds to the stimuli the artist makes potentially effective as "images" for aesthetic experience. An initial condition for making of the experience itself a mood is thus satisfied, but the significant issue truly arises because of the intervention of technique. The object or event is made and the artist controls both the total number of effective stimuli in the work and the frequency with which any one or related group of images is exhibited within the whole work of art. In addition, and not alone in the temporal arts, the artist controls the order in which the images of the total situation are presented for aesthetic experience.

Regarding the total number of stimuli intended to evoke productive imagination in aesthetic experience, it is sufficient to say that the rules of profoundly moving art clearly enforce upon the adept craftsman at least the restrictions imposed by economy. Within the unified work of art, the materials should ideally be interpenetrated by the primary and related symbols of feeling. And, on grounds of intelligibility, the aesthetic percipient may well demand no more images than can be presented without confusion in the work of art.

Of greater significance in the artistic task of stimulating productivity in aesthetic experience and of reducing practical or theoretical compulsions laid upon the percipient is the fact that the craftsman may control the frequency with which a given or related symbol of feeling is reiterated. In this, the aesthetic potentialities of the material play no small role. In non-aesthetic experience, there may or may not be possible some alleviation of too intense feeling. Ordinarily, however, there is a monotonous and wearing repetition of the same or of a similar conatively "toned" idea or situation. It is the intense and consequently shocking character of emotional or passionate situations, such as fear or hatred, that puts them beyond the possibility of all but the minimum of objectification and consequently makes them difficult to endure or, indeed, to reflect upon.

A similar dis-ease not infrequently manifests itself in the experience of a drama, a symphony, or a painting in which the artist has failed to compensate for the intensity of feeling aroused if one emotional situation or idea is concentrated upon largely to the exclusion of all others. The structure and material of art permit wide variety, while yet permitting advantage to be taken of the need for conflict and intense feeling as presuppositions of the mood. There is, for example, no more moving dramatic scene than the conclusion to *Othello*. Yet, there are presented images of a variety of symbols for feeling, integrated, but because of diversity in unity, allowing the percipient to escape the discomfort consequent upon too great attention to any one image. If the symbol is not varied and at the same time unified, the intensity of feeling may lead either to distress, to insensibility, or to laughter.

The artist may avoid these disruptive consequences of too strong concentration upon one feeling by the use of numerous technical devices. He may alternate, as Shakespeare does, tragic and comic scenes in his tragedies or may lighten the brooding menace of peril or fear by recourse to the lyric. He may show the variety of character in his dramatic subject, making of him no type or monstrosity, but evidencing in speech and in action a varied nature centered upon the core which is the source of primary interest. He may employ the extended metaphor, as Milton does, to introduce symbols of the vast panoply of earth and heaven and so lend variety to the unity of the story of man's fall. The artist may, in the spatial arts, follow the suggestion of Lessing that the climax of the dramatic event be avoided and so allow for imagination's full play. By selection, the artist averts the intrusion of the accidental and the irrelevant. He integrates events and ideas with the primary symbols. But because the artist's imagination is productive, hackneyed rules may not circumscribe his technique in using symbols. It is integral to great art that the artist rules his own domain within the limitations of the meaning of the symbols but that he actualizes interrelations and connections not apparent before in them. Thus, the use of drapery in Greek sculpture at the highest stage of its development does not conceal but reveals the contour and tactile qualities of the body. Similarly, Gothic architecture makes actual potentialities of feelings concerning space undreamed of in classical architecture.[6]

That the work of art is an *idem in alio* permits the diminution not only of practical compulsion in the aesthetic mood but the satisfaction of the demand for the resolution of theoretical problems as well. The potentialities of the material in which the artist incorporates the non-aesthetic symbols of feeling are almost without limit but, nonetheless, both symbol and material have unity. There is possible, in consequence, a kind of rhythm in art which, by use of subtle variation of theme or motif, permits in the most striking instances of fine art an almost complete clarification of the meaning of the familiar generic symbol itself. To achieve this is part of the task of the artist and for the task he has to hand the initially attractive sensuous factors of the material—color, patina, pleasing sound, etc. Diverse modes of presentation within the unified object—lines leading our vision to other and related lines in the painting, masses of dark shades balancing masses of figures, themes in musical compositions attacked again and again with variations of theme and sound—help to clarify for the aesthetic percipient of the best instances of fine art the meaning of the original symbol.

Various possibilities for variety of light and shade, of color and hue, various possible coherent intonations of sound, the variety of effects that may be produced by technique operating upon wood or marble or bronze, encourage the artist to the repetition with subtle variation of musical theme, architectural motif, tragic narrative, or central situation, idea, or event. The material lends itself to the artistic interrelations of lines in paintings, the balancing of heavy and light colors or masses, and the repetition of content. But the primary importance of these technical operations upon material is this, that the same generic but now individualized symbol of feeling may be presented again and again from related but varied standpoints, in the course of which the potentialities of the material are increasingly objectified and clarified. One consequence is that the symbol of feeling for which the percipient has a predisposition in experience is made, in the fulfillment of the aesthetic mood, com-

[6] Cf. W. Worringer, *Form in Gothic*.

pletely manifest in its meaning. And it is the agency of variety in unity to which the material contributes that effects this result.[7]

In general terms, then, the formula of *idem in alio*, as it is put into effect, minimizes the compulsion of practical necessitation, as well as the need for theoretical speculation in aesthetic experience. Its proper employment in art is not, however, merely negative. It enables the artist also to present for productive imagination a "total situation" immeasurably enriched, once the essential condition of variety in unity implicit in the conjoining of symbol and material is satisfied. Craft actualizes potentialities in the material itself.

The technical processes of art may be directed to material in such manner that the number and frequency of unified stimuli which become "images" for the aesthetic percipient are again affected. The consequence may be primarily to diminish in aesthetic experience the significance of practical and theoretical activity. Craft has, however, a more significant proximate end than this. The materials—the words and silences of poetry,[8] the colors, shades and tints of painting, the tactile and visual properties of bronze and wood—become in the completed work of art stimuli for imagination with aesthetic potentialities of their own. Their values transcend but presuppose the material's worth in the initial task of communicating symbols and enrich the "total situation" in which productive imagination in aesthetic experience operates.

The ground for this enrichment is evident in the following quotation from the writings of Gerard Manley Hopkins, although the means are varied and the principle must be altered *mutatis mutandis* in application to works in other arts. Hopkins, asking why, on Wordsworth's principle, "the accentuation" is used in "verse and never in prose" offers this suggestion: "It is because *where the structure forces us to appreciate each syllable* it is natural and in the order of things for us to dwell on all modifications affecting the

[7] This appears to be the significant answer to the question that remained after our examination of Zeller's interpretation of *katharsis*. On Zeller's theory it would be difficult to offer a reason for the diminution in aesthetic experience of intense feeling. See above, pp. 301-302.

[8] Sir Walter Raleigh, *Style*, p. 115: Words, "coloured by the neighborhood of silence. . . ."

general result or type which the ear preserves and accordingly with such as are in themselves harmonious we are pleased, but in prose where syllables have none or little determinate value to emphasize them is unmeaning."[9] The artist discovers in the material itself precisely those values which make craftsmanship in fine art more than a technique for construction, and he takes advantage of those values because the product of the technique comes to be integral to a "total situation."

To have presented seriatim the divergent factors that enter among others upon the work of art may also have suggested that the object made is a mere aggregate. But symbols and materials are organically formed or unified in a whole and because of this the number of stimuli and the frequency of their display in the work of art as an "image" become factors in a new principle, in which variation is aesthetically effective only under the rule of unity in terms of end.

III

THE aesthetic experience begins with the object of fine art. As the aesthetic percipient turns to a product made by the artist, the experience is of a symbol rich in potentialities for productivity. The artist has exerted his control over the total number, the order, and the frequency of the diverse but interrelated images which constitute the symbol and he has lavished his skill upon the materials. The result is a whole that provides a "total situation," integrated to the extent that at the outset of aesthetic experience the operations of imagination are circumscribed. Productive imagination at this stage makes effective the stimuli within the presented symbol and, as Bosanquet remarks, "*the feeling is submitted to the laws of an object.*"[10]

In a realm made familiar by reproductive imagination, the productive aspect of feeling is free to make evident the interrelation of

[9] *The Note-Books and Papers of Gerard Manley Hopkins*, p. 94. (Italics are mine.) By permission of Oxford University Press, New York.

[10] Bernard Bosanquet, *Three Lectures on Aesthetic*, p. 8.

parts, the subtle nuances of interpretation, the sublime or delicate power of expression, effects of dexterity and technical skill, and the profundity or inclusiveness of conception actualized in varying measure and with varying degrees of success in all profoundly moving works of art. The initial exaltation of spirit accompanying the free operation of productive imagination is sustained. The work is unified and the energies of the perceiver are concentrated. What may be the merely irritating and irrelevant characteristics of ordinary feeling do not disrupt the peripheral behavior of mood which is complete, although it is not overt action.

The energy released by feeling and made available for productive imagination serves to sustain the creativity that is part of the aesthetic mood and that consists, as does all such productivity of feeling, in making effective stimuli in a "total situation." Consequently, the empathists insist correctly that the aesthetic experience is contemplative—a conclusion anticipated by Kant in these words: "We *linger* over the contemplation of the beautiful because this contemplation strengthens and reproduces itself."[11] As imagination proceeds in its operations, maintains itself and makes effective stimuli within the presented art object, there ensues an experience characterized by the "temporal spread" that marks off mood from instinct or emotion. At least in this aspect, the aesthetic mood is analogous to the "fusion of feeling" that characterizes artistic creativity.

It is, nonetheless, impossible to rest content with the foregoing description, despite the fact that it is sound within limits and accords with a well-respected tradition of aesthetic experience. The fact is that aesthetic experience, tradition to the contrary, is not fulfilled by "resting in the image," by mere contemplation. Its productivity transcends the art object. The reason for this is evident. All conative experiences, and aesthetic experience is no exception to the rule, are characterized by disequilibrium. All truly productive experiences of this kind—those which end neither in depression nor in automatic response to extrinsic stimuli—are instances, as well, of restored equilibrium.

For several reasons—and for one fundamentally important reason

[11] *K.d.U.*, Sec. 12.

that will be plain—aesthetic experience resembles Bergson's description of mystical experience,[12] in that the equilibrium is established at another level. The proximate reasons for this are not difficult to discover or to state. Among the aspects to be considered is that aesthetic experience is a mood of courage consequent upon the memory of past triumph. Courage is no doubt of value in itself, as Aristotle argues, but it is principally valuable as a means to an end. The tendency of the exalted mood of courage is to go beyond the limits imposed for the experience by the art object.[13]

The instrumentality of courage is, however, not the most significant even of the proximate conditions for aesthetic experience's transcendence of the object of art. Equally important, certainly, is the paradox that the internal controls by means of which the artist directs the percipient's imagination to the object and attempts to cause it to "rest in the image" also so enriches the symbol of feeling that productive imagination simply follows its own nature, that of maintaining and continuing creativity.[14]

But the most important proximate condition for the transcendence turns upon the differences between artistic and aesthetic creation. It is true, certainly, as Housman implies, that making is incomplete without the peculiar function of transmitting feeling, i.e., of evoking aesthetic experience. It is also true that both artistic creation and aesthetic productivity are not fully comprehended without consideration in each instance of the end of art. There are, however, two conditions of artistic creativity which are not implicated in aesthetic experience. The first is this, that although there is a "fusion of feeling" called mood which permits the artist to communicate and which is analogous to the aesthetic mood, the mood of artistic creativity is preceded by conditions quite different from those presupposed by aesthetic productivity. The second is this, that artistic creativity, i.e., the making, is immediately fulfilled in

[12] Cf. below, pp. 512 ff.

[13] See next chapter.

[14] One may certainly have a specific experience of an individual object of art and concentrate upon that object, while yet the experience goes beyond the direct relation of subject and object. Moreover, although reproductive imagination is generic feeling, there is also a generic productivity of feeling in contrast to its specific manifestations.

"making," while within the total structure of art no object, event, or symbol made by craft corresponds to the artistic object as the completion of the aesthetic percipient's activity.

Biographies and autobiographies of artists are replete with descriptions of the trials, struggles, and miseries that not infrequently precede the act of creating. The act of creation begins in feeling and may be emotional to a degree that, before "fusion of feelings," the artist suffers shock. The conflict is resolved for the aesthetic percipient or reduced to a mere overtone of admonition. For the artist it is evident, however, that crises may actually warn of inadequacies to face the situation presented by inner conflict. Moreover, in artistic creation is presupposed the task of evaluating generic symbols and judging their adequacy for communication. For the aesthetic percipient, the choice has been made and the problem solved. The artist must select the materials and know and use the best techniques for the task. Finally, making is physical, mental, and technical effort actually expended.

The artist, then, actually makes or produces a work of art. The experience of the symbol produced is a conative act that makes energy available. The conative experiences prior to artistic making and in making utilize the artist's powers and energies. There is so little need for the energy made available by aesthetic experience that behavior has been called "tentative" and, indeed, there is no need in the aesthetic mood for more than tentative movement or preparation for action. As we have observed, the energy derived from feeling is not employed to resolve theoretical problems presented in the symbols. The conflicts which the artist has expressed in the generic symbol are resolved so that practical action is not needed. The meaning of the symbol has been clarified in the variety in unity of the product of art and the problem of expressing the symbol in material has been undertaken by the artist. The work of art is, in this sense, a problem solved.[15]

Another factor in the experience of profoundly moving art which induces productive imagination to transcend the object is the "temporal spread" by which the latter is distinguished from instinct or

[15] Cf. above, p. 122 for Kant's analogous inference.

emotion. It is this extension of the experience in time that furthers the tendency towards continuation of the experience and lends itself to the maintenance of productivity once the subject's contemplation of the object is concluded. By this means, also, the essence of productive imagination, the making effective of stimuli in a total situation, combines with an investigation of analogous feeling stimuli.

The latter suggestion concerning productive imagination is significant for the aesthetic mood's actual transcendence of the art object. Productive imagination is, in contrast to reproductive, directed neither to the generic nor to the typical. Productivity in feeling functions as creativity and is manifested in the discovery of the individual and the unique. As we have observed, productive feeling enables the artist to give the generic symbol the mark and stamp of his own unique interpretation. The identical productivity of imagination which enables the artist to make an art object unmistakably his own is not and cannot be satisfied in aesthetic experience in the percipient's mere recreation of an artist's "images." However subtle and complete the latter may be, however interrelated and however significant, they do not suffice to satisfy the individual aesthetic percipient's productive imagination. Even the productive recreation of the artist's individualized symbol is insufficient for this purpose. Aesthetic experience is no more completely reproductive than is the gifted musical conductor's interpretation of profoundly moving music. And, more significantly, productivity of imagination, to which pertains the generic function of making effective stimuli in a "total situation," is specified in each productive act in part according to the nature of the individual who feels.

To accept this inference, it is not necessary to deny that aesthetic experience is grounded in profoundly moving works of art; nor is it to deny what was previously argued, that fine art is inexhaustible. It is simply to consider inexhaustibility as the reason for our return to the work of fine art, rather than as a demand to be satisfied by constant and uninterrupted contemplation. The object of art is at once the *locus* of our interest and the point of departure for our own productive powers. It is thus dual in nature and the creativity it evokes may not be circumscribed by even complex works like Titian's "Descent from the Cross" or Beethoven's *Eroica.* Nor is it alone the fact that productive imagination is the imagination of an individual which leads to transcendence. Men are creatures of desires which are satisfied in action related to ends and purposes. The usual use of their energy takes place in the fields of action, in making, and in speculation.

In consequence of all these factors in art and in productive imagination, as well as in their preconditions, we are carried beyond the art object. The mood of creativity persists to be utilized. The mood is sufficiently extended in time to permit its utilization, precisely as the "fusion of feeling" allows the artist to make and to communicate. Associated images and the percipient's natural endowments may lead the moralist from aesthetic contemplation to ethical speculation or practical activity, as they may lead the scientist to attempt to extend his control over nature, the critic to criticism, and the artist to the creation of works of art.[16] Equilibrium is re-

[16] By way of illustration, it may be argued that the Biblical scholar who remarks that the Christ depicted in Raphael's "Christ among the Money Changers" is too young to accord with the evidence of the New Testament is offering an irrelevant criticism. This is true and yet his error is a natural one. Granted that he has been moved aesthetically, his productive imagination employs itself subsequently with material the potentialities of which he knows and with which he works. His remark is evidence of the creative power of art. But because the imagination is thus creative, its operation has erroneously led to the assumption that the painting necessarily teaches and is intended to teach, in this case, Biblical lore. The instance cited is, however, no more irrelevant to the problem than is the assumption that art criticism is integral to aesthetic experience. In fact, the critic's assumption that his criticism of technique or materials employed is more relevant than is the Biblical critic's is erroneous. The critic and the scholar alike have been inclined by aesthetic experience to the fields of their natural inclinations and training and to the pursuit of the activity they normally follow. It is the strength of Croce's aesthetic that it insists upon the irrelevance of art criticism and art history to the aesthetic experience. It is the theory's weakness that it fails properly to analyze the grounds for their frequent confusion. By way of illustration, the artist is inspired to the production of works of art by the exaltation of the aesthetic mood. His production of works of art is not aesthetic experience. Pater produces a work of art in his essay on *La Gioconda.* The painting inspires him to his own production of a work of art but it might equally well have inspired him to his essays on Platonism.

It is quite another matter, however, to argue that the critic and the moralist,

established at another level. From that other level, we may again return enriched to the experience of the work of art.

Many experiences other than that of art evoke feeling, release energy, and establish moods of creativity. But fine art is the realm of true imagination and is the unique image for it, in part because by its means neither the artist nor the symbol coerces the will or the intellect to undertake a specific task. There is in aesthetic experience freedom from the compulsion to specific non-aesthetic ends. In this, fine art differs from its near kin, oratory. The work of art specifies neither by teaching, by illustration, by dogma, by theology, nor by the display of scientific truth, the particular mode of action or the particular direction of speculation in which the productivity it evokes will be utilized. If it is argued that men will turn naturally for aesthetic gratification to works of art which do offer precept and guidance in their own fields of endeavor, it may be replied that they may equally well act by contraries or, if not, that they run the risk of stultifying aesthetic experience before it begins.

Profoundly moving art is "freeing" art. It is "freeing" art not only in that it liberates us from the need for action defined in terms of the ends of science, morality, and religion but also in this, that it causes productive imagination to transcend the art object and enter upon new "total situations" in which the ends of action are not specified. The individual so moved presents to himself effective stimuli in ideas, objects, events, and situations other than the work of art. Aesthetic experience provides the energy for further action. But, in addition, it is a mood of courage needed to enable us to attack the new problems which present themselves in the new situation. It is in consequence of these facts that art is perhaps the

once led to criticism and moral practice, are unlikely to have a fuller aesthetic experience, once they return to a work of art. Their enriched experience makes of the work of art the *locus* for a richer experience. The subtlety of the experience derives from the specific symbols of art and these are not known by predisposition but by means of scholarship, learning, and information. But however much one may bring to specific symbols of art and however rich the experience, productivity is not fulfilled in the direct relation of the percipient to the object.

most effective "energizer" of man's spirit.[17] Because imagination is "all of a piece," because it is fulfilled in "total situations," its productivity will make effective stimuli in ideas, events, objects, and situations with the "images" of which the scientist, the moralist, the theologian, and the artist, *qua* scientist, moralist, theologian, and artist, will work.

Regarding the operations of imagination's productive powers, it must be reiterated that men do not differ as men of imagination and of no imagination. The artist is, as we pointed out early in this essay, not the only imaginative creator.[18] Men differ, rather, in terms of the materials in which their individual imaginations are effectively employed. Each man is by temperament prone to work in specific ways and with specific materials. In the particular material in which a man's imagination discovers its appropriate domain and by means of the particular techniques in which he is trained, the individual will be inspired by art to expend the energy derived from the experience of art in the field of the vocation natural to him. The courage implicit in aesthetic experience will be used to encourage unremitting effort to resolve the particular problems and to overcome the particular difficulties in science, in morality, in art, and in the practical activities of life which are obstacles to the attainment of the objects of the individual's deepest desires. This is not to argue that all men are specialists, "cut off from one another as if by an axe." Art will inspire the great man, the Leonardo, the Michelangelo, the Aristotle, as well as the "Jack-of-all-trades" to display his powers in many fields and it will likewise inspire all men to effort in various activities. Art "creates the creator." This is its end. It inspires the creator by the recall of past triumphs to continue in the task presented endlessly to him.

The artist, no less than other men, derives from the experience of fine art the inspiration for his own making of profoundly moving art. His "making" is a τέχνη no less difficult to master and one demanding no less skill than that of the mathematician or of the scientific theologian. The artist's productive imagination naturally

[17] Cf. above, Chap. VII.
[18] Cf. above, pp. 6-7.

makes effective stimuli in materials. Particular skills are required to satisfy the material's requirements. Nonetheless, productive imagination follows its pattern of creativity in artistic employment as it does in entering upon man's non-aesthetic activities. It functions to present alternative "images" in the "total situation," to reveal the potentialities of symbol and material. It makes manifest alternative modes for "making" in the new situation into which it is projected.

It is at this stage that imagination is truly creative and it is because of this creativity that art is not properly characterized merely by the familiar and the generic. The Chaucer who inherits the tale of Troilus and Cressida from Boccaccio discovers in that symbol of love new and unique possibilities for psychological analysis of human character under stress. The sculptors of the Nike Temple parapet work in a tradition with precise symbols and an inherited technique. Yet the individual artists have left figures that vary to the degree that one sculptor's work is rigid and lifeless, one creative and alive. All excellent makers discover alternative modes for making in the material of their art, some to the degree that at times makes it appear possible for them to ignore the requirements of stone or sound or word itself. Yet, on analysis, each work is evidence of the truth that Yellin, an able fashioner of metal, once expressed: "No work is good unless the material is used in the way it should be, and the designs made to suit the material." The art of a master converts restrictions laid upon lesser artists into paths to freedom within the law of the material. Theirs is the power of a productive imagination to discover new and alternative ways of actualizing unrealized potentialities in symbol and material.

The master craftsman often appears to develop a "second nature," an understanding of his craft and materials. It is because of this that art achieves its proper freedom. Rigid rules laid down for art by artist or critic cannot withstand the productivity of artistic feeling. Thus, Lessing lays down the rule that the ugly is destructive of beauty in the spatial art of sculpture. Rodin demonstrates in the most direct way possible that even a sculptured figure with gaping mouth may be portrayed effectively if only the appearance of life and movement is made explicit in a material capable of displaying them. Realism lays down rules for painting which, if followed, would make of it *mimesis*. Impressionism discovers potentialities in technique and material which shatter the rule. The fact appears to be, indeed, that material presents almost infinite possibilities for technical expression. The limitations it imposes upon the artist are limitations which restrict caprice and the vagaries of a fancy that would fain find freedom only by ignoring all rules derived from material's potentialities. Great an artist as is Shakespeare, even his craft encounters the obstacle that the human material for dramatic action does not easily encompass the paragon of virtue. The poet's failure to recognize in this instance that the potentialities for dramatic action are limited destroys *Measure for Measure* as a tragedy. Working within the limitations of material, Shakespeare in *Hamlet* and in *Othello* is again the master.

It is small wonder, in view of the impact of individual creativity in the production of forms for artistic material, in the interpretation of generic symbols, and in the advances in the techniques of crafts, that historians of art and artists themselves have sought for the sources of profound art in art itself. It is intelligible to argue that the products of a truly creative imagination frequently give rise to imitation, copying, and schools. The artist of great stature makes evident certain "lines" to be followed in working out the potentialities of materials, in the employment of new media, in coping with the problem of form as the unification of hitherto dissociated ideas or events, and in the developments and uses of technique. Indeed, so strong is the influence of tradition that a once-established "form" is not infrequently used to unify or express content bearing little resemblance to that which the form was originally intended to express.[19]

There are, however, limitations upon the self-nourishment of art. Form, as Rebecca West has written, is not "a decorative adjustment" but, rather, "a cup in which life can be poured and lifted to the lips and be tasted." The initial inspiration departs from schools as the power of generic symbols of feeling to move us comes to be stultified by custom, repetition, and usage. The deft technique

[19] Cf. E. Panofsky, *Studies in Iconology*, e.g., pp. 121 ff.

comes to be detached from the living symbol it was primarily intended to express and may become mere "skill for skill's sake." But art does not live wholly upon itself. Seminal influences are needed to restore vigor to artistic production and to revive aesthetic interest, seminal influences which derive from the non-aesthetic symbols of feeling, from science, morality, and religion, to the "images" of which feeling has attached. Art receives willingly, because feeling attaches easily to the "images" "squeezed out" by science. Art cherishes that to which the "life of reason" no longer pertains.

Men retain in the faith sustained by deep feeling the familiar vestiges of old science, old theology, old social usage, and old morality and customs. The artist, as we have observed, uses these, the "referrents," for the generic symbols of art. Not all events or objects of the kind become symbols for art, although so powerful is man's creative imagination that it would be impossible to predict that any specific vestigial form of an ancient science could not at some time be given individual and moving interpretation in symbolic form and so effect aesthetic experience. There is no more abstruse theology than that of St. Thomas. But, understood and familiarized in the stories of martyrs and saints, it evokes feeling and enters the artistic symbolism of Dante and the Renaissance.

"Art creates the creator." It supplies him with the energy, the courage, and the inspiration to direct the productivity which its profound symbols evoke for use in man's endless task of controlling himself and nature. The sciences by which he controls nature, himself, and society enrich the art that in turn makes possible the continued efforts of the scientist, moralist, and theologian. Truly profoundly moving art is rare but there are many intimations of its power in art that approximates to the ideal. Perhaps one should say of works of art with power to evoke genuine aesthetic experience that they, like "all noble things are difficult as they are rare." Infrequently as they may be made, the nobility of the experience they do evoke is beyond doubt. The aesthetic mood does bespeak the truth spoken by the ancient poet: "Many a wonder lives and moves, but the wonder of all is man." Aesthetic experience can occur because of the wonders that man and his ancestors have wrought. "With patient furrows," man "wears and wears away . . . Earth, supreme of mighty gods, eldest, imperishable." In consequence of these, his efforts, he may enjoy in profoundly moving art the symbols of his achievements.

Conclusion

Chapter XIX

The Tragic and the Comic

Before the vision of a new time can shape itself in the intellect, the sense of repulsion that had all along been upon us takes on an assurance of constancy: whithersoever we tend, we know we can never turn back. *This I call the tragic moment. That it is not without sadness, is true; that it is all made of sadness, is not. Whatever* fœtidi et horribilis *there may be in the end of the tragic* story *(regarded as an integral thing), such words have no last say in telling of the tragic* mood. *For only when the tragic moment is inspired of* beauty *have we the tragic mood.*

—EDGAR A. SINGER, JR.[1]

THE main purpose of this essay has been to consider the nature and significance of aesthetic experience. From the beginning, however, it has been evident that philosophy of art is no more successful in isolating aesthetic experience from the "total structure" of art than in abstracting "aesthetic surface" or "beautiful forms" from the contexts in which alone they are meaningful. Consequently, it has been essential to our purpose to write of the end of fine art and, as well, of the symbols of art.

It has been assumed throughout that fine art is implicated in feeling and, in fact, that one of the criteria for the evaluation of any aesthetic symbol is that it moves us profoundly. It has been urged that aesthetic experience proffers energy and inspiration for creativity. We have argued that the antinomic aspects of fine art and

[1] Edgar A. Singer, Jr., *On the Contented Life*. (By permission of Henry Holt and Company, publishers.)

of aesthetic experience derive from the generic and specific symbols of art and from the reproductive and productive aspects of feeling.

To be profoundly moved, it was observed, effects a disequilibrium. To be profoundly moved by fine art effects disequilibrium and a restoration of equilibrium at a higher level. We are so restored in aesthetic experience, but not wholly so in reproducing the artist's creativity in the work of art. Rather, we are restored in the mood that fulfills its own creativity in a new "total situation."

Professor Singer observes in his essay on "Esthetic and the Rational Ideal" that the man moved by fine art is "moved out of himself." One so moved is "changed as to one's purpose; it is to enter on a world in which things are revalued." It is in the process of such revaluation that equilibrium is restored. The presuppositions of revaluation are manifold. Among those that condition aesthetic experience, not the least significant is discontent with the past expressed in the artist's generic symbols and with the ineffectuality of feeling as an instrument for the control of nature.

In an essay written not alone to analyze aesthetic experience but to make evident its presuppositions, and, in consequence, one in which emphases are placed upon generic rather than specific symbols in art, there is a natural tendency to relate the aesthetic mood to the "ideal," to the "limiting conception" of fine art. In actual, as contrasted to ideal, aesthetic experience, the discontent evoked by the work of art may derive from varied sources. Sound criticism of specific works of art not infrequently shows that the artist lacks technical skill; that he has failed to exclude symbols, ornaments, meanings, or facile techniques that remain external to the unity of the art object; that his work is insincere or that it is a display of mere virtuosity; that there is evidence of insensibility, lack of profound insight, or indelicacy of feeling; that the artist has subordinated his art to the achievement of a non-aesthetic end; that he is unable to make a coherent whole of the ingredients in the completed work of art; that he has produced only an obvious imitation of a form or symbol incompletely comprehended. One might continue almost *ad infinitum*, recognizing in each instance a sound reason for dissatisfaction.

Yet, however serious may be the defect that obscures what may well be aesthetic qualities in the object and so obstructs aesthetic experience, the systematic causes for discontent in the aesthetic mood are due rather to the nature of the aesthetic problem than to specific imperfections in the work of art. It is of such a systematic problem that Professor Singer writes:

> If in the movement of the artist's art the sense of direction takes a homeward turning—the moment is comic; or rather its mood is so, when art exalts the exile's sense of returning and warms the lover's glow of reconciliation. But if the artist's impulsion, though not toward any new world, has so turned from the old as to let form in the heart a vague "irrevocable," then the way is open to tragedy. . . . When, then, art has brought us to the moment we have called *the tragic*, the moment when a movement out of the old self and its time-out-of-joint has "set" in the sense of never-returning, then if the mood is heroic, its energy creative, I call the work of art *beautiful*.[2]

If, then, in the aesthetic recreation of the artist's productivity, following in the art object an imagination that has been at work individuating the generic symbol of feeling, it is discovered that the values have been obliterated and destroyed, equilibrium cannot be restored by a reversion to the past symbolized in the work of art. This is the precondition of tragic art. In the realm of the comic, however, it is notable that, start where they will, analyses of laughter, of wit, of satire, humor, and the like, constantly conclude that the artist is intent upon man's idiosyncrasies, upon his peculiarities, quirks, and eccentricities—in most cases upon aberrations from a social or cultural standard.[3] The field of the comic has been a battleground for speculation precisely because the comic merges with the corrective. Nor is the reason for this far to seek. However severe the strictures laid by the comic artist upon the ideas, situations, objects, events, or characters he symbolizes, the comic as a form of art permits no complete destruction of the values inherent in the symbol or in its "referrent." There is always in the art

[2] Edgar A. Singer, Jr., "Esthetic and the Rational Ideal," *On the Contented Life*, pp. 51-53. (By permission of Henry Holt and Company, publishers.)

[3] Cf. Bergson, Plato, Gregory, Freud, and Meredith.

actuated by the comic spirit an offer of possible return to the same level of evaluation as that with which the artist began or, indeed, a reversion to a lower level. Ben Jonson and Molière, Brueghel and Hogarth, are masters in art that rids symbols of inflated egos, exaggerations, and aberrations. This they do by a breath of the comic spirit. The old values are shaken but reaffirmed. There is disequilibrium but there is equilibrium restored. It is not strange that society which necessarily maintains itself by the conservatism of its institutions has discovered in laughter and in comedy powerful weapons in its armory against the eccentricity which may threaten the accepted norm and, consequently, society's continuation in an accustomed mode.

The comic most nearly inspires the artist to produce profoundly moving art in the comedy of manners and in those similar *genres* which evoke the smile and not the "carcajada" of the Spaniard. George Meredith's essay upon the comic spirit is brilliant precisely because its author knew that the truth lay in this direction. Yet a great artist may escape such restrictions and extricate his art from the toils. Burlesque and parody do, in consequence, sometimes excel the comic intent of an inferior workman.

It is true, also, as Singer implies, that much that is significant in the terms tragic and comic has been overlooked by evaluating a work of art as if it were integral in respect of one or the other: "unmixed laughter and unmixed sweetness are offered us less commonly than we may suppose." Yet, there is a comic spirit. I should suggest that its genesis is to be traced to the same evolution of man from the brute that is the presupposition of the making and experience of profoundly moving tragic art. For, granted that there are distinctions and discriminations to be made between tragic art and comic art, both have this in common, that they arouse the feelings and that in their experience there is productivity, reflection, and diminution of overt behavior. It is true that the tragic mood is the mood of courage, that in it man's recollection of past triumphs is integral. It is no less true that the comic mood reminds us that the course of man's evolution to manhood and of his development into a social entity does not constitute a chronicle of unbroken progress. Man has suffered defeats and his progressive development has been purchased at the price of retrogression and reversion. The comic spirit seizes upon defeat, obstacle, and reversion. Its masters do this, not to depress our spirits but rather to re-establish and ground more firmly the primarily communal and social values by which the continuity of race and culture were and are maintained in the face of adversity and defeat.

This is, in turn, however, but one manifestation of the forces emerging in comedy and in the comic. The re-establishment of the old values by a society forced to use the weapons of satire implies only that changes and reforms in the social structure occur more slowly and are more difficult to effect than are those which mark the progress of science. Man is reminded, by the comic, that he is not all-conquering, that he is not omniscient, that he is not master of the universe with forward path unimpeded. Courage and fortitude are essential for the constant struggle but they do not always avail against the obstacles in the way. Man is reminded, constantly, that in the last resource, in the crisis, there remains the "wisdom of the body" which effects emergency action.

Man is, as John Palmer suggests, "an angel in the body of a beast."[4] The comic spirit levels man's too pretentious assumptions of omnipotence and omniscience. Humanity's progress from the life of the brute is subject for a sublime chronicle, "As year by year the ploughshares turn and turn." The Chorus of *Antigone* recounts in magnificent phrase man's conquests of sea, of air, and of earth. We hear of "Wise utterance and wind-swept thought and civil, social ways." But man has nonetheless not divested himself of all traces of his brute ancestry. In the comic, as in the tragic, awareness of that ancestry makes art possible. The tragic and the comic alike reflect man's sublimity, the first because it is a sign of his heroism, the second because, although the gall of defeat may be bitter upon his lips, the aesthetic mood permits him to smile at his everpresent plight, man being "an angel in the body of a beast." This, too, is

[4] John L. Palmer, *Comedy*, p. 26. (This quotation from Mr. Palmer's book and those which follow are used by permission of Martin Secker, Limited, publishers.)

heroism but, as Palmer knows, "not till we have left an appreciable gap between ourselves and our prognathous ancestors did we fall beneath the comic eye."

The comic character is, at times, laughed *at*, but he is more significantly smiled *upon*. We know him to be ourselves—and of those selves, it has been truly said:

> We laugh away the grossness of the flesh. We are creatures of divine intelligence and immortal souls; we reach at beauty; we push spiritually towards heaven; we grasp infinity and measure the suns of space; but still we are clay that must be voided and fed; that stumbles in the dirt and grows fat. Gargantuan laughter is man's answer to the fate which imprisoned him in blood and bone, submitting the expression of his finest emotions to hazards of the body.[5]

What emerges in aesthetic experience may be either a tragic or a comic revelation. The mood partakes somewhat of both. Whether it is dominantly tragic or pre-eminently comic, profoundly moving art speaks primarily of sublimity. There is exaltation in the experience of all art that moves men profoundly and gives them courage to face a world always to some degree and, at times, brutally inimical to their desires. In the recognition of this, I should suggest, Nietzsche brought to a close *The Birth of Tragedy*. His words, likewise, may well conclude this essay:

> In walking under high Ionic colonnades, looking upwards to a horizon defined by clear and noble lines, with reflections of his transfigured form by his side in shining marble, and around him solemnly marching or quietly moving men, with harmoniously sounding voices and rhythmical pantomime, would he not in the presence of this perpetual influx of beauty have to raise his hand to Apollo and exclaim: "Blessed race of Hellenes! How great Dionysus must be among you, when the Delian god deems such charms necessary to cure you of your dithyrambic madness! . . ." To one in this frame of mind, however, an aged Athenian, looking up to him with the sublime eye of Æschylus, might answer: "Say also this, thou curious stranger: what sufferings this people must have undergone, in order to be able to become thus beautiful! But now follow me to a tragic play, and sacrifice with me in the temple of both the deities!"

[5] *Ibid.*, p. 27.

Bibliography

BIBLIOGRAPHY

The list of books and articles which follows is intended to provide bibliographical information concerning publications quoted or cited in the text and to indicate material for additional reading, more particularly in aspects of the subject for which the general bibliographies in aesthetic are not wholly adequate. For readers especially interested in the literature of the fine arts, William A. Hammond, *A Bibliography of Aesthetics and of the Philosophy of the Fine Arts* (Longmans, Green & Company, 1934) and the bibliography in David M. Robb and J. J. Garrison, *Art in the Western World* (Harper & Brothers, 1942) are recommended.

Abell, W., *Representation and Form.* New York, Charles Scribner's Sons, 1936.

Abercrombie, L., *The Theory of Poetry*. London, Martin Secker, 1924.

Adrian, E. D., *The Basis of Sensation.* New York, W. W. Norton & Company, Inc., 1928.

Aeschylus, *The Oresteia*, translated by Gilbert Murray. London, George Allen & Unwin, 1928.

Aeschylus, *Tragœdiæ*, edited by G. Hermannus. Berlin, Weidmann, 1859.

Alexander, S., *Art and Instinct*. Oxford, The Clarendon Press, 1927.

Alexander, S., *Beauty and Other Forms of Value*. London, Macmillan and Co., 1933.

Alison, A., *Essays on the Nature and Principles of Taste*. Edinburgh, A. Constable, 1825.

Allen, Grant, *Physiological Aesthetics.* New York, D. Appleton & Company, 1877.

Allport, F. H., *Social Psychology*. Boston, Houghton Mifflin Company, 1924.

Amsden, C., *Navaho Weaving*. Santa Ana, Calif., The Fine Arts Press, 1934.

Angell, J. R., *Psychology*. New York, Henry Holt & Company, Inc., 1906.

Aristotle, *Aristotelis Opera*, edited by I. Bekker. Berlin, Academia Regia Borussica, 1831-1870.

Aristotle, *De Anima*, translated by R. D. Hicks. Cambridge, Cambridge University Press, 1907.

Aristotle, *The Works of Aristotle Translated into English*, edited by J. A. Smith and W. D. Ross. Oxford, The Clarendon Press, 1908-1931.

Arréat, L., *Mémoire et Imagination*. Paris, F. Alcan, 1895.

Augustine, Saint, *A Select Library of the Nicene and Post-Nicene Fathers of the Christian Church*, edited by P. Schaff. New York, The Christian Literature Co., 1886-1890.

Augustine, Saint, *De Ordine*, translated by R. P. Russell, O. D. New York, Cosmopolitan Science and Art Service Co., 1942. (*See also* Russell, R. P.)

Augustine, Saint, *Opera Omnia*, edited by J. P. Migne. Paris, Garnier Fratres, 1841-1877.

Barr, A. H., Jr. (ed), *Cubism and Abstract Art*. New York, Museum of Modern Art, 1936.

Baessler, A., *Ancient Peruvian Art*. Berlin, A. Ascher and Co., 1902-1903.

Basch, V., *Essai Critique sur l'Esthétique de Kant*. Paris, J. Vrin, 1927.

Baumgarten, A. G., *Aesthetica*. Bari, J. Laterza and Sons, 1936.

Bell, C., *Art*. London, Chatto and Windus, 1914.

Bell, C., "Negro Sculpture," *Arts and Decoration*, Vol. 13, 1920.

Berenson, B., *The Central Italian Painters of the Renaissance*. New York, G. P. Putnam's Sons, 1909.

Bergson, H., *L'Évolution Créatrice*. Paris, F. Alcan, 1907.

Bergson, H., *Matière et Mémoire*. Paris, F. Alcan, 1908.

Bergson, H., *Matter and Memory*, translated by N. M. Paul and W. S. Palmer. New York, The Macmillan Company, 1912.

Bergson, H., *Le Rire, Essai sur la Signification du Comique*. Paris, F. Alcan, 1931.

Bergson, H., *Les Deux Sources de la Morale et de la Religion*. Paris, F. Alcan, 1932.

Bergson, H., *The Two Sources of Morality and Religion*, translated by R. A. Audra, C. Brereton, and W. H. Carter. New York, Henry Holt & Company, Inc., 1935.

Bernays, J., *Zwei Abhandlungen über die Aristotelische Theorie des Drama*. Berlin, W. Hertz, 1880.

Berthaud, A., *St. Augustini doctrina de pulchro ingenuisque artibus ex variis illius operibus excerpta*. Poitiers, Académie de Besançon, 1894.

Birkhoff, G. D., *Aesthetic Measure*. Cambridge, Harvard University Press, 1933.

Blanc, C., *Grammaire des Arts du Dessin, Architecture, Sculpture, Peinture, etc.* Paris, V. J. Renouard, 1867, 1870.

Blümel, Carl, *Griechische Bildhauerarbeit*. Berlin, Verlag für Kunstwissenschaft, 1927.

Boas, F., "The Decorative Art of the Indians of the North Pacific Coast," *Bulletin of American Museum of Natural History*, Vol. 9, 1897.

Boas, F., "Decorative Designs of Alaskan Needlecases," *Proceedings, U. S. National Museum*, 1906.

Boas, F., *Primitive Art*. Cambridge, Harvard University Press, 1927.

Bosanquet, B., "Croce's Aesthetic," *Proceedings of the British Academy*, Vol. 9. London, H. Milford, Oxford University Press, 1914.

Bosanquet, B., *Three Lectures on Aesthetic*. London, Macmillan and Co., 1923.

Bosanquet, B., *A History of Aesthetic*. London, G. Allen and Unwin, 1934.

Bradley, A. C., *Oxford Lectures on Poetry*. London, Macmillan and Co., 1926.

Bragg, Sir William, *The Universe of Light*. New York, The Macmillan Company, 1927.

Breasted, J. H., *A History of Egypt*. New York, Charles Scribner's Sons, 1912.

Bréhier, E., *La Philosophie de Plotin*. Paris, Boivin et Cie., 1928.

Bridges, R., "On English Homophones," *S.P.E. Tract No. 2*. Oxford, The Clarendon Press, 1919.

Broad, C. D., *Five Types of Ethical Theory*. New York, Harcourt, Brace & Company, Inc., 1930.

Brown, G. Baldwin, *The Fine Arts*. New York, Charles Scribner's Sons, 1891.

Browne, Sir Thomas, *The Works of Sir Thomas Browne*, edited by G. Keynes. London, Faber and Gwyer, 1928-1931.

Bullough, E., "Psychical Distance as a Factor in Art and an Aesthetic Principle," *British Journal of Psychology*, Vol. 5, 1912-1913.

Bunzel, R., *The Pueblo Potter*. New York, Columbia University Press, 1929.

Burke, Edmund, *A Philosophical Enquiry into the Origin of Our Ideas on the Sublime and Beautiful*. London, J. Dodsley, 1770.

Burnet, J., *Early Greek Philosophy*. London, A. and C. Black, 1920.

Burnet, J., *Greek Philosophy: Thales to Plato*. London, Macmillan and Co., 1932.

Butcher, S. H., *Aristotle's Theory of Poetry and Fine Art*. London, Macmillan and Company., 1932.

Buytendijk, F. J. J., *El Juego y su Significado*. Madrid, Revista de Occidente, 1935.

Bywater, I., *Aristotle on the Art of Poetry*. Oxford, The Clarendon Press, 1909.

Callahan, J. L., *A Theory of Aesthetic According to the Principles of St. Thomas Aquinas*. Washington, Catholic University of America, 1927.

Cannon, W. B., "The James-Lange Theory of Emotions: A Critical Examination and an Alternative Theory," *American Journal of Psychology*, Vol. 39, 1927.

Cannon, W. B., "Neural Organization for Emotional Expression," *Feelings and Emotions, The Wittenberg Symposium*. Worcester, Clark University Press, 1928.

Cannon, W. B., *Bodily Changes in Pain, Hunger, Fear and Rage*. New York, D. Appleton-Century Company, Inc., 1929.

Cannon, W. B., "Again the James-Lange and the Thalamic Theories of Emotion," *Psychological Review*, Vol. 38, No. 4, 1931.

Carpenter, R., "Dynamic Symmetry: A Criticism," *American Journal of Archaeology*, Series 2, Vol. 25, 1921.

Carpenter, R., *The Esthetic Basis of Greek Art of the 5th and 4th Centuries B. C.* Bryn Mawr, Bryn Mawr College, 1921.

Carpenter, R., *The Sculpture of the Nike Temple Parapet*. Cambridge, Harvard University Press, 1929.

Carpenter, R., "The Spirit of Classic Art," *Historical Aspects of the Fine Arts*. Oberlin, Oberlin College, 1938.

Carpenter, R., "The Basis of Artistic Creation in the Fine Arts," *The Bases of Artistic Creation*. New Brunswick, Rutgers University Press, 1942.

Carriere, M., *Aesthetik*. Leipzig, F. A. Brockhaus, 1859.

Carritt, E. F., *The Theory of Beauty*. London, Methuen and Co., 1923.

Carritt, E. F., *Philosophies of Beauty*. New York, Oxford University Press, 1931.

Casson, S., *XXth Century Sculptors*. London, H. Milford, Oxford University Press, 1930.

Casson, S., *The Technique of Early Greek Sculpture*. Oxford, The Clarendon Press, 1933.

Cellini, Benvenuto, *The Life of Benvenuto Cellini*. New York, Charles Scribner's Sons, 1903.

Chapman, I., *St. Augustine's Philosophy of Beauty*. New York, Sheed & Ward, Inc., 1939.

Cheney, S., *A Primer of Modern Art*. New York, Tudor Publishing Company, 1924.

Cicero, M. Tullius, *Ad M. Brutum*, edited by H. Sjogren. Upsala, 1910.

Clouzot, H. and Level, A., *L'Art Nègre et l'Art Oceanien.* Paris, Devambez, 1919.

Cochez, M., "L'Esthétique de Plotin," *Revue Néo-Scolastique,* Vol. 20, 21, 1913-1914.

Cohen, H., *Ästhetik des Reinen Gefühls.* Berlin, B. Cassirer, 1912.

Cohn, J., *Allgemeine Ästhetik.* Leipzig, W. Engelmann, 1901.

Coleridge, S. T., *The Poetical Works of Samuel Taylor Coleridge,* edited by J. D. Campbell. London, Macmillan and Co., 1903.

Collingwood, R. G., *Outline of a Philosophy of Art.* Oxford, The Clarendon Press, 1925.

Collingwood, R. G., *The Principles of Art.* Oxford, The Clarendon Press, 1938.

Collins, H. B., "Prehistoric Art of the Alaskan Eskimo," *Smithsonian Institution Report.* Washington, 1929.

Combarieu, J., *Histoire de la Musique.* Paris, A. Colin, 1920.

Conway, W. M., *The Literary Remains of Albrecht Dürer.* Cambridge, Cambridge University Press, 1889.

Cornford, F. M., *The Origin of Attic Comedy.* London, E. Arnold, 1914.

Cornford, F. M., *Plato's Cosmology.* New York, Harcourt, Brace & Company, Inc., 1937.

Croce, B., *Estetica come Scienza dell' Espressione e Linguistica Generale.* Bari, G. Laterza e Figli, 1908.

Croce, B., *Breviario di Estetica.* Bari, Laterza e Figli, 1913.

Croce, B., *The Essence of Aesthetic,* translated by Douglas Ainslie. London, W. Heinemann, 1921.

Croce, B., *Aesthetic,* translated by Douglas Ainslie. London, Macmillan and Co., 1929.

Culin, S., "Negro Art," *Brooklyn Museum Quarterly,* Vol. 10, 1923.

Cushing, F. H., "A Study of Pueblo Pottery as Illustrative of Zuñi Culture Growth," *Fourth Annual Report, Bureau of Ethnology.* Washington, D. C., 1886.

Dabney, J. P., The Musical Basis of Verse. New York, Longmans, Green & Company, 1901.

Dali, Salvador, *Paintings, Drawings, Prints: Salvador Dali,* edited by James Thrall Soby. New York, Museum of Modern Art, 1941.

Dante Alighieri, *The Divine Comedy,* translated by H. F. Cary. New York, Willey Book Co., 1901.

Daremberg, C. V., Saglio, E., and Pottier, E., *Dictionnaire des Antiquités Grecques et Romaines.* Paris, Hachette, 1881-1919.

Darwin, Charles, *The Expression of the Emotions in Man and Animals.* New York, D. Appleton & Company, 1873.

De Laguna, F., "A Comparison of Eskimo and Palaeolithic Art," *American Journal of Archaeology*, Vols. 26-27, 1932-1933.

De Laguna, T., "Notes on the Theory of Ideas," *Philosophical Review*, Vol. 43, No. 5, 1934.

De Quincey, T., *The Collected Works of Thomas De Quincey*, edited by D. Masson. Edinburgh, A. and C. Black, 1889-1897.

Descartes, R., *The Method, Meditations . . . Principles of Descartes*, edited by John Veitch. London, W. Blackwood and Sons, 1925.

Dessoir, M., *Ästhetik und Allgemeine Kunstwissenschaft*. Stuttgart, F. Enke, 1906.

Dessoir, M., "Aesthetics and the Philosophy of Art in Contemporary Germany," *The Monist*, Vol. 36, 1926.

Dewey, J., "The Theory of Emotions," *Psychological Review*, Vol. 1, No. 6, Vol. 2, No. 1, 1894-1895.

De Wulf, M., "Les Theories Esthétiques propres à S. Thomas," *Revue Néo-Scolastique*, Vol. 2, 1895-1896.

De Wulf, M., *Études Historiques sur l'Esthétique de S. Thomas*. Louvain, Institut Supérieur de Philosophie, 1896.

De Wulf, M., *L'Oeuvre d'Art et la Beauté*. Paris, F. Alcan, 1920.

De Wulf, M., *History of Mediaeval Philosophy*. London, Longmans, Green and Co., 1926.

Diels, H., *Die Fragmente der Vorsokratiker*. Berlin, Wiedmann, 1906-1910.

Dionysius Areopagita, *Opera Omnia, edited by B. Corderius* [in *Patrologiæ Cursus Completus . . . Græca,* edited by J. P. Migne]. Paris, 1857-1884.

Dionysius Areopagita, *The Works of Dionysius the Areopagite*, translated by The Reverend John Parker. London, J. Parker and Co., 1897.

Douglas, F. H., "Apache Basketry," *Publications, Denver Art Museum*, 1934.

Douglas, F. H., "Basketry Construction Technics," *Publications*, Denver Art Museum, 1935.

Dryden, John, *Essays of John Dryden*, edited by W. P. Ker. Oxford, The Clarendon Press, 1900.

Dumas, G., *Traité de Psychologie*. Paris, F. Alcan, 1923-1924.

Dunham, B., *A Study in Kant's Aesthetics*. Lancaster, Science Press, 1934.

Dürer, A., *The Literary Remains of Albrecht Dürer*, translated by W. H. Conway. Cambridge, Cambridge University Press, 1889.

Egan, R. F., "The Genesis of the Theory of 'Art for Art's Sake'

in Germany and England," *Smith College Studies in Modern Languages*, Vol. 2, Nos. 4-5, 1924.
Einstein, C., *Negerplastik*. Munich, K. Wolff, 1920.
Einstein, C., *Afrikanische Plastik*. Berlin, E. Wasmuth, 1921.
Eliot, T. S., *The Use of Poetry and the Use of Criticism*. Cambridge, Harvard University Press, 1933.
Emerson, R. W., "Courage," *Society and Solitude*. Boston, Houghton Mifflin Company, 1883.
Emmons, Lieut. G., "The Basketry of the Tlingit," *Memoirs, American Museum of Natural History*, Vol. 3, Pt. 2, 1903.
Eschweiler, K., *Die Ästhetischen Elemente in der Religionsphilosophie d. hl. Augustin*. Munich, Euskirchener Volkszeitung, 1909.
Euripides, *Elektra*, *Medea*, and *Trojan Women*, translated by Gilbert Murray. New York, Oxford University Press, 1907.
Euripides, *Euripides, the Athenian Drama*, translated by Gilbert Murray. New York, Longmans, Green & Company, n.d.
Euripides, *Tragœdiæ*, edited by G. Hermannus. Leipzig, Weidmann, 1837-1841.
Evans, V. Burdwood, "A Scholastic Theory of Art," *Philosophy*, Vol. 8, No. 29, 1933.
Fechner, G. T., *Vorschule der Ästhetik*. Leipzig, Breitkopf und Härtel, 1876.
Fewkes, J. W., "Ancient Zuñi Pottery," *Putnam Anniversary Volume*, New York, 1909.
Ferguson, A. S., "Plato and the Poet's ΕΙΔΩΛΑ," *Philosophical Essays Presented to John Watson*. Kingston, Queen's University, 1922.
Firth, R. W., "The Maori Carver," *Journal of the Polynesian Society*, Vol. 34, 1925.
Flaccus, L. W., *The Spirit and Substance of Art*. New York, F. S. Crofts & Co., 1941.
Fleure, H. J., and Peake, H., *Hunters and Artists*. Oxford, The Clarendon Press, 1927.
Foat, F. W. G., "Anthropometry of Greek Statues," *Journal of Hellenic Studies*, Vol. 35, 1915.
Frazer, Sir George B., *The Golden Bough*. London, Macmillan and Co., 1911-1915.
Freud, S., *Wit and Its Relation to the Unconscious*. New York, Moffat, Yard, and Co., 1916.
Freud, S., *Totem and Taboo*. New York, Moffat, Yard, and Co., 1918.
Frobenius, L., "Die bildende Kunst der Afrikanen," *Mitteilungen der Anth. Gesellschaft*. Vienna, A. Hölder, 1897-1898.

Frobenius, L., *Die Masken und Geheimbunde Afrikas*. Halle, A. Graesel, 1898.

Galen, C., *De Placitis Hippocratis et Platonis*, edited by I. Müller. Leipzig, G. Teubner, 1874.

Gauguin, P., *Noa Noa*. Paris, Crès, 1924.

Ghyka, M. C., *Esthétique des Proportions dans la Nature et dans les Arts*. Paris, Gallimard, 1927.

Gilbert, K. E., *Studies in Recent Aesthetic*. Chapel Hill, University of North Carolina Press, 1927.

Gilbert, K. E., and Kuhn, H., *A History of Esthetics*. New York, The Macmillan Company, 1939.

Gill, Eric, *Art Nonsense*. London, Cassell and Co., 1929.

Gilson, E. H., *The Philosophy of St. Thomas Aquinas*. Cambridge, W. Heffer and Sons, 1929.

Gollancz, I., *The Sources of Hamlet*. London, H. Milford, Oxford University Press, 1926.

Gomperz, T., *Greek Thinkers*, translated by L. Magnus. London, John Murray, 1920.

Goodenough, E. R., *By Light, Light*. New Haven, Yale University Press, 1935.

Goodenough, E. R., *Religious Tradition and Myth*. New Haven, Yale University Press, 1937.

Gordon, G. B., "Conventionalism and Realism in Maya Art at Copan," *Putnam Anniversary Volume*. New York, 1909.

Gordon, K., *Esthetics*. New York, Henry Holt & Co., Inc., 1909.

Green, W. C., "Plato's View of Poetry," *Harvard Studies*, Vol. 1, 1918.

Gregory, J. C., *The Nature of Laughter*. New York, Harcourt, Brace & Company, Inc., 1924.

Griggs, E. H., *The Philosophy of Art*. New York, B. W. Huebsch, 1913.

Groos, K., *The Play of Animals*, translated by E. L. Baldwin. New York, D. Appleton & Company, 1897.

Groos, K., *The Play of Man*, translated by E. L. Baldwin. New York, D. Appleton & Company, 1901.

Grosse, E., *The Beginnings of Art*. New York, D. Appleton & Company, 1897.

Guillaume, E., "Doryphore," *Monuments de l'Art Antique*, edited by O. Rayet. Paris, A. Quantin, 1884.

Guillaume, E., *Études de l'Art Antique et Moderne*. Paris, A. Quantin, 1888.

Guillaume, P., and Munro, T., *Primitive Negro Sculpture*. New York, Harcourt, Brace & Company, Inc., 1926.

Guthe, C. E., "Pueblo Pottery Making," *Papers, Phillips Academy.* New Haven, 1925.

Guyau, M. J., *Les Problèmes de l'Esthétique Contemporaine.* Paris, F. Alcan, 1884.

Haldane, E. S., *Descartes, His Life and Times.* New York, E. P. Dutton & Co., Inc., 1905.

Hall, H. U., "Notes on Some Congo and West African Wood Carvings," *The Museum Journal,* Vol. 14, 1923.

Hall, H. U., "Some Shields of the Plains of the Southwest," *The Museum Journal,* Vol. 17, 1926.

Hambidge, J., *Dynamic Symmetry.* New Haven, Yale University Press, 1920.

Hamilton, A., *The Art Workmanship of the Maori Race.* Wellington, New Zealand Institute, 1926.

Hammond, W. A., *A Bibliography of Aesthetics and of the Philosophy of the Fine Arts from 1900 to 1932.* New York, Longmans, Green & Company, 1934.

Hamsun, K., *The Growth of the Soil,* translated by W. W. Worster. New York, Alfred A. Knopf, Inc., 1921.

Hanslick, E., *Vom Musikalisch-Schönen.* Leipzig, J. A. Barth, 1896.

Hartmann, E. von, *Philosophie des Unbewussten.* Berlin, C. Duncker, 1882.

Hartmann, E. von, *Die deutsche Aesthetik seit Kant.* Leipzig, W. Friedrich, 1888.

Hartmann, E. von, *Philosophy of the Unconscious.* London, Kegan Paul, Trench, Trübner & Co., 1893.

Hazlitt, W., *Characters of Shakespeare's Plays.* Oxford, The Clarendon Press, 1924.

Heard, Gerald, *The Social Substance of Religion.* New York, Harcourt, Brace & Company, Inc., 1931.

Hegel, G. W. F., *The Introduction to Hegel's Philosophy of Fine Art,* translated by B. Bosanquet. London, Kegan Paul, Trench, Trübner & Co., 1905.

Hegel, G. W. F., *The Philosophy of Fine Art,* translated by F. P. B. Osmaston. London, G. Bell and Sons, 1920.

Hegel, G. W. F., *Sämtliche Werke.* Stuttgart, F. Frommann, 1927-1940.

Heilbrunn, L. V., *An Outline of General Physiology.* London, W. B. Saunders, 1938.

Hildebrand, A., *Das Problem der Form in der bildenden Kunst.* Strassburg, J. H. E. Heitz, 1918.

Hirn, Y., *The Origins of Art.* New York, The Macmillan Company, 1931.

Hoffman, W. J., "The Graphic Art of the Eskimos," *Annual Report, U. S. National Museum*, 1897.

Hogarth, W., *The Analysis of Beauty*. London, W. Strahan, 1772.

Holmes, W. H., "Origin and Development of Form and Ornament in Ceramic Art," *Fourth Annual Report of the Bureau of Ethnology*, Washington, 1886.

Holmes, W. H., "Study of Textile Art in its Relation to Form and Ornament," *Sixth Annual Report of the Bureau of Ethnology*. Washington, 1888.

Hooton, E. A., *Up from the Ape*. New York, The Macmillan Company, 1931.

Hopkins, Gerard Manley, *The Correspondence of Gerard Manley Hopkins and Richard Watson Dixon*. London, Oxford University Press, 1935.

Hopkins, Gerard Manley, *The Letters of Gerard Manley Hopkins to Robert Bridges*. London, Oxford University Press, 1935.

Hopkins, Gerard Manley, *The Note-Books and Papers of Gerard Manley Hopkins*. London, Oxford University Press, 1937.

Hopkins, Gerard Manley, *Further Letters of Gerard Manley Hopkins*. London, Oxford University Press, 1938.

Housman, A. E., *The Name and Nature of Poetry*. Cambridge, Cambridge University Press, 1933.

Hutcheson, F., *An Inquiry into the Original of Our Ideas of Beauty and Virtue*. London, R. Ware, 1753.

James, William, "What Is an Emotion?" *Mind*, Vol. 9, 1884.

James, William, "The Physical Basis of Emotion," *Collected Essays*. New York, Longmans, Green & Company, 1894.

James, William, *Principles of Psychology*. New York, Henry Holt & Company, Inc., 1918.

James, William, *Collected Essays and Reviews*. New York, Longmans, Green & Company, 1920.

Jenness, D., "Eskimo Art," *Geographical Review*, Vol. 12, No. 2, 1922.

Jespersen, J. O. H., *Growth and Structure of the English Language*. Oxford, B. Blackwell, 1935.

Johnson, Samuel, *The Rambler*. London, Tegg, 1826.

Jowett, B. (tr.), *The Dialogues of Plato*. Oxford, The Clarendon Press, 1892.

Jowett, B. (tr.), *Politica of Aristotle*. Oxford, The Clarendon Press, 1921.

Joyce, T. A., *Maya and Mexican Art*. London, The Studio, 1927.

Kant, I., *Kant's Kritik of Judgment*, translated by J. H. Bernard. London, Macmillan and Co., 1892.

Kant, I., *Immanuel Kants Werke*, edited by Ernst Cassirer. Berlin, Wode Gruyter and Co., 1922.

Kant, I., *Kant's Theory of Ethics*, translated by T. K. Abbott. London, Macmillan and Co., 1927.

Kant, I., *Kant's Critique of Pure Reason*, translated by N. K. Smith. London, Macmillan and Co., 1929.

Kant, I., *Kant's Lectures on Ethics*, translated by Louis Infield. London, Methuen and Co., 1930.

Kelly, I. T., "The Carver's Art of the Indians of Northwestern California," *University of California Publications in American Archaeology and Ethnology*, 1930.

Kennard, E. A., *Hopi Kachinas*. New York, J. J. Augustin, Inc., 1938.

Ker, W. P., *The Art of Poetry*. Oxford, The Clarendon Press, 1909.

Kidder, A. V., "Pottery of the Pajarito Plateau and Some Adjacent Regions in New Mexico," *Memoirs of the American Anthropological Association*, Lancaster, 1915.

Knight, W. A., *The Philosophy of the Beautiful*. London, John Murray, 1916.

Knox, I., *The Aesthetic Theories of Kant, Hegel, and Schopenhauer*. New York, Columbia University Press, 1936.

Köhler, W., *The Mentality of Apes*. New York, Harcourt, Brace & Company, Inc., 1925.

Krakowski, E., *Une Philosophie de l'Amour et de la Beauté. L'Esthétique de Plotin et son Influence*. Paris, E. de Boccard, 1929.

Lalo, C., *Introduction à l'Esthétique*. Paris, A. Colin, 1912.

Lamb, Charles, *Essays of Elia*. London, Moxon, 1853.

Lange, K., *Das Wesen der Kunst*. Berlin, G. Grote, 1901; 2nd ed., 1907.

Langfeld, H. S., *The Aesthetic Attitude*. New York, Harcourt, Brace & Company, Inc., 1920.

Lee, Vernon (Violet Paget), *Beauty and Ugliness*. London, John Lane, 1912.

Lee, Vernon (Violet Paget), *The Beautiful*. Cambridge, Cambridge University Press, 1913.

Lehmann, W., and Soering, H., *The Art of Old Peru*. London, E. Benn, 1924.

Lemaitre, G., *From Cubism to Surrealism in French Literature*. Cambridge, Harvard University Press, 1941.

Leonard, W. E., *The Fragments of Empedocles*. Chicago, The Open Court Publishing Company, 1908.

Leonardo da Vinci, *The Literary Works of Leonardo da Vinci*, edited by Jean Paul Richter. London, Oxford University Press, 1939.

Leonardo da Vinci, *The Notebooks of Leonardo da Vinci*, edited by Edward McCurdy. New York, Reynal & Hitchcock, Inc., 1938.

Lessing, G. E., *Laokoon*. Berlin, H. Blümner, 1880.

Lipps, Theodor, "Einfühlung, innere Nachahmung und Organenempfindungen," *Archiv für die Gesamte Psychologie*, Vol. 1, 1903.

Lipps, Theodor, *Ästhetik*. Leipzig and Hamburg, L. Voss, 1903-1906.

Lipps, Theodor, "Weiteres zur Einfühlung," *Archiv für die Gesamte Psychologie*, Vol. 4, 1904-1905.

Listowel, Earl of, *A Critical History of Modern Aesthetics*. London, G. Allen and Unwin, 1933.

Loeb, Jacques, *The Mechanistic Conception of Life*. Chicago, University of Chicago Press, 1912.

Longinus, C., *De Sublimitate*, ed., Otto Iahne. Bonn, Marcus, 1867.

Longinus, C., *On the Sublime*, translated by W. R. Roberts. Cambridge, Cambridge University Press, 1899.

Longinus, C., *On the Sublime*, translated by W. H. Fyfe. London, W. Heinemann (The Loeb Classical Library); Cambridge, Harvard University Press, 1927.

Lotze, R. H. *Geschichte der Ästhetik in Deutschland*. Munich, J. G. Cotta, 1868.

Lotze, R. H., *Microcosmus*, translated by E. Hamilton and E. E. C. Jones. Edinburgh, T. and T. Clark, 1887.

Lowes, J. L., *The Road to Xanadu*. Boston, Houghton Mifflin Company, 1927.

Lucretius, T., *De Rerum Natura*, translated and edited by H. A. J. Munro. Cambridge, Cambridge University Press, 1893.

McCurdy, G. G., *Human Origins*. New York, D. Appleton-Century Company, Inc., 1924.

McDougall, William, *An Introduction to Social Psychology*. Boston, J. W. Luce and Co., 1921.

McDougall, William, *An Outline of Psychology*. New York, Charles Scribner's Sons, 1923.

MacKay, Ernest, "Proportion Squares on Tomb Walls in the Theban Necropolis," *Journal of Egyptian Archaeology*, Vol. 4, 1917.

Mackenna, Stephen, *Plotinus*. London, The Medici Society, Ltd., 1917-1926.

McKeon, R. P., "Literary Criticism and the Concept of Imitation in Antiquity," *Modern Philology*, Vol. 34, 1936.

Malone, Kemp, "The Literary History of Hamlet," *Anglistische Forschungen*, Vol. 59, 1923.
Malory, Sir Thomas, *Le Morte d'Arthur*. New York, E. P. Dutton & Co., Inc., 1926.
Maritain, Jacques, "Notes sur St. Thomas et la Théorie de l'Art," *Revue des Jeunes*, No. 10, 1920.
Maritain, Jacques, *The Philosophy of Art*, translated by J. O'Connor. Ditchling, St. Dominic's Press, 1923.
Maritain, Jacques, *Art et Scolastique*. Paris, Louis Rouart et Fils, 1927.
Maritain, Jacques, *Art and Scholasticism*, translated by J. F. Scanlan. New York, Charles Scribner's Sons, 1930.
Maritain, Jacques, "Sign and Symbol," *Journal of the Warburg and Courtauld Institutes*, Vol. 1, 1937-1938.
Marshall, H. R., "Some Modern Aestheticians," *Mind*, Vol. 29, 1920.
Marshall, H. R., *Pain, Pleasure, and Aesthetics*. London, Macmillan and Co., 1894.
Mason, J. A., "Eskimo Pictorial Art," *The Museum Journal*, Vol. 18, 1927.
Mason, J. A., "A Remarkable Stone Lamp from Alaska," *The Museum Journal*, Vol. 19, 1928.
Maspero, Sir G. C. C., *Life in Ancient Egypt and Assyria*. New York, D. Appleton-Century Company, Inc., 1930.
Matthews, Washington, *Navaho Legends*. Boston, Houghton Mifflin Company, 1897.
Matthews, Washington, "Night Chant, a Navaho Ceremony," *Memoirs of the American Museum of Natural History*. New York, 1902.
Maude, Aylmer, *Tolstoy on Art*. London, Oxford University Press, n.d.
Mauron, Charles, *Aesthetics and Psychology*. London, Hogarth Press, 1935.
Mead, C. W., "Prehistoric Bronze in South America," *Anthropological Papers, American Museum of Natural History*, Vol. 12, 1915.
Mead, C. W., "Conventionalized Figures of Ancient Peruvian Art," *Bulletin, American Museum of Natural History*, Vols. 12, 15, 1916.
Mead, C. W., *Old Civilizations of Inca Land*. New York, American Museum of Natural History, 1924.
Mead, M., *The Maoris and Their Arts*. New York, American Museum of Natural History, 1928.

Megdyes, L., "The Art of the African Negro," *International Studio*, Vol. 76, 1922.

Meier-Graefe, Julius, *Modern Art*, translated by F. Simmonds. New York, G. P. Putnam's Sons, 1908.

Menéndez y Pelayo, D. M., *Historia de las Ideas Estéticas en España*. Madrid, Hernando, 1896-1912.

Mercier, Cardinal, *Métaphysique Générale, ou Ontologie* (*Cours de Philosophie*, Vol. 7). Louvain, Institut Supérieur de Philosophie, 1923.

Meredith, George, *An Essay on Comedy and the Uses of the Comic Spirit*. New York, Charles Scribner's Sons, 1923.

Millay, Edna St. Vincent, *The Harp-Weaver and Other Poems*. New York, Harper & Brothers, 1923.

Milton, John, *The Poetical Works of John Milton*, edited by H. C. Beeching. London, Oxford University Press, 1921.

Molsdorff, W., *Die Idee des Schönen in der Weltgestaltung bei Thomas von Aquino*. Jena, G. Neuenhahn, 1891.

Morgan, T. H., *A Critique of the Theory of Evolution*. Princeton, Princeton University Press, 1916.

Morris, Bertram, *The Aesthetic Process*. Evanston, Northwestern University Press, 1943.

Mössel, E., *Die Proportion in Antike und Mittelalter*. Munich, C. H. Beck, 1926-1931.

Müller, Valentin, "The Prehistory of the 'Good Shepherd,'" *Journal of Near Eastern Studies*, Vol. 3, No. 2, 1944.

Munnynck, M., "L'Esthétique de S. Thom. d'Aquino," *San Tommaso d'Aquino*. Milan, Soc. Ed. Vita e Pensiero, 1923.

Mure, G. R. G., *Aristotle*. London, E. Benn, 1932.

Murray, Gilbert, "Excursus," in *Themis*. Cambridge, Cambridge University Press, 1912.

Murray, Gilbert, *Hamlet and Orestes; A Study in Traditional Types*. New York, Oxford University Press, 1914.

Murray, Gilbert, *The Classical Tradition in Poetry*. Cambridge, Harvard University Press, 1927.

Nahm, Milton C. (ed.), *Selections from Early Greek Philosophy*. New York, F. S. Crofts & Co., 1934.

Nahm, Milton C., "The Philosophical Implications of Some Theories of Emotion," *Philosophy of Science*, Vol. 6, No. 4, 1939.

Nahm, Milton C., "The Function of Art," *Art: A Bryn Mawr Symposium*. Bryn Mawr, Bryn Mawr College, 1940.

Nahm, Milton C., "Form in Art," *Art: A Bryn Mawr Symposium*. Bryn Mawr, Bryn Mawr College, 1940.

Newman, E. B., Perkins, F. T., and Wheeler, R. H., "Cannon's

Theory of Emotion: A Critique," *Psychological Review*, Vol. 37, No. 4, 1930.

Newman, W. L., *The Politics of Aristotle*. Oxford, The Clarendon Press, 1924.

Nietzsche, F., *The Birth of Tragedy*, translated by W. A. Haussman. Edinburgh, T. N. Foulis, 1910.

Oates, W. J., and O'Neill, Eugene, Jr., *The Complete Greek Drama*. New York, Random House, Inc., 1938.

Obermaier, H., *Fossil Man in Spain*. New Haven, Yale University Press, 1924.

Ogden, R. M., *The Psychology of Art*. New York, Charles Scribner's Sons, 1938.

Orchard, W. C., "Fine Line Decoration of Ancient Southwestern Pottery," *Indian Notes, Museum of the American Indian*. New York, 1925.

Palmer, John L., *Comedy*. London, Martin Secker, 1914.

Panofsky, E., *Dürers Kunsttheorie*. Berlin, G. Reimer, 1915.

Panofsky, E., *Studies in Iconology*. New York, Oxford University Press, 1939.

Panofsky, E., *Albrecht Dürer*. Princeton, Princeton University Press, 1943.

Paredes, B., "Idéas Estéticas de Santo Tomas," *La Ciencia Tomista*. Madrid, 1911.

Parker, DeWitt H., *The Principles of Aesthetic*. New York, Silver, Burdett & Company, 1920.

Pascal, B., *Pensées*. New York, E. P. Dutton & Co., Inc., 1931.

Pater, Walter, *Studies in the History of the Renaissance*. London, Macmillan and Co., 1873.

Pater, Walter, "Style," *The Writer*, Vol. 11, No. 1, 1898.

Pater, Walter, *The Renaissance*. London, Macmillan and Co., 1919.

Paton, H. J., *Kant's Metaphysic of Experience*. London, G. Allen and Unwin, 1936.

Pavlow, I. P., *Conditioned Reflexes*. London, Oxford University Press, 1927.

Pavlow, I. P., *Lectures on Conditioned Reflexes*. New York, International Publishers Co., Inc., n.d.

Peake, H., and Fleure, H. J., *Hunters and Artists*. Oxford, The Clarendon Press, 1927.

Phillpotts, B. S., *The Elder Edda and Ancient Scandinavian Literature*. Cambridge, Cambridge University Press, 1920.

Phillpotts, B. S., *Edda and Saga*. London, T. Butterworth, 1931.

Picasso, P., "Statement by Picasso: 1935," *Picasso, Forty Years of*

His Art, edited by A. H. Barr, Jr. New York, Museum of Modern Art, 1939.

Piéron, H., "Emotion in Animals and Man," *Feelings and Emotions, The Wittenberg Symposium.* Worcester, Clark University, 1928.

Plato, *Hippias Major*, translated by H. N. Fowler (The Loeb Classical Library). London, W. Heinemann; Cambridge, Harvard University Press, 1926.

Plato, *The Hippias Major*, edited by D. Tarrant. Cambridge, Cambridge University Press, 1928.

Plato, *Opera Omnia*, edited by G. Stallbaum. Gothae, Hennings, 1857-1885.

Plato, *Philebus*, translated by H. N. Fowler (The Loeb Classical Library). London, W. Heinemann; Cambridge, Harvard University Press, 1925.

Plato, *Symposium*, translated by W. R. M. Lamb (The Loeb Classical Library). London, W. Heinemann; Cambridge, Harvard University Press, 1925.

Plato, *The Dialogues of Plato*, translated by B. Jowett. Oxford, The Clarendon Press, 1892.

Plato, *The Laws of Plato*, translated by A. E. Taylor. London, J. M. Dent and Sons, 1934.

Plato, *The Republic of Plato*, translated by J. L. Davies and D. J. Vaughan. London, Macmillan and Co., 1907.

Plato, *Timaeus and Critias*, translated by A. E. Taylor. London, Methuen and Co., 1929.

Pliny the Elder, *The Elder Pliny's Chapters on the History of Art in the Historia Naturalis*, translated by K. Jex-Blake. London, Macmillan and Co., 1896.

Plotinus, *Ennéades*, edited by E. Bréhier. Paris, University of France, 1924-1938.

Plotinus, *Plotinus*, translated by Stephen Mackenna. London, The Medici Society, Ltd., 1917-1926.

Plutarch, *Miscellanies and Essays*, translated by W. W. Godwin. Boston, Little, Brown & Company, 1898.

Pope, Arthur, "A Quantitative Theory of Aesthetic Value," *Art Studies: Mediaeval, Renaissance, and Modern*, Vol. 3, Cambridge, Harvard University Press, 1925.

Portnoy, Julius, *A Psychology of Art Creation.* Philadelphia, University of Pennsylvania, 1942.

Poussin, N., *Correspondance de Nicolas Poussin.* Paris, H. Champion, 1911.

Prall, D. W., *Aesthetic Judgment.* New York, The Thomas Y. Crowell Company, 1929.

Prall, D. W., *Aesthetic Analysis.* New York, The Thomas Y. Crowell Company, 1936.

Pratt, C. C., *The Meaning of Music.* New York, McGraw-Hill Book Company, Inc., 1931.

Puffer, E. D., *The Psychology of Beauty.* Boston, Houghton Mifflin Company, 1905.

Puttenham, George, *The Arte of English Poesie.* Cambridge, Cambridge University Press, 1936.

Rader, M., *A Modern Book of Esthetics.* New York, Henry Holt & Company, Inc., 1935.

Radin, Paul, *Primitive Religion.* New York, Viking Press, Inc., 1937.

Raleigh, Sir Walter, *Style.* London, E. Arnold, 1901.

Rapaport, David, and Weber, A. O. "Teleology and the Emotions," *Philosophy of Science*, Vol. 8, No. 1, 1941.

Read, Herbert, *Art and Society.* London, Macmillan and Co., 1937.

Reichard, G., and Newcomb, F., *Shooting Chant; Sandpaintings of the Navajo.* New York, J. J. Augustin, Inc., 1937.

Richards, I. A., *Principles of Literary Criticism.* New York, Harcourt, Brace & Company, Inc., 1924.

Richter, G. M. A., *The Sculpture and Sculptors of the Greeks.* New Haven, Yale University Press, 1930.

Ritter, Constantin, *Die Kerngedanken der platonischen Philosophie.* Munich, E. Reinhardt, 1931.

Robb, D. M., and Garrison, J. J., *Art in the Western World.* New York, Harper & Brothers, 1942.

Robertson, D. S., *A Handbook of Greek and Roman Architecture.* Cambridge, Cambridge University Press, 1929.

Robin, L., *La Théorie Platonicienne des Idées et des Nombres.* Paris, F. Alcan, 1908.

Robin, L., *Platon.* Paris, F. Alcan, 1935.

Rodin, Auguste, *L'Art*, edited by P. Gsell. Paris, B. Grasset, 1911.

Rodin, Auguste, *Art*, translated by R. Fedden. London, Hodder and Stoughton, 1912.

Russell, R. P., *Divine Providence and the Problem of Evil* (translation of St. Augustine's *De Ordine*). New York, Cosmopolitan Science & Art Service Co., 1942.

St. Exupéry, Antoine de, *Wind, Sand and Stars.* New York, Reynal & Hitchcock, Inc., 1939.

Saintsbury, G. E. B., *A History of English Prosody.* London, Macmillan and Co., 1910.

Santayana, G., *The Sense of Beauty*. New York, Charles Scribner's Sons, 1896.

Saxo Grammaticus, *The Danish History*, translated by Oliver Elton. London, Oxford University Press, 1894.

Schadow, J., *Polyclet oder von den Maassen des Menschen*. Berlin, Sachse und Comp., 1834.

Schasler, M. A. F., *Ästhetik als Philosophie des Schönen und der Kunst*. Berlin, Sachse und Comp., 1872.

Schellhas, P., "Representation of Deities of the Maya Manuscripts," *Peabody Museum Papers*. Cambridge, 1904.

Schiller, J. C. F., *The Philosophical and Aesthetic Letters and Essays of Schiller*, translated by J. Weiss. London, J. Chapman, 1845.

Schiller, J. C. F., *Sämmtliche Werke*, edited by Goedecke. Stuttgart, J, G. Cotta, 1871.

Schiller, J. C. F., *Complete Works*, edited by C. J. Hempel. Philadelphia, I. Kohler, 1881.

Schiller, J. C. F., *Letters upon the Aesthetical Education of Man*, in *Essays Aesthetical and Philosophical*. London, G. Bell and Sons, 1882.

Schoen, Max, *Art and Beauty*. New York, The Macmillan Company, 1932.

Schopenhauer, A., *The World as Will and Idea*, translated by R. B. Haldane and J. Kemp. London, Kegan Paul, Trench, Trübner & Co., 1883-1896.

Schuhl, P. M., *Platon et l'Art de son Temps*. Paris, F. Alcan, 1933.

Scott, G., *The Architecture of Humanism*. London, Constable and Co., 1914.

Semper, G., *Der Stil in den technischen und tektonischen Künsten*. Munich, Bruckmann's Verlag, 1860-1863.

Senk, H., "Der Kopf als Einheit des ägyptischen Proportionskanons," *Archiv für Orientforschung*, Vol. 13, 1940.

Shakespeare, William, *The Arden Shakespeare*. London, Methuen and Co., 1899-1924.

Shelley, Percy, *A Defence of Poetry*. Oxford, B. Blackwell, 1923.

Sherrington, Sir Charles, "Experiments on the Value of the Vascular and Visceral Factors for the Generation of Emotions," *Proceedings, Royal Society of London*, Vol. 66, 1900.

Sherrington, Sir Charles, *The Integrative Action of the Nervous System*. New York, Charles Scribner's Sons, 1906.

Sherrington, Sir Charles, *Man on His Nature*. Cambridge, The University Press, 1941.

Shorey, Paul, *The Unity of Plato's Thought* (University of Chicago

Decennial Publications). Chicago, University of Chicago Press, 1903.

Shorey, Paul, *What Plato Said.* Chicago, University of Chicago Press, 1933.

Shorey, Paul, *Platonism, Ancient and Modern.* Berkeley, University of California Press, 1938.

Singer, Edgar A., Jr., "Philosophy of Experiment," *The Symposium,* Vol. 1, No. 2, 1930.

Singer, Edgar A., Jr., "On a Possible Science of Religion," *Philosophical Review,* Vol. 40, No. 2, 1931.

Singer, Edgar A., Jr., "Beyond Mechanism and Vitalism," *Philosophy of Science,* Vol. 1, No. 2, 1934.

Singer, Edgar A., Jr., "Esthetic and the Rational Ideal," *On the Contented Life.* New York, Henry Holt & Company, Inc., 1936.

Singer, Edgar A., Jr., *On the Contented Life.* New York, Henry Holt & Company, Inc., 1936.

Singer, Edgar A., Jr., "Logico-Historical Study of Mechanism," *Studies in the History of Science.* Philadelphia, University of Pennsylvania Press, 1941.

Skelton, John, *Poetical Works,* edited by A. Dyce. London, T. Rodd, 1843.

Skinner, H. D., "Evolution in Maori Art," *Journal of the Royal Anthropological Institute,* Vol. 46, 1916.

Skinner, H. D., "The Origins and Relationships of Maori . . . Decorative Arts," *Journal of the Polynesian Society,* Vol. 33, 1924.

Smith, Henry Bradford, "Postulates of Empirical Thought," *Journal of Philosophy,* Vol. 25, No. 12, 1928.

Sollas, W. J., *Ancient Hunters.* London, Macmillan and Co., 1911.

Sophocles, *Tragœdien,* edited by F. W. Schneidewin. Leipzig, Weidmann, 1853-1857.

Sophocles, *Oedipus,* translated by G. Murray. New York, Oxford University Press, 1911.

Sophocles, *The Antigone,* translated by G. Murray. New York, Oxford University Press, 1941.

Speck, Frank, "Central Eskimo and Indian Dot Ornamentation," *Indian Notes, Museum of the American Indian,* 1925.

Spencer, Herbert, *Principles of Psychology.* New York, D. Appleton Company, 1885-1886.

Spinden, H. J., *A Study of Maya Art, Peabody Museum Memoirs,* Vol. 6. Cambridge, 1913.

Spingarn, J. E., *A History of Literary Criticism in the Renaissance.* New York, The Macmillan Company, 1899.

Springer, A. H., *Handbuch der Kunstgeschichte*. Leipzig, A. Kröner, 1923.
Stewart, J. A., *Notes on the Nicomachean Ethics of Aristotle*. Oxford, The Clarendon Press, 1892.
Stewart, J. A., *The Myths of Plato*. London, Macmillan and Co., 1905.
Stewart, J. A., *Plato's Doctrine of Ideas*. Oxford, The Clarendon Press, 1909.
Sullivan, J. W. N., *Beethoven: His Spiritual Development*. New York, Alfred A. Knopf, Inc., 1927.
Susemihl, F., and Hicks, R. D., *Aristotle's Politics*. London, Macmillan and Co., 1894.
Svoboda, K., *L'Esthétique de Saint Augustin et ses Sources*. Brno, Masarykova Universita, 1933.
Sweeney, J. (ed.), *African Negro Art*. New York, Museum of Modern Art, 1935.
Swindler, Mary H., *Ancient Painting*. New Haven, Yale University Press, 1929.
Sydow, E. von, "Das Tier in der Afrikanischen Plastik," *Der Ararat*, Vol. 2, 1921.
Sydow, E. von, *Exotische Kunst, Afrika und Ozeanien*. Leipzig, Klinkhardt und Biermann, 1921.
Sydow, E. von, *Handbuch der Afrikanischen Plastik*. Berlin, B. Reimer, 1930.
Taine, H. A., *Philosophie de l'Art*. Paris, Hachette, 1901.
Tarrant, D. (ed.), *The Hippias Major*. Cambridge, Cambridge University Press, 1928.
Taylor, A. E., *Plato: The Man and His Work*. New York, Dial Press, Inc., 1927.
Taylor, A. E., *A Commentary on Plato's Timaeus*. Oxford, The Clarendon Press, 1928.
Taylor, A. E., *Timaeus and Critias*. London, Methuen and Co., 1929.
Taylor, A. E., *The Laws*. London, J. M. Dent, 1934.
Thomas Aquinas, Saint, *Opera Omnia*. Rome, T. di Propaganda, 1882-1889.
Thorburn, J. M., *Art and the Unconscious*. London, Kegan Paul, Trench, Trübner & Co., 1925.
Tolstoy, Leo N., "What Is Art?" in *Tolstoy on Art*, translated by Aylmer Maude. London, Oxford University Press, n.d.
Trollope, A., *An Autobiography*. Edinburgh, William Blackwood and Sons, 1883.
Trumbull, Robert, *The Raft*. New York, Henry Holt & Company, Inc., 1942.
Utitz, E., *Aesthetik*. Berlin, R. Heise, 1923.

Utitz, E., *Geschichte der Ästhetik*. Berlin, Junker und Dunnhaupt, 1932.

Vacant, A., and Mangenot, E., *Dictionnaire de Théologie Catholique*. Paris, Letouzey et Ané, 1900-1905.

Vaillant, G. C., *Indian Arts in North America*. New York, Harper & Brothers, 1939.

Valentine, C. W., *Introduction to the Experimental Psychology of Beauty*. London, T. C. and E. C. Jack, 1913.

Vallet, P., *L'Idée du Beau dans la Philosophie d'Aquin*. Paris, Roger et Chernoviz, 1887.

Van Gogh, V., *Letters to Emile Bernard*, translated by Douglas Lord. New York, Museum of Modern Art, 1939.

Venturi, L., *History of Art Criticism*. New York, E. P. Dutton & Co., Inc., 1936.

Verral, A. W., *Euripides, the Rationalist*. Cambridge, Cambridge University Press, 1895.

Vinaver, E., *Malory*. Oxford, The Clarendon Press, 1929.

Vischer, F. T. von, *Aesthetik*. Leipzig, C. Mäcken, 1845-1857.

Vitruvius Pollio, M., *De Architectura*, edited by F. Krohn. Leipzig, Teubner, 1912.

Vitruvius Pollio, M., *The Ten Books on Architecture*, translated by M. H. Morgan. Cambridge, Harvard University Press, 1914.

Volkelt, J., *System der Ästhetik*. Munich, Beck, 1925-1927.

Wallace, William, *Lectures and Essays on Natural Theology and Ethics*, edited by E. Caird. Oxford, Frowde, 1898.

Watt, H. J., *The Foundation of Music*. Cambridge, The University Press, 1919.

Weber, A. O., and Rapaport, D., "Teleology and the Emotions," *Philosophy of Science*, Vol. 8, No. 1, 1941.

West, Rebecca, *Black Lamb and Grey Falcon*. New York, Viking Press, Inc., 1941.

Whittaker, Thomas, *The Neo-Platonists*. Cambridge, Cambridge University Press, 1918.

Williams, C. R., *The Decoration of the Tomb of Per-nēb*. New York, The Metropolitan Museum, 1932.

Wilson, Thomas, "Prehistoric Art: or, The Origin of Art as Manifested in the Works of Prehistoric Man," *Annual Report . . . Smithsonian Institution, Report of the U.S. National Museum*, 1898.

Wind, E., "The Subject of Botticelli's 'Derelitta,'" *Journal of the Warburg and Courtauld Institutes*, Vol. 4, Nos. 1-2, 1940-1941.

Windle, B. C. A., *The Proportions of the Human Body*. London, Ballière, 1889.

Wissler, C., "Harpoons and Darts in the Stefánsson Collection," *Anthropological Papers, American Museum of Natural History*, Vol. 22, 1918.

Worringer, W., *Form in Gothic*. London, G. P. Putnam's Sons, 1927.

Yerkes, R. M., *Almost Human*. New York, D. Appleton-Century Company, Inc., 1925.

Zeising, A., *Aesthetische Forschungen*. Franfurt a.m., Meidinger, 1855.

Zeller, E., *Plato and the Older Academy*. London, Longmans, Green and Co., 1876.

Zeller, E., *Aristotle and the Earlier Peripatetics*. London, Longmans, Green and Co., 1897.

Index